American
Regional Folklore

American Regional Folklore

A SOURCEBOOK AND RESEARCH GUIDE

Terry Ann Mood

A B C ✦ C L I O

SANTA BARBARA, CALIFORNIA   DENVER, COLORADO   OXFORD, ENGLAND

Library of Congress Cataloging-in-Publication Data
Mood, Terry Ann, 1945–
American regional folklore : a sourcebook and research guide / Terry Ann Mood.
p. cm.
Includes bibliographical references and indexes.
ISBN 1-57607-620-2 (alk. paper)   ISBN 1-57607-621-0 (e-book)
1. Folklore—Research—United States. 2. Folklore—United States—Classification.
3. Folklore—United States—Handbooks, manuals, etc. 4. United States—Social life and
customs—Handbooks, manuals, etc. I. Title.
GR105.34.M66   2004
398'.072'073–dc22
2004014737

04 05 06 07 ⁊ 10 9 8 7 6 5 4 3 2 1

This book is also available on the World Wide Web as an e-book.
Visit abc-clio.com for details.

ABC-CLIO, Inc.
130 Cremona Drive, P.O. Box 1911
Santa Barbara, California 93116-911

This book is also available on the World Wide Web as an eBook.
Visit www.abc-clio.com for details.

This book is printed on acid-free paper.
Manufactured in the United States of America.

To John

Contents

Chapter Three

The South and Southern Highlands, 151

Alabama, Arkansas, Florida, Georgia, Kentucky, Louisiana,
Mississippi, North Carolina, South Carolina, Tennessee,
Virginia, West Virginia

Chapter Four

The Midwest, 215

Illinois, Indiana, Iowa, Kansas, Michigan, Minnesota,
Missouri, Nebraska, Ohio, Wisconsin

Chapter Five

The Southwest, 265

Arizona, New Mexico, Oklahoma, Texas

Chapter Six

The West, 311

California, Colorado, Nevada, Utah, Wyoming

Acknowledgments

$\mathcal{I}$ WOULD LIKE TO THANK my colleagues at the Auraria Library, University of Colorado at Denver, who pitched in to help with some of my duties at the library, while I was working on this book.

Thank you, too, to the staff in the Interlibrary Loan department of Auraria Library, who worked diligently to obtain the books I examined for this bibliography.

Introduction

What Is Folklore?

There are probably as many definitions of folklore as there are folk-lorists, or at least as many definitions as there are encyclopedias, dictionaries, and other reference works in folklore. To Charles Haywood, the eminent scholar who compiled the still standard *A Bibliography of North American Folklore and Folksong* (New York: Dover, 1961), folklore is "the sum total *traditional* heritage of a people" (p. xv). Jan Brunvand, in *American Folklore: An Encyclopedia* (New York: Garland, 1998), quotes the nineteenth-century scholar William J. Thomas's definition of folk-lore: "the Lore of the People . . . [comprising] the manners, customs, observances, superstitions, ballads, proverbs, etc. of the olden time" (pp. 285–286). Brunvand goes on to say that contemporary folklorists haven't changed the definition much; they have only broadened it a bit to include modern, urban, and technologically advanced folklore along with the rural and the old-fashioned. *The Penguin Dictionary of American Folklore* (New York: Penguin Reference, 2000) says that folklore "has been traditionally associated with the past in general and with the rural life of the past in particular" and that "to qualify as an example of folk-lore, a tale or dance or song or belief or method of building or what-ever must the be the product of essentially oral transmission or infor-mal demonstration, that it must be identifiable as the product of tradition, and that the item can be shown to be a variation of some rec-ognizable, traditional typo" (p. 199). Tristram Coffin writes in *Uncertain Glory: Folklore and the American Revolution* (Detroit, MI: Folklore Associ-ates, 1971), "Folklore is, of course, individually created art that a homo-geneous group of people who don't, won't, or can't preserve, vary, and recreate as they pass it along from mouth to ear and ear to mouth" (p. 2). He goes on to say that folklore includes "myths, legends, tales, songs, proverbs, riddles, superstitions, rhymes, and other forms of literary expression" (p. 2).

Standard dictionaries echo the theme of the oral tradition. *Webster's Third New International Dictionary of the English Language* defines folklore as "Traditional customs, beliefs, dances, songs, tales, or sayings preserved orally and unreflectively among a people." *The World Book Dictionary* defines it as "The beliefs, legends, customs, and the like, of a people, tribe, or other group." And that arbiter of word history and definition, *The Oxford English Dictionary,* defines folklore as "The traditional beliefs, legends, and customs, current among the common people; the study of these."

So although the specific wording of the definition varies from scholar to scholar and from publication to publication, the same themes emerge: Folklore is an oral tradition that is handed down rather than written down and is changed as it is passed on. Folklore appears to be a living literature, able–even eager–to change as the specific need for the tradition changes, or as the tradition–tale, riddle, joke–moves from one locale to another. It also seems to encompass many types of stories, tales, songs, and games.

Are all ghosts stories folklore? No. But some are, such as those that are associated with a particular place or time. Is all folklore fictional? No again. Often folktales have a basis in fact. Many folk characters are historical figures who have become part of our national folklore. Davy Crockett, Paul Revere, and Annie Oakley, for example, are all real historical figures, but the stories and legends about their lives have turned them into folk characters as well.

The stories and tales of various ethnic groups, although traditionally automatically categorized as folklore, are now often accepted as components of religion. In the early days of collecting tales, various people who worked particularly with Native American groups labeled all the stories and tales they heard from these people as folklore. Charles Godfrey Leland collected Native American tales in the northeast and compiled them in *The Algonquin Legends of New England; or, Myths and Folk Lore of the Micmac, Passamaquoddy, and Penobscot Tribes* (Boston: Houghton Mifflin, 1884; repr., Detroit, MI: Singing Tree Press, 1968) and *Kuloskap the Master: And Other Algonquin Poems* (New York: Funk and Wagnalls, 1902). Silas T. Rand did the same in *Legends of the Micmacs* (New York: Longmans, Green, 1894; repr., New York: Johnson Reprint, 1971). Many of the tales these men published in their collections are more accurately seen as stories of the religious traditions of the Algonquins and the Micmacs, gospel rather than lore. They are creation stories–stories of how the world came to be and of humanity's place in it. Henry R. Schoolcraft worked with Midwestern tribes, collecting their stories in *The Myth of Hiawatha; and Other Oral Legends, Mythologic and Allegoric, of the North American Indians* (Philadelphia: J. B. Lippincott, 1856; repr., AuTrain, MI: Avery Color Studios, 1984). Again, the stories he recounted are now recognized as being part of the tribes' religious tradition. By contrast with these early collectors and interpreters of folklore, one can look at something like Percy Bullchild's *American Indian Genesis: The Story of Creation* (Berkeley, CA: Seastone Press, 1998), in which he retells the Blackfoot story of creation, clearly labeling it as a religious story, not folklore.

The definition of folklore used in the present text incorporates elements of both scholarly and dictionary definitions. It is an inclusive definition: Sources listed in the bibliography include stories that are based in fact and those that are purely imaginative. The bibliography includes many collections of Native American stories, because they were considered folklore at the time they were collected, researched, and written down; although they are now recognized as records of religion, they remain the stories, history, and wisdom of a people. The bibliography also includes some ghost stories, some tall tales, stories of shipwrecks and sea serpents, of giants and little people. In short, the bibliography contains the stories of the people or folk, recounted throughout generations, changing as the needs of the story and of the people change, and passing "from mouth to ear and from ear to mouth."

Scope of the Book

The first two chapters discuss the general outlines of research in the field of American folklore and provide tips on locating additional folklore sources, both through library research and through other scholarly and community sources. Chapter 1 concentrates on research in the library. This chapter presents information on how to locate libraries that will be helpful for folklore research and lists major sources that can be found within them. This chapter also provides information on how to navigate the difficulties and frustrations—and the discoveries and joys—of library research. Chapter 2 goes beyond the library, to discuss other ways of locating useful information. Historical societies, museums, and local organizations are all fruitful places to explore.

Part 2 of the book (chapters 3 through 9) consists of an annotated bibliography of both classic and contemporary sources on American folklore. Part 2 begins with a general chapter, which treats the United States as a whole and includes works that encompass folklore in the entire country, such as general handbooks and encyclopedias, or collections of folktales not limited to one region. Following this general chapter are eight chapters, each concentrating on a specific region of the United States. The regions are those defined by Charles Haywood, already mentioned as the author of the classic work *A Bibliography of North American Folklore and Folksong*:

* Northeast: Connecticut, Delaware, Maine, Maryland, Massachusetts, New Hampshire, New Jersey, New York, Pennsylvania, Rhode Island, Vermont, Washington, D.C.
* South and Southern Highlands: Alabama, Arkansas, Florida, Georgia, Kentucky, Louisiana, Mississippi, North Carolina, South Carolina, Tennessee, Virginia, West Virginia
* Midwest: Illinois, Indiana, Iowa, Kansas, Michigan, Minnesota, Missouri, Nebraska, Ohio, Wisconsin
* Southwest: Arizona, New Mexico, Oklahoma, Texas
* West: California, Colorado, Nevada, Utah, Wyoming

* Northwest: Idaho, Montana, North Dakota, Oregon, South Dakota, Washington
* Alaska
* Hawaii

These bibliographic chapters are organized as follows. Each of the eight regional chapters opens with a brief checklist of authors, folk characters, and the titles of major collections of tales, which the reader can consult for a quick summary of the folklore of a specific region. The chapter is then introduced by an essay written by a scholar in the field. These introductions discuss the folklore of the particular region, often pulling together various themes and historical trends and relating the folklore to our lives today. The essay writers also mention sources not included in the annotated bibliography. Following this introductory essay is the main portion of each of the chapters—an annotated bibliography of sources about the folklore of each region, or in the case of the general chapter, of the United States as a whole. The bibliographies are divided into the following subject categories:

* History and Study: works that will assist the student of folklore to understand the field
* Treasuries: works, often anthologies, that include folklore of many different types, such as poetry, tales, and folksong
* Tales and Legends: the stories of folklore
* Folk Music: both words and music, often with a specific focus, such as songs of a particular trade
* Folk Belief and Ritual: folk medicine and superstition

* Material Culture: works that describe the artifacts and activities of folklore
* Folklore for Children: works specifically written for children

Finally, following the annotated bibliography of materials comes some additional material:

* A list of literary authors who incorporate folklore themes in their writings, together with a brief list of some of their major works
* A list of regional museums, with addresses and phone numbers
* A mention of journals that treat the folklore of a particular region
* A list of relevant Web sites

None of these supplementary lists is meant to be complete. The field is simply too vast to make that claim. They are, rather, representational, and will perhaps whet the reader's appetite for locating more. The chapters on library research and on research beyond the library should be useful in that continuing search.

The books included in the bibliography were chosen according to the following criteria:

* Most of the references contain an account of the folklore itself, rather than scholarly studies of it. Because a serious student of folklore should be acquainted with some of the older scholarly works, some works of folklore scholarship are listed, particularly classic ones, in the "History and Study" section of each chapter. But the preponderance of the material in the bibliography

consists of books in which one can read folklore rather than read about it.

* Most of the books are either in print or are well known and popular enough to be readily available in many libraries. I have not included obscure publications–often locally produced and quite interesting and valuable–because of the difficulty in obtaining them.

* I have included some items that probably fall under the somewhat scornful term *fakelore,* a word coined by Richard Dorson. By fakelore, Dorson means popular literature that has been written for the marketplace, rather than tales that have grown spontaneously from people's experiences and memories. For instance, Dorson includes Stephen Foster songs and the stories of Paul Bunyan under the rubric fakelore. For the purposes of this book, which is meant to be a source particularly for people wishing to explore a bit of the folklore of their own region, state, town, or neighborhood, including so-called fakelore seemed appropriate. Whether or not Paul Bunyan stories grew spontaneously or were helped along with a little marketing seems irrelevant; the point is that they have become well-known and loved legends of the Midwest.

* I have included material about real people and events: those that have been absorbed into our national memory and have become folk characters or happenings. Davy Crockett and Paul Revere are examples.

As with any bibliography, the final choice of what to include was an individual one. Some of the items contained in the bibliography might not fit a particular definition of folklore, but if I found a source appealing and felt it would contribute to an individual's knowledge and appreciation of folklore, I included it.

Certain types of items I have not included:

* Journal articles. To prepare a bibliography of journal articles on the subject of American folklore would be a lifetime project.

* Books that present an individual folktale, usually written for children. Again, these are too numerous to include. Collections of folktales are included; single tales published as books are not.

* Books that are primarily reminiscences of days gone by. If these reminiscences included detailed information about an older way of life–descriptions of old occupations, ways of farming, furnishings, and crafts, for example, I included them under the heading "Material Culture." I did not include books that were not as detailed.

* Fiction, short stories, or novels. A number of authors explore folklore themes in their fiction. I have not included these works in the bibliography, but a list of such literary authors can be found at the end of each regional chapter.

* Urban folklore–those legends that once appeared in chain letters and now can be found on the Internet: the department store said to charge

a customer hundreds of dollars for a cookie recipe, or the dying boy who wanted to receive greeting cards. Most of these legends have been around only a short time and have yet to acquire the status of tales passed down through generations.

* Theses and dissertations.
* As previously mentioned, items that are either not in print or are not easily obtainable from a library.

Reading an Entry

Each entry in the bibliography begins with an entry number. Entries within each section of a chapter (e.g., Treasuries or Folklore for Children) are listed alphabetically by author, editor, or compiler. Books with no author, editor, or compiler are listed alphabetically by title. Publication information follows: place of publication, publisher, and date, along with paging. I have listed the various components of each book, such as illustrations, index, bibliography, glossary, or appendixes. Both LC (Library of Congress) number and ISBN (International Standard Book Number) are included when available. The intent of all this information is to make it easier for the reader to obtain a particular book from a bookstore or library. The ISBN can be particularly valuable; often two books have the same title or at least quite similar ones. An ISBN is unique to the book and should make retrieval easier.

Each entry contains a brief description of the book's contents. Descriptions might include a mention of the geographic area covered, themes explored, types of tales or music included, or folklore characters described.

Audience

A student of folklore should find the beginning chapters helpful. In addition to providing guidance in doing research in a library, chapter 1 will acquaint the student with the major sources of folklore study and provide an entry point into the study of the field. The advent of computer research has in some ways made library research much easier, but has also added to the complexity of the process. Numerous databases exist, as well as openly accessible Internet sites, which must be learned and examined, in addition to print resources. Much material on folklore has not yet found its way into computerized databases and must be searched for in the old-fashioned way, using printed bibliographies, catalogs, and indexes to periodicals. Much material is held in small collections, or in manuscript form, and must be ferreted out with effort and imagination.

People who want to incorporate folklore into a project they're doing make up the second major group that will find this book useful. Perhaps you are a teacher who wants to expose students to the fun of learning about local legends and legendary characters. Or perhaps you belong to an organization that wants to celebrate an anniversary, and you must create a display or put on a program concerning local legends and folklore. The sources in this book should help you to do that.

Folklore Today

Folklore binds us together and connects us to our past. Legends that have been told for generations, often with adaptations and additions to fit the legend to whatever time it is told in, can be shared among families and social groups. At the same time, regional folklore can differentiate us. In this time of superhighways and franchising, when most of us see the same things as everyone else on our cable televisions and on the Internet, regional folklore, with its talk of Paul Bunyan or Johnny Appleseed, of miners' legends or lumberjack songs, reminds us of our individuality as well as of our oneness.

I echo numerous folklore scholars by saying that old ways and old days disappear rapidly and constantly. Before one realizes that a story, a dialect, a country remedy is disappearing, remembered by only a few, it has already vanished. Collecting, reading, and appreciating folklore, or "the oral tradition of the folk," can serve to hold these days and ways a little closer, for a little longer.

PART ONE

Library Research

Not that long ago, pursuing a research project at a library was comparatively simple. Perhaps the results weren't guaranteed, perhaps it was difficult to find references to your topic, or, having found them, to locate the actual sources. The process in itself, however, was rather straightforward: Locate a nearby library, go there, look through their card **catalog** (*Note:* words in bold type are defined in the Glossary that appears at the end of this chapter) for books on your subject, consult the printed **periodical indexes** on the shelves, ascertain which **periodicals** the library subscribed to, find the appropriate issues, and you'd pretty much exhausted the available resources. You might go the extra step and see if there were **government publications** available, or ask about either going to another library or acquiring materials from it, but the card catalog and periodical indexes were the major tools. The amount of material you found on a given topic depended on the size of the library's **collections**.

Now, with the rapidly expanding availability of computer searching, electronic access, electronic delivery of documents, and the Internet, all that has changed. On the surface, it would seem that computers would make the researcher's job easier. In some ways that is true; in others, their effect is quite the opposite. Although it is true that electronic searching makes more material available to the researcher, it is equally true that it multiplies the choices that a researcher needs to make, and thus adds to the complexity of the search. Even a medium-sized library often has electronic access to items beyond its own walls, and a large research library offers a truly astonishing scope of resources. Of course, the library user must have some minimal computer skills: be comfortable using a computer keyboard, be able to read a computer screen, be able to operate a mouse, and have some facility **downloading** information either through a printer or onto a disc.

Using the Internet or the Library?

The Internet is truly a valuable source for all sorts of information, including information on folklore. There is, however, some confusion over what the Internet can do, and there are some downsides to using it. Confusion is common concerning the difference between the Internet and the World Wide Web. Briefly, the Internet is a delivery device for many kinds of information, including information available on the World Wide Web. Information available on the Web is only a portion of what is available through the Internet. The very short history of the Internet, which follows, will show how quickly it developed and will indicate how quickly it has become a major force in information gathering.

The Internet began in the late 1960s, when the United States was concerned it was falling behind the Soviet Union in the space race. A combined project of the Department of Defense and the Advanced Research Projects Agency looked for a way to link computers so that scientists could share research projects and work together. The result was ARPANET, which linked computers at four universities: University of Utah, Stanford Research Center, University of California at Los Angeles, and University of California at Santa Barbara.

In time, more and more universities joined the network, and other networks developed, including USENET and BITNET. Different networks used different computers, which again made communication difficult. This difficulty was alleviated with the development of TCP/IP, or Transmission Control Protocol/Internet Protocol. TCP/IP was a way to tell computers how to break down information into small, transmittable packets, send it to its proper location, and reassemble the packets. During all this development, the personal computer, or PC, was also becoming available, which made computers accessible to individuals as well as to cor-

porations and universities. Individuals wanted to be able to access the Internet as well.

Up to this time, most of the people using the Internet were the ones who had entered information onto it, and they were naturally able to retrieve that information. But, as individuals began accessing the Internet, it became obvious that search techniques needed to be developed so that people could find what was stored there. Enter Gophers, early search engines. These search engines, developed at universities, were text-only—the graphical search engines, which most people use today, hadn't yet been designed. Three early Gophers were Archie, Veronica, and Jughead, named for comic book characters. Archie originated at McGill University, Veronica at the University of Nevada, and Jughead at the University of Manchester. These Gophers operated with menus: The first page would list broad categories, such as Arts, Science, Mathematics, and News. Entering the menu for Arts might bring up a subsequent menu with smaller categories, such as visual arts, dance, theater, and music. Eventually, by working through these menus, you would arrive at information targeted to a topic. It was not a very specific or quick way to search for information. If you were looking for material on folklore, you might enter through an Arts menu, which in turn might have led you to a literature section, or even directly to a folklore section.

While Gophers were being used, the World Wide Web was developed by the European Laboratory for Particle Physics in Switzerland as another means of searching for information on the Internet. It pioneered the concept of linking various databases, or sources of information. While reading a file, you would see numbers embedded within it. Typing in one of those numbers would send you to a file of pertinent information. For example, if you were reading a file on the early history of the United States, a reference to George Washington might have the number 1 next to it. Typing that number into a designated space would open a file on Washington. This version of the World Wide Web was text only, with no graphics or pictures. Graphics came with the introduction of Mosaic, the first graphical Web browser, or **graphical user interface**. With the use of Mosaic, Internet users could see pictures. Linking from site to site became easier as well; you could link from a picture or know a link was there because of the color. The development of the mouse at the same time accelerated the use of these changes.

All these inventions and developments led to what we now know as the World Wide Web on the Internet, with its graphics, color, linking capabilities, and search engines such as Yahoo and Google.

Using the Internet, or more specifically, the searching capabilities of the World Wide Web, has many advantages:

* It's easily accessible, available from home, from terminals at a library or school, from Internet cafés, even from handheld devices.
* It's quick and relatively easy to use.
* You can almost always find something on your topic.

There are, however, downsides to Internet searching:

* The Web is not fully indexed.

Search engines search only some of the information available.
* Sometimes a search will yield too many results to be useful. A search on the word *folklore,* for example, on the Google search engine, yields more than 862,000 results. Limiting the search by adding the word *American* still gives more than 270,000 results, or "hits." Such a large set of results is very difficult to sort through.
* Search engines search only for a match between the words you type in and the words in a site. They don't search for synonyms. While searching the Web, it is necessary to use as many descriptive words and terms as you can think of.
* Search engines search only material on the Web, material that is usually free. Much of the material available through the Internet is available only through purchase or subscription, and some is not available to individuals.
* Some of the material on the Web is put up by individuals or organizations with an agenda; sorting out the objective and reliable can be difficult.

But certainly the Web is an easy, available source for information and contains much of value.

Sometimes searching a library—or libraries—is a better choice, although there are pros and cons to this as well. On the upside, libraries:

* Index and catalog their collections, which helps you do a more complete search.

* Purchase materials that individuals cannot afford or do not want to purchase.
* Provide access to computer databases, available through the Internet, that are either not available for purchase by individuals, or are too costly for most individuals to purchase.
* Provide help to individuals searching for materials, including help in making the most efficient use of material on the Net.
* House and preserve a great deal of written material that is not available on the Net.

Downsides to using libraries might be:

* Difficulty of getting to a library
* Inconvenient hours
* Restrictions on who may use the library
* Large collections that make it difficult to locate specific material

If you're interested in doing a thorough search, you'll probably want to use both the Net and one or more libraries.

Searching the Internet

Searching the Internet is a comparatively simple process. All you need is your computer and an **Internet service provider (ISP).** Log on to a **search engine,** and type in your search. The number and names of search engines change frequently; it is impossible to list them all. A few to try are

* Google
* Alta Vista
* Lycos
* Dogpile
* Yahoo
* The search engine associated with your Internet service provider, such as MSN or AOL

The words you type into the search engine will of course be specific to your search. Some suggestions:

* *Folklore* or *folk,* coupled with the name of your state or locality
* A folk character such as Johnny Appleseed
* A historic event that has become legend, such as Paul Revere's ride
* The name of an author with whose works you are familiar

If you're a newcomer to the Net, try reading one of the many books that serve as an introduction to it—*The Internet for Dummies* (IDG Books Worldwide, 2000), *Internet Basics without Fear: Quick-Start Guide for Becoming Internet-Friendly in Just a Few Easy Steps* (Final Draft Publications, 2000), *Understanding the Internet: A Clear Guide to Internet Technologies* (Butterworth-Heineman, 2000), or *The Complete Idiot's Guide to the Internet* (Prentice Hall, 2001).

Searching a Library—or Libraries

When researchers are looking for information on a fairly obscure topic, or want to do a thorough search on a topic, it is a good idea to look for information at a library, or libraries. You'll use similar methods to access information that you would at home using the Net. You'll no doubt use a computer, you'll access information from a variety of sources, and you'll type in subject words that describe your topic. The differences, however, can be enormous. Librarians choose what items to collect, house, and make available, based on their clientele's interests and needs. By contrast, the Net is open to information posted or submitted by anyone. Libraries organize their collections so that specific items within them can be retrieved using certain methods; libraries have access to **databases** that contain scholarly information on a variety of subjects and that, unlike many of the sites on the Internet, are paid for by the library.

Sometimes a search on the Web will lead you to a library. In your Web search, you may locate a library Web site that will list and describe items that sound germane to your search. Often the text of the items won't be on the Web—copyright restrictions might prevent a library from putting the text of an item itself on the Web, the library can't afford to digitize the material, or the material might be so fragile that digitization isn't possible. To view the items you have to visit the library itself.

Selecting a Library

The researcher's first task is to choose a library or libraries to explore. Perhaps your first instinct is to head for the largest library to which you have access, such as a large public library in the area or a nearby college or university library. That's not always the wisest course. Sometimes bigger isn't better. Much depends on the size and scope of your project, as well as the particular subject area you have interest in. Perhaps a smaller but more specialized library will be more on target for your needs. In addition to the large public and

university libraries, consider the following:

* A local historical society. Many have libraries or collections of material on their area.
* A small public library. Many have special collections that concentrate on the town, county, or region in which they're located.
* A local museum. They often have their own libraries.

For help in locating such smaller libraries, try the yellow pages; there's often a listing for libraries. Or try a search on the Web, looking for a page about your local area, or a home page for a library. If this doesn't help, try consulting the *Directory of Special Libraries and Information Centers* (Detroit: Gale). This is an annual listing of libraries throughout the country that specialize in collecting on one or more subjects. Many are located in businesses and collect information specific to that business. Others are in museums, government agencies, historical societies, historic buildings, genealogical societies, or private clubs. This book may give you a lead to libraries with collections on subjects in which you're interested. You can find a copy of the directory in most medium to large public libraries.

Scoping Out a Library

It is probably everyone's instinct upon entering a library, eager and ready to find materials on a certain subject, to go immediately to whatever computer one encounters just beyond the front door. This is often not the most efficient use of time or the best way of finding materials. It is worth your while to take some time to scope out the library and to ask a few questions. Find out:

* How is the library organized? By departments? By type of material?
* What access methods are available? Computers? An old-style card catalog? Printed indexes to parts of the collection?
* What electronic databases are available? Access to search engines on the Web? Paid databases that specialize in history? A homegrown database on the local area?
* What are its hours of operation? Weekends as well as weekdays? Evenings?
* What services are available? Consultation and reference help? Materials available for checkout? Photocopying facilities?

Library Organization

It's best to have a general idea of how a particular library is organized before trying to use it. If you don't, you'll waste time wandering about looking for things in the wrong places—or looking for things that don't exist at all! Most libraries try to be logical in their organization and place items in certain places for specific reasons. Remember, however, that libraries are constantly growing and changing, as new materials are received and technology changes, and that sometimes placement is a matter of necessity, driven by available space rather than by strict logic. You might ask why there is no photocopier located near the journals. Perhaps the answer is as simple as that no electrical out-

lets exist in that vicinity or the ones there are already at peak capacity and that to add another electrical appliance would overload the system. It might also be true that the library staff is working diligently behind the scenes to remedy the situation. Remember that all researchers' needs are different and that what seems to you like an illogical placement of certain materials might be much appreciated by a researcher in another field.

First take a look around and see what departments exist. Perhaps there is a map or a floor plan that has this information. Some things to look for:

* Are there departments devoted to certain types or formats of material, such as periodicals, reference books, media materials?
* Are there departments that house materials in a certain subject area?
* Is there a department or section for current fiction, or a broad subject category such as business or humanities?
* Are there departments with more specialized materials, particularly such areas as genealogy or local history?

Taking a few moments to familiarize yourself with a library's general layout will keep you from going to a history department to ask for folklore journals, if you're in a library that keeps all its journals, no matter on what topic, in a periodicals department. See if your library has floor plans or other location guides.

During this preliminary stage, you might also investigate if some materials, particularly older ones, are kept in a specialized format or location:

* Are old issues of journals and newspapers kept on microfilm or microfiche?
* What about older records of a specific locale, such as city or county records? Are some or even all materials kept in a closed area, accessible only by special permission or pass or requiring retrieval by a library staff member?
* Are some materials shelved off-site?

In either of the latter two cases, you will need to request such materials in advance. This will take some time, either hours or a day or two. Knowing this in advance will avoid frustration at the time when you actually want the items.

You might want to investigate checkout privileges:

* Are you a qualified borrower?
* Can all materials leave the library, or must some be used only in house?

Some libraries limit checkout to their own clientele, such as residents of the city or students at the university. Special libraries, belonging to an organization, often limit circulation to their members. Some large research libraries require that an individual be working on a bona fide research project before using some or all of the collections. Sometimes if you arrange in advance for access, by writing or phoning ahead with a description of your project, you can gain privileges that would be denied you if you were to walk in cold. Take some time to familiarize yourself with the rules of the institution you wish to use. Often these rules will be posted on the library's Web page. Re-

member, a polite inquiry concerning the rules and limitations usually brings a better response than a blunt or impatient demand for services to which you are not entitled by the rules of the institution. Your local public library might be able to help you obtain materials from a library that has more limited access. Sometimes a library will lend material to another library rather than directly to an individual.

Access Methods

Almost all libraries have a main access point, or guide to the bulk of their collections. Sometimes this is a card catalog, but almost always now it is a computer, or **online catalog**, sometimes called a **PAC (public access catalog)** or **OPAC (online public access catalog)**. It is certainly worth taking some time to explore the setup and search methods employed by the computer system used by a particular library, because all online catalogs are definitely not alike. Commands, searching capabilities, printing and downloading capabilities, and display of information differ among the various catalogs.

If you are completely unfamiliar with computers, or merely unfamiliar with a particular computer system, look first to see if the library offers printed guides to the system, online help screens, and classes or instruction sessions. Many libraries offer one or more of these aids. Instruction sessions are often run by volunteers who have been taught by librarians. A few minutes spent reading over printed guides or scrolling through preliminary help screens can save much frustration later. And remember that librarians and library staff are almost always friendly and helpful—ask them if you're stuck.

The next step is to explore the system itself. With the increase in computer capacity and speed, many libraries offer computer access to more than the physical and digital materials housed in their own building. See if the system you're working with has a list of databases. Most libraries have a catalog to their own collections, as well as databases that index and often provide full text of magazine articles. Many of these concentrate on material in a certain subject, perhaps business or science. There may even be a database of local materials listing items of interest to your area. Make sure you're looking at a database that is germane to your interests.

Not all databases are equal. Obvious differences involve the information or material the database helps you find, but other differences exist as well. You may find a database that is only an entry point for multiple other databases. For example, choosing a database named *Colleges* might open up a list of the catalogs of numerous area colleges. Some databases require a **password** for access, which is often available only to registered users of the library.

Off-Site Access

Many libraries offer access to their databases through a home computer. This way, you do not have to be in the library to find out what they own—or at least some portion of their **holdings**. To access libraries through your computer, you will need a modem and a communications package, which allows you to connect to other computers. Consult the manual for your communications package for advice on setting up your computer. You might also call the library you wish to access; the librarians can help you connect to their system.

Sometimes, when you connect to a library's catalog through your home computer, you will have access to only some of their online offerings. Some databases may require a password for off-site access. In the case of a public library, this usually means you must be a resident of the community and have a library card; your library card number often serves as the password to databases. In the case of a college or university library, passworded databases are usually available only to students and faculty of the institution. Check with the library to see if you are eligible to use password access.

National Databases

WorldCat is a database offered by many, but not all, libraries. WorldCat offers author, title, and subject access to millions of records. You can enter a subject term—for example, the word *folklore* paired with your state name—and retrieve a listing of books on the subject. FirstSearch will tell you which libraries own a book. It also allows you to limit your search by language, by year of publication, by type of material (book, video, etc.), and by various other parameters. This means, for example, that you can retrieve a list of books on the folklore of Maine published only since 1990 and written in English. It is an invaluable tool, one worth checking for.

Periodical Indexes

A number of **periodical indexes** exist, in a variety of formats:

* Printed indexes
* Online databases
* CD-ROMs

All do the same thing—they allow you to locate articles in magazines or journals. Most work on a subject format, meaning that you look up a subject, and the index lists articles in various journals that relate to that subject. Most indexes give you the following information:

* *Author and title* of article
* *Title* of magazine
* *Date and volume number* of the magazine
* *Pages* on which the article is located

Online databases and **CD-ROMs** are simply electronic versions of the same type of source and give you the same type of information. Most people find online indexes the easiest to use and CD-ROMs the next easiest. Print indexes seem more cumbersome to most people. Online indexes are often accessible off-site. However, as previously noted, you should find out if you're eligible for such off-site access. In addition, both online and CD-ROM versions of indexes some-times—again not always—provide the *full text* of the articles listed. Print indexes do not. However, there are times when print indexes are the only source available or are the best for your topic. Electronic indexes often

* Cover only very recent material.

If you think material published many years ago will be useful, print indexes may be your only source.
* Are more costly, in most cases, than print indexes; many libraries cannot afford to replace print indexes with electronic in all cases.
* Cover only material of wide interest. If you are looking for information about a very local character or event, you might need to use print indexes.

Explore your library and ask questions of the library staff to find out what indexes are available.

Some indexes to inquire about, which might be available in any of the formats, are the following:

* *Abstracts of Folklore Studies*
* *Humanities Index*
* *America: History and Life*
* *Poole's Index* (for nineteenth-century material)
* *MLA International Bibliography of Books and Articles.* Volume 5 in the print version covers folklore topics. The online version also covers folklore.

If you are using a print index, or the full text is not provided by the online index, you will have to locate the actual article. Take down the information about the article provided by the index (title, author, title of magazine, date, and pages). It's also a good idea to note down which index you were using and even what library you're in. That way, you can retrace your steps if necessary, to double-check something or if your topic changes slightly and you want to do your search again.

Journals on Folklore

A number of journals specifically devoted to folklore topics exist. Some regional journals are listed in this book, within the appropriate chapter. To locate others, try consulting *Ulrich's International Index of Periodicals* (New Providence, N.J.: Bowker). *Ulrich's* is available in many libraries and is an extensive listing of published journals.

Some very small, local journals on folklore may not be listed in *Ulrich's*. Try contacting your local community college, local library, or historical association to see if such publications exist in your area. Some high school classes occasionally have class projects on local folklore and publish the results. Since the success of *Foxfire*, a project in the 1970s undertaken by high school students in Georgia, such projects have expanded.

To locate specific information in such small journals, you will probably have to browse through the various issues. Most of these very small publications are not indexed in any of the commercial periodical indexes. Occasionally, a library or historical society will maintain a locally produced index to a local journal.

Natural Language versus Controlled Vocabulary

To really use an index efficiently you need to speak its language. Many people, when confronted with a computer keyboard and a subject to search, begin typing immediately, entering terms and phrases that describe the subject they are searching. When searching a paper index, they turn immediately to the most common word that describes their topic. This works sometimes, but a more efficient method for using many indexes and databases is available. If using a database, find out if the database you are searching uses

* **natural language** or
* **controlled vocabulary**

Natural language means the computer will search each record contained in the database for any occurrence of the word or words entered. This seems like the best method, but it can be risky. There are usually numerous ways to describe a particular topic. If you're searching for stories of buried treasure and sunken pirate ships in your area, for instance, you might type in those terms to search. But what if the book or article that fits your needs perfectly uses the words *brigands* or *buccaneers* in its title, rather than the words you chose? You will not retrieve it.

For that reason, many databases use a controlled vocabulary and attach **subject terms** to each record. Identical subject terms are assigned to each book or article that is about the same subject, which means that if you in turn search by a subject heading, you will retrieve all items labeled that way. Almost all library catalogs use such subject terms. If you're searching for books, using the accepted subject term is the best way to get the most results for your time—and retrieve the greatest number of books. To discover subject terms, use *The Library of Congress Subject Heading Guide* (Washington, D.C.: Library of Congress). This set of books lists all subject terms established by the Library of Congress. You can look up a term that describes your topic and see if it is a recognized subject term. If it is not, the *Library* *of Congress Subject Heading Guide* will refer you to the correct term. It will also give you a list of related terms, which often helps in devising a search method.

Most libraries use Library of Congress subject headings for their book database. One trick is to use natural language for your first search of a book database, then look at the records you retrieve. The library record will probably list the approved subject headings that are attached to these records. You can then do a subsequent search using these terms, which are often more specific than the first ones you entered.

Many databases of magazine articles do not use the Library of Congress subject headings. When searching a magazine database, oftentimes the best method is to start with natural language. Type in a broad subject term, again such as *folklore* paired with your state or locale, and look through the list of retrieved articles. Often in addition to listing the title, author, magazine, date, and pages, a database will identify the subject headings under which the article is indexed. If so, you can do a new search using one or more of these subject terms.

Print indexes will sometimes have a **thesaurus** available, listing subject terms. Ask a library staff member if such a thesaurus is available.

Government Publications

The U.S. government is a major publisher. The Government Printing Office publishes the *Congressional Record,* the *Federal Register,* IRS forms, census forms, congressional documents such as committee reports, and material from the executive and legislative branches. The GPO Fact Sheet, available online at *http://www. accessgpo.gov/public-affairs/5-99facts.html,* states that it is the largest industrial employer in Washington, D.C. Many early ethnological and anthropological studies were first published by the U.S. government, in such publications as *Bulletin of the Smithsonian Institution, Bureau of American Ethnology.* Since then, the government has continued to publish in all areas.

Government publications are well indexed in a variety of ways, but the major entry point is *Monthly Catalog of U.S. Government Publications.* Recent documents, from 1994 forward, are indexed in an online version, titled simply *The Catalog of U.S. Government Publications.* It is available free at *http://www.gpoaccess.gov/cgp/ index.html.* For earlier online indexing, back to 1976, you must use a database titled *Monthly Catalog.* This is a subscription database and is subscribed to by some libraries. Indexing from 1976 forward is also sometimes available on a CD-ROM. Another online source that indexes some but not all older government documents is *WorldCat,* also available as a subscription through some libraries. Even earlier indexing, for documents published between 1895 and 1940, is in two print publications, *The Catalog of the Public Documents of the Congress and of All Departments of the Government of the United States* (popularly known as the *Document Catalog)* and *The Monthly Catalog of the United States Government Publications.* After 1940, *The Monthly Catlog* became the sole source of indexing.

The online or print *Catalog* works like other indexes: Look up a subject, and the *Catalog* will list publications related to it. You can do a search by subject or for a particular title. Try searching for the name of a local folklore character or place, or put in such terms as *folklore, folk literature,* or *folk tales,* paired with the name of your state, city, or region; or with an ethnic group such as Indians, Blacks, or Italian Americans.

Remember that government publications are often kept in a different section of the library from books, and are not always catalogued in the library's main catalog, especially those documents published earlier than 1976. They also often have a call number different from those given to books, called the Superintendent of Documents call number. Be sure to note this number in order to facilitate locating the document itself.

In addition, a number of standard search engines do a good job of searching for government publications. Try:

* www.google.com/unclesam
* www.FirstGov.com
* www.SearchGov.com

Remember, too, to check out the Web sites of various government agencies. The Library of Congress Web site, at *www.loc. gov,* provides many documents in full text, and indexes others. Established by President John Adams in 1800, the Library of Congress began with an appropriation of $5,000 to buy books suitable for the needs of Congress. In 1802, President Thomas Jefferson appointed the first librarian of Congress and extended the privilege of the library, including the privilege of borrowing books, to the executive branch. Those privileges were soon extended to the judiciary and to other government agencies. Jefferson had another enormous impact on the Library when, in 1815, he sold his personal collection of books to the Library of Congress. This purchase expanded the scope of the Library's collections. From being a collection that concentrated on historical and legal works, suitable for the needs of the government, it now contained works on philosophy, literature, and the arts. From these modest beginnings the Library of Congress has grown to a collection of more than 10 million items, employing more than 5,000 people. You can read a complete—and fascinating—history of the Library of Congress at its Web site, *www.loc.gov.*

The Library of Congress is many things to many people. It still serves as the actual library for members of Congress and their staffs and is used as a research library for legislative issues. It is also a major research library for scholars of all disciplines and is open to the public. The Library of Congress also provides services to libraries throughout the country and the world; many new books receive their cataloging from the Library of Congress. Not least, it serves as a cultural center, presenting artistic programs throughout the year.

One arm of the Library of Congress is its extensive folklore collection, the American Folklife Project, which includes oral histories, published material, manuscripts, and photographs. The collections are searchable online, and the full text of many of the materials within the collections is available at the Web site. For example, the American Memory Project, part of the American Folklife Center, contains full text collections on such topics as ranching in Nevada in the mid-twentieth century, Virginia folk tunes, and oral histories from the Depression of the 1930s. Folk music collections are particularly strong, with collections of music from Woody Guthrie and the Lomaxes, both well-known names in folk music. If anything, the Library of Congress site is so rich in material that it might be overwhelming to the novice researcher. Go to the site for a look at the truly splendid resources available in the field. You can directly access the Library of Congress folklore site, the American Folklife Center, at *www.loc.gov/folklife.*

Other government agencies have Web sites useful for folklore studies. National parks, monuments, or historic sites often have their own Web sites. These usually have historical information about the site, including information on folklore connections. If you'll be visiting a national park or historic site, use a search engine to locate Web addresses for these sites and agencies.

In addition to publications put out by the federal government, there are many documents published by state governments. A state agency, such as the state library, the education department, the state archives department, or perhaps an agency charged with preserving the history of the state, might publish documents relating to local history and folklore. Indexing and distribution of these documents varies by state. Often the state Web site (usually at *www.state.abbreviation ofstatenamehere.us;* for example, *www.state. ms.us,* or *www.state.ak.us*) will have links to various documents and publications, or to the state library. The Web sites will vary from state to state, both in their appearance and organization and in what can be found there. Many do not yet have the documents they publish indexed or available on their Web site. In general, the state library of your state, or a major public library, will have information about locating state documents.

Once you've identified documents you wish to use, the next step is locating the documents themselves. Although most libraries own some documents, only the very largest own a great number. First find out if your local library owns the documents you're interested in. Many libraries have documents listed in their online catalogs, or OPACs, intermingled with other books. Other libraries might have a specific listing for documents and might shelve them in a separate area of the building. Documents related to the particular town or state might be in a special collection. The best plan is to ask at your local library. For many U.S. documents, you may need to visit a **depository library.** Beginning in 1813, the Federal Depository Library Program, or FDLP, has designated various major public and academic libraries in each state as depositories. These libraries receive an enormous number of documents from the government for free. In return, they pledge to keep the documents accessible and allow all U.S. residents access.

State documents can be more complicated, because publication and distribution of state documents are controlled and funded by individual states. In most cases, libraries purchase only those state documents that suit their collections and clientele. Ask at your local library about finding state documents.

Search Strategy

Establishing a **search strategy** is important. Knowledge of all the databases and search techniques can't make up for the lack of a search strategy. As already discussed, failure to know the layout of the particular library you're using, not knowing what databases are available, or confusion about the differences between natural language and controlled vocabulary can make research less efficient or can result in a less-successful search. In other words, lack of understanding the basics of research can add greatly to the searcher's frustration level. Lack of a clear definition of your research topic can also lead to frustration. Searching an inappropriate database, having to repeat searches because you've thought of additional subject terms, or changing the focus of your research midway can all add to the time it takes to research your subject—and add to your frustration as well. Some repetition and change is inevitable when doing research. After all, the search process itself leads to new discoveries—otherwise, why do it?—and such discoveries naturally lead you down new paths. But some aggravation can be avoided with a little forethought. After learning the general organization and focus of the library you're using, the next step—before actually searching a database—is to think specifically about your topic and where you are likely to find information about it. It might be a good idea to jot down two columns of information: Subject Terms and Databases, or Search Points. Under Subject Terms, list all the terms, words, and phrases that describe your subject. Indicate which are controlled vocabulary and which are natural language. Under Databases, or Search Points, list all the databases you will search using these terms. Also list any special collections that might not be available as a database,

that you plan to search. For instance, you might want to search the *Monthly Catalog* for government documents or browse through file boxes in an archives or special collections room. For a search on the subject of pirate treasure, your list might look like this:

Subject Terms	Databases, or Search Points
Pirates	book database for library
Buccaneers	WorldCat
Pirate ships	*Abstracts of Folklore Studies* (print)
Buried treasure	Local archives room
Bluebeard	*Humanities Index* (print)
	Poole's Index (print)

As you search each database or location, you can check that you are searching all subject terms on your list.

Again, keep detailed notes, not only of the information you find but also of how and where you find it. A piece of information might prove invaluable from another point of view as you progress through your research. If you need to find the same piece of information a second time, it will be much easier if you have noted the exact path you took to find it the first time. This is particularly important if you're using more than one library.

Retrieving Material

Once you've used the library catalog, indexes, and databases and have identified books, articles, or other material you want to look at, you then have to find the actual items. Many databases contain the full text of the articles they index; with these databases, searching and locating articles is accomplished in one step. Other databases, however, will only index an article, giving you the information you need to locate it. You might need to locate items in another database, or in print form. A book you've found using the library's catalog should be available in that library. Consult the floor plan or map to find its location. It might be in a special area, such as a reference department or archives. If the book is checked out to someone else, most libraries let you put a hold on it; you'll be notified when the item is returned and available.

To find a journal article, first see if the library provides a list of the journals that it owns. If the library owns the journal you're interested in, your search is over. If not, ask a staff member to help you find the journal at another library.

For either books or journal articles you've identified that your library doesn't own, you might need to explore library consortia or use interlibrary loan.

Library Consortia

More and more libraries are combining forces and joining with each other to form consortia. Oftentimes people who have privileges at one member library have privileges at all of the members of the consortia. You can borrow books from all member libraries, or use their meeting facilities. Sometimes, too, you can request books from another member library through your library's computer system. If you find that your own library does not own a specific book, you can sometimes request a wider search, on the databases of several libraries. If a member

library owns the book, you can request that it be sent to your home library for you to pick up.

Interlibrary Loan

Many, if not most, libraries are part of a worldwide interlibrary loan system, through which you can obtain books and articles not owned by your local library. Either the entire book, or in the case of a journal article, a photocopy of the article, is obtained by your local library for your use. When you are through with it, you return the item to your library, which in turn returns it to the lending library. Through this system, books and articles can be obtained from all over the world.

Your responsibility, of course, is to abide by the rules. Your responsibilities include

* Providing your library with clear bibliographic information concerning the item you wish them to locate—author, title, publisher, date, in the case of a book; author, title, name of journal, date, and page numbers, in the case of a journal article.
* Providing your library with your information: name, address, phone number, library identification number.
* Returning items on time. If you don't, you risk losing not only your own borrowing privileges through this service but the privileges of other users of your library. If too many registered borrowers at a specific library are late in returning interlibrary loan items—or lose them

altogether—other libraries will stop lending items to that library.

* Paying any associated costs. In most cases this service is free, although sometimes photocopies must be paid for.

Sometimes this service is restricted to registered borrowers only, or to people enrolled at the school offering the service. Ask about the rules in advance. Also allow plenty of time for this service. Although electronic access has made the asking for materials much quicker and easier, there is still time needed to send items through the mails and to process the necessary paperwork. Don't expect to place an interlibrary loan order one day and receive the material the next.

Some Major Folklore Sources

The bibliography in this book lists sources of folklore information, based on geography. The first chapter in Part 2 lists and describes books that either discuss folklore of the entire United States or offer folktales from throughout the country. The remaining chapters do the same for specific geographic regions of the country. If you want simply an overview of folklore, to learn a bit more about it or investigate whether it's a field of study you want to pursue, you might consult one or more of the following major sources, all of which are annotated in the chapter covering the entire United States.

Brunvand, Jan. *American Folklore: An Encyclopedia*
Brunvand, Jan. *The Study of American Folklore: An Introduction*

Dorson, Richard M. *Buying the Wind*
Dorson, Richard M. *Handbook of American Folklore*
Green, Thomas A., ed. *Folklore: An Encyclopedia of Beliefs, Customs, Tales, Music and Art*
Larousse Dictionary of World Folklore

Sets and Series

In addition to the books listed in the regional bibliographies, there are several sets or series of books that can be helpful in folklore studies. These are series that were published some time ago, but whose information is still valuable. They cover the entire United States; usually each book in the series concentrates on a particular region in the country.

American Guidebook Series

First among these series has to be the American Guidebook series put out in the 1930s by the Works Progress Administration. Each state has a guidebook, each of which gives a history of the state and usually a discussion of the government, educational system, topography, and industry of the time. In addition, most also discuss local folklore, either in a chapter dedicated to the subject or in references throughout the book. For example, the New Jersey guidebook from the Federal Writers' Project, *New Jersey: A Guide to Its Past and Present* (New York: The Viking Press, 1939), contains a chapter on "Folklore and Folkways," on pages 126–133. It recounts the history and doings of the Leeds devil, a creature "with the head of a collie dog, the face of a horse, the body of a kangaroo" (p. 126); tales of pirates; stories of ghosts; and tales of farming, including one of a farmer who captured a shark, saddled and bridled it, and then made a living by riding the shark to deliver mail along the river. The second half of the chapter, on folkways, recounts some of the old ways of the various groups that made up the state's early population. As with other Federal Writers' Project guidebooks, this provides a quick survey of the rich treasure of folklore associated with the state, and readers can use it as a starting point.

Another guidebook in the same series, *Maryland, A Guide to the Oldtime State* (New York: Oxford University Press, 1940), does not contain a chapter titled "Folklore." However, the introductory chapter, "Maryland, My Maryland" (pp. 3–9), serves the same function. It describes customs and superstitions specific to Maryland; tells of annual events such as jousting tournaments; introduces the "snallygaster," a bird of prey that carries off small children and sometimes adults to its lair in the mountains; and details certain patterns of speech and expressions. As do the other guidebooks in the series, this one provides an excellent introduction to a specific region's folklore, namely, Maryland. It also provides the customary bibliography and timeline of events important to the state's history.

Some of the guidebooks, such as *Pennsylvania: A Guide to the Keystone State* (New York: Oxford University Press, 1940), do not recount legends or tales. They do, however, give a flavor of the area. The Pennsylvania guidebook includes sections on arts and crafts, music, and industry, all of which help the reader get a sense of the early days of the state and how it developed.

Each of the guidebooks includes a final chapter describing tours in various sections of the given state. Obviously the road designations and directions have changed a great deal since the guidebooks were written, but the information provided about places worth seeing is often still true and often mentions local legends.

In addition, the guidebooks provide a bibliography of sources covering various state features, including folklore. Although old, these bibliographies are still valuable.

American Folkways Series

The general editor for the series American Folkways was Erskine Caldwell. Nearly thirty titles were eventually published, each by a different author and each highlighting a different section of the country, such as the Blue Ridge country or the Mormon country. The books present an overview of many of the stories and customs of the particular region. *Blue Ridge Country,* by Jean Thomas, for example, concerns itself with the area of the Blue Ridge encompassing parts of Kentucky, Tennessee, North Carolina, South Carolina, Georgia, and Alabama, and all of West Virginia. The first section deals with the land itself and its people, including stories of such legendary settlers as Daniel Boone. Later sections describe feuds, such as the one between the Hatfields and McCoys; traditional work like timbering; crafts of the country; customs of marriage and of funerals; superstitions; and ghost stories. See the box for a list of titles in this series.

AMERICAN FOLKWAYS SERIES

Adirondack Country, William C. White, 1954

Big Country: Texas, Donald Day, 1947

Blue Ridge Country, Jean Thomas, 1942

Corn Country, Homer Croy, 1947

Deep Delta Country, Harnett T. Kane, 1944

Desert Country, Edwin Corle, 1941

Far North Country, Thames Williamson, 1944

Golden Gate Country, Gertrude Atherton, 1945

Gulf Coast Country, Hodding Carter and Anthony Ragusin, 1951

High Border Country, Eric Thane, 1942

High Sierra Country, Oscar Lewis, 1955

Lower Piedmont Country, H. C. Nixon, 1946

Mormon Country, Wallace Stegner, 1942

Niagara Country, Lloyd Graham, 1949

North Star Country, Meridel Le Sueur, 1945

Old Kentucky Country, Clark McMeekin, 1957

Other Illinois, Baker Brownell, 1958

Ozark Country, Otto Ernest Rayburn, 1941

Palmetto Country, Stetson Kennedy, 1942

Pinon Country, Haniel Long, 1941

Pittsylvania Country, George Swetnam, 1951

Redwood Country, Alfred Powers, 1949

Rocky Mountain Country, Albert N. Williams, 1950

Short Grass Country, Stanley Vestal, 1941

Smoky Mountain Country, North Callahan, 1952

Southern California Country, Carey McWilliams, 1946

Town Meeting Country, Clarence M. Webster, 1945

Wheat Country, William Bracke, 1950

Rivers of America Series

Much folklore developed along rivers, among their rapids and sandbanks, passed along by the people who plied them and lived along their shores. The series Rivers of America spotlights the history of America's rivers, including their folklore. A good portion of each title in this series deals with the industry and development that took place along a river, but much folklore material is included as well. Some titles provide a retelling of various legends associated with a particular river. Arthur Bernon Tourtellot begins *The Charles* (New York: Farrar and Rinehart, 1941) by retelling some old Algonquin legends. He continues with stories recorded by John Winthrop, stories that have assumed the status of legends, and other early tales of Boston and its citizens. Harry Emerson Wildes, author of *The Delaware* (New York: Farrar and Rinehart, 1940), includes tales of Henry Hudson. And *The St. Lawrence* (New York: Farrar and Rinehart, 1942), by Henry Beston, incorporates several tales of French Canada.

Some well-known authors contributed books to this series, including Edgar Lee Masters, Robert Peter Coffin, and Carl Carmer. See the box for a list of titles in this series.

American Customs Series

Each volume in the American Customs series describes various customs and folkways. The volumes often have a great deal of information about occupations

The Allagash, Lew Dietz, 1968

The Allegheny, Frederick Way, 1942

The American: River of El Dorado, Margaret Sanborn, 1974

The Arkansas, Clyde Brion Davis, 1940

The Brandywine, Henry Seidel Canby, 1941

The Cape Fear, Malcolm Ross, 1965

The Chagres, River of Westward Passage, John Easter Minter, 1948

The Charles, Arthur Bernon Tourtellot, 1941

The Chicago, Harry Hansen, 1942

The Colorado, Frank Waters 1946

The Columbia, Stewart Hall Holbrook, 1956

The Connecticut, Walter R. Hard, 1947

The Cumberland, James McCague, 1973

The Cuyahoga, William Ellis, 1975

The Delaware, Harry E. Wildes, 1940

The Everglades: River of Grass, Marjory Stoneman Douglas, 1947

The Fraser, Bruce Hutchinson, 1950

The French Broad, Wilma Dykeman, 1955

The Genesee, Henry W. Clune, 1963

The Gila, River of the Southwest, Edwin Corle, 1951

The Housatonic: Puritan River, Chard Powers Smith, 1946

The Hudson, Carl Lamson Carmer, 1939

The Humboldt, Highroad of the West, Dale Lowell Morgan, 1943

The Illinois, James Gray, 1940

The James, from Iron Gate to the Sea, Blair Niles, 1939

The Kaw: The Heart of a Nation, Floyd Streeter, 1941

Kennebec, Cradle of Americans, Robert Coffin, 1937

The Kentucky, Thomas D. Clark, 1942

A Log to New York City, Warren E. Brant, 1985

Lower Mississippi, Hodding Carter, 1942

The Mackenzie, Leslie Roberts, 1949

The Merrimack, Raymond Holden, 1958

The Minnesota: Forgotten River, Evan Jones, 1962

The Missouri, Stanley Vestal, 1945

The Mohawk, Codman Hislop, 1948

The Monongahela, Richard Bissell, 1952

The Niagara, Donald Braider, 1972

The Ohio, Richard Banta, 1949

The Potomac, Frederick Gutheim, 1949

Powder River: Let'er Buck, Maxwell S. Burt, 1938

River of the Carolinas: The Santee, Henry Savage, 1956

Rivers of the Eastern Shore, Hulbert Footner, 1944

The Sacramento, River of Gold, Julian Dana, 1959

The St. Croix: Midwest Border River, James Taylor Dunn, 1965

The St. Johns, A Parade of Diversities, James B. Cabell, 1943

The St. Lawrence, Henry Beston, 1942

The St. Lawrence, Henry Beston, 1951

The Salinas: Upside-Down River, Anne B. Fisher, 1945

Salt Rivers of the Massachusetts Shore, Henry Forbush Howe, 1951

The Sangamon, Edgar Lee Masters, 1942

The Saskatchewan, Marjorie Elliott Wilkins Campbell, 1950

The Savannah, Thomas Stokes, 1951

The Shenandoah, Julia Davis Adams, 1945

Songs of the Rivers of America, Carl Lamson Carmer, 1942

The Susquehanna, Carl Lamson Carmer, 1967

Suwannee River, Strange Green Land, Cecil Matschat, 1938

The Tennessee, Donald Davidson, 1946

Twin Rivers, the Raritan and the Passaic, Harry E. Wildes, 1943

Upper Mississippi, a Wilderness Saga, Walter Havighurst, 1937

The Wabash, William Wilson, 1940

The Winooski, Heartway of Vermont, Ralph Nading Hill, 1949

The Wisconsin, River of a Thousand Isles, August Derleth, 1942

The Yukon, Richard Mathews 1968

AMERICAN CUSTOMS SERIES

It's an Old California Custom, Lee Shippey, 1948

It's an Old Cape Cod Custom, Edwin Mitchell, 1949

It's an Old New England Custom, Edwin Mitchell, 1946

It's an Old New Orleans Custom, Lura Robinson, 1948

It's an Old Pennsylvania Custom, Edwin Mitchell, 1947

It's an Old State of Maine Custom, Edwin Mitchell, 1949

It's an Old Wild West Custom, Duncan Emrich, 1949

SOCIETY IN AMERICA SERIES

The Amiable Baltimoreans, Francis F. Beirne, 1951

The Lusty Texans of Dallas, John William Rogers, 1951; 1960

Memphis Down in Dixie, Shields McIlwaine, 1948

The Proper Bostonians, Cleveland Amory, 1947; 1983

The Serene Cincinnatians, Alvin F. Harlow, 1950

The Spectacular San Franciscans, Julia Cooley Altrocchi, 1949; 1979

Washington Cavalcade, Charles Hurd, 1948

AMERICAN TRAILS SERIES

The Bloody Bozeman: The Perilous Trail to Montana's Gold, Dorothy M. Johnson, 1971

The California Trail: An Epic with Many Heroes, George Rippey Stewart, 1962

The Devil's Backbone: The Story of the Natchez Trace, Jonathan Daniels, 1952; 1971

Doomed Road of Empire: The Spanish Trail of Conquest, Hodding Carter, 1963; 1971

The El Dorado Trail: The Story of the Gold Rush Routes across Mexico, Ferol Egan, 1970

The Gathering of Zion: The Story of the Mormon Trail, Wallace Earle Stegner, 1964; 1971

The Golden Road: The Story of California's Spanish Mission Trail, Felix Riesenberg, 1962; 1971

The Great North Trail: America's Route of the Ages, Dan Cushman, 1966; 1971

The Great Wagon Road: From Philadelphia to the South, Parke Rouse, 1973

The National Road, Philip Dillon Jordan, 1948

The Old Post Road: The Story of the Boston Post Road, Stewart Hall Holbrook, 1962; 1971

The Overland Trail, Jay Monaghan, 1947

Western Vision: The Story of the Oregon Trail, David Sievert Lavender, 1963; 1971

The Wilderness Road, Robert L. Kincaid, 1947; 1955

Winner Take All: The Trans-Canada Canoe Trail, David Sievert Lavender, 1977 and daily life. See the box for a list of the titles in the series.

Society in America

Published by E. P. Dutton during the 1940s, each title in the Society in America series titles profiles a different city.

American Trails Series

Historical trails are profiled in the American Trails Series published by McGraw-Hill. Hodding Carter and Wallace Stegner are among the authors.

American Lakes Series

Each book in this series, published by Bobbs-Merrill, profiles an American lake. Geologic history is included, as well as information about early inhabitants and explorers.

American Mountain Series

Books in this American Mountain Series contain chapters by various authors, all experts in the particular areas they write about. Chapters include information on the geology and geography of the mountain range, history of the area, flora and fauna, and activities such as skiing, hiking, or climbing. Vanguard Press published this series.

AMERICAN LAKES SERIES

The Great Salt Lake, Dale Lowell Morgan, 1947
Lake Erie, Harlan Henthorne Hatcher, 1945
Lake Huron, Fred Landon, 1944
Lake Michigan, Milo Milton Quaife, 1944
Lake Okeechobee, Wellspring of the Everglades, Alfred Jackson Hanna, 1948
Lake Ontario, Arthur Pound, 1945
Lake Pontchartrain, Walter Adolphe Roberts, 1946
Lake Superior, Grace Lee Nute, 1944
Sierra-Nevada Lakes, George Henry Hinkle, 1949

AMERICAN MOUNTAIN SERIES

The Berkshires: The Purple Hills, Roderick Peattie, 1948
The Black Hills, Roderick Peattie, 1952
The Cascades: Mountains of the Pacific Northwest, Roderick Peattie, 1949
The Friendly Mountains: Green, White, and Adirondacks, Roderick Peattie, 1942
The Great Smokies and the Blue Ridge: The Story of the Southern Appalachians, Roderick Peattie, 1943
The Inverted Mountains: Canyons of the West, Roderick Peattie, 1948
The Pacific Coast Ranges, Roderick Peattie, 1946
The Rocky Mountains, Wallace Walter Atwood, 1945
The Sierra Nevada: The Range of Light, Roderick Peattie, 1947

American Adventurer Series

This series consists of titles published for children, each one profiling an American adventurer.

AMERICAN ADVENTURER SERIES

Buffalo Bill, Frank Lee Beals, 1947
Cowboys and Cattle Trails, Shannon Garst, 1948
John Paul Jones, Vinson Brown, 1958
Kit Carson, Frank Lee Beals, 1943
The Rush for Gold, Frank Lee Beals, 1946
Wild Bill Hickok, S. M. Anderson, 1947

Sources Outside the Library

Libraries can provide much valuable material. Some of it is a bit buried and requires a diligent search, but treasures are available for those who look. Libraries aren't the only source of folklore material; there are wonderful finds waiting other places as well. The next chapter discusses some of these other sources.

Glossary

catalog: List of materials in a library's collection. In the past, catalogs were made up of printed cards, each card representing a particular item. Now, most catalogs are computerized.

CD-ROM: Stands for compact disc, read-only memory. This compact disc format holds data and graphics that can be viewed on a computer.

collection: The items a particular library owns: books, periodicals, videos, documents, and so forth. Sometimes the term is used to refer to items in a specific department of a library, such as an archives department or a department with local information

controlled vocabulary: Words and phrases agreed on in advance to describe items on a certain subject. A controlled vocabulary used in an index or a catalog allows you to retrieve all items on a particular subject, even if the titles of these items use various terminologies. All should have the same words or phrases used to describe them.

database: Information divided into separate records and collected together, with a system in place to retrieve individual items within it. Usually the term *database* refers to a computerized collection of information.

depository library: Some 1,300 libraries in the United States are designated by the U.S. government as depository libraries. These libraries receive, free of charge, documents published by the U.S. government. Such libraries undertake to make the documents available to the general public.

downloading: Moving or transferring information (a record, an item) from a database to a smaller, personal file, usually a personal computer.

government publications: Items published by a government. Both the United States and the United Kingdom are large publishers, as are many states.

graphical user interface (GUI): A way to communicate or talk to a computer or database using pictures rather than text. Abbreviated GUI and pronounced "gooey."

holdings: Items owned or housed in a library. Often the term *holdings statement* is used to list the specific issues of a magazine a library owns. For example, "*Time* magazine, 1926–1998" means the library owns the issue of *Time* between those dates.

Internet service provider (ISP): A company that provides a connection from a personal computer to the Internet.

natural language: A term usually used in reference to a computerized database, meaning that when searching for information in the database, you use ordinary terms, not specifically designated, consistent index terms. See **controlled vocabulary.**

online catalog: A listing of a library's items in a computerized format. Usually accessible not only from the library building itself but also from outside, via phone lines.

online public access catalog (OPAC): Another term for online catalog.

password: A word or set of letters used to identify a user and allow access to a restricted database.

periodical index: Listing of information in magazines and journals, usually alphabetical and arranged by subject and author.

periodicals: A publication that appears on a regular schedule, such as weekly or monthly.

public access catalog (PAC): A third term for online catalog. Online catalog, online public access catalog (OPAC), and public access catalog (PAC) are used interchangeably.

search engine: A computer program that allows a remote user to search for Web sites on specific subjects. The user enters keywords into the search engine and the search engine retrieves relevant Web sites.

search strategy: A plan for searching for information. A search strategy usually involves a listing of subject terms to search and places to search–specific libraries, collections, databases, or indexes.

subject terms: A word or phrase that describes a particular topic; all articles on the topic that are listed in a particular index are listed under that subject.

thesaurus: A book of words and their synonyms, usually concentrating on a particular subject. In the case of a thesaurus attached to a database, the thesaurus lists the specific words that are used to describe particular subjects.

Research beyond the Library

In addition to using standard techniques of library research to locate books and other materials on a folklore-related subject, folklore seekers can use myriad other sources. Some of the following suggestions do involve library research; they are intended to help you locate directories or other books that will in turn lead to further sources.

Museums and Historical Societies

Museums and historical societies store a wealth of information on folklore. To locate museums or historical societies in your area, the easiest method is to consult your local yellow pages, under a variety of listings, such as museums, historical centers, organizations, and associations. Remember that yellow pages are compiled by various companies, using different terminologies, so be creative in your search. Also remember that many museums and historical societies are run by governmental agencies, so consult your phone book under the government listings as well. There are a multitude of directories to help locate state and local museums, either geographically or by subject area. Try consulting the catalog of your local public or academic library under "Museums, directories" and the name of your state or city. Some of the most widely available and helpful are the following:

Blacks in Museums: A Directory of African American Museums and Museum Programs, 4th ed. (Wilberforce, OH: African American Museums Association, 1993).

Encyclopedia of Associations (Detroit, MI: Gale Press, annual). The entries listed in this encyclopedia include the name, address, phone, and fax number for various associations throughout the United States, organized by subject. Following that basic information comes a brief history of the organization and a thumbnail sketch of what its purpose and activities are, as well as a list of its publications. The book contains two indexes, one organized by keyword and the other organized by state.

Hispanic Resource Directory (Juneau, AK: Denali Press, 1996). This directory lists associations, research centers, libraries, and museums having a Hispanic emphasis.

Official Museum Directory (Washington, DC: American Association of Museums, 1980–. 31st edition: 2001). This directory lists museums located throughout the country, giving their names, addresses, and telephone numbers and a brief description of the museums. The directory is organized by state, then city within the state, making it easy to locate museums within your geographic area. An index by institution name lets you locate a particular museum, while an index by category allows you to find museums of special interest. Categories of interest to the folklore student include:

History–Historic Houses and Historic
    Buildings
History–Historic Sites
History–Historical and Preservation
    Societies
History–Historical Society Museums
History–Preservation Projects
Art–Folk Art Museums

Libraries having collections other than books:
    Specialized–Antiques
    Specialized–Costume
    Specialized–Furniture

World of Learning (London: Europa Publications, annual since 1947). This text lists libraries, universities, research organizations, learned societies, and museums worldwide. It is arranged by country, and under the United States, it is arranged by state. The listings for the country or state are arranged by

category: universities, research organizations, and so on.

Local Festivals, Fairs, and Celebrations

Many localities host festivals or fairs that celebrate the history of the area. These can be valuable resources for those seeking information on local folklore. One way to discover groups and individuals who sponsor such events in other areas of the country is to contact your local historical society. The staff may be able to assist you in identifying such events.

A sourcebook that identifies such local efforts is Frances Shemanski, *A Guide to Fairs and Festivals in the United States* (Westport, CT: Greenwood, 1984). This selective guide to fairs and festivals throughout the United States is arranged by state, then city. Each entry contains information on the history, special features, and date of a fair or festival. An appendix lists these fairs by broad category.

Many other sources describe festivals and holidays and discuss the folklore associated with them. The listings in the first chapter of Part 2 of this book describe many of them. Two of the major sources are described below.

Hennig Cohen and Tristram P. Coffin, eds., *The Folklore of American Holidays,* 3d ed. (Detroit, MI: Gale Press, 1999).

This source is arranged by date, moving chronologically through the year. An index by subject helps locate customs of a particular nature (for example, food or religious customs), and the table of contents is quite detailed and helpful in locating holidays that include customs of interest. Holidays noted run a gamut: well-known and widely celebrated American holidays (Fourth of July, Thanksgiving); regional or ethnic holidays (Bastille Day, Cinco de Mayo, Kentucky Horse Day); modern holidays (the anniversary of Elvis Presley's death, Kwanza); or religious holidays (Ascension Day, Purim). Try this source for everything from the somewhat obvious like Chinese New Year's celebrations or Easter egg hunts to ones known only to locals, such as the Florida Seminole Green Corn Dance, the pancake races on Shrove Tuesday, or Turtle Days in Churubusco, Indiana.

The editors of this work are well-known authorities on American folklore.

Robert H. Griffin and Ann H. Shurgin, eds., *The Folklore of World Holidays,* 2d ed. (Detroit, MI: Gale Press, 1998).

A companion volume to *The Folklore of American Holidays,* listed above, this source follows a similar chronological arrangement. Under each date—or approximate date, as some holidays move from year to year—are listed customs from all over the world, arranged by country. This is a good place to look if you're interested in expanding your knowledge of the rich folk culture associated with holidays. It will show you how some of your local customs originated and evolved.

Programs and Courses in Folklore

If you're interested in pursuing folklore as an academic study, you can find colleges and universities that offer either a degree in the field or an area of emphasis within another field by consulting *The College Blue Book,* 25th ed. (New York: Macmillan, 1995). *The College Blue Book,* a multi-volume reference source for information

on colleges and universities, will help if you are looking for an entire program in folklore, not merely one or two courses. *The Blue Book* lists which schools offer degrees in particular fields. Use the volume "Degrees Offered by Colleges and Subjects," consult the section arranged by subject, and look up "Folklore."

You can also check the Internet at *www.lcweb.loc.gov/folklife/source/grad.html* for a list of colleges and universities offering programs in folklore. This source only lists those organizations that offer complete programs, not schools that only offer a course or two.

Perhaps you just want to take a course or two in the field or a course that emphasizes the folklore of your locale. Many local colleges and universities have courses in folklore, either for college credit or through an adult education program offering no credit. To find out what's available locally, the first thing to do is simply contact the college(s). Ask for the folklore department, but remember that many colleges do not have a full department. Other departments that might offer courses or programs in folklore include history, literature or English, psychology, sociology, women's studies, African American studies, Hispanic studies, and ethnic studies.

To obtain more information about a particular school's programs and courses, you can contact the admissions office of the school and ask that a catalog be sent. Often there is a small charge for it, but having a catalog at hand allows you to explore course offerings thoroughly.

You can also use the Internet to obtain information on schools in your areas. Almost all colleges now have a home page, and many have their catalogs or course offerings listed on the Web. Often, although not always, the Internet address for a college or university is *http://www.schoolname.edu.*

Studying Online

Several colleges and universities present their entire curriculum online, over the Internet. Students can take courses online, often at their own pace, using a home computer. They complete coursework, submit papers, and talk to their instructors and fellow students online. In addition, almost all colleges and universities now offer at least some of their courses on-line, sometimes including history and folklore.

You can try a Web search for folklore courses, using an Internet search engine such as Yahoo or Google. You can also search Fathom.com, OnlineLearning.net, R1edu.org, or CyberU.com to get directories and links to online programs and courses. These sites allow searches by keyword and connect you with institutions that offer online courses in the fields you search.

Other Places to Study Folklore

A number of other organizations often offer adult education courses in folklore. They include:

* Local historical societies
* Churches
* Adult education programs run by the public school district
* Public libraries
* YMCA, YWCA, or similar groups

Often a local paper has weekly listings of such course offerings.

National and State Parks and Monuments

Both national and state park and monument sites are often planned around areas of local interest. Sometimes these sites have connections to local folklore. Moreover, the state and local agencies responsible for these sites often have printed literature available that describes each site and its history. One way of locating local sites of interest is through the government pages of a telephone directory, under either the state or the federal government listings; look under National Parks in the federal government listings.

In addition, there are a number of directories that list national and local parks and monuments. Some are listed below.

American Automobile Association. *AAA Guide to the National Parks.* Compiled by Doreen Russo. New York: Collier Books, Macmillan, 1994, 0-02-062049-7. Two features of this book make it of interest to folklore searchers. One is the introductory material on each park. Such material often contains a capsule history of the area, including information on local folklore. The other is the section entitled "Other Points of Interest (Museums, Historic Sites, etc.)," which directs you to other sites nearby that would be of interest. Such sites might include historic buildings, farms, factories, villages, or museums, any of which might be of interest to those pursuing local folklore connections.

Curtis, Nancy C. *Black Heritage Sites: An African American Odyssey and Finder's Guide.* Chicago: ALA, 1996. This is a guide to sites of historical significance to African Americans, many of which are connected to folklore characters and legends. It also lists historic sites related to such African American folklorists as Zora Neale Hurston. Its listings of sites that explicate the African American's life from earlier days make it useful from a material culture standpoint.

National Register of Historic Places 1966– 1991. Nashville, TN: American Association for State and Local History, 1991. This voluminous, closely printed text is a complete listing of all sites listed on the National Register of Historic Places. Obviously many, perhaps most, of the places listed will not be of interest to someone looking for folklore studies. However, because the list is arranged by state and then by county within each state, it is easy enough to scan the listings for a particular geographic area. Some sites are connected with local characters and personages. The text's front matter lists state historic preservation officers for each state. These people and their offices might prove to be a valuable resource.

Smith, Darren L., ed. *Parks Directory of the U.S.: A Guide to 3,700 National and State Parks, Recreation Areas, Historic Sites, Battlefields, Monuments, Forests, Preserves, Memorials, Seashores, and Other Designated Recreation Areas in the United States Administered by National and State Park Agencies,* 2d ed. Detroit: Omnigraphics, Inc., 1994. The lengthy title is indicative of the wealth of information contained in this volume.

It is arranged by state. Many of the sites listed are purely recreational in nature, with hiking trails or campsites, but some have folklore connections as well. For example, Fort Tejon State Historic Park in Friant, California, has a museum of local history and army life. Fort Boonesborough State Park in Richmond, Kentucky, is a reconstructed fort of the Daniel Boone era, which tells his story and the story of that time. Craftsmen on site demonstrate old crafts. The Fort Abraham Lincoln State Park in Mandan, North Dakota, has a museum with exhibits on the life of the Mandan Indians. Numerous other sites present activities related to folklore.

Again, the Internet will be useful in a search for information about national, state, and local monuments. Two Web sites to explore are the National Park Service site, maintained by the U.S. government, and the home page for your own state. The National Park Service site is at *www.nps.gov/.* It leads to information about national parks and national historical landmarks. You can search by a state and get a listing of sites in that state, or you could also search by a subject or interest, for example:

* Battlefields
* American presidents
* Early explorers

And by specific ethnic groups, for example:

* African American
* Alaskan Native
* Pacific Islander

You can combine those two searches to get information about a certain subject area that emphasizes a particular ethnic group.

The general Web site address for a state home page is *www.state.statenamehere.us,* with the two-digit ZIP code abbreviation for the state inserted in the statenamehere placeholder. For example, to reach the home page for Massachusetts, you would use as an address *www.state.ma.us;* for California, *www.state.ca.us.* Explore the homepage for the state or states you're interested in. Each is set up slightly differently, but many have links to information about the history of the state, or to sites of historical interest. Don't forget that if you don't have access to the Internet at home, your local public library probably does.

Newspapers

Investigate local newspapers, both daily and weekly. Try regional ones if the town you're interested in doesn't have one. Many small town or regional newspapers include or have included stories about local characters or events in folklore. A resident might write a weekly or monthly column on folklore or happenings of local interest. Occasionally the author will compile these columns and publish them as a book; some of these books are listed in the bibliography. Locating specific stories might take a bit of effort and legwork. Many newspapers will allow access to old issues, either on microfilm or in paper copy, but accessing them is not always easy. Problems in accessing newspaper stories include

* Old issues could be missing, because of destruction of the newspaper building itself in a fire or flood
* Old issues might not have been kept
* Old issues could have been printed on paper that is now deteriorating

A major obstacle to accessing old newspapers is a lack of indexing. Some newspapers, particularly major ones like the *New York Times* or *Washington Post,* are thoroughly indexed. You can find either print or computer indexes of these major newspapers at large and medium-sized libraries. Sometimes the index will be specific to an individual paper; however there are indexes covering hundreds of publications. One of these larger indexes is the Lexis-Nexis system, which indexes both magazines and newspapers. Many libraries subscribe to this service. Other, similar, computerized indexes exist. Ask at your library to see what they offer. In general, indexes of newspapers are similar to those of magazines and provide the following information:

* Author of article, if available
* Title of article
* Title of newspaper
* Date the article appeared
* Pages on which the article appeared

Most computerized newspaper indexes allow you to limit your search to information from a particular paper or articles published on a certain date. If you know that information, be sure to enter it as part of your search. If you're looking only for information on a certain topic, or material related to a specific geographic area, you can do a keyword or subject search to retrieve relevant articles.

In some cases, the full text of the article will appear in the index. If this is not the case, you will have to locate the actual article. To do this you will need to copy down the information about the article provided by the index (title, author, title of magazine, date, and pages).

A good source for small newspapers is a state historical society. They sometimes preserve various newspapers from throughout the state.

Storytelling

The art of storytelling has always endured, despite the development of rivals such as radio, television, and movies. Today, even with such competition as video games and the Internet, storytelling is enjoying a resurgence in popularity. Perhaps our fast-paced, electronic world has fueled a new interest in the personal, intimate art of storytelling. Storytellers are available to entertain or to speak at conferences or at such activities as community meetings or church events. Some of their stories are based on local legends. Many storytellers teach courses that can help you discover the stories that live in your own experiences and families. Most storytellers have spent years collecting stories. They have a great deal of information to share and can put you in touch with some of their sources.

There are a number of storytelling societies. Contact one; a member might be able to put you in touch with local groups. Your local historical society might also be of help in locating local storytellers.

Storytelling organizations include:

By Word of Mouth Storytelling Guild (*http://shorock.com/folk/bwom/9th/ contact.html*)
Box 56

Frankford, MO 63441
314-784-2589

International Order of E.A.R.S.
(*http://www.cornislandstorytelling festival.org*)
12019 Donohue Ave.
Louisville, KY 40243
502-245-0643

Jewish Storytelling Coalition
(*http://www.ultranet.com/~jewish/story. html*)
63 Gould Road
Waban, MA 02168

National Association of Black Storytellers (*http://www.nabsnet.org/*)
P.O. Box 67722
Baltimore, MD 21215
410-947-1117

National Story League
c/o Virginia Dare Shope
1342 4th Ave., Juniata
Altoona, PA 16601
814-942-3449

National Storytelling Network
(*http://www.storynet.org*)
P.O. Box 309
Jonesborough, TN 37659
423-753-2171

Books on storytelling can provide hints on telling your own story—how to get started, possible triggers to loosen memories, settings that are more conducive than others to successful storytelling sessions—and detail how storytelling can help bind families and friends together.

Cooper, Patsy. *When Stories Come to School: Telling, Writing, and Performing*

Stories in the Early Childhood Class Room. New York: Teachers and Writers Collaborative, 1993.

Davis, Donald. *Telling Your Own Stories: For Family and Classroom Storytelling, Public Speaking, and Personal Journaling.* Little Rock, AR: August House, 1993.

Greene, Ellen. *Storytelling: Art and Technique,* 3d ed. New Providence, NJ: R. R. Bowker, 1996.

Hayes, Joe. *Here Comes the Storyteller.* El Paso, TX: Cinco Punto Press, 1996.

Meyer, Richard J. *Stories from the Heart: Teachers and Students Researching Their Literary Lives.* Mahwah, NJ: Lawrence Erlbaum Assoc., 1996.

National Directory of Storytelling. Jonesborough, TN: National Association for the Preservation and Perpetuation of Storytelling, 1994.

National Storytelling Association. *Tales as Tools: The Power of Story in the Classroom.* Jonesborough, TN: National Storytelling Press, 1994.

Personal Contacts

Throughout your search, you can find people who can help you. You'll find experts as well as people just starting out on the search. All of them might have information or enthusiasm to share. As you search, remember to ask questions of:

* Professors and teachers who teach in the field
* Local authors whose characters, settings, or plots are based on local incidents or people
* Librarians in history departments or societies
* Children's librarians who run story hours
* Journalists who have researched interesting or bizarre happenings, or well-known local characters
* Elderly, longtime residents of the area, who always have fascinating stories to tell

Especially for Children

Children might need to participate in a folklore research project, or simply be interested in finding information about their local area. Some reasons for children to get involved in such research include:

* A project for school
* A project for Scouts or other youth groups
* Participation in a local festival or celebration
* Discovering more information on a favorite character

If your child is involved in a folklore project, some things to do might be:

* Check the appropriate regional section of this bibliography for the subsection "Folklore for Children," to get a listing of folklore sources written for children
* Read stories about folklore characters such as Pecos Bill or Paul Bunyan
* Look for children's activities books that feature folklore subjects
* Play old-fashioned games and sing the old songs
* Find old jokes and riddles
* Cook using old recipes

* Talk to elderly relatives and friends and hear their stories of the old days
* Visit your public library
* Visit a local historical society
* Visit nearby sites of historical interest

And of course, there's the Internet. Most children enjoy using a computer, and what seems tedious in a book might be more enticing on a computer screen. Some things to be aware of when allowing your child to search the Net for material include:

* As discussed previously, the Internet contains information from a variety of sources and people. Some sources will be valid and believable, others will not. Children might not be able to differentiate between the reliable and the bogus.
* Much of the material retrieved could be too advanced and complicated for a child to understand.
* And finally, some material on the Internet isn't suitable for viewing by children, because of sexual or violent content. Even a search for an innocent topic in folklore could turn up unsuitable material.

To counteract the last difficulty, some libraries and individuals have installed filters on their computers, which blocks access to questionable material. There are pros and cons to this solution. On the positive side, filters will prevent access to a lot of undesirable material, but no filter is completely effective, and some material you might think unsuitable for your child could still be retrieved. Filters also can block out harmless and potentially useful sites that happen to match the parameters set up for blocking. Using a filter to block certain portions of the Internet is a personal decision.

Using This Bibliography

The material that follows in this bibliography should help you locate sources helpful to your project or to your geographic area. Sources are arranged geographically, with a section for each area of the country. All sources are described and range from the classic, old-but-still-valuable to the very recent. Examples of the former include Henry R. Schoolcraft's *The Myth of Hiawatha, Other Oral Legends, Mythologic and Allegoric, of the North American Indians* (Philadelphia: J. B. Lippincott, 1856) and numerous works by Cecil Sharp, who collected folk music of the Appalachians. Both of these authors represent early attempts to collect and preserve the oral traditions of "the folk." More recent entries in the bibliography are Rudolfo Anaya's *Maya's Children: The Story of La Llorona* (New York: Hyperion Books for Children, 1996) and Claudine Burnett's *Strange Sea Tales along the California Coast* (Long Beach, CA: Historical Society of California, 2000). Anaya retells the story of La Llorona for an audience of modern children, whereas Burnett retells the always-fascinating stories of sea monsters. All of these texts show the continuing interest in folklore and the tradition on which it rests.

PART TWO

United States

United States: Checklist

Look for tales on folk characters:

    Cowboys
    Frontiersmen and women
    Miners, loggers, and fishermen
    Railroad engineers
    Riverboat captains
    Sailors

Look for collections and studies by:

    Benjamin Botkin
    Jan Harold Brunvand
    Tristram Potter Coffin
    Richard M. Dorson
    Alan Dundes
    Stith Thompson

Find music collections by:

    Woody Guthrie
    Alan Lomax
    John Lomax
    Carl Sandburg

Explore the rich folklore heritage of ethnic groups:

    African Americans
    Asian Americans
    European Americans
    Latin Americans
    Native Americans

Find various types of folklore:

    Games
    Jokes
    Rhymes
    Riddles
    Songs
    Tales of heroes and heroines
    Tall tales

Consult journals:

    Folk Music
    Journal of American Folklore
    Material Culture

Bibliography

History and Study

1. Bronner, Simon J., ed. *Folk Nation: Folklore in the Creation of American Tradition.* Wilmington, DE: SR Books, 2002. xiv, 283p. Bibliog. (American Visions, no. 6). 2002-21206. 0-8420-2891-9; 0-842028927pa.

As general editor, Bronner brings together essays and articles from a variety of sources, folklore scholars, and time periods in a book that "explores the intellectual and cultural uses of folkness to cultivate the idea of an American nation and people" (Preface, p. xi).

Contributors include such well-known folklorists as John A. Lomax, Benjamin A. Botkin, Ruth Suckow, and Richard Dorson. Essays are on a variety of topics, including folk art, folk arts and crafts, and folk music. Two essays from the 1990s explore the idea of folklore as a strength of a multicultural society.

2. Brown, Joseph Epes. *Animals of the Soul: Sacred Animals of the Ogalala Sioux.* Rockport, MA: Element, 1992. xiii, 145p. Illus. Appendix A: The Ogalala and Siouan Speaking Groups. Appendix B: Uses of the Bison. Appendix C: Qualities Associated with Animals. Appendix D: Mammals, Birds, and Insects. Appendix E: Ogalala Names Relating to Animals or Birds. Notes. Bibliog. 91-29083. 1-85230-343-3; 1-85230-297-6.

Brown discusses both the everyday role of animals in Ogalala life and their spiritual significance. He also presents information about the significance of animals in Ogalala art. Throughout, he indicates the central importance of animals to Ogalala life and religion.

3. Brunvand, Jan Harold. *The Study of American Folklore, An Introduction,* 4th ed. New York: Norton, 1998. xxiv, 640p. Index. 97-26188. 0-393-97223-2.

This fourth edition of the classic first published in 1968 describes and discusses many elements of folklore. Brunvand begins with a discussion of "What Is Folklore?" In this, he discusses "fakelore," the imposed tradition not truly passed down in oral tradition. His definition of folklore is an oral tradition that exists in different versions and is anonymous. He considers folklore to be useful in rite of passage traditions and ceremonies. Subsequent chapters are on:

Folk Speech
Proverbs
Riddles and Other Verbal Puzzles
Rhymes and Folk Poetry
Myths and Legends
Folktales
Folksongs
Ballads
Superstitions
Customs
Folk Dances
Folk Games
Gestures
Folk Architecture
Folk Crafts and Art
Folk Costumes
Folk Foods

Brunvand divides folklore into verbal folklore (tales and legends, myths), partly verbal folklore (dances, games, customs, festivals), and nonverbal folklore (gestures, music, arts and crafts).

This is an excellent introduction to the study of folklore.

4. Brunvand, Jan Harold, ed. *American Folklore: An Encyclopedia.* New York: Garland, 1996. xviii, 794p. Illus. Index. Bibliog. (Garland Reference Library of the Humanities, vol. 1551). 95-53734. 0-8153-0751-9.

Jan Harold Brunvand offers a collection of broadly based articles on folklore. The encyclopedia includes articles on various groups (African Americans, Jewish Americans); activities (folk dance, folk art); holidays; and categories of folk material (ghost stories, tall tales). The inclusion of biographies of noted folklorists such as Zora Neale Hurston and Richard M. Dorson is particularly valuable.

The articles have bibliographies appended.

This is a good one-volume introduction to folklore, which will lead a student to other sources for more detail.

5. Carney, George O. *Baseball, Barns, and Bluegrass: A Geography of American Folklife.* Lanham, MD: Rowman and Littlefield, 1998. xxxvi, 287p. Illus. Index. Bibliog. 97-42879. 0-8476-8600-0; 0-8476-8601-9pa.

Carney has collected nineteen essays by cultural geographers, previously published in journals. Essays cover six different "folklife traits":

Architecture
Food and Drink
Music
Sports and Games
Religion and Cemeteries
Medicine

Essays explore these various themes in one of the eleven "folklife regions" defined and described by Terry G. Jordan:

Acadian French: southwestern Louisiana

Yankee: New York, Vermont, New Hampshire, and southern Maine

Pennsylvania: Amish country in Pennsylvania, Maryland, and Virginia

Upland South: Appalachian sections of West Virginia, Kentucky, Tennessee, Virginia, North Carolina, South Carolina, Alabama, Georgia, Illinois, Indiana, and Ohio; the Ozark sections of Missouri, Arkansas, Oklahoma; and the Texas hill country

Mexican: parts of Texas, Arizona, and New Mexico

Highland Hispanic: parts of New Mexico and Colorado

Mormon: Utah and parts of Idaho

African American/Lowland South: parts of North Carolina, South Carolina, Georgia, Alabama, Mississippi, Arkansas, Louisiana, and Texas

Mountain West: parts of Colorado and Idaho

Southwestern Native American: parts of Arizona and New Mexico

Plains Ranch: Western Kansas and Oklahoma; parts of Texas, New Mexico, Arizona, Nebraska, South Dakota, Wyoming, Montana, Nevada, California, and Oregon

Carney provides a map detailing these folklife regions.

6. Coffin, Tristram Potter. *Uncertain Glory: Folklore and the American Revolution.*

Detroit, MI: Folklore Associates, 1971. 270p. Name and subject index. Index to Song and Poem Texts. Index to themes. Illus.

Coffin's thesis is that folklore changes with the times and survives in a particular form in a particular age because a tale or story provides "reaffirmation, ethic, wisdom, and comfort needed by 'men born of woman'" (Introduction, p. 17). In other words, folklore provides necessary fundamental truths.

He explores this theme using folklore from the American Revolution, showing how the soldiers of that war used folktales to give themselves the comfort of familiar things in an unfamiliar world. Now tales of that war have become our own folklore and provide a sense of unity and of history.

Coffin distinguishes between folklore and *fakelore*, a term he borrows from Richard Dorson. The latter he defines as popular literature, rooted in Madison Avenue and the mass media, and usually created for the mass market, to sell something or for sale itself, rather than the oral literature rooted in the actual "folk." Such people as Stephen Foster, George Gershwin, and Bob Dylan—and their creations—he considers fakelore.

Fakelore, however, can become folklore. An item like "Paul Revere's Ride" by Longfellow, although created more from imagination than from historical fact in its details, has become the average person's standard source of knowledge about that event. Although it began as fakelore, with retelling in various forms, it has attained the status of folklore.

Helen Archibald Clarke, in *Longfellow's Country* (New York: Baker and Taylor, 1909), makes a similar point about Longfellow: that his works, founded in legend, have themselves become folklore.

7. Crawford, Richard. *America's Musical Life: A History.* New York: Norton, 2001. xv, 976p. Illus. Index. Notes. Bibliog. 99-047565. 0-393-04810-1.

Crawford emphasizes three strains of American music: classical, popular, and folk. In the folk music vein, he explores the history of Native American music, colonial music, military music, African American music, and music with a religious theme.

Arrangement is chronological.

8. Dorson, Richard M. *America in Legend: Folklore from the Colonial Period to the Present.* New York: Pantheon Books, 1973. xvi, 336p. Index. Notes. Bibliog. 0-394-46140-1.

"It is the thesis of this book that the vital folklore and especially the legends of a given period in American history reflect the main concerns and values, tensions and anxieties, goals and drives of the period." (Foreword, p. xiv).

Thus Richard Dorson states his belief in the essential truth of folklore, even if most tales are not completely accurate. He arranges his material chronologically, beginning with colonial tales of witchcraft and the devil, on through the cunning and canny Yankee, unschooled but clever. Later tales focus on Western themes of mining and ranching.

Throughout the tales, Dorson intersperses his own commentary, in which he attempts to reveal the truths that the tales convey.

Like Tristram Potter Coffin in *Uncertain Glory: Folklore and the American Revolution* (Detroit, MI: Folklore Associates, 1971), Dorson makes a distinction between folklore and fakelore, popular literature written for the marketplace rather than tales that grow spontaneously from people's experiences and memories. Dorson is the originator of the term *fakelore*, a fact that Coffin freely acknowledges.

In his last chapters, Dorson gives some examples of "urban legends," modern day tales and stories that are attaining folklore status.

9. ——. *American Folklore*. Chicago: Univ. of Chicago Press, 1959. ix, 328p. Bibliographic notes. Table of Motifs and Tale Types. Index. (The Chicago History of American Civilization). 59-12283.

Dorson's introduction to this work presents his view of folklore as "the oral traditions channeled across the centuries through human mouths" (p. 2). He also uses the introduction to present his distinction between true folklore, founded on oral tradition, and *fakelore* (his coined word), a "contrived, romantic picture of folklore" (p. 4), usually concocted for the mass market.

The rest of the book follows the natural development of our national and regional folklores, tracing the origin of various stories and characters. He also looks at immigrant folklore, African American folklore, and folk heroes.

The bibliographic notes are extensive, listing numerous invaluable sources for the study of folklore.

10. Dorson, Richard M., ed. *Handbook of American Folklore*. Bloomington: Indiana Univ. Press, 1983. xix, 584p. Illus. Bibliog. Index. 82-47574. 0-253-32706-7.

Dorson has compiled a scholarly book of readings by various authors. Section headings are Topics of Research (American Experiences, American Cultural Myths, American Settings, American Entertainments, and American Forms and

Performers), Interpretation of Research, Methods of Research, and Presentation of Research. This is concerned with the study of folklore and how to collect and interpret it, rather than with the tales themselves.

11. Dundes, Alan. *Mother Wit from the Laughing Barrel*. Englewood Cliffs, NJ: Prentice-Hall, 1973. xiv, 673p. Bibliog. 77-164923. 0-13-603019-x; 0-13-603001-7.

Some of the best known names in both folklore studies and African American studies are represented in this collection of essays, among them Zora Neale Hurston, Richard M. Dorson, Eldridge Cleaver, Alan Dundes, Claude Brown, Charles W. Chesnutt, Alan Lomax, and Langston Hughes. The book is not a collection of tales, but a discussion of African American folklore.

The various essayists discuss the tale, folk humor, folk song and music, folk belief, folk art, and the origins of folktales and beliefs.

This is an important look by many different people, who look at different aspects of folklore.

12. Green, Thomas A., ed. *Folklore: An Encyclopedia of Beliefs, Customs, Tales, Music, and Art*. Santa Barbara, CA: ABC-CLIO, 1997. 2 vol. Illus. 97-25924. 0-87436-986-x.

This two-volume encyclopedia has brief articles on folklore theories and subjects. Beginning students can obtain a great deal of information here.

13. Gutiérrez, Ramón A., and Geneviève Fabre. *Feasts and Celebrations in North American Ethnic Communities*. Albuquerque: Univ. of New Mexico Press, 1995. xiv, 195p. Index. Chapter notes. 94-42710. 0-8263-1593-3.

Festivals and celebrations, both historical and current, are not only described here, but are also discussed in the context of how they contribute to the building of a community. Celebrations in African American, Hispanic, Filipino, and Caribbean communities are included, from New York City, New Orleans, New Mexico, and the South.

14. Jones, Alison. *Larousse Dictionary of World Folklore.* New York: Larousse, 1995. ix, 493p. Illus. Bibliog. Biographical notes on prominent folklorists. List of ethnographical and folklore museums throughout the world. A Calendar of Festivals and Folkloric Events throughout the World. 94-73124. 0-7523-0012-1.

Obviously of wider scope than North American folklore, this still has much of interest. An entry on North American folklore gives a brief overview of some of the major relevant themes and characters. Other entries follow up on this article, with more information on characters and regions. For instance, there are entries for such folk figures as John Henry, Johnny Appleseed, and Paul Bunyan; as well as for historical figures who have become folk figures, such as Jesse James and Davy Crockett. The appendix of museums can help locate nearby museums with valuable collections.

15. Jones, Michael Owen, ed. *Putting Folklore to Use.* Lexington: Univ. Press of Kentucky, 1994. 264p. Index. Chapter Bibliographies. 93-2101. 0-8131-1825-5; 0-183108187pa.

A series of essays by different authors all address the issue of folklore's role and value in today's world. The essays are presented under three subheadings:

Promoting Learning, Problem Solving,
    and Cultural Conservation

Improving the Quality of Life
Enhancing Identity and Community

Part I includes essays on such cultural institutions as museums, homeless shelters, and schools. In Part II essays explore folklore's role in the business world: in an office situation, in the tourism industry, and in medicine. Part III concerns itself with identity issues, from the aged to craftspeople working in folk arts.

This book does much to move folklore from the category of arcane, historical study to a position in the forefront of society.

16. MacDonald, Margaret Read. *The Storyteller's Sourcebook: A Subject, Title, and Motif Index to Folklore Collections for Children.* Detroit, MI: Gale Group, 2001. xii, 712p. 00-48395. 0-8103-0471-6.

Both folktale collections and picture books are indexed here. MacDonald indexes folktale titles that are listed in *Children's Catalog,* as well as other titles that have proved enduringly popular with children's librarians and with storytellers. The motif index allows storytellers to identify and locate stories with a particular theme.

17. *Places of Folklore and Legend.* Pleasantville, NY: Reader's Digest, 1997. 144p. Illus. Index. (Explore America). 96-40045. 0-89577-9056.

Not strictly folklore, this book explores the places that have become legendary. Places included are

the route of Paul Revere's ride
Nantucket, the whaling center
the sites of John Brown's raid
the lost colony of Roanoke
Daniel Boone territory
the sites of the Texas revolution,
    including the Alamo

Cody, Wyoming, home to Buffalo Bill
the area where the transcontinental
    railroad joined together
the Klondike
the volcanoes of Hawaii

A gazetteer adds briefer information on another twenty-five sites.

The full-color illustrations include photographs of the sites in the present day as well as renditions of associated artifacts.

18. Price, Charles Edwin. *A Student Guide to Collecting Folklore.* Johnson City, TN: Overmountain Press, 1996. 30p. Illus. 1-57072-056-8pa.

This slim volume is geared toward high school students. It gives helpful hints on collecting recent folklore. Price suggests fruitful topics for research, such as interviewing local craftspeople about how their techniques differ or resemble techniques from earlier days; talking to their grandparents about their childhoods; or asking a local firefighter or police officer about a disaster or crime. He also offers hints about breaking down a research topic into manageable bites and organizing information. Some of the hints seem obvious, but would be useful to a young student. For example, show up on time for a scheduled interview and be polite!

19. Probert, Thomas. *Lost Mines and Buried Treasures of the West: Bibliography and Place Names, from Kansas West to California, Oregon, Washington, and Mexico.* Berkeley: Univ. of California Press, 1977. xviii, 593p. Index. 76-24596. 0-520-03327-2.

Fifteen states, in the West, Southwest, Midwest, and Northwest regions, and parts of Mexico are covered in this bibliography of lost treasure. Each state is dealt with in a separate section. Within each section, Probert has listed specific lost treasures, identifying each by its most accepted name. Under each entry of a lost treasure is a brief description of location; Probert uses present-day place names to locate the treasure. The description is followed by a listing of printed sources about the treasure.

The index allows access by alternate names for treasures. The index also lists authors of the references.

States covered are Arizona, California, Colorado, Idaho, Kansas, Montana, Nevada, New Mexico, Oklahoma, Oregon, South Dakota, Texas, Utah, Washington, and Wyoming; Mexico is included in its own separate section.

20. Roth, John E. *American Elves: An Encyclopedia of Little People from the Lore of 380 Ethnic Groups of the Western Hemisphere.* Jefferson, NC: McFarland, 1997. xii, 329p. Maps. Bibliog. Dictionary of Ethnic or Linguistic Groups. 95-5886. 0-89950-944-4.

Roth has collected information about the little people lore of 380 ethnic groups in North and South America. The information comes from personal interviews, oral histories, letters, memoirs, and archival research. Information about each group includes the habitat of the little people, the specific magical powers they are said to possess, and their social structure. He also gives information on specific characters in each group.

Roth provides maps to indicate where a particular ethnic group lives.

21. Sherman, Josepha, and T. K. F. Weisskopf. *Greasy Grimy Gopher Guts: The Subversive Folklore of Childhood.* Little Rock, AR: August House Publishers, 1995. 248p. Notes. Bibliog. 95-34555. 0-087483-423-6; 0-87483-444-9pa.

The authors have collected rhymes from children, relating to various fears and taboos that children have. Their premise is that folklore has long been used to mock and thus control these fears. Rhymes concern a host of childhood fears:

"Gopher Guts and Other Gross-Outs"
Sex, pregnancy, childbirth
Bodily functions
Relatives, friends, and enemies
Institutions—church, school, and
    camp—and rebellion against them
Holidays
Advertising
Television and other popular culture
Barney

Although many of the rhymes are commonly known among children, and indeed have been popular over several generations, the compilers made sure that each rhyme in this collection is still being said today. Each rhyme was told to the collectors by a particular child. Most of the rhymes are recorded in several versions.

22. Turnbaugh, William A., and Sarah Peabody Turnbaugh, eds. *Basket Tales of the Grandmothers: American Indian Baskets in Myth and Legend*. Peace Dale, RI: Thornbrook Pub., 1999. xv, 210p. Illus. Notes. Index. 99-71002. 0-9628314-1-7.

In their preface, the Turnbaughs state that their aim is to "recontextualize" Native American baskets, a word they admit is a buzzword. They mean that rather than looking at baskets only for their design and artistry, as artifacts, their intent is to wed them again to the stories they traditionally told and the role they played in other stories.

Throughout this book, the Turnbaughs blend descriptions and photographs of baskets with stories, both stories of the makers of the baskets and legendary stories in which a basket is featured or has a role.

Baskets and tales from throughout the United States are included, with a heavy emphasis on the Northeast, the West, and the Southwest.

The photographs and the stories of the makers build an impressive picture of this art.

Treasuries

23. Battle, Kemp P., comp. *Great American Folklore: Legends, Tales, Ballads, and Superstitions from All Over America*. New York: Barnes and Noble Books, 1986. xxiv, 646p. Bibliog. Index of Tall Tales and Legends. Index of Ballads and Verse. Index of Superstitions and Miscellaneous Lore. 0-88029-902-9.

Great American Folklore is in the tradition of such books by Benjamin Botkin as *Treasury of American Folklore* or *Treasury of Southern Folklore*. It is a compendium of tales, stories, songs, jokes, and superstitions, most drawn from such classic sources and folklorists as Mody Boatright, Carl Carmer, Frank Dobie, Richard Dorson, Zora Neale Hurston, Vance Randolph, and Botkin himself. The result is a collection full of well-known folk characters such as John Henry, Paul Bunyan, and Davy Crockett. Many of the tales are short—only a page or less—suitable for reading aloud or storytelling.

In his introduction, Battle deals with the dilemma of "folklore" that is more manufactured by popular media than it is spontaneously generated and transmitted by word of mouth. Unlike Richard Dorson, who deplores this manufactured folklore—or "fakelore"—as he called it, Battle believes that folklore is a product of both print and word of mouth, that "American folklore flows from mouth to print and back again. History blurs with folk legends and folklore feeds off history" (Introduction, p. xxi).

24. Botkin, Benjamin A. *The American People: Their Stories, Legends, Tales, Traditions, and Songs.* London: Pilot Press, 1946; repr., New Brunswick, NJ: Transaction Publishers, 1998. xxvi, 405p. Introduction by Louis Filler, which is a brief biography of Botkin. 97-27086. 1-56000-984-5.

Botkin compiles one of his typical collections: stories of folk heroes, tall tales, rhymes, jokes, and songs. There are animal tales, stories of witches and ghosts, tales for children. Stories of folk heroes include those of Davy Crockett, Casey Jones, Paul Bunyan, Buffalo Bill, and Johnny Appleseed. Songs are those of sailors and river men, lumberjacks, cowboys, miners, farmers, prisoners, tramps, and songs from African American culture.

25. ——. *A Treasury of American Folklore: The Stories, Legends, Tall Tales, Traditions, Ballads and Songs of the American People.* New York: Crown Publishers, 1944. xxvii, 932p. Foreword by Carl Sandburg. Index.

Both tales and songs are included in this compendium, by one of America's foremost folklorists. The tales are from all over the country, of heroes such as John Henry and Paul Bunyan; of witches and ghosts; of cowboys and outlaws. They include stories that are based in fact, tall tales, animal tales, and children's stories. The songs often include music transcribed.

This is a good introduction to the richness of American folklore, with something for every geographic area.

26. Botkin, Benjamin A., and Alvin F. Harlow, eds. *A Treasury of Railroad Folklore: The Stories, Tall Tales, Traditions, Ballads and Songs of the American Railroad Man.* New York: Crown Publishers, 1953. xiv, 530p. Index. 52-9973.

Both a historian and a folklorist took part in this compilation. According to the introduction, written by Botkin, Harlow, the historian, concentrated on material that illustrated the beginning of, the history of, and the jobs done on the railroads, including actual working methods. The folklorist, Botkin, concentrated on stories, tales, legends, songs, and poetry, such as those told and retold by the railroaders themselves.

27. Bronner, Simon J., ed. *American Children's Folklore.* Little Rock, AR: August House, 1988. 281p. Illus. Bibliog. (The American Folklore Series). 88-23469. 0-87483-068-0pa.

It seems that every kind of childhood tradition that most of us remember from our school days is included here. Traditional speech, such as taunts and insults, rhymes, autograph album inscriptions, song parodies, jokes and riddles, tales and legends, beliefs and customs, games, and toys, are all here. Tales and legends include horror stories, ghosts stories, and camp legends. The section on language includes information on secret languages developed by children to confound the adult world, such as pig Latin, and others much more confusing. Jokes are often of the cruel variety.

In his introduction, Bronner gives a brief look at the literature of children's folklore.

28. Coffin, Tristram Potter. *Folklore from the Working Folk of America.* Garden City, NY: Doubleday, 1973. xxxviii, 464p. Notes. Index. 79-97699. 0-385-038747.

Although most collections of folklore approach the subject regionally or geographically, this one approaches it through vocation or occupation. Coffin makes the point that much of folklore, particularly American folklore, is rooted in occupation: the folklore of mining, for example, or of lumbering. He divides the material in this book by genre—tales, songs, verses, riddles, superstitions, sayings, games, and dance—but labels each with an occupational description. Occupations run from the obvious (logging, fishing) to the obscure (circus performer, chimney sweep) to categories not normally thought of as occupations (college student, housewife).

The notes indicate sources for all material and provide relevant asides and explanations.

29. ——. *Folklore in America: Tales, Songs, Superstitions, Proverbs, Riddles, Games, Folk Festivals with 17 Folk Melodies.* New York: Doubleday, 1966; repr., New York: Univ. Press of America, 1986. xxiii, 256p. Notes on sources. Index. 86-9249. 0-8191-5355-9pa.

This was originally printed in 1966 under the title *Folklore in America: Tales, Songs, Superstitions, Proverbs, Riddles, Games, Folk Drama and Folk Festivals.* The subtitle indicates the various sections of the book.

In his introduction, Coffin provides a useful discussion of the differences between the literary tradition, the popular tradition, and the oral tradition. Literary tradition is written material, through which people of education transmit their culture. The oral tradition is preserved by those without the ability to read and write, who transmit the important information of their culture by word of mouth. The popular tradition is neither; rather it is a literature created specifically for mass consumption. Often this popular tradition mimics folk literature, as with the stories and songs of such manufactured folk heroes as Paul Bunyan and Pecos Bill, or the pseudo folk songs of Stephen Foster. Coffin is a bit more forgiving of the impetus to create this popular tradition than is Richard Dorson, who scornfully refers to such created folklore as "fakelore."

Coffin maintains that the oral tradition and the popular tradition are ever changing, and that at times, items created as popular tradition can be altered through the oral tradition until they become folklore.

All the material in this book was previously published in the *Journal of American Folklore.* Coffin provides sources of all the material and indicates what tradition a particular piece belongs to.

30. Dance, Daryl Cumber, ed. *From My People: 400 Years of African American Folklore.* New York: Norton, 2002. xliii, 736p. Illus. Bibliog. Index. 2001-44843. 0-393-04798-9.

Unlike Dance's earlier book, *Shuckin' and Jivin': Folklore from Contemporary Black Americans* (Bloomington: Indiana Univ. Press, 1978), which concentrated mainly on folktales, this monumental compendium of African American folklore collects the entire gamut of genres. Starting with a collection of folktales, including Br'er Rabbit tales and Tar Baby tales, it continues with a collection of folk music—spirituals, blues, and ballads. Dance then presents a collection of essays about the African American experiences, including essays by Willie Morris, Paul Lawrence Dunbar, Alan Lomax, Ralph Ellison, and Harriet Beecher Stowe. A section on folk arts and crafts follows, copiously illustrated with both black-and-white and color photographs. A selection of sermons is followed by a selection of personal memories. Also included are sections on soul food, proverbs, rhymes and songs, riddles and jokes, superstitions, and folk beliefs.

Dance has collected an enormous amount of folklore from different genres and presents it in an entertaining and informative way.

31. Emrich, Duncan. *Folklore on the American Land*. Boston: Little, Brown, 1972. xix, 703p. Illus. Index. Bibliographic notes. 72-161865.

Emrich includes some of everything in this anthology: tales and legends, rhymes and games, street cries, folk songs, beliefs and superstitions. He agrees with Richard Dorson's differentiation between true folklore of oral tradition and the "fakelore" of mass-produced heroes and tales and includes here none of the latter—no stories of Paul Bunyan, for instance. He also limits himself to folklore in English. Although he acknowledges a vast body of material contributed by and important to various immigrant groups (Pennsylvania German folklore, for example), he says he is trying here to provide folklore that can appeal to the broadest possible segment of the population.

He also does not include any physical folklore, any mention or description of such things as arts and crafts, rural industries, or cooking.

What is left is a satisfying anthology of mainstream American folklore, a joy to explore, whether to recognize loved favorites or to discover new ones.

32. Taylor, Colin F., editorial consultant. *Native American Myths and Legends*. New York: Smithmark, 1994. 144p. Illus. Index. Bibliog. 0-8317-6290-x.

This is more than a book of tales. Photographs of artifacts are included, in color as well as in black and white; and religious and traditional ceremonies are described and pictured. Many of the photographs are from the nineteenth century.

The book is divided into the following sections:

The Southeast
The Southwest
The Plains
Plateau and Basin
California
The Northwest Coast
The Subarctic
The Arctic
The Northeast

Each section is written by a scholar of the area.

In the introduction, Colin F. Taylor gives an overview of Native American mythology, making the point that "North American Indian mythology is intertwined with religion and can be separated into two major groups—that which concerns the tribe or clan, and that which relates to the individual. However, most important was the belief in the existence of a higher power, far superior to the natural qualities of Man" (p. 6).

33. Thompson, Stith. *Motif-Index of*

Folk-Literature: A Classification of Narrative Elements in Folktales, Ballads, Myths, Fables, Mediaeval Romances, Exempla, Fabliaux, Jest-Books and Local Legends, rev. and enlarged. Bloomington: Indiana Univ. Press, 1955–1958. 6 vols.

From the title, it is obvious that this work encompasses more than American folklore. It is one of, if not the only, major reference works in folklore studies. Thompson's purpose, in his own words, was to "arrange in a single logical classification the elements that make up traditional narrative literature" (vol. 1, p. 11). Building upon previous motif indexes, which were limited geographically, Thompson compiled an index that covered material worldwide.

Under extremely narrow topics headings, Thompson lists all the tales that relate to that topic. Scholars and students can use the Thompson motif index to locate stories and tales that deal with the same theme. Newly discovered folk literature is organized using these same headings and descriptions.

34. Thompson, Sue Ellen, ed. *Holiday Symbols: A Guide to the Legend and Lore Behind the People, Places, Food, Animals, and Other Symbols Associated with Holidays and Holy Days, Feasts and Fasts, and Other Celebrations, Covering Popular, Ethnic, Religious, National, and Ancient Events, as Observed in the United States and Around the World.* Detroit, MI: Omnigraphics, 1998. xiii, 558p. Index. 97-40379. 0-7808-0072-9.

Although this book addresses holidays worldwide, much of it concerns U.S. holidays and celebrations. Short entries describe the various holidays and the customs associated with them. Both religious and secular holidays, such as Father's Day, are included.

Tales and Legends

35. Barrick, Mac E. *German-American Folklore.* Little Rock, AR: August House, 1987. 264p. Bibliog. (The American Folklore Series). 87-14449. 0-87483-036-2.; 0-87483-037-0pa.

Although most people think that German American folklore centers around the Pennsylvania Dutch, this book shows that it has a much broader reach. Barrick explores the proverbs, riddles, rhymes, songs, folk narrative, games, customs, foodways, superstitions, folk art, and folk architecture of German Americans in all regions of the United States.

The introduction is a bibliographic essay that refers to numerous additional sources on German American folklore.

36. Bord, Janet, and Colin Bord. *The Bigfoot Casebook.* Harrisburg, PA: Stackpole Books, 1982. 254p. Index. Bibliog. 81-14586. 0-8117-0303-7.

The Bigfoot Casebook is divided into two parts. Part 1 is a chronological discussion of various Bigfoot sightings, with extensive quotations from various documented cases. Part 2 is also a chronological listing, with much briefer information on many more sightings than were covered in Part 1. The authors do not include any events that consisted merely of seeing a Bigfoot footprint; all cases documented included actual reported sightings.

The Bords state that Bigfoot, far from being a creature confined to the Northwest as is commonly believed, has been sighted in all states but three: Delaware, Rhode Island, and South Carolina.

37. Botkin, Benjamin A. *A Civil War Treasury of Tales, Legends and Folklore.* Secaucus, NJ: Blue and Grey Press, 1985.

xx, 625p. Notes on sources. Index. 81-81150. 0-89009-967-7.

Botkin has put together a collection of stories and anecdotes of the Civil War, culled from newspapers and magazine accounts, personal reminiscences of soldiers, papers of various historical societies, and a host of other firsthand accounts. Stories center not only around the famous, such as Lincoln and Lee, but also around the ordinary soldier or civilian whose life was touched or forever changed by the war. Botkin indicates sources for all the stories.

38. Botkin, Benjamin A., ed. *A Treasury of American Anecdotes: Sly, Salty, Shaggy Stories of Heroes and Hellions, Beguilers and Buffoons, Spellbinders and Scapegoats, Gagsters and Gossips, from the Grassroots and Sidewalks of America.* New York: Random House, 1957. xxix, 321p. Index. Notes. 57-10053.

The title of this book indicates at once that this is a typical Botkin work: a compendium, a collection, a melange of what he likes to call "floating literature"—literature without a known author or a fixed form, which changes in the telling or transmitting. Botkin divides this volume into sections and describes the sections as follows:

Country Wit and Humor
Boasting and Boosting
Hick vs. City Slicker
Humor of Minority Groups
Tricksters and Tricksters Fooled
Wise Fools and Foolish Wise
Artistic Liars or Whoppers
Preachers and Their Flocks
Hero Worship
Politics and Politicians
Symbolic and Allegorical Stories

Bizarre Stories
Bedroom and Backhouse Humor
Shaggy Dog Stories

The anecdotes are short, less than a page, and notes indicate the origin of each story.

39. Chittick, V. L. O., ed. *Ring-Tailed Roarers: Tall Tales of the American Frontier 1830–60.* Caldwell, ID: Caxton Printers, 1946. 316p. Illus. by Lloyd J. Reynolds. Notes on authors and sources.

A variety of frontier heroes, from a variety of American locations, appear in this book. Davy Crockett and Mike Fink are the best known, but also included are Joe Meriweather, Billy Harris, Sally Hooter, Mike Hooter, Arch Coony, and Dick Harlan. In addition, there are stories about archetypes such as the riverboat captain and the bear fighter.

40. Coffin, Tristram Potter, ed. *Indian Tales of North America: An Anthology for the Adult Reader.* Philadelphia: American Folklore Society, 1961. xvii, 157p. Notes to the Tales. Index of material on the North American Indian in *Journal of American Folklore.* (Bibliographical and Special Series). 61-11866. 029-273506-5.

Coffin has gathered these tales from ones previously printed in the *Journal of American Folklore.* He includes tales from many groups. They include animal tales, tales of creation, and trickster tales. His introduction provides background to the tales and an explanation of how an understanding of both the tales and the Native American way of life can enrich our own culture. The Notes to the Tales gives the original publication information for each tale.

41.——. *Parade of Heroes: Legendary Figures in American Lore.* Garden City, NY:

Anchor Press, Doubleday, 1978. xxxviii, 630p. Notes. Index. 77-80881. 0-385-09711-5.

Coffin brings together legendary figures from throughout the United States, from Daniel Boone and Davy Crockett in the East to Paul Bunyan in the Midwest. Many of the heroes here are not as well known.

Coffin includes tricksters, such as Br'er Rabbit and High John; larger-than-life figures, such as Davy Crockett; sports figures like Babe Ruth; outlaws, such as Jesse James and Billy the Kid; storytellers; and singers. He also includes some folksong in the volume.

42. Courlander, Harold. *A Treasury of Afro-American Folklore.* New York: Crown, 1976. xx, 618p. Index. Bibliog. Appendices. 75-31952.

The subtitle of this work is "The Oral Literature, Traditions, Recollections, Legends, Tales, Songs, Religious Beliefs, Customs, Sayings, and Humor of Peoples of African Descent in the Americas." It is indeed a compendium of many different types of folklore, and from all the Americas. He divides the material into folklore from the Caribbean, from Central and South America, and from the United States.

Courlander presents the material alone, without any accompanying commentary or criticism, beyond a brief introduction to each section.

Appendices tell the African stories that are prototypes of the tales told here.

43. Cunningham, Keith. *American Indians: Folk Tales and Legends.* Ware, Hertfordshire: Wordsworth, 2001. 400p. Sources for Stories. 1-84022-505-x.

For this collection of tales and legends from many Indian tribes, Cunningham

culled and chose from the extensive tales published in the early years of the *Journal of American Folklore,* between 1888 and 1934. In his introduction, Cunningham indicates that this was the time period when America as a nation "began to see what had been lost and what was in danger of being lost as a result of the American experience and expansion" (p. 17). One consequence of this realization was an increased attention on collecting the stories and traditions of various groups.

Cunningham includes one or more stories from thirty-five different groups: Abenaki, Achomawi, Acoma, Arapaho, Blackfoot, Carrier, Cheyenne, Chipewyan, Comanche, Coos, Cree, Eskimo, Flathead, Fox, Hopi, Huron, Iroquois, Mandan, Mojave, Navajo, Ojibwa, Papago, Piegan, San Luisenos, Shasta, Shawnee, Shoshone, Sioux, Tahltan, Tewa, Ute, Western Mono, Winnebago, Yavapai, and Zuni.

The collection is useful and valuable for two reasons. First, it presents a wide variety of tales, showing the breadth and sweep of Native American tradition. Secondly, Cunningham's introduction eloquently expresses the reason why such stories remain essential today: "Each story embodies a world view and way of life and relationships recorded by their teller and collectors. They are flesh made word" (p. 21). The Sources for Stories section gives the original citation in *Journal of American Folklore* for each story.

44. Dance, Daryl. *Shuckin' and Jivin': Folklore from Contemporary Black Americans.* Bloomington: Indiana Univ. Press, 1978. xxii, 390p. Biographies of major contributors. Notes. 77-23635. 0-253-35220-7.

Folktales form the bulk of this collection, although Dance also includes some proverbs and superstitions.

Tales include the following categories:

Tales of origin and naming
Tales of heaven and hell
Ghost tales
Conjure tales
Tales about religion
Self-degrading tales
Tales about white women and black
    men
Tales about women
Tales about marital infidelity
Ethnic jokes
Tales about the cruelty of white
    people
Tales about outsmarting white people
Outlaw tales
Animal tales
Risqué tales

45. DeSpain, Pleasant. *Sweet Land of Story: Thirty-Six American Tales to Tell.* Little Rock, AR: August House, 2000. 176p. Illus. Notes on the Stories. 00-056543. 0-87483-569-0; 0-87483-600-xpa.

DeSpain is a professional storyteller, who collected these tales from a variety of sources. The thirty-six tales are from various regions of the country:

Northeast
Southeast
Midwest
Gulf States
Rocky Mountain
Pacific Coast

Ghosts, outlaws, lovers, folk characters, and historical figures are all here. Folk characters include Paul Bunyan and Pecos Bill; historical figures are Jesse James, John Chapman—or Johnny Appleseed—and Calamity Jane.

The stories are meant to be read aloud or told.

46. Dorson, Richard M. *American Negro Folktales.* Greenwich, CT: Fawcett, 1956. x, 384p. Bibliog. Index of tale types. Index of motifs.

Here Dorson reprints almost all the material from two of his previous publications: *Negro Folktales in Michigan* (Cambridge, MA: Harvard Univ. Press, 1956) and *Negro Tales from Pine Bluff, Arkansas and Calvin, Michigan* (Bloomington: Indiana Univ. Press, 1958). He arranges the tales thematically into the following sections:

Animal and Bird Stories
Old Marster and John
Colored Man and White Man
Hoo-Doos and Two Heads
Spirits and Hants
Witches and Mermaids
The Lord and the Devil
Wonders
Horrors
Protest Tales
Scare Tales
Fool Tales
Lying Tales
Preachers
Irishmen

Most of the tales are extremely brief, half a page or less.

Dorson provides information about sources and about parallel tales. He himself, in his book *Handbook of American Folklore* (Bloomington: Indiana Univ. Press, 1983), says that the tales in *American Negro Folktales* are "conscientiously documented."

47. ——. *Buying the Wind.* Chicago: Univ. of Chicago Press, 1964. xvii, 574p. Illus. Subject, Places, Persons, and Title Indexes. Index of Tale Types. Index of Motifs. Index of Informants. Index of Collectors. Bibliog.

Dorson divides his book into seven geographical sections:

Maine Down-Easters
Pennsylvania Dutchmen
Southern Mountaineers
Louisiana Cajuns
Illinois Egyptians
Southwest Mexicans
Utah Mormans

All the tales transcribed here are directly from an oral source: Dorson writes down the exact conversation he had with each informant. Tales center on the sea, witchcraft, and a character named Barney Beal. Dorson also includes jokes, or what he calls "jocular tales," and ballads. Dorson supplies headnotes to the stories, in which he gives information on motifs and themes, and traces similar tales in other areas of the country or in other cultures. In addition to an index of subjects, places, people, and titles, Dorson provides an index of motifs, based on Stith Thompson, and one of tale types. He also lists all informants and the names of other collectors from whom he acquired tales.

His introduction is worth reading on its own; it gives much information on the methods employed by folklore collectors.

48. ——. *Man and Beast in American Comic Legend.* Bloomington: Indiana Univ. Press, 1982. xix, 184p. Introduction by Alan Dundes. Afterword by Jeff Dorson. Notes. 81-48622. 0-253-33665-1.

Dorson was working on this book at the time of his death in 1981. The bulk of the book was completed; Dorson had yet to write the introduction and conclusion. Alan Dundes, another eminent folklorist, provides the introduction, and Dorson's son, Jeff Dorson, contributes the afterword.

Dorson's own material is divided into two sections: one of fantastic animal creatures, the other of tall tales about people who are true historical figures but whose lives and deeds have been exaggerated into folklore.

Animals described are

The Windham Frogs
The Guyuscutus
The Sidehill Dodger
The Hugag
The Hodag
Oscar the Turtle
The Jackalope
The Hoopsnake
The Sea Serpent
Bigfoot

People are:

Jim Bridger
Oregon Smith
John Darling
Gib Morgan
Len Henry
Jones Tracy
Daniel Stamps
Hathaway Jones

In his introduction, Dundes speculates on the meaning of these creatures: Is the search for mythical creatures such as sea serpents a reflection of the romantic American nature? Is the preponderance of hybrid creatures, such as the Jackalope, a metaphor for the mixture of peoples that make up American society? Is the fact that so many American folk heroes are larger than life and perform impossible deeds a comment on America's sense of inferiority to an older Europe?

Both the introduction and Jeff Dorson's afterword give much biographical information about Richard Dorson, a giant in American folklore studies.

49. Erdoes, Richard, and Alfonso Ortiz, eds. *American Indian Myths and Legends.* New York: Pantheon Books, 1984. xv, 527p. Illus. by Richard Erdoes. Index. Bibliog. Appendix. 84-42669. 0-394-50796-7.

Tales come from all Indian tribes. They are grouped as follows:

Tales of Human Creation
Tales of World Creation
Tales of the Sun, Moon, and the Stars
Monsters and Monster Slayers
War and the Warrior Code
Love and Lust
Trickster Tales
Animals
Ghosts and the Spirit World
Death and the Afterlife

An appendix describes the various tribes.

50. Feldmann, Susan. *The Storytelling Stone: Traditional Native American Myths and Tales.* New York: Dell, 1965; repr., 1999. xi, 288p. Bibliog. 0-385-33402-8pa.

Creation stories, trickster stories, and tales of heroes and the supernatural make up this collection. Tales are from the Zuni, Seneca, Mono, Wintun, Blackfoot, Winnebago, Eskimo, Tlingit, Tsimshian, Micmac, Comanche, Malecite, Yokuts, Onondaga, Modoc, Menominee, Cheyenne, Pawnee, Bellacoola, Crow, Okanagon, Cherokee, Wishram, Ojibwa, Arapaho, Chilcotin, Quinault, and Tewa cultures.

51. *Folktales of the American Indian: 24 Stories from the Original Legends.* New York: Gramercy Books, 1916; repr., 1997. 303p. Illus. 0-517-18354-4.

First published in 1916 as *The Indian Fairy Book,* this presents twenty-four tales from a variety of Native American cultures. Tales deal with magic powers, with animals and birds, and with how various things in the natural world came to be. No background information on any of the tales is provided, nor is the culture from which the tales originate identified.

52. Green, Archie. *Calf's Head and Union Tale: Labor Yarns at Work and Play.* Urbana: Univ. of Illinois Press, 1996. 283p. Illus. Index. Bibliog. 95-50190. 0-252-02248-3; 0-252-06553-0pa.

Green has collected folktales concerning the workplace. He defines a folktale as a story that has traveled, that has survived generations, that transmits cultural wisdom, and that "ties personal history to community memory" (p. 7). According to Green, this collection of tales "amplifies the many accents in which American workers caress and curse their tools, troubles, and triumphs" (p. 5).

He maintains that many of these tales go back to ancient days. Modern day steelworkers have roots in the ancient god Vulcan, whereas today's sailors still listen to echoes of both Sinbad and Captain Ahab.

Tales come from all walks of life: blue-collar, pink-collar, and professional.

53. Hamilton, Virginia. *Her Stories: African American Folktales, Fairy Tales, and*

True Tales. New York: Blue Sky Press, 1995. xiii, 112p. Illus. by Leo and Diane Dillon. Bibliog. 94-33055. 0-590-47370-0; 0-590-56603-2, limited ed.

Folktales and true tales mingle in this book. Here are folktales of tricksters and fairies, of female giants with magical powers, and vampires. Here, too, are three tales of real life heroines, Millie Evans, Lettice Boyer, and Mary Lou Thornton. Evans tells about her life as a slave and describes her thoughts and actions when she was told about emancipation. Boyer talks about Depression times and about the courage and hard work that was necessary to survive those times. Finally, Thornton tells about her early days in Ohio and her family's struggles.

All the tales are told with the intent of giving a view of African American women's past and of connecting today's women with that past.

The illustrations are in full color.

54. Hughes, Langston, and Arna Bontemps, eds. *The Book of Negro Folklore.* New York: Dodd, Mead, 1958. xv, 624p. 58-13097.

The editors tried to collect folklore representing many strains: the well-known animal stories of the Br'er Rabbit variety; preacher stories; tall tales; stories of work, such as the John Henry saga; and reminiscences of slavery. They include also songs and poetry.

The last sections contain more contemporary material in the same tradition. The stories, songs, and poetry in these sections are by well-known artists: Brownie McGhee, Paul Laurence Dunbar, Richard Wright, Ralph Ellison, Alice Childress, and Langston Hughes.

55. Jameson, W. C. *Buried Treasures of the Atlantic Coast: Legends of Sunken Pirate Treasures, Mysterious Caches, and Jinxed Ships, from Maine to Florida.* Little Rock, AR: August House, 1998. 192p. Maps. Glossary. Bibliog. 96-38773. 0-87483-484-8.

Wrecks, treasures, and mysteries from both New England and the southern states are described here. Blackbeard is the most familiar tale in this collection; others are of a silver treasure lost off the coast of Delaware, a mysterious light off the Barrier Islands of North Carolina, and a pirate stash on Barron's Island in New York. Other states with stories to tell are Maine, New Hampshire, Massachusetts, Rhode Island, Connecticut, New Jersey, Maryland, Virginia, South Carolina, Georgia, and Florida. The maps are simple line maps showing an approximate location for the story.

56. Jones, James Athearn. *Tales of an Indian Camp.* London: Henry Colburn and Richard Bentley, 1829. 3 vol.

The preface of the 1829 edition is a lengthy rigmarole about a group of French aristocrats who have an interest in the native peoples of the American continent. They commission a French priest of great learning to study the tribes and ascertain, among other things, whether the American Indians share ancestry with the Tartars and whether the languages of the two groups are related. This priest, after much travel and study, convenes a gathering of all Indian tribes. It is at the gathering that the tales are told.

In the preface to the second edition, titled *Traditions of the North American Indian* and published in 1830, Jones states that the story of the French priest was false, written only to provide a framework for the tales. In this preface, he is more specific as to the tales' origins. Some he heard while growing up, others he solicited during his own travels in America, and still others he took from written sources. His references to these written sources are detailed.

The tales themselves concern the creation of the world and include themes of death, hunting, fertility, and love. This is a valuable early collection of tales from many tribes.

57. Kroeber, Karl. *Artistry in Native American Myths.* Lincoln: Univ. of Nebraska Press, 1998. xi, 292p. Index. Notes. 97-51506. 0-8032-2737-x; 0-8032-7785-7pa.

Myths and stories from a variety of Native American cultures are told here: Blackfoot, Yurok, Tlingit, Beaver, Cherokee, Kiowa, Chinook-Clackamas, Winnebago, Navajo, Nez Percé, Lipan Apache, Sioux-Dakota, Chinook-Wishram, Chemehuevi, and Sioux-Lakota.

The "artistry" in the title refers to the author's conviction that these stories are meant to be performed more than read, and that the performance adds to the experience. Because of this conviction, he has added commentaries to each section of the book, which are intended to help the reader experience the stories more as performance and thus feel the emotional component.

58. Leeming, David, and Jake Page. *Myths, Legends, and Folktales of America: An Anthology.* New York: Oxford Univ. Press, 1999. xi, 221p. Illus. Index. Bibliog. 97-48607. 0-19-511783-2.

Leeming and Page present various types of myths, legends, and tales, all of which have grown out of the American experience. They begin with creation myths, stories of goddesses, and trickster tales from various Native American groups. Next come stories from the early European settlers, both Hispanic and Anglo. Some of these are what Leeming and Page call "sociological myths," myths that helped a new country explain itself. Such myths as that of the self-made man are told here, as well as tales of such archetypes as the cowboy and the outlaw. Juxtaposed are stories of real people, such as Billy the Kid and Johnny Appleseed, who have become folk characters, and tall tale characters, such as Pecos Bill and Paul Bunyan.

Tales from both African American and Asian American traditions fill out the volume, including slave tales, tales of Br'er Rabbit—a variation of the trickster tales—and stories of modern-day heroes, such as Martin Luther King Jr.

Leeming and Page contend that all these tales and stories have gone into the American consciousness and have helped make Americans what they are.

59. Matson, Emerson N., comp. *Legends of the Great Chiefs.* Nashville, TN: Thomas Nelson, 1972. 125p. 72-5870. 0-8407-6242-9.

Creation stories are a major part of this collection, myths from Indian tribes of Idaho, Montana, Nebraska, North Dakota, Oregon, South Dakota, Washington, and Wyoming. Also here are tales of Coyote, of Sasquatch, and stories of real-life legends Sitting Bull and Crazy Horse.

60. McNeese, Tim. *Illustrated Myths of Native America: The Northeast, Southeast, Great Lakes, and Great Plains.* London: Blandford, 1998. 160p. Illus. by Richard Hook. Index. Bibliog. 0-7137-2666-0.

McNeese retells the stories, many of them creation stories, of a number of Native American peoples. Included are tales of the Penobscot, Passamaquoddy, Micmac, Iroquois, Wabanaki, Algonquin, Yuchi, Natchez, Creek, Cherokee, Tuskegee, Seminole, Choctaw, Caddo, Biloxi, Alabama, Chippewa, Ottawa, Ojibwa, Great Lakes Sioux, Winnebago, Cheyenne, Blackfoot, Pawnee, and the Iowa.

Like its companion volume, *Illustrated Myths of Native America: The Southwest, Western Range, Pacific Northwest and California,* this is illustrated by Richard Hook in vibrant full color.

61. ——. *Illustrated Myths of Native America: The Southwest, Western Range, Pacific Northwest and California.* New York: Sterling, 1999. 176p. Illus. by Richard Hook. Index. Bibliog. 00-550564. 0-7137-2700-4.

Like its companion volume, *Illustrated Myths of North America: The Northeast, Southeast, Great Lakes, and Great Plains,* this book tells the ancient stories of the groups mentioned in the title. Many are creation stories; others are tales of animals.

Each geographic section is prefaced by a brief discussion of the life lived by these ancient peoples: their religion, their domestic life, their relationship with their neighbors, and their economy.

The volume is beautifully illustrated with full-color, full-page illustrations.

62. Roberts, Nancy. *The Gold Seekers: Gold, Ghosts and Legends from Carolina to California.* Columbia: Univ. of South Carolina Press, 1989. xviii, 265p. Illus. Bibliog. 89-22563. 0-87249-657-o; 0-87249-658-9pa.

Ghosts, lost treasures, and legendary mining characters, such as George Walter, who salted his mine with gold, populate this book. There is the girl who died tragically and is seen walking in the woods, tales of voodoo, and tales of fortunes lost in gambling. Most of the tales take place

either in California or in South Carolina, but Alabama, Georgia, North Carolina, and Virginia are also featured.

63. San Souci, Robert D. *Cut from the Same Cloth: American Women of Myth, Legend, and Tall Tale.* New York: Puffin Books, 2000. xvi, 140p. Illus. by Brian Pinkney. Bibliog. 92-5233. 0-399-21987-01 0-698-11811-1pa.

San Souci organizes these tales of women by region: Northeast, South, Midwest, Southwest, and West. The women are from various cultures, African American, Anglo American, Mexican American, and Native American (Chippewa, Eskimo, Hawaiian, Miwok, Pueblo, and Tewa).

San Souci describes the women as follows: "These are women who controlled the power of fire and lighting (Hiiaka and Pale-Faced Lightning); women who were giant-slayers (Hekeke and Old Sally Cato); 'sisters under the fur' (Molly Hare and Sister Fox), who are every bit as spunky and clever as their counterpart, Br'er Rabbit; and women who were strong enough to triumph over the heat and thirst of alkali deserts along the California trail (Sweet Betsy) or the cold and near-starvation of the Arctic winter (Otoonah)" (p. xiii).

The illustrations are black and white, in a woodcut style. The illustrator, Pinkney, also provides a map of the United States, also in woodcut style, with the locations of the various stories indicated.

64. Skinner, Charles M. *American Myths and Legends.* Philadelphia: J. B. Lippincott, 1903; repr., Detroit, MI: Gale Research, 1974. vol. 1: 352p.; vol. 2: 345p. Illus. 78-175743. 0-8103-4036-4.

Skinner was an early enthusiast for legends and myths. This is his second collection; it follows *Myths and Legends of Our Own Land* (Philadelphia: J. B. Lippincott, 1896; repr., Detroit, MI: Singing Tree Press, 1969) and is a supplement to it. Unlike the first one, this is not arranged geographically, or indeed by any other method. The tales simply follow one another with no categories.

Tales are a mix of ghost stories, stories about local characters, love stories, and stories about unusual happenings. He includes Native American legends and stories as well as those of the later settlers.

65. ——. *Myths and Legends of Our Own Land.* Philadelphia: J. B. Lippincott, 1896; repr., Detroit, MI: Singing Tree Press, 1969. vol. 1: 318p.; vol. 2: 335p..

At the time he compiled his collection, Skinner believed that most people felt the United States was too young to have a body of legend. He disagreed, believing that such men as Washington and Franklin were our own legendary figures and that tales of spirits, of heroic battles, and of homespun virtue had grown over the history of the country and had become legend. Like other writers who collected folklore at that time, Skinner believed that some tales were already disappearing, victims of growth, urbanization, and homogenization, and he compiled this collection partly to preserve them.

He divides his collection geographically, beginning with tales of the Northeast, such as those of the Hudson and of Henry Hudson, then continues with such New England tales as those of Paul Revere, Miles Standish, and Mt. Katahdin. He continues across the country, with tales from the South, the Central States, the Rocky Mountains, and the Pacific Coast. This is a major collection of tales from all areas of the country.

66. Smith, Jimmy Neil, ed. *Homespun: Tales from America's Favorite Storytellers.* New York: Avon, 1988. xxi, 390p. Bibliog. 87-32989. 0-517-56936-1.

More than stories or tales fill this book. It is also a resource book for people who wish to become storytellers, or at least to enrich their lives and the lives of their families and friends through the telling of stories. The tales themselves fill the first two-thirds of the book and are told by a variety of tellers. Some are of the supernatural, some are tales of traditional American characters, and some are humorous stories.

The last third of the book concerns the craft of storytelling. Various storytellers tell how they developed and honed their talent, how they discover the stories they tell, and how they work to improve the telling of them. They also explain how storytelling can be of practical use in the world. Stories can sometimes reach people closed off to other communication: elderly, uncommunicative people in nursing homes, troubled children, people whose past has been painful.

The editor adds a list of American storytellers, a bibliography of books about storytelling, a list of storytelling organizations, and one of storytelling events and festivals that include storytelling.

67. Spies, Karen. *Our Folk Heroes.* Brookfield, CT: Millbrook Press, 1994. 48p. Illus. Index. Bibliog. (I Know America). 93-35013. 1-56294-440-1.

In this slim book, Spies packs information on sixteen American folk characters. The entries are obviously brief–two or three pages for each character. However, they are attractively presented, with copious illustrations, and provide the salient information. Characters included are

Ethan Allen
Molly Pitcher
Old Stormalong
Francis Marion
Mike Fink
Johnny Appleseed
Davy Crockett
High John
John Henry
Jesse James
Calamity Jane
Deadwood Dick
Pecos Bill
Hiawatha
Paul Bunyan
Iktomi

68. Squier, Emma-Lindsay. *Children of the Twilight: Folk-Tales of Indian Tribes.* New York: Cosmopolitan Book Corp., 1926. 257p.

Squier includes no explanation or historical background for these tales. Most are from the West and Southwest, and most involve animals and the Indians' relationship with them.

69. Thompson, Stith. *Folk Tales of the North American Indians.* Bloomington: Indiana Univ. Press, 1929; repr., [1966]. 66-22898. 0-253-20091-1pa.

Stith Thompson presents these tales in his usual scholarly fashion, with extensive notes, an index of motifs, and a bibliography. He arranges the tales by tale type rather than by geographic area, although the notes give ample information about geographic origins. Tales are in the following groups:

Mythological stories
Mythological incidents
Trickster tales
Hero tales

Journeys to the other world
Animal wives and husbands
Miscellaneous tales
Tales borrowed from Europeans
Bible stories

The tales are from the entire North American continent.

Folk Music

70. Dugaw, Dianne, ed. *The Anglo-American Ballad: A Folklore Casebook.* New York: Garland, 1995. xxii, 337p. Index. Bibliog. (Garland Folklore Casebooks). 94-24348. 0-8153-1747-6.

Two centuries' worth of writing on the Anglo-American ballad are collected here, beginning with two essays from *The Spectator,* written in 1711 by Joseph Addison, and ending with a piece on the relationships between African and Anglo traditions, written in 1984. The essays examine how the ballad has traditionally been used to cement a feeling of national or group identity.

The Garland Folklore Casebook series is edited by Alan Dundes, a noted American folklorist.

71. Lomax, Alan. *The Folk Songs of North America in the English Language.* Garden City, NY: Doubleday, 1960. xxx, 623p. Melodies and guitar chords transcribed by Peggy Seeger. Illus. by Michael Leonard. Bibliog. Banjo and guitar guide to chords and picking. Discography. Index of song titles. Map on endpapers. 60-15185. 0-385-04844-0.

Lomax has divided this book into four geographic parts: The North, The Southern Mountains and Backwoods, The West, and The Negro South. Within each section, songs are arranged also by theme, such as working songs, railroad songs, soldiers, or cowboys.

The introduction discusses the place and importance of music in American life and history.

72. Lomax, John A., and Alan Lomax. *American Ballads and Folk Songs.* New York: Macmillan, 1934; repr., New York: Dover Publications, 1994. xxxix, 625p. Index to titles. Bibliog. 94-17510. 0-486-28276-7pa.

Originally published in 1934, this is a collection of songs of "the cowboy, the miner, the tramp, the lumberjack, the Forty-niner, the soldier, the sailor, the plantation Negro (as also his sophisticated city cousin), the sailor on the Great Lakes, and even the boatman in the early days of the Erie Canal" (Introduction, p. xxvii), all those who settled and built America. Hundreds of songs are included, many with music transcribed, arranged by category:

Railroad Songs
Levee Camps
Southern Chain Gangs
Negro Bad Men
White Desperadoes
Songs from the Mountains
Cocaine and Whiskey
The Blues
Creole Negroes
Reels
Minstrel Types
Breakdowns and Play Parties
Childhood
Vaqueros of the Southwest
Cowboy Songs
Overlanders
The Miner
The Shanty-Boy

The Erie Canal
The Great Lakes
Sailors and Sea Fights
War and Soldiers
White Spirituals
Negro Spirituals

73. Lomax, John A., and Alan Lomax, collectors and compilers. *Our Singing Country: A Second Volume of American Ballads and Folk Songs.* New York: Macmillan, 1941. xxxiv, 416p. Ruth Crawford Seeger, Music Editor. Index of Songs. Index of First Lines. Bibliog.

A sequel to *American Ballads and Folk Songs* (New York: Macmillan, 1934; repr., New York: Dover Publications, 1994), this contains songs in the following categories:

Religious songs
Social songs (dance and game songs, lullabies, courting and love songs, tall tale songs)
Working songs
Outlaw songs
Blues

The Music Preface contains some suggestions on how to sing the songs: in as natural a way as possible, with or without accompaniment, keeping time with your foot, with or without harmonization.

74. Lornell, Kip. *Introducing American Folk Music: Ethnic and Grassroot Traditions in the United States.* Boston: McGraw-Hill, 2002. xviii, 302p. Illus. Index. Selected Song Index. 2001-44320. 0-07-241421-9pa.

Lornell begins with an introductory section of information about the place of music in American culture and the influence of mass media. He follows this with sections on various threads of American traditional music: Anglo-American secular folk music, Anglo-American sacred folk music, African American religious folk music, African American secular folk music, Native American traditional music, and Chicano music.

He spends some time on various folk revivals, including the popular folk music of the 1960s, interpreted by such performers as Bob Dylan, Tom Paxton, and the Limelighters. He also discusses how such music has been used to advance various causes such as civil rights and workers' rights.

Lornell includes a CD of various songs that he discusses in the book.

75. *The People's Song Book.* New York: Boni and Gaer, 1948. 128p. Foreword by Alan Lomax. Preface by Benjamin A. Botkin.

This is a friendly songbook—more than a hundred songs that have been sung and enjoyed by many people over many years. There are songs of the labor movement, political songs, songs of various working groups—farmers, railway workers, soldiers.

A guitar chord chart at the back helps a beginning guitar student get started.

76. Sandburg, Carl. *The American Songbag.* New York: Harcourt, Brace and World, 1927. xxiii, 495p. Index of song titles.

The introduction states that this book is "rich with the human diversity of the United States" (p. vii). In it are 280 songs and ballads from all regions. There are songs of lumberjacks and railroad workers, prisoners on chain gangs and sailors on ships, people in war and people at parties. It is a collection of the songs of all people.

77. ———. *The New American Songbag.* New York: Associated Music Publishers, 1950. 107p. Index.

About sixty songs, with music transcribed, are included in this volume, an update of Sandburg's *The American Songbag* (New York: Harcourt, Brace and World, 1927). The songs tell about many American themes: work, the cowboy, tall tales, love, and heroes.

78. Santelli, Robert, Holly George-Warren, and Jim Brown, eds. *American Roots Music.* New York: H. N. Abrams, 2001. 232p. Foreword by Bonnie Raitt. Illus. 2001–2511. 0-8109-1432-8; 0-8109-2139-1pa.

Blues, folk, Tejano, country, and rock and roll all feature prominently in this book. There are chapters, too, on African American musical traditions and Native American music.

Numerous photographs pepper the book, mostly of performers and performances.

79. *Songs of the Workers: To Fan the Flames of Discontent.* 34th. ed. Chicago: Industrial Workers of the World, 1973. 64p.

The title says it all: These are songs calculated to motivate workers to strive for better conditions, better pay, and a better life. No music is transcribed in the text, although many of the songs have an indication as to what tune should be used.

Folk Belief and Ritual

80. Castle, Sue. *Mother Knows Best? The Truth about Mom's Well-Meaning (But Not Always Accurate) Advice.* Secaucus, NJ: Citadel Press, 1995. 141p. Illus. 94-41190. 0-8065-1631-3pa.

Superstitions of all sorts make up this book, along with information either confirming or debunking them. Superstitions explored are on pregnancy and childbirth, sickness, the weather, pets, child care, and even exercise.

81. Engle, Peter. *Sneezing after Sex Prevents Pregnancy.* New York: St. Martin's Press, 1996. 97p. Illus. 96-27926. 0-312-14696-5.

Seventy old wives' tales concerning health are described and either confirmed or debunked in this book. It's not true that lemon juice will get rid of freckles. Nor is it true that crocodiles grab your shadow and pull you into the water. On the other hand, it is true that you lose most body heat through your head, so wearing a hat in cold weather is indeed a good idea.

As can be seen, the range of tales considered is broad, some well known and some quite obscure.

82. Gourse, Leslie. *Native American Courtship and Marriage Traditions.* New York: Hippocrene Books, 2000. vi, 178p. Index. Bibliog. 0-7818-0768-9.

Gourse intends this book to be helpful for couples planning weddings, adding hints on how to incorporate various Native American customs into the ceremony. Customs detailed are from the following groups:

Hopi
Navajo
Cherokee
Iroquois
Oglala Sioux

Gourse discusses food traditions, jewelry worn during a ceremony, rituals, and clothing worn.

83. Huson, Paul. *Mastering Herbalism: A Practical Guide.* New York: Stein and Day, 1974; repr., Lanham, MD: Madison Books, 2001. 371p. Illus. Index. Glossary. Bibliog. 2001-18324. 1-56833-181-9.

Huson includes more than the folklore of herbs, although that is a facet of this book. All aspects of working with herbs are included: growing herbs, where to buy them, and how to use them. Huson pays much attention to the traditional medical uses of herbs. One chapter, "Witchcraft and Wortcunning," discusses the magical uses of herbs.

Illustrations are black-and-white line drawings of various plants.

84. Jones, Leslie. *Happy Is the Bride the Sun Shines On: Wedding Beliefs, Customs, and Traditions.* Chicago: Contemporary Books, 1995. xi, 178p. Bibliog. 95-5084. 0-8092-3432-7.

Jones presents a potpourri of wedding customs and superstitions, from wearing a penny sewn into the wedding dress for good luck to putting three pieces of bread under the bridal bed, to ensure good luck for your children. No explanations or history of the superstitions are given.

85. Lys, Claudia de. *A Treasury of Superstitions.* New York: Philosophical Library, 1948; repr., New York: Gramercy Books, 1998. 494p. Index. Bibliog. 96-47411. 0-517-18130-4.

First published as *A Treasury of American Superstitions,* this book describes and gives background on a host of folk beliefs related to:

Birds
Flowers and insects
Snakes
Fish
Animals

Physiology and gestures
Women
Love
Courtship and marriage
Pregnancy, childbirth, and babies
Foods
Death and funerals
Clothing
Jewels and gems
Dreams
Sickness
Holidays
Work
Water
Sun, moon, stars, and planets
Good luck charms
Numbers

De Lys explores the background of many superstitions and explains why they have such a hold over many of us today.

86. Menard, Valerie. *The Latino Holiday Book: From Cinco de Mayo to Dia de los Muertos–The Celebrations and Traditions of Hispanic-Americans.* New York: Marlowe and Co., 2000. xvi, 174p. Bibliog. Directory of Latino Organizations in the United States. 00-21889. 1-56924-646-7pa.

Menard concentrates on the holiday traditions of three major Latino groups in the United States: Mexican American, Cuban American, and Puerto Rican. She organizes her materials by season of the year, with a section for each spring, summer, fall, and winter. Within each section she discusses the history and the customs surrounding various holidays. The major religious holidays–Christmas, Easter, Feast of the Virgin of Guadalupe–are here; as well as historical celebrations–Cinco de Mayo, National Puerto Rican Day, Cuban Independence Day; and family celebrations such as Quinceañera, the celebration of a girl's fifteenth birthday.

87. Rinzler, Carol Ann. *The Dictionary of Medical Folklore.* New York: Crowell, 1979. 243p. Index. 78-69518. 0-690-01704-9.

Rinzler has collected more than 500 items about folk medicine. She has arranged these alphabetically under general categories, so that all items about alcohol, for example, or chocolate or food poisoning are grouped together. She has attempted to establish the efficacy of each treatment or the truth of each statement.

An index helps locate desired information.

88. Santino, Jack. *All Around the Year: Holidays and Celebrations in American Life.* Urbana: Univ. of Illinois Press, 1995. xxi, 227p. Illus. Index. Bibliog. Notes. 93-1516. 0-252-02049-9; 0-252-06516-6pa.

Santino describes customs of well-known, widely celebrated holidays such as Christmas and Thanksgiving. He also gives attention to holidays celebrated in particular cultures, such as Laskiainen, a Finnish-American holiday celebrated in northern Minnesota. In addition, he spends some time describing some "homegrown" holidays and rituals, in which individuals, families, businesses, or communities create a holiday around a local celebration or event.

The first chapter places holidays in the American context, explaining why they continue to be meaningful.

89. Walker, Barbara, ed. *Out of the Ordinary: Folklore and the Supernatural.* Logan: Utah State Univ. Press, 1995. x, 218p. Index. Bibliog. 95-4422. 0-87421-191-3; 0-87421-196-4pa.

The authors of the essays in this volume believe that a belief in the supernatural influences our behavior in many ways. Various folklore practices reflect this. Essays here deal with precognition of events; folklore knowledge that influences farming practices; ghosts and hauntings; séances and attempts to communicate with the spirit world; and folk healing. Two essays explore specific folk cultures: the Hawaiian belief, shared by many, in the goddess Pele, and American Hmong folk beliefs.

90. Wyman, Walker D. *Mythical Creatures of the U.S.A. and Canada: A Roundup of the Mythical Snakes and Worms, Insects, Birds, Fish, Serpents, and Mermaids, Animals and Monsters That Have Roamed the American Land.* Revised and enlarged. River Falls: Univ. of Wisconsin-River Falls Press, 1978. x, 105p. Illus.

Wyman presents chapters on different types of mythical creatures: Snakes and Worms; Insects; Birds; Fish, Serpents, and Mermaids; Animals and Monsters; and Sasquatch and Other Ape-like Creatures. Within these categories he lists such creatures as Milking Snakes, which offer an explanation as to why one cow among a herd is dry; the Pinnacle Grouse, which is born with one wing and thus flies only in circles; and the Bog Hop, half beaver and half moose.

The lack of an index makes this more a book to dip into for enjoyment rather than one to use as reference.

Illustrations are sketches of the various animals.

Material Culture

91. Camp, Charles. *American Foodways: What, When, Why and How We Eat in America.* Little Rock, AR: August House, 1989. 128p. Illus. Notes. Bibliog. (The American Folklore Series). 89-33486. 0-87483-096-6.

Camp begins this volume with an overview of the literature in folklore scholarship concerning food. He continues with a discussion of the meaning of food in society and how food has become integrated into social situations and functions.

Specific chapters follow, on the place of food in:

Origin tales
Tall tales
Legends
Jokes
Songs
Rhymes

He also discusses the traditional calls from food vendors and how food figures in beliefs, customs, architecture, and crafts. Camp then broadens his scope with chapters on such folk-related aspects of food as table setting, the roles of hosts and guests, and the importance of timing in eating.

His final chapters look at food in celebrations and religious events.

92. Carlson, Barbara. *Food Festivals: Eating Your Way from Coast to Coast.* Detroit, MI: Invisible Ink Press, 1997. xiv, 428p. Cook-offs and Recipe Contests Index. Date Index. Food Type Index. General Index. Glossary. 97-971. 1-57859-003-5pa.

Arranged by state, this directory lists and describes food festivals throughout the United States. Carlson makes no claim to completeness; she states that a directory of Oktoberfests alone would be a volume equal in size to this one. The indexes are particularly useful, allowing one to locate festivals featuring a particular type of food or taking place in a specific month.

93. West, Amanda B. *Main Street Festivals: Traditional and Unique Events on America's Main Events.* New York: J. Wiley and Sons, 1998. xix, 214p. Illus. Index by Month. Subject Index. 97-33058. 0-471-19290-2pa.

The festivals described here "celebrate [the] local history, agriculture, music, food, and culture" (p. xi) of the towns in which they are located. Information about each festival includes location, description, dates, admission fees, and contacts.

94.Wilson, David Scofield, and Angus Kress Gillespie, eds. *Rooted in America: Foodlore of Popular Fruits and Vegetables.* Knoxville: Univ. of Tennessee Press, 1999. xiii, 239p. Illus. Index. Chapter bibliographies. 98-58096. 1-57233-052-x; 1-57233-053-8pa.

Ten fruits and vegetables have a place of honor here:

Apples
Bananas
Corn
Cranberries
Hot peppers
Oranges
Pumpkins
Tobacco
Tomatoes
Watermelon

They come from a variety of regions of the country, or from other countries. All have significance in our lives; "They have slipped into our minds and hearts as sym-

bols of what we value about ourselves and about the places we live" (p. xi).

Essays discuss the symbolism these products have in our lives.

Folklore for Children

95. Botkin, Benjamin A., and Carol Withers. *The Illustrated Book of American Folklore: Stories, Legends, Tall Tales, Riddles, and Rhymes.* New York: Grosset and Dunlap, 1958. 99p. Illus. by Irv Docktor. Title index.

Botkin and Withers include many forms of folklore in this compendium for children: stories, tall tales, riddles, jokes, and rhymes. Many of the selections are for reading aloud; others are participatory. Stories come from many cultures and countries, but have become American stories over time. In the words of the introduction:

There are simple but authentic stories that carry us into American Indian worlds quite different from our own—here long before America was "discovered." There are Negro stories brought from Africa and adapted to their New World setting. There are Spanish stories from the Southwest and Puerto Rico; stories from the Pennsylvania Germans and the Louisiana French; a story brought by Portuguese fishermen to Cape Cod; Russian, Italian and Jewish stories told in New York City; Norwegian stories from Wisconsin; Chinese and Japanese stories from California. Some of them still keep the flavor of the lands from which they came. Yet they are all American stories because they have been told and heard in America. American folklore is a tree with its roots in many times and places and its branches in the here and now. (p. 7)

96. Caduto, Michael J., and Joseph Bruchac. *Keepers of the Night: Native American Stories and Nocturnal Activities for Children.* Golden, CO: Fulcrum, 1994. xxii, 146p. Illus. by David Kanietakeron Fadden. Index. Glossary. 94-2602. 1-55591-177-3pa.

Caduto and Bruchac tell, and Fadden illustrates, stories from a variety of Native American cultures and traditions: Anishinabe, Okanagan, Onondaga, Paiute, and Shoshone. All the stories feature nocturnal animals. Accompanying the stories are suggestions and instructions for a variety of activities to do with children outdoors: building and tending a campfire, observing stars, watching an eclipse, and seeking out night-blooming plants. Throughout the book the authors weave information about the various cultures from which the tales are drawn.

97. Field, Rachel L., comp. *American Folk and Fairy Tales.* New York: Charles Scribner's Sons, 1929. xiv, 302p. Illus. by Margaret Freeman.

Paul Bunyan stories, Louisiana folktales, Native American tales, Uncle Remus tales, and southern mountain stories are all part of this old but still engaging anthology of folktales for children. It also contains "Rip Van Winkle" and Nathaniel Hawthorne's "Great Stone Face."

98. Malcolmson, Anne. *Yankee Doodle's Cousins.* Boston: Houghton Mifflin, 1941. xiv, 268p. Glossary.

Malcolmson compiled this collection of American folklore for children because, in her words, she felt American folklore had been "snubbed" by teachers who preferred to share British and European folklore with their classes. This book is written for children of middle school age.

It is divided into four geographic sections: The East, The South, The Mississippi Valley, and The West.

The book's glossary includes not only words peculiar to folklore but also words and terms deemed to be unknown by middle schoolers.

99. Mason, Jane. *Paul Bunyan and Other Tall Tales.* New York: Scholastic, 2002. 107p. (Scholastic Junior Classics). 0-439-29154-2.

Mason has adapted tales about folk characters and real people who have attained the status of folk legends. Stories are about Paul Bunyan, Sal Fink, Stormalong, Bess Call, John Henry, Annie Oakley, and Johnny Appleseed.

100. Osborne, Mary Pope. *American Tall Tales.* New York: Alfred A. Knopf, 1991. 115p. Illus. by Michael McCurdy. 89-37235. 0-679-80089-1.

Osborne's stories are of American icons:

Davy Crockett
Sally Ann Thunder Ann Whirlwind
Johnny Appleseed
Stormalong
Mose
Febold Feboldson
Pecos Bill
John Henry
Paul Bunyan

She prefaces each tale with "Notes on the Story," which gives what biographical and factual information is available on the character. McCurdy's vibrant, full-page woodcuts illustrate all the stories. Osborne says that one of the characters,

Sally Ann Thunder Ann Whirlwind, is a composite of many American frontierswomen.

The bibliography is divided into sections, with a listing for each character, and provides an easy way to gather more material on the individuals whose tales are told here.

101. Raczek, Linda. *Stories from Native North America.* Austin, TX: Raintree Steck-Vaughn, 2000. 48p. Illus. by Richard Hook. Bibliog. Glossary. 99-048317. 0-7398-1336-6; 0-7398-2033-8pa.

Stories are from the Southwest, Alaska, the Rocky Mountains, the Great Plains, and the Upper Great Lakes. Two tales involve Coyote, the trickster.

Illustrations are full page and full color.

102. San Souci, Robert D. *Larger than Life: The Adventures of American Legendary Heroes.* New York: Delacorte Press, 1991. 59p. Illus. by Andrew Glass. 0-385-32180-5pa.

San Souci presents for children tales of five American heroes: John Henry, Stormalong, Pecos Bill and his romance with Slue-Foot Sue, Strap Buckner, and Paul Bunyan. The illustrations, in color, often cover a double page and are sure to delight.

103. Sieling, Peter. *Folk Music.* Broomall, PA: Mason Crest Publishers, 2003. 101p. Illus. Glossary. Index. Bibliog. (North American Folklore). 2002-154737. 1-59084-342-8.

Sieling begins with a definition and explanation of American folk music. He relates it to contemporary times by printing more recent words to traditional tunes such as "Battle Hymn of the Republic." Many of the examples he uses are those that are often sung by schoolchildren.

Subsequent chapters discuss stringed instruments, the roots of American folk music, African American folk music, Cajun music, the music of Appalachia, Hispanic folk music, and the folk music revival of the twentieth century.

Seiling uses illustrations generously, both drawings and photographs. He also sprinkles brief boxed information throughout the text: biographies, descriptions of instruments, or technical information about how to play a specific instrument.

This book would be suitable for middle school age–children.

104. *Tall Tales.* Austin, TX: Steck-Vaughn, 1990. 80p. Illus. (Folktales from around the World). 89-11504. 0-8114-2406-5. 0-8114-4156-3pa.

Although some of these folktales are from countries other than the United States, the bulk of them are American. Here are tales of Paul Bunyan, Pecos Bill, Sally Ann Thunder Ann Whirlwind, Davy Crockett, Mike Fink, and John Darling. Each tale is very brief, only a page or two, so this is not the place to find extensive information on any of these characters. However, the illustrations are colorful and the short length of the tales makes it ideal for reading aloud.

105. Walker, Paul Robert. *Big Men, Big Country: A Collection of American Tall Tales.* San Diego, CA: Harcourt Brace Jovanovich, 2000. 79p. Illus. by James Bernardin. Bibliog. 91-45126. 0-15-207136-9.

Walker retells the stories of nine American heroes: Davy Crockett; Old Stormalong; Big Mose, the legendary fireman in New York; John Darling from the Catskills, who was carried to China and back again by giant mosquitoes; Ol' Gabe, nickname of Jim Bridger; Paul

Bunyan, John Henry, Gib Morgan, the oil driller, and Pecos Bill.

Walker provides some background on each of the stories, explaining a bit how the legend came to be. Bernardin's illustrations are full color and full page.

106. Young, Richard, and Judy Dockrey Young. *Race with Buffalo: And Other Native American Stories for Young Readers*. Little Rock, AR: August House, 1994. 172p. Illus. by Wendell E. Hall. Notes. Glossary. 94-6145. 0-87483-343-4; 0-87483-342-6pa.

Tales from many Native American tribes are retold here for children. Each tale has a headnote indicating where it originated. Stories are grouped into sections, headed:

In Ancient Times
Young Heroes
Magical Beasts
Laughing Stories
How and Why Stories
Trickster Stories
The Spirit World

107. Zorn, Steven. *Classic American Folk Tales*. Philadelphia: Courage Books, 1992. 56p. Illus. 91-58125. 0-56138-062-8.

Zorn retells the stories of several American folk heroes, both historical and imaginary:

Paul Bunyan
Johnny Appleseed
Br'er Rabbit
John Henry
Davy Crockett
Pocahontas
Pecos Bill

Each tale is illustrated by a different artist.

Museums: A Selected List

Museums that feature everyday life abound in all regions of the country. Through the display of clothing, farm implements, household goods, industrial tools, or entire houses, workshops, and communities, these museums can help people of today understand and appreciate the lives lived by those who came before. The list below is not a complete list of museums in the United States, but by browsing through it, one can get a glimpse of the richness of museum offerings. Explore on your own and discover even more fascinating museums.

Museums listed in this chapter are a sampling of those that display and highlight American folklore in general, rather than folklore devoted to a particular region. Museums concentrating on a specific region are listed in the chapter of the appropriate region.

District of Columbia

Daughters of the American Revolution
    Museum
1776 D Street, N.W.
Washington, D.C. 20006
202-879-3241
http://www.dar.org

National Museum of American History
14th St. and Constitution Avenue,
    N.W.
Washington, D.C. 20560
Mailing address:
Smithsonian Institution
Washington, D.C. 20560
202-357-2700
http://americanhistory.si.edu/

Smithsonian Institution
1000 Jefferson Drive, S.W.
Washington, D.C. 20560
Mailing address:
1000 Jefferson Drive, S.W. Rm 370,
    MRC033
Washington, D.C. 20560
202-357-2700
http://www.si.edu

Maine

Lubec

Roosevelt Campobello International
    Park Commission
P.O. Box 129
Lubec, Maine 04652
506-752-2922
http://www.fdr.net

Maryland

Annapolis

United States Naval Academy Museum
118 Maryland Avenue
Annapolis, Maryland 21402
410-293-2108
http://www.usna.edu/museum

Baltimore

Fort McHenry National Monument and
    Shrine
End of E. Fort Avenue
Baltimore, Maryland 21230
410-962-4290
http://www.nps.gov/fomc

New Mexico

Santa Fe

Museum of International Folk Art
706 Camino Lejo
Santa Fe, New Mexico 87505
Mailing address:
P.O. Box 2087
Santa Fe, New Mexico 87504
505-476-1200
http://www.moifa.org

New York

Hudson

American Museum of Fire Fighting
Firemen's Home
125 Harry Howard Avenue
Hudson, New York 12534
518-828-7695
http://www.artcom.com/museums

Kings Point

American Merchant Marine Museum
United States Merchant Marine Academy
Kings Point, New York 11024
516-773-5515
http://www.usnma.edu

New York

American Folk Art Museum
45 W. 53rd Street
New York, New York 10019
Mailing address:
555 W. 57th Street
New York, New York 10019

800-421-1220
http://www.folkartmuseum.org

West Point

West Point Museum
United States Military Academy, Bldg.
   2110
West Point, New York 10996
845-938-2203
http://www.usma.edu

Pennsylvania

Carlisle

United States Army Military History
   Institute
22 Ashburn Drive
Carlisle, Pennsylvania 17013
717-245-3611
http://carlisle-www.army.mil/usamhi

Philadelphia

Independence National Historic Park
313 Walnut Street
Philadelphia, Pennsylvania 19106
215-597-8787
http://www.nps.gov/inde

Washington Crossing

Washington Crossing Historic Park
1112 River Road
Washington Crossing, Pennsylvania
   18977
Mailing address:
P.O. Box 103

Washington Crossing, Pennsylvania 18977
215-493-4076
http://www.spiritof76.org

Rhode Island

Newport

Naval War College Museum
686 Cushing Road
Coasters Harbor Island
Newport, Rhode Island 02841
401-841-4052
http://www.nwc.navy.mil/museum

Vermont

Shelburne

Shelburne Museum, Inc.
5555 Shelburne Road
Shelburne, Vermont 05482
Mailing address:
P.O. Box 10
Shelburne, Vermont 05482
802-985-3346
http://www.shelburnemuseum.org

Virginia

Charlottesville

Monticello, Home of Thomas Jefferson
Route 53 Thomas Jefferson Parkway
Charlottesville, Virginia 22902
Mailing address:
P.O. Box 316
Charlottesville, Virginia 22901
804-984-9801
http://www.monticello.org

Mount Vernon

George Washington's Mount Vernon
End of George Washington Parkway
  South
Mount Vernon, Virginia 22121
Mailing address:
George Washington's Mount Vernon
P.O. Box 110
Mount Vernon, Virginia 22121
703-780-2000
http://www.mountvernon.org

Journals of Folklore:
A Selected List

The journals in the list below publish articles on folklore. Some are scholarly; others are more popular. Many other journals and newsletters exist, published by museums, historical societies, folklore organizations, community groups, and schools. Explore your own area to see what other publications of folklore exist. Folklore journals specific to a region are listed in the appropriate chapter.

The Folklore Society of Greater Washington,
  Newsletter
Folklore Society of Greater Washington
307 Broadleaf Drive N.E.
Vienna, Virginia 22180
703-281-2228

Journal of American Folklore
American Anthropological Association
4350 North Fairfax Drive, Suite 640
Arlington, Virginia 22203
703-528-1902

Journal of Cultural Geography
225 Scott Hall

Oklahoma State University
Stillwater, Oklahoma 74078

Material Culture
Pioneer America Society
C/o Dr. Charles F. Calkins
Department of Geography
UW Center Waukesha
Waukesha, WI 53188

Pioneer America Society Newsletter
University of Akron
Department of Geography
302 E. Buchtel Mall
Akron, OH 44325

Web Sites: A Selected List

Below is a list of a few Web sites dealing with folklore. You can find other Web sites by doing an Internet search on a search engine such as Google or Yahoo!, or by looking on the Web sites of various folklore organizations with which you are familiar. Web sites germane to folklore of a specific region are listed in the appropriate chapter.

Aadizzookaanag, http://www.kstrom.net/
  isk/stories/myths/html
Traditional stories, legends, and myths of various Native American groups.

American Folklife Center, Library of
  Congress, http://www.loc.gov/folklife/
The Web page for the Folklife Center, which contains collections on folklore and folklife worldwide.

American Folklore Society, http://www.
  afsnet.org/
Web site of the American Folklore Soci-

ety, including calendar of events, bylaws, membership information, and a list of publications. Links to other folklore sites are provided.

Archive of Folk Culture of the U.S. Library of Congress, http://www.lcweb.loc.gov/ folklife/archive.html
Access to materials in the Archive of Folk Culture at the Library of Congress, which includes manuscripts, recordings, photographs, and moving images.

Folklife and Fieldwork: A Layman's Introduction to Field Techniques, http:// www.lcweb.loc.gov/folklife/fieldwk.html
The text of the book by this title. Contains information on interviewing and fieldwork techniques.

Kevin Barry Perdue Archive of Traditional Culture, University of Virginia, http://faculty.minerva.acc.virginia.edu/ ~tradcult/
The site describes the holdings of the archive, which collects manuscripts, re-

cordings, books, journals, and student papers on folklore.

Smithsonian Center for Folklife and Cultural Heritage, http://www.folklife.si.edu/
Not only American folklore, but folklore from around the world is the focus of this Web site. It lists and describes folklore events such as festivals and exhibitions.

Teacher's Guide to Folklife Resources for K–12 Classrooms, http://www.lcweb.loc.gov/ folklife/teachers.html
Contains the 1994 publication *A Teacher's Guide to Folklife Resources for K–12 Classrooms*, prepared by American Folklife Center of the U.S. Library of Congress.

Traditional Arts Programs Network (TAPNET), http://afsnet.org/tapnet/
Links to many sites of folklore and folk arts, compiled by the National Council for the Traditional Arts of the National Endowment for the Arts. Programs maintained at both the federal and local levels are listed.

The Northeast

Connecticut, Delaware, Maine, Maryland, Massachusetts, New Hampshire, New Jersey, New York, Pennsylvania, Rhode Island, Vermont, and Washington, D.C.

The Northeast: Checklist

Look for tales on:

Native American legends of the earth's
   beginnings, of paradise, of heroes
Tales of the Revolution
Sea stories, of ghost ships, sea
   serpents, and fishermen
Witchcraft and the devil

And for characters such as:

Glooskap, the "Lord of Beasts and
   Men"
Mashop
Captain Kidd

Historical characters such as:

Paul Revere, Ethan Allen, and
   Nathan Hale
Little Jack
Passaconnaway
Mikumwessak, or dwarfs
Lox, the mischief maker
Wanagamaswak, or fairies
Chocorua

Read classic authors such as:

Samuel Adams Drake
Horace Beck

Charles Leland
John Josselyn
Benjamin Botkin
Richard Dorson
Charles M. Skinner
Silas T. Rand

And journals such as:

Northeast Folklore
Maine Folklife

Explore:

Your local library
Nearby university and college libraries
Local historical societies

Acquaint your children with:

Stories of heroes and heroines
Tales of the earth's beginning
Seafaring adventures
Ghost stories
Tall tales of the lumberjacks

THE NORTHEAST: INTRODUCTION

The designation Northeastern United States—Connecticut, Delaware, District of Columbia, Maine, Maryland, Massachusetts, New Hampshire, New Jersey, New York, Pennsylvania, Rhode Island, and Vermont—is arbitrary and primarily a cartographer's initiative. Within the area's 176,020 square miles live, according to a 2001 census estimate, 60,546,341 people, or about 343 persons per square mile. To speak only in terms of demographics and statistics, however, belies the diversity of multicultural traditions that make the Northeast unique. The diversity I refer to includes Amerindian lore, traditions transplanted by immigrants from around the world, and native, Northeastern lore that could only have developed from the region's own geographical, cultural, political, and historical realities.

More than a century and a half ago, the English scholar William Thoms coined the word *folk-lore,* in an article he published in the British journal *The Athenium* (1846). He suggested using it in place of the then current phrase *popular antiquities.* This phrase refers to what scholars and laypeople alike consider survivals from the distant past, including popular beliefs, unusual customs still practiced in peasant society, old ballads, and tales. Forty-two years later, with the formation of the American Folklore Society in 1888—in the Northeast, at Boston, Massachusetts—American scholars sought to professionalize the study of American folk cultures. They urged the society's members to document what they saw as fast vanishing traditions, namely, "relics" of English traditions, African American lore in the southern states, traditions from Indian tribes, and the lore of French Canadians, Mexicans, and other migrant groups. In time, folklorists expanded their field of study to include regional lore that arose within the United States. In fact, the latter, as this bibliography clearly shows, has become in the Northeast a major focus of folklore study.

The study of folklore, then, was rooted in a curiosity about the past and how it survived in the beliefs and practices of people often in rural settings and out of mainstream culture. In time, the scope of what folklorists and laypeople alike studied expanded significantly, as this bibliography suggests. Lore was not simply relics from the past, but vital cultural markers that pointed to a conservation of traditions.

Scholars contribute to folkloristics how to collect, identify, catalogue, and analyze items of folklore within the context of professionalism. They bring to bear on lore the discipline's theories and analytic methodologies as well as those developed by cultural anthropologists, archaeologists, historians, literary critics, psychologists, and sociologists. Laypeople bring a sense of the local community that the professional might not have, quick access to local resources, which the outsider might spend months trying to locate, and a deep desire to preserve and share a community's local traditions. Although there are professionals with specific expertise, there remains in the study of folklore plenty of room for the nonprofessional. In fact members of many local folklore and history societies in the Northeast are not professionals, and, nevertheless, they contribute significantly to the study of their region's folklore.

This bibliography includes book-length publications by literary authors, professional scholars, regional writers, and laypeople interested in preserving and popularizing regional traditions. Despite this book's emphasis on regions, we cannot ignore a few basic studies about American folklore that can help to provide a broader context for looking at Northeastern lore. A valuable overview of folklore in the United States is Jan Brunvand's *The Study of American Folklore*, 4th ed. (New York: W. W. Norton and Co., 1998). His text provides an excellent introduction to the many genres of folklore and includes extremely useful bibliographies at the end of each chapter. Any serious researcher will need to consult Cathleen C. Flanagan and John T. Flanagan's *American Folklore: A Bibliography 1950–1974* (Metuchen, NJ: Scarecrow Press, 1977) and the "Folklore" section in the annual *International Bibliography of Books and Articles on the Modern Languages and Literatures* (New York: The Modern Language Association of America). College and university libraries probably have an on-line edition of this extremely important bibliography that is updated annually.

Because this book is a bibliography of other books, it only lists those subjects that are treated in book length. Thus, the titles included here do not begin to exhaust the resources available to the diligent researcher. Thousands of journal articles have been written about lore in the Northeast. In addition to *Northeast Folklore,* which is listed in "Journals in Folklore of the Region," I add *New York Folklore Quarterly,* the *Potash Kettle* (the quarterly of the Vermont Folklore Society), and *Visit'n* (the annual of the Vermont Folklife Center). The numerous publications from The Dublin Seminar for New England Folklife (Boston: Boston University Press) are extremely valuable.

Moreover, this collection, following older visions of what constitutes folklore, generally ignores—except for a small handful of works—lore in the major cities of the Northeast. Urban centers are very fertile areas for folk traditions. This collection also focuses little on the lore of immigrant populations—African Americans, Greek Americans, Italian Americans, Jewish Americans, Welsh Americans, and so on. Two ethnic groups, Amerindians and the Pennsylvania Dutch, are treated. Indeed, most of all of these groups have been the subject of numerous studies, scholarly and popular.

I refuse to use the term *melting pot* to describe the folk traditions and culture of the Northeastern United States. The flavors of its many traditions have not stewed together long enough so that they have lost their distinctiveness. Ethnic, regional, and local pride keeps traditions alive and keeps them singular. This bibliography of the Northeast testifies to the enduring strength of local traditions, unique to their distinctive regions.

There are, however, a few traditions that can be found throughout the entire Northeast. For example, the Yankee appeared in the latter part of the eighteenth century. His earliest manifestation was a country bumpkin, ill fitted to cope with urban life and the social pretenses of high society. As a figure representing a British bias against colonists, the Yankee was satirized in the Revolutionary War with the ditty "Yankee Doodle." Nevertheless, Americans, quick to laugh at themselves, took up the song with great aplomb and spread it across the newly founded nation. Gregarious, curious, and naive about anything beyond his own village, the Yankee became a beloved figure in lore and popular literature. Eventually he evolved into one of this nation's greatest stock stage figures. By the mid-nineteenth century, the term *Yankee* began to be applied indiscriminately and pejoratively, by Southerners, to anyone who lived north of the Mason-Dixon line. Finally, the world adopted the term to refer to any American, and Americans gladly sang the refrain "The Yanks are coming." The evolution of the Yankee reflects a cultural process of transforming regional traits into a caricature that becomes a folk and popular hero. Both the enduring Yankee and the pejorative Puritan have become staples in American speech and lore. Dorson, in his book *Jonathan Draws the Long Bow* (1946), annotates the curious career of this figure. A more detailed history of this figure is found in his *American in Legend* (New York: Pantheon Books, 1973). This book also outlines the meteoric rise of other Northeastern folk heroes.

Many Americans and Northeasterners know about Paul Revere's midnight ride and the ghost of Sleepy Hollow. Both of these are set in the Northeast and by now might seem to many people as a part of regional or national lore. Nevertheless, they are well-known literary creations, without any traditional folk precedents. They remain part of the American consciousness through the efforts of accomplished writers, diligent anthology editors, and zealous pedagogues. Bound to print, these accounts have become *the* story, regularized and standardized by repeated printings and reprinting, rather than originating in and maturing through the eccentricities of folk and popular traditions.

Many of the sources cited in this bibliography represent folklore retold by Northeasterners who take pride in re-creating and reshaping their regional lore for mass audiences. Some mirror fakelore, that is, they attempt to pass off new and original material as if it were real folklore. A good example of this is the several books published by Maurice Jagendorf. Much of what he wrote is unrepresentative of authentic oral traditions. Nevertheless, his works have been read as examples of American folklore, which they are not. Despite the inclusion of such material, the bibliography also provides leads to scholarly publications in which the authors seek to maintain the authenticity of the lore without extravagantly polishing it. Some excellent examples of true scholarship are George Carey's books on Maryland folklore.

Another common tradition in the Northeast can be found among Amerindians. This is ironic, because many people, including scholars, once believed that Amerindian lore had virtually vanished from the Northeast. It was erroneously assumed that European and American settlers and colonizers successfully eradicated all vestiges of Indian culture. In fact, Northeastern Amerindian culture went "underground," as it were, but it was kept alive by people tenaciously and proudly intent on not allowing it to vanish. Today, it is emerging and beginning to occupy a deserved place in the folklore of the Northeast. A very important general bibliography is William Clements and Frances Malpezzi's *Native American Folklore, 1879–1979* (Athens:

Swallow Press and Ohio UP, 1984). In addition, a number of regional publications feature detailed studies on Northeast Amerindian material culture, ranging from traditional basket weaving and woodcarving skills to homeopathic medicine and traditional beliefs.

The Northeast is home to more than twenty Amerindian tribes. Not all of the lore from all of the groups has received the attention its deserves. In these pages, the Abanaki, Algonquin, Deleware, Malecite, Iroquois, Micmac, Passamaquoddy, Penosbscot, Pequot, Seneca, and Wampanoag are represented. The quality of the material, however, varies. Older accounts might contain biases that create unrealistically romantic views of American life and traditions. Some recent novels and books for children reflect the growing spirit of pan-nativism. Authors might misrepresent the traditions of one tribe by uncritically incorporating into their fictions lore from other—sometimes very distant—tribes. Such writers who intentionally take literary license as they purport to retell traditional myths, legends, and tales serve the needs of neither their audience nor the groups about which they are writing. Every source cited in any bibliography must be critically evaluated. Caveat emptor.

Despite different languages and customs among the Northeastern Amerindians, there are some common elements of lore. One mythic figure found throughout the region is the cultural hero who is often also the trickster. Glooscap (Gluskap, Kluscap, Gluskabe) is widely found throughout the Woodland region of the Northeast. He has other names in tribes farther south. As both a cultural hero and a trickster, he plays a prominent role in the region's folklore. He reshapes the landscape and destroys supernatural creatures haunting the woodlands so that humans can eventually live in safety. His natural curiosity and naïveté may get him into trouble, but he usually manages to survive harrowing encounters with monsters and the unfriendly animistic landscape. A number of authors have rewritten the antics and exploits of the trickster for children, censoring out the more ribald and violent dimensions of this figure. Eleven of the twenty titles in the section "Folklore for Children" are on Native American subjects. Each should be considered with care for their accuracy and completeness in presenting Amerindian lore.

A notable source for Northeastern Amerindian traditions is William Simmons's *Spirit of the New England Tribes: Indian History and Folklore, 1620–1984* (1986). This work is complemented by a number of studies dealing with the lore of individual tribes, ranging from the Delaware to the Eastern and Western Abenaki. An additional source worth consulting is Charles Haywood's *A Bibliography of North-American Indian Folklore and Folksong* (1951; New York: Dover Publications, 1961). In addition, members of the American Folklore Society published in the early years of the society's existence a considerable body of Indian lore. These important texts appeared in early issues of the *Journal of American Folklore*.

In recent times, with mounting interest in natural healing, Amerindian medical practices are receiving new attention. Fortunately, writers in the nineteenth and twentieth centuries, intrigued by nonprofessional medical practices, made considerable efforts to document medical lore.

Silver Raven Wolf's *American Folk Magick* (1998) and Gladys Tantaquidgeon's two books *Folk Medicine of the Delaware* (1972; 1995) and *A Study of Delaware Indian Medical Practices* (1942; 1980) are extremely valuable resources. Two books edited by Wayland Hand—*American Folk Medicine: A Symposium* (Los Angeles, CA: UCLA Center for Study of Comparative Folklore and Mythology, 1976) and *Magical Medicine* (Berkeley: University of California Press, 1980)—are very useful for an overview of folk medicine. Although neither book deals exclusively with Northeastern Amerindian folk medicine, both provide insights into the general topic of folk medicinal customs and practices in America.

Amerindian lore is a vital part of folk culture in the Northeastern states. Some of it—especially its religious-oriented myths, customs, and rituals—survived separate from the lore European immigrants brought to the Northeast. One area, however, in which there is some overlap deals with the supernatural. As explorers and settlers encountered the New World, they were both exhilarated with the economic and political possibilities that lay ahead of them and frightened by the vastness of the land and strangeness of what they encountered. No doubt early settlers, who themselves brought a whole range of European beliefs to the New World, were intimidated by Amerindian beliefs in a spirit world. The Puritans were quick to point out that from their perspective Indian beliefs were signs that the devil was at work in the New World.

John Josselyn, an early coastal explorer, and the Puritan preacher Increase Mather provided numerous accounts and observations that can be labeled legends because they portray the subject matter with such a degree of realism that the narratives and statements beg to be believed. They recount with a remarkable sense of certainty what they either observed themselves or gathered from persons whom they considered reliable witnesses. A good addition to these works is Richard Dorson's compilation of colonial text entitled *America Begins* (Chicago: Ayer Publishing Co., 1972).

Josselyn perhaps can be credited with introducing the European motif of a sea serpent onto the northeastern coast. Amerindian tales already spoke of a great sea monster. Tales of such a creature stimulated New Englanders' imaginations for more than three centuries. The Cape Ann Serpent is certainly the most famous of all American sea monsters. Horace Beck's *Folklore and the Sea* (1973; 1999) provides a good overview of the sea serpent tradition in general, but J. P. O'Neill, in her *The Great New England Sea Serpent* (1999), provides plenty of eyewitness testimonies and newspaper accounts of this Massachusetts wonder in particular. An observant peruser of this bibliography will also note that other parts of the Northeast and the United States have their own aquatic monsters, many linking Amerindian and European traditions. Vermont and upstate New York share "Champ," the monster of Lake Champlain, and Delaware and New Jersey have "Chessie," the serpent of the Chesapeake Bay.

Mather, in his *Remarkable Providences* (1683; 1890), recounts the early experiences of Puritan settlers who saw the hand of God in everything that befell them, good and bad. To verify the ways of God to man, Mather garnered together numerous anecdotes about strange occurrences, which he and his fellow believers interpreted as proof for witches with their black magic, warlocks, and the devil living in the colonies. Yet his claims are essentially supernatural beliefs transplanted from Europe, where they took deep root, sometimes nourished by tales learned from the Indians. Extended quotes from Mather's work can be found in Dorson's *America Begins.*

New Jersey, however, lays claim to one of the Northeast's most important supernatural figures–the Jersey Devil. No less than five anthologies of New Jersey lore describe this Piney Barren monster, and two works treat it in some depth.

Devil figures and sea monsters are simply two of the many supernatural creatures about which there is some lore or, at the least, a fanciful, literary imagination. The Northeast has its own Bigfoot, vampires, haunted houses and graveyards, mysterious sailing ships, and thousands of local spots where people claim to have seen ghosts. Basic to research is Peter Benes's *Wonders of the Invisible World, 1600–1900* (Boston: Boston University Press, 1995). Louis C. Jones's *Things That Go Bump in the Night* (New York: Hill and Wang, 1959) is a superb anthology of New York ghost legends and belief. Faye Ringel's excellent study *New England's Gothic Literature* (1995) provides rich insights into the play between supernatural folk creatures and literary efforts to depict them. Joe Citro's two books *Green Mountains, Dark Tales* (1999) and *Passing Strange* (1996) are good examples of an author using folklore to create wonderful, literary short stories. A recent, fascinating study of Northeastern vampires can be found in Michael E. Bell's *Food for the Dead: On the Trail of New England's Vam-*

pires (New York: Carroll and Graff, 2001). It is a balanced approach to the study of vampire traditions and has an excellent bibliography.

Although this bibliography provides access to a variety of specialized studies, ranging from Amerindian lore to tales of ghosts and other monsters, many of the entries are good places to start in order to get a general knowledge about the Northeast's folk traditions. Richard Dorson's *Jonathan Draws the Long Bow* (1946) is a good introduction to New England traditions that appeared chiefly in nineteenth- and early twentieth-century popular publications. Ben Botkin's *Treasury of New England Folklore* (1947; 1965) is equally useful. However, both works are less critical about their sources. They may reproduce or summarize an item from the popular media of the day without specifically verifying whether the item is folklore or the creative outpourings of a literary imagination. Nevertheless, both, used carefully, are invaluable.

Well-represented in this bibliography are anthologies of lore from individual states. During the Great Depression, the federal government provided work for writers by asking that each state produce a volume on the state. In most of these, one can find passages dealing with local traditions and lore. Subsequently, scholars and popularizers have written newer "biographies" of individual states. Some, such as Vermont and Connecticut, are not as well represented as are Maryland and Maine, not because there is less lore found in these places, but because less of it has been published in easily accessible, book-length sources. Notable for their thoroughness, are George Carey's *Maryland Folklore* (1989) and *Maryland Folklore and Folklife* (1970). David Cohen in *Folklore and Folklife of New Jersey* (1983) does for the Garden State what Carey did for the Diamond State.

Pennsylvania is well represented, due to the efforts of collectors such as George Korson and Henry Wharton Shoemaker (the latter is represented by seven books) and the members of the Pennsylvania German Folklore Society. The so-called Pennsylvania Dutch is the one Northeastern ethnic group receiving the most attention, except for the Amerindians, in this bibliography. Because these German immigrants, with their strict religious and cultural beliefs, remained somewhat isolated from mainstream American and northeastern cultures, they retained many Old World beliefs and customs. Whether one is interested in the group's medicinal practices (Brendle and Unger's *Folk Medicine of the Pennsylvania Germans* [1935]), its religious beliefs (Wentz's *Pennsylvania Dutch: Folk Spirituality* [1993]), or its domestic and agricultural practices (Kirchner's *In Days Gone By* [1996]), there is plenty of material included in this bibliography.

An often-neglected folklore, that dealing with industrialization in the Northeast, receives some treatment in Tristram Coffin and Hening Cohen's *Folklore from the Working Folk of America* (1973; New York: Doubleday-Anchor 1974). This study gives a general overview of industrial lore, not limited to traditions in the Northeast. Historically, it was in the Northeast that the first American mills using what was, in the nineteenth century, considered modern technology were built. Mill towns get some treatment especially with Brigitte Lane's *Franco-American Folk Traditions and Popular Culture in a Former Milltown* (1990). In recent decades, there has been renewed interest in the kinds of lore found in industrialized centers. For example, with the creation of the first urban national park in Lowell, Massachusetts, researchers have taken on the task of collecting oral traditions, including life histories and mill songs and legends. Publications of their findings are often available on-site.

All of the states in the northeast, except Vermont, either lie along the eastern seaboard or have relatively easy access to the Atlantic Ocean. It is not surprising, then, that a considerable body of lore related to the sea evolved in the region. Among these the most important is Horace Beck's *Folklore and the Sea* (1973; 1999). Also useful is Samuel Drake's *A Book of New England Legends* (1901; 1969), but it must be used with caution, because Drake was not above rewriting his material for a literary audience. Edward Snow's three books are again useful but are literary retellings of tradition material. A slightly dated but very useful source for maritime lore including the Northeast is Peter Bartis (comp.), *Maritime Folklore Resources: A Directory and Index* (Washington, DC: American Folklife Center, Library of Congress, 1980).

Another major industry in the Northeast was logging, and the songs and tales of the lumberjacks have been well documented. Robert Bethke's *Adirondack Voices* (1981) and Roland Gray's collection of songs entitled *Songs and Ballads of the Maine Lumberjacks* (1924; 1969) are extremely important studies of lumberjack songs. One of the best studies of a legendary lumberjack is Roger Mitchell's *George Knox; From Man to Legend* (Orono, ME: Northeast Folklore Society, 1969).

Coal mining also spawned rich tale and ballad traditions. The various publications by the Pennsylvania collector George Korson are invaluable, not only for the collections themselves, but also for Korson's commentary.

Yankee folksay—unique words, proverbs, riddles, metaphors—with its droll wit, continues to intrigue. This bibliography has a number of works that seek to lay out to the public the linguistic oddities of Northeasterners. The ongoing *Dictionary of American Regional English* (Cambridge, MA: Belknap Press of Harvard University Press, 1985–) is a superb place to explore regional terms and phrases that pop up in everyday speech. Carl Withers's revision of Clifton Johnson's *What They Say in New England* (1963) remains a valuable study. Collections such as David Cohen's *Folklore and Folklife of New Jersey* (1983) and Brigitte Lane's *Franco-American Folk Traditions* (1990) have chapters or passages that focus on the colorful expressions and ways of speech that characterizes some parts of the Northeast. New England proverbs are also beginning to receive serious study through the efforts of Wolfgang Mieder. Particularly useful is his *New England Proverbs* (Shelburne, VT: New England Press, 1989), both for the texts and a brilliant introduction.

As the books listed in this section of the bibliography suggest, most people think that folklore consists of oral tales, ballads, beliefs, and customs that are thought to be threatened by modern culture. A vast area that is often overlooked is what folklorists refer to as *folklife*. This is a catchall term that is gaining strong support in professional folklore circles as a possible substitute for the more commonly used *folklore*. At one time folklife meant those types of lore that were not passed down by oral traditions. For example, it included folk architecture, folk clothing, ways of preparing and preserving food, and practices associated with everything from hunting to religious rituals. Bits and snatches of folklife are represented in this collection, but there are several studies dealing with folklife studies that deserve special attention. One of the most significant omissions is Henry Glassie's *Pattern in the Material Culture of the Eastern United States* (Philadelphia: University of Pennsylvania, 1969). This study deals with everything from folk architectural forms to domestic pottery. Although the book does not exclusively analyze material culture in the Northeast, the region does receive considerable attention. Other omissions include Scott Hastings's *The Last Yankees: Folkways in Eastern Vermont and the Border Country* (Hanover: UP of New England, 1990), which is a superb study of material folk customs along the upper Connecticut Valley. *Salt Book* (Garden City, NY: Anchor Press, 1977) and *Salt 2* (Garden City, NY: Anchor Press/Doubleday, 1980), both edited by Pamela Wood, offer plenteous examples of Maine coastal customs, ranging from lobstering practices to sail making and river driving. Publications by the Northeast Folklore Society have, over the years, introduced many readers to the customs and material culture of loggers in Maine. Very significant are the annual proceedings of the Dublin Seminar for New England Folklife, published by Boston University.

Folklore has been a wellspring for many literary authors. In the nineteenth century, writers such as Hawthorne and

Melville recognized a wealth of ideas in folk customs and oral traditions, ripe for their creative use. Hawthorne took a particular interest in his community's past and preserved local legends and beliefs in a number of his works. Particularly noteworthy are his *Twice-Told Tales* (1837) and *Mosses from an Old Manse* (1846). Melville drew upon the lore of the sea for major works such as *Moby-Dick* (1851) and several of his short stories. Kevin J. Hayes's *Melville's Folk Roots* (Kent, OH: Kent State University Press, 1999) explores in some detail Melville's debt to folk traditions. Washington Irving found useful some New York traditions, but he did not also hesitate to incorporate into his short stories and essays material extracted from non-American literary sources or from tales he probably learned while living in Europe. He casually recasts them for his American audiences by resetting them in upstate New York. His famous headless horseman and the snoozing Rip Van Winkle have become staples of American literary culture, but unfortunately for our purposes have little to do with northeastern folk culture of Irving's time. Nevertheless, local Chambers of Commerce in the Catskills ardently seek to convince tourists about the folk authenticity of these literary tales. Robert Frost, except for one or two poems, did not deal with Northeast folklore, although he did incorporate in his poetry a broad sense of some of the character traits of the rural Yankee. Vermont's Rowland E. Robinson, on the other hand, provides a treasure of northern Vermont's Anglo and French-Canadian lore. Writing in Yankee dialect, Robinson recreated pre–Civil War life in a rural Vermont village, using extensively local lore and customs. Ronald Baker's

Folklore in the Writings of Rowland E. Robinson (Bowling Green, OH: Bowling Green University Popular Press, 1973) is a model study of the relationship between regional folklore and local-color writing. Several other northeastern writers have received attention from folklorists. A basic, although dated, research tool, however, is Steven Swann Jones's *Folklore and Literature in the United States: An Annotated Bibliography of Studies of Folklore in American Literature* (New York: Garland Publishers, 1984). Determining whether an author is "inventing" lore for his works or drawing on actual lore requires some intriguing research into a region's language, customs, and narratives viable at the time the author was writing. Joseph Citro's tales of strange happenings in the Green Mountain State is a combination of local anecdotes and creative imagination. This is equally true for Joseph C. Allen's *Fireside Tales Told 'Longside the Stove in Sanderson's*, Marillis Bittinger's *Tall Tales of Cape Cod*, Thomas Howard's *Folklore from the Adirondack Foothills*, and others authors listed in this collection. Some lesser-read Northeastern authors, such as Ann Stephens, Seba Smith, and Frances Whitcher, tapped into the spirit of Northeastern folklore and popular traditions, transforming them into wonderful pieces of popular literature. All of these writers, however, share a common love for traditions—folk and popular—of the northeastern United States. Whoever wants to use them to learn more about regional traditions must be particularly careful, drawing from these writers no more than what each can offer. Nevertheless, excellent and valuable works by popular writers and authors make valuable contributions to our knowledge about a region's folklore. The least useful for serious folklore purposes are popularizers and writers who do not discriminate between lore and their own creative imagination. These, however, are often wonderful examples of literary art and of popular culture.

Sometimes the least useful resources are material written especially for children.

George Browne's *Real Legends of New England* (1930) are retellings of texts that are more literary than folk. Washington Irving's "Legend of Sleepy Hollow" and "Rip Van Winkle," as I mentioned, have never been a part of folk traditions in the Northeast but have become a staple of children's literature and are regularly included in anthologies of American literature. Perhaps their ubiquitous nature alone leads many to believe erroneously that they are a part of Northeastern folklore. It is telling that Amerindian publications dominate the "Folklore for Children" section of the bibliography. Such lore, particularly tales involving animals or myths dealing with the re-creation of the world by a culture hero, is recast, however, to emphasize modern messages about current concerns, such as the wise use of natural resources. It is possible that the original texts were less concerned with such an issue, but the retelling of them for modern audiences who are concerned with such issues has breathed new life into the stories. Among these publications, however, are several that deliberately seek to retain the authentic voice of the traditional storyteller and to present authentic oral narratives.

Children's lore deserves more attention by professionals and laypeople alike. One significant collection of children's lore from the Connecticut River Valley is Scott Hastings's *Miss Mary Mac All Dressed in Black* (1990). I could only wish that more contextual information were included, thus making this valuable resource even more important. Brian Sutton-Smith's *Children's Folklore: A Source Book* (New York: Garland Publishers, 1995) does not deal specifically with the Northeast, but it does provide a valuable bibliography and a collection of superb essays that can add to the knowledge of the scholar, teacher, and layperson interested in this amazingly rich area of American folklore.

As this bibliography clearly shows, there is a considerable body of lore in the Northeast. However, this bibliography does not begin to exhaust the published resources that are available. Moreover, there remains an enormous amount of modern lore, ranging from urban legends to ethnic customs and traditions, that have not been wholly documented by either professional scholars or interested laypeople. Lore flourishes throughout the Northeast, and much of it remains to be collected and studied.

Richard Sweterlitsch

REFERENCES AND FURTHER READING

Allen, Barbara. "Regional Folklore." *American Folklore: An Encyclopedia*. Ed. Jan Brunvand. New York: Garland, 1996. 618–619.

Bonner, Simon J. "Middle Atlantic Region." *American Folklore: An Encyclopedia*. Ed. Jan Brunvand. New York: Garland, 1996. 479–480.

Lightfoot, William. "Regional Approach." *Folklore: An Encyclopedia of Beliefs, Customs, Tales Music, and Art*. Ed. Thomas Green. Santa Barbara, CA: ABC-CLIO. Vol. 2. 698–706.

Morley, Linda, and Eleanor Wachs. "New England." *American Folklore: An Encyclopedia*. Ed. Jan Brunvand. New York: Garland, 1996. 510–513.

THE NORTHEAST: BIBLIOGRAPHY AND OTHER RESOURCES

Bibliography

History and Study

108. Abrams, Ann Uhry. *The Pilgrims and Pocahontas: Rival Myths of American Origin*. Boulder, CO: Westview Press, 1999. xxii, 378p. Illus. Index. Notes. Bibliog. 99-10926. 0-8133-3497-7.

Although the characters in these stories are real (Pocahontas, Virginia settlers, the Pilgrims), both the stories and characters have become mythic. Abrams's thesis is that two myths competed to be the defining myth of America. The Pocahontas myth contributed to an image of Virginia as a center of culture; the Pilgrim myth promoted Massachusetts as an area inhabited by hardworking, pious people. As the United States moved toward the Civil War, these myths extended to embrace the entire North and South and were used by partisans of both sides to bolster their beliefs in their cause.

Throughout the history of this country, writers and artists have explored these myths. Abrams discusses the iconography that has developed around these competing myths.

109. Allen, Ray, and Nancy Groce, eds. *Folk and Traditional Music in New York State*. Newfield: New York Folklore Society, 1988. iii, 200p. Special issue of *New York Folklore*, v. 14, no. 3–4, 1988. ISSN 0361-204x.

This special issue of *New York Folklore* takes as its premise that New York from its beginning was the home of various ethnic groups and that all these groups had their own native music. All these traditions have made New York a state with a diverse musical culture.

Before European settlement, both the Leni-Lenape and the Iroquois Native Americans, each tribe with its own musical tradition, lived in the region. Later came the Dutch, the English, German, Irish, Scotch-Irish, Jews, Italians, Poles, Ukrainians, Greeks, Russians, Slovaks, Chinese, Arab, Korean, South American, and Afro-Caribbean immigrants. The essays in this issue examine the contributions of each ethnic group.

No actual songs are transcribed.

110. Bartholomew, Paul, Bob Bartholomew, William Brann, and Bruce Hallenbeck. *Monsters of the Northwoods: An In-Depth Investigation of Bigfoot in New York and Vermont, Documenting Encounters from Historical Encounters with Early Settlers and Indian Folklore to Today*. Whitehall, NY: Paul Bartholomew, 1980. 120p.

The Bartholomews report on sightings of Bigfoot, or Sasquatch, starting with Samuel de Champlain's reported sighting in 1603, up to sightings in 1991. They report the words and descriptions of many eyewitnesses.

111. Bonner, Willard Hallam. *Pirate Laureate: The Life and Legends of Captain Kidd*. New Brunswick, NJ: Rutgers Univ. Press, 1947. xvi, 239p. Bibliographical notes.

Bonner attempts in this book to separate fact from fiction in the stories of Captain Kidd. It is his contention that

Kidd has been maligned by history, the victim of political and commercial interests that turned his exploits, supported at the time by people in power, into dishonest and dangerous ones.

Bonner tells the story of Kidd's life as truly as he can, piecing it together from contemporary documents. He then describes the way in which his actions were condemned, a sham trial was held, and execution swiftly carried out. Throughout this process, Kidd was being turned into a folk character, as was typical of that time. On the day of his execution, broadsides were sold purporting to carry the words of his dying confession. Bonner traces the development of this legendary Kidd—a development that started even before his death—and tries to separate it from the fact.

The second section of the book is titled "Literary Uses" and retells some of the tales written about Kidd by such shapers of American literature as Washington Irving, James Fenimore Cooper, and Harriet Beecher Stowe. In his retelling and explication of these tales, Bonner reveals how the legend of the infamous Captain Kidd became embedded in the American consciousness.

112. Clarke, Helen Archibald. *Longfellow's Country*. New York: Baker and Taylor, 1909. 252p. Illus.

Clarke views and critiques Longfellow's poetry through the filter of the folklore he so often used.

She divides her work into six chapters and discusses the poetry that fits into each:

Coastal
The Nova Scotia area, including his tales and references to Glooskap
The historical stories he used, such as that of John Alden and Priscilla Mullins, or of Paul Revere's ride
Religious persecution, particularly of Quakers, and witchcraft
The Hiawatha legend
Stories of Cambridge

The last concentrates mostly on the poet's own life and family, but some of his poems, such as "The Village Blacksmith," have themselves become part of folklore.

Clarke is less a critic than she is an admirer of Longfellow's poetry; her book is not unbiased. But her exposition of how Longfellow uses the folklore of New England is of interest, as is her retelling of some of the tales he used. It's an interesting look at how one poet intertwined literature and folklore, and in so doing, became part of folklore himself.

Illustrations are black-and-white photographs of sites mentioned in the poetry and of places Longfellow lived.

113. Cohen, David Steven. *Folk Legacies Revisited*. New Brunswick, NJ: Rutgers Univ. Press, 1995. x, 151p. Index. Notes. 94-16185. 0-8135-2138-6; 0-8135-2139-4pa.

Cohen examines four different contemporary ethnic groups in America. One is composed of Native Americans in New Jersey, with some African American ancestry. These people were "detribalized" by white majority America, who saw people with any African American ancestry as being black; they are now redefining themselves as Native American. The second is an Afro-Dutch group in New York, with Dutch and African ancestry, who have their own culture, customs, and folk beliefs. The third are the Pineys of New Jersey, a group often scorned and marginalized. The fourth are the Angel Dancers, a small religious sect also in New Jersey, who during the late 1800s and early 1900s were reviled and persecuted.

Cohen's thesis is that all these marginalized groups are as American as anyone in the mainstream, because it is from all these different groups that the mainstream develops and changes.

114. ——. *Folklore and Folklife of New Jersey*. New Brunswick, NJ: Published as a project of the Folklife Program of the New Jersey Historical Association by Rutgers Univ. Press, 1983. xviii, 253p. Illus. Notes. Bibliog. Index. 82-5203. 0-8135-0964-5. 0-8135-0989-0pa.

The chapter headings give an indication of how complete Cohen intends this work to be:

The Jersey Joke
A Lenape Indian Myth
Names
Folk Speech
Legend
Folk Belief
Folk Medicine
Folk Music, Folk Song, and Folk
    Dance
Folk Painting
Folk Sculpture
Traditional Boats
Folk Architecture
Folk Furniture
Quilts, Coverlets, and Samplers
Pottery, Basketry, and Glass
Foodways
Games and Recreation
Festivals, Ceremonies, and Rituals

Within each chapter, Cohen both gives an overview of the subject and cites numerous examples. He chooses numerous illustrations of crafts and skills such as boats, houses, pottery, and glass to illuminate his explanations.

Anyone wanting a complete survey of folklore in New Jersey would do well to begin here.

115. Dorson, Richard Mercer. *Jonathan Draws the Long Bow*. Cambridge, MA: Harvard Univ. Press, 1946. viii, 274p. Bibliographical footnotes.

The "long bow" of the title is another term for tall tale, and Jonathan is a generic name used in many New England stories. Thus, "Jonathan draws the long bow" means "Jonathan tells the tall tale or folktale."

Dorson has collected tales that appeared in print, whether in town histories, in early newspapers or journals, or as adaptations in poetry or short stories. He avoids tales that are current in speech only; although, as his introductory chapter makes clear, he believes that the New England folktale developed simultaneously in speech and in writing, and that both methods of transmittal contributed to its survival.

The book's tales are arranged thematically:

Tales of the supernatural—witches,
    ghosts, and hauntings
Yankee characters
Tall tales, including those of sea
    serpents and other mythical
    creatures
Local legends, including those of
    Indians
Literary tales of such authors as
    Whittier

Dorson does not reproduce the tales. He prints extended excerpts, interspersing them with his own historical explanation of their origins and route of transmittal and survival, and with his analysis of their place in our national character.

116. Hoberman, Michael. *Yankee Moderns: Folk Regional Identity in the Sawmill Valley of Western Massachusetts, 1890–1920.* Knoxville: Univ. of Tennessee Press, 2000. liii, 162p. Illus. Index. Notes. Bibliog. 00-008138. 1-57233-087-2.

Hoberman has lived in the Sawmill Valley area of Massachusetts for years. Here he interviews seventeen residents about their lives in the area during the early part of the twentieth century. He contends that folk beliefs or folkways develop not only because of local geography and isolation but also from interaction—sometimes unwanted and sometimes even violent—with other areas. He disputes the theory that isolated populations are backward and resistant to change, saying instead that these populations adapt to changes and developments as well as urban populations do.

117. Korson, George Gershon. *Pennsylvania Songs and Legends: A Folklore Anthology.* Baltimore: Johns Hopkins Univ. Press, 1949. 466p. Illus. by Charles P. Allen. Index.

Korson has edited a collection of essays on Pennsylvania legends and folk music, written by various experts, including Henry W. Shoemaker, Howard C. Frey, and Korson himself. The essays discuss the development of the different strands of folklore in the state and discuss its importance to Pennsylvania's history. Some of the essays discuss a particular ethnic group: British, Pennsylvania Dutch, German, Native American, or Amish. Others concentrate on the folklore of a particular industry or trade: wagoners, canal workers, railroaders, lumber-

jacks, raftsmen, coal miners, and oilmen. A chapter on tall tales rounds out the collection.

Some tunes are transcribed in the various essays on folk music.

118. Lane, Brigitte Marie. *Franco-American Folk Traditions and Popular Culture in a Former Milltown.* New York: Garland, 1990. xxvii, 599p. Edited by Albert B. Lord. Notes. Bibliog. Appendices. (Harvard Dissertations in Folklore and Oral Tradition). 90-39059. 0-8240-2674-8.

Lane's Ph.D. dissertation is here reprinted. She did the fieldwork for the thesis in the early 1980s, studying the Franco-American communities of Lowell, Massachusetts. These "little Canadas" retained many of the folk traditions and customs of French Canada.

Her first section gives a history of the French American community and a summary of its intellectual and cultural accomplishments. She then presents a series of discussions of various cultural forms:

Traditional narratives and popular literature
Short forms such as children's songs, riddles, and proverbs
Jokes and anecdotes
Oral history; and song, including dance

In each of these sections she presents not only examples of the form but a discussion of how it developed and how it was being maintained at the time. Many of the examples, as might be expected, are in French.

Appendices include a number of longer examples of the various genres discussed: several folktales, some children's songs, and a collection of adult songs.

Throughout the book, she emphasizes the fact that at the time of her research, these communities were losing their cohesiveness and their connection to their traditions, because of the pressures of modern life. Television, improved communication in general, improved transportation, increased reliance on English on the part of younger people, and consequent loss of skill in the French language all contributed to the end of the "little Canadas."

119. O'Neill, J. P. *The Great New England Sea Serpent: An Account of Unknown Creatures Sighted by Many Respectable Persons between 1638 and the Present Day.* Camden, ME: Down East Books, 1999. 256p. Illus. Bibliog. and Web sites. Appendices. 0-89272-461-7pa.

O'Neill recounts all the sightings of sea serpents during the last three and a half centuries, principally in the Gulf of Maine and adjacent waters. She pulls together newspaper accounts, journals, and the testimony of eyewitnesses. She has attempted to correct past mistakes in transcription.

Two appendices are provided. One is a table of all sightings, giving date, location, where viewed from, and names of witnesses. This appendix also serves as an index, as it gives the page numbers on which information about that particular sighting can be found. The second appendix is a recording of the questions asked by the New England Linnaean Committee of witnesses to a sighting of a sea serpent in August 1817. Their investigation was the first attempt to investigate by scientific means the mythical creature.

120. Ringel, Faye. *New England's Gothic Literature: History and Folklore of the Supernatural from the Seventeenth through the Twentieth Centuries.* Lewiston, NY: E. Mellen Press, 1995. v, 267p. Index. Bibliog. (Studies in American Literature, Volume 6). 94-34973. 0-7734-9047-7.

Witches, sea serpents, vampires, and mysterious creatures of the forest are all topics for Ringel. She discusses the literature associated with each of these mythical beings.

121. Simmons, William S. *Spirit of the New England Tribes: Indian History and Folklore, 1620–1984.* Hanover, NH: Univ. Press of New England, 1986. xi, 331p. Illus. Index. Bibliog. 85-40936. 0-87451-372-3.

Simmons arranges New England folklore into several categories:

Stories based on the first encounters between Native American and Europeans
Christianity; shamans and witches
Ghosts
Treasures, related either to the devil or to pirates
Giants
Little people
Dreams

Within each section he reprints early tales in their exact words, either whole or in part, and adds exposition and explanation from later scholarship. The result is a thorough look at the folklore of this region, from both the perspective of the early oral and written traditions and that of later study and scholarship.

In addition to the subject and name index, Simmons adds a motif index. In it he lists folk motifs and gives their motif number in either Stith Thompson's *Motif Index of Folk-Literature (1955–58)* or Ernest Baughman's *Type and Motif-Index of the Folktales of England and North America (1966)*. He has assigned his own motif number to a few motifs. The motif index also gives the page numbers in Simmons's book on which various motifs are discussed.

Simmons also adds an appendix of tales and tale fragments that he deemed did not fit into any of his major categories and which consequently he did not include in the main text of his book. He felt, however, that they were too interesting to leave out and therefore includes them as an appendix.

Treasuries

122. Botkin, Benjamin Albert. *Treasury of New England Folklore; Stories, Ballads, and Traditions of the Yankee People.* 1947; rev., New York: Crown, 1965. xxii, 618p. 64-17848.

Botkin's book, first published in 1947, has been reissued and reprinted a number of times. The copy examined was the revised edition of 1965.

This is a broad collection of tales about people, places, traditions, mysteries of ghosts and specters, witches and devils, historical tales of such figures as John Alden and Priscilla Mullins, Ethan Allen, Calvin Coolidge, and P. T. Barnum, and even recipes. There is information about crafts and rural industries such as sugaring, building a stone wall, samplers and quilting; information about courting customs—bundling and courting sticks; and information and stories about holidays. Some information and stories about word and phrase derivation is also included.

Reading this cover to cover or dipping into it for a brief sample will give an idea of the rich oral and written tradition of this area of the country, its history, and its people.

It is an invaluable collection of a variety of folkways and folk arts.

123. Carey, George Gibson. *A Faraway Time and Place: Lore of the Eastern Shore.* Washington, DC: Robert. B. Luce, 1972; repr., New York: Arno Press, 1977. 256p. 77-70586. 0-405-10086-8.

Carey has written several books of folklore. Here he concentrates his folklore-collecting energies on the watermen of a region on the Eastern Shore of Maryland, between the Nanticoke and the Pocomoke rivers. He includes tales, jokes, and information on beliefs and superstitions.

124. ——. *Maryland Folklore.* Centreville, MD: Tidewater Publishers, 1989. xii, 163p. Bibliog. 89-40302. 0-87033-396-8.

In this work, Carey expands on the material he presented in three earlier books, *Maryland Folklore and Folklife* (Cambridge, MD: Tidewater Publishers, 1970), *Maryland Folk Legends and Folk Songs* (Cambridge, MD: Tidewater Publishers, 1971), and *A Faraway Time and Place: Lore of the Eastern Shore* (Washington, DC: Robert. B. Luce, 1972; repr., New York: Arno Press, 1977). He notes in his introduction that he does not reprint in this text the folk songs that appear in the earlier works, but he does reprint and expand on legends, riddles, jokes, children's rhymes and games, and other folklore. He also adds lengthy sections on screen painting, rug weaving, and boat building. Taken all together, Carey's four books present a valuable look at the folklore of one area of Maryland.

125. ——. *Maryland Folklore and Folklife.* Cambridge, MD: Tidewater Publish-

ers, 1970. x, 98p. Illus. Notes. Bibliog. 71-142189. 0-87033-154-xpa.

Carey's book is a true potpourri of folk information collected in Maryland. He begins with a chapter on material culture, in which he gives information on crafts, architecture, farming, and various Maryland occupations, such as oyster fishing. He follows this with sections on legends; tall tales; jokes; folk songs; proverbs; riddles; children's games; folk beliefs, such as weather beliefs and customs surrounding courtship, marriage, childbirth, and death; and folk medicine.

In short, he presents a bit of every aspect of Maryland folklore. The material collected here is the result of a government-supported study of Maryland folklore.

126. Cutting, Edith E. *Lore of an Adirondack County.* Ithaca, NY: Cornell Univ. Press, 1943. 86p. Index. (Cornell Studies in American History, Literature, and Folklore, Vol. I).

Folklore of a very local sort is the subject of this book. Cutting has assembled the folklore she remembers growing up in the Adirondacks. A variety of forms appear—tales, tall tales, weather lore, songs and ballads, proverbs, and games. Cutting lived with her family in Essex County, New York.

127. Kirchner, Audrey Burie. *In Days Gone By: Folklore and Traditions of the Pennsylvania Dutch.* Englewood, CO: Libraries Unlimited, 1996. xiv, 123p. Illus. Bibliog. (World Folklore Series). 95-48860. 1-56308-381-7.

Both folklife and folklore are covered in this book. Under folklife, the authors discuss the Plain People and the Church People, Pennsylvania German dialect, family and home life, occupations (farming, woodworking, weaving, manufacturing, and iron), the Conestoga wagon, the Pennsylvania rifle, folk arts (Scherenschnitte, Fraktur, quilting, needlework, tinware, pottery, basketry), holidays (New Year's Day, Fastnacht Day (or Shrove Tuesday), Easter, Ascension Day, Harvest Home, Christmas), and Brauche (healing) and Hexe.

Under folklore are examples of children's rhymes, plant legends, tall tales, folktales, and tales of Eileschpiggel, or the trickster character.

A third section contains traditional recipes.

128. McMahon, William H. *Pine Barrens Legends, Lore, and Lies.* Wilmington, DE: Middle Atlantic Press, 1980. 149p. Illus. Bibliog. Index. 80-23518. 0-912608-19-6.

The Pine Barrens is an area in New Jersey covering about a million acres of "mysterious sand hills, restless pines and cedars, ruins of forgotten settlements, exotic flowers and ferns, various wee creatures, winding streams of matchless beauty and cold, pure water—the last great wilderness between New England and the Virginias" (p. 13). Traditionally, the people living there, called Pineys, were an isolated people with their own traditions.

Here McMahon collects some of the traditions and stories of this area. Most of the book consists of legends and tall tales. There is also, however, some information on early industries, such as the iron industry and glass blowing, on household maintenance, on local folk remedies, on local jargon, and on regional music.

McMahon brings things up to date with some information on local people who are trying to continue—or in some cases resuscitate—old customs.

129. Thompson, Harold William. *New York State Folktales, Legends and Ballads.* New York: J. B. Lippincott, 1939; repr., New York: Dover, 1967. 530p. Index. Appendix. 65-7559. 0-486-20411-1pa.

This reprint was originally titled *Body, Boots & Britches: Folktales, Ballads and Speech from Country New York.* It contains tall tales, stories of heroes of the early frontier, stories of tricksters, murderers, sailors, soldiers, pirates, and mountaineers. Stories on various traditional trades are included, such as lumbering and whaling. A great many folk songs are included, although without music transcribed.

The Appendix, titled "Who Told You?" gives information on the people who provided the stories.

130. Whitney, Annie Weston, comp. *Folk-lore from Maryland.* New York: American Folklore Society, 1925; repr., New York: Kraus Reprint, 1969. 239p. Index. (Memoirs of the American Folklore Society, vol. 18).

The folklore collected here is more than tales, including sayings, customs, superstitions, folk medicine, children's rhymes—all the snippets of information and custom that make up folklore. It is presented without explanation or source. It is classified according to Wuttke's "Deutscher Volksaberglauben." Thus items to do with the same subject, be it wedding customs or weather signs, cooking or holidays, are collected together. An index also helps locate items on a particular subject.

Charles Haywood, author of the authoritative *Bibliography of North American Folklore,* describes this volume as "What every state should have."

Tales and Legends

131. Adams, Charles J., III. *Bucks County Ghost Stories.* Reading, PA: Exeter House Books, 1999. 186p. Illus. 1-880683-13-xpa.

Adams and a research partner, David J. Siebold, research and write books about local lore, such as ghosts and shipwrecks. This book concerns ghost stories in Bucks County, near Philadelphia.

Adams describes his research methods as follows:

"We plod through dusty documents, historical societies and museums; we probe newspaper morgues, spend countless hours on the internet, and then spend months wandering streets or roads to keep appointments with those who have stories to share." (p. 4)

Most of the ghosts here have been seen in buildings, rather than in open country.

132. Adams, Charles J., III, and David J. Siebold. *Pocono Ghosts, Legends, and Lore, Book Two.* Reading, PA: Exeter House Books, 1995. 115p. Illus. 1-880683-08-3pa.

The publication of Adams and Siebold's first collaboration, *Pocono Ghosts, Legends, and Lore* (which is listed here under Siebold as author) naturally led to communications from still more people who had seen ghosts or lived in haunted houses. This supplementary collection is presented here.

133. Adams, Richard C. *Legends of the Delaware Indians and Picture Writing.* Washington, DC, 1905; repr., Syracuse, NY: Syracuse Univ. Press, 1997. xiv, 115p. Edited and with an introduction by Deb-

orah Nichols. Illus. Bibliog. (The Iroquois and their Neighbors). 97-23740. 0-8156-0487-4.

Richard Adams, himself part Delaware Indian, was fascinated by the stories and traditions of his tribe. *Legends of the Delaware Indians and Picture Writing* contains several legends of the Delaware as he transcribed them, as well as an explanation of an autobiography of one John Hill, which was originally done in pictographs. Adams deciphers and explicates the various pictures that tell this story.

In this reprint, several of the legends are printed in the original Lenape language. Here also is a biography of Richard Adams himself, which tells of his other efforts on behalf of the Delaware people. In addition to preserving their stories, he worked to gain them legal rights and standing.

134. Allen, Joseph C. *Fireside Tales Told 'Longside the Stove in Sanderson's*. New Bedford, MA: George H. Reynold, 1933. 59p.

Sanderson's was the name of a general store on Martha's Vineyard, a place that "carried a stock of everything necessary to the comfort and happiness of the residents of the place and constituted a club-room for the male population beside" (Foreword). Allen sat in this "club-room" and collected the tales told by its members. He tells them in rhyme, using the local dialect. They are tall tales: of a whale so big that it had an entire ship in its mouth; of a goose shot by hunters so often that when it was finally shot dead, its entire body was found to be made of lead.

135. Anastas, Peter. *Glooskap's Children: Encounters with the Penobscot Indians of Maine*. Boston: Beacon Press, 1973. 216p. 72-75534. 0-8070-0518-5.

Anastas presents his material in four different formats:

Documents related to Indian history such as newspaper articles, letters, accounts of early voyages
Voices, or transcripts of interviews he conducted with members of the Penobscot Tribe
Journal, or excerpts from the journal that he kept while living on Indian Island
Legends, or Indian tales and stories

The four types of writing are interspersed within the book; not all the legends are printed together. Most are reprinted from Horace Beck's *Gluskap the Liar* (Bond Wheelright Company, 1966).

The legends are interesting as a counterpoint to the other material included in the book, but this is not an essential collection. The legends are better read in Beck's book.

136. Asfar, Dan. *Ghost Stories of Pennsylvania*. Edmonton, Alberta: Ghost House Books, 2002. 207p. Illus. 1-894877-08-x.

Haunted houses, battlefield ghosts, spirits wandering the countryside, and ghosts that haunt public buildings all mingle in this collection of ghost tales. Asfar interviewed many of the people who have reported seeing these ghosts.

One he did not interview was Thomas A. Edison, who became fascinated with the stories associated with one home in Pittsburgh. So interested was he in the phenomena that he began work on an electrical machine that would allow people to communicate with the dead. Unfortunately, Edison himself died before the machine became operative.

Black-and-white photographs of some

of the haunted sites provide the illustrations.

137. Bartlett, John H. *The Legend of Ann Smith, a New England Story in Verse.* Chicago: M. A. Donohue, 1931. 90p.

Although there are other poems in this volume besides "The Legend of Ann Smith," it is the only one that can be classified as legend or folklore. The others are mostly sketches of local characters or types.

The Ann Smith legend tells the story of a six-year-old girl traveling in a snowstorm with her family, on their way to settle in the wilderness that was New Hampshire. Ann is swept away by the storm but is restored to her family by Sootanore, a hitherto fierce chief who is touched by her plight. Her near death brings about a reconciliation and peace between the settlers and the Native Americans.

This legend, as well as the other stories in the collection, is in verse.

138. Beauchamp, William M. *Iroquois Folk Lore: Gathered from the Six Nations of New York.* Port Washington, NY: Ira J. Friedman, 1965. 251p. Index of the tales. (Empire State Historical Publication XXXI).

Beauchamp, a charter member of the American Folk Lore Society, founded in 1888, collected these tales from many sources and over many years. He states that he wrote them down from oral accounts of Native Americans. His first is a chronology of the history of the Six Nations, told by David Cusick in 1825. Other tales center on various creation stories, animals, war, alliances, and the natural world.

The tales are well told and intriguing. However, there is little if any explanatory material fitting the stories together. This is not the book for those looking for a chronological account, an explanation of where certain stories originated, or biographical sketches of gods or heroes. The tales are told on their own.

139. Beck, Horace P. *Folklore and the Sea.* Middletown, CT: Wesleyan Univ. Press, published for The Maine Historical Association, 1973; repr., Edison, NJ: Castle Books, 1999. xvii, 463p. Bibliog. Index. (The American Maritime Library, v.6). 0-7858-1119-2.

The reader has to dig for tales of New England in this book, for Beck covers folklore of the sea from around the world. Much of it is from the British Isles, particularly the islands of Scotland and Ireland. But what is found of New England is choice. Most of the New England stories relate to ghost ships, wrecked ships whose crews return to sail again, dead sailors who reappear to bid good-bye to relatives, and ships that are seen endlessly reenacting their own last moments. Other lore concerns seafaring language, superstitions (ships' figureheads developed so that a ship would always have eyes and thus be able to help in her own navigation), and sea serpents.

The index helps locate pertinent information, but a basic knowledge of New England geography is helpful. There is no listing in the index for Massachusetts or Rhode Island, for example, but there are references to the city of Gloucester, Massachusetts, to Baker's Island, which is located off the coast of Salem, Massachusetts, and to Block Island, off Rhode Island.

Beck has brought together an amazing amount of curious and historical lore of the sea. Sea lovers and folklore lovers alike will enjoy this book.

140. ——. *The Folklore of Maine*. Philadelphia: Lippincott, 1957. xvi, 284p. Bibliog. Illus.

More than a collection of tales, this places folktales in a historical context. Beck writes sustained chapters on coastal place names; on John Josselyn, who wrote of New England flora, fauna, and folklore in the 1670s, thus becoming Maine's first folklorist; on the sea and islands; and on lumbering. Each chapter mentions various tales and legends, but rather than recounting them fully, Beck weaves them into a more comprehensive history of the place.

Beck includes superstitions, descriptions of customs, and songs—some with music transcribed—in his account. The result is more than a collection of separate tales; it is, rather, an assessment of Maine's history using folklore as a prism.

141. ——. *Gluskap the Liar and Other Indian Tales*. Freeport, ME: Bond Wheelright Company, 1966. x, 182p. Bibliog. Illus.

Beck devotes the first third of this book to a discussion of the archaeology and history of the Native Americans of Maine. He concentrates primarily on the largest group, the Penobscot, with some attention to the Passamaquoddy. However, he points out that these were nomadic peoples, who paid little attention to strict national boundaries, and that these two groups frequently interacted with each other and with two other tribes, the Micmac and the Malecite. The tales in this book are principally from the Penobscot, with tales from the others included if they relate to the Penobscot.

The tales themselves were chosen to illuminate the life of the Penobscot, and Beck states that it is not a complete collection, but rather one culled from much more extensive field notes. He has changed the strictly oral nature of the traditional folktale to one more literary in style, but has tried to "make the tales and other material flow as they would normally in an evening's conversation."

Many of the tales are about Gluskap the giant, a section is devoted to tricksters and transformers, and one to magic. Later tales have European elements, although with Indian heroes and Indian customs. Many of these center around N'Jacques, or Little Jack, a poor boy known in Irish and French folktales as well as in these. Another section highlights tales of war, and a final section has medicine as a theme.

Beck adds a brief appendix in which he discusses some of the themes that the tales illuminate. He also adds a list of folk motifs according to the Stith Thompson Motif Index system and indicates what themes appear in particular tales.

Although not pretending to be a complete collection of tales, this is representative. Beck's discussion of motifs as well as of the historical background of the tales makes this extremely valuable as well as entertaining.

142. Bierhorst, John, ed. *White Deer and Other Stories Told by the Lenape*. New York: W. Morrow, 1995. xi, 137p. Illus. Bibliog. Glossary. 94-30962. 0-688-12900-5.

The Lenape, or Delaware, people are the native people of New Jersey. Although few live in New Jersey now—most are in Ontario and Oklahoma—folk narratives still preserve stories of the old people. Here Bierhorst presents stories of creation, "hero tales, star myths, animal stories, and trickster stories" (p. 8).

These tales were for the most part collected between 1907 and 1984. Bierhorst's introduction explains the tradition of storytelling among the Lenape and some of the customs surrounding storytelling.

143. Bisbee, Ernest E. *State o' Maine Scrap Book of Stories and Legends of "Way Down East."* Lancaster, NH: Bisbee Press, 1940. 70p. Illus.

Although more a brief history of Maine than a collection of legends, some legends are incorporated in this text. Some are well known (the story of Norumbega; the legend of the marriage between Katahdin, the spirit of the mountain, and a young Indian woman that resulted in the birth of a baby with stone eyebrows); others are less common (the stories of Jack the Ripper, a logger who made a pact with the devil for success and fortune; of Judge Jonathan Bucks, who wrongly convicted and hanged a man for the mutilation of a young woman, and whose gravestone was years later mysteriously marked with the outline of a woman's leg).

Such a short book obviously contains only brief accounts, but they are charmingly presented. Reading through the whole chronological account of Maine, from the prehistoric Red Paint people to the early twentieth century, one gets some sense of how legends are intertwined with history.

Illustrations are black-and-white photographs.

144. Bittinger, Marillis. *Tall Tales of Cape Cod.* Plymouth, MA: The Memorial Press, 1948. 93p. Illus.

Bittinger makes no distinction between tales she read, tales she heard from others, and tales she wrote herself. There is no indication of where a tale comes from or whether it is authentic or not. Tales are on a variety of subjects, most involving seafarers and local characters.

145. Bowman, Don. *Go Seek the Pow Wow on the Mountain: And Other Indian Stories of the Sacandaga Valley.* Greenfield Center, NY: Greenfield Review Press, 1993. xxi, 93p. Edited by Vaughn Ward. Illus. by Deborah Delaney. Bibliog. (Bowman Books, No. 6). 93-78205. 0-912678-87-9pa.

In 1930, the Sacandaga River valley in Saratoga County, New York, was flooded as part of a flood control project. Whole settlements, "cranberry bogs on the Big Vly, covered bridges, factories, schools, stores, blacksmith shops and churches" (pp. xiii–xiv) were wiped out. The people who lived there came from a variety of backgrounds—Indian, German, and British. The stories that survived the loss of those communities show the same mixture—stories of creation that blend Native American mythological beings with Sunday school stories, stories of healing and witchcraft, stories that tell a lesson vital to all.

These stories are here retold by Don Bowman, who worked on the construction projects related to the flood control project. They include creation stories, stories with a moral lesson attached, and ghost stories of doomed lovers.

146. Brendle, Thomas R., and William S. Troxell. *Pennsylvania German Folk Tales, Legends, Once-upon-a-Time Stories, Maxims, and Sayings.* Norristown: Pennsylvania German Society, 1944. xxiv, 238p. (Pennsylvania German Society, Volume L).

Published as part of the Proceedings and Addresses of the Pennsylvania German Society, this compilation presents tales of treasure, legends surrounding plants, stories of the devil and the people who made pacts with him, proverbs, stories of special days, hex stories, and stories of ministers. Each section of the book is preceded by a brief introduction that gives the background of that type of tale.

Richard Dorson, in his *American Folklore*, mentions this as an "excellent collection" of folk narrative.

147. Brenizer, Meredith M. *The Nantucket Indians: Legends and Accounts before 1659.* Nantucket, MA: Poets Corner Press, 1976. 45p. Bibliog. Illus.

The tales in this small booklet are brief—from half a page to two pages. The first ones concern the making of the island Nantucket and Martha's Vineyard. One tells of a giant named Mashop who fell asleep on a Cape Cod beach and when half asleep kicked his sand-filled moccasins into the sea. One became the Vineyard and one became Nantucket. Other tales tell of how particular places were named, explain phenomena such as fog, describe Indian life and customs, or simply tell the story of a particular event.

Its brevity obviously precludes the booklet from being a major work. However, the tales are charming, the printing is attractive, and line drawings illustrating many of the tales make it interesting.

148. Brinton, Daniel Garrison. *Lenâpé and their Legends: With the Complete Text and Symbols of the Walam Olum, a New Translation, and an Inquiry into Its Authenticity.* Philadelphia, 1884; repr., New York: AMS Press, 1977. viii, 262p. Index. Vocabulary. Notes. (Brinton's Library of Aboriginal American Literature, Number 5). 77-102641.

The language, way of life, and stories of the Lenape are all told and explored here. Stories include creation stories, migration stories, and stories of the hero Michabo.

The Walam Olum is a pictograph story of great deeds. It was first recorded in the mid-1800s by Constantine Samuel Rafinesque-Schmaltz. There has been a question as to whether Rafinesque produced this writing himself; Brinton maintains it is authentic.

Brinton here reproduces the pictograph, provides the text in the Lenape language and in English, and discusses both the story and the language itself.

149. Bronner, Simon J. *Popularizing Pennsylvania: Henry W. Shoemaker and the Progressive Uses of Folklore and History.* University Park: Pennsylvania State Univ. Press, 1996. xxii, 277p. Illus. Index. Bibliog. 95-15354. 0-271-01486-5; 0-271-01487-3pa.

"Few regions have had as energetic and influential a promoter as Henry Shoemaker" (p. xiii). Thus begins the introduction to this book, a biography of Shoemaker and a retelling of some of the legends he promoted. The biography section comprises fully two-thirds of the book. The latter third consists of a few legends: The Legend of Penn's Cave, Nita-nee, The Indian Steps, and Wildmannli.

Bronner examines the question of whether Shoemaker did too much embellishing of local legends, at the expense of accurate transcribing.

The bibliography is extensive and valuable.

150. Carey, George Gibson. *Maryland Folk Legends and Folk Songs.* Cambridge, MD: Tidewater Publishers, 1971. viii, 120p. Index of Folk Motifs. 75-180857. 0-87033-158-2pa.

Carey defines a folk group as any group of people connected by one or more commonalities—religion, occupation, geography, or ethnicity. He defines folk material as legends, songs, or other material transmitted orally—and usually changed and adapted with each telling.

He maintains that the legends and songs recounted here have little literary merit, for he has set them down as he or others heard them during twenty years of collecting. Most of the material is from the Eastern Shore or from western Maryland.

The legends concern local characters, ghosts, witchcraft, the devil, and urban legends. Songs span the gamut—love songs, songs concerning a particular occupation, military songs, songs of history.

151. Citro, Joseph A. *Green Mountains, Dark Tales.* Hanover, NH: Univ. Press of New England, 1999. xx, 229p. Index. 98-33105. 0-87451-863-6.

Citro describes this collection as being made up of "Eccentrics, ghosts, monsters, the unexplained and the unexplainable" (p. xx). He divides his stories into three sections:

People, including witches, angels, and
    Mary Mable Rogers, a woman who
    was hanged for murder—twice
Places, centering on mysterious events
    in schools, universities, and houses
Things, which tells the stories of
    treasures, mysteriously moved
    stones, and mysteriously appearing
    images

152. ——. *Passing Strange: True Tales of New England Hauntings and Horrors.* Boston: Houghton Mifflin, 1996. 320p. Geographic index. 96-32202. 1-57630-018-8.

According to Citro, New England has a long history of tale telling and ghosts. Both Nathaniel Hawthorne, an author from the early days of American literature, and Stephen King, one from contemporary days, claimed to have seen a ghost. Hawthorne's was a man he saw reading the newspaper at the Boston Athenaeum. To his surprise, a member told him that the man, a Doctor Harris, had been dead for years. King's encounter happened at a party; he saw a ghostly figure in the bedroom where the coats of the party guests had been kept.

Citro has collected numerous stories of ghost sightings from everyday New Englanders. Spirit writing, communication from beyond, vampires, and sightings in graveyards are among the kinds of tales collected. Citro provides a city index to help identify stories that take place in particular locales.

153. Cox, William T. *Fearsome Creatures of the Lumberwoods: With a Few Desert and Mountain Beasts.* Washington, DC: Press of Judd & Detweiler, 1910. 47p. Illus.

Cox provides one-page descriptions of some of the mythical beasts celebrated by lumbermen: the gemberoo, the splinter cat, the wapaloosie. All tales are accompanied by black-and-white drawings of the creature discussed.

Many of these tales are told in areas other than New England, wherever loggers worked.

154. Curtin, Jeremiah. *Seneca Indian Myths.* New York: E. P. Dutton, 1922; repr., New York: Dover, 2001. xii, 516p. Glossary. 2001-22026. 0-486-41602-x.

In the late 1880s, Jeremiah Curtin, who had long had an interest in "philology and mythology" (p. v), began a position with the Bureau of Ethnology. He studied the Seneca language and spent several years on the Seneca Reservation in Versailles, New York. While there, he collected the stories of the inhabitants, which he said even at the time were being forgotten. Only the elders of the Seneca were able to tell him these stories; they had been forgotten or ignored by younger members.

Tales are of the natural world, of interaction between humans and animals, and of instances in which humans are helped or rescued by either animals or spirits.

155. Dahlgren, Madeleine Vinton. *South Mountain Magic: Tales of Old Maryland.* Boston: J. R. Osgood, 1882; new ed., Maple Shade, NJ: Lethe Press, 2002. viii, 126p. (America Obscura). 1-59021-003-4pa.

Dahlgren wrote this book after being widowed in 1876 and purchasing a residence in Maryland; she became intrigued by the legends and stories of the area and began collecting them. Many of the stories in this book deal with the occult, witchcraft, and ghosts and hauntings. She also includes a chapter on folk medicine and cures.

Some of the stories are from Native American traditions, and others date to the early settlers of the region, many of whom were of German origin.

Dahlgren's prose is flowery and romantic, a bit difficult for modern ears.

156. Day, Holman. *Up in Maine: Stories of Yankee Life Told in Verse.* 2d. ed. Boston: Small, Maynard, 1900. xv., 209p. Illus.

A few of the poems in this collection are sailors' yarns, of shipwrecks and killer fish. The poems are written in Maine dialect.

157. Digges, Jeremiah [pseudonym]. *Bowleg Bill the Sea-Going Cowboy, or Ship Ahoy and Let 'Er Buck!* New York: Viking Press, 1938. 188p. Illus. by William Gropper.

Josef Berger wrote both *Bowleg Bill the Sea-Going Cowboy* and *The Cape Cod Pilot* (Boston: Northeastern Univ. Press: 1985) under the same assumed name, Jeremiah Digges. This book is a compilation of tall tales about Bowleg Bill, born a cowboy in Wyoming, who became a sailor and shipped out of Boston, San Francisco, and various ports on Cape Cod. He never became an able-bodied seaman–he was too much the cowboy and too unskilled at sailing for that, but he had many adventures. He lures a whale to his ship with music; he captures a mermaid; and he takes part in a mutiny.

These are the tall tales of seagoing.

158. ——. *The Cape Cod Pilot.* Provincetown, MA: Modern Pilgrim Press, 1937; repr., Boston: Northeastern Univ. Press, 1985. xii, 401p. Illus. Index.

Josef Berger was a writer for the Works Progress Administration (WPA) during the Depression. He wrote *Cape Cod Pilot* not as a WPA writer but in his free time and published it under the pseudonym Jeremiah Digges. Written as a guidebook, it is arranged by town, taking the reader on a journey "down Cape" from Sandwich to the tip of Provincetown and back again to Barnstable and finally Falmouth on Buzzards Bay. It is not a guidebook of old churches and museums, although they are mentioned. It is instead a book of anecdotes, tall tales, and yarns, gathered by the author from the old people of that time, those who remembered the Cape as a center of fishing, whaling, glass manufacturing, and salt making; before it became the tourist center of the 1930s and later.

Tales concern the weather, witchcraft, sea serpents, sea captains, and shipwrecks. The geographic organization of the book means that tales with a certain theme are not grouped together, but the subject index helps locate stories on a particular subject.

159. Drake, Samuel Adams. *A Book of New England Legends and Folk Lore in Prose and Poetry.* New and revised. Boston: Little, Brown, 1901; repr., Detroit, MI: Singing Tree Press, 1969. xvi, 477p. Index. Illus.

Drake's book, revised and reprinted numerous times, is a classic in the field. He believed that legend, tale, and myth have something deep and important to say about society, which scientific explanation cannot always reveal. Such tales can explain what motivates and moves society. He collected these tales, which are in both poetry and prose, from all over New England. Some are rooted in historical fact but are embellished a bit by time and repetition.

This 1901 edition is divided geographically:

Boston, Cambridge, Lynn and
   Nahant, Salem, Marblehead, Cape
   Ann, Ipswich and Newbury (all in
   Massachusetts)
Portsmouth and Hampton in New
   Hampshire
York, Maine
Plymouth, again in Massachusetts
Rhode Island
Connecticut
Nantucket
The White Mountains

Each section begins with a one- or two-page description of the area, its land, history, and people. The description sets the scene for the legends.

160. ——. *Heart of the White Mountains, Their Legend and Scenery.* New York: Harper and Brosl, 1882. 340p. Illus.

Drake wrote this book not only as a guidebook, but as a book for the entertainment of the traveler. He hoped that in addition to providing practical information on travel and information on what to see in the area, it would also be enjoyable and interesting to read. It is thus part guidebook, part history, and part anecdote.

The legends retold here are scattered throughout the book, as Drake writes about particular areas. An index entry "legends" leads the reader to specific pages.

Drake tells the legend of a general who made a pact with the devil for riches. The devil undertook to fill the general's boots with gold each month. One month the greedy general cut the soles from his boots, so that they were bottomless. Furious at being tricked, the devil burned down the house, destroying the gold in the process. Indian legends include the story of Chocorua, recounted in many books, who leaped to his death from the mountain that now bears his name; of Passaconnaway, a Pennacook chief, who ascended to heaven in a chariot of fire; the story of the deluge, in which only Powaw and his wife were saved when all the earth was covered in water, and who when the waters subsided sent forth a hare to see if it was safe to venture forth; the tradition of the Indians' heaven, which was believed to be beyond the White Mountains; the lovers who leaped to their deaths over Glen Ellis Falls rather than be separated; and the Indian maiden who disappeared and was thought dead, but had really gone to marry the spirit of the mountain.

He tells, too, the horrific tale of the sacking of the village of St. Francis de Sales, an Indian settlement under the protection of a French missionary. The American force of rangers, after killing all the inhabitants, stole a silver image of the Virgin Mary before leaving. They never returned to their base camp, but perished in the mountains, flinging away from them at the last the silver statue, which they blamed for their misfortune. The statue was never found.

161. Early, Eleanor. *Adirondack Tales.* Boston: Little, Brown, 1939. 247p. Illus. Index.

Early says in her introduction that she takes the essential information about a place and dresses it up "with chocolate-covered facts to make a local history" (p. 8). She also maintains that her books are as accurate as she can make them, through extensive research and conversation with local historians.

She writes a guidebook, with information on specific places to visit. But interspersed with this tourist information are details designed to make tourists want to visit—the stories of local characters, well-known ones such as Diamond Jim Brady and Rip Van Winkle, and lesser-known ones such as Campbell's ghost at Ticonderoga. The writing is lighthearted and makes interesting reading.

162. ——. *New England Sampler.* Boston: Waverly House, 1940. xii, 372p. Illus.

Most of this book consists of sketches of real people and events, from the Salem witch hysteria to Lizzie Borden, Lydia Pinkham (maker of an early patent medi-

cine and an early believer in the power of advertising and marketing), and John L. Sullivan. One chapter, however, gives a précis of several New England ghost stories. Early recounts the story of the ghost ship of New Haven, Connecticut, which left New Haven for London in the depth of winter in the late seventeenth century. It was never seen or heard from again until a year from the following June, when it sailed in during a mighty thunderstorm, sailing dead against the wind. When it had come as close to shore as the depth of water allowed, it vanished. First its sails and masts, then its hull dissolved into mist.

Early also recounts the tale of Ocean Born Mary. This child's mother was on a ship captured by the pirate Philip Babb. The mother's fright brought on the birth. Babb was so touched by the helplessness of the newborn girl that he released the ship, requesting that the child be named Ocean Born Mary. The mother kept her promise. When Ocean Born Mary was grown, herself a mother and a widow, Babb provided a house for her. It is this house, in Henniker, New Hampshire, that Mary haunts.

The last ghost story concerns Jonathan Moulton, who had two wives, Abigail and Sarah. Sarah, the second wife, had a most unpleasant experience on her wedding night: The ghost of Abigail, the first wife, appeared and removed the wedding rings from Sarah's hand. The rings were never seen again.

Illustrations are black-and-white drawings.

163. English, J. S. *Indian Legends of the White Mountains.* Boston: Rand, Avery, 1915. 92p.

English retells twelve legends, which

he says he received both from the records of local historical societies and from individuals. All the tales are of the White Mountains. Many concern early contracts between Anglo settlers and Native Americans, and others have love as their theme. The tales are short.

164. Federal Writers' Project of the Works Progress Administration. *New Jersey, a Guide to Its Present and Past.* New York: The Viking Press, 1939. xxxii, 735p. Illus. Index. Classified bibliography. Chronology of significant events in New Jersey history. (American Guide Series).

The New Jersey guidebook from the Federal Writers' Project contains a chapter on "Folklore and Folkways," on pages 126–133. These pages recount the history and doings of the Leeds devil, a creature "with the head of a collie dog, the face of a horse, the body of a kangaroo, the wings of a bat, and the disposition of a lamb" (p. 126); tales of pirates; stories of ghosts; and tales of farming, including one of a farmer who captured a shark, saddled and bridled it, and made a living delivering mail while riding it along the river. The second half of the chapter, on folkways, recounts some of the old ways of the various groups that made up the state's early population. As with other Federal Writers' Project guidebooks, this provides a quick survey of the rich treasure of folklore associated with the state, and readers can use it as a starting point. The bibliography, as with the other guidebooks, is excellent, though old.

Again as with the other guidebooks in the series, the last half of the book describes tours one can take by car through the state, again mentioning local legends as they pertain to the particular area.

165. Frazier, Jeffrey R. *The Black Ghost of Scotia and More Pennsylvania Fireside Tales: Origins and Foundations of Pennsylvania Mountain Folktales and Legends, Vol. II.* Lancaster, PA: Egg Hill Publications, 1997. xxii, 169p. Illus. Notes. Bibliog. 97-169510. 0-9652351-1-4pa.

Frazier found the reception to his first book of Pennsylvania tales, *Pennsylvania Fireside Tales* (Lancaster, PA: Wickersham Printing Co., 1996), so encouraging that he continued collecting and published a second volume. The tales in this volume treat of the old days and celebrate the hardy pioneer spirit that settled the state. In his introduction, Frazier repeats his conviction that even in this day of television and other electronic entertainment, people still appreciate the old tales.

166. ——. *Pennsylvania Fireside Tales.* Lancaster, PA: Wickersham Printing Co., 1996. 149p. Illus. Notes. Bibliog. 0-9652351-0-6pa.

Witches, ghosts, and criminals are among the characters in these tales from Pennsylvania. Frazier interviewed longtime residents and perused old newspaper issues for stories, which he says are the ones that were told around the fire in the days before the existence of such entertainment as television and video games.

167. Gardner, Emelyn Elizabeth. *Folklore from the Schoharie Hills.* Ann Arbor: Univ. of Michigan Press, 1937. xv, 351p. Illus. Index. Bibliog. List of Informants.

Gardner collected these stories and songs in the early part of the twentieth century, over about a six-year period starting in 1912. She includes tales, ghost stories, superstitions, rhymes and games, and folk songs.

In addition to the tales themselves, the introductory material is also of interest. Gardner writes of the methods she employed in collecting her material, traveling by stage and hired carriage into the hills, staying in people's houses, and encountering their distrust and suspicion. People were unwilling to be photographed, fearing that the picture would steal their soul; one woman became enraged when she saw Gardner making notes, thinking she was practicing witchcraft; many people simply refused to speak with her, as any stranger was suspect. These were people who seldom went farther than five miles from home, who had never seen a train, much less ridden on one, and who referred to the Atlantic Ocean as "a big river" and to Pennsylvania, only fifty miles away, as "furrin' parts."

In this book, Gardner has indeed preserved a way of life now vanished.

168. Geller, L. D. *Sea Serpents of Coastal New England*. Plymouth, MA: The Pilgrim Society, 1970. 10p. (Pilgrim Hall Series on New England Folklore).

These few pages print excerpts from an 1817 report, *Report of a Committee of the Linnaean Society of New England Relative to a Large Animal Supposed to Be a Sea Serpent Seen Near Cape Ann, Massachusetts, in August 1817* (Boston, 1817). The report collected first-person accounts of sightings of a sea serpent seen by numerous people—most of whom were reputable, reliable people—near Gloucester, Massachusetts. The accounts agreed on the size, shape, color, and behavior of the creature.

169. Glimm, James York. *Flatlanders and Ridgerunners: Folktales from the Mountains of Northern Pennsylvania*. Pittsburgh, PA: Univ. of Pittsburgh Press, 1983. xxxi, 199p. Illus. Notes. 82-10895. 0-8229-3471-x; 0-8229-5345-5pa.

Glimm is originally from Long Island (where, he says in his preface, the closest thing to nature is the golf course) and came to the mountains of northern Pennsylvania to teach at Mansfield State College. He became intrigued with the folklore and stories of the region and began collecting them. His interest led him to study folklore seriously, including a year's sabbatical study and work with Richard Dorson.

In this book he presents more than a hundred tales and anecdotes. The tales concern

Local activities, such as hunting and
    fishing
Customs
The supernatural
Tall tales

Many are told in the form of personal anecdotes, as if the event had happened to the speaker.

Glimm remarks in his introduction that while men told mostly tales of adventure, including yarns and tall tales, the women's stories were concerned mostly with folk belief, folk medicine, signs, and portents.

The tales here are short—often less than a page—but numerous. Glimm assures the reader that they are transcribed faithfully in the teller's voice, with his own interpolations, questions, and comments excluded.

Notes tell the sources of the tales.

170. ——. *Snakebite: Lives and Legends of Central Pennsylvania*. Pittsburgh, PA: Univ. of Pittsburgh Press, 1991. xii, 256p. 90-49473. 0-8229-3667-4; 0-8229-5444-3pa.

Glimm, the author of *Flatlanders and Ridgerunners* (Univ. of Pittsburgh Press,

1983), divides the tales in this follow-up book into three categories:

Folktales, or "anonymous story(ies) that circulate(s) by word of mouth" (p. 2)

Local legends and superstitions, or stories that may have started out as true, but have been embellished through many tellings

True stories, of disasters, hard times, and everyday life

Glimm has a somewhat different take on days gone by. Although many think of the old days as infinitely more stable, quiet, and peaceful than our own time, Glimm makes a convincing case for the theory that people in the early part of this century lived through more amazing change than we have: the change from an agrarian to an industrial society, improvements such as electricity and telephones, change in the status of women, inventions such as movies and television, and an increasingly diverse society.

All the stories told here were collected in central Pennsylvania, in the area around the West Branch of the Susquehanna River.

171. Goerlich, Shirley Boyce. *Legends and Reality: Based on Stories from Chenango, Delaware and Otsego Counties, Central New York State.* Bainbridge, NY: RSG Publishing, 1990. ii, 55p. Illus. 90-092242. 0-9614858-3-3.

Goerlich collected legends from Chenango, Delaware, and Otsego counties in central New York. Many of them concern stories of people who were buried in unusual ways—and sometimes came back to haunt the area.

172. Gore, Mrs. M. F., and Mrs. G. E. Speare. *More New Hampshire Folk Tales.* Plymouth, NH: Mrs. Guy E. Speare, 1936. xv, 287p.

Rather than the chronological arrangement of tales as in the first volume by Mrs. Gore and Mrs. Speare, these tales are loosely grouped by theme:

Tavern Tales
Along the Seacoast
Pioneers
Scotch-Irish Tales
School Days
Anecdotes from various New Hampshire towns

Most of the stories are true, although somewhat changed in the telling over the years. They include reminiscences of early residents, collected and written down by members of New Hampshire women's clubs. A few qualify as tall tales.

173. ——. *New Hampshire Folk Tales.* Plymouth, NH: New Hampshire Federation of Women's Clubs, 1932. xvi, 265p.

As so many collections of folklore are, this is a mixture of truth and fiction—sometimes truth and fiction in the same tale. It is chronologically arranged. The first tales are Native American ones of various places in New Hampshire—Winnepesaukee; Indian Leap, or Ahwannega; Salmon Falls; Squam Lake; Lake Sunapee. Then come stories of Indian battles and captivity by Indians. Tales of people, places, and events in the American Revolution follow a section on pioneer life and the pioneers' encounters with the natural world of animals and topography. The last two sections encompass stories of superstition, such as ghosts, witches, and demons; and of famous people who lived in or visited New Hampshire.

The tales are almost all quite short, usually one or two pages. The ones that purport to be true may be embellished by time (one tale is cherished by two different families as family lore), but this makes them even more part of folklore, even if less of history.

174. Hale, Duane K., ed. *Cooley's Traditional Stories of the Delaware.* Anadarko, OK: Delaware Tribe of Western Oklahoma Press, 1984. ix, 81p. Illus.

The Lenape, or Delaware, people lived originally in the eastern United States, before being forced into Oklahoma. The arrangement of this book of their stories is very simple and very effective. Biographies of the storytellers come first. Then come the stories themselves—in English and also in the Delaware language. Finally comes a word list of Delaware words.

Most of the stories concern animals.

Hale, the editor of this volume, also edited *Turtle Tales: Oral Traditions of the Delaware Tribe of Western Oklahoma* (Delaware Tribe of Western Oklahoma, 1984), listed in the chapter on folklore of the Southwest.

175. Halpert, Herbert Norman. *Folktales and Legends from the New Jersey Pines; a Collection and a Study.* Indiana Univ., 1947. 762p. Bibliog.

An early collector of legends from the New Jersey Pine Barrens, Halpert worked there during the 1930s and 1940s. For part of this time, he was a doctoral candidate at Indiana University; this is his doctoral thesis.

One aim of his study was to explore the relationship of these tales, told in a specific section of the United States, to European tales, and this takes up much of his thesis. He also, however, presents the stories themselves as he heard them. He divides the tales into the following categories:

The Fiddler and the Devil
The Wizard of the Pines
Devils, Witches, and Spirits
Strong Men and Tall Tales
Fools and Clever Fellows
Tricksters and Clever Fellows

With each tale he gives the name of the narrator and the date the tale was collected.

176. Harris, Harold. *Treasure Tales of the Shawangunks and Catskills.* [Ellenville, NY:] H. Harris, 1955. 127p. Illus. Bibliog.

Harris lived in New York City for the beginning of his adult life. Work took him to the area of the Shawangunks and Catskills, where he says he found a home. He developed an interest in the legends of the area and talked to longtime residents to collect these. One of the legends even has to do with Captain Kidd, not a name usually associated with this part of New York.

This book was reissued in 1998, but the new edition is difficult to obtain from libraries.

177. Hitakonanu'laxk. *The Grandfathers Speak: Native American Folk Tales of the Lenape People.* New York: Interlink Books, 1994. x, 134p. Glossary. Bibliog. (International Folk Tales). 93–39771. 1-56656-129-9; 1-56656-128-0pa.

These tales of the Lenape people, or Delaware, tell their creation story and the story of their development as a people, including how they came to live in what is now the eastern United States. Some of the stories have a moral lesson to teach; others expound on the history of the Lenape people. Still others are told just for fun and entertainment.

Hitakonanu'laxk, or Tree Beard, gives in his introduction a history of the

Lenape people, a look at their traditional way of life, information about their first meeting with Europeans, and a discussion of their spiritual life.

178. Hommell, Pauline. *Teacup Tales: Folklore of the Hudson Valley.* New York: Vantage Press, 1958. 99p.

Twenty-five tales, each only a few pages in length, make up this little book. All focus on the Hudson Valley.

179. Irving, Washington. *The Sketch Book of Geoffrey Crayon, Gentleman.* Boston: Twayne, 1978. xxxii, 510p. (The Complete Works of Washington Irving). 77-0134130. 0-8057-8510-8.

Most of the essays in *The Sketch Book* concern Irving's travels in England, but it also contains his two immortal folklore creations, "Rip Van Winkle" and "The Legend of Sleepy Hollow," both of which have become folklore classics. As with other volumes in the Twayne's Complete Works series, this contains Explanatory Notes and "A List of Emendations," or a list of all differences in the texts of various editions of this work.

The author of these tales, Washington Irving himself, as well as the purported author, Diedrich Knickerbocker, have become folk characters as well.

180. Jameson, W. C. *Buried Treasures of New England: Legends of Hidden Riches, Forgotten War Loots, and Lost Ship Treasures.* Little Rock, AR: August House Publishers, 1998. 192p. Glossary. Bibliog. 96-39749. 0-87483-485-6.

All of the New England states have their stories of lost treasures, and Jameson chronicles four or five from each state. As one might expect, many of these are treasures sunk at sea, but others are the hidden—and then forgotten—loot of robberies or of smuggling.

Jameson provides an outline map of each state, with the approximate location of each treasure marked.

181. Klees, Emerson. *Legends and Stories of the Finger Lakes Region: The Heart of New York State.* Rochester, NY: Friends of the Finger Lakes Pub., 1995. 144p. Illus. Bibliog. 95-60906. 0-9635990-5-4.

Stories from a variety of sources make up this book, some true, some rooted in truth but embroidered, and some invented. Many Native American tales and legends of the area are included. Also here are tales of sea serpents sighted in the lakes; ghosts; romances; and heroes. True tales include some about inventions (the invention of ice cream sundaes); historical events (the day an aqueduct failed and as a consequence the Erie Canal ran dry); and stories of how various towns came to be named.

182. Leland, Charles Godfrey. *The Algonquin Legends of New England; or, Myths and Folk Lore of the Micmac, Passamaquoddy, and Penobscot Tribes.* Boston: Houghton Mifflin, 1884; repr., Detroit, MI: Singing Tree Press, 1968. vii, 379p. Illus. Bibliog.

This Singing Tree Press publication is a reprint of Leland's 1884 book. He began collecting the legends contained in it in 1882. They are of the New England Algonquin Indians, also known as the Wabanaki or Abenaki. They include the Passamaquoddies and Penobscots and the Micmacs.

Leland includes legends of Glooskap, the central god; his twin brother, Malsumsis, who represents evil; Lox, the mischiefmaker; and Chenoo, the human with an icy heart.

Leland does more than recount the legends themselves. In his introduction and in notes within the legends, he comments on the parallels he sees between these Algonquin legends and other mythological structures. He compares the Algonquin legends with the well-known Norse legends of Thor and Oden, and with Eskimo legends.

183. Leland, Charles Godfrey, and John D. Prince. *Kuloskap the Master: And Other Algonquin Poems.* New York: Funk and Wagnalls, 1902. 370p. Index. Illus.

Charles Leland is the author of *The Algonquin Legends of New England* (1884; repr. Detroit, MI: Singing Tree Press, 1968). In this book he teams up with John D. Prince, a linguist with knowledge of the Algonquin language, to present Algonquin legends in poetic form. Some of the legends told here are also in *Algonquin Legends of New England;* others are unique to this volume.

About two-thirds of this volume is devoted to legends of Kuloskap, "The Lord of Beasts and Men." They describe his birth, his creation of the world, his kindness to the creatures he created, and his battles with evil forces.

Another section presents legends of witchcraft, and the final segment is composed of lyric poems.

This presentation of the Kuloskap—or Glooskap—legends gives a flavor of how they were meant to be told—as chanted sagas.

184. Lunt, C. Richard K. *Jones Tracy: Tall-Tale Hero from Mount Desert Island.* Orono, ME: Northeast Folklore Society, 1969. 74p. Bibliog. Notes. Index of informants. (Northeast Folklore, vol. X).

Jones Tracy lived all his life (1856–1939) in Maine as a farmer. He became well known locally as a teller of tall tales. Lunt here presents a brief biography of

Tracy and a number of his tales, all retold by people who had heard Tracy tell them. The tales concern local activities and places. In one, Tracy had only one bullet, but saw two wild turkeys he wanted to shoot. He solved the problem by aiming for a rock that was in between the two turkeys; the bullet hit the rock, split, and each half of the bullet killed one turkey. In another, he had an apple tree that was not bearing sweet fruit. Having heard that adding iron to the soil would improve the crop, he buried a number of horseshoes at its base. The next year, the tree bore "two armored cruisers and a battleship" (p. 40).

Tracy is similar to Hathaway Jones, the teller of tall tales in Oregon, in *Tall Tales from Rogue River: The Yarns of Hathaway Jones* (Corvallis: Oregon State Univ. Press, 1990).

185. MacIver, Kenneth A., and William Thomson. *Tales for a New England Night.* Cape Neddick, ME: Nor'easter Heritage Publications, 1980. 88p. Illus. by Robert J. Neary. pa.

The area north of Boston is the locale for most of these ghost stories. Essex, Salem, and Gloucester all have their resident ghosts, and MacIver describes them here.

186. McCloy, James F., and Ray Miller Jr. *The Jersey Devil.* Wallingford, PA: Middle Atlantic Press, 1976. 121p. Illus. Index. Bibliog. 75-32056. 0-912608-05-6.

McCloy and Miller give a history of the Jersey Devil, that mythical creature seen most often in southern New Jersey. They include accounts of sightings and of hoaxes.

187. ———. *Phantom of the Pines: More Tales of the Jersey Devil.* Moorestown, NJ: Middle Atlantic Press, 1998. x, 166p. Illus.

Index. Bibliog. Chronology. 98-13684. 0-912608-95-1.

A second book by McCloy and Miller about the Jersey Devil. Since the publication of their first book, *The Jersey Devil,* they continued to collect material and anecdotes, which they publish here. First they give a history of the Devil's appearances in New Jersey and of its relation to other folk creatures, such as Bigfoot. They continue with accounts of more recent sightings.

They add a chronology of sightings of the large, fire-breathing creature known as the Jersey Devil.

188. McCutchen, David M., trans. *Red Record: The Wallam Olum: The Oldest Native North American History.* Garden City Park, NY: Avery Pub. Group, 1993. xvi, 222p. Illus. Maps. Notes. Bibliog. Index. 92-23247. 0-89529-525-3pa.

The Red Record is a Delaware chronicle, the story of creation as seen by the Delaware, and a record of the group's crossing of the American continent in ancient times. Linda Poolaw, who at the time McCutchen wrote this book was the Grand Chief of the Delaware Nation Grand Council of North America, Inc., wrote in the Foreword: The Red Record is a song "sung by my ancestors, as they traveled thousands of miles in search of that place where the Sun wakes up" (p. x).

McCutchen presents the story in several ways. He first presents the story as poetry, in the pictures and words of the Delaware language. He then translates the poetry into poetry written in English. Finally, he offers a prose translation of the sense of the narrative.

The Red Record gives a look at the ancient history of one Native American tribe, its everyday life, and its travels. It also reveals the story of its first meeting with European colonists.

189. Mead, Alice, and Arnold Neptune. *The Giants of the Dawnland: Eight Ancient Wabanaki Legends.* Cumberland Center, ME: Loose Cannon Press, 1996. 73p. Illus. Bibliog. 1-888-034-01-7pa.

First collected and written down between 1870 and 1884, the stories here tell of the early days of the Micmac, Penobscot, and Passamaquoddy people in Maine, when hunting and fishing were the means to survival. Here are the tales of Gluskape, or Glooskap, the beginnings of the world, how rivers, lakes, and hills came to be, and how the country was freed of monsters and serpents.

190. Mechling, William H. *Malecite Tales.* Ottawa: Government Printing Bureau, 1914. vi, 133p. (Canada. Department of Mines. Geological Survey Branch, Memoir 49, Anthropological Series.)

Mechling collected tales of the Malecite Indians, those living both in Maine and in Quebec and New Brunswick. The first fifty pages consist of Glooskap tales. Another group is about the wise woman Poktcinskwes. The rest are miscellaneous tales of war, adventure, animals, and plants. The two last tales are from the Micmacs.

191. Nichols, Robert E., Jr. *Birds of Algonquin Legend.* Ann Arbor: Univ. of Michigan, 1995. xvi, 149p. Illus. by Linda Hoffman Kimball. Index. Bibliog. 95-19668. 0-472-10611-2.

The tales and legends recounted here are from the various tribes of the Algonquin people. All concern birds and their significance in Algonquin society. Nichols adds headnotes to explain various facts of natural history that modern people are often unacquainted with and that help illumine the point of each tale. He also gives the attribution of each story, both the name of the original storyteller, if known, and the first printed source.

192. Nicolar, Joseph. *The Life and Traditions of the Red Man.* Bangor, ME: C. H. Glass, 1893; repr., Fredericton, N.B.: Saint Annes Point Press, 1979. xvi, 150p. Bibliog. C79-094292-5.

Nicolar was a member of the Penobscot Nation. He tells here the tales of Glooscap, although somewhat transformed to bring them into line with his Christian beliefs. He omits the characteristics of Glooscap that show him as a trickster, concentrating instead on his role as the creator of the world.

193. Parsons, Elsie Clews. *Folk-Lore from the Cape Verde Islands.* Cambridge, MA: American Folklore Society, 1923. 2v.

Collected in the early 1900s, these tales are from a group of Portuguese immigrants from the Cape Verde Islands to the United States. Volume 1 prints the stories in English; Volume 2 uses the Portuguese dialect of the islands. Some tales are European in origin; others are African.

194. Rand, Silas T. *Legends of the Micmacs.* New York: Longmans, Green, 1894; repr., New York: Johnson Reprint, 1971. xlvi, 452p. 70-184257.

Silas Rand, a missionary among the Micmac Indians of Nova Scotia and Prince Edward Island in the nineteenth century, collected and transcribed these stories about them during that time. The Micmacs also inhabited northern Maine. These are the stories of Gluskap and Chenoo, of chiefs and magic animals. Many later scholars of Native American myths made use of Rand's work, including Charles Leland in his *Algonquin Legends of New England* (1884; repr., Detroit, MI: Singing Tree Press, 1968).

This book is a very early transcription of these ancient legends, written by someone who spoke the Micmac language and who lived among those people.

195. Rapp, Marvin A. *Canal Water and Whiskey: Tall Tales from the Erie Canal Country.* Revised and expanded. Buffalo: Western New York Heritage Institute, Canisius College, with the support of the Lockport Savings Bank, 1992. viii, 398p. Illus. List of sources. Index. 1-878097-07-5.

Rapp grew up on the Erie Canal; his grandfather worked for the Buffalo Creek Railroad, which serviced the canal. Rapp's childhood was spent steeped in the workings of the canal. Here he recounts the stories the old-timers told him, people who worked on the canal and who in turn had heard stories from even older workers. The stories date back to the 1820s, when the canal was being built.

Stories concern the workers—diggers, towpath workers, lock operators; people who were involved peripherally—entertainers, storekeepers, tavern owners; life on and beside the canal; and various mysteries and ghost stories that the canal has engendered.

196. Rash, Bryson B. *Footnote Washington: Tracking the Engaging, Humorous, and Surprising Bypaths of Capital History.* McLean, VA: EPM Publications, 1983. 127p. Illus. 83-1572. 0-914440-62-4.

Some of the vignettes in this collection are truly historic notes—the history of how the area now known as Washington, D.C., was chosen as the capital of the United States, for example. Others have the ring of folklore—the story, for instance, of Henry Wilson, vice president under U. S. Grant, who was called from his bath to attend to urgent business, caught a chill, and died. He can now be seen walking along the corridor leading to his office in the Senate, wrapped in a towel. It should be noted that at the time, bathtubs were located in the basement of the House and the Senate, and were used by all members; it was from this bathtub that Wilson was called.

Rash arranges his anecdotes geographically, in the following sections:

The Capitol
The White House
The Washington Monument
The Lincoln Memorial
Pennsylvania Avenue and the Mall
Statues and Plaques
Washington National Cathedral
Georgetown
Nearby Washington
Cemeteries

All in all, this is a slight but charming book, well worth a browse.

197. Reynard, Elizabeth. *The Narrow Land: Folk Chronicles of Old Cape Cod.* 3d. ed. Boston: Houghton Mifflin, 1978. xiv, 343p. Bibliog. Illus.

Originally published in 1934, Reynard's book has seen many editions. All the threads that made up the fabric of Cape Cod are apparent here: tales from Indian legends, tales of witches from the days of early European settlement, pirate stories, sea serpents, and ghost ships. Some are familiar tales common to most cultures with a particular setting. Others are based on Cape Cod's own history and are more specific: for example, stories of the gaffers at the glass factory in Sandwich and the tales they spin.

198. Rondina, Christopher. *The Vampire Hunter's Guide to New England.* North Attleborough, MA: Covered Bridge Press, 2000. vi, 186p. Notes. Bibliog. 0-58066-055-xpa.

According to Rondina, New England possesses the greatest tradition of vampire lore outside Eastern Europe. The explanation seems to be that just after the Revolutionary War, a mysterious epidemic plagued New Englanders. They called it the wasting disease, or consumption. In an attempt to explain why and how it was devastating families, they reached back to the tradition of vampires and concluded that the undead were preying on the living.

Rondina says that many of the stories of vampires died with the last surviving member of the family that told it. But here he has reconstructed and retells nine stories with roots in the late eighteenth and early nineteenth centuries. He also gives a timeline of the vampire legend; discusses various film representations; and reprints two literary approaches to the vampire, one a poem by Amy Lowell, and one a story by Edgar Allan Poe.

199. ——. *Vampire Legends of Rhode Island.* North Attleborough, MA: Covered Bridge Press, 1997. xv, 80p. Illus. Bibliog. 0-924771-91-7pa.

Rhode Island has a rich legacy of vampire stories. Most of them are set in the years between 1796 and 1892 and have a foundation in fact. During that period, families who lost several members often believed that the grave of the recently deceased housed a vampire that would in turn kill another member of the family. Families would exhume a body in order to destroy the vampire and end the curse.

Rondina tells the various legends of the areas, often adding reprints of contemporary newspaper accounts to these chilling stories.

200. Sams, Jamie. *Other Council Fires Were Here before Ours: A Classic Native American Creation Story as Retold by a Seneca Elder.* San Francisco: HarperSanFrancisco, 1991. 147p. 90-55307. 0-06-250763-xpa.

A Seneca elder and her granddaughter retell the Seneca creation story, the creation of the worlds of spirit, love, ice, water, separation, illumination, and prophecy. The story makes the case that in order to survive and prosper, humans must live in harmony with the entire world.

An appendix illustrates and explains the symbols of the Seneca language.

201. Shaw, Edward Richard. *Legends of Fire Island and the South Side.* Reissue. Port Washington, NY: Ira J. Friedman, 1969. 212p. Illus. Notes explaining some place names. (Empire State Historical Publications Series no. 76). 72-101021. 87198-076-2.

This is a reissue of an 1895 publication, published by Lovell, Coryell & Co. In it, Shaw tells seven legends of the area.

202. Shoemaker, Henry Wharton. *Black Forest Souvenirs, Collected in Northern Pennsylvania.* Reading, PA: Bright-Faust Printing, 1914; repr., Baltimore: Gateway Press, 1991. xix, 404p. Illus. New index by Spencer Kraybill. 91-72080.

Shoemaker made his first visit to this region as a young man in 1898. He made subsequent visits in the following four years, always talking to people there and collecting notes of the stories they told. He next revisited in 1907 and found a changed area—in his words, one of "slashings, fire-swept wastes, emptiness, desolation, ruin. . . . Gone were the hemlocks, beeches, maples and pines; gone the sweet singing birds, the balmy breezes, gone even were the lumbermen with their red or blue shirts, the lumber camps, the stemwinder log railways, gone was everything but ruin" (Preface, pp. xv–xvi). It was then that he decided to write down the stories he had heard. This collection is the result. It was published after his earlier successes, *Pennsylvania Mountain Stories* and *More Pennsylvania Mountain Stories,* and tells the stories of a different area of the state.

The illustrations are photographs of logging camps.

203. ——. *The Indian Steps and Other Pennsylvania Mountain Stories.* Reading, PA: Bright Printing, 1912. ix, 427p. Illus.

The Indian steps of the title refer to steps carved from the Tussey Mountains in central Pennsylvania. They were to aid a group of fighters from the southern part of the area in crossing the mountains to attack their northern rivals. Other legends are also included.

In his introduction, Shoemaker states that some of the stories included here are of "more human interest than folklore" (p. vi) and defends their inclusion by saying that "[a]ny story which relates to human beings will sooner or later become folklore" (p. vi–vii). It is true that many of the stories here are of people contemporary with Shoemaker; it is equally true that now, some eighty-five years later, they have the ring of legend.

204. ——. *Juniata Memories: Legends Collected in Central Pennsylvania.* Reading, PA: J. J. McVey, 1916. xv, 395p. Illus. Bibliog. of Shoemaker's works.

This book concentrates on the legends of the southern part of the Juniata Valley in Pennsylvania. In an earlier book, *In the Seven Mountains,* Shoemaker collected and published legends of the northern part of the same area. These legends were collected between 1911 and 1913, and Shoemaker takes pains to state in his preface that he has written them down exactly as they were told to him. He changed some names if, he writes, the particulars of the story would embarrass the individual's descendants. Many of the legends concern lost loves and ghosts.

205. ——. *More Allegheny Episodes: Legends and Traditions Old and New. Gathered among the Pennsylvania Mountains.* Altoona, PA: Mountain City Press, 1924. vol 1—pp. 1–262. vol. 2—pp. 263–544. 2 vol. (Vol. XII, Pennsylvania Folklore Series).

These two volumes are typical of Shoemaker's work in folklore–a mixture of ghost stories, tales of pioneer days, anecdotes, and legends.

206. ——. *More Pennsylvania Mountain Stories.* Reading, PA: Bright Printing, 1912. xv, 405p. Illus.

Books previously published by Henry Shoemaker include *Wild Life in Western Pennsylvania* and *Pennsylvania Mountain Stories,* both predecessors to this volume, both collections of folklore of central Pennsylvania. This third volume concentrates on stories of ghosts and of witchcraft.

207. ——. *South Mountain Sketches; Folk Tales and Legends Collected in the Mountains of Southern Pennsylvania.* Altoona, PA: Times Tribune, 1920. 332p. Illus.

Shoemaker compiled and published many volumes of folklore from Pennsylvania. He wrote down the tales told him and transcribed them in the words of the speaker. In the introduction to this volume he laments his own lack of literary imagination that prevented him from rewriting the tales in a more literary style. Of course, the present reader of folklore does not share that regret.

Shoemaker collected these tales from 1907 to 1919.

208. ——. *Susquehanna Legends, Collected in Central Pennsylvania.* Reading, PA: Bright Printing, 1913. xviii, 389p. Illus.

As in so many other of Henry Shoemaker's collections of Pennsylvania folklore, the major themes of this collection are lost loves, ghosts, and Native American legends. Also as in others, he states that he has recorded each legend as it was told to him.

209. ——. *Tales of the Bald Eagle Mountains in Central Pennsylvania.* Reading, PA: Bright Printing, 1912. xx, 490p. Illus.

Like so many chroniclers of folklore, Shoemaker in his introduction to *Tales of the Bald Eagle Mountains* laments the fact that no earlier collectors worked in this geographic area, during times when local legends were more plentiful, remembered, and easily recorded. Despite his unhappiness, however, he managed to collect and publish numerous collections. In this one, he set out to locate and publish a tale for each mountain in the Bald Eagle chain.

The stories are similar to those in some of his earlier books: Native American legends, tales of love, and ghost stories.

210. Siebold, David J., and Charles J. Adams III. *Pocono Ghosts, Legends, and Lore.* Reading, PA: Exeter House Books, 1991. 115p. Illus. Bibliog. 1-880683-00-8pa.

This is the first book of ghost stories that Siebold and Adams collaborated on; they have gone on to publish several more. This one centers on the Poconos. All stories are told from the point of view of the person or persons who reported seeing the ghost.

Illustrations are black-and-white photograph of the scenes of the ghost sightings.

211. Simmons, William S. "The Mystic Voice: Pequot Folklore from the Seventeenth Century to the Present," in *The Pequots in Southern New England,* by Laurence M. Hauptman and James D. Wherry, eds. (Norman: Univ. of Oklahoma Press, 1990), 141–175. Index. Bibliog. 90-50135. 0-8061-2286-2.

Simmons is known for his book *Spirit of the New England Tribes* (Univ. Press of New England, 1986). In *The Pequots in Southern New England,* he contributes one chapter, on the history and the contemporary life of the Pequots. He recounts legends found both in historical manuscripts and in interviews with present-day members of the Pequots. The legends include those of the god Wetucks, or Maushop—alternative names for the same god—and of his wife, Squant. Other tales of people he recounts are those of the Devil, the Little People, and the Wooden People, a fairy people who live in the woods. He also includes tales of animals, planting, weather, and witchcraft and of encounters between Native Americans and the early settlers.

Simmons believes that understanding the meaning of legends leads us to a greater understanding of truth.

212. Snow, Edward Rowe. *Fantastic Folklore and Fact: New England Tales of Land and Sea.* New York: Dodd, Mead, 1968. x, 270p. Illus. Index. 68-54451. 0-396-05844-2.

The author of numerous books of New England stories and tales, Snow presents his usual mixture of fact and fiction: some true tales of shipwrecks, murders, and daring rescues; some legends and tall tales of ghosts, mythical beasts, and walking corpses.

All his books are entertaining.

213. ——. *Incredible Mysteries and Legends of the Sea.* New York: Dodd, Mead, 1967. 266p. Illus. Index. Bibliographical footnotes. 67-26146.

This is a mixed bag of sea stories—shipwrecks, pirates, mermaids and mermen, and ghost ships. Snow has researched these stories as much as possible and presents extensive quotes from contemporary accounts, interviews with parties concerned or with those who knew them. His stories come not just from New England but from other seafaring areas as well.

Thoroughly entertaining, this provides many leads for further investigation in Snow's notes.

214. ——. *The Islands of Boston Harbor, Their History and Romance, 1626–1935.* New York: Dodd, Mead, 1971. xiv, 274p. Illus. Index.

The first edition of Snow's book was published in 1936 and sold out. He brings it up to date in this 1971 edition.

Most of the book is a history of the many islands in Boston Harbor and the role they played in colonial, revolutionary, and later times. He mentions two ghost stories: "The Lady in Black," and "The Lady in Scarlet." The Lady in Black is the ghost of a young woman whose husband, a Confederate soldier, was a prisoner of war on George's Island. She dressed in men's clothes and slipped past sentries to visit him and help him escape, but their escape attempt was discovered. The husband was killed, and his wife was hanged. Her ghost is now seen on the island. The Lady in Scarlet was with her husband on a British ship during the Revolution. The ship was bombarded by American fire, and the woman died. Buried on shore rather than at sea, as was her dying request, she rests uneasily and occasionally appears to people on Long Island in the harbor.

215. Steese, Mark, and Sam McPheeters. *Traveler's Tales: Rumors and Legends of the Albany-Saratoga Region.* 2d. ed. Albany, NY: M. Steese and S. McPheeters, 1982. 66p. Illus. by Mark Steese. Index. Bibliog. pa.

According to the authors, this began as a travel guide, but became instead a book of local legends. The territory covered is the Albany-Saratoga region of New York and includes Albany, Rensselaer, Saratoga, Schenectady, and Washington counties. The legends range from ones extant during colonial days to more recent tales of mysterious murders. There are numerous ghost stories. All the legends are extremely brief, usually less than a page in length.

216. Taft, Lewis A. *Profile of Old New England: Yankee Legends, Tales, and Folklore.* New York: Dodd, Mead, 1965. xiii, 271p. Bibliog. 65-10462.

Taft says that earlier collections of folklore were abridged so that they lost their entertainment value. He hopes this collection restores that.

He includes love stories, supernatural tales, crime, and Indian tales. Many are tales of Colonial days. A few discuss the origin of place names.

217. Thomas, Howard. *Folklore from the Adirondack Foothills.* Prospect, NY: Prospect Books, 1958. viii, 150p. Illus.

Tales of murder, violent death, and ghosts make up the bulk of the stories in this book. Other stories involve everyday life, and many are based on real incidents

and real people—stories of a country doctor, a mad priest, and a sawmill. Even the story about a local sea serpent has a basis in fact.

Thomas rounds out the collection with four frankly fictional stories.

218. Woods, Caroline. *Haunted Delaware: Delightfully Dreadful Legends of the First State.* Bryn Mawr, PA: Buy Books on the Web.Com, 2000. i, 73p. Illus. Bibliog. 0-7414-0345-5pa.

This volume comprises ten tales of haunted Delaware. Some are only a page or two long. Woods gives what background she can, but often there is no explanation of the apparition or knowledge of the history of the event. Illustrations are black-and-white photographs of the scenes of the hauntings.

219. Workers of the Federal Writers' Project of the Works Progress Administration in the State of New York. *New York, a Guide to the Empire State.* New York: Oxford Univ. Press, 1940. xxxi, 782p. Illus. Index. Classified Bibliography. Chronology of significant dates in New York history.

Pages 111 to 117 of this book contain a chapter on folklore. In it the authors touch the major themes of New York folklore. The tales of Washington Irving are mentioned, as are Dutch tales of pirate ships and lost treasure. Indian tales include those of doomed young lovers as well as of Hiawatha, who brought peace to the Iroquois. Witches, goblins, and spirits are also plentiful in New York folklore and are mentioned here. The folklore section, although obviously brief, gives enough information for the uninformed to begin exploration.

Other sections of the book give an overview of the state's history in such areas as education, religion, and the arts. The latter half consists of tours to take in various sections of the state. Although obviously the road designations and directions are much changed, the descriptions of places worth seeing are often still true and often include information about local legends.

Folk Music

220. Bethke, Robert D. *Adirondack Voices: Woodsmen and Woods Lore.* Urbana: Univ. of Illinois Press, 1981. xii, 148p. Illus. Index. Bibliographic notes. 80-24054. 0-252-00829-4.

The first half of this book concerns the vanished way of life of the woodsman, the logger, of the early twentieth century. In interviews with men from this tradition, Bethke illuminates their life. He also quotes them at length, telling some of the old tales.

The second half concerns folk music and the music and songs of the lumber camps. Bethke again describes the life of the lumbermen, often quoting them at length, and intersperses his descriptions and his quotes with transcriptions of songs, both words and music.

221. Cazden, Norman, Herbert Haufrecht, and Norman Studer. *Folk Songs of the Catskills.* Albany: State Univ. of New York Press, 1982. 650p. Index of titles and first lines. 0-87395-580-3. 0-87395-582-2pa.

Between 1941 and 1962, the music directors of Camp Woodland in New York, a summer camp for children, made an extensive collection of the folk music of the Catskills. It is their collection that is codified and presented here.

The songs are arranged into categories, as denoted by the chapter headings:

Lumbering and Rafting
Songs of War and Battle
Ballads of True Love
Courting Too Slow
Love Meets Obstacles
Tragedies, Legends
Religious Songs
Pioneer Days
Working and Hard Times
Shabby-Genteel Songs
Outlaws and Ruffians
Scrapes and Escapades
Merry Ditties
Nonsense Songs
Catskill Scene

The songs' backgrounds are explained and many, though not all, have their music transcribed. In his foreword, Pete Seeger, like so many folk writers before him, makes a plea that we not forget the old days and the old ways, as only by remembering them can we build a worthwhile present and future.

222. Eckstrom, Fannie Hardy, and Mary Winslow Smyth, eds. *Minstrelsy of Maine: Folk-Songs and Ballads of the Woods and the Coast.* Boston: Houghton Mifflin, 1927; repr., Ann Arbor: Gryphon Books, 1971. xvi, 390p. Index.

The editors spent some twenty years collecting songs and ballads in Maine. This collection they limited to songs of the woods and songs of the sea, thereby eliminating, they say, "all our local historical, early American, Revolutionary, naval and Civil War songs; songs of disasters, prize-fights, animals, and murders; Forty-Niner songs, of which we have found a dozen; temperance, Masonic, and prison songs; dance and game songs; and most important of all and largest in number, all our English and Irish traditional songs" (p. viii). What is left, however, forms an impressive body.

The tales in verse and song tell of unrequited love, of love lost to death, of shipwrecks and lumbering tragedies, of love and friendship betrayed, of war and hardship. As much as prose tales, these tell of a people.

223. Gray, Roland Palmer, collector and ed. *Songs and Ballads of the Maine Lumberjacks.* Cambridge, MA: Harvard Univ. Press, 1924; repr., Detroit, MI: Singing Tree Press, 1969. xxi, 191p. 73-75944.

These were collected mostly in the late teens and early twenties of the twentieth century. The editor makes the point in his introduction that "soon it will be too late to gather them (the ballads); those who know them are rapidly passing on. Even now the type of lumberjack of fifty years ago is hard to find" (p. xx). Therefore Gray collected and preserved them "with a sense of obligation to American literature."

About fifty ballads and songs are included. Despite the title, some of the songs concern ships and seafaring.

Some ballads are about battles, others love (usually sad and unrequited), still others the working day. All tell us something about not only the specific event sung about but about the people who made them up and sang them.

224. Korson, George. *Coal Dust on the Fiddle.* 1943; repr., Hatboro, PA: Folklore Associates, 1965. 460 p. Index. Bibliog. Appendix.

Korson collected these songs over five years, from 1938 to 1943. He uses the songs collected and transcribed here to il-

lustrate and illuminate the miners' way of life. Chapters concern:

Life in the coal camps
The economic reality of the company store
Love, courtship, and the role of women
Recreation
Tall tales and superstitions
Disasters
The union
Strikes

Each chapter interweaves songs on these themes with narrative and description. Music is transcribed as well as lyrics.

The appendix provides brief biographies of the singers.

225. Korson, George Gershon. *Minstrels of the Mine Patch. Songs and Stories of the Anthracite Industry.* Philadelphia: Univ. of Pennsylvania Pres, 1938; repr., Hatboro, PA: Folklore Associates, 1964. xx, 332p. Index. Bibliog. Glossary.

Korson was one of the early collectors of urban and industrial folklore, concentrating his efforts on the anthracite coal miners of Pennsylvania. Here he collects hundreds of songs, ballads, humorous songs, songs of strikes, labor disputes, and union organizing, and songs of accidents and deaths.

He includes a few stories, mostly humorous.

226. Shoemaker, Henry Wharton. *Mountain Minstrelsy of Pennsylvania.* Rev. and enlarged. Philadelphia: McGirr, 1931; repr., Ann Arbor, MI: University Microfilms, 1969. 319p. Index of titles. 31-28899.

Shoemaker divides the songs here into the following categories:

Songs and Ballads
Folk Songs by the Fireside
Songs of the Civil War Period
English Folk Songs
Echoes of Early Songs and Ballads of
    the Mountaineers of Southern
    Germany

The bulk of the songs are in the first category, Songs and Ballads.

Shoemaker's introduction gives some history of the ballad form in this area and information as well about the people living there at the time of his work—the late nineteenth and early twentieth centuries. Like many early collectors of folklore and folk song, Shoemaker hoped that his collections would stir an interest in the study of unique populations, with their old customs and ways.

Folk Belief and Ritual

227. Bonfanti, Leo. *Strange Beliefs, Customs, and Superstitions.* Pride Pub, 1980. 48p.

Bonfanti writes brief, one- or two-sentence explanations of various superstitions. The superstitions are grouped by category:

Witches
Halloween
Christmas
Weather
Folk Medicine
Thanksgiving
Marriage
Dreams
Sailors' Beliefs

As there is neither an index nor a table of contents, it is not possible to locate particular categories or superstitions without browsing. On the other hand, the book is so brief that the reader can flip through it in very little time.

Bonfanti includes no information on where the beliefs originate.

The book is, however, full of interesting tidbits: If a shark swims close to a ship, a crew member or a passenger will die; at least one couple in a double wedding will be divorced within five years; don't eat a hot boiled lobster with a glass of milk as it causes sickness.

Although not a scholarly work, this is an enjoyable one, the kind of book one can pick up and open at random, sure of finding something interesting.

228. Brendle, Thomas R., and Claude W. Unger. *Folk Medicine of the Pennsylvania Germans: The Non-Occult Cures.* Norristown, PA: Pennsylvania German Society, 1935. xlviii, 303p. Illus. Bibliog. (Pennsylvania German Society, Volume XLV).

Brendle and Unger used three major sources for their collection of folk remedies: interviews with people who still remembered and/or used the old folk remedies; perusal of written remedies passed down in families either in special books or as notes in a family Bible or other book; and early medical books, almanacs, newspapers, and broadsides printed in early Pennsylvania German printing shops.

The material presented here consists first of a discussion of the origin of diseases (acts of God, inherited, contagious, evil spirits or other supernatural powers, human agency such as witches, charms, and spells). Second comes a discussion of various folk remedies and cures, grouped by type of disease or complaint—tumors, rashes, abscesses, heart problems, and so on. The remedies are presented without explanation, justification, or judgment.

229. Dow, Elaine. *Simples and Worts: Being All About the Herbs of Our Puritan Forefathers (and Mothers), with Additional 17th and 18th Century Miscellany.* Topsfield, MA: Historical Presentations, 1982. 80p. Illus. by David Workman. Bibliog. Glossary.

Very similar to *Herbs and Herb Lore of Colonial America* (New York: Dover, 1995) in both content and format, this is an alphabetical list of plants with descriptions of their medicinal uses. Some of these remedies have now become folk medicine: Some plants were believed to protect against evil, others were known as love potions. The book is attractively illustrated with line drawings of the plants by David Workman. The glossary defines terms used in herbal medicine, such as *infusion* or *posset*.

230. Fogel, Edwin Miller. *Beliefs and Superstitions of the Pennsylvania Germans.* 2d revised printing. 1915; repr., Millersville, PA: Center for Pennsylvania German Studies, Millersville Univ., 1995. 242p. Bibliog. 95-70731. 1-883294-24-x.

Fogel first published this study in 1915. It is a collection of sayings, culled from individuals in southeast Pennsylvania. There is no index, but the sayings are collected into categories, and the table of contents indicates the categories. Many of the sayings concern farming and superstitions and beliefs connected with the rhythm of farm life. Others concern human relationships, weather, hunting and fishing, medical superstitions and cures, dreams, and death.

231. *Herbs and Herb Lore of Colonial America.* Compiled by the Grounds Committee of the National Society of the Colonial Dames of America in the State of Connecticut. Wethersfield, CT: National Society of the Colonial Dames of America in the State of Connecticut, 1970; repr., New York: Dover, 1995. vi, 74p. Illus. 94-48527. 0-486-28529-4pa.

Where does botany or medicine leave off and folklore or literature begin? This book blends them all. A series of one- or two-page descriptions of the uses of each plant, along with a line drawing, blends all the disciplines. Although the bulk of the information is on early medicinal use of plants, there are other uses described as well. For instance, the forget-me-not was given to anyone starting a journey on February 29. The peony was dug up only at night so that the digger could avoid being observed by woodpeckers. Anyone observed by woodpeckers while digging up peonies, it was believed, would become blind.

The editors give information on how a particular plant was introduced to the new world, its early uses, and whether it was native. There are many references to John Josselyn, the early New England folklorist and natural historian.

This was first published in 1970 as *Simples, Superstitions and Solace: Plant Material Used in Colonial Living: Drawings and Quotations Taken from Early Herbals.*

In appearance and content, this book is similar to *Simples and Worts* by Elaine Dow (Topsfield, MA: Historical Presentations, 1982).

Illustrations are black-and-white line drawings of the plants.

232. Herr, Karl. *Hex and Spellwork: The Magical Practices of the Pennsylvania Dutch.* York Beach, ME: Red Wheel/Weiser, 2002. xii, 144p. Bibliog. 2002-8481. 1-57863-182-3pa.

Karl Herr is the pseudonym of someone who has written extensively on magic and spells. Here the author takes on the persona of the *Hexenmeister,* or spell master, to discuss various magic and traditional practices of the Pennsylvania Dutch. Herr includes chapters on healing practices; the magic of hex signs; spoken magic in spells and charms; the *Himmelbrief,* or heavenly letter, a letter written to a departed loved one or to God; and magic worked with natural objects such as stones or shells.

Herr includes diagrams of various painted hex signs.

233. Janos, Elisabeth. *Country Folk Medicine: Tales of Skunk Oil, Sassafras Tea, and Other Old-Time Remedies.* 1990; repr., New York: Galahad Books, 1995. ix, 150p. Index. Bibliog. 90-42571. 0-88365-903-4.

Janos interviewed some 3,000 people at senior centers and nursing homes to gather material for this book. From them she garnered information on self-treatment in rural New England and New York State.

She begins with a look at "some unusual healing substances": resins and turpentine; kerosene; skunk oil; snake oil; flannel; and sewage pharmacology. The rest of the book is divided into remedies for various types of ailments:

Respiratory problems
Digestive problems
Musculoskeletal problems
Neurological problems
Eye, ear, nose, mouth, and throat
External injuries
Skin conditions
Influenza and fevers
Problems of infancy and childhood
Female concerns
Preventive medicine

234. Jarvis, DeForest Clinton. *Arthritis and Folk Medicine.* 1960; repr., New York: Galahad Books, 1997. 179p. Index. 96-79820. 0-88365-983-2.

Jarvis wrote this book as an answer to the letters he received after his first book, *Folk Medicine, A Vermont Doctor's Guide to Good Health* (New York: Galahad Books, 1996), was published. He concentrates here on arthritis and mostly on ways to cure or alleviate it through diet.

235. ——. *Folk Medicine: A Vermont Doctor's Guide to Good Health.* New York: Henry Holt, 1958; repr., New York: Galahad Books, 1996. 191p. Appendices. 95-81983. 0-88365-940-9.

Jarvis made an almost lifelong study of the folk remedies and preventive care of Vermont. In this book he explains much of what he discovered, suggesting various remedies for particular conditions—such as gargling with vinegar to relieve a sore throat—and explains in medical or biological terms why such remedies often work. He believes that much of folk medicine is based on sound empirical knowledge that we have lost as we have become more urbanized and less in touch with the wisdom and rhythms of nature.

Appendices are five: One details some studies Jarvis made of animal disease; the second is a list of uses to which Vermonters put cider vinegar; the third details a cure for hangover (liberal intake of honey); the fourth chemically analyzes kelp; and the fifth is titled "Helpful Bacteria and Alkalinity."

236. Johnson, Clifton. *What They Say in New England: A Book of Signs, Sayings, and Superstitions.* Boston: Lee and Shepherd, 1896. 263p.

Johnson was a well-known and successful writer in the late nineteenth and early twentieth centuries. He wrote children's books, travel books, and books of folklore. This book is a product of years of traveling around western Massachusetts, talking to all people, collecting stories, sayings, cures, and rhymes. The bulk of the book is a collection of folk wisdom on a variety of topics: friendship, weather, dreams, fortune telling, money, death, animals. Want to rid yourself of unsightly freckles? Catch a frog and rub it—live— over your face. Want to retain a friendship? Never give to or receive from a friend a knife, scissors, or other sharp-edged tool. It will cut the friendship. Want to make money? Say "Money before the week is out" three times when you see a shooting star, and you'll have money before the week is over.

Johnson finishes the collection with rhymes, songs, and a few tales or stories.

This is considered one of the earliest attempts to record directly what people said, without the filter of scholarship.

Johnson gives no sources for his sayings.

237. ——. *What They Say in New England, and Other American Folklore*, edited and with an introduction by Carl Withers. New York: Columbia Univ. Press, 1963. xxiv, 289p.

Withers has added material to Johnson's classic 1896 book, *What They Say in New England* (Boston: Lee and Shepherd). In his introduction, he gives biographical and critical information on Johnson, explaining Johnson's contribution to folklore study. He adds to the body of the work other material written by Johnson, published in periodicals and in his travel books. Finally, he includes a bibliography of Johnson's writings.

This reprint of Johnson's work, with additional material, makes *What They Say in New England* more accessible to more people.

238. Lindholdt, Peter J. *A Critical Edition of John Josselyn's 1674 Account of Two Voyages to New England*. Pennsylvania State Univ., 1985. x, 387p. Ph.D. thesis, 1985.

Josselyn was one of the first European visitors to New England to write an account of its appearance and wonders based on observation. Various critics have described him as a naturalist, a medical man, a humorist, a travel writer, or an ethnologist. Horace P. Beck in *The Folklore of Maine* (Philadelphia: Lippincott, 1957) terms him a *folklorist*. This claim has validity, for Josselyn writes of the natural world from his own seventeenth-century perspective. He intersperses his descriptions of the natural world with folk remedies using plants and animals. He describes the Indians he meets as being closer to nature than his own people. Paul J. Lindholdt gives a critical presentation of Josselyn's classic work, in which he explains many of Josselyn's archaic references.

239. Mather, Increase. *Remarkable Providences: Illustrative of the Earlier Days of American Colonization*. London: Reeves and Turner, 1890. xix, 262p.

Not strictly folklore, this was written as fact, by a man who believed all the stories he gathered and wrote down. In his introduction to this 1890 edition of a book first published in 1683, George Offer says that Mather had an "implicit faith in the power of the invisible world to hold visible intercourse with man;—not the angels to bless poor erring mortals, but the demons imparting power to witches and warlocks to injure, terrify, and destroy" (p. x).

Thus Mather, pastor of the North Church in Boston for sixty-two years in the late seventeenth and early eighteenth centuries, gathered tales of deliverances at sea, of miraculous healings, of people saved from dangerous and extreme weather conditions, of demons, and of witchcraft. Mather saw all happenings as works of either God or the devil. Therefore, deliverance from dangerous weather was a sign of God's mercy and affliction with some illnesses such as epilepsy could be the result of possession by the devil.

Although Mather wrote what he considered the truth, some of these stories have with time become the basis for folklore, particularly his stories of what sounds like activity by poltergeists.

240. RavenWolf, Silver. *American Folk Magick: Charms, Spells and Herbals.* St. Paul, MN: Llewellyn, 1998. xx, 291p. Illus. Index. Bibliog. 98-26297. 1-56718-720-xpa.

A history of the Powwow begins this book, both in Europe and in the New World. By *Powwow,* RavenWolf does not mean the current image of Native Americans sitting around a council fire. Instead, her more historical meaning of the term is of the "oldest of the American magickal system(s) created by the European settlers. It stems from Pagan Witchcraft . . . melded with Native American magicks" (xiii).

This book is a "practical" guide to such magic, offering recipes, chants, information on herbs used in magic, and even some advice on keeping records of charms, rituals, and spells. RavenWolf also includes specific charms for specific situations—banishing garden pests, catching a criminal, and reversing a charm.

Throughout the book, she tries to show that ancient principles can be applied today to modern problems.

This book was published previously under the title *HexCraft* (St. Paul, MN: Llewellyn, 1995).

241. Tantaquidgeon, Gladys. *Folk Medicine of the Delaware and Related Algonkian Indians.* 1972; repr., Harrisburg: Pennsylvania Historical and Museum Commission, 1995. 145p. Index. Bibliog. (Pennsylvania Historical and Museum Commission, no. 3). 0-911124-07-5.

Two major sections make up this book. One, concerning the Delaware, was first published in 1942; the other, concerning the Mohegan, was first published in 1928. The section on the Delaware discusses their theories on the causes of disease and their response to it through the use of plants. Tantaquidgeon also gives information on the Delawares' attitudes and use of witchcraft and dreams; their signs and omens; and their foodways.

Similar information is given for the Mohegan. An appendix lists plants used in healing, identifying the botanical name, the common name, native use, part of plant used, and type of medicine.

242. ——. *A Study of Delaware Indian Medicine Practice and Folk Beliefs.* Commonwealth of Pennsylvania, Department of Public Instruction, Pennsylvania Historical Commission, 1942; repr., New York: AMS Press, 1980. 91p. Index. Bibliog. 76-43864. 0-404-15724-6.

This was originally published in 1942 by the Commonwealth of Pennsylvania, Department of Public Instruction, Pennsylvania Historical Commission. The author was a Mohegan Indian who learned the use of plants in medicine from her grandmother and others. She studied the uses of such plants by the Delaware in the Pennsylvania–New Jersey area at the behest of the Department of Anthropology, University of Pennsylvania. The information is mostly from a practitioner of the techniques, Witapanoxwe, or "Walks with Daylight."

This study is full of detail of particular plants used for particular conditions.

Three appendices contain:

Nanticoke Folk Beliefs
Uses of Medicinal Plants among the
   Canadian Delaware
Three Oklahoma Delaware Myths:
   "The Boy Who Lived with a Bear,"
   "The Woods Dwarf," "The Seven
   Wise Men."

Three tables are also included, listing plant use among three different groups:

Plants and Plant Uses of the
   Oklahoma Delaware
Plants and Plant Uses of the Delaware
   Munsee, Six Nations Reserve,
   Ontario
Plants Used by the Nanticoke of
   Indian River, Sussex County,
   Delaware

243. Wentz, Richard E., ed. *Pennsylvania Dutch: Folk Spirituality*. New York: Paulist Press, 1993. vi, 329p. Index. (Sources of American Spirituality). 92-33184. 0-8091-0439-3.

In this series of essays by various authors, Wentz brings together a look at the folk belief of the Pennsylvania Dutch. Such beliefs exist outside the formal structure of church belief, but are nevertheless crucial, helping people cope both with everyday life and with crises.

Wentz provides essays that look at the preacher's role in promoting folk belief, at folk customs around the Christmas celebration, folk beliefs related to healing, folk beliefs as expressed in arts and crafts, and finally some literary expressions of folk belief.

Material Culture

244. Cady, Daniel Leavens. *Rhymes of Vermont Rural Life*. 4th ed. Rutland, VT: Tuttle, 1922. 279p.

Cady's poems reflect activities in rural Vermont in the early part of the century—making soap, dipping candles, making maple syrup. He writes, too, of Vermont residents—the hired man, schoolchildren, the proprietor of a country store. Although he does not write first-class poetry, he does evoke the old way of life. What Cornelius Weygandt does for New Hampshire in such titles as *The White Hills* (New York: Henry Holt, 1934) and *November Rowen* (New York: D. Appleton-Century, 1941), Cady does for Vermont.

245. Dodge, N. S. *Sketches of New England, or Memories of the Country*. New York: French, 1842. vi, 286p.

Dodge writes a series of essays about the old days and the old ways of New England. In them the reader will find information on holiday celebrations, particularly Thanksgiving, that most New England of days; of early medicine; of courting customs; and of religious practices. Interspersed are love stories.

246. Federal Writers' Project of the Works Progress Administration of the State of Maryland. *Maryland, a Guide to the Old Time State*. New York: Oxford Univ. Press, 1940. xxviii, 561p. Illus. Bibliog. Chronology of significant dates in the history of Maryland. (American Guide Series).

Unlike other books in the series, this one does not contain a chapter titled "Folklore." The introductory chapter, however, "Maryland, My Maryland" (pp. 3–9), serves that function. It describes customs and superstitions; tells of annual events such as jousting tournaments; introduces the "snallygaster," a bird of prey that carries off small children and sometimes adults to its lair in the mountains; and details certain patterns of speech and expressions. As with the other guidebooks, this provides an excellent introduction to specifically Maryland folklore. It provides also the customary bibliography and timeline of events important to the state's history.

The tours that make up the latter half of the book again mention local legends, as they are appropriate.

247. Federal Writers' Project of the Works Progress Administration for the State of Pennsylvania. *Pennsylvania: A Guide to the Keystone State.* New York: Oxford Univ. Press, 1940. xxxii, 660p. Illus. Bibliog. Index. Chronology of significant dates in the history of Pennsylvania.

Unlike some others in the Federal Writers' Project series of guidebooks that retell certain legends and tales, this does not. What it does do is give a flavor of the area. It includes sections on arts and crafts, music, and industry, all of which help the reader get a sense of the early days of the state and how it developed.

248. Hastings, Scott E. *Last Yankees: Folkways in Eastern Vermont and the Border Country.* Hanover, NH: Univ. Press of New England, 1990. 143p. Illus. Appendix of Archaic Words and Terms. 89-24785. 0-87451-510-6; 0-87451-511-4pa.

The information in this book was collected by Scott E. Hastings as part of his research for the development of the Vermont Folklife Research Project, a project sponsored by Laurence Rockefeller. He did his oral research in an area he calls the Yankee Highlands, on the border of Vermont and New Hampshire. The book

is a series of essays, most describing country industries such as sawmilling or threshing; or country crafts such as building walls or the cutting of tanbark for use in the tanning industry. All the information comes from individuals who practiced the specific trades or crafts. The essays are filled with lengthy quotations from the people interviewed.

In his introduction, Hastings sounds the same lament and the same hope that earlier folklorists—Botkin and Skinner among them—sounded: that the way of life portrayed here, transcribed in the words of those that lived it, was fast vanishing, and needed to be preserved.

249. Kopp, Joel, and Kate Kopp. *American Hooked and Sewn Rugs: Folk Art Underfoot.* New York: Dutton, 1985; repr., Albuquerque: Univ. of New Mexico Press, 1995. 141p. Illus. Index. Bibliog. 94-38607. 0-8263-1616-6.

Both a history of hooked and sewn rugs and a visual display of them, this book presents hundreds of full-color pictures of such rugs. The text shows an appreciation of the meaning of the rugs, the way in which they enabled often isolated and hardworking women, with little leisure time and no entertainment, to bring color and beauty into their lives.

A separate section gives diagrams of the various techniques used in rug making.

250. Korson, George Gershon. *Black Rock; Mining Folklore of the Pennsylvania Dutch.* Baltimore: Johns Hopkins Press, 1960; repr., New York: Arno Press, 1979. xi, 453p. Index. Source Notes. (Johns Hopkins University Press Reprints). 78-19326. 0-405-10607-6.

Korson attempts here to describe the transition of the Pennsylvania Dutch people from an agricultural people to an industrial one, and how they eased that transition by holding on to their customs and their beliefs. He describes courting customs, speech patterns, religious practices, folk medicine, and games. He also talks about everyday life in the mines, on the canals and railroads, and in the factories, all of which were worked by the Pennsylvania Dutch.

The last two sections contain legends, often concerned with labor leaders, and folk songs.

251. Ladd, C. E., and E. R. Eastman. *Growing Up in the Horse and Buggy Days.* New York: Nesterman, 1943. 263p.

Ladd and Eastman grew up on farms in New York State, during the time that mechanized farming was just beginning to take over from age-old methods. Their reminiscences show the reader the old ways; they write of farming, going to school, recreation, hunting–the everyday life of a vanished time.

252. Macneal, Patricia M., Bonelyn L. Kyofski, and Kenneth A. Thigpen, eds. *Headwaters and Hardwaters: The Folklore, Cultural History and Traditional Arts of the Pennsylvania Northern Tier.* Mansfield, PA: Northern Tier Cultural Alliance, 1997. iv, 197p. Illus. 96-70566. 0-9654340-0-1pa.

The counties of Potter, Tioga, Bradford, Cameron, Clinton, Lycoming, and Sullivan make up the Northern Tier of Pennsylvania. This collection of essays, written with the help of a grant from the Pennsylvania Council on the Arts, the Pennsylvania Heritage Affairs Commission, and the Pennsylvania Heritage Parks Program, highlights various aspects of the region's cultural heritage. Many local folk artists were involved in the project, as well as the three main editors.

Essays are varied. They deal with both local industries (lumbering and coal min-

ing) and with crafts (rifle making, spinning, weaving, and quilting). There is also an essay on musical traditions.

253. Mitchell, Edwin Valentine. *It's an Old New England Custom.* New York: Vanguard Press, 1946. 277p.

These 277 pages are an easy read. The reader can dip in at will, quickly skimming chapters of interest. Chapters are on a variety of subjects, not all of which are folklore related: bundling; the great age attained by many New England residents; customs surrounding Thanksgiving; and various foods common to New England. Chapters most relevant to folklore are those on haunted houses, ghost ships, and place names.

254. ——. *It's an Old Pennsylvania Custom.* New York: The Vanguard Press, 1947. 262p.

Mitchell describes customs relating to music, courtship and marriage, work life, witchcraft, dress, and dwellings. He also touches on the lives of the Amish.

255. Weygandt, Cornelius. *The Blue Hills: Round and Discoveries in the Country Places around Pennsylvania.* New York: Henry Holt, 1936. xxi, 434p. Illus.

Weygandt writes one of his signature books, this time about the Blue Hills of his native Pennsylvania. His essays tell of old days and old ways, focusing on the everyday, such as foods, household items, modes of travel, and clothing.

256. ——. *Down Jersey: Folks and Their Jobs, Pine Barrens, Salt Marsh and Sea Islands.* New York: D. Appleton-Century, 1940; repr., Union City, NJ: William H. Wise/Books about New Jersey, 1980. xii, 348p. Illus. Index. 80-51866. 0-8349-7544-0.

Once again, Weygandt writes a book about a time and place he knew well and that has appeal today. This one is about the Jersey shore, another place where Weygandt often spent the summer. Many of the essays treat of the seaside; others talk of old crafts and trades, such as glassblowing and raising cranberries. In others he writes of pastimes, such as hunting and the fiddlers of the "Piney" area.

All of his essays contain the flavor of bygone days, with tantalizing mentions of peddlers, coal wagons, and glass bottles designed to be carried in saddlebags.

257. ——. *The Heart of New Hampshire.* New York: G. P. Putnam and Sons, 1944. xvi, 210p. Illus. Index.

In *The Heart of New Hampshire,* Weygandt writes many sketches of people pursuing the old skills and crafts of country people—basket making, gardening, furniture making. As with his other books, this one evokes a lost time.

258. ——. *New Hampshire Neighbors.* New York: H. Holt, 1937. xv; 368p.

New Hampshire Neighbors is another of Weygandt's books about the old ways and the old people. In a series of sketches he describes country characters and ways of life that are now vanished. One can learn the minutiae of life from Weygandt's books, what was eaten for dinner, what trees grew by the roadsides, and what devastation an epidemic could bring to a single family.

259. ——. *November Rowen.* New York: D. Appleton-Century, 1941. xiv; 308p. Illus. Index.

Like his earlier books, *The White Hills* and *New Hampshire Neighbors,* this one treats of the old days. In a series of essays, Weygandt writes of the people and places of a bygone New Hampshire. He describes farming and gardening, cooking, social customs, and people themselves. Many of the chapters deal with country crafts, such as handmade autograph albums or collections of ornaments made from hair.

Despite the age of the book, and the fact that it is about an even earlier age, one sentiment Weygandt expresses is true today: a wish for the slower pace and greater beauty of a lost era. He describes a handmade autograph book as having a "gentility it would be better the world had more of today."

260. ——. *The White Hills.* New York: Henry Holt, 1934. xi, 399p. Illus. Index.

Weygandt, a Philadelphian, writes here about New Hampshire, where he spent many of his summers. He describes the people, the way of life, the speech patterns, the old skills and crafts—a way of life now gone.

261. Wilbur, C. Keith. *The New England Indians.* 2d ed. Old Saybrook, CT: Globe Pequot Press, 1996. 123p. Illus. Index. Bibliog. 96-21202. 1-56440-993-7pa.

Black-and-white line drawings illustrate various artifacts used by Native Americans in New England. Farming implements, implements of war, canoes, cooking materials, and materials used in hunting and fishing are all described and illustrated.

Wilbur also discusses the changes in Native American culture that occurred and developed because of their contact with settlers.

262. Yoder, Don. *Discovering American Folklife: Essays on Folk Culture and the Pennsylvania Dutch.* Ann Arbor, MI: UMI Research Press, 1990; repr., Mechanicsburg, PA: Stackpole Books, 2001. xiii, 314p. Illus. Chapter notes. Index. Bibliog. 00-056333. 0-8117-2743-2pa.

A longtime professor at the University of Pennsylvania, Yoder made a major study of Pennsylvania Dutch folklife. He was instrumental in the growing use of the word *folklife* as opposed to *folklore*. In his opinion, *folklife* is a more inclusive term, which encompasses all aspects of a culture: oral tradition, written documents, material culture, and spiritual dimensions.

The thirteen essays here concentrate on the Pennsylvania Dutch and discuss such varied aspects of the culture as folk medicine, religion, cookery, costume, harvest customs, and witchcraft.

Folklore for Children

263. Browne, George Waldo. *Real Legends of New England.* Chicago: A. Whitman, 1930. 264p. Illus. by Alexander Key. (Young Heart Historical Romance Library).

Here Browne retells for children many well-known legends based on fact. The stories are arranged chronologically, starting with colonial times, on through the Revolution and the beginning of the industrial age. Many well-known stories are here: the story of Hannah Dustin's capture by and escape from Indians; Paul Revere's ride; Nathan Hale's sacrifice for his country. Also included are some lesser-known ones: a baby whose birth on board ship so touched the heart of a marauding pirate that he withdrew from his attack and requested that the baby be named Ocean Born Mary; a young soldier in the Revolutionary army who swam across Lake Champlain with a message for an American commander; two sisters in the War of 1812 who played the fife and drum and deceived the British into thinking an entire regiment defended their town.

The book is illustrated with black-and-white drawings.

264. Bruchac, Joseph. *The Boy Who Lived with the Bears, and Other Iroquois Stories.* New York: HarperCollins Publishers, 1995. 63p. Illus. by Murv Jacob. 94-9829. 0-06-021287-x; 0-06-021288-8lib bdg.

Bruchac, a storyteller himself, retells six stories of the Iroquois nation for children. All the stories concern animals. The stories are meant to teach life lessons; in them, the animals learn the importance of cooperation and responsibility. The full-color, full-page illustrations are charming.

265. Curry, Jane Louise. *Turtle Island: Tales of the Algonquin Nations.* New York: Margaret K. McElderry Books, 1999. 145p. Illus. by James Watts. 98-20393. 0-689-82233-2.

The Algonquin nations lived from what is now the Middle Atlantic states up through Canada. They included the Abenaki, Blackfoot, Cree, Cheyenne, Fox, Lenape, Malecite, Menomini, Miami, Micmac, Montauk, Narraganset, Naskapi, Ojibway, Passamaquoddy, Penobscot, Pequot, Shawnee, and Wampanoag.

Curry compiles twenty-seven tales from various members of the Algonquin nations. The creation story is here, told by the Lenape, or "the real people," as they were known to other members of the Algonquin nations; as well as Glooskap; tales of the struggle between good and evil; and tales of the natural world.

Watts illustrates many of the tales with black-and-white line drawings; while Curry adds notes about the stories and the storytellers.

266. Fritz, Jean. *The Good Giants and the Bad Pukwudgies.* New York: G. P. Putnam's Sons, 1982. 40p. Illus. by Tomie de

Paola. 81-17921. 0-399-20870-4; 0-399-20871-2pa.

Fritz retells the story of the giant Maushop and his wife, Quant. Maushop forms Buzzard's Bay while taking a nap and burrowing in the sand; he throws his moccasins into the bay and thus forms Nantucket and Martha's Vineyard Islands. When his five sons are killed, their bodies, buried in the bay, form the Elizabeth Islands.

Also in the story are Quant, Maushop's wife; Squant, a sea woman with green hair, square eyes, and a siren's song; and the Pukwudgies, mischievous small creatures who torment the First People, or Wampanoag Indians, who live on the Narrow Land, or Cape Cod.

In an endnote, Fritz explains that she obtained her information on these legends form Elizabeth Reyard's *The Narrow Land* (Boston: Houghton Mifflin, 1978). Here she retells those legends for children.

The illustrations are imaginative and colorful.

267. Hastings, Scott E., Jr. *Miss Mary Mac All Dressed in Black: Tongue Twisters, Jump-Rope Rhymes, and Other Children's Lore from New England.* Little Rock, AR: August House, 1990. 159p. 90-36299. 0-87483-156-3pa.

Most of the items collected here are from children, although there is one section of "Rhymes from Adult Vermonters." Hastings divides the verses into sections:

Jump-Rope Rhymes
Counting-Out Rhymes
Everyday Rhymes
Tongue Twisters
Rhymes from Adult Vermonters

Most are short, some only a few lines; others are a stanza or two.

Hastings provides a list of sources: No names of the children from whom he obtained a particular rhyme are included, but their ages and the town or city they lived in are listed. He also includes an essay on how to collect such folklore, with suggestions like having children work alone rather than in groups or pairs, so that they do not influence each other.

268. Ha-yen-doh-nees (Leo Cooper). *Seneca Indian Stories.* Greenfield Center, NY: Greenfield Review Press, 1995. xx, 62p. Illus. by Beth Ann Clark. 94-75711. 0-912678-89-5.

Ha-yen-doh-nees was a Seneca living on the Allegheny Reservation. He heard these tales from his parents and grandparents, told them in his turn to children and grandchildren, and finally put them in writing. Like so many other Native American tales, these concern the natural world, how animals and birds came to be named and to look like they do.

269. Hill, Kay. *Glooscap and His Magic: Legends of the Wabanaki Indians.* New York: Dodd, Mead, 1963. 189p. Illus. by Richard Kennedy. Glossary.

Glooscap is the most revered god in the Abenaki tradition. Here Hill concentrates on his magical abilities, whether as creator of the earth, as trickster, or as the one who found summer and thus provided warm, productive weather for the earth.

Hill focuses on the main thread of each story, suppressing the subplots that sometimes make the traditional stories hard to follow for a modern audience.

270. ——. *More Glooskap Stories: Legends of the Wabanaki Indians.* New York: Dodd, Mead, 1970. 178p. Illus. by John Hamberger. Glossary. 79-99180.

Hill retells many of the Glooskap tales for children. Tales are about the creation of the world, about Glooskap's intervention to save and help mankind, and about other giants and gods.

271. Irving, Washington. *The Legend of Sleepy Hollow*. Drexel Hill, PA: Bell Publishing, 1928; repr., New York: William Morrow, 1990. 106p. Illus. by Arthur Rackham. (Books of Wonder). 90-592. 0-688-05276-2.

There have been numerous editions of Irving's classic tale, *The Legend of Sleepy Hollow*. This 1990 edition contains the color illustrations done by Arthur Rackham for a 1928 edition. Their detail and quality of fantasy evoke the German fairy tales that were the origin of both the tale and the illustrations.

272. ———. *Rip Van Winkle*. Philadelphia: David McKay, 1921. 86p. Illus. by N. C. Wyeth.

The illustrations by N. C. Wyeth are what distinguish this edition of *Rip Van Winkle* from the many others that exist. Both the black-and-white sketches and the full-color plates are engaging.

This makes a good companion to the edition of *The Legend of Sleepy Hollow*, published by Bell Publishing Company in 1928, and reissued by William Morrow in 1990. The illustrations in that edition are by Arthur Rackham.

273. Jagendorf, M. A. *The Ghost of Peg Leg Pete, and Other Stories of Old New York*. New York: Vanguard Press, 1965. 125p. Illus. by Lino S. Lipinsky. Historical notes on the tales. Transcriptions of songs of New York. 65-17371.

Here are tales of the old New York, from the days when it was New Amsterdam through more recent times. Characters include such well-known folk figures as Peter Stuyvesant and lesser-known

ones like the patriotic Mrs. Murray, who used her charm to delay the British general Howe long enough for General Washington and his troops to escape New York.

Historical notes provide context for the tales, and some old songs are transcribed with both words and music.

274. Jagendorf, Moritz A. *The Marvelous Adventures of John Darling*. New York: Vanguard Press, 1949. xiii, 239p. Illus. by Howard Simon.

John Caesar Cicero Darling was a storyteller who lived in the Catskill Mountains, and whose main subject was himself. As Jagendorf, the editor of this collection, tells it, Darling's stories "grew out of seeds of his own life, incidents from his farm and his work and his travels. In most of the tales there is the germ of actuality" (p. 230). Darling tells stories larger than life, a story of killing a wolf by ramming his fist so hard inside the animal's mouth that he caught hold of the tail and turned the wolf inside out; a story of felling a hollow tree so that it lay across a raging river and a stranded family could drive its wagon straight through; and the story of the giant mosquitoes from which he fashioned a chariot to fly him around the world.

275. ———. *New England Bean-Pot: American Folk Stories to Read and to Tell*. New York: Vanguard Press, 1948. xviii, 272p. Illus. by Donald McKay.

Jagendorf calls these tales, written for children, "folk stories." Unlike collectors, who find their tales from the people who tell them, and who are careful to record the circumstances in which a tale was "collected," Jagendorf has written these himself, basing them on authentic folklore. He found the tales in various places, in newspaper accounts, town or county records, or from individuals. To these Jagendorf has added "proverbs, customs, and weather lore, and sometimes even local happenings from where the stories take place" (p. x). The result is a collection of tales with more plot and detail than many folktales that are more authentically preserved. These are perhaps more pleasing to the modern ear. B. A. Botkin, a noted folklorist, provides a brief foreword. Tales are grouped by state.

276. Macmillan, Cyrus. *Glooskap's Country, and Other Indian Tales.* New York: Oxford Univ. 1956. 273p. Illus. by John A. Hall. 0-19-540058-5.

Macmillan's book contains a number of tales of Glooskap, written for children.

277. Manitonquat (Medicine Story). *The Children of the Morning Light: Wampanoag Tales.* New York: Macmillan, 1994. 72p. Illus. by Mary F. Arquette. 92-32328. 0-02-765905-4.

A traditional storyteller, Manitonquat here commits to print for the first time the stories he told, so that more people will be able to know them. The stories are of the Wampanoag Indians of southeastern Massachusetts. They tell of the creation of the earth and the birth of twins Maushop and Matahdou. Maushop made all good things in the world, and Matahdou made all the evil and dangerous things. The stories go on to tell of the creation of various islands, including what is now Martha's Vineyard, and finally of the human race. The illustrations are full page and in full color.

278. Miller, Marian. *Iroquois Legends.* Batavia, NY: Genesee County History Department, 1997. 75p. Illus.

Marian Miller was a Seneca, who learned her tales from her parents and grandparents. She wrote them down so that "school children and others can en-

joy reading them" (p. viii). Like so many Native American legends, these involve animals and the natural world.

279. ——. *Iroquois Legends, Volume II.* Batavia, NY: Genesee County Historical Department, 1998. 83p. Illus. by Aaron Mosier. pa.

Miller has prepared a second volume of Iroquois legends, suitable for reading aloud to children. The Genesee County historian, in an introduction, makes the point that these are transcribed just as Miller tells them, to preserve the authentic voice of the storyteller. Legends concern creation and such natural wonders as how birds got their colors.

280. Partridge, Emelyn Newcomb. *Glooscap the Great Chief, and Other Stories: Legends of the Micmacs.* New York: Macmillan, 1919. 293p. Illus. Glossary of Micmac words.

Partridge here tells for children various Micmac legends. In her preface she says that she has used Silas T. Rand's earlier work, *Legends of the Micmacs* (1894; New York: Johnson reprint, 1971), and Charles Leland's *The Algonquin Legends of New England* (1884; repr., Detroit, MI: Singing Tree Press, 1968) and *Kuloskap the Master* (New York: Funk and Wagnalls, 1902) for her sources.

She tells animal tales, fairy tales, and of course, tales of Glooscap, the creator.

In the introduction, Partridge gives some sketchy information about the culture of the Micmacs, and some information on the life of Silas T. Rand.

281. Shenandoah, Joanne-Tekalibwa:kbwa, and Douglas M. George-Kanentiio. *Skywoman: Legends of the Iroquois.* Santa Fe, NM: Clear Light Publishers, 1998. 108p. Illus. by John Kahionkes Fadden and David Kanietakeron Fadden. 96-32488. 0-940666-99-5.

These legends of the Iroquois in New York tell stories of the natural world—how the various constellations came to be and why evergreens never lose their leaves. Also here are stories about the healing powers the Iroquois learned from the little people.

Some illustrations are in full color; others are black and white.

282. Willington, Louisa Penn. *Aunt Louisa's Rip Van Winkle*. New York: Hart Publishing, 1977. 24p. Illus. 77-79198. 0-8055025-79.

Full-page color drawings and smaller black-and-white sketches illustrate this children's version of the legend of Rip Van Winkle. This version of the Washington Irving tale is told in verse. The color illustrations are detailed and imaginative.

A brief biographical note of Washington Irving follows the poem.

283. Wilson, Gilbert L. *Indian Hero Tales*. New York: American Book Company, 1916. 203p. Illus. Notes. Glossary of Indian Words.

Based on the books published by Silas T. Rand and Charles Leland, this is another telling of the legends of the great Glooscap, the Abenaki creator.

A supplemental section gives information to young people of the time on camping, from how to make and set up an Indian tent to how to safely store supplies.

Literary Authors: A Selected List

Below is a selected list of authors who reflect and interpret the history and atmosphere of their region. These are authors of novels, poems, short stories, or reminiscences. Through reading the works of these authors, one can acquire knowledge of the history, people, and flavor of the region. This is not a complete list, either of authors, or of their works, but rather one calculated to start readers exploring and discovering their own favorites.

Frost, Robert, 1874–1963

> "Birches"
> *Collected Poems of Robert Frost*
> *In the Clearing*
> "Stopping by Woods on a Snowy Evening"
> *A Swinger of Birches: Poems of Robert Frost for Young People*

Hawthorne, Nathaniel, 1804–1864

> *Complete Novels and Selected Tales of Nathaniel Hawthorne*
> *The House of the Seven Gables*
> *Mosses from an Old Manse*

Irving, Washington, 1783–1859

> *The Complete Tales of Washington Irving*
> *Diedrich Knickerbocker's A History of New York*
> *The Legend of Sleepy Hollow*
> *Rip Van Winkle: And Other Stories*
> *Spectre Bridegroom*

Jewett, Sarah Orne, 1849–1909

> *The Best Stories of Sarah Orne Jewett*
> *The Country of the Pointed Firs*

Longfellow, Henry Wadsworth, 1807–1882

> *The Complete Poetical Works of Longfellow*
> *Evangeline: A Tale of Acadie*
> "Hiawatha"
> "The Midnight Ride of Paul Revere"

Ogilvie, Elisabeth, 1917–

The Ebbing Tide
High Tide at Noon
My World Is an Island
Storm Tide

Whittier, John Greenleaf, 1807–1892

"Barbara Frietchie"
*The Complete Poetical Works of John
    Greenleaf Whittier*
*The Poetical Works of John Greenleaf
    Whittier*
"Snowbound"

Museums of the Region: A Selected List

Museums that feature everyday life abound in all regions of the country. Through the display of clothing, farm implements, household goods, industrial tools, or entire houses, workshops, and communities, these museums can help people of today understand and appreciate the lives lived by those who came before. The list below does not mention all museums in the region, but by browsing through it, one can get a glimpse of the richness of museum offerings. Explore on your own and discover even more fascinating museums.

Connecticut

Bridgeport

The Barnum Museum
820 Main Street
Bridgeport, Connecticut 06604
203-331-1104
http://www.barnum-museum.org

Bristol

New England Carousel Museum
95 Riverside Avenue
Bristol, Connecticut 06010
860-585-5411
http://www.thecarouselmuseum.com/

East Granby

Old New-Gate Prison and Copper Mine
Newgate Road
East Granby, Connecticut 06026
Mailing address:
59 South Prospect Street
Hartford, Connecticut 06106
860-566-3005
http://www.chc.state.ct.us

East Windsor

Connecticut Trolley Museum
58 North Road
East Windsor, Connecticut 06088
Mailing address:
P.O. Box 360
East Windsor, Connecticut 06088
860-627-6540
http://www.ceraonline.org

Greenwich

Putnam Cottage
243 East Putnam Avenue
Greenwich, Connecticut 06830
203-869-9697
*http://www.museumsusa.org/data/museums/
    CT/76071.htm*

Hamden

Eli Whitney Museum, Inc.
915 Whitney Avenue
Hamden, Connecticut 06517
203-777-1833
http://www.eliwhitney.org

Hartford

The Old State House
800 Main Street
Hartford, Connecticut 06103
860-522-6766
http://www.shareCT.org

Manchester

Lutz Children's Museum
247 South Main Street
Manchester, Connecticut 06040
860-649-2838
http://www.lutzmuseum.org/links.asp

Mystic

Mystic Seaport
75 Greenmanville Avenue
Mystic, Connecticut 06355
Mailing address:
P.O. Box 6000
Mystic, Connecticut 06355
860-572-0711
http://www.mysticseaport.org

Norwich

The Leffingwell House Museum
348 Washington Street
Norwich, Connecticut 06360

Mailing Address:
P.O. Box 13
Norwich, Connecticut 06360
860-889-9440
http://www.visitnewengland.com

Ridgefield

Keeler Tavern Museum
132 Main Street
Ridgefield, Connecticut 06877
Mailing Address:
P.O. Box 204
Ridgefield, Connecticut 06877
203-438-5485
http://www.keelertavernmuseum.org/

Stonington

Old Lighthouse Museum
7 Water Street
Stonington, Connecticut 06378
860-535-1440
http://www.stoningtonhistory.org/
    light.htm

Willimantic

Windham Textile and History Museum
157 Union-Main Street
Willimantic, Connecticut 06226
203-456-2178
http://www.millmuseum.org

Delaware

Dover

Delaware Agricultural Museum and Village
866 North Dupont Highway

Dover, Delaware 19901
302-734-1618
http://www.agriculturalmuseum.org

Milford

Milford Museum
121 South Walnut Street
Milford, Delaware 19963
302-424-1080
http://www.visitdover.com/tours/
   attractmilfordmus.html

Seaford

Governor Ross Plantation
North Pine Street
Seaford, Delaware 19973
Mailing Address:
Route 1
Box 393
Seaford, Delaware 19973
302-628-9500
http://www.sussexcountyonline.com/
   towns/seaford/ross.html

Winterthur

The Henry Francis Du Pont Winterthur
   Museum, Inc.
Route 52
Winterthur, Delaware 19735
302-888-4600
http://www.winterthur.org

District of Columbia

Dumbarton House
2715 Q Street, N.W.
Washington, D.C. 20007

202-337-2288
http://www.dumbartonhouse.org/

Ford's Theatre National Historic Site
   (Lincoln Museum)
511 10th Street, N.W.
Washington, D.C. 20004
202-426-6924
http://www.nps.gov/foth

Frederick Douglass National Historic Site
1411 W Street, S.E.
Washington, D.C. 20020
Mailing address:
c/o National Parks–East
1411 W Street, S.E.
Washington, D.C. 20020
202-426-5691
http://www.cr.nps.gov/csd/exhibits/
   douglass

Mary McLeod Bethune Council House
   National Historic Site
1318 Vermont Avenue, N.W.
Washington, D.C. 20005
202-673-2402
http://www.nps.gov/mamc

Maine

Ashland

Ashland Logging Museum, Inc.
P.O. Box 866
Ashland, Maine 04732
207-435-6039
http://www.townofashland.com

Bath

Maine Maritime Museum
243 Washington Street

Bath, Maine 04530
207-443-1316
http://www.bathmaine.com

Boothbay

Boothbay Railway Village
Route 27
Boothbay, Maine 04537
Mailing address:
P.O. Box 123
Boothbay, Maine 04537
207-633-4727
http://www.railwayvillage.org

Camden

Old Conway Homestead Complex and
    Museum
U.S. Route 1
Camden-Rockport Lane
Camden, Maine 04843
Mailing address:
P.O. Box 747
Rockport, Maine 04856
207-236-2257
http://conwayhouse.home.mc.org

Dover-Foxcroft

Blacksmith Shop Museum
100 Dawes Road
Dover-Foxcroft, Maine 04426
207-564-8618
http://www.mainemuseums.org/htm/
    museumdetail.php3?orgID=196

Isleboro

Sailor's Memorial Museum
Grindle Point
Isleboro, Maine 04848
Mailing address:
P.O. Box 76
Isleboro, Maine 04848
207-734-2253
http://www.lighthouse.cc/grindle/
    history.html

Kennebunkport

Seashore Trolley Museum
195 Log Cabin Road
Kennebunkport, Maine 04046
Mailing address:
P.O. Box A
Kennebunkport, Maine 04046
207-967-2712
http://www.trolleymuseum.org

New Gloucester

Shaker Museum
707 Shaker Road
New Gloucester, Maine 04260
207-926-4597
http://www.shaker.lib.me.us

Owls Head

Owl's Head Transportation Museum
Route 73
P.O. Box 277
Owls Head, Maine 04854
207-594-4418
http://www.ohtm.org

Patten

Patten Lumberman's Museum
61 Shin Pond Road
Patten, Maine 04765
Mailing address:
P.O. Box 300
Patten, Maine 04765
207-528-2650
http://www.mainerec.com/logger.html

Pemaquid Point

The Fishermen's Museum
Lighthouse Park
Pemaquid Point, Maine 04554
Mailing address:
3007 Bristol Road
New Harbor, Maine 04554
207-677-2494
http://www.lighthouse.cc/pemaquid

Rockland

Shore Village Museum
104 Limerock Road
Rockland, Maine 04841
207-594-0311
http://www.lighthouse.cc/shorevillage

Searsport

Penobscot Marine Museum
5 Church Street
Searsport, Maine 04974
Mailing address:
P.O. Box 498
Searsport, Maine 04974
207-548-2529
*http://www.penobscotmarinemuseum.
org*

Stockton Springs

Fort Knox State Historic Site
711 Fort Knox Road
Stockton Springs, Maine 04981
207-469-7719
fortknox.maineguide.com/

Thomaston

Montpelier–The General Henry Knox
  Museum
Route 1 and Route 131
Thomaston, Maine 04861
Mailing address:
P.O. Box 326
Thomaston, Maine 04861
207-354-8062
http://www.generalknoxmuseum.org

Maryland

Accokeek

The Accokeek Foundation, Inc.
3400 Bryan Point Road
Accokeek, Maryland 20607
301-283-2113
http://www.accokeek.org

Baltimore

Baltimore Maritime Museum
Piers 3 and 5
Pratt Street
Baltimore, Maryland 21202
Mailing address:
802 South Caroline Street
Baltimore, Maryland 21231
410-396-3453
http://www.baltomaritimemuseum.org

Baltimore Streetcar Museum, Inc.
1901 Falls Road
Baltimore, Maryland 21211
Mailing address:
P.O. Box 4881
Baltimore, Maryland 21211
410-547-0264
http://www.baltimoremd.com/streetcar

Brunswick

Brunswick Railroad Museum and Visitor
   Center
40 West Potomac Street
Brunswick, Maryland 21716
301-834-7100
http://www.brunswickmuseum.org

Cumberland

George Washington's Headquarters
Greene Street
Cumberland, Maryland 21502
Mailing address:
Parks/Recreation City Hall
P.O. Box 1702
Cumberland, Maryland 21502
301-759-6636
http://www.ohwy.com/md/g/geowashq.htm

Saint Michaels

Chesapeake Bay Maritime Museum
Mill Street
Saint Michaels, Maryland 21663
Mailing address:
P.O. Box 636
Saint Michaels, Maryland 21663
410-745-2916
http://www.cbmm.org

Sharpsburg

Chesapeake and Ohio Canal Tavern
   Museum
16500 Shepherdstown Park
Sharpsburg, Maryland 21782
301-739-4200
http://www.nps.gov/choh

Massachusetts

Barnstable

Olde Colonial Courthouse, Tales of
   Cape Cod
Olde Colonial Courthouse
Main Street
Route 6A
Barnstable, Massachusetts 02630
Mailing address:
P.O. Box 41
Barnstable, Massachusetts 02630
508-375-6468
http://www.capehistory.com

Boston

Ancient and Honorable Artillery
   Company
Armory
Faneuil Hall
Boston, Massachusetts 02109
617-227-1638
http://www.ahacsite.org/

Boston Fire Museum
344 Congress Street
Boston, Massachusetts 02210
617-482-1344
http://www.bostonfiremuseum.org

Paul Revere House/Paul Revere
   Memorial Association
19 North Square
Boston, Massachusetts 02113
617-523-2338
http://www.paulreverehouse.org

Charlestown

Bunker Hill Museum
43 Monument Square
Charlestown, Massachusetts 02129
Mailing address:
P.O. Box 1776
Charlestown, Massachusetts 02129
617-242-1843
http://www.paulreverehouse.org/

Deerfield

Historic Deerfield, Inc.
The Street
Deerfield, Massachusetts 01342
Mailing address:
P.O. Box 321
Deerfield, Massachusetts 01342
413-774-5581
http://www.historic-deerfield.org

Duxbury

Alden House Museum
105 Alden Street
Duxbury, Massachusetts 02332
781-934-9092
http://www.alden.org

Essex

Essex Shipbuilding Museum
66 Main Street
Essex, Massachusetts 01929
Mailing address:
P.O. Box 277
Essex, Massachusetts 01929
978-768-7541
*http://www.essexshipbuildingmuseum.
   com*

Hadley

Hadley Farm Museum
147 Russell Street
Hadley, Massachusetts 01035
Mailing address:
164 South Maple Street
Hadley, Massachusetts 01035
413-586-1812
*http://www.hadleyonline.com/
   farmmuseum*

Harvard

Fruitlands Museums
102 Prospect Hill Road
Harvard, Massachusetts 01451
978-456-3924
http://www.fruitlands.org

New Bedford

New Bedford Whaling Museum
18 Johnny Cake Hill
New Bedford, Massachusetts 02740
508-997-0046
http://www.whalingmuseum.org

Newbury

Coffin House
14 High Road
Route 1A
Newbury, Massachusetts 01951
Mailing address:
141 Cambridge Street
Boston, Massachusetts 02114
978-462-2634
http://www.spnea.org

Pittsfield

Hancock Shaker Village
Route 20
West Housatonic Street
Pittsfield, Massachusetts 01202
Mailing address:
P.O. Box 927
Pittsfield, Massachusetts 01202
413-443-0188
http://www.hancockshakervillage.org

Plymouth

Plimoth Plantation, Inc.
137 Warren Avenue
Plymouth, Massachusetts 02362
Mailing address
Box 1620
Plymouth, Massachusetts 02362
508-746-1622. ext. 8249
http://www.plimoth.org

Salem

Peabody Essex Museum
E. India Square
Salem, Massachusetts 01970

978-745-1876
http://www.plem.org

Sandwich

Sandwich Glass Museum
129 Main Street
Sandwich, Massachusetts 02563
Mailing address:
P.O. Box 103
Sandwich, Massachusetts 02563
508-888-0251
http://www.sandwichglassmuseum.org

Saugus

Saugus Ironworks National Historic Site
244 Central Street
Saugus, Massachusetts 01906
781-233-0050
http://www.nps.gov.sair

Sturbridge

Old Sturbridge Village
1 Old Sturbridge Village Road
Sturbridge, Massachusetts 01566
508-347-3362
http://www.osv.org

New Hampshire

Canterbury

Canterbury Shaker Village
288 Shaker Road
Canterbury, New Hampshire 03224
603-783-9511
http://www.shakers.org

Enfield

Lockehaven Schoolhouse Museum
Lockehaven Road
Enfield, New Hampshire 03748
Mailing address:
P.O. Box 612
Enfield, New Hampshire 03748
603-632-7740
http://www.newhampshire.com/pages/
   museumlist/cfm

Hampton

Tuck Museum
40 Park Avenue
Hampton, New Hampshire 03842
Mailing Address:
P.O. Box 1601
Hampton, New Hampshire 03843
603-926-2543
http://www.nhultranet.com/~hhs/
   hhshome.htm

Laconia

The Belknap Mill Society
The Mill Plaza
Laconia, New Hampshire 03246
603-524-8813
http://www.specialplaces.org/
   2001belknapmill.htm

Milton

New Hampshire Farm Museum, Inc.
Route 125
Plummer's Ridge
Milton, New Hampshire 03851

Mailing address:
P.O. Box 644
Milton, New Hampshire 03851
603-652-7840
http://farmmuseum.org

Portsmouth

John Paul Jones House Museum
43 Middle Street
Portsmouth, New Hampshire 03801
Mailing address:
P.O. Box 728
Portsmouth, New Hampshire 03802
603-436-8420
http://www.portsmouthhistory.org/
   jpjhouse.html

South Sutton

South Sutton Old Store Museum
12 Meeting House Hill Road
South Sutton, New Hampshire 03273
Mailing address:
P.O. Box 555
South Sutton, New Hampshire 03273
603-938-5843

Tamworth

Remick Country Doctor Museum and
   Farm
58 Cleveland Hill Road
Tamworth, New Hampshire 03886
Mailing address:
P.O. Box 250
Tamworth, New Hampshire 03886
603-686-6117
http://www.remickmuseum.org

New Jersey

Allaire

Historic Allaire Village Inc.
Allaire State Park
Route 254
Allaire, New Jersey 07727
Mailing address:
P.O. Box 220
Allaire, New Jersey 07727
732-938-2253
http://www.allairevillage.org

Batsto

Historic Batsto Village
Route 542
Batsto, New Jersey 08037
Mailing address:
Wharton State Forest
4110 Nesco Road
Hammonton, New Jersey 08037
609-561-0024
http://www.batstovillage.org

Millville

Museum of American Glass at Wheaton
    Village
1501 Glasstown Road
Millville, New Jersey 08332
856-825-6800
http://www.wheatonvillage.org

Morristown

Fosterfields Living Historical Farm
73 Kahdena Road
Morristown, New Jersey 07960

973-326-7644
http://www.parks.morris.nj.us

Parsippany

Craftsman Farms Foundation
2352 Route 10 West
Manor Lane
Parsippany, New Jersey 07950
Mailing address:
2352 Route 10 West
Box 5
Morris Plains, New Jersey 07950
973-540-1165
http://www.parsippany.net/
    craftsmanfarms.html

Piscataway

East Jersey Olde Towne, Inc.
River Road and Hoes Lane
Piscataway, New Jersey 08855
Mailing address:
P.O. Box 661
Piscataway, New Jersey 08855
732-463-9077
http://www.cultureheritage.org/village.asp

Somerville

Old Dutch Parsonage
71 Somerset Street
Somerville, New Jersey 08876
908-725-1015
http://www.ohwy.com/nj/o/oldupshs/htm

Titusville

Johnson Ferry House Museum

Washington Crossing State Park
355 Washington Xing Penn Road
Titusville, New Jersey 08560
609-737-2515
http://www.fieldtrip.com/nj/97370623.htm

New York

Albany

Shaker Heritage Society
875 Watervliet–Shaker Road, Suite 2
Albany, New York 12211
518-456-7890
*http://www.crisny.org/not-for-
    profit/shakerwv*

Chittenango

Chittenango Landing Canal Boat
    Museum
7010 Lakeport Road
Chittenango, New York 13037
315-687-3801
http://www.canalboatmuseum.org

Clayton

The Antique Boat Museum
750 Mary Street
Clayton, New York 13624
315-686-4104
http://www.abm.org

Cold Spring Harbor

Cold Spring Harbor Whaling Museum
Main Street

Cold Spring Harbor, New York 11724
Mailing address:
P.O. Box 25
Cold Spring Harbor, New York 11724
631-367-3418
http://www.cswhalingmuseum.org

East Aurora

Elbert Hubbard-Roycroft Museum
363 Oakwood Avenue
East Aurora, New York 14052
Mailing address:
P.O. Box 472
East Aurora, New York 14052
716-652-4735
http://www.roycrofter.com/museum.htm

Elizabethtown

Adirondack Center Museum
Court Street
Elizabethtown, New York 12932
Mailing address:
P.O. Box 428
Elizabethtown, New York 12932
518-873-6466
http://www.adkhistorycenter.org

Fabius

Pioneer Museum
Highland Forest Route 80
Fabius, New York 13063
Mailing address:
P.O. Box 146
Liverpool, New York 13088
315-453-6767
*http://www.co.onondaga.ny.us/
    parks.htm*

Fort Hunter

Schoharie Crossing State Historic Site
129 Schoharie Street
Fort Hunter, New York 12069
Mailing address:
P.O. Box 140
Fort Hunter, New York 12069
518-829-7516
http://nysparks.state.ny.us/cgi-bin/
   cgiwrap/nysparks/historic.cgi?p+23

Katonah

John Jay Homestead State Historic Site
400 Route 22/Jay Street
Katonah, New York 10536
Mailing address:
P.O. Box 832
Katonah, New York 10536
914-232-5651
http://www.nysparks.com

Kingston

Trolley Museum of New York
89 East Strand
Kingston, New York 12401
Mailing address:
P.O. Box 2291
Kingston, New York 12402
845-331-3399
http://tmny.org

Monroe

Museum Village
1010 Route 17 M
Monroe, New York 10950
845-782-8247
http://www.museumvillage.org

Mumford

Genesee Country Village and Museum
1410 Flint Hill Road
Mumford, New York 14511
Mailing address:
P.O. Box 310
Mumford, New York 14511
716-538-6822
http://www.gcv.org

New York

Fraunces Tavern Museum
54 Pearl Street
New York, New York 10004
212-425-1778
http://www.frauncestavernmuseum.org

The South Street Seaport Museum
207 Front Street
New York, New York 10038
212-748-8725
http://www.southstseaport.org

Old Chatham

The Shaker Museum and Library
88 Shaker Museum Road
Old Chatham, New York 12136
518-794-9100, ext. 100
http://www.shakermuseumandlibrary.org

Rome

Erie Canal Village
5789 New London Road
Route 46 and 49 West
Rome, New York 13440
888-374-3226
http://www.eriecanalvillage.com

Ticonderoga

Fort Ticonderoga
Fort Road
Ticonderoga, New York 12883
Mailing address:
P.O. Box 390
Ticonderoga, New York 12883
518-585-2821
http://www.fort-ticonderoga.org

Water Mill

Water Mill Museum
41 Old Mill Road
Water Mill, New York 11976
Mailing address:
P.O. Box 63
Water Mill, New York 11976
631-726-4625
http://www.watermillmuseum.org

Pennsylvania

Allentown

Leni Lenape Historical Society/
  Museum of Indian Culture
2825 Fish Hatchery Road,
Allentown, Pennsylvania 18103
610-797-2121
http://www.lenape.org

Altoona

Railroaders Memorial Museum
1300 9th Avenue
Altoona, Pennsylvania 16602
814-946-0834
http://www.railroadcity.com

Ambridge

Old Economy Village
14th and Church Streets
Ambridge, Pennsylvania 15003
724-266-4500
http://www.oldeconomyvillage.org

Bethlehem

Moravian Museum of Bethlehem, Inc.
66 West Church Street
Bethlehem, Pennsylvania 18018
Mailing address:
459 Old York Road
Bethlehem, Pennsylvania
610-867-0173
http://www.historicbethlehem.org

Birdsboro

Daniel Boone Homestead
400 Daniel Boone Road
Birdsboro, Pennsylvania 19508
610-582-1744
http://www.berksweb.com/boone.html

Chadds Ford

Brandywine Battlefield
U.S. Route 1
Chadds Ford, Pennsylvania 19317
Mailing address:
Box 202
Chadds Ford, Pennsylvania 19317
610-459-3342
http://www.ushistory.org/brandywine

Easton

National Canal Museum, Hugh Moore
   Historical Park and Museums
30 Centre Square
Easton, Pennsylvania 18042
610-559-6613
http://canals.org

Eckley

Eckley Miners' Village
Main Street
Eckley, Pennsylvania 18255
Mailing address:
R.R. 2, Box 236
Weatherly, Pennsylvania 18255
570-636-2070
http://www.phmc.state.pa.us

Galeton

Pennsylvania Lumber Museum
U.S. Route 6
Galeton, Pennsylvania 16922
Mailing address:
P.O. Box 239
Galeton, Pennsylvania 16922
814-435-2652
http://www.lumbermuseum.org

Green Lane

Goschenhoppen Folklife Library and
   Museum
Route 29
RedMen's Hall
Green Lane, Pennsylvania 18054
Mailing address:
P.O. Box 476
Green Lane, Pennsylvania 18054

610-367-8286
http://www.goschenhoppen.org

Harleysville

Mennonite Heritage Center
565 Yoder Road
Harleysville, Pennsylvania 19438
Mailing address:
P.O. Box 82
Harleysville, Pennsylvania 19438
215-256-3020
http://www.mhep.org

Kutztown

Pennsylvania German Cultural Heritage
   Center at Kutztown University
P.O. Box 306
Kutztown, Pennsylvania 19530
Mailing address:
P.O. Box 30
Kutztown, Pennsylvania 19530
610-683-1589
http://www.kutztown.edu/community/
   PGCHC

Media

Colonial Pennsylvania Plantation
Ridley Creek State Park
Media, Pennsylvania 19063
610-566-1725
http://www.de.psu.edu/cpp/index.htm

Philadelphia

The African American Museum in
   Philadelphia
701 Arch Street

Philadelphia, Pennsylvania 19106
215-574-0380
http://www.aampmuseum.org/aamp.html

Betsy Ross House and Flag Museum
239 Arch Street
Philadelphia, Pennsylvania 19106
215-686-1252
http://www.ushistory.org/betsy

Independence Seaport Museum
Penn's Landing Waterfront
211 South Columbus Boulevard at
    Walnut Street
Philadelphia, Pennsylvania 19106
215-925-6713
http://seaport.philly.com

Steamtown

Steamtown National Historic Site
Cliff Street off Lackawanna Avenue
Scranton, Pennsylvania 18503
570-340-5200
http://www.nps.gov/stea

Strasburg

Railroad Museum of Pennsylvania
300 Gap Road
Strasburg, Pennsylvania 17579
Mailing address:
P.O. Box 15
Strasburg, Pennsylvania 17579
717-687-8629
http://www.rrmuseumpa.org

Stroudsburg

Quiet Valley Living Historical Farm
1000 Turkey Hill Road

Stroudsburg, Pennsylvania 18360
570-992-6161
http://www.quietvalley.org

York

Industrial and Agricultural Museum,
    York County Heritage Trust
217 West Princess Street
York, Pennsylvania 17403
Mailing address:
250 East Market Street
York, Pennsylvania 17403
717-848-1587
http://www.yorkheritage.org

Rhode Island

Bristol

Coggeshall Farm Museum
Route 114
Poppasquash Road
Bristol, Rhode Island 02809
Mailing address:
P.O. Box 562
Bristol, Rhode Island 02809
401-253-9062

Jamestown

Jamestown Museum
92 Narragansett Avenue
Jamestown, Rhode Island 02835
Mailing address:
P.O. Box 156
Jamestown, Rhode Island 02835
401-423-0784

Newport

Bellcourt Castle
657 Bellevue Avenue
Newport, Rhode Island 02840
401-849-1566
http://www.belcourtcastle.com/

The Preservation Society of Newport
    County/Newport Mansions
424 Bellevue Avenue
Newport, Rhode Island 02840
401-847-1000
http://www.newportmansions.org

Pawtucket

Slater Mill Historic Site
Roosevelt Avenue
Pawtucket, Rhode Island 02860
Mailing address:
P.O. Box 696
Pawtucket, Rhode Island 02862
401-725-8638
http://www.slatermill.org

Providence

Culinary Archives and Museum,
    Johnson and Wales University
315 Harborside Boulevard
Providence, Rhode Island 02905
401-598-2805
http://www.culinary.org

The John Nicholas Brown Center for the
    Study of American Civilization
357 Benefit Street
Providence, Rhode Island 02903
Mailing address:
Box 1880
Brown University

Providence, Rhode Island 02912
401-272-0357

Vermont

Bellows Falls

Adams Old Stone Grist Mill
Mill Street
Bellows Falls, Vermont 05101
Mailing address:
47 Atkinson Street
Bellows Falls, Vermont 05101
802-463-3734

Bennington

The Bennington Museum
West Main Street
Bennington, Vermont 05201
802-447-1571
http://www.benningtonmusuem.com

Middlebury

Vermont Folklife Center
Masonic Hall
3 Court Street
Middlebury, Vermont 05753
Mailing address:
P.O. Box 442
Middlebury, Vermont 05753
802-388-4964
http://www.vermontfolklifecenter.org

Springfield

Eureka School House
State Route 11
Springfield, Vermont 05156

Mailing address:
Historic Preservation
National Life Building
Drawer 20
Montpelier, Vermont 05620
802-828-3051
http://www.historicvermont.org

Vergennes

Lake Champlain Maritime Museum
4472 Basin Harbor Road
Vergennes, Vermont 05491
802-475-2022
http://lcmm.org

Woodstock

Billings Farm and Museum
River Road and Route 12
Woodstock, Vermont 05091
Mailing address:
P.O. Box 489
Woodstock, Vermont 05091
802-457-2355
http://www.billingsfarm.org

Journals in Folklore of the Region: A Selected List

Other journals and newsletters besides the one listed below exist. These are often smaller and more local, published by museums, historical societies, folklore organizations, community groups, and schools. Explore on your own to see what other publications on folklore exist.

Northeast Folklore

Web Sites: A Selected List

Below is a list of a few Web sites dealing with folklore of the region. You can find other Web sites by doing an Internet search on a search engine such as Google or Yahoo!, or by looking for the Web sites of various folklore organizations with which you are familiar.

Amish, the Mennonites, and the Plain People,
    http://www.800padutch.com/amish.html
Profiles the way of life of the Amish and Mennonites: dress, education, social structure.

Center for Folklore and Ethnography,
    University of Pennsylvania,
    http://www.sas.upenn.edu/folklore/
Basic information about the department.

Folklore: Harvard University,
    http://www.fas.harvard.edu/~folkmyth/
As well as giving information about folklore programs at Harvard, this links to other sites on folklore, including electronic journals, folklore centers, and folklore societies.

George Korson Collection,
    http://www.lcweb.loc.gov/spcoll/137.html
Korson was a collector of folk music, mostly of working people. This Web site describes the Korson collection at the Library of Congress.

Helen Hartness Flanders Ballad Collection,
    http://www.middlebury.edu/~lib/FBC/
Helen Hartness Flanders was the donor of this collection of folk music and folklife materials to Middlebury College.

The Maine Folklife Center,
    http://www.umaine.edu/folklife/

Information about the Maine Folklife Center, including mailing address, phone number, E-mail, and information about collections and programs.

New York Folklore Society,
    http://www.nyfolklore.org/
Information on the society, including membership information and publications.

Salem, Massachusetts: What about Witches?
    http://www.salemweb.com/guide/witches.
    htm
Provides information about the seventeenth-century witchcraft trials in Salem, Massachusetts, including links to other Web sites.

University of Pennsylvania: Department of
    Folklore and Folklife: Research Annex,
    http://ccat.sas.upenn.edu/annex/
Information about the department, including research being done. Links to other Web sites.

Witchcraft in Salem Village,
    http://etext.virginia.edu/salem/
    witchcraft/index.html
Provides information about the seventeenth-century witchcraft trials in Salem, Massachusetts.

The South and Southern Highlands

Alabama, Arkansas, Florida, Georgia,
Kentucky, Louisiana, Mississippi,
North Carolina, South Carolina, Tennessee,
Virginia, West Virginia

Look for tales on:

Horse racing
The Civil War
Shipwrecks
Pirate treasure
Roanoke, the lost colony
African American folktales
Br'er Rabbit and Br'er Fox

And for characters such as:

Davy Crockett
Daniel Boone
John Henry
High John, Little John, Foolish John
Blackbeard
Casey Jones

Look for collections by:

Joel Chandler Harris
Richard Chase
Julius Lester
Ruby Pickens Tartt
Zora Neale Hurston

Find music collections by:

Richard Chase
Arthur Kyle Davis Jr.

John Jacob Niles
Vance Randolph

Introduce children to:

Uncle Remus
Casey Jones
The Jack Tales
The books of Lois Lenski

Explore the rich literature of the region with:

Erskine Caldwell
Ellen Glasgow
Samuel Clemens (Mark Twain)
Marjorie Kinnan Rawlings
Jesse Stuart

Consult journals:

Appalachian Heritage
Mid-American Folklore
Southern Folklore
Southern Folklore Quarterly

THE SOUTH AND
SOUTHERN HIGHLANDS: INTRODUCTION

When referring to the South and the Southern Highlands, one is speaking about at least one region (Southern Highlands) within a larger region (the South). Moreover, if one is looking for a homogeneous area characterized by people who share exactly the same culture from one to another, then neither the South nor the Southern Highlands can be considered a region. As commonly used, *Southern Highlands* means the southern Appalachians; for the purposes of this text, it also includes most of northern Arkansas, which is in the Ozark Mountains. Despite the belief, mainly held by people from Appalachia, that the Ozarks is not "Appalachia West," it is much more interesting than that. Northern Arkansans owe their primary allegiance not to southern Appalachia but to the Ozarks, meaning most of northern Arkansas, southern Missouri, eastern Oklahoma, and small portions of southeastern Kansas and southwestern Illinois. But, in this chapter, northern Arkansas is grouped with West Virginia and sections of Alabama, Georgia, Kentucky, North Carolina, South Carolina, Tennessee, and Virginia as part of the Southern Highlands.

Although no homogeneous culture exists in the South and Southern Highlands, there is at least one historical event that even today, almost a century and a half after it ended, has a strong presence in the two regions. That is the Civil War, whose memory is kept alive primarily by legends and folksongs. Often the legends deal not with regular soldiers but with guerrilla groups, such as the jayhawkers, who became notorious for their burnings and killings. One tale told in Arkansas concerns jayhawkers stealing and killing a baby. Another narrative says that the jayhawkers hung and killed a young boy who started to berate them. In later years the boy's ghost haunted the place of his unjust execution. A family living near Pleasant Hill, Louisiana, where a Civil War battle occurred in 1864, told of being troubled by a ghost looking for its teeth, which one member of the family had found.

Sometimes Civil War legends involve ongoing feuds; this is true of a tale told in Johnson County, Tennessee. Two competing feud factions spent a great deal of time capturing and torturing victims. Usually they were released unharmed, but badly bruised and shaken. On one occasion, though, a man was killed. Ever since, the ghost of casualty reenacts his execution in such an eerie manner that people are afraid to go near the place of his death.

On other occasions legends are set during the Civil War but have no connection with battles. Instead, they deal with the fact that some people in the South were anti-Confederate. This is true of a tale told in Georgia about a Union sympathizer who got into an argument with a pro-Confederate member of the community. The Union man helped one of the Confederate's slaves to escape and then killed the slave owner. He was hung for the murder, and the millhouse where he was executed soon supernaturally disappeared.

Some other legends are family sagas showing that loyalty during the war was not always what we would believe. A South Carolina narrative points this out in an interesting way. According to the yarn, two brothers began the war as Confederates but switched sides while they were in Virginia. They were reportedly starving when their troop passed by a farm with a large orchard. Although ordered not to steal any apples, one of the brothers disobeyed, and while he was up in a tree pulling down the fruit, the commanding officer shot him in the arm. Forthwith the brothers became Union soldiers, remaining on the Federal side until the end of the war. As one of their descendants recently said, "That story may not be true, but if it isn't it ought to be."

Famous generals figure very little in Southern folk narratives about the Civil War. Their role is usually tangential, as in the story kept alive in a North Carolina family who speak with pride about their great-grandfather. His claim to fame is that he was with Robert E. Lee when he surrendered at Appomattox.

There is a particularly strong tradition of songs about the Civil War. Some, such as "The Battle of Shiloh Hill," about a conflict that took place in 1862, which has been collected in North Carolina and Mississippi, recount the horrors of the battle in general terms, concluding with the hope that there will never again be such a slaughter. Others, such as "The Battle of Mills Springs," which has been collected in Arkansas, North Carolina, Tennessee, Virginia, and West Virginia; "The Drummer Boy of Shiloh," collected in North Carolina; and "The Last Fierce Charge," collected in Arkansas, Georgia, Kentucky, and North Carolina, all point out the horrors of war for individual soldiers. Others, such as "The Battle of Bull Run," collected in Arkansas, and "The Battle of Shiloh," collected in Virginia, take a partisan Southern stance referring

to "cowardly Yankees" and "brave Southern soldiers." A few, such as "The Rebel's Escape," collected in Kentucky and Tennessee, emphasize an individual soldier's craftiness in escaping from prison. Even famous generals figure in folk ballads about the Civil War. Thus, in West Virginia, they still celebrate Phil Sheridan's ride at the Battle of Cedar Creek in October 1864.

Throughout the twentieth century many different collectors recorded and published the folksongs of the South and the Southern Highlands. Now, all the states in the two regions have at least one printed work devoted to their vocal music traditions. The mammoth work among all these is *The Frank C. Brown Collection of North Carolina Folklore* (1952–1964), a seven-volume work, of which four volumes deal with folksongs and ballads. Brown (1870–1943), a Duke University professor, and his students collected this material between 1913 and 1943. Even more impressive is Vance Randolph's *Ozark Folksongs* (1946–1950), the largest published work compiled by a single individual, which was collected between 1911 and 1944. Byron Arnold and Ray Browne published collections from Alabama, John Harrington Cox's *Folk-Songs of the South* (1925) consists of materials from West Virginia, and Josiah Comb's *Folk-Songs of the Southern United States* (1926; revised 1967) contains items exclusively from Kentucky. In 1929 and 1960 Arthur Kyle Davis published books of ballads from Virginia collected by members of the Virginia Folklore Society, and in 1949 he published an index of non-ballad materials in the society's archives. Alton Morris published a collection of folksongs from Florida, Arthur Palmer Hudson did the same for

Mississippi, George Boswell for Tennessee, Art Rosenbaum for Georgia, and Reed Smith for South Carolina. Smith, though, was so biased in favor of Child ballads, the 305 ballads that Francis James Child canonized in his ten-volume *The English and Scottish Popular Ballads* (1882–1898), that he excluded all other songs. This prejudice surfaced as recently as 1956 when Richard Chase insisted in introductory remarks to his *American Folk Tales and Songs* that a "true folk ballad" is a variant or version of one of the 305 Child ballads, no more or less. Fortunately, most collectors didn't take such a narrow view; if they had, our knowledge of folksinging would be far less today than it is.

Some collectors became performers; eventually the latter activity overshadowed the former. So it is with John Jacob Niles (1892–1980), who spent considerable time in the 1920s and 1930s collecting ballads and folksongs in southern Appalachia. Much of this material was published in *Ballad Book* (1960). Earlier he had published *Singing Soldiers* (1927) and *Songs My Mother Never Taught Me* (1929), which contained both folk and popular songs, and two collections of traditional music, *Impressions of a Negro Camp Meeting* (1925) and *Seven Kentucky Mountain Songs* (1928). At about the same time he began publishing these works, Niles started giving concerts, where he did very nontraditional performances of traditional songs, most of which he had collected from folksingers. Later he began focusing on original compositions; throughout his career he produced three "in the style of folk music" that were based on an element of traditional music and which many people assume are of anonymous origin: "Go 'Way from My

Window," "I Wonder as I Wander," and "Black Is the Color."

All of the publications mentioned thus far are primarily concerned with Anglo-Saxon materials. Irene Therese Whitfield's *Louisiana French Folk Songs* (1939) deals with a different ethnic group—the Louisiana Cajuns. Their name is a colloquial rendering of Acadian, a reference to Acadia in Nova Scotia where these people lived before being expelled in 1755 when the French lost most of their New World holdings to England. Some of the ballads in Anglo-Saxon tradition also found their way into Cajun lore, albeit with Cajun titles. Thus, "A Paper of Pins" became "Un Paquet d'Epingles," and "Billy Boy" became "Billy Garcon." Then there are such items as "Le Mariage Anglais," about the marriage between an English king and a French princess, which comes from French tradition, and "Jolie Blon," which seems to be of Cajun origin.

Another ethnic group—African Americans—have been the subject of several folksong collections. Guy B. Johnson and Howard W. Odum wrote two volumes, *The Negro and His Songs* (1925) and *Negro Workaday Songs* (1926). Newman Ivey White also produced *American Folk-Songs* (1928), made up largely of material he collected in Alabama and North Carolina. There have also been a number of less voluminous works on the subject as well as studies of individual ballad heroes, such as John Henry. That is appropriate because the "steel-drivin' man" is the fictional character most often associated with black folk traditions. Supposedly, he died sometime between 1870 and 1872 at the Big Bend Tunnel near Hinton, West Virginia, after competing with a steam drill in a test of the practicality of the device. Actually, there is no proof that John Henry ever existed, and, according to some, if he did he was not from West Virginia but from places far removed, such as Jamaica. Regardless of the hero's origins, the ballad about John Henry is widely known throughout the South and much of the rest of the United States.

Although John Henry is a black, probably fictional, hero popular in both white and black folk tradition, Casey Jones was white and definitely a real historical figure popular in both black-and-white tradition. John Luther ("Casey") Jones (1863–1900) was an engineer on the Illinois Central Railroad who died April 30, 1900, at Vaughan, Mississippi, when his train crashed into a freight train. Shortly before the wreck he warned his Negro fireman, Sim Webb, to jump from the cab and save his life. Casey pulled on the brakes, but it was too late. Official sources placed some blame on Jones for the fatal wreck, because he reportedly failed to heed a warning flag a thousand feet in front of the train he hit. Even so, in popular imagination, Casey is the ultimate hero who thought first of protecting his crew and passengers at the expense of his own life. For some reason, his wife has not fared so well. According to the lines of one song, at the time of her husband's death, she was having an affair with another railroad worker. There is no historical basis for this charge.

Narratives about many topics are rife throughout the two regions, those that are told as true events are called legends; those related as fiction are called folktales. Few folktales associated with the South and Southern Highlands have gained more attention than the Jack tales.

First reported in 1925 by Isabel Gordon Carter, they gained more popular acclaim after Richard Chase, a Virginia schoolteacher, published *The Jack Tales* (1943), *Grandfather Tales* (1948), and *American Folk Tales and Songs* (1956). These collections of European magic and wonder—tales featuring a hero named Jack—were all gathered from one family, that of Council Harmon, in Watauga County, North Carolina. Interested in attracting a wider audience for the tales, Chase rewrote many of them to increase their appeal and readability.

Even more famous are the Uncle Remus tales popularized in the late nineteenth century by Joel Chandler Harris (1848–1908). A journalist, Harris became interested in writing his narratives featuring the avuncular figure Uncle Remus relating animal fables to the little white boy from the big house after reading an article on Southern Negro folklore that he found inaccurate. He drew upon his own recollections of yarns he had heard from blacks before the Civil War, combining them with materials obtained from ex-slaves. With no prior knowledge of folklore, Harris, spurred by the runaway success of *Uncle Remus: His Songs and His Sayings* and its sequels, became an unintentional folklorist. When his second volume, *Nights with Uncle Remus,* appeared, Harris was pointing out connections between his Br'er Rabbit cycle and Kaffir, Hottentot, Amazon Indian, and Creek animal tales. He erred in insisting that these tales were of remote African origin, when they really were a mix of African and European elements.

Although from a purely folklore standpoint Harris's publications were often wrongheaded, they did have a positive influence by inspiring subsequent collections of African American folklore. Most immediately, they motivated the collections of Charles C. Jones and Mrs. A. M. H. Christensen, both of them emphasizing animal fables. Zora Neale Hurston (1903–1960) corrected this tendency with *Mules and Men* (1935), a collection of narratives Hurston, a black, recorded from African American Floridians and Alabamians between 1929 and 1931. She also had lots of animal tales but also Jack tales and nonfiction items. Hurston later included black folklore in several novels and collections. In all of these she successfully positions herself as mediator between the black folk community and her largely white reading audience.

A number of folktale characters found throughout the South and Southern Highlands are known by the name John. Some of these, such as yarns about Foolish John, are numskull narratives involving the protagonist making ridiculous actions. An example is a tale found in French American tradition that is derived from the Grimm Brothers' clever Hans. In this narrative, John is left alone by his mother, who tells him to put parsley in the soup. It so happens that the French word for parsley sounds a great deal like the name Percy. In John's house there is a dog named Percy, which, to the animal's great displeasure, he proceeds to put in the boiling hot soup.

High John de Conquer was the opposite of Foolish John, in that far from being a buffoon, he was a hero who gave black slaves hope to endure, and has not walked among blacks as a real man since slavery ended. Even so, he waits just out of sight and is able to return wherever blacks need him to help overcome things they could not accomplish otherwise. No matter how bad things look now for blacks, things will soon be much worse for their oppressors, because of John's interference. High John also brought laughter, and most of the tales about him are humorous. In one example, the master began to suspect John of stealing his pigs, which had started disappearing from the plantation. So he decided to catch him at the theft and came to High John's house, where John was cooking a pig. After an extended argument, the master insisted John give him whatever was cooking in the pot. John maintained it was a possum, but after his hand was forced, he said, "I put this thing in here a possum, but if it comes out a pig, it ain't no fault of mine."

Another set of African American tales set in antebellum times are the John and Old Master narratives. They reflect the physical circumstances of slave life and the complex attitude of both love and hate many bondsmen held toward their owners. There are four main categories of these narratives: the deceptive, roguish John; tales in which Old Master gets the best of John; yarns where John bests Old Master; and those texts in which John acts foolish. Without question the best known of the John and Old Master tales is one that puns with a pejorative term for Blacks. Known as "Coon in the Box," this yarn is traditional in Africa and the Caribbean. In this narrative John has convinced his boss he knows everything, so his owner bets with other parties that he can guess what is in a box (a coon). John finally decides to admit he is stumped and says, "You got the old coon at last." John's answer, of course, is correct, and Master wins his bet without realizing that he has been duped. In another popular text John scares off another tough slave by kissing his master's wife and kicking his master in the rear. Sometimes this yarn is applied to Little John, another folktale trickster.

There are a wide variety of stories and songs dealing with actual historical figures, few of these are more popular than tales about Davy Crockett (1786–1936). This frontier personality's legendry received a boost in the mid-1950s when Walt Disney made two movies about him and several recordings of a ballad concerning him were popular. One hundred twenty years earlier Crockett was the subject of numerous folk anecdotes, many of which were published anonymously in *The Life and Adventures of Colonel David Crockett of West Tennessee* (1833). The author was probably Matthew St. Clair Clarke, clerk of the House of Representatives from 1832 to 1833, a staunch Whig and close friend of Crockett. Despite its title, this book is hardly a biography; instead it is a collection of tales reportedly told by the "colonel" and anecdotes circulating about him. The 1833 book was followed by an autobiography written by Crockett and Thomas Chilton, a Kentucky Whig congressman, and a series of almanacs issued annually between 1835 and 1856. All of these publications contributed to the backwoodsman's legendary status.

In the *Life and Adventures of Colonel David Crockett of West Tennessee,* Clarke recounted three kinds of yarns with Crockett as the protagonist: accounts of experiences hunting bear, elk, and panthers; "Dutch" (i.e., German) dialect stories; and humorous anecdotes and tall tales. The hunting stories were not folktales, al-

though some seemed fantastic, and occasionally bore a hint of the supernatural, as in one narrative where he hunted bear instead of turkey because he had dreamed the night before of having a battle with a bear. He reasoned, "in a bear country I never know'd such a dream to fail." The dialect stories focused on mistakes resulting from the Dutchman's faulty understanding of English. All of them are very politically incorrect today. The best known comic anecdote associated with Crockett recounted in *The Life and Adventures of Colonel David Crockett of West Tennessee* and by countless folk raconteurs concerns his trickery with a coonskin. In the backwoods, animal skins often served in lieu of money. According to the narrative, on one occasion while campaigning for election, Crockett wished to treat his company to some strong drink. In this particular place a coonskin would buy a quart of whiskey. Having only one coonskin, he threw it on the counter and loudly called for its value in whiskey. After measuring out the purchase, the merchant threw the coonskin in the loft. Crockett took out his ramrod, and when the merchant wasn't looking, retrieved the coonskin and put it back in his pocket, and kept repeating the retrieval until the crowd's thirst was quenched.

Other historical figures contemporary with Crockett, such as Daniel Boone (1734–1820), didn't enjoy as much folk popularity as the "colonel." Boone, however, served popular literature as a dramatic symbol of frontier ingenuity in opening up areas of the country not previously settled by whites. Stories that circulated about him emphasized his abilities as a hunter, but even here he was no match for Crockett. Although famous,

Boone did not run for any political office and had no "biographers" pushing his legend in a huge series of publications. His esteem, however, catapulted him into the novels of James Fenimore Cooper, where he appeared in fictional guise as an intrepid Indian fighter and wilderness scout alternately called Natty Bumpo, Deerslayer, Hawkeye, and Leatherstocking. With modification this generic figure has remained popular to the present day in movies and television programs.

Crockett and Boone may be said to be positive historical personalities, but there are a number of legends about unpleasant real people. Coastal areas of the South have numerous tales about pirates. These raiders were said to have the ability to raise storms, but, of course, they mainly occupied their time overtaking and looting ships. On the Atlantic coast, the most notorious such personality was Edward Teach (1680–1718), or Thatch, or Tatch. An imposing figure reputed to be almost seven feet tall with a jet black beard that extended to his waist, the latter feature resulted in his being called Blackbeard. A ladies' man, he is credited with having had thirteen wives, but he is mainly remembered as a pirate. He staked out the Atlantic as his territory, and he roamed it at will, sinking or manning the ships he captured with a select group of his men. When he was killed, his head was cut off and placed on the bowsprit of the *Ranger,* one of the ships used in capturing him. It remained on the boat until the vessel returned to Virginia, from whence it had originally come. Teach's mutilated body was tossed overboard, where tradition says it swam three times around the two ships, *Ranger* and *Adventure,* used in bringing Blackbeard to his end.

Teach has been dead for almost three centuries now, but in legends, he lives on. Most of these narratives concern the Teach lights, which are sometimes reflected in the waters of Pamlico Sound; Teach's Hole, where the headless apparition of the pirate searches for its lost head; his phantom ship that brings doom to all who see it; and treasure chests hidden in numerous places. It is said that anyone who follows the Teach lights until they come to rest will find Blackbeard's buried treasure, but they will also find disaster, because they will also meet the devil, who, as Teach's sworn partner, guards the cache. This tradition hasn't stopped numerous people from searching for the treasure and, according to one legend, it was actually discovered in Edenton, North Carolina. The problem was that no one was to say anything until the riches were brought out of the ground. Unfortunately, those digging for it couldn't abide by the rule, and every time they struck the iron ring on the top of the chest, they would talk and immediately the treasure would disappear.

While supposed buried pirate loot has given rise to many tales, not all buried treasure legends are associated with sea raiders. Members of a North Carolina family had a persistent dream about a treasure buried under a tree. The dreams included a warning not to mention the dreams or the treasure to anyone or they would never find the valuable buried cache. When the first two sons attempted to dig it up, they were scared away by a dozen headless men. The story ended happily, which rarely happens with yarns of this type. Telling his fiancée he had a secret that he could only reveal to her after their marriage, the third son discussed the dream immediately after the wedding. The young couple went to the tree, saw the headless men, but weren't scared off. They found the treasure, became very wealthy, and lived happily ever after.

North Carolina's Outer Banks has been a place of numerous mysteries, one occurring less than one hundred years after Columbus discovered the New World. In 1587 a group of settlers came from England to settle on Roanoke Island. In that year Virginia Dare became the first white child born in North America. Governor John White soon returned to England for supplies, but, unfortunately, he was unable to come back to America for three years. When he did return in 1590, the entire colony was gone, vanished without a trace. The letters *CRO* were carved into a nearby oak tree, and it is generally believed this was the beginning of an attempt to name the people responsible for doing away with the colonists. Most people assumed that a band of hostile, local Indians led by one Wanchese had massacred the settlers. Their actual fate, however, has remained unsolved.

There are no folk legends about the "Lost Colony" per se, although, owing to an outdoor pageant of the same name, the colony remains well known more than four hundred years after it passed into oblivion. A pseudo-Indian narrative circulated in the late twentieth century about Virginia Dare. According to this tale, she was idolized by local Indians, who called her Winona-Ska. A tribesman named Chico cast a spell on her, changing her into a white deer. Her Indian paramour, Okisko, shot a silver-headed arrow into her heart, transforming her to human form again, but this rescue was short-lived, because a rival Indian loosed

his own magic arrow, which killed her. Thereafter, she haunted the island as a white deer.

Throughout the South and Southern Highlands ghost narratives abound, far and away the most popular being the Vanishing Hitchhiker, a legend derived from European tales about the Wandering Jew and the Flying Dutchman. There are many variations on the story, but, in general, it consists of a young man driving down a lonely road, usually while it is raining, when he sees a young girl dressed in white by the roadside. He stops to give her a ride, she gets in the backseat of his car, and she tells him where she wants to go. When the car arrives at its destination, the young man opens the door to help the girl out, but in the meantime, she has disappeared. He then knocks on the door of the house that the young girl asked him to drive to and explains his situation to the woman who answers the door. The woman announces that the apparition was her daughter, who was killed years before in a car wreck on that particular date. Each year on the anniversary of her death, the same incident occurs.

Throughout coastal portions of the South, tales of shipwrecks are commonplace. One interesting such narrative concerns a murder-robbery that occurred in the Graveyard of the Atlantic in the eighteenth century. Wealthy Palatines on their way to the New World were murdered and robbed of the wealth they were carrying by the captain and crew of the ship they were traveling on. The ship was set on fire after the passengers had been divested of their treasures. The murderer-robbers were drowned when the boat in which they were attempting to get to shore capsized. It is said that since then, the phantom of the burning ship appears periodically. There are also numerous accounts of sightings of other spectral ships that have wrecked. The *Carroll M. Deering*, which broke up in 1921, was sighted after it went down, and the screams of people who were on board the ship can still be heard, especially during storms.

Horse and dog racing are popular in some parts of the South and Southern Highlands. These activities often generate talk about whose horse or dog is the fastest, but few of these comments result in widely told tales. There is, however, one horse race that gave rise to a ballad reported from Kentucky and Arkansas, but it is probably more widely known because it has appeared on several commercial records. On July 4, 1878, in the last four-mile heat match in American horse-racing history, the Kentucky thorough-bred Ten Broeck defeated the mare Miss Mollie McCarthy. The ballad "Ten Broeck and Mollie," or "Mollie and Tin Brooks" (it is known by both titles), provides an account of the race, but in it, Ten Broeck is talking to his rider, which makes the account unrealistic. According to the song Mollie dies at the end of the race.

Considering the great cultural variety in the South and Southern Highlands, it is not surprising that the two regions have produced a varied literature, ranging from the work of Erskine Caldwell (1903–1987) to the now largely forgotten publications of Alice French, who used the pseudonym Octave Thanet, to the books of Jesse Stuart, among others.

Caldwell's short stories and novels have been described by one critic as being "about poverty," primarily because of his two biggest successes—*Tobacco Road* (1932) and *God's Little Acre* (1933). These novels about economic conditions among Georgia sharecroppers, tenant farmers, and mill workers were spiced up with incidents of lust, rape, murder, and degrading poverty. Some people considered them so violent and horrific that many places censored the books. Caldwell's 1944 novel *Tragic Ground* brought an obscenity charge against him.

Along with his violent, horrific books, Caldwell had another side. In the 1930s he produced several works of social criticism, including *Some American People* (1935), *Tenant Farmer* (1935), and *You Have Seen Their Faces* (1937). For many Caldwell's best book is *Georgia Boy* (1944), a classic of American boyhood that has been favorably compared to Mark Twain's *The Adventures of Huckleberry Finn*. This novel, with its account of twelve-year-old William Stroup, demonstrates the author's unique gift for comedy rising out of the terrible. Young Stroup looks at the antics of his shrewd but shiftless father, Morris, his mother, Martha, and their trouble-prone yard boy, Handsome Brown.

Alice French (1850–1934) was one of the early regionalists, her writings focused on the canebrake country of Arkansas. French developed a simple, clear, realistic style that made her popular from 1887, when she published her first regional novel, *Knitters in the Sun*, until 1911, when *Stories That End Well* was issued. Today her work is generally forgotten, except by short-story anthologists.

That is not the case with Samuel Langhorne Clemens (1835–1910), who used the pseudonym Mark Twain. A prolific author, Twain is of interest here because of his *The Adventures of Huckleberry Finn* (1884), the finest regional novel ever written in the United States and one containing a great deal of folklore. Unfortunately, Twain was not a resident of the regions under consideration here, and his novel only tangentially deals with them, so it is outside the realm of the present discussion.

One of the most prolific regional writers was Kentucky's Jesse Stuart (1907–1984), the author of more than sixty books, four hundred and fifty short stories, and two thousand poems. He started out as an educator, but after the success of his book of poems, *Man with a Bull-Tongue Plow* (1934), he turned his attention primarily to writing. In 1936 a collection of short stories, *Head O'W-Hollow,* was published, followed by *Beyond Dark Hills* (1938), an autobiography, and *Trees of Heaven* (1940), a novel. These four books were all in different genres, providing examples of his versatility. Stuart's unique talents include describing the special relationship between farm people and animals. One story, "Dawn of Remembered Spring," consists of snake tales and legends, and his novel *Mongrel Mettle* (1944) is the autobiography of a dog. Stuart's other great gift is for depicting mountain people who may seem foolish to "civilized society," but whose human dignity and rural values enable them to eventually triumph over difficult circumstances.

Stuart's *The Thread That Runs So True,* about his experiences as a one-room schoolteacher, was selected by the National Education Association as the best book of 1949. *Taps for Private Tussie* (1943), a novel about Army bungling and the havoc it unleashes on a down-on-their-luck family, which has been called an American classic, and *Foretaste of Glory*

(1946), a tale about what happens when a local preacher prophesies the end of the world, are the most critically acclaimed of Stuart's several books. He increases the local color by a liberal use of folklore. His extensive resort to folk traditions is thoroughly explored in Mary Washington Clarke's *Jesse Stuart's Kentucky* (1968).

Whereas Jesse Stuart's focus was on Kentucky, the books of Ellen Glasgow (1874–1945) depicted life in Virginia. Her books about the state can be divided into three main groups. Her early novels, such as *The Voice of the People* (1900) and *The Deliverance* (1904), are historical accounts of the Commonwealth, that is, Virginia. A second group, including *The Romantic Comedians* (1926) and *They Stooped to Folly* (1929), deal with life and manners in Richmond. A third, and final, group, including *Barren Ground* (1925) and *Vein of Iron* (1935), deal with the country, meaning the area west of the Tidewater. Four main themes are developed in her books: the old South and the new; woman's position in both; human failings; and the inner hardness she called the "vein of iron." Glasgow said her theme was the same in all her books, the struggle between nature and human nature, between biology and civilization. For her, defeat is not tragic, surrender is—an assessment she applied to both the South and individuals.

Glasgow, who patterned her style after that of the great English and French novelists, in particular Balzac, Flaubert, and De Maupassant, had a very stylized manner of writing that emphasized form and language. She was enough of a realist that she saw the ironic and tragic in life and accurately depicted manners and foibles. She shied away, however, from anything approaching the brutal or fierce. Her books are primarily remembered for her accounts of women, characters who embody her ideals.

Whereas Glasgow wrote about her native area, Marjorie Kinnan Rawlings (1896–1953) represents the outsider who publishes books about their adopted native area. Born in Washington, D.C., she grew up in Wisconsin and eventually came to live in upstate New York. She gained acclaim as a regional writer only after she moved to the Florida backwoods. Almost immediately she identified with the region and started writing with knowledge and sympathy about its landscape and people. Rawlings was that rare writer able to straddle two worlds. To the Florida "crackers" she wrote about, she was an outsider they could accept, while to her northern readers, she was still one of their own and thus was considered objective. In *The Yearling* (1938), which won a Pulitzer Prize, *When the Whippoorwill* (1941), *Cross Creek* (1942), and *Cross Creek Cookery* (1942), Rawlings delineated in a sympathetic manner life in the Florida backwoods. Her most important role, however, was in leading the way for a reassessment of Southern regional writing that helped rescue many regionalists from literary oblivion.

The regional writer who writes about not one but many areas in the South and Southern Highlands and doesn't live in any of the sections she writes about is rare. This is the distinction claimed by Lois Lenski (1893–1974), author of a series of regional books for what she called "middle-aged" children. The Ohio native, who spent most of her adult life in Connecticut, had previously written several books for children before initiating her regional series with *Bayou Suzette* (1944),

a story of the French-speaking people of Louisiana. This book won the Ohioana medal and was followed by *Strawberry Girl* (1946), about a Florida "cracker," that is, white family, which won the Newbery Medal. *Blue Ridge Billy* (1946), about a North Carolina mountain family, and *Judy's Journey* (1947), about sharecroppers, followed. The latter volume won the award of the Children's Book Committee of the Child Study Association, because it faced with honesty and courage real problems encountered by young people in today's world.

Although the general perception is that children's books don't require much research, this was certainly not the case with Lenski's publications. She spent time in the localities described in her books, listening to stories told by people living there, making sketches of them, their houses, and surroundings, details later incorporated in the book, either as text or illustrations. Thus, in effect, she did collecting much like any folklorist.

W. K. McNeil

THE SOUTH AND SOUTHERN HIGHLANDS: BIBLIOGRAPHY AND OTHER RESOURCES

Bibliography

History and Study

284. Bordelon, Pamela, ed. *Go Gator and Muddy the Water: Writings by Zora Neale Hurston from the Federal Writers' Project.* New York: Norton, 1999. xvi, 199p. Illus.

Index. Notes. 98-28585. 0-393-04895-8; 0-393-31813-3pa.

During 1938–1939, Hurston worked in Florida as a writer with the Federal Writers' Project. Much of the writing she did during this time was published anonymously; some was never published at all but resided only in state archives. Bordelon has collected all these writings and publishes them here, along with a lengthy biographical essay.

Some of the writings are essays on the art of collecting folklore, on race relations, on African American artists. Some are her versions of folktales from Florida. And some are stories of the work world of people she interviewed, mainly African American workers in the turpentine and citrus industries.

These early tales show the roots of much of Hurston's fictional works.

285. Brown, Virginia Pounds, and Laurella Owens. *Toting the Lead Row: Ruby Pickens Tartt, Alabama Folklorist.* University: Univ. of Alabama Press, 1981. xi, 180p. Index. Bibliog. Notes. Biographical sketches of singers and storytellers of Sumter County, Alabama. 81-4902. 0-8173-074-0.

This is a biography of Ruby Pickens Tartt, a woman who collected folklore all her life from African Americans in Alabama. She worked for the Works Progress Administration as well as with John Lomax on his song collecting. This book, however, isn't folklore. It concerns her life, with some reminiscences, and contains life stories of blacks in the area, including some former slaves.

286. Chappell, Louis W. *John Henry: A Folk-Lore Study.* 1933; repr., Port Washington, NY: Kennikat Press, 1968. 144p. Index. Bibliog. Appendix. 68-25202.

Similar to Guy B. Johnson's study of the John Henry story, this is a discussion of the development of the story and a look at the evidence of whether the story and the character are based on real events. The appendix contains a large collection of variant John Henry songs and ballads. Chappell includes variants of some 200 songs, including hammer songs and songs about John Hardy, the man who some think provided the true-life model for John Henry.

287. Clarke, Kenneth W. *Uncle Bud Long: The Birth of a Kentucky Folk Legend.* Lexington: Univ. Press of Kentucky, 1973. 77p. Illus. by Harold Rigsby. List of informants. 73-77252. 0-8131-1290-7.

Uncle Bud Long and his family lived at Clark's Landing in western Kentucky, in the early part of this century. They were well known by their neighbors, but not for good reasons. Instead, they were held up as an example of how not to live, as they were considered stingy, crude, and primitive. Legends and fragments of legends about the family still existed in the area when Kenneth Clark lived there in the 1970s and began listening and collecting.

In this book he doesn't retell the tales as much as he tells the story of the origin of the tales and of their continuing evolution. He contends that legends and folklore are the forerunner to written literature. Here, he says, is a chance to examine these underpinnings of literature before the written word has supplanted them. He compares this with the development of the Davy Crockett and Daniel Boone legends, which are both now so obscured with modern day literary adaptations that their origins are hard to discern.

288. Henry, Jacques M., and Sara Le-Menestrel, eds. *Working the Field: Accounts*

from French Louisiana. Westport, CT: Praeger, 2003. vi, 188p. Illus. Index. 2002-29761. 0-89789-836-2.

A collection of essays by various folklorists and anthropologists, *Working the Field* makes the case for a continuation of field anthropology. The editors' contention is that field research enhances theoretical research.

289. Johnson, Guy B. *John Henry: Tracking Down a Negro Legend.* 1929; repr., New York: AMS Press, 1969. viii, 155p. Bibliog. 75-80720.

This is a reprint of the 1929 edition. Johnson not only collects here various songs and ballads of John Henry but also discusses the history and development of the legend. He sorts through the evidence of whether the character of John Henry is based on a real person, John Hardy, and traces the development of the story.

290. Lofaro, Michael A., ed. *Davy Crockett: The Man, the Legend, the Legacy, 1786–1986.* Knoxville: Univ. of Tennessee Press, 1985. xxiii, 203p. Illus. Index. 84-25737. 0-87049-459-7; 0-87049-507-0pa.

The various essayists in this volume discuss the ways in which Davy Crockett has left the pages of history to become a character not only in folklore but in what Richard Dorson calls "fakelore." Crockett died in 1836; in 1837 *Crockett's Free-and-Easy Songbook* was published. Even before that time, Crockett himself contributed to the legend with the publication of an autobiography and of the *Crockett Almanacs,* tales written by professional writers using him as a character but not based in fact. Since that time, the Crockett character has appeared in books, songs, theatre, movies, and television.

291. McNeil, W. K., ed. *The Charm Is Broken.* Little Rock, AR: August House,

1984. 201p. Illus. Chapter Notes. 83-71902. 0-935304-66-5; 0-935304-67-3pa.

McNeil has assembled a collection of articles from various journals treating folklore of Arkansas and Missouri. Articles are written by a variety of eminent folklorists, both from the nineteenth century and more contemporary times.

Folk music, social customs, traditional work methods, games and leisure activities, place names, and folk art are among the topics considered in the essays. In addition, he includes an essay on the contemporary topic of oral traditions that develop on college campuses.

292. McNeil, W. K., and William M. Clements, eds. *An Arkansas Folklore Sourcebook.* Fayetteville: Univ. of Arkansas Press, 1992. 281p. Ill. Chapter notes. Bibliog. Discography. 92-5544. 1-55728-254-4.

In a series of essays, both the editors of this volume and other contributors examine the place that traditional folklore and folkways have in the life of contemporary Arkansans. Music, tales, vernacular architecture, traditional medicine, foodways, and festivals and celebrations are among the themes examined.

293. Mould, Tom. *Choctaw Prophecy: A Legacy of the Future.* Tuscaloosa: Univ. of Alabama Press, 2003. xxxvi, 263p. Illus. Notes. Index. Bibliog. (Contemporary American Indian Studies). 2002-15812. 0-8173-1225-0; 0-8173-1226-9pa.

Prophecy and storytelling are a way of life for the Choctaw of Mississippi. Mould presents a thorough discussion of the history and role of prophecy. He discusses various types of prophecy, gives information on their origin, and presents the role of the storyteller. He also demonstrates the importance of this tradition in the modern world, discussing how prophecy is used as a teaching tool.

An appendix summarizes the prophecies that he collected and recorded.

294. Patterson, Daniel W. *A Tree Accurst: Bobby McMillon and Stories of Frankie Silver.* Chapel Hill: Univ. of North Carolina Press, 2000. xii, 224p. Illus. Notes. Index. Bibliog. 00-036385. 0-8078-2564-6; 0-8078-4873-5pa.

In 1833, Frankie Silver, a young married woman, was executed for the ax murder of her husband, Charlie. Her story has become a folk legend, with many versions. Stories and songs have been written about the incident, which many believe was a miscarriage of justice.

Bobby McMillon, a singer and collector of folk songs, has also collected many of the stories about the case. This book is a combination of a biography of McMillon and a retelling of the various tales about Frankie Silver that he has collected. It attempts to tell the true story of the crime, reconstructed from the various documents about it—court records, newspaper accounts, old stories—that exist. Whether it is indeed the true story, and whether the true story will ever be known, will be up to the reader.

295. Ray, Celeste. *Highland Heritage: Scottish Americans in the American South.* Chapel Hill: Univ. of North Carolina Press, 2001. xix, 256p. Index. Notes. Bibliog. Glossary. 00-060722. 0-8078-2597-2; 0-8078-4913-8pa.

During his days as a student at the University of Edinburgh, Ray was not interested in the Jacobite period of Scottish history. That is the era that people most often associate with Scotland and the era that has provided most symbols of Scotland—the tartan, the bagpipes, and the kilt. When he returned to North Carolina, however, struck by the strong ties that present-day North Carolinians felt with their Scottish ancestry, he began to explore those associations.

In this book he describes the various ways in which individuals and families maintain their Old World ties. He discusses dress, Highland games, the importance of family or clan, and the eagerness with which residents of the region participate in planned tours of Scotland.

296. West, Victor Royce. *Folklore in the Works of Mark Twain.* Lincoln: Univ. of Nebraska, 1930. 87p. Index. Bibliog.

This is a master's thesis. In it, West discusses how Mark Twain uses folklore. Chapter headings include Ghostlore; Demonology; Witchcraft; Luck; Signs, Portents, and Omens; Proverbs; and Superstitions.

297. Williams, Brett. *John Henry: A Bio-Bibliography.* Westport, CT: Greenwood Press, 1983. xiii, 175p. Illus. Index. (Popular Culture Bio-Bibliographies). 82-12056. 0-313-22250-9. ISSN: 0193-6891.

Williams explores both the "life" of John Henry and the legend built around the name. She brings together old interviews with people who purported to know the actual John Henry; examines all the art, literature, and music that represented him; and recaps scholarly discussions of the role this folk character has played in American life. She ends with a bibliography of printed materials about John Henry, and a discography of recordings.

Treasuries

298. Botkin, Benjamin A. *Lay My Burden Down: A Folk History of Slavery.* Chicago: Univ. of Chicago Press, 1968. xxi, 297p. Illus. Index.

Workers with the Federal Writers' Project in the 1930s and 1940s collected this material. Botkin served as chief editor of the Writers' Unit and planned and supervised the material for deposit at the Library of Congress. The present book is a selection of the material collected.

All are first-person narratives of former slaves. They range from brief folktales to reminiscences. The narratives are authentic sounding, with many recollections of punishments, slave auctions, and the like.

Taken together, the narratives give a picture of life during those times, with many references to specific tasks and work, such as weaving, soap making, and cooking, as well as glimpses of various customs of marriage, birth, and death.

299. ——. *A Treasury of Mississippi Folklore: Stories, Ballads, Traditions and Folkways of the Mid-American River Country.* New York: Crown Publishers, 1955. xx, 620p. Index of Authors, Titles, and First Lines of Songs. Index of Subjects, Names, and Places. 55-10172.

Similar to Botkin's *A Treasury of Southern Folklore,* this contains stories and songs of the Mississippi River. Some are rooted in fact, such as those of Abraham Lincoln, Davy Crockett, and Jim Bowie; some are pure fancy. Characters include pirates, fishermen, riverboat captains and workers, settlers, farmers, and trappers. This is the story of "Big Muddy" told in imaginative ways. The last section contains songs.

300. ——. *A Treasury of Southern Folklore: Stories, Ballads, Traditions, and Folkways of the People of the South.* New York: Crown Publishers, 1949. xxiv, 776p. Index of Authors, Titles, and First Lines of Songs. Index of Subjects, Names, and Places.

Botkin likens his book to a dinner ordered à la carte—you may sample what you will, rather than eating a set meal. As with that meal, the reader of this book may read at will, sampling only what is of interest.

Like his *Treasury of New England Folklore,* this one is a broad collection of tales, folk beliefs, historical figures, such as Daniel Boone and Henry C. Calhoun (as well as more modern figures such as Pretty Boy Floyd), humor, and plenty of songs. Casey Jones is here, as well as Barbara Frietchie and Harriet Tubman, pirates Blackbeard and Jean Laffite, and a host of Revolutionary War and Civil War figures. The section on folk music includes many songs with music transcribed.

Like *The Treasury of New England Folklore* this is an invaluable collection.

301. Johnson, F. Roy. *Tales from Old Carolina: Traditional and Historical Sketches of the Area between and about the Chowan River and Great Dismal Swamp.* Murfreesboro, NC: Johnson Publishing, 1965. vii, 248p. Illus. 65-8878.

Both tales and folk belief mingle in this book. Tales concern both historical figures such as George Washington and more ordinary folk, whereas folk belief involves various superstitions, folk cures, and witchcraft.

Some of the material gives a good picture of everyday life on the Carolina frontier, such as housing, recreation, and local industries.

302. Killion, Ronald G., and Charles T. Waller, eds. *A Treasury of Georgia Folklore.* Atlanta: Cherokee Publishing, 1972. xv, 267p. Illus. by Maureen O'Leary. Index. 72-88901.

The material in this book has been pieced together by the editors from material collected in the 1930s by field-workers of the Federal Writers' Project. The material so collected was never put into print at the time; instead, uncollated and unorganized notes were deposited in various libraries in the state. Only some of the 3,000 manuscript pages survived; of those that did, only some of the material is in this book.

The editors organized this raw material into a topic arrangement. Chapters are on

Folktales
Conjure
Conjure Tales
Folk Medicine
Superstitions and Beliefs
Folk Wisdom
Beliefs and Customs: Man and His
   Environment
Beliefs and Customs: Love, Courtship,
   Marriage, and Death
Children's Lore
Folk Songs

In their preface, the editors state that personal judgment swayed many of their decisions as to what to include and exclude: When several versions of the same tale existed in the notes, they included their own favorite. With the wealth of material available to them, these decisions were necessary. The result is a varied concoction of stories, songs, tales, and poetry that give a flavor of the folklore of Georgia.

303. Lacey, T. Jensen. *Amazing North Carolina: Fascinating Facts, Entertaining Tales, Bizarre Happenings, and Historical Oddities from the Tarheel State.* Nashville: Rutledge Hill Press, 2003. ix, 246p. Illus. Index. Bibliog. 2002-153074. 1-55853-965-4pa.

History and legend are blended in this book. On the serious side, Lacey gives information about the early struggles of the civil rights movement, including the sit-ins at the Greensboro Woolworth lunch counter, and about the Civil War. He provides, too, basic information about the state, such as a list of the state symbols (flower, bird, fish, etc.; there is even an official North Carolina fruit, the scuppernong grape), a list of movies made or set in North Carolina, and a chapter of sports trivia.

To this, he adds tales of ghosts—there's even one in the governor's mansion; burial and grave customs; traditional medicine and cures; and the history of various unusual town names.

This is a book to dip into, rather than read through.

The bibliography is one of Web sites concerning North Carolina.

304. Parsons, Elsie Clews. *Folk-Lore of the Sea Islands, South Carolina.* American Folk-Lore Society, 1923; repr., Chicago: Afro-Am Press, 1969. xxx, 217p. Bibliog. List of informants or writers of the tales. 79-99401. 8411-0071-3.

The first two-thirds of this book consists of tales told by residents of the Sea Islands just off the coast of South Carolina. They were collected by the author in the early part of the century and first published in 1923 by the American Folk-lore Society. Many of the tales are of Br'er Rabbit and Br'er Fox, but there are others as well.

In addition to the tales, Parsons includes games and rhymes, riddles, and a section on folkways, such as marriage customs, dress, dreams, death, and medicine.

Notes with the tales indicate origins and variants.

305. White, Newman Ivey, general ed. *Frank C. Brown Collection of North Carolina Folklore. In Seven Volumes.* Durham, NC: Duke Univ. Press, 1952–1964. vol. 1, xiv, 712p.; vol. 2, xxiii, 747p.; vol. 3, xxx, 709p.; vol. 4, xliv, 420; vol. 5, xli, 639p.; vol. 6, lxxi, 664p.; vol. 7, xxxiii, 677p. Indexes. vol. 1, 52-10967; vol. 2, 52-10967; vol. 3, 52-10967; vol. 4, 57-8818; vol. 5, 57-8818; vol. 6, 52-10967; vol. 7, 52-10967.

These seven volumes, each with a different editor, represent a mammoth job of collating and organizing the enormous collection of folklore of Dr. Frank C. Brown, a professor at Duke University and founder of the North Carolina Folklore Society. The seven volumes contain information on: vol. 1: Games, Speech, Customs, Proverbs Riddles, Tales; vol. 2: Folk Ballads; vol. 3: Folk Songs; vol. 4: The Music of the Ballads; vol. 5: The Music of the Folk Songs; vols. 6 and 7: Popular Beliefs and Superstitions.

The collection is exhaustive and scholarly.

Tales and Legends

306. Abrahams, Roger D., ed. *African American Folktales: Stories from Black Traditions in the New World.* New York: Pantheon, 1985; repr., 1999. xxii, 327p. Illus. Index. Bibliog. Notes on sources. (The Pantheon Fairy Tale and Folklore Library). 84-16601; 98-42200. 0-394-52755-0; 0-394-72885-8pa; 1999: 0-375-70539-2pa.

Abrahams has collected folktales from many black communities in the western hemisphere, but the bulk of them come from the American South. Many of the stories are tales told to encourage moral behavior.

In his lengthy introduction, Abrahams discusses the history of black folklore and demonstrates how, despite its association with the slavery days, it can still be appreciated and valued today.

307. Allsopp, Frederick William. *Folklore of Romantic Arkansas.* Kansas City, KS: The Grolier Society, 1931. 2 vols. Illus. Index. vol. 1: xx, 333p; vol. 2: xvi, 371p.

Allsopp arranges the material in this ample two-volume work by time period and by theme. Some of his chapters concentrate on tales of a certain time: Prehistoric Days, Missionary Days, and Early Days in Arkansas. Others are collections of tales with a common theme: Romantic Legends, Legends of Places, Lost Mines, and Hidden Treasures. Within each chapter are short tales—only a page or two each—on the given theme.

In his preface, Allsopp writes of the tales of Native Americans, who "evidence a spirit of adventure and romance." He includes many of these tales as well as a chapter of black folklore.

Allsopp offers no provenance for his tales; they stand alone. His two volumes present a rich collection of tales from a state once considered remote and "backwoods."

308. Ancelet, Barry Jean. *Cajun and Creole Folktales: The French Oral Tradition of South Louisiana.* Jackson: Univ. Press of Mississippi, 1994. lxxii, 2224p. Originally published in hardcover in 1994 by Garland, as Volume 1 of the World Folktale Library. Index of Tale Types. Index of Motifs. Index of Narrators. Bibliog. 93-31848 (Garland); 93-48885 (Univ. of Mississippi.). 0-8153-1498-1 (Garland); 0-87805-709-9pa. (Univ. of Mississippi).

Ancelet presents these folktales in both French and English, on facing pages. He divides the stories into the following categories:

Animal Tales
Magic Tales
Jokes
Lies and Tall Tales
Pascal Stories
Legendary Tales
Historical Tales

(Pascal tales are a specialized form of spontaneous tall tale, centering around the character of Pascal and his wondrous exploits—he is said to have ridden his bicycle on the ocean from Louisiana to Paris, starting out at the same time Lindbergh took off on his historic flight, and reaching Paris before the aviator!)

Ancelet also provides a history of the folktale in this region and a discussion of the ways in which the French language has influenced its development.

Earlier tellers of French folktales include Alcée Fortier in the nineteenth century, whose publications are difficult to obtain, and Corinne Saucier, author of *Folk Tales from French Louisiana* (Baton Rouge: Claitor's Publishing Division, 1962).

309. Aswell, James R., and others. *God Bless the Devil! Liars' Bench Tales.* Chapel Hill: Univ. of North Carolina Press, 1940. xi, 254p. Illus.

The Liars' Bench of the title refers to the place in any town where people congregate to tell stories, some true, some embellished, some outright whoppers. The stories told here were collected and transcribed by writers of the Tennessee Writers' Project of the Works Projects Administration. In the preface, William R. McDaniel, state supervisor of the writers'

group, divides the tales into three groups: those with a definite local origin; those more universal in nature, echoing those told in Europe; and whoppers or tall tales.

310. Barden, Thomas E., ed. *Virginia Folk Legends.* Charlottesville: Univ. Press of Virginia, 1991. xiv, 347p. Notes to the Legends. Appendices. 91-12422. 0-8139-1331-4. 0-8139-1335-7pa.

Barden has mined these legends from the thirty file boxes of material collected by WPA workers in the 1930s. They represent all geographic areas of Virginia. All are tales or legends that had an oral circulation, whether only within a family or to a wider public. Categories that Barden uses are

Animals
Beginnings (creation or origin stories)
Civil War and Emancipation
Conjure and Witchcraft
Ghosts
Haunted Houses
Indians
Legendary People
Murder and Violence
Place Names
Simon Kenton
Spirit Dogs
Supernatural Events
Treasure
Unusual Events

Appendices note the names of both the tellers of the tales and of the collectors, as well as geographic locations of the tales. Barden's scholarly introduction discusses the process of collection and the categorization of the tales.

311. Bell, Charles Bailey. *The Bell Witch, a Mysterious Spirit.* Nashville, TN: Lark Bindery, 1934. 228p. 72p.

Bell tells the stories of his forebears, who settled in Tennessee in the early 1800s. Several members of the family, including his own father, were supposedly visited by a witch or spirit, who played tricks, disrupted gatherings, but also foretold the future.

312. Bennett, John. *Doctor to the Dead: Grotesque Legends and Folk Tales of Old Charleston*. 1946; repr., Columbia: Univ. of South Carolina Press, 1995. xxix, 260p. 94-35199. 1-57003-040-5.

Bennett collected these tales in the early part of the twentieth century, from elderly African American residents of Charleston. They are tales based on the Gullah traditions of the area. Many of the stories center on death, fear of death, and the possibility of visits from the dead.

This reprint includes photographs of seven of the storytellers. These photographs are reproductions of the originals included by Bennett himself in a copy of the book he presented to good friends at the time of publication.

313. Blair, Walter, and Franklin J. Meine, eds. *Half Horse Half Alligator: The Growth of the Mike Fink Legend*. Chicago: Univ. of Chicago Press, 1956. vii, 289p. Illus. Bibliog. 56-10082.

In this volume, Blair and Meine bring together all the stories they could find in original sources about Mike Fink, the legendary Mississippi River keelboatman. They found their stories in books, magazines, almanacs, and newspapers. For all stories, the editors give the source, author, and date.

An introduction gives the bare facts of Fink's life as known and outlines the growth of the legend.

314. ——. *Mike Fink, King of Mississippi Keelboatmen*. 1933; repr., Westport, CT: Greenwood Press, 1971. xii, 283p. Illus. Bibliog. 74-138143.

Mike Fink is a hero in the tradition of Daniel Boone or Davy Crockett, a real person who over time has become larger than life, given heroic characteristics, written about, and glorified. He represents the Mississippi river men who helped the Western movement succeed by transporting both goods and people. Mike Fink, according to legend, was an Indian scout, an accomplished hunter and marksman, a man who could capture outlaws and outwit gamblers. In this book. Blair and Meine retell some of the Mike Fink stories.

315. Bradley, Bob. *This Here's Country: Legends and Folklore from East Tennessee's Hill Country*. Bristol, TN: Bob Bradley, 1996. 110p. Illus.

Many of the tales told here are based in Civil War history—tales of hidden caches of weapons or coins. Other tales are of natural disasters, such as floods or lost mines. Many were told to the author by old-timers, who had been told the story in their turn by an even older resident.

316. Browne, Ray B., coll. and ed. *"A Night with the Hants" and Other Alabama Folk Experiences*. Bowling Green, OH: Bowling Green Popular Press, 1976. xxi, 263p. Bibliog. Index of informants. List of Tales with Distinguishable Motifs. Index of Motifs. 76-43449. 1-87972-075-1.

In his introduction, Browne categorizes the folklore of Alabama into three divisions: tales of death, hauntings, and the supernatural; tales told for amusement; and anecdotes purported to be true. Browne recounts many of all types, in many cases indicating the source of the tale. He marks tales that have parallel versions and gives the parallels in a separate section.

This is a book for both the scholar and the casual, interested reader of folklore. The scholar will appreciate the indexing of motifs and the presentation of parallel tales, and others will simply enjoy the stories.

317. Bruce, Annette J. *Tellable Cracker Tales*. Sarasota, FL: Pineapple Press, 1996. 103p. Illus. Index of Places and Names. 95-41668. 1-56164-094-8.

Annette Bruce is a storyteller. Here she adapts some of the stories she has told at schools, libraries, and festivals into written versions. Included are Cracker Jack tales (most famously collected by Richard Chase), historical tales, and tall tales and nonsense stories. Also included are folktales with themes that are common throughout the world, here told with Florida characters, dress, and customs; and so-called gator tales, which are fanciful tales not necessarily including an alligator.

The book is meant to be a guide for other storytellers, in addition to being a source to be read. Bruce adds hints to each tale as to how the tale should be told, the time it takes to tell, and its intended audience.

318. Burrison, John A., ed. *Storytellers: Folktales and Legends from the South*. Athens: Univ. of Georgia Press, 1989. vii, 261p. Illus. Indexes: Storytellers; Collectors; Tale Types; Tale Titles. Bibliog. 88-37143. 0-8203-1099-9.

Burrison's 92 students in folklore at Georgia State University collected these tales from 112 narrators. In all, 260 tales are included. They come from the Georgia Folklore Archives, a collection of stories gathered by successive classes of Burrison's students. This selection aims at

being representative of the folklore of the southern states. He includes tales of tricksters, ghost stories, tall tales, bawdy tales, and tales with a moral. He also includes stories from various groups: African American folktales, Cherokee Indian Myths, swamp yarns from the Okefenokee. Each section of the book begins with a brief headnote written by Burrison, putting the tales in context and giving some information about the collecting method.

319. Campbell, Marie. *Tales from the Cloud Walking Country*. Bloomington: Indiana Univ. Press, 1958; repr., Athens: Univ. of Georgia Press, 2000. 270p. Illus. Notes. Bibliog. 99-35649. 0-8203-2186-9pa.

During the 1920s and 1930s, Marie Campbell lived and worked in the mountain region of Kentucky. At that time, the region was still isolated from the rest of the country, although with such innovations as radio, improved transportation, and increased numbers of schools, the old ways were fast changing. Before they disappeared, Campbell heard the old stories, often local variations of such tales as Cinderella and Snow White, and participated in old-time activities, such as quilting bees or square dancing.

Tales from the Cloud Walking Country tells some of the stories as she heard and recorded them.

320. Carmer, Carl. *Stars Fell on Alabama*. New York: Farrar and Rinehart, 1934. xiv, 294p. Illus. by Cyrus LeRoy Baldridge.

Most of the chapters in this book are sketches of individuals rather than folktales. However, interspersed among these are a few tales and ghost stories, including some Br'er Rabbit tales.

As an appendix, Carmer adds a section titled "From the Author's Notebook." In it he includes a number of jottings: a list of fiddlers' tunes, a list of quilt patterns, lists of local superstitions, and brief Br'er Rabbit tales.

Unfortunately, the book also recounts stories from the darkest days of segregation.

321. Christensen, Abigail M. H. *Afro-American Folk Lore, Told Round Cabin Fires on the Sea Islands of South Carolina.* Boston: J. G. Cupples, 1892; repr., Freeport, NY: Books for Libraries Press, 1971. xiv, 116p. (The Black Heritage Library Collection). 71-157364. 0-8369-8802-7.

According to the author's introduction, these are South Carolina variants of the Br'er Rabbit legends told in Georgia and published as the Uncle Remus stories by Joel Chandler Harris.

322. Claudel, Calvin Andre. *Fools and Rascals: Folktales of Louisiana and Their Background.* Baton Rouge: Legacy Publishing, 1978. 78p. Illus. by Lauren Cunningham. Bibliog. 0-918784-18-2.

Claudel has collected numerous tales from Louisiana and grouped them by category: tales of numskulls, such as Foolish John or Jean Sot; of clever or stupid animals; of rascals and rogues; and of heroes and heroines involved with magic. Each category begins with a brief introduction giving a bit of background.

After each tale, Claudel gives the tale type, taken from Aarne and Thompson's *The Types of the Folk-tale;* the name of the person who collected the tale; and the parish from which the tale was collected.

He also includes a bibliography of sources.

323. Coleman, Christopher Kiernan. *Strange Tales of the Dark and Bloody Ground: Authentic Accounts of Restless Spirits, Haunted Honky-Tonks, and Eerie Events in Tennessee.* Nashville, TN: Rutledge Hill Press, 1998. 254p. 98-34829. 1-55853-661-2pa.

Ghost tales and hauntings from the Appalachian Mountains, the Cumberland Valley, Nashville, the Tennessee Valley, and Memphis are included here. Some are stories from the eighteenth and nineteenth centuries, but more modern ghosts are also represented, including several appearances by Elvis.

324. Curry, Jane Louise. *The Wonderful Sky Boat: And Other Native American Tales of the Southeast.* New York: Margaret McElderry Books, 2001. 142p. Illus. 00-040207. 0-689-83595-7.

Curry has collected tales from a variety of Native American tribes in the South: Yuchi, Caddo, Catawba, Chitimacha, Yamassee, Cherokee, Choctaw, Seminole, Creek, Natchez, Hitchiti, Eastern Cherokee, Koasati, Biloxi, Apalachee, Tunica, and Alabama. She also adds information about the storytellers, and brief source notes.

Stories are meant to be told as well as read.

325. Derr, Mark. *The Frontiersman: The Real Life and the Many Legends of Davy Crockett.* New York: Quill/William Morrow, 1993. 304p. Index. Bibliographic Notes. 92-41921. 0-688-13798-9pa.

A distant cousin of Davy Crockett, Derr states in his introduction that he has long had an admiration for his ancestor. Like other biographers of Crockett, including Richard Hauck and Richard Dorson, Derr attempts to sort out the facts of Crockett's life from the fiction. His biography interweaves the two, but makes clear when he is reporting facts and when he is interpreting the legend.

326. Dorson, Richard M. *The Tall Tales of Davy Crockett: The Second Nashville Series of Crockett Almanacs, 1839–1841.* Enlarged

facsimile. Knoxville: Univ. of Tennessee Press, 1987. xlviii, 116p. Illus. Index. 86-30831. 0-87049-525-9; 0-87049-526-7pa.

Dorson here reprints, with illustrations, three of the *Crockett Almanacs*, which mixed astronomical data such as times of sunrises and sunsets, with tall tales of Davy Crockett. They were immensely popular in the early 1800s. Dorson's introduction discusses the role the *Almanacs* played in the development of Crockett as folk hero.

327. Dorson, Richard M., ed. *Davy Crockett, American Comic Legend*. New York: Spiral Press for Rockland Editions, 1939. xxvi, 171p. Illus. Notes. Introduction by Howard Mumford Jones.

These are tales taken from the *Crockett Almanacs* published between 1835 and 1856. Most of the tales are of Crockett himself, a Crockett obviously larger than life who weighed 200 pounds when he was eight years old, beat a Mississippi River steamer in a canoe he hollowed out from a log, and even got the earth moving again one cold morning when it froze on its axis—he killed a bear and used the "hot ile," or hot oil, from it as grease. Dorson includes stories of members of Crockett's family as well, his aunt, his sister, his uncle, his grandmother, and of various women friends, all as brave and able as he. His grandmother is said to have had a cough so loud it caused the cider barrels to roll against each other in the cellar.

328. Edmunds, Pocahontas Wight. *Tales of the North Carolina Coast*. Raleigh: Edwards and Broughton, 1986. 179p. Illus. Index. 86-91218.

Edmunds arranges her tales geographically, grouping together tales from a particular part of North Carolina. Tales concern the lost colony of Roanoke, pirate treasure, lost ships, ghosts, and various battles and wars. Some of the stories are not strictly folktales, but instead are brief vignettes of famous North Carolinians.

329. Ewing, James. *A Treasury of Tennessee Tales*. 1985; Rev. ed. with additional stories by James Crutchfield. Nashville, TN: Rutledge Hill Press, 1997. 191p. Illus. Index. Bibliog. 96-29912. 1-55853-451-2pa.

The stories told here are for the most part true—although some have had some embellishment over the years. The characters are from real life, but have become part of our folk culture. Here are Casey Jones, Jesse James, the moonshiner, and the "revenooers," and Nathan Bedford Forrest. Pioneers, outlaws, and politicians mingle here.

330. Floyd, Blanche W. *Ghostly Tales and Legends along the Grand Strand of South Carolina*. Winston-Salem, NC: Bandit Books, 2002. 134p. Illus. 1-878177-12-5.

The varied heritage of the South is reflected in this book of ghost tales. Inhabitants came from a variety of places and left their ghosts behind. Irish ghosts are here, as well as ones from the traditions of Africa, Wales, Scotland, England, France, and Native America.

In addition to geographic variety, there is also the variety of time span; ghost stories arise from the Revolutionary War, the Civil War and Reconstruction, and of course from the long history of piracy along the Carolina coast.

331. Fortier, Alcée. *Louisiana Folk-Tales*. Boston: Published for the American Folklore Society by Houghton, Mifflin, 1895. xi, 122p. Notes. (Memoirs of the American Folklore Society, vol. II).

These tales, collected and transcribed by one of Louisiana's most respected early folklorists, are told both in Creole and in English. Fortier states in his introduction that the translations are not literal, but are faithful to the spirit and sense of the tales. He groups the tales into two major sections, Animal Tales and Märchen. This book could be usefully contrasted with the modern one by Barry Jean Ancelet, *Cajun and Creole Folktales: The French Oral Tradition of South Louisiana* (Univ. Press of Mississippi, 1994).

332. Fraiser, Jim. *Mississippi River Country Tales: A Celebration of 500 Years of Deep South History.* Gretna, LA: Pelican, 2000. 167p. Illus. Bibliog. 91-60522. 0-9627737-1-9pa.

Many of the characters and events here are historical: the conquistadores, Jefferson Davis, William Faulkner. Others are historical but have attained the status of folk events or heroes: steamboat disasters, riverboats, Jim Bowie, gamblers, buccaneers, and traveling salesmen. He also tells some stories from Native American traditions, and some stories of witches and hauntings.

With the help of all these characters and events, Frasier tells the story of the South along the Mississippi.

333. Fullman, Lynn Grisard. *Haints, Ghosts and Boogers: Chillbump Stories from Alabama after Dark.* Birmingham, AL: Seacoast, 1995. 119p. Illus. 1-8785-61-22-7pa.

The first tale in this book is one with many variations, told in many places. It is the tale of a young girl, dead in a violent death, who walks country roads and who often asks for a ride from a stranger. Sometimes, as in this version, the stranger later talks to the girl's parents, telling them their daughter was out alone, only to learn that the girl had been dead for some years.

The other tales in this book span time; many are from the 1800s, and others are from the 1960s, 1970s, and 1980s. All tell of apparitions.

334. Garrison, Webb B. *Southern Tales: A Treasury of Stories from Virginia, North Carolina, South Carolina, Georgia, Florida, Alabama, Kentucky, Tennessee, and Mississippi.* New York: Galahad Books, 1997. ix, 498p. Illus. 97-73425. 0-88365-963-8.

All the stories in this treasury are of real people, but many of the people have become folk legends. Such characters as Miss Sally Louisa Tompkins, who founded and ran a civilian hospital for wounded soldiers, are here. After issuing orders that all hospitals must be run by the army, Jefferson Davis found a way to let her continue her work: He made her a captain in the Confederate Army. Other better-known subjects are Daniel Boone, William McGuffy of McGuffy Reader fame, Booker T. Washington, Elizabeth Blackwell, Dorothea Dix, the Grimké sisters, Aaron Burr, Juan Ponce de León, Tecumseh, Davy Crockett, Sam Houston, and John James Audubon. More recent characters include Franklin Delano Roosevelt and Eudora Welty.

Not strictly folklore, this book still evokes the region and is full of people who have become part of our folk memory.

335. Haley, Gail E. *Mountain Jack Tales.* New York: Dutton Children's Books, 1992. x, 131p. Illus. by Gail E. Haley. Glossary. Bibliog. 92-6432. 0-525-44974-4. Paperback, Boone, NC: Parkway, 2002. 2001-37445. 1-887-90551-0pa.

Haley uses a character called Poppyseed to speak these retellings of the Jack tales. Many of the tales are Southern variations on ageless fairy tales, in which Jack outsmarts the witch or is assisted by a beautiful young girl. He often wins his way through charm and wit.

336. Hammons, Ann. *Wild Bill Sullivan, King of the Hollow.* Jackson: Univ. Press of Mississippi, 1980. viii, 144p. Bibliog. Index. Genealogical chart. 80-19625. 0-87805-127-9.

Hammons, a descendant of Wild Bill Sullivan, writes a book that is part biography, part family story, part a look at the way of life in nineteenth-century Sullivan's Hollow. Some of the stories about Wild Bill, a legendary fighter who feuded with both family and neighbors, have been enough exaggerated to become legend. Particularly interesting is the material on the way life was lived: farming methods, household management, and recreation.

337. Harris, Joel Chandler. *The Complete Tales of Uncle Remus.* Boston: Houghton Mifflin, 1955. xxxii, 875p. Compiled by Richard Chase. Illus. Glossary. 54-12233. 0-395-06799-5.

There have been numerous editions of the Uncle Remus stories since their first publication in 1880. In this text, the tales from all nine Uncle Remus collections are reprinted. The editor, Richard Chase, is a well-known folklorist and also the compiler of *The Jack Tales.*

The Uncle Remus tales are from *Uncle Remus: His Songs and His Sayings; Nights with Uncle Remus; Daddy Jake, the Runaway: And Short Stories Told after Dark; Uncle Remus and His Friends: Old Plantation Stories, Songs, and Ballads with Sketches of Negro Character; Told by Uncle Remus; Uncle Remus and Brer Rabbit; Uncle Remus and the Little Boy; Uncle Remus Returns;* and *Seven Tales of Uncle Remus.* The original introductions are included, and the tales are illustrated with the original illustrations by Arthur Burdette Frost, Frederick Stuart Church, J. M. Condé, Edward Windsor Kemble, and William Holbrook Beard.

In his foreword, Chase states that this edition preserves the original tale, with its dialect, as much as possible. Chandler used many variant spellings, from book to book and often within the same book. Chase has let the variant spellings remain in different books, but has tried to spell a word consistently within a single book.

Chase believes the tales remain popular because they "grew up in the soil of our nation" and "came from the soul of a people" (Foreword, p. xxx). Like so many other folklorists, he believes that knowing and remembering the old tales help us remain united as a nation.

338. Hauck, Richard Boyd. *Davy Crockett, a Handbook.* 1982; repr., Lincoln: Univ. of Nebraska Press, 1986. xxi, 169p. Illus. Index. Bibliog. 86-6933. 0-8032-7230-8pa.

Hauck attempts in this book to present the stories of both the real, historical David Crockett, and of the legend that grew out of that life. He presents the facts of Crockett's life as they are known, with extensive documentation; and then discusses the growth of the legend. There is much information here on the legend and on how and why it came about—who promoted it, who benefited from it, and why it was necessary to the American character.

This was first published under the title, *Crockett: A Bio-Bibliography.*

339. Heatwole, John L. *Supernatural Tales: Ghosts, Poltergeists, Phantom Animals and Unusual Occurrences.* Bridgewater, VA: The Mountain and Valley Series, 1998. i, 57p. Illus. Sources. (The Virginia and

West Virginia Mountain and Valley Folklife Series).

Most of the brief stories here are of
gentle ghosts, whose appearances are reas-
suring rather than frightening. They center in the Shenandoah Valley of Virginia
and West Virginia.

340. Hendricks, W. C., ed. *Bundle of
Troubles and Other Tarheel Tales.* Durham,
NC: Duke Univ. Press, 1943. ix, 206p.
Notes on origin of tales.

About 40 tales, of the more than 200
collected and written down by the North
Carolina Writers' Project, are in this
book. In the words of the introduction,
they are stories of "witches, ghosts, and
queer characters, tall tales, and hunting
and fishing yarns." They are on universal
themes—tricksters, ghosts and haunts, animal stories. Some concern the well-
known John Henry, the "steel driving
man."

341. Hurston, Zora Neale. *Mules and
Men.* San Bernadino: Borgo Press, 1990.
xxiii, 309p. Bibliog. 89-45672. 0-06-
091648-6.

Hurston collected these tales in
Florida in the late 1920s and early 1930s.
She has arranged them into two sections:
one of tales, including Jack tales and tales
of High John; and one of voodoo.

Hurston was and still is considered one
of the foremost collectors of black folklore. This is her classic contribution.

Sorrow's Kitchen (New York: Collier,
1993) by Mary Lyons tells the story of
Hurston's life; *Adventures of High John the
Conqueror* (New York, Dell: 1992) by
Stephen Sanfield tells some of the High
John stories and gives much information
about Hurston's life.

342. Jackson, Thomas William. *On a
Slow Train through Arkansaw.* Lexington:
Univ. Press of Kentucky, 1903; repr.,
1985. xi, 137p. Edited by W. K. McNeil.
Notes. 85-8557. 0-8131-1543-4.

W. K. McNeil has edited a classic book
of American regional humor, Thomas
Jackson's 1903 book *On a Slow Train
through Arkansaw.* The book is a compilation of jokes and humorous stories, all
with a regional flair.

McNeil adds an introduction, in which
he discusses briefly the history of American regional humor, and a biography of
Jackson. He also provides notes on the
text.

343. Johnson, F. Roy. *Legends, Myths,
and Folk Tales of the Roanoke-Chowan.*
Murfreesboro, NC: Daily News, 1962.
viii, 105p. Illus.

Tales of Indians, early settlers, pirates,
animals, and even the devil mingle in this
book of briefly told legends from a particular area of North Carolina. No attri-
butions are given.

Numerous hand-drawn maps indicate
the locale of various tales.

344. ——. *The Lost Colony in Fact and
Legend.* Murfreesboro, NC: Johnson Pub-
lishing, 1983. 104p. Illus. by Eugenia
Johnson. 0-930230-46-9.

Johnson first gives what facts are
known about the lost colony of Roanoke,
Virginia. He then pulls together all the
stories that have grown up to explain the
colony's disappearance. None is authen-
ticated.

345. Johnson, Guy B. *Folk Culture on
St. Helena Island, South Carolina.* Chapel
Hill: Univ. of North Carolina Press,
1930; repr., Hatboro, PA: Folklore Associates, 1968. xxi, 183p. Index. Bibliog.

Although the main thrust of this book
is a study of the folk music and folklore
of the Sea Islands off the coast of South

Carolina, its value to the present bibliography is in the tales it retells. The first section is a discussion of Gullah, the dialect of the area; the second is a discussion of the origin of folk songs. But in the third and shortest section, various tales are retold. These are brief, most only a few paragraphs. Many are of the Br'er Rabbit genre.

346. Jones, Charles C., Jr. *Negro Myths from the Georgia Coast Told in the Vernacular.* Boston: Houghton Mifflin, 1888; repr., Detroit, MI: Singing Tree Press, 1969. x, 171p. Glossary. 68-21779.

Jones gives credit in his preface to Joel Chandler Harris for bringing "to public notice the dialect and folk-lore in vogue among the negroes of Middle Georgia." His book, he says, attempts to do the same for the folklore of the swamps of Georgia and the Carolinas.

These tales are of Br'er Rabbit and Br'er Bear and the other creatures familiar from the Chandler works. They are written in dialect, which makes them difficult to read.

347. Jones, Charles Colcock. *Gullah Folktales from the Georgia Coast.* 1888; repr., Athens: Univ. of Georgia Press, 2000. xxxv, 192p. Glossary. 99-089728. 0-8203-2216-4pa.

Jones was a slaveholder from Georgia who fought in the Civil War. After the war, he began chronicling the history of the South, publishing accounts of the history of his local area and other areas of Georgia. Joel Chandler Harris, who by then had published some of his Uncle Remus tales, asked Jones to collect tales from his area. This Jones proceeded to do.

Many of the tales have the same characters and themes as the Uncle Remus tales: Br'er Rabbit and Br'er Fox, trickery and cleverness. The tales are told in dialect.

There is no explanation from Jones about where the tales were collected, who told them, or the circumstances in which they were gathered. Nor is there any background on the tellers.

This new edition contains a brief biography of Jones.

348. Jump, Sean. *Ghosts in the Hills: Tales of Mystery and the Supernatural in East Kentucky.* Corbin, KY: Inferno Books, 1997. 124p. Illus. 98-100085.

Murdered babies, witches, and ghostly visitors are only a few of the apparitions described in this book. All were seen or heard in east Kentucky; all are documented.

349. Kitchens, Ben Earl. *Tomatoes in the Treetops: The Collected Tales of Harry Rhine.* Florence, AL: Thornwood Book Publishers, 1983. 72p. Illus. 82-16980.0-943054-39-7.

Kitchens has collected the tall tales of Harry Rhine, a resident of Tishomingo County, Mississippi. He apparently regaled the residents for years with these tales of fishing, hunting, farming, and traveling. The tales themselves are quite short, most only a paragraph.

350. Lankford, George E., ed. *Native American Legends: Southeastern Legends: Tales from the Natchez, Caddo, Biloxi, Chickasaw, and Other Nations.* Little Rock, AR: August House, 1987. 265p. Illus. Notes. Bibliog. (American Folklore Series). 87-1144. 0-87483-038-9; 0-87483-039-7pa.

The major themes of Native American tales are here: creation stories, explanations of the natural world, heroes, and tricksters. Tales are from the Natchez, Yuchi, Tunica, Biloxi, Chitimacha, Cherokee, Caddo, Alabama, Hitchiti, Menomini, Ojibwa, Creek, Koasati, Sumu, Carib-Arawak, Choctaw, Kashita, Taskigi, Atakapa, Tukabahchee, Seminole, Abnaki, Skidi Pawnee, Mandan, Dakota, Iowa, Ashanti, Fan, Bakongo, and Ibo.

351. Lee, Fred J. *Casey Jones: Epic of the American Railroad*. Kingsport, TN: Southern Publishers, 1939. xiv, 298p. Illus. Appendix.

This is a biography of Casey Jones rather than a study of the folklore that has grown up around him, but it provides useful information about his life. The appendix gives information on how the song "Casey Jones" came to be composed.

352. MacKaye, Percy. *Tall Tales of the Kentucky Mountains*. New York: George H. Doran, 1926; repr., Westport, CT: Greenwood, 1973. vii, 181p. Illus. by E. MacKinstry. 73-9375. 0-8371-7010-9.

MacKaye retells tales of the Kentucky mountains, using the voice of Solomon Shell, a wandering mountain man who enthralled adults and children alike with his tales.

The stories are told in dialect.

353. Martin, Howard N. *Myths and Folktales of the Alabama-Coushatta Indians of Texas*. Austin, TX: The Encino Press, 1977. xxxvii, 114p. Index. Glossary. Bibliog. Appendix. 0-88426-052-6.

Martin collected these tales in the 1930s, from the "Old Ones," people who, under the pressure of advancing settlement, had moved from their homes in Florida, Georgia, and Alabama, to the group's final home in East Texas. These Old Ones remembered and were able to tell stories about the times before white settlement, stories of the days when people, animals, and gods shared the land, and stories of the old ways of life.

The tales are arranged thematically: mythological tales, including creation myths; animal and bird stories; stories of the afterworld; trickster stories; stories of cannibals, ghosts and witches, monsters, and marriage between humans and animals; stories of heroes; and historical tales.

The appendix gives tale types and motifs.

354. Martin, Margaret Rhett. *Charleston Ghosts*. Columbia: Univ. of South Carolina Press, 1963. x, 105p. Illus. 63-22508.

Martin used both archival research and personal accounts—one of them her own—to compile these stories. All, she says, are based in fact.

355. McCarthy, William Bernard, ed. *Jack in Two Worlds: Contemporary North American Tales and Their Tellers*. Chapel Hill: Univ. of North Carolina Press, 1994. xlvi, 290p. Illus. with black-and-white photographs of storytellers. Bibliog. Place and Name Index. Subject Index. 93-35592. 0-8078-2135-7; 0-8078-4443-8pa.

The Jack tale is a long-standing, centuries-old tradition in both British and American folklore. Richard Chase collected them in his *The Jack Tales* (Houghton Mifflin, 1943). Here they are retold with explanatory material. Eight Jack tales are presented here, along with an essay about each tale and information about the particular storyteller who tells it.

The introduction tells the history of the Jack tale tradition.

356. McNeil, W. K., comp./ed. *Ghost Stories from the American South*. Little Rock, AR: August House, 1985. 170p. Notes. Index of Southern Localities. 84-45638. 0-935304-83-5; 0-935304-84-3pa.

In his introduction, McNeil states that the material collected here is mainly previously unpublished, passed down through oral tradition. His categories include haunted houses and other haunted places, headless ghosts, treasure stories, traveling ghosts, malevolent ghosts, and witches and banshees.

All the tales are representative of the ghost literature of the region.

The notes give information on the recounter of the tale and on how and when the tale was related to the editor.

357. McNeil, W. K., ed. *Ozark Mountain Humor: Jokes on Hunting, Religion, Marriage and Ozark Ways.* Little Rock, AR: August House, 1989. 212p. Notes. Bibliog. (The American Folklore Series). 89-400. 0-87483-085-0; 0-87483-086-9pa.

McNeil defines the Ozarks as northern Arkansas, southern Mississippi, and parts of eastern Oklahoma, Kansas, and Illinois. Roughly the area is bounded by the Arkansas, the Missouri, the Mississippi, and the Neosho rivers.

Jokes are presented in the following categories:

Tall Tales
Local Characters
Husbands, Wives, and Lovers
Foolish
Wise
Religion
Heaven and Hell
Drinking, Gambling, and Other Vices
Eerie Humor

In addition to the jokes themselves, McNeil gives a lengthy introduction on the history and meaning of humor, with particular emphasis on Ozark humor traditions. He also provides notes on the jokes themselves, including biographical facts about his various informants.

358. Montague, Margaret. *Up Eel River.* New York: Macmillan, 1928. 225p.

Eel River is a fictitious river in West Virginia, which was used to indicate that something said was untrue or an exaggeration—as in, "Oh, that must have happened up Eel River." Montague tells four stories of Tony Beaver, a giant of a lumberman in the Paul Bunyan tradition, who lived up Eel River. His exploits include roping time itself and changing it to suit his needs. Tony's sister, Betsy Beaver, also figures in the tales. She is as outsized as is Tony. She saved the camp from destruction more than once, including a time when a lumberjack mistakenly cut a sugar maple that was a bleeder—and the camp nearly drowned in maple sugar water.

359. Mooney, James. *Myths of the Cherokee.* 1900; repr., New York: Dover, 1995. 576p. Illus. Index. Glossary. 95-22350. 0-486-28907-9pa.

The Cherokee area was located in Tennessee, Kentucky, Virginia, South Carolina, and North Carolina. This reprint of a 1900 *Nineteenth Annual Report of the Bureau of American Ethnology* gives a history of the Cherokee people, including a lengthy discussion of their often unhappy relations with the U.S. government. It then goes on to retell various stories of the Cherokee, including creation stories; stories of animals, birds, snakes, fish, and insects; tales of heroes; and tales of historical events.

360. Moore, Tom. *Mysterious Tales and Legends of the Ozarks.* Philadelphia: Dorrance and Co., 1938. 148p.

Moore tells eight tales of ghosts, foretelling the future, and mysterious apparitions in the Ozarks.

361. Powell, Jack. *Haunting Sunshine.*

Sarasota, FL: Pineapple Press, 2001. 174p. Illus. Index. Bibliog. 00-050215. 1-56164-220-7pa.

All the ghost tales told here are set in Florida. Powell, a retired physician, organizes the tales by setting:

Theatres
Houses
Historic Buildings
Churches
Restaurants
Schools
Military Installations
Hotels

362. Price, Charles Edwin. *Demon in the Woods: Tall Tales and True from East Tennessee.* Johnson City, TN: The Overmountain Press, 1992. ix, 64p. 0-932807-82-8pa.

In addition to a Cherokee tale of creation and tales of weird and wonderful creatures of the forest, this book contains tales of "a witch who drove people mad, a personal account of a miraculous cure, lost civilizations in the middle of Cherokee National Forest, and a host of death and burial superstitions" ("About the Tales," vii).

Most of the tales concern legendary creatures of the frontier: fish thirty feet long, a four-foot-tall cat that walks on its hind legs, a bewitched horse. All are from eastern Tennessee.

363. Randolph, Vance. *The Devil's Pretty Daughter, and Other Ozark Folktales.* New York: Columbia Univ. Press, 1955. xvi, 239p. Illus. by Glen Rounds. Bibliog. Notes on sources.

Randolph spent years collecting the folklore of the area. Here he presents a broad collection.

364. ———. *Pissing in the Snow and Other Ozark Folktales.* Urbana: Univ. of Illinois Press, 1976. xxxiii, 153p. Bibliog. 76-18181. 0-252-00618-6.

Randolph collected these tales at the same time he was collecting tales for his other works, however, they were not published at the same time as the others because of their bawdy nature; editors were reluctant to include them. Some twenty years after most of his work was printed, these tales with a sexual or scatological content became available.

Annotations after each tale by Frank A. Hoffman comment on the tales and give references to variants.

365. ———. *Sticks in the Knapsack.* New York: Columbia Univ. Press, 1958. xvii, 171p. Illus. by Glen Rounds. Bibliog. Notes on sources.

More folktales collected by this dean of the folklore of the region.

366. ———. *The Talking Turtle and Other Ozark Folk Tales.* New York: Columbia Univ. Press, 1957. xviii, 226p. Illus. by Glen Rounds. Bibliog. Notes on sources.

More folktales appear here, from Randolph's large collection.

367. ———. *We Always Lie to Strangers: Tall Tales from the Ozarks.* New York: Columbia Univ. Press, 1951. viii, 309p. Illus. Bibliog. Index.

This is another of Vance Randolph's collections of Ozark lore, this one concentrating on tall tales. The tales included concern themselves with the physical geography of the area, with monsters, farming, hunting, fishing, snakes, heroes, and weather.

368. ———. *Who Blowed up the Church House?* New York: Columbia Univ. Press, 1952. xix, 232p. Illus. Index. Bibliog. Notes.

Some of the tales here are reprinted from Randolph's earlier works, *The Ozarks* and *Ozark Mountain Folks*. Others are from various periodical publications, and still others are published for the first time here. In his introduction, Randolph assures the reader that he has set down the tales accurately, only spelling some words differently than they were pronounced in the spoken version.

369. Reneaux, J. J. *Cajun Folktales*. Little Rock, AR: August House, 1992. 176p. Glossary. 92-18627. 0-87483-283-7; 0-87483-282-9pa.

Reneaux presents these folktales in four sections:

Animal Tales
Fairy Tales
Funny Folktales
Ghost Stories

His brief introduction gives a short history of the region and the various cultural and linguistic influences on it.

370. ———. *Haunted Bayou and Other Cajun Folk Stories*. Little Rock, AR: August House, 1994. 164p. Illus. by Wendell E. Hall. Glossary. 0-87483-384-1. 0-87483-385-xpa.

Only three of the thirteen tales that Reneaux tells here are traditional tales. The others he says he has "pieced together," adding his own interpretation and imagination to fragments heard during his collecting. All, he says, try to accomplish the usual role of ghost stories: to acknowledge fears and the unknown, and in so doing to build defenses against these things. They represent, "our universal quest to understand the mysterious, eternal cycle of life, death, and life again." (Introduction, p. 11)

371. Rhyne, Nancy. *More Tales of the South Carolina Low Country*. Winston-Salem, NC: J. F. Blair, 1984. 121p. 84-21710. 0-89587-042-8pa.

This is Rhyne's second book of Low Country tales; her first was *Tales of the South Carolina Low Country*. Like the first, it is filled with ghosts, witch doctors, and mysterious happenings.

372. ———. *Tales of the South Carolina Low Country*. Winston-Salem, NC: J. F. Blair, 1982. xii, 93p. 82-9710. 0-89587-027-4pa.

Ghosts, mermaids, and voodoo doctors are among the characters in this collection of tales from South Carolina.

373. Roberts, Leonard W. *South from Hell-fer-Sartin: Kentucky Mountain Folk Tales*. Lexington: Univ. of Kentucky Press, 1955. 287p. List of informants. Index of Type Numbers. Index of Motif Numbers. 55-7002.

Roberts collected these tales in eastern Kentucky, in Leslie and Perry counties. He writes in his introduction that he has transcribed them faithfully as he heard them, preserving the various ways of speech and colloquialisms. He divides the stories into animal tales, ordinary tales (wonder tales, religious tales, romantic tales, tales of the stupid ogre), jokes and anecdotes, and local legends.

The *Hell-fer-Sartin* of the title refers to a creek name. His journey in this area took him south from Hell-fer-Sartin Creek.

374. Roberts, Nancy. *Civil War Ghosts and Legends*. Columbia: Univ. of South Carolina, 1992; repr., New York: Metro-Books, 2002. 183p. Illus. 1-58663-566-2.

John Brown continues to walk in Harper's Ferry. Other Civil War figures, too, although not so famous, walk here. Roberts tells two stories in each chapter. She recounts a scene of the Civil War, one that led to violent death. Then she brings the scene into the present day and recounts contemporary encounters with the ghosts of those killed.

375. ——. *Ghosts of the Carolinas.* Columbia: Univ. of South Carolina Press, 1967. 116p. Illus. 0-87249-568-8; 0-87249-587-6pa.

Stories here are evenly divided between North and South Carolina. Most of the tales are of human hauntings, but there is also a tale of a ghostly dog and some of ghostly phenomena such as mysterious lights. As with others of Roberts's books, this is illustrated with black-and-white photographs.

376. ——. *Ghosts of the Southern Mountains and Appalachia.* Columbia: Univ. of South Carolina Press, 1978. vi, 150p. Illus. 88-20836. 0-87249-597-3; 0-87249-598-1pa.

Roberts here collects ghost tales from Appalachia. She indicates which town or area each tale comes from. Illustrations are black-and-white photographs of various locales.

377. ——. *North Carolina Ghosts and Legends.* Rev. ed. Columbia: Univ. of South Carolina Press, 1991. viii, 122p. Illus. 91-14469.0-87249-764-X. 0-87249-765-8pa.

First published under the title *An Illustrated Guide to Ghosts and Mysterious Occurrences in the Old North State* (1967), Roberts presents an expanded version here. Many of the stories told here are ghost stories. All concern the land and the coastline of North Carolina. This makes a good companion to Roberts's *South Carolina Ghosts: From the Coast to the Mountains* (Columbia: Univ. of South Carolina Press, 1983).

378. ——. *South Carolina Ghosts: From the Coast to the Mountains.* Columbia:

Univ. of South Carolina Press, 1983. vii, 152p. Illus. Bibliog. 0-87249-428-4; 0-87249-429-2pa.

In this book, ghosts populate colleges, castles, roads, and even slaughter yards. According to Roberts, all the tales are based in fact. This makes a good companion to Roberts's *North Carolina Ghosts and Legends* (Columbia: Univ. of South Carolina, 1991).

379. ——. *This Haunted Southland: Where Ghosts Still Roam.* Columbia: Univ. of South Carolina Press, 1970. 125p. Illus. 88-26096. 0-87249-588-4; 0-87249-589-2pa.

Many of the ghost stories told here relate to railroads. Others take place in mines and on boats. Illustrations are black-and-white photographs.

380. Russell, Randy, and Janet Barnett. *The Granny Curse, and Other Ghosts and Legends from East Tennessee.* Winston-Salem, NC: J. F. Blair, 1999. xii, 146p. 99-046957. 0-89587-185-8.

This volume comprises twenty-five ghost tales from east Tennessee. The "Granny Curse" of the title refers to an old granny, one skilled in magic and herb medicine, who enabled her grandson to marry by placing a curse on his sweetheart's parents, who had opposed the match. It was a nonlethal curse, and lifted when the match had been made.

381. Saucier, Corinne L. *Folk Tales from French Louisiana.* Baton Rouge: Claitor's Publishing Division, 1962. 138p. Motif Index. Published Variants of the Tales. Bibliog. 62-13679.

Saucier, considered one of the premier folklorists of Louisiana, divides this collection into four categories: semi-legendary, fairy, comical, and animal stories. She includes tales of both Little John and Foolish John, as well as some Br'er Rabbit tales.

The tales were collected at two distinct times: 1923 and 1949. Although the tales were collected in Avoyelles Parish, in central Louisiana, Saucier makes the point that they are told all over the state.

382. Saxon, Lyle, Robert Tallant, and Edward Dreyer. *Gumbo Ya-Ya: A Collection of Louisiana Folktales*. Boston: Houghton Mifflin, 1945. xiii, 581p. Illus. Index. Appendix A: Superstitions. Appendix B: Colloquialisms. Appendix C: Customs. (Louisiana Writers' Project Publications).

Members of the Louisiana Writers' Program of the Work Projects Administration collected this material. It includes Creole and Cajun folklore and folkways, as well as that of African Americans. Information is about musical festivals and celebrations, wedding customs, river lore, ghosts, everyday working life, and religious holidays.

383. Sergent, Donnie, Jr., and Jeff Wamsley. *Mothman: The Facts behind the Legend*. Point Pleasant, WV: Mothman Lives, 2002. 164p. Illus. Bibliog. 2001-119432. 0-9667246-7 4.

In November 1966, two young couples reported seeing a mysterious creature near Point Pleasant, West Virginia. One of the women described it for this book in this way: "It was about seven feet tall. It had wings that were visible on its back, the tips of the wings could be seen above its shoulders. The body of it was like a slender, muscular man, and was flesh-colored. It's [sic] wings were an ashen white in color. The wings looked like angel wings. Its face couldn't be seen, because the eyes simply hypnotized you when you looked into them" (p. 20).

Their report caused a media frenzy and

a flurry of interest in the phenomenon. Since then, various theories have been expounded to explain the mysterious creature: marsh gas, a large bird, an effort on the part of the U.S. government to hide various activities connected with power generation, or a genuine otherworldly creature.

The authors of this book bring together transcripts of eyewitness accounts of sightings, newspaper clippings, and correspondence concerning the phenomena.

384. Solomon, Jack, and Olivia Solomon, comps. *Ghosts and Goosebumps: Ghost Stories, Tall Tales, and Superstitions from Alabama*. Athens: Univ. of Georgia Press, 1994. xiii, 202p. Notes for further study. List of Alabama Folk Tales in the Library of Congress. 93-40015. 0-8203-1634-2pa.

Most of the stories and superstitions collected here are from two sources: Some were collected between 1958 and 1962 by folklore students at Troy State University, others by workers in the National Writers' Project, Folklore Division, of the WPA. Some material comes from investigations of folklore students at Alexander City State Junior College, from 1972 to 1977. All material concerns central and southeastern Alabama.

Material is arranged in three major groups. First come the tales, all extremely short—some only a paragraph—and all with the contributor's name noted. Next come the superstitions, on death, birth, marriage, weather and farming, good and bad luck. Last comes the section of WPA material, which consists of narratives by former slaves.

All sections are introduced by a discussion of the material, including references to eminent folklorists and their work.

The "Notes for Further Study," at the back of the book (pp. 186–198) is a bibliographic essay on major sources for the study of American folklore.

385. Sport, Kathryn, and Bert Hitchcock. *De Remnant Truth: The Tales of Jake Mitchell and Robert Wilton Burton.* Tuscaloosa: Univ. of Alabama Press, 1991. viii, 247p. 91-27203.0-8173-0515-7pa.

These tales, first published in newspapers between 1885 and 1894, were the result of a collaboration between a white bookstore owner and a black former slave. Jake Mitchell told the tales and Robert Wilton Burton transcribed them and had them published. The tales center on "Jake," a resident of Marengo County, and on his conviction that everything in Marengo County was superior to things anywhere else.

An introduction gives biographical information on both Burton and Mitchell and sets the tales in context, explaining the social forces that shaped them and showing how they can still be of value today. It is the contention of the editors that one can discard the "husk" and retain the "kernel" of the tale itself.

386. Stouff, Faye. *Sacred Beliefs of the Chitimacha Indians.* Rev. ed. Baton Rough, LA: Nashoba Tek Press, 1995. 82p. Illus. by Margot Soulé. Edited by Maureen Pitre. 95-74716. 1-887875-01-8.

This is a revised edition of a book published by Twitty and Twitty in 1971. It sets down the legends or religious beliefs of the Chitimacha Indians of Louisiana, which the author first heard when living on a Chitimacha reservation in the 1920s. They recount beliefs relating to the beginnings of the earth, to the supreme being, and to the spirits of animals and plants and the help they give to people.

One can look at these stories as expressions of faith or as legends. Either way, they express the beliefs and ways of life of a particular group of people.

387. Tackett, Sarah Jane Turnbow. *Alabama's Favorite Folk Tales.* Birmingham, AL: Seacoast, 1998. 143p. Illus. 1-878561-56-1pa.

Each of the tales included in this volume is preceded by a note of where the story is set and followed by notes on the sources of the story, whether it is a traditional tale, one told by a particular individual, or one first seen by the author in a newspaper or magazine.

There are many stories here of apparitions and mysterious happenings. All of them are meant to be told as well as read.

388. Tanenbaum, Linda Duck, and Barry McGee. *Ghost Tales from the North Carolina Piedmont.* Winston-Salem, NC: Bandit Books, 2002. 116p. Illus. 2002-108815. 1-878177-13-3.

Ghosts apparently still walk the halls and stairways of many buildings in the Piedmont area of North Carolina. Tanenbaum and McGee gather some of them together here: children who died violently, men killed in the course of their professional duties, young women seeking to avenge the death of a child. None of the ghosts seem violent themselves, although they are unpleasant to meet.

Lydia is here as well, the young woman who figures in ghost stories from many areas of the United States. Killed in a car accident, she presumably waits by the side of the road and hitches a ride home, only to disappear abruptly when her driver lets her out. If the driver seeks out the house she has asked to be taken to for an explanation, he is often met by a woman who says her daughter was killed years before, often on the anniversary of the day of her appearance.

389. Tartt, Ruby Pickens. *Dim Roads and Dark Nights: The Collected Folklore of Ruby Pickens Tartt.* Kingston, AL: Livingston Univ. Press, 1993. iii, 200p. Edited by Alan Brown. Bibliog. Appendices. 0-942979-10-9; 0-942979-11-7pa.

Ruby Pickens Tartt, a white woman living in Sumter County, Alabama, collected folklore from Blacks in the area in the 1930s and 1940s. Some of her collecting was for the WPA Writers' Project. Most of the material she collected remained as unsorted papers at Livingston University. Now Alan Brown has collated and organized her writings, with this book as the result.

Folktales include many animal tales, some anecdotes of local characters, slave narratives, and preacher tales. All are presented the way she wrote them down, except for some changes in the spelling of certain words.

Even during her lifetime Tartt was considered a foremost collector of folklore; Alan Lomax, the renowned folksinger and folk song collector, urged her to publish her work. This collection proves the staying power of her work.

Appendices include a tribute to Ruby Pickens Tartt written by another eminent folklorist, Carl Carmer, author of *Stars Fell on Alabama,* and a glossary.

390. Tatham, Robert L. *Ozark Treasure Tales.* Raytown, MO: R. L. Tatham, 1979. 31p. Illus. Maps. pa.

Tatham gives information on eight lost treasures. In his introduction, he tells readers that it is unlikely they will find any of the treasures—although they do indeed exist—but that the hunt will be enjoyable.

391. Thompson, Rose, coll. *Hush, Child! Can't You Hear the Music?* Edited by Charles Beaumont. Athens: Univ. of Georgia Press, 1982. xxxiii, 94p. Illus. 81-10442. 0-8203-0588-X.

Rose Thompson collected these tales during the 1930s and 1940s, when she worked for the Farm Security Administration as a home supervisor—a program that helped rural women learn more efficient ways of gardening, food preparation, and other farm activities. The tales fall into three categories: Mr. Rabbit and the Devil; tales with a religious theme; and songs and music.

The introduction explains much about the collecting of the stories and the people who told them.

392. Whedbee, Charles Harry. *Blackbeard's Cup and Stories of the Outer Banks.* Winston-Salem: J. F. Blair, 1989. 175p. 89-32193. 0-89587-070-3.

Whedbee's short stories are a mixture of those entirely imagined and those based on local legend. All concern the outer banks of North Carolina.

393. Writers' Program of the Work Projects Administration in the State of South Carolina. *South Carolina Folk Tales: Stories of Animals and Supernatural Beings.* Columbia: Bulletin of the Univ. of South Carolina, 1941. xi, 122p. Index. Bibliog.

All these tales were collected by workers of the Works Projects Administration. The introduction makes clear that many different collecting styles and abilities were present, which accounts for the unevenness in the presentation of the tales. Animal tales include many of the Br'er Rabbit genre. Supernatural tales are of ghosts, witches, treasures, the devil, witch doctors, and conjuring.

Although the tales were recorded as

spoken, some changes in spelling have been made to make the tales more readable.

Folk Music

394. Arnold, Byron, ed. *Folk Songs of Alabama.* University: Univ. of Alabama Press, 1950.xiii, 193p. Bibliog. Index of titles. Index of first lines. Index of Old English ballads. Index of Negro folk songs. Index of play party songs.

Arnold's indexes indicate the type of songs he collected: Old English ballads, Negro folk songs (spirituals and work songs), and play party songs. In addition to these three types, he notes in his introduction that he also collected a large number of songs of American and Alabama origin. He arranges the songs not by type, but by the person from whom he collected them. Thus all songs collected from one singer are grouped together, some with footnotes giving information on variants collected from another singer. Sections are preceded by biographical information about the singer. Thus the user of this book can see what songs came from a particular geographic area. Arnold collected all songs in this volume during a six-week time period in 1945, while traveling throughout the state. He maintains that the songs were part of everyday life for the singers, used as lullabies or as accompaniments to household tasks.

395. Boyd, Joe Dan. *Judge Jackson and The Colored Sacred Harp.* Montgomery: Alabama Folklife Association, 2002. 159p. Illus. Index. Index of Songs. Bibliog. 2002-8855. 0-9672672-5-0.

Judge Jackson, born in 1883, wrote *The Colored Sacred Harp* in 1934. It was an extension of *The Sacred Harp,* published in 1902, a songbook that facilitated singing by giving each printed note a different shape. *The Sacred Harp* was widely popular, incorporating religious songs, camp songs, and other popular tunes of the day, and gave rise to the phenomenon of shape singing, by which people learned to sing using these shaped notes. Shape singing groups abounded, at churches and in community groups.

Jackson took this idea and turned it into an expression of the African American experience and history, emphasizing spirituals. The technique and the book itself permeated African American culture in the South.

Boyd traces two histories: Jackson's life and the life of the book, which Jackson "nurtured to publication, against all odds, during the Great Depression" (Intro., p. 12). He also discusses the continuing tradition of shape singing, which he hopes will "survive modern media's persistent attempts to homogenize our musical culture" (p. 124).

The included CD contains music recorded from the 1930s through the 1970s. Boyd gives notes on the recording sessions.

396. Chapell, Louis Watson. *Folk-Songs of Roanoke and the Albemarle.* Morgantown, West Virginia: The Ballad Press, 1939. 203p. Index to song titles.

Chapell presents songs from the Albemarle, an area in eastern North Carolina that includes the tidewater region of Roanoke Island and the Albemarle Sound. He divides the songs into British Ballads, Sea Ballads, Other Ballads, Nell Cropsey Songs, and Religious Songs, as well as a miscellaneous category. Nell

Cropsey was a young woman of the area who disappeared in 1901 and whose body was discovered several weeks later; her lover was convicted of her murder.

A number of the songs concern John Henry. Chapell provides music for a few of the songs.

397. Chase, Richard, comp. *American Folk Tales and Songs: And Other Examples of English-American Tradition as Preserved in the Appalachian Mountains and Elsewhere in the United States.* New York: Dover Publications, 1971. 240p. Title Index. Bibliog. 72-140231. 0-486-22692-1pa.

Part 1 consists of tales, including Jack Tales and Irishman Tales; Part 2 consists of songs and ballads. Some of the songs have music transcribed.

All the material is from the English American tradition.

398. Combs, Josiah H. *Folk-Songs of the Southern United States* (Folk-Songs du Midi des Etats-Unis). Austin: Univ. of Texas Press, 1967. xxvii, 254p. Index of Titles and First Lines of Song Texts. Appendix. 67-65344.

First published in 1925, in French, these are songs collected by Josiah H. Combs in Kentucky, Virginia, West Virginia, Tennessee, Arkansas, Oklahoma, and Texas. D. K Wilgus, the present editor, worked with the draft of a manuscript in English that Combs had prepared to produce this volume. Songs included are of British and Native American origin. The appendix is an index to the Combs Collection of songs and rhymes housed at the University of California, Los Angeles.

399. Davis, Arthur Kyle, Jr. *More Traditional Ballads of Virginia: Collected with the Cooperation of Members of the Virginia Folklore Society.* Chapel Hill: Univ. of North Carolina Press, 1960. xxvii, 371p. Bibliog. Index of Titles and First Lines.

Following the 1929 publication of *Traditional Ballads of Virginia* (Cambridge, MA: Harvard Univ. Press, 1929), the editor and various assistants and collaborators continued to collect more ballads in the area. This collection is a follow-up to the original. Davis refers to the original publication in his introduction and urges people to read that material for background information. This newer collection also presents ballads extant at the time of publication. Like the earlier work, Davis presents variants of the ballads, as well as tunes if available. Headnotes give historical information on a particular ballad as well as information on its collection.

Forty-six ballads are included in the collection.

400. ——. *Traditional Ballads of Virginia.* Collected under the auspices of the Virginia Folk-Lore Society. Cambridge, MA: Harvard Univ. Press, 1929. xviii, 634p. Illus. Index of titles.

All fifty-one ballads in this volume are genuine English or Scottish ones, still extant in Virginia at the time of collecting. Although fifty-one ballads does not seem like a great number, the editor collected all known variants as well, making this a formidable volume both in size and in scholarship. The first section sets out the words of the ballad, along with variants and notes on collecting; the second section transcribes the music. Here are the standard traditional ballads: "Barbara Allen," "Lord Randall," "The Cherry Tree Carol," and "Gypsy Laddie."

Despite its age, this volume is still a valuable one for lovers of the ballad.

401. Fussell, Fred C. *Blue Ridge Music*

Trails: Finding a Place in the Circle. Chapel Hill: Univ. of North Carolina, 2003. xxx, 255p. Illus. Index. 2002-154136. 0-8078-5459-xpa.

Fussell believes that visitors to North Carolina and Virginia can understand and connect to the culture of the region by listening to its indigenous music. This music—bluegrass, gospel, blues, and country and western—is still enthusiastically and widely played at "community centers, coffee shops, barbecue restaurants, music stores, fast-food joints, shopping malls, community festivals, street fairs, barbershops, school auditoriums, and town parks" (Preface, p. xx).

Dividing the area into eight regions, Fussell describes many of these locations and musical events. He gives locations (including driving directions) and contact information for dozens of traditional music venues and events in the particular region.

Numerous photographs, many in color, fill the book, of performers and performances. The photographs are by Cedric N. Chatterley.

402. Helms, Karen G. *Hand-Me-Down Songs: Traditional Music of Union County, North Carolina.* Monroe, NC: Ambassador Press, 1982. 25p. spiral binding. Illus.

Helms has included more than songs in this brief paperback. Historical sketches, descriptions of rural crafts such as basket weaving and of rural remedies for such things as kidney trouble and earache, and even recipes are interspersed with the songs. Helms has provided a few blank pages at the back for readers to note their own known snippets of folklore.

403. Joyner, Charles W. *Folk Song in South Carolina.* Columbia: Univ. of South Carolina Press, 1971. viii, 112p. Bibliog. (Tricentennial Booklet Number 9). 70-164707. 0-87249-227-3.

Ballads, Religious Songs, and Secular Songs are the three divisions Joyner uses to present these South Carolina folk songs. Some of the songs are familiar ("Barbara Allen" and "Michael Row the Boat Ashore" are examples), whereas others are lesser known. Joyner often gives a line of music with the song.

404. McNeil, Keith, and Rusty McNeil. *Civil War Songbook, with Historical Commentary.* Riverside, CA: WEM Records, 1999. 104p. Illus. Index of songs. Bibliog. 1-878360-24-8pa.

According to the McNeils' introduction to this book, the Civil War coincided with an upsurge in the availability of popular music. Pianos were commonly owned, sheet music was easily printed and cheaply purchased, and certain songs were popular throughout the United States. The Civil War naturally inspired much songwriting, both for and by soldiers for morale purposes, and for the civilians left behind.

The McNeils arrange the songs chronologically. There are four sections, each with appropriate songs: The War Begins, The Realities of War, The Changing War, and The Union Forever. Many of the songs are familiar today: "The Yellow Rose of Texas," "The Battle Hymn of the Republic," "Goober Peas," "We Are Coming, Father Abraham," "Go Down Moses," and "John Brown's Body" are all here. All the songs have music transcribed, as well as a brief historical note explaining the impetus for the particular song.

Illustrations are contemporary black-and-white renditions.

405. McNeil, W. K. *Southern Folk Ballads*. Little Rock, AR: August House, 1987–1988. vol. 1, 219p.; vol. 2, 224p. Index of titles. Index of first lines. Index of locations. Index of informants. Bibliodiscography. (The American Folklore Series). vol. 1, 87-751904; vol. 2, 87-751904. vol. 1, 0-87483-038-9; 0-87483-039-7pa. vol. 2, 0-87483-047-8; 0-87483-046-xpa.

War, Crime and Criminals, Lovers, and Cowboys and Pioneers are the categories of songs collected in Volume 1 of this compilation. Volume 2 adds Humorous Ballads, Murder Ballads, Tragedies and Disasters, Supernatural Topics, and Death and Dying to the list.

Ballads come from throughout the South. Most have music transcribed.

406. ——. *Southern Mountain Folksongs: Traditional Songs from the Appalachians and the Ozarks*. Little Rock, AR: August House, 1993. 235p. Bibliog. Bibliodiscography. (The American Folklore Series). 92-36617. 0-87483-284-5; 0-87483-285-3pa.

Hundreds of songs of the southern mountains, Appalachia, and the Ozarks, make up this book. McNeil arranges them into six chapters:

Songs about Love and Lovers
Religious Songs
Children's Songs
Songs for Special Occasions
Songs of Work
Comic Songs

Many of the songs have music transcribed.

The Biblio-discography at the end of the book lists each song, books that contain information about the song, and recordings of the song.

407. Niles, John Jacob. *The Ballad Book of John Jacob Niles*. New York: Bramhall House, 1961. xxii, 369p. Bibliog. Index of Song Titles. Index of Explanatory Material. 60-002.

The songs collected here are from Virginia, West Virginia, and Kentucky. There are only sixty-five songs in the collection, but each one has been meticulously researched and explained. In addition to the words and the tune, Niles includes a history of the song, notes on variations, and details about how he collected it.

408. Perdue, Charles L. *Don't Let the Devil Outtalk You: Folksongs, Rhymes, Chants, and Other Musical Material from the WPA Collection of Georgia Folklore and Ex-Slave Interviews*. Charlottesville: Univ. of Virginia, 1970. ii, 146p. Index.

Perdue prepared this as a paper for an independent studies project for the University of Pennsylvania. He collected material "of a musical nature" from that in the WPA collection of Georgia folklore and interviews with ex-slaves. He provides an index to the material and indicates sources.

409. Randolph, Vance. *Ozark Folksongs*. Columbia: Univ. of Missouri Press, 1980. 4 volumes. Bibliog. vol.1 0-8262-0297-7; vol. 2 0-8262-0298-5; vol. 3 0-8262-0299-3; vol. 4 0-8262-0300-0.

Vance Randolph wrote a number of books on Ozark folklore. He entrusted his immense collection of Ozark folksongs to the State Historical Society of Missouri, which published the collection in 1946. This 1980 edition is a reprint of the first edition. The four volumes contain a wealth of folk songs. Volume 1 is British Ballads and Songs; Volume 2 is Songs of the South and West; Volume 3 is Humorous and Play-Party Songs; and Volume 4 is Religious Songs and Other Items. As noted in the introduction in

Volume 1, there is some overlap among volumes; volumes other than 1 might contain some songs of British origin, for example. For people interested in music of this area, this book is invaluable.

410. Sharp, Cecil James. *English Folk Songs from the Southern Appalachians, Composing Two Hundred and Seventy-Three Songs and Ballads with Nine Hundred and Sixty-Eight Tunes.* London: Oxford Univ. Press, 1932. vol. 1: xxxvii, 436p.; vol. 2: xi, 411p. 2 volumes. Bibliog. Index of titles.

Sharp is known mostly for his studies of English folk song and dance, but in 1916, 1917, and 1918, he made several trips into the southern Appalachians to collect songs of English origin. This collection, of 273 songs and ballads, and an earlier collection, consisting of 122 songs and ballads, are culled from the more than 500 songs he collected. He gives several variants for each song, noting the date of collection and the individual who sang the song. Sharp, like so many other collectors of folklore, made the point in his introduction that it was essential to collect and record such material before encroaching mass culture wiped out individual regional differences. The older, 1917, collection is not easily attainable.

411. Smith, Reed, coll. and ed. *South Carolina Ballads.* Cambridge, MA: Harvard Univ. Press, 1928; repr., Spartanburg, SC: Reprint Company, 1972. x, 174p. Appendix: List of Ballad Titles with Their Number in the Child Collection Noted. 74-187374. 0-87152-102-4.

Instead of merely presenting a collection of ballads, Smith attempts to define the form, discuss its use, and examine the origin and variants of a number of particular ballads.

412. Tartt, Ruby Pickens. *"Honey in the Rock": The Ruby Pickens Tartt Collection of* *Religious Folk Songs from Sumter County, Alabama.* Macon, GA: Mercer Univ. Press, 2001. xxxvi, 176p. Edited and with preface, introduction, and bibliographic essays by Olivia Solomon and Jack Solomon. Index to First Lines. Bibliographical Essays: General Bibliog.; Ruby Pickens Tartt; Discography of Alabama Afro-American Folk Songs. 90-42394. 0-86554-336-4.

As a WPA worker in the 1930s, Ruby Pickens Tartt traveled through Sumter County, Alabama, to collect and transcribe the African American folk songs of the area. Those in this edition of her collection are religious in nature.

The introductory essay by Olivia Solomon and Jack Solomon discusses the ways in which this music helped African Americans of the time come to terms with their history of bondage.

No music is transcribed with the songs.

413. Wolfe, Charles K., ed. *Folk Songs of Middle Tennessee: The George Boswell Collection.* Knoxville: Univ. of Tennessee Press, 1997. xxi, 186p. Index. Bibliog. List of Major Informants for This Collection. 96-10011. 0-87049-957-2; 0-87049-958-0pa.

Eastern Tennessee has long been a Mecca for folk song collectors, beginning with Cecil Sharpe at the beginning of the twentieth century. Middle Tennessee, the home of Nashville, was neglected for some time, thought of as a place of popular rather than traditional music. George Boswell, in the 1950s, set out to disprove that and to collect the traditional music and songs of middle Tennessee.

This collection is based on Boswell's work. Here are British ballads and songs, including the well-known "Barbara Allen" and "Lord Randall"; Native American ballads; Civil War songs; songs from specific localities; popular songs; comedy songs; lyrics and laments; and religious songs.

Music is transcribed with all the songs, along with information as to where and from whom the particular song was collected.

Folk Belief and Ritual

414. Bolinger, Bonnie May Fancher. *Madison County Folklore: Collections of Bonnie May Fancher Bolinger.* Albany, OR: Burr and Ada Fancher, 1995. 80p. Edited by Burr "Doc" Fancher. 1-887335-00-5.

A teacher for many years in Madison County, Arkansas, Bonnie Bolinger collected these sayings, poems, and remedies from her fourth grade classes between 1959 and 1961. After her death, her brother, Burr "Doc" Fancher, edited them.

The sayings have to do with health, weather, love and marriage, and agriculture. There are also aphorisms about ambition, minding your own business, honesty, thrift, and other bedrock virtues. The ballads and songs often depict a true event from the past, or are rhymes for children's play.

Bolinger provides brief information about each of her fourth grade informants, most of whom got the information from parents and grandparents, and indicates which poems and sayings were acquired from which child.

Although brief, this book is charming in its authenticity.

415. Brunson, Marion Bailey. *Pea River Logic: Hand Me Downs from Grandpa's Trunk.* Tuscaloosa, AL: Portals Press, 1986. xiii, 161p. Illus. by Mary B. Rollins.

Brunson has collected superstitions,

sayings, weather lore, slang, and dream signs in this book. None of the sayings or expressions is attributed or explained, simply presented. But it is an interesting compilation of folklore and folk sayings from one area of the country.

416. Federal Writers' Project. *Drums and Shadows: Survival Studies among the Georgia Coastal Negroes.* Athens: Univ. of Georgia Press, 1940; repr., Ann Arbor, MI: Univ. Microfilms, 1969. xx, 274p. Foreword by Guy B. Johnson. Illus. Index. Bibliog. Glossary. List of informants. Notes on customs and traditions.

The Federal Writers' Project is responsible for many contributions to folklore study. This is a collection of beliefs and tales from a somewhat geographically isolated area, the Georgia coast. Many of the inhabitants of this area during the time of the study were former slaves, or the children or grandchildren of slaves. Moreover, the foreword makes clear that because the slave population of this area was continually augmented not from native-born people but from new slaves imported from Africa, the connection between African customs and beliefs and those practiced in this region was continuously reinforced. Thus the customs discussed here can be seen as closely related to customs practiced in Africa. The book itself is organized geographically. Actual tales are not retold, but much information is given about folk medicine, folk belief, the influence of both good and bad spirits, and the power of "bad mouth," or a curse put upon one by an enemy. Notes in an appendix indicate parallels between customs practiced here and those practiced in Africa.

417. Gaudet, Marcia G, and James C. McDonald, eds. *Mardi Gras, Gumbo, and Zydeco: Readings in Louisiana Culture.* Jack-

son: Univ. Press of Mississippi, 2003. xv, 179p. Illus. Index. Bibliog. 2002-9708. 1-57806-529-1; 1-57806-530-5pa.

The collected essays here concentrate on southern Louisiana, in particular Creole and Cajun traditions. Foodways are represented by the King Cake tradition in New Orleans at Epiphany and by an essay on the importance of the crawfish to the Cajun culture. Other essays concentrate on Christmas traditions; religion and anticlerical humor; witches; and of course the now nationally known celebration of Mardi Gras.

The editors add a section of discussion questions geared to each essay, so that the book can be used in classrooms.

418. Heatwole, John L. *Old Sayings, Proverbs, Riddles and Conundrums.* Bridgewater, VA: The Mountain and Valley Series, 2000. 47p. Illus. (The Virginia and West Virginia Mountain and Valley Folklife Series, no. 15). 1-893934-07-1pa.

Some of the sayings in this book are in the form of advice or morals; some are in rhyme. Heatwole also presents various word games, riddles, and tongue twisters from the region.

419. ——. *Superstitions.* Bridgewater, VA: The Mountain and Valley Series, 1996. i, 26p. Illus. Sources. (The Virginia and West Virginia Mountain and Valley Folklife Series). 1-893934-01-2pa.

Bad luck, good luck, weather lore, foretelling the future, and using signs to make decisions are all captured in short, pithy sayings from Virginia. Many of the sayings date from the early days of settlement.

420. Mitchell, Faith. *Hoodoo Medicine: Gullah Herbal Remedies.* Columbia, SC: Summerhouse Press, 1999. xi, 113p. Illus. Index. Bibliog. 98-29389. 1-887714-33-2.

Mitchell gives a history of the Sea Is-

lands, including an explanation of how the Gullah people adapted their knowledge of herbal medicine in Africa to their new environment. She then presents a directory of herbs of the area, alphabetically arranged, with a description of each and the uses to which it is put in medicine. Illustrations are both black-and-white photographs of the area, and line drawings of the various plants.

421. Montell, William Lynwood. *Ghosts along the Cumberland.* Knoxville: Univ. of Tennessee Press, 1975. xiv, 240p. Index of collectors. Index to tale types and motifs. Subject index. Glossary. Bibliog. 74-32241. 0-87049-165-2.

Montell, along with his students at Campbellsville College, collected this lore between 1958 and 1968. The material is divided into three sections. Part I concerns portents of death, those happenings that foretell a death. Part II relates the rituals that surround death. Part III tells ghost stories, the stories of apparitions and hauntings.

422. Pinckney, Roger. *Blue Roots: African-American Folk Magic of the Gullah People.* St. Paul, MN: Llewellyn, 1998. xii, 170p. Illus. Index. Bibliog. 98-27091. 1-56718-524-x.

The Sea Islands off the coasts of South Carolina and Georgia were the home of the Gullah, originally slaves brought from Africa. Because of the isolation of the islands, much of their African culture survived into the twentieth century. Roger Pinckney had much exposure to this culture, both through his own family and through the people who worked for his family. He accompanied his grandmother, a freelance writer, who also worked for the South Carolina welfare department, on her excursions to interview possible welfare recipients; he listened to the stories of his nurse, an elderly woman with a store of religious lore to share; he heard his father, the county coroner, tell tales of death caused—inexplicably—by hex.

In *Blue Roots*, Pinckney first tells the history of the islands, including the various waves of exploration, discovery, and settlement that changed the islands from their natural state to slaveholding plantations, then to small farms owned and worked by the former slaves, and then—in many cases—to retreats for people fleeing from urban crowds. He then describes the activities and importance of the root doctors, who used both faith and the healing powers of plants to effect cures. He tells of various amazing cures and also of the battles between the root doctors and the more traditional practitioners of medicine.

423. Puckett, Newbell Niles. *Folk Beliefs of the Southern Negro*. 1926; repr., New York: Greenwood, 1968. xiv, 644p. Illus. Bibliog. Index. List of informants. 68-55912.

Puckett collected his material in the 1920s, using a combination of interviews and questionnaires. Chapters are

Burial Customs, Ghosts, and Witches
Voodooism and Conjuration
Charms and Cures
Taboos
Signs and Omens
Christianity and Superstition.

424. Randolph,Vance. *Ozark Superstitions*. New York: Columbia Univ. Press, 1947. viii, 367p. Illus. Index. Bibliog.

Randolph collected this material while living in the Ozarks during the 1920s and later. He states in his introduction that the people who told him the various charms, customs, and warnings truly believed them. Superstitions are on a variety of topics, as seen in the list of chapter headings:

Weather Signs
Crops and Livestock
Household Superstitions
Water Witches
Mountain Medicine (mostly herbal)
Power Doctors (people who cure
    through charms and portents)
Courtship and Marriage
Pregnancy and Childbirth
Ghost Stories
Animals and Plants
Ozark Witchcraft
Death and Burial

Chapters are narrative, rather than merely lists of charms and superstitions. Randolph usually indicates where and how he came by a particular piece of information.

425. Teaford, Ruth Romaine. *Southern Homespun*. Huntsville, AL: Strode Publishers, 1980. 127p. 79-91431. 0-87397-158-2.

This slender volume contains a glossary of words and phrases used in Walker County, Alabama; a list of folk remedies; and a section of superstitions. A brief section of ghost stories follows the superstitions.

426. Wood, Cedric Stephen, ed. *Cracker Cures: A Compendium of Cures, Concoctions, Potions, Remedies, Magic, Old Wives' Tales, Omens, Luck Signs, and Talismans*. Arcadia, FL: Peace River Valley Historical Society, 1976. viii, 43p. Illus. Bibliog. This brief book lists cures for various ailments and conditions, mostly based on local herbs, superstitions, customs relating to healing,

and good and bad luck charms. An appendix describes various plants.

A brief disclaimer at the beginning warns against using these cures without proper medical advice, and a skull and crossbones precedes the listing for those cures that have been shown to have severe side effects.

Material Culture

427. Alvey, R. Gerald. *Kentucky Bluegrass Country.* Jackson: Univ. Press of Mississippi, 1992. xxiv, 322p. Illus. Bibliog. notes. Index. (Folklife in the South Series). 91-48029. 0-87805-510-X. 0-87805-544-4pa.

As might be expected from a book on Bluegrass country, the horse and its culture dominates this one. There are chapters on the Gentleman Farm, Horse Farm Procedures, Riding to Hound, the Code Duello, and Folk Traditions of the Bluegrass World. There is also information on local architecture and buildings, mills and taverns of the area, gambling, fishing and hunting, bourbon, tobacco, and foods.

428. Ancelet, Barry Jean, Jay D. Edwards, and Glen Pitre. *Cajun Country.* Jackson: Univ. Press of Mississippi, 1991. xxiv, 253p. Illus. Bibliog. Index. (Folklife on the South Series). 90-28931. 0-87805-466-9. 0-87805-467-7pa.

For those interested both in the history of the Cajun people and in their ongoing, still resonant traditions, this book would be a good choice. Part 1 contains a history of the people, from their first settling in the Nova Scotia area in the early seventeenth century, their expulsion from that area in 1755, and their eventual settlement in Louisiana from 1765 on.

Later sections discuss their family organization, religious rites and traditions, folk medicine, law and justice, architecture, food, music, games, and oral traditions.

In the section on oral traditions, traditional tales are told in both French and English.

429. Arpy, Jim. *The Magnificent Mississippi.* Grinnell: Iowa Heritage Gallery/Publications, 1983. 134p. illus. 0-910381-07-0.

Fact and legend are mingled in this book. Lavishly illustrated with black-and-white photos, this depicts such disparate professions as rafting and rafters, the steamboat world of Mark Twain, and the circus. It depicts too the natural world of floods and earthquakes.

The copious illustrations, combined with the informal, reportorial style of writing, make this an engaging book.

430. Bucuvalas, Tina, Peggy A. Bulger, and Stetson Kennedy. *South Florida Folklife.* Jackson: Univ. Press of Mississippi, 1994. xvii, 254p. Illus. Bibliog. Index. (Folklife in the South Series). 93-29928. 0-87805-659-9. 0-87805-660-2pa.

Unlike others in this series, which are organized along subject lines, with chapters on such topics as domestic industries and recreation, this book is organized by ethnic group. Each one discusses the folk traditions of a group that has at various times influenced the culture of south Florida. Chapters are on the Seminole and Miccosukee, the Crackers, the Cubans, and the Nicaraguans and Islanders.

Other chapters are on traditional skills and occupations, on Florida's tropical islands, and on the traditions created by and for tourists.

431. Coggeshall, John M. *Carolina Piedmont Country.* Jackson: Univ. Press of

Mississippi, 1996. xviii, 271p. Illus. Bibliog. essay. List of informants. Index. (Folklife in the South Series). 95-49438. 0-87805-766-8; 0-87805-767-6pa.

Coggeshall discusses both the changes in and the contemporary state of folklife in the Carolina Piedmont area. He includes chapters on speech, cultural values, beliefs, social gatherings and play, foods, traditional occupations, and material culture.

432. Cooper, Horton. *North Carolina Mountain Folklore and Miscellany.* Murfreesboro, NC: Johnson Publishing, 1972. 160p. Illus.

Miscellany is the proper title for this book. It contains superstitions on healing, death, courting customs, friendship; songs; jokes; a glossary of mountain speech; descriptions of everyday life and its activities. Cornhuskings are described, as are quilting bees and the custom of "dumb suppers," during which young girls prepare a meal in total silence, then sit down to eat it with an empty chair between each two girls. If a man comes in and sits in one of the chairs, it is thought that he will marry the girl he sits next to.

Cooper makes the point, as so many other authors have done, that the automobile and modern communications have changed the southern mountains forever, destroying their uniqueness. His descriptions of everyday life help preserve that way of life, at least in print. His descriptions bring to life a vanished time.

433. Harlow, Alvin F. *Weep No More, My Lady.* New York: Whittlesy House/McGraw-Hill, 1942. x, 455p. Illus. Index.

The original jacket blurb for *Weep No More, My Lady* states, "It is not a history, not a travel book, not a volume of reminiscences, but a thoroughly enjoyable amalgam of all three." It treats such subjects as education, food, social mores, as well as more serious ones such as agriculture, economics, and the Civil War. It reflects the darker side of the South as well, with reminiscences of the system of slavery that paint a prettier picture than the reality.

Altogether, it gives a picture of one part of the South during a particular time.

434. Hoebing, Phil. *Wildcat Whistle: Folklore, Fishing and Hunting Stories from the Mississippi River Valley.* Quincy, IL: Franciscan Press, 1997. xxii, 121p. Illus. 98-11304. 0-8199-0989-0.

The stories told here are by and of the real Mike Finks, the men who either worked on the Mississippi as river men, or who used it for recreation. To these men, the river was a way of life.

Most of the stories are true ones, of the old ways of fishing and hunting. They talk of early modes of transportation, such as Model T's, their first guns, their first dogs—and sometimes their first brushes with the law for illegal hunting and fishing. Some are tall tales, about spectacular catches, and some are true tales of fish and game no longer seen in the area.

One chapter discusses the folklore associated with snakes.

435. Hurst, Samuel Need. *The Mountains Redeemed: The Romance of the Mountains etc.* Appalachia, VA: Hurst, 1929. xvii, 384p. Illus.

It is the author's stated intention to portray accurately the Blue Ridge Mountain area and its people. He describes customs of the eighteenth and nineteenth centuries, using as his vehicle the lives of Allen and Nancy, at first a young couple seen during their courtship and wedding, then later through their married life, their ever-increasing family, Allen's service during the Civil War (about which he knew nothing, living in a remote area without access to newspapers or much interest in the world beyond his own), and later prosperity. The tale continues by following their descendants.

Using this scheme, Hurst describes courtship and wedding customs, farming and homemaking methods, religious and leisure activities of the area, schooling and medicine. He goes on to describe the increasing industrialization of the area, owing to the coming of the railroad and increasing mechanization of mining.

All in all, he paints a detailed picture of life in rural southwest Virginia during its early history.

436. McNeil, W. K. *Ozark Country.* Jackson: Univ. Press of Mississippi, 1995. xiv, 194p. Illus. Bibliog. Index. (Folklife in the South Series). 95-14859. 0-87805-728-5. 0-87805-729-3pa.

Like other books in this series, this one looks both at historical customs and at how customs have changed and adapted for the present day. The book first discusses the early days in the Ozarks and some of the earliest inhabitants. McNeil goes on to discuss family life, with a look at such home industries as architecture, furniture making, clothing, quilting and other needlework, foodways, and soap making. Then he takes a look at such traditional livelihoods as blacksmithing, pottery, gunsmithing, basket making, wood carving, broom making, coopering, doll making, musical instrument making, and pearling. Later chapters deal with such things as courting customs and those connected with death, folk medicine, games and entertainment, and storytelling.

All the material is seen from a contemporary perspective, how the older customs have evolved and are still vital today.

McNeil builds on the early work of Vance Randolph, an earlier folklorist of the region.

437. Montell, William Lynwood. *Upper Cumberland Country.* Jackson: Univ. Press of Mississippi, 1993. xix, 187p. Illus. Bibliographic Notes. Index. (Folklife in the South Series). 93-6972. 0-87805-630-0. 0-87805-631-9pa.

Montell blends the old and the new in this book, discussing first the history of this border area between Kentucky and Tennessee. He goes on to explore family structure and importance, the role of schools and churches in the community, traditional medicine, and death customs. He ends with a discussion of current-day folk practices, often founded on older traditions, and often involving young people. For example, he writes about the teenage custom of cruising the local main street, a custom he says grew out of older traditions of young people visiting and courting in horse and buggy.

He ends with a look at intergenerational activities.

438. Randolph, Vance. *The Ozarks: An American Survival of Primitive Society.* New York: The Vanguard Press, 1931. ix, 310p. Illus.

Randolph's book is full of information about the old days: the place of women, religious customs, household routines, buildings, farming, amusements, and superstitions. It is an invaluable look at a vanished way of life.

439. ——. *Ozark Mountain Folks.* New York: The Vanguard Press, 1932. ix, 279p. Illus.

Ozark Mountain Folks is a good companion piece to Randolph's earlier work, *The Ozarks*. Both discuss everyday life in the Ozarks. This volume has chapters on schooling; locally meted out justice; household duties, particularly women's responsibilities such as making clothes; hunting; and witchcraft.

The book is illustrated with black-and-white photographs.

440. Reed, John Shelton. *1001 Things Everyone Should Know about the South.* New York: Doubleday, a division of Bantam Doubleday Dell Publishing Group, 1996. viii, 310. Illus. Index. 95-41854. 0-385-47441-5.

There are indeed 1001 entries in this encyclopedia-like book, 1001 brief entries about everything from geography to television shows, all about the South. Sections are

Geography and Environment
Origins and Folkways
Agriculture, Culture, and Industry
The Confederacy and Its Legacy
Race and Politics
Writers and Literature
Music and Dance
Southern Cuisine
Architecture and Art
Religion and Higher Education
Sports and Tourism
The South of the Mind (the Mythic
    South)

Snippets of folklore are buried throughout, information on folk medicine, on place names, on local characters, on foods, songs, and customs of all descriptions. Although this does not provide a narrative history of folklore or long folktales, it is delightful as a place to browse.

441. Roberts, Leonard W. *Up Cutshin and Down Greasy: Folkways of a Kentucky Mountain Family.* Lexington: Univ. of Kentucky Press, 1959. viii, 165p. Illus. Index. Appendix. 59-10277.

Roberts, the author of *South from Hell-fer-Sartin* (Univ. of Kentucky Press, 1955), here allows various members of the Couch family of Kentucky to tell their own stories. In a series of informal interviews—more visits than interviews—Jim and Dave Couch tell the stories of their families, both their birth families and the families they created with their wives and children. They tell of farming ways in the early part of the twentieth century, of housekeeping techniques, of recreation such as storytelling and singing. They tell, too, of their moonshining days, including some specific information on how it is done.

All in all, this is a book full of information about the way of life in rural Kentucky before electricity and the automobile changed things. Here one can learn how clothing was made, how beans were shelled, what songs were sung, what farming methods were used. One gets a sense of a life that was full of work, but full of family as well.

The final section of the book contains some folktales and songs.

442. Sheppard, Muriel Earley. *Cabins in the Laurels.* Chapel Hill: Univ. of North Carolina Press, 1935. 313p. Illus.

Sheppard tells the stories of the everyday lives of the people of the Toe River Valley, between the Blue Ridge Mountains in North Carolina and the Tennessee line. She writes about farming, hunting, schooling, leisure activities, courtship and marriage—all the stuff of life. She often interjects the words of a folk ballad to illustrate a particular story or theme, as with her use of the ballad "The Quiltin'," despite its name a tale of jealousy and murder, to illustrate the story of a mountain woman who killed her husband with an axe.

443. Wigginton, Eliot, ed. *The Foxfire Book.* New York: Anchor Books, Doubleday, 1972. 384p. Illus.

Material from various editions of *Foxfire,* a folklore magazine published by students at a Georgia high school, make up the contents of this book. Most of the material concerns customs and everyday life: soap making, hog killing, churning, weather, country crafts such as furniture making and basket making, hunting, faith healing, and moonshining.

Foxfire as a project and a publication sparked many similar projects in towns throughout the United States.

444. Williams, Michael Ann. *Great Smoky Mountains Folklife.* Jackson: Univ. Press of Mississippi, 1995. xviii, 216p. Illus. Bibliographical notes. Index. (Folklife in the South). 95-13341. 0-87805-792-7.

Williams says in her introduction that the folklife of the Great Smoky Mountains, in Tennessee and North Carolina, is so rich and varied that this book makes no pretense at completeness. It is instead selective.

In it, Williams presents an introductory section on the history of settlement of the area, and how the region's folklife was identified and studied during the late nineteenth and early twentieth centuries. The bulk of the book is a look at various aspects of folklife: music and dance; material folk traditions (architecture, basketry, and quilting); food, drink, and medicine; and verbal lore. In this section she points out various changes that have

occurred within the folklife of the region, stating correctly that such changes are inevitable, as folklife changes continually. The final section of the book looks at the impact that tourism, especially the creation of the national park, has had on the development of folklife traditions.

445. Wilson, Charles Morrow. *Backwoods America.* Chapel Hill: Univ. of North Carolina Press, 1935. 209p. Illus. by Bayard Wootten.

Wilson writes of the country people of Arkansas and Missouri in the Ozarks. He maintains that life there has not changed between Elizabethan times and the times he writes of. His chapters include information on local language, leisure time pursuits, such as music and hunting, humor, justice, crafts, religion and folk belief, and professions. Taken together, the chapters present a look at a way of life still current in the 1930s but almost vanished today.

446. Windham, Kathryn Tucker. *Alabama: One Big Front Porch.* Tuscaloosa: Univ. of Alabama Press, 1975. 158p. Illus. Index. 75-30455. 0-87397-089-6. Windham's book is a mixture of stories of historical characters, superstitions, information about the ways followed in the old days, tales of mythical animals, such as the hoopsnake, and even old recipes. It is profusely illustrated with photographs of present-day people and places. The whole package evokes a way of life in a particular section of the country.

Folklore for Children

447. Causey, Beth G. *South Carolina Legends.* Mount Pleasant, SC: Hope Publishing Co., 1969. 64p. Illus. by Janet Thurston.

Causey retells four legends of the area for children. Two of the legends concern the American Revolution.

448. Chase, Richard. *The Jack Tales.* Boston: Houghton Mifflin, 1943. xiii, 202p. Illus. by Berkeley Williams Jr. Index. Glossary. Appendices: Brief essay giving a history of the interest in the folktale in this country.

Explanations of sources of the tales are included in this book, as is a discussion of parallels between these tales and others. Most people know the tale "Jack and the Bean Stalk." Here are many more tales of Jack, such as the time he set off to ask the North Wind not to blow. They are tales told by families in North Carolina, in the southern Appalachians. They tell the stories of Jack, an ordinary boy who has fantastic adventures and meets frequently with magical beings, but who always returns to his plain life.

According to Herbert Halpert, who wrote the appendix, Jack is in some ways the opposite of one American hero: the hardworking man who succeeds due to perseverance and honesty. By contrast, Jack is a trickster, who succeeds partly through his wits, but mostly through luck.

449. Doucet, Sharon Arms. *Lapin Plays Possum: Trickster Tales from the Louisiana Bayou.* New York: Melanie Droupa Books/Farrar, Straus and Giroux, 2002. 64p. Illus. by Scott Cook. Glossary. 2001-29387. 0-374-34328-4.

Br'er Rabbit and Br'er Fox, who originated in Africa and who "quarreled all the way to French-speaking Louisiana" (Author's note, p. 63), here appear as Compère Lapin and Compère Bouki. Lapin plays his usual tricks, once more enrages Bouki, and escapes as always into the briar patch.

The full-color illustrations are detailed and appealing.

450. Hamilton, Virginia. *When Birds Could Talk and Bats Could Sing: The Adventures of Bruh Sparrow, Sis Wren, and Their Friends.* New York: Blue Sky Press, 1996. 63p. Illus. 95-15307. 0-590-47372-7.

All the stories here have morals. The hummingbird lost its voice when the wind became angry at hummingbird's spying on him; the wind took hummingbird's voice. Moral: Don't interfere in other people's business. The buzzard is bald because, after following an old, sick horse for years, waiting for it to die, the horse in its last act kicked the buzzard and tore all the feathers off its head. Moral: Don't pick on the poor and weak.

The tales are charmingly told with bold, full-color, full-page illustrations. Here are illustrations of birds in straw hats, a buzzard in a stovepipe hat, and a peacock in a top hat. This is definitely a read-aloud book.

451. Jaquith, Priscilla. *Bo Rabbit, Smart for True: Folktales from the Gullah.* New York: Philomel Books, 1981. 55p. Illus. by Ed Young. Bibliog. 80-13275. 0-399-20793-7. 0-399-61179-7lib binding.

Jaquith retells four Gulluh tales. Her telling of the tales is based on the tales as transcribed by Albert H. Stoddard, a native of Daufuskie Island off South Carolina's coast. He recorded the tales years after transcribing them, for the Archive of Folk Song of the Library of Congress.

Jaquith provides notes on the origin of each tale.

452. Johnston, Marianne. *Casey Jones.* New York: PowerKids Press, 2001. 24p. Illus. Index. Glossary. 2001-274568. 0-8239-5582-6.

Other titles in this series for children

are entitled *Johnny Appleseed, Daniel Boone, Jim Bowie, Paul Bunyan,* and *Davy Crockett.* All contain a brief life story of the individual, information geared to encouraging children to learn about heroes and folk characters, and a page explaining how the character is remembered today.

An index and a glossary of unfamiliar words help children become familiar with the organization of academic books.

453. ——. *Daniel Boone.* New York: PowerKids Press, 2001. 24p. Illus. Index. Glossary. (American Legends.) 2001-274569. 0-82395579-6.

One of a series, this brief book gives highlights from Boone's life, from his birth in Pennsylvania to his death at age eighty-five in Missouri. Johnston also gives information on "what is a legend" and why legends are important and enjoyable. Other books in the series are entitled *Jim Bowie, Davy Crockett, Casey Jones,* and *Johnny Appleseed.*

454. ——. *Davy Crockett.* New York: PowerKids Press, 2001. 24p. Illus. Index. Glossary. (American Legends). 2001-274567. 0-8239-5581-8.

Like the others in this series, this book encourages children to become acquainted with legends and legendary characters. The biographical information, from his birth in Tennessee to his death at the Alamo, is brief and heavily illustrated. Johnston also gives information about how Crockett is memorialized today.

Other books in the series are entitled *Jim Bowie, Daniel Boone, Casey Jones,* and *Johnny Appleseed.*

455. Lenski, Lois. *Blue Ridge Billy.* New York: J. B. Lippincott Company, 1946. 203p. Illus. by Lois Lenski. 46-6400.

Lenski wrote a series of children's books about various regions of the United States, including the Newbery Medal–winning *Strawberry Girl. Blue Ridge Billy* concerns a boy in North Carolina, his life, his adventures, his family and neighbors. The story allows Lenski to describe farming methods, household duties, family relationships, hunting, and such country crafts as basket making.

456. ——. *Judy's Journey.* New York: J. B. Lippincott Company,1947. 212p. Illus. by Lois Lenski. 47-4504. 0-397-30131-6.

Judy's Journey, another in Lenski's regional series for children, concerns a family forced by the Depression to travel as farmworkers, often living in migrant labor camps, and sometimes in their car. The story takes them from Alabama through Georgia, Florida, the Carolinas, Virginia, and Maryland into New Jersey. Lenski's story shows the warmth of family life that prevails in spite of hardships. It also shows the way of life common to people in this situation at this time. Woven into the story is much information about both farming and schooling.

457. ——. *Strawberry Girl.* Philadelphia: J. B. Lippincott Company, 1945. xii, 194p. Illus. by Lois Lenski. 45-7609.

One of Lenski's regional stories, about children who live in various parts of the United States, this is about a "strawberry family" in Florida, who grow strawberries and other crops. The oldest girl in the family longs for a wider world than that offered on the farm. Through the telling of the story of this girl, with her dreams, her feud with a neighboring family, her work on the farm, Lenski paints many unique scenes. She writes of a taffy pull; of a traveling animal doctor who tends to the teeth of both animals and family members; of a church social; and of education in a one-room school. The black-

and-white illustrations add to the reality of the book.

Even though old, this still tells a fascinating story for today's children. Lenski received the Newbery Medal, for excellence in children's literature, for this book.

458. Lester, Julius. *Further Tales of Uncle Remus: The Misadventures of Brer Rabbit, Brer Fox, Brer Wold, the Doodang, and Other Creatures.* New York: Dial, 1990. 148p. Illus. by Jerry Pinckney. 88-20223. 0-8037-0610-3;0-8037-0611-1lib binding.

459. ——. *The Last Tales of Uncle Remus.* New York: Dial, 1994. xvi, 156p. Illus. by Jerry Pinckney. 93-7531. 0-8037-1303-7; 0-8037-1304-5lib binding.

460. ——. *More Tales of Uncle Remus: Further Adventures of Brer Rabbit, His Friends, Enemies, and Others.* New York: Dial, 1988. xvi, 143p. Illus. by Jerry Pinckney. 86-32890. 0-8037-0419-4; 0-8037-0420-3lib binding

461. ——. *The Tales of Uncle Remus: The Adventures of Brer Rabbit, His Friends, Enemies, and Others.* New York: Dial, 1988. xxi, 151p.Illus. by Jerry Pinckney. 85-20449. 0-8037-0271-X; 0-8037-0272-8lib binding.

These are beautiful and valuable books. In four volumes, Lester retells the stories told by the Uncle Remus character, of Br'er Fox, Br'er Wolf, and the beloved Br'er Rabbit, the small, weak animal who always triumphs. In Lester's words, "Brer Rabbit is us" (Introduction, *More Tales of Uncle Remus,* viii). He states that even though Br'er Rabbit sometimes uses methods that are less than ethical, this reflects the human condition—we are bad as well as good, and Br'er Rabbit indicates this. Br'er Rabbit reflects the "whole" of humanness, not an unattainable perfection.

Lester's introductions are as interesting as the tales themselves. He discusses his decision to retell the tales, and more specifically to retain at least in name the character of Uncle Remus, with its echo of slavery and plantation days. His explanation is that the character provides a voice for the tales, one that he has updated by using some contemporary black English and contemporary references. He contends further that it is the character, the voice, which has made the tales endure. However, he uses the character principally in the titles of the volumes, providing a historical link to the tales recounted by Joel Chandler Harris. The tales themselves are told by a voice, which make them truly tales to be read aloud or told by a storyteller, but the voice is not necessarily that of Uncle Remus.

Lester states that these tales comprise "the largest single collection of Afro-American folktales ever collected and published" (Foreword, *The Tales of Uncle Remus,* xiii), collected with integrity and told with an effort to put the authentic language on paper.

Pinckney's illustrations, many in full color, are a delight.

These four volumes of tales, told by an eminent Afro-American folklorist and illustrated by a winner of both the Caldecott Honor Book award and the Coretta Scott King Award for Illustration, are not to be missed.

462. Lyons, Mary E. *Sorrow's Kitchen: The Life and Folklore of Zora Neale Hurston.* New York: Collier, 1993. xiii, 144p. Illus. Index. Bibliog. (Charles Scribner's Sons Books for Young Readers). 90-8058. 0-684-19198-9.

Lyons has written a biography of Hurston, interweaving her own research and words with long passages from

Hurston's own writings. None of the tales Hurston collected is reproduced, but there are many passages concerning her experiences in collecting folklore.

This is written for middle school– and high school–age readers, and would be a good introduction to young people of this eminent folklorist.

463. Reneaux, J. J. *How Animals Saved the People: Animal Tales from the South.* New York: HarperCollins, 2001. 64p. Illus. by James Ransome. Glossary. Bibliog. 99-52379. 0-688-16253-3, trade; 0-688-16254-1, library binding.

Reneaux retells eight tales from the South. Categories are Appalachian, African American, Native American, Creole, and English, Scots-Irish, and German. Some are humorous; others are scary.

Illustrations are in full color.

464. Sanfield, Steve. *The Adventures of High John, the Conqueror.* New York: Dell, 1992. xii, 113p. Illus. by John Ward. Bibliog. 0-440-40556-4.

Zora Neale Hurston collected many of the High John tales in her book *Mules and Men.* High John was a human cousin of Br'er Rabbit, the small, weak creature who survived by being cleverer than his enemies. He played tricks on the slaveholders to such an extent that they never knew whether he was working for them or against them—and that was just the way he wanted it. In these tales, High John fools not only the master but many times his fellow slaves as well.

Sanfield, a storyteller for many years, calls High John "that hope-bringer, that will-to-dream" (Introduction, p. 7).

465. Scheer, George F., ed. *Cherokee Animal Tales.* 2d. Tulsa, OK: Council Oak Books, 1998. 80p. Illus. by Robert Frankenberg. 91-73537. 0-933031-59-9; 0-933031-60-2pa.

In 1997, James Mooney spent time with the Cherokee of North Carolina, studying their language and their stories. He gathered myths and folk beliefs, and set them down in English. The tales he transcribed, of Rabbit the trickster, of the Deer, the Mole, the Possum, and the Red-bird, are told here in his words, with very little change. The illustrations make them appealing for younger readers.

An introduction, also by Scheer, tells the history of the Cherokee, from their time in the North Carolina area, through various "relocations" by the American government, including their journey along the infamous Trail of Tears.

466. Van Laan, Nancy. *With a Whoop and a Holler: A Bushel of Lore from Way Down South.* New York: Atheneum Books for Young Readers, an imprint of Simon and Schuster Children's Publishing Division, 1998; repr., New York: Aladdin Paperbacks, 2001. vii, 102p. Illus. by Scott Cook. 96-24336. 0-689-81061-x; 0-689-84474-3pa.

The titles of these tales are enough to make you laugh: "How Come Ol' Buzzard Boards," "Mister Grumpy Rides the Clouds," "Did You Feed My Cow?" Van Laan's intent in this collection was to recreate the southern stories she heard in childhood and to write them so that they could be told out loud and enjoyed by children today. The stories are divided up regionally: the Bayou (Louisiana); the Deep South (Mississippi, Alabama, and parts of Georgia, South Carolina, and North Carolina); and the Mountains (parts of Georgia, South Carolina, North Carolina, and Virginia).

She includes a couple of Uncle Remus stories and a Jack tale, because, she says, "these are so universally identified with Southern folk literature" (p. vii), but she includes other less-familiar ones, and rhymes, riddles, and superstitions as well. Many of the stories involve animals, both wild animals such as possum and farm animals—chickens, mules, and goats.

The illustrations, in full color, are fanciful and appealing.

467. Vencill, Jerry. *Old Jonah's Book of Tales.* Pounding Mill, VA: Henderson, 1997. 59p. Illus. by Ken Henderson. Glossary. 1-891029-00-2.

Vencill is a storyteller who tells his stories in the persona of Old Jonah, a mountainman dressed in buckskin and carrying a rifle. The tall tales here are ones he has told; they are from the Clinch Mountains in southwest Virginia. They are told in Appalachian dialect and illustrated with black-and-white line drawings. In one of the tall tales, Old Jonah goes to the moon and back, riding on a buzzard.

468. ——. *Old Jonah's Book of Tall Tales.* Pounding Mill, VA: Henderson, 1998. 136p. Illus. by Ken W. Henderson. Glossary. 1-891029-01-0.

This second book of tales from Jerry "Old Jonah" Vencill is, like the first, written in the dialect of the Appalachian Mountains. All are told in the first person, the persona of Old Jonah.

Vencill adds a glossary of mountain words.

469. Weintraub, Aileen. *Blackbeard: Eighteenth-Century Pirate of the Spanish Main and Carolina Coast.* New York: PowerKids Press, 2002. 24p. Illus. Glossary. Index. (The Library of Pirates). 00-11240. 0-8239-5794-2.

Each page of text of this brief book tells one story about Blackbeard: his blockade of Charleston, South Carolina, or the hardships sailors of that time endured.

The glossary and index make this book an introduction to research and study techniques for children.

Literary Authors: A Selected List

Below is a selected list of authors who reflect and interpret the history and atmosphere of their region. These are authors of novels, poems, short stories, or reminiscences. Through reading the works of these authors, one can acquire knowledge of the history, people, and flavor of the region. This is not a complete list, either of authors or of their works, but rather one calculated to start readers exploring and discovering their own favorites.

Cabell, James Branch, 1879–1958

> *The Devil's Own Dear Son: A Comedy of the Fatted Calf*
> *The Eagle's Branch*
> *Something About Eve: A Comedy of Fig-Leaves*

Cable, George Washington, 1844–1925

> *The Cavalier*
> *Creoles and Cajuns: Stories of Old Louisiana*
> *Gideon's Band: A Tale of the Mississippi*
> *The Grandissimes: A Story of Creole Life*
> *The Silent South*

Caldwell, Erskine, 1903–1987

> *Complete Stories*
> *The Earnshaw Neighborhood*
> *God's Little Acre*
> *Tobacco Road*

Chesnut, Mary Boykin, 1823–1886

A Diary from Dixie

Chesnutt, Charles Waddell, 1858–1932

Collected Stories of Charles W. Chesnutt
The Conjure Woman
The Short Fiction of Charles Chesnutt
Stories, Novels, and Essays
The Wife of His Youth: And Other Stories
of the Color Line

Chopin, Kate, 1851–1904

The Awakening
Bayou Folk

Clemens, Samuel Langhorne
(Mark Twain) 1835–1910

The Adventures of Huckleberry Finn
The Adventures of Tom Sawyer
The Celebrated Jumping Frog of Calaveras
County and Other Sketches
Life on the Mississippi

Crockett, David, 1786–1836

An Account of Colonel Crockett's Tour to
the North and Down East, in the Year of
Our Lord One Thousand
A Narrative of the Life of David Crockett,
of the State of Tennessee

Faulkner, William, 1897–1962

Absalom, Absalom!
Collected Stories
Go Down, Moses
The Hamlet
Light in August
Sanctuary

Glasgow, Ellen, 1873–1945

The Deliverance: A Romance of the
Virginia Tobacco Fields
The Freeman
The Voice of the People

Green, Paul, 1894–1981

In Abraham's Bosom
Land of Nod: And Other Stories

Harris, Joel Chandler, 1848–1908

Free Joe, and Other Georgian Sketches
Nights with Uncle Remus: Myths and
Legends of the Old Plantation
On the Plantation: A Story of a Georgia
Boy's Adventures during the War
Uncle Remus, His Songs and His Sayings:
The Folklore of the Old Plantation

Lanier, Sidney, 1842–1881

The Centennial Edition of the Works of
Sidney Lanier
Poems of Sidney Lanier
Tiger-Lilies: A Novel

McCullers, Carson, 1917–1967

The Ballad of the Sad Café and Other
Stories
The Member of the Wedding
Reflections in a Golden Eye

Murfree, Mary Noailles
(Charles Egbert Craddock), 1850–1922

In the Tennessee Mountains
The Prophet of the Great Smoky
Mountains

Rawlings, Marjorie Kinnan, 1896–1953

Cross Creek
The Sojourner
The Yearling

Read, Opie, 1852–1939

An Arkansas Planter
The Carpetbagger
A Kentucky Colonel
On the Suwanee River
A Tennessee Judge
The Waters of Caney Fork: A Romance of
Tennessee

Russell, Irwin, 1853–1879

Christmas-Night in the Quarter and Other
Poems
Poems

Simms, William Gilmore, 1806–1870

Beauchampe or, The Kentucky Tragedy:
A Sequel to Charlemont
Border Beagles: A Tale of Mississippi
Charlemont or, The Pride of the Village,
a Tale of Kentucky
Guy Rivers: A Tale of Georgia
Katharine Walton, or, The Rebel of
Dorchester

Stuart, Jesse, 1906–1984

Cradle of the Copperheads
A Jesse Stuart Harvest
Men of the Mountains
My Land Has a Voice

Warren, Robert Penn, 1905–1989

All the King's Men

At Heaven's Gate
Night Rider

Welty, Eudora, 1909–2001

The Collected Stories of Eudora Welty
Delta Wedding
The Golden Apples

Wolfe, Thomas, 1900–1938

Look Homeward, Angel
Of Time and the River: A Legend of
Man's Hunger in His Youth
The Web and the Rock
You Can't Go Home Again

Wright, Richard, 1908–1960

Black Boy: A Record of Childhood and
Youth
Native Son

Young, Stark, 1881–1963

The Pavilion: Of People and Times
Remembered, of Stories and Places
So Red the Rose
River House

Museums of the Region: A Selected List

Museums that feature everyday life abound in all regions of the country. Through the display of clothing, farm implements, household goods, industrial tools, or entire houses, workshops, and communities, these museums can help people of today understand and appreciate the lives lived by those who came before. The list below does not mention all museums in the region, but by browsing through it, one can get a glimpse of the richness of museum offerings. Explore on your own and discover even more fascinating museums.

Alabama

Florence

Pope's Tavern Museum
203 Hermitage Drive
Florence, Alabama 35630
256-760-6439
http://www.ohwy.com/al/p/poptavmu.htm

Mobile

Historic Mobile Preservation Society
300 Oakleigh Place
Mobile, Alabama 36604
334-432-6161
http://www.historicmobile.org

Arkansas

Berryville

Heritage Center Museum
1880 Court House on Square
Berryville, Arkansas 72616
Mailing address:
P.O. Box 249
Berryville, Arkansas 72616
870-423-6312
http://www.ohwy.com/ar/c/caroctyh.htm

Eureka Springs

Gay Nineties Button and Doll Museum

Off Route 62
Eureka Springs, Arkansas 72632
Mailing address:
Route 2, Box 452
Berryville, Arkansas 72616
501-253-8588
http://www.arkansaskids.com/
*   detail.asp?ID=745*

Springdale

Shiloh Museum of Ozark History
118 West Johnson Avenue
Springdale, Arkansas 72764
501-750-8165
http://www.springdaleark/shiloh

Florida

Bradenton

Manatee Village Historic Park
604 15th Street
Bradenton, Florida 34208
941-749-7165
http://www.clerkofcourts.com

Coral Gables

Coral Gables Merrick House
907 Coral Way
Coral Gables, Florida 33134
Mailing address:
C/o Historic Preservation Department
City of Coral Gables
City Hall
405 Biltmore Way
Coral Gables, Florida 33134
305-460-5361
http://www.citybeautiful.net

Dade City

Pioneer Florida Museum Association,
    Inc.
15602 Pioneer Museum Road
Dade City, Florida 33526
Mailing address:
P.O. Box 335
Dade City, Florida 33526
352-567-0262
http://www.dadecity.com/museum

Delray Beach

Cornell Museum of Art and History
51 North Swinton Avenue
Delray Beach, Florida 33444
407-243-7922
http://www.oldschool.org/oldschool

Key West

Key West Lighthouse Museum
938 Whitehead at Truman
Key West, Florida 33041
305-294-0012
http://www.kwahs.org

Pensacola

Historic Pensacola Village
120 Church Street
Pensacola, Florida 32501
Mailing address:
P.O. Box 12866
Pensacola, Florida 32576
850-595-5985
http://www.historicpensacola.org

Georgia

Albany

Thronateeska Heritage Foundation, Inc.
100 Roosevelt Avenue
Albany, Georgia 31701
912-435-1572
http://www.heritagecenter.org

Columbus

Historic Columbus Foundation, Inc.
700 Broadway
Columbus, Georgia 31901
Mailing address:
P.O. Box 5312
Columbus, Georgia 31906
706-322-0756
http://www.historiccolumbus.com

Crawfordville

Confederate Museum
456 Alexander Street
Crawfordville, Georgia 30631
Mailing address:
P.O. Box 310
Crawfordville, Georgia 30631
706-456-2221
http://www.g-net.net/~ahssp/

Rossville

The Chief John Ross House
200 East Lake Avenue
Rossville, Georgia 30741
Mailing address:
826 Chickamauga Avenue
Rossville, Georgia 30741
706-861-3954

Stone Mountain

Georgia's Stone Mountain Park
Highway 78
Stone Mountain, Georgia 30086
Mailing address:
P.O. Box 778
Stone Mountain, Georgia 30086
404-498-5690
http://www.stonemountainpark.org

Kentucky

Danville

McDowell House and Apothecary Shop
125 South 2nd Street
Danville, Kentucky 40422
606-236-2804
http://www.mcdowellhouse.org

Frankfort

Kentucky Historical Society
100 West Broadway
Frankfort, Kentucky 40601
502-564-1792
http://www.kyhistory.org

Lexington

Mary Todd Lincoln House
578 West Main
Lexington, Kentucky 40507
Mailing address:
P.O. Box 132
Lexington, Kentucky 40588
859-233-9999
http://www.cr.nps.gov/nr/travel/lexington/
   mtl.htm

Louisiana

Bermuda

Beaufort Plantation Home
4078 Highway 494 and Highway 119
Bermuda, Louisiana 71456
Mailing address:
919 Parkway
Natchitoches, Louisiana 71457
318-352-9580

Melrose

Melrose Plantation Home Complex
Melrose Plantation House Complex
Melrose General Delivery
Melrose, Louisiana 71452
Mailing address:
P.O. Box 2248
Natchitoches, Louisiana 71457
318-379-0055
http://www.natchitoches.net/melrose

New Orleans

The Historic New Orleans Collection
533 Royal Street
New Orleans, Louisiana 70130
504-523-4662
http://www.hnoc.org

New Orleans Pharmacy Museum
514 Rue Chartres
New Orleans, Louisiana 70130
504-565-8027
http://www.pharmacymuseum.org

Shreveport

Pioneer Heritage Center
One University Place
Shreveport, Louisiana 71115
318-797-5332
http://www.lsus.edu

Mississippi

Hattiesburg

Turner House Museum
500 Bay
Hattiesburg, Mississippi 39401
601-582-1771
*http://www.museumsusa.org/data/
    museums/MS/159129.htm*

Pascagoula

Old Spanish Fort and Museum
4602 Fort Street
Pascagoula, Mississippi 39567
228-769-1505
http://www.ohwy.com/ms/o/olspstmu.htm

Vaughan

Casey Jones Museum
Main Street
Vaughan, Mississippi 39179
Mailing address:
10901 Vaughan Road, #1
Vaughan, Mississippi 39179
662-673-9864
*http://www.trainweb.org/caseyjones/home/
    html*

North Carolina

Asheville

Southern Highland Craft Guild at the
    Folk Art Center
Milepost 382
Blue Ridge Parkway
Asheville, North Carolina 28805
Mailing address:
P.O. Box 9545
Ashville, North Carolina 28815
828-298-7928
http://www.southernhighlandguild.org

Bailey

The Country Doctor Museum
6629 Vance Street
Bailey, North Carolina 27807
Mailing address:
P.O. Box 34
Bailey, North Carolina 27807
919-235-4165
http://www.ohwy.com/nc/c/cntydrmu.htm

Cullowhee

Mountain Heritage Center
Western Carolina University
Cullowhee, North Carolina 28723
828-227-7129
http://www.wcu.edu/mhc

Winston-Salem

Museum of Early Southern Decorative
    Arts
924 South Main Street
Winston-Salem, North Carolina 27101

Mailing address:
P.O. Box 10310
Winston-Salem, North Carolina 27108
336-721-7360
http://www.mesda.org

South Carolina

Bennettsville

Jennings-Brown House Female Academy
123 South Marlboro Street
Bennettsville, South Carolina 29512
Mailing address:
P.O. Box 178
Bennettsville, South Carolina 29512
843-479-5624

Charleston

Old Exchange and Provost Dungeon
122 East Bay Street
Charleston, South Carolina 29401
843-727-2165
http://www.oldexchange.com

Columbia

South Carolina Confederate Relic Room
and Museum
World War Memorial Building
920 Sumter Street
Columbia, South Carolina 29201
803-898-8095
http://www.state.sc.us/cr

Tennessee

Athens

McMinn County Living Heritage
Museum
522 West Madison Avenue
Athens, Tennessee 37303
Mailing address:
P.O. Box 889
Athens, Tennessee 37303
423-745-0329
http://www.usit.com/livher/

Chattanooga

Chattanooga African Museum/
Bessie Smith Hall
200 East Martin Luther King Boulevard
Chattanooga, Tennessee 37403
Mailing address:
P.O. Box 11493
Chattanooga, Tennessee 37401
423-266-8658
http://www.caamhistory.com

Hermitage

The Hermitage:
Home of President Andrew Jackson
4580 Rachel's Lane
Hermitage, Tennessee 37076
615-889-2941
http://www.thehermitage.com

Memphis

Mississippi River Museum at
Mud Island River Park
125 North Front Street

Memphis, Tennessee 38103
901-576-7230
http://www.mudisland.com

Morristown

Crockett Tavern Museum
2002 Morningside Drive
Morristown, Tennessee 37814
615-587-9900
*http://www.morristowncityhall.com/
    tavern.htm*

Virginia

Alexandria

Gadsby's Tavern Museum
134 North Royal Street
Alexandria, Virginia 22314
703-838-4242
http://www.gadsbystavern.org

Clifton Forge

Allegheny Highlands Arts and Crafts
    Center, Inc.
439 Ridgeway Street
Clifton Forge, Virginia 24422
Mailing address:
P.O. Box 273
Clifton Forge, Virginia 24422
703-862-4447
*http://www.members.aol.com/ahchamber/
    areaeven.htm#ARTCRAFT*

Newport News

Virginia Living Museum

524 J. Clyde Morris Boulevard
Newport News, Virginia 23601
757-595-1900
http://www.valivingmuseum.org

Staunton

Frontier Culture Museum
1290 Richmond Road
Staunton, Virginia 24401
Mailing address:
P.O. Box 810
Staunton, Virginia 24402
540-332-7850
http://www.frontiermuseum.org

West Virginia

Fairmont

Prickett's Fort
Route 3
Box 407
Fairmont, West Virginia 26554
304-363-3030
http://www.prickettsfort.org

Harpers Ferry

Harpers Ferry National Historical Park
Fillmore Street
Harpers Ferry, West Virginia 25425
Mailing address:
P.O. Box 65
Harpers Ferry, West Virginia 25425
304-535-6224
http://www.nps.gov/hafe/home.htm

Journals on Folklore of the South: A Selected List

The journals in the list below publish articles on folklore of the region. Some are scholarly; others are more popular. Many other journals and newsletters exist. Often, these are smaller, of more local interest, and published by museums, historical societies, folklore organizations, community groups, and schools. Explore your own area to see what other publications of folklore exist.

Appalachian Heritage
The Daily Clog
Florida Folklife Resource Directory
Folk Arts Notes
Foxfire
Louisiana Folklore Miscellany
Mid-America Folklore
Mississippi Folklife
North Carolina Folklore Journal
Southern Folklore

Web Sites: A Selected List

Below is a list of a few Web sites dealing with folklore of the region. You can find other Web sites by doing an Internet search on a search engine such as Google or Yahoo!, or by looking for the Web sites of various folklore organizations with which you are familiar.

Adventures of Colonel Daniel Boone, Formerly a Hunter: Containing a Narrative of the Wars of Kentucky, http://www.earlyamerica.com/lives/boone/index.html
Full text of the 1784 publication that es-

tablished Daniel Boone as a hero and legend.

Appalshop, http://www.Appalshop.org
Appalshop is a cultural center that facilitates study about the Appalachian Mountains. They produce theatre, radio, and television programs and help create and promote festivals of folklife.

Augusta Heritage Center, Davis and Elkins College, http://www.augustaheritage.com/
The Augusta Heritage Center conducts workshops in various traditional crafts and activities. The site provides information and a registration form.

Frank C. Brown Collection, http://www.lcweb.loc.gov/spcoll/036.html
The Frank C. Brown Collection, at the Library of Congress, contains recordings made by Brown of North Carolina folk songs.

Ghosts of Sweet Briar College, http://ghosts.sbc.edu/
Ghost stories about Sweet Briar College in Sweet Briar, Virginia.

Gumbo Pages, http://www.gumbopages.com/index.html
Information about cuisine, music, cultural attractions of New Orleans and Louisiana. Provides recipes and links to other culinary and music sources.

Joseph S. Hall Collection, http://www.lcweb.loc.gov/spcoll/105.html
The collection is of recordings of people who lived at one time within the Great Smoky Mountains National Park. Recordings contain folktales, local history, information about customs, and songs.

Lower Mississippi Delta: African American Heritage, http://www.cr.nps.gov/delta/afriamer/heritage.htm
Sponsored by the U.S. National Park Service, this site provides information on the history and culture of African Americans from the Lower Mississippi River Delta in Louisiana, including information on folklore.

Seminole Tribe of Florida, http://www.seminoletribe.com/
Information about the Seminole Tribe, including legends.

Southern Folklife Collection, http://www.lib.unc.edu/mss/sfc1/
Information on materials at the Southern Folklife Collection in the Manuscripts Department at the University of North Carolina at Chapel Hill. The collection has much information about traditional Southern music.

Uncle Remus: Social Context and Ramifications, http://xroads.virginia.edu/~UG97/remus/remus.html
Both information about Joel Chandler Harris, the creator of the Uncle Remus stories, and some of the tales themselves, with commentary, are included.

University of Arkansas Collection, http://www.lcweb.loc.gov/spcoll/249.html
Information about the Library of Congress collection on the University of Arkansas, including recordings of traditional music: ballads, work songs, prison songs, and spirituals.

Vance Randolph Collection, http://www.lcweb.loc.gov/spcoll/193.html
A description of The Library of Congress's Vance Randolph Collection, including recordings of Ozark folk songs. Also includes field notes, photographs, and some of Randolph's correspondence and papers.

Virginia Folklore Society, http://minerva.acc.virginia.edu/~vafolk/
Web site for the society, including information about activities and membership information.

William Leonard Eury Appalachian Collection, http://www.library.appstate.edu/appcoll/
Information about the William Leonard Eury Appalachian Collection at Appalachian State University Library in Boone, North Carolina. The collection contains materials about the Southern Highlands, including information about Appalachian folklore.

Works Progress Administration (WPA) Life Histories, http://eagle.vsla.edu/wpa/
Contains about 1,300 life histories, including interviews with former slaves. Interviews were conducted by workers with the Works Progress Administration.

CHAPTER FOUR

The Midwest

Illinois, Indiana, Iowa, Kansas, Michigan,
Minnesota, Missouri, Nebraska, Ohio, Wisconsin

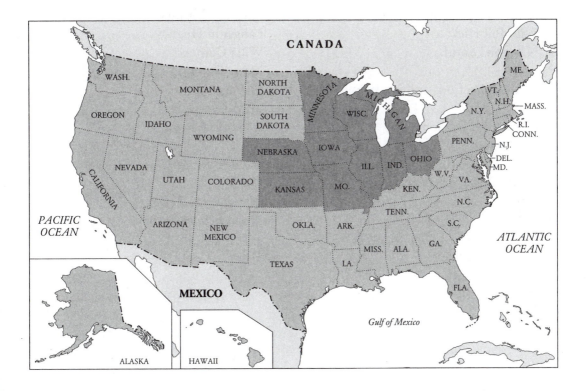

The Midwest: Checklist

Look for tales on:

Tricksters
Mackinac Island
Loggers and logging camps
Buried treasure

And for characters such as:

Paul Bunyan
Mike Fink
Johnny Appleseed
Wild Bill Hickok
"Oregon" Smith

Look for collections and works by:

Richard M. Dorson
Opie Read
Roger L. Welsch
Henry Rowe Schoolcraft

Find music collections by:

Earl Clifton Beck
Mary O. Eddy

Introduce children to:

French tales
Tales of the Arikara, the Chippewa,
   the Winnebago
The Hodag
The Alligator Horse

Explore the rich literature of the region
with:

Sherwood Anderson
Langston Hughes
Willa Cather
Mark Twain
Wallace Stegner
Theodore Dreiser
Edna Ferber

Consult journals:

Mid-America Folklore
Midwestern Folklore

THE MIDWEST: INTRODUCTION

The forms and functions of Midwestern folklore are universal, however, Native American cultures, settlement patterns, historical circumstances, occupations, and the physical environment contributed to a blend of folk traditions unique to the Midwest. As in other regions of the United States, the earliest known examples of Midwestern folklore are Native American traditions. From Schoolcraft's *Myth of Hiawatha* (1856) to Douglas Parks's *Traditional Narratives of the Arikara Indians* (1991), Native American folklore, especially narrative folklore, is well represented in the Midwestern section of this sourcebook. (Sources mentioned in this introductory essay without complete bibliographic information can be found in the Bibliography section of this chapter.) Mentor L. Williams edited a collection of *Schoolcraft's Indian Legends* (1956), including tales of Manabozho (also called Manabush, Nanabozho, Nanabush, Wenabozho, Winabojo, and Winabijou, as the name varies among tribes and villages of the upper Midwest and Great Lakes area). Manabozho is not simply a prankster and clown, like some of the tricksters in Bernice G. Anderson's *Trickster Tales from Prairie Lodgefires* (1979); he also is a culture hero, the creator of life and ruler of the earth, as Victor Barnouw's *Wisconsin Chippewa Myths and Tales and Their Relation to Chippewa Life* (1977) shows. Manabozho's stories explain the origin of the world as well as the characteristics of plants, animals, and other natural features. In the Upper Peninsula of Michigan, Dorson (1952) collected secular tales of this ancient mythological trickster.

Native Americans freely borrowed and adapted European tales and influenced at least one type of traditional narrative told by all Midwesterners—place-name legends (traditional accounts of the origin of topographic names), exemplified in Dorothy Moulding Brown's popular little book, *Wisconsin Indian Place-Name Legends* (1948). As this sourcebook illustrates, many compilers of Native American tales have reworked the narratives for popular and/or juvenile audiences, but European settlers generally did not borrow and adapt Native American oral tales. The exception, however, might be early French traders, missionaries, travelers, and settlers, who fraternized with Native Americans, sharing traditions and adapting many aspects of Native American cultures, notably material culture. Because of the impact of the environment on culture, immigrant groups generally borrow more material culture traits from indigenous groups than local groups borrow from immigrants. Accordingly, European settlers borrowed extensively from Native American material culture in the areas of subsistence, hunting, fishing, travel, medicine, and costume—some temporarily, some permanently. French trappers, for example, borrowed and adapted the skin shirts, leggings, moccasins, and breechclouts of Native Americans as well as their birch-bark canoes and their hunting, fishing, and trapping practices. The environment also influenced the material culture of later settlers. In forested areas of the Midwest, trees played an important role in traditional arts, crafts, and architecture, but in the Great Plains, where trees are scarce, grass, rushes, and sod were used instead of wood. Two books illustrating that the nature of Midwestern traditional arts, crafts, and architecture is essentially determined by environment are Warren Roberts's *Log Buildings of Southern Indiana* (Blooomington, IN: Trickster Press, 1996) and Roger Welsch's *Sod Walls: The Story of the Nebraska Sod House* (1968). The physical environment also has had an impact on Midwestern narratives. For example, Danielson (in *Sense of Place: American Regional Cultures*, ed. Barbara Allen and Thomas J. Schlereth, Lexington: Univ. Press of Kentucky, 1990) examines Midwestern legends and personal experience tales about tornados and their relation to regional consciousness and identity. Tales range from serious ones, about a woman sucked up a chimney by a tornado, to humorous ones, about an airborne police car caught in a twister.

A good guide for locating some Midwestern traditional artists and craftspeople is Dvorachek and Saltzman's *Iowa Folklife Resource Directory: Performing Arts, Material Culture, Occupations, Display Events, Ethnic and Regional Museums and Cultural Organizations, Researchers/Consultants* (1997). Though limited to a single Midwestern state, the resource book is useful to those working in other states, as it identifies some traditional occupations that might be overlooked—including auctioneers, firefighters, butchers, horse trainers, and meat packers—as well as more recognizable traditional craftspeople, such as blacksmiths, cabinet makers, carpenters, farmers, woodworkers, and musical instrument makers. The material culture of Midwestern religious and ethnic groups, too, is well documented in the Midwestern section of this encyclopedia: planting and beekeeping in the Amana Colonies; dairy farming, sturgeon fishing, and birch-bark canoes in Wisconsin; covered bridges and stone walling in Indiana; carvers, furniture makers, and basket weavers in Missouri; folk arts and architecture of Amish and Moravians in Ohio; potters and quilters in Iowa; and hunting, fishing, and county fairs in Michigan.

The French established Midwestern settlements in Detroit, Kaskaskia, Chaokia, Vincennes, St. Genevieve, and St. Louis, where they sang songs, told tales, practiced customs, and performed other folklore they brought with them from Europe. French settlers brought with them, among other forms of folklore and folklife, folktales of 'Tit Jean and legends of the *loup garou* (werewolf), *lutin* (diminutive night riders), *chasse galerie* (phantom canoe), and *feu follet* (will-o'-the-wisp), setting some of these old-world tales in the Midwest. Carrière (1937) collected folktales about 'Tit Jean from French descendants in Old Mines, Missouri, and Rosemary Hyde Thomas presents these tales for general readers in *It's Good to Tell You: French Folktales from Missouri* (1981). Celia Ray Berry preserves some old French folk songs (French texts with tunes and English translations) performed in the Midwest in *Folk Songs of Old Vincennes* (Chicago: H. T. Fitz-Simons, 1946). The French in Vincennes sang these songs from the old country, probably via French Canada, in most social contexts to while away the hours. Very popular at King's Balls and other festivities were "Les moutons egares," "A la claire fontaine," "Au clair de la lune," and "Adam et Eve au Paradis," among many others. Old French customs, entertainments, and material culture as well as folktales, including supernatural and historical legends, can be found in Baker's

French Folklife in Old Vincennes (Terre Haute: Indiana Council of Teachers of English, 1989; reprint 1998). Dorson (1952) collected versions of old French folktales from descendants of French-Canadians who moved from Quebec Province to the Upper Peninsula of Michigan in the 1880s and 1890s to work in the lumber camps.

After the Revolution a stream of Scotch-Irish Southerners brought Jack tales and other narratives, British and Irish folk songs, and other forms of folklore across the Alleghenies into the southern parts of Ohio, Indiana, Illinois, and later into parts of Missouri. With similar kinds of folklore, settlers from Maryland and Pennsylvania followed another path, the Ohio River, into Ohio, Indiana, and Illinois. In the Midwest, British and Irish Jack tales lose some of their magical motifs, and Jack relies more on his own abilities or on some rich benefactor rather than on supernatural helpers or magical objects, though sometimes he is simply lucky. British ballads and songs change in the Midwest, too. Midwestern versions of English and Scottish traditional ballads generally are shorter, often localized, and sometimes modernized. For instance, Midwestern dialects and place-names might replace British speech and place-names, guns might replace swords, and landlords might replace lords. Midwestern versions of ballads also move from narrative to lyric, with tunes, often more attractive to Midwestern singers and their audiences, dominating texts. Midwestern versions of imported ballads often become humorous, and supernatural and gory elements tend to disappear. For instance, in the Midwest, the serious English ballad

"Three Ravens," or its cynical Scottish variant "Twa Corbies," becomes a comic song, "The Three Crows" or "Crow Song," with a dead horse replacing a slain knight. A happy tune and a comic refrain replace the hopefulness of English versions and the despair of Scottish versions. Morals sometimes are added to Midwestern versions of imported ballads, perhaps influenced by the broadside tradition, whereas in traditional British versions, especially those in Francis James Child's collection of English and Scottish ballads, morals may be implicit but are not spelled out. British broadsides and Irish tunes have been especially influential on Midwestern balladry and folk song, but Midwesterners have given their own stamp to imported songs. Fortunately, from most Midwestern states there are good collections of both imported and regional songs and ballads, including Belden's Ballads and Songs Collected by the Missouri Folk-Lore Society (1940; reprint 1955), Eddy's Ballads and Songs from Ohio (1939; reprint 1964), Brewster's Ballads and Songs of Indiana (1940; reprint 1981), and Gardner and Chickering's Ballads and Songs of Southern Michigan (1939; reprint 1967). The latter includes a variety of songs about such topics as love, war, religion, occupations, disasters, and crime.

Folk beliefs and legends also are well represented in collections from Midwestern states. For example, Allen (1963) preserves legends and beliefs of southern Illinois; Taylor (1999) devotes a chapter to ghost stories related to Abraham Lincoln; and from the region called "Little Egypt" in southern Illinois, Neely (1938; reprint 1973) offers a variety of legends and songs, including admirably collected ghost and witch tales and a local outlaw ballad, "The Death of Charlie Burger." From one county in Illinois, Hyatt (1935) gathered all kinds of folk beliefs and edited the best and most representative of the early collections of Midwestern folk beliefs. Though he covers a larger geographical area, Koch (1980) edited a similar collection of superstitions from Kansas. Gard and Sorden (1962) cover legends, beliefs, cures, jokes, proverbs, and names in Wisconsin; and Wisconsin ghost lore is well represented in Boyer's collection (1996) of supernatural legends and Matson and Stotts's collection (1996) of personal experience tales about encounters with ghosts. Sackett and Koch (1961) include a wide variety of folklore from Kansas, including customs, sayings, proverbs, riddles, verse, folk songs, dances, games, speech, and foodways in addition to legends and beliefs; and Heitz (1997) surveys Kansas ghost stories. Pound (1959) brings together legends, customs, games, foodways from Nebraska; and later Welsch (1966) surveys Nebraska songs, dances, tales, customs, beliefs, and foodways. From Indiana, Baker surveys humorous narratives (1986) as well as legends (1982) and place-names and their stories (1995). Each state has its hero stories, but legends of some heroes, such as the outlaw Jesse James, are found in several Midwestern states, including Missouri, where he was born, Minnesota, where he robbed a bank, and Indiana, where he supposedly had some hideouts. Midwestern heroes are featured in several books, including Rosa's discussion of the life and legends of Wild Bill Hickok (1996) and Katz's treatment of Ohio legends about Johnny Appleseed (1994).

The tall tale, a humorous narrative of lying and exaggeration, was especially popular on the Midwestern frontier, particularly among hunters, fishermen, farmers, and boatmen, as these whoppers frequently deal with hunting, fishing, rough weather, fertile soil, big crops, and fabulous animals. Many Midwestern tall tales deal with the legendary logger Paul Bunyan, who quickly passed from a folk hero of lumberjacks to a mass culture hero of many Americans, mainly in advertising and children's literature, as Daniel Hoffman shows in *Paul Bunyan: Last of the Frontier Demigods* (1952). Printed texts of Bunyan's exploits in children's literature fail to capture the tall tale's art, which, as Mark Twain suggests in "How to Tell a Story," lies in its manner of telling, not especially in its content. Hoffman also examines the limited use of Paul Bunyan in the poetry of Robert Frost and Carl Sandburg and other formal literature. Jansen's *Abraham "Oregon" Smith: Pioneer, Folk Hero, and Tale-Teller* (1947, repr. 1977) more accurately conveys the repertoire of a Midwestern tall tale teller, who, in turn, became a folk hero and the subject of tales.

More authentic lumberjack folklore than most of the Bunyan material can be found in ballads and other folk songs collected in the Midwest. The great forests of the Midwest impressed the first settlers, who first cleared the trees for space and then cut more trees to build houses, barns, and fences. Because of the abundance of trees in the upper Midwest, the logging industry moved from Maine and passed through Michigan, Wisconsin, and Minnesota on its way to Washington and Oregon. Historically, no other country experienced what Franz Rickaby, a major source of Peters's collection, *Folk Songs out of Wisconsin* (1977), has called the "Golden Age of American Lumbering" (1870–1900). Although many of the tunes of lumberjack songs were borrowed from Irish street ballads, the texts were unique. The songs celebrated cutting trees; hauling, rolling, and driving logs; breaking logjams; and the romance between a logger and a town girl, often ending in tragedy. Midwestern loggers preserved all kinds of songs, though, including some not dealing with their occupation, because they came from a variety of ethnic and occupational backgrounds and didn't have much else to do to while away their time in the lumber camps except play checkers, tell stories, and sing songs. Beck's *Lore of the Lumber Camps* (1941) not only preserves a variety of songs sung in Michigan lumber camps, but it also sets lumberjack songs, tall tales, and naming traditions in their historical contexts.

Over seven years Franz Rickaby collected songs from loggers in Michigan, Wisconsin, and Minnesota, and published them in *Ballads and Songs of the Shanty-Boy* (1926). He claimed that no group celebrated itself in folk song more than the lumberjack. According to Rickaby, the woods songs were composed by individuals who consciously set out to create them and, unlike other early collectors of folk songs, stressed the importance of tunes. According to Rickaby, the text of a song without its tune was ineffective; consequently, he emphasized the musical tradition of loggers' songs, providing tunes as well as texts of "Jack Haggerty's Flat River Girl," "The Shanty-Boy on the Big Eau Claire," "Michigan-I-O," and other woods songs.

In parts of the Midwest, mining was another important occupation that pro-duced a body of folklore, especially stories and songs but also speech, beliefs, naming, and other traditions. Though Cornish miners were brought to southwestern Wisconsin to work in copper mines, coal miners generated most of the mining lore, because more Midwesterners worked in coal mining than in lead, gold, silver, or copper mining, simply because of environmental resources. Coal miners' songs are especially important for historical and sociological interests, for unlike the songs of lumberjacks and of other occupational groups in the Midwest, coal mining songs represent mass protest; there is a growing passion for unionism that doesn't show up in many of the songs of other occupational groups. Miners' songs tell of greedy bosses, long hours, dangers of work, poor working conditions, and disasters. In addition, miners lived with their families close to the shafts, so miners' songs reveal a domestic life that doesn't appear in songs of lumberjacks and other occupational groups. George Korson's *Coal Dust on the Fiddle: Songs and Stories of the Bituminous Industry* (1943) includes songs, tales, folk medicine, and superstitions of miners in three Midwestern states: Ohio, Indiana, and Illinois. The book is significant because Korson places the texts in the context of the coal camp. Among other things, he provides background information on company houses, camp schools, company stores, camp saloons, mine disasters, camp bards, mine pets, family life, and the struggle for a better life through unionism.

Steamboats on the great Midwestern rivers and ore boats on the Great Lakes generated all kinds of folklore, including tall stories. Along the Mississippi, Missouri, and Ohio Rivers, comic legends were told of keelboatmen and ringtailed roarers, especially about Mike Fink, king of Midwestern boatmen. In *Western Rivermen, 1763–1861: Ohio and Mississippi Boatmen and the Myth of the Alligator Horse* (1990), Allen traces the life of the river man in oral history and written documents and shows how the Midwestern river man in heroes like Mike Fink—half horse, half alligator—developed into an American hero. B. A. Botkin's *A Treasury of Mississippi River Folklore: Stories, Ballads, Traditions, and Folkways of the Mid-American River Country* (1955) provides broader coverage of Mississippi River folklore. Welsch's three collections of tall tales, many culled from *The Nebraska Farmer,* clearly show how international narratives have been adapted to regional climate, topography, and conditions, as chapter headings in *Shingling the Fog and Other Great Plains Lies* (1972) include Rough Weather, Fabulous Lands, and Hard Times.

Though the tall tale has lost some of its appeal, humorous folk narratives still are among the most popular folktales in the Midwest. As Baker's *Jokelore* (1986) illustrates, besides tall tales, humorous folk narratives include jokes about animals, married couples, drunks, lazy people, ethnic and regional groups (frequently incorporating international motifs of the wise and foolish), the clergy and religious groups, occupational groups, and contemporary recreations, such as golf. James Leary's *Midwestern Folk Humor* (Madison: Univ. of Wisconsin Press, 1991; reprinted as *So Ole Says to Lena,* 2001) shows that many upper Midwestern jokes have European and other American versions, but have been adapted to Midwestern people,

places, and events. Besides jokes about ethnic and occupational groups, Leary includes contemporary dialect jokes about the Scandinavian stock characters, Ole and Lena, and their Finnish counterparts, Eino and Toivo.

As Richard M. Dorson illustrates in *Negro Folktales in Michigan* (1956), African Americans moving North before and after the Civil War brought with them a variety of traditional songs, dances, beliefs, speech, rhymes, and narratives, including many animal tales, in which animals talk and act like humans. Mary Alicia Owen reworks a number of traditional animal tales set in a frame story and retold in dialect in *Voodoo Tales, as Told among the Negroes of the Southwest* (1893; reprint 1969). Animal tales often deal with a clever animal tricking a stupid animal or explain physical or behavioral characteristics of a particular animal, such as why rabbits have long ears and long hind legs. Children's storybooks and animated cartoons have replaced the functions of some of the old animal tales, but off-color jokes about animals, generally breaking some social taboo, remain popular in the Midwestern oral tradition.

Around the turn of the nineteenth century, other settlers from New York and New England came to the Midwest by way of the Great Lakes and settled in Ohio, Michigan, Wisconsin, Iowa, and the northern parts of Indiana and Illinois. These English-speaking settlers were joined by Germans, who by 1850 accounted for a large percentage of the foreign-born population in the Midwest. First in their native language and later in English dialect, German settlers told stories about coming to the Midwest, personal and place naming, deals and bets, women's power, pioneer preachers and priests, witches and the devil, politics, and tragedies, as Eberhard Reichmann shows in *Hoosier German Tales* (Indianapolis: German-American Center & Indiana German Heritage Society, 1991). Three fifty-two-page booklets produced by Stanley A. Kaufman and the German Culture Museum in Walnut Creek, Ohio, treat other aspects of German folklife in the Midwest: *Amish in Eastern Ohio* (1991) provides a brief history of Amish in Ohio with information on furniture, architecture, and folk arts; *Germanic Folk Culture in Eastern Ohio* (1996) examines the history of Germans in eastern Ohio and their architecture, furniture, quilts, coverlets, Fraktur, metalwork, costume and household crafts; and *Moravians in Ohio* (1987) deals with the architecture, furniture, music, Fraktur, metalwork, textiles, and toys of the earliest Germanic group in Ohio. Since the country was the field for most folklorists in the past, consequently, much folklore collected in the Midwest comes from rural areas and reflects an older traditional way of life characterized by interdependence and cooperation for both work and play. Many hands make light work, and Midwestern pioneers living a mile or two away were always willing to help one another at various bees (or work parties). Logging bees, or log rollings, were held when logs were cut and ready for piling and burning, as Botkin documents in "The Indiana Log-Rolling" (in *Folk-Say: A Regional Miscellany,* Norman: Univ. of Oklahoma Press, 1929). Raising bees, which Midwestern Amish still hold, were held when a house or barn was ready for erecting. Generally in the spring or fall when someone had a building to move, neighbors with their

oxen formed a drawing bee and moved the building on skids. Midwestern pioneers also pitched in at harvesting and haying. Husking bees were held in the fall, sometimes in an open field lighted by a great bonfire, but often in a barn. In late autumn or early winter, paring bees, or apple cuts, were held. Bushels of apples were peeled, quartered, cored, and strung for drying.

The various bees also served as settings for eating, drinking, and entertainment as well as for communal work. Meals and refreshments were served at most bees at noon and/or after the work was done. If the bees were an all-day event, women pitched in and prepared a huge meal at midday; then in the evening after work was done, games were played, stories were exchanged, and refreshments were served. Work parties illustrate how the various genres of folklore intermingle in traditional settings. The work party, itself, is a folk custom where material culture, foodways, song, dance, storytelling, and conversational genres are performed. Because of the social function of work bees, collective jobs were continued for social reasons long after the need for collectively performed tasks disappeared. Other customs revolving around the calendar (Easter, Thanksgiving, Christmas) and rites of passage (birth, marriage, death) also served as occasions for pioneer families to get together and share folklore.

Midwestern pioneers depended on their own resources for amusement even when work was not involved. As Leah Jackson Wolford shows in *The Play-Party in Indiana* (Indianapolis: Indianapolis Historical Society, 1959), one major form of country entertainment was the play party, a kind of camouflaged dance that served as one of the few occasions where young people could get together. Although sometimes performed at bees and other gatherings, the play party often was held independent of other functions. Usually the play party was open to the whole community and was attended by the entire family, though the active participants were young people of high school and marriageable age and young married couples. Old folks and children generally were spectators, though children might play their own games, such as drop-the-handkerchief. The nature of play party games distinguished them from other gatherings. Many Midwestern settlers—often Quakers, Presbyterians, Methodists, Baptists—thought dancing was wicked and that the fiddle was the devil's instrument; therefore, young people played singing and swinging games, which didn't require instrumental music and weren't considered dancing. The players provided their own music by singing, and they swung each other by hands, as swinging by waist was generally taboo, though some were forfeit games, in which a kiss was the payment. The young people danced until about midnight, when generally light refreshments were served, although well-to-do families might serve an entire dinner. As Philip Martin shows in *Farmhouse Fiddlers: Music and Dance Traditions in the Rural Midwest* (1994), not all Midwesterners objected to music and dancing and held traditional fiddling and dancing in homes. The play party and home dances disappeared, however, with the coming of the automobile, radio, and other forms of entertainment.

From 1880 to 1920 immigrants from northern, southern, and central Europe as well as another stream of immigrants from Britain and Ireland settled in the Midwest to work in mills, mines, factories, and farms. Later in the twentieth century, other immigrants from Europe, Asia, and Mexico joined them with still other bodies of folklore in other languages, including that of the Hmong of Laos in Minnesota and that of Mexican Americans and other Spanish speakers in several Midwestern cities. Dorson's *Land of the Millrats* (1981) deals with the urban and occupational folklore of some of these ethnic groups in the Calumet Region (Gary, East Chicago, Hammond, and Whiting) of Indiana. In *Folklore of the Calumet Region* (Carpenter, ed., 1980; reprinted from *Indiana Folklore* [1977]), Dorson contrasts the folklore of the city in northwest Indiana with the fieldwork he undertook in the 1940s in a rural area of the Upper Peninsula of Michigan. Different from country folklore, the folklore of the region reflects urban experiences there: crime on the streets, flight from the city, and working conditions in the steel mills. In "Is There a Folk in the City?" Dorson (*Journal of American Folklore* 83 [1970], 207–215) notes the paucity of conventional folklore genres in Gary and East Chicago, but writes of the richness of personal experience stories and other cultural traditions, such as the African American church, European calendar customs, ethnic dances, and ethnic cooking. Ethnic groups display traditional artifacts, old-world costumes, portraits of national heroes, and musical instruments; and they reinforce their ethnic cultures through regular correspondence and visits to the home country.

Midwestern folk cultures, of course, share traits with other cultures—formal and popular cultures as well as other regional cultures. Some African American traditions were bred in the South and nourished in the Midwest. African Americans who migrated from the rural South to the Midwest brought with them their folk beliefs and customs as well as folktales. Practitioners of hoodoo in urban Midwestern cities continue to heal and get revenge as they did in Southern communities, though with some changes. In the Midwest, southern root doctors often profess religious affiliations and become spiritualists or psychics. Reflecting an urban, commercial environment, practitioners of hoodoo in Midwestern cities also advertise and market their alleged powers, merging folk and popular cultures.

Family and age groups also play an important role in maintaining Midwestern traditions. Regional culture is first encountered within the family, and families transmit, vary, and integrate traditions among the many different folk groups living within a region. Family reunions and other celebrations not only provide continuity to family relationships, but they also link family members to the community. Many family stories, easily collected today in the Midwest, are either legends or memorates. Dorson's sagamen in *Bloodstoppers and Bearwalkers* boast about their strength, endurance, and cleverness in personal experience tales from the Upper Peninsula. Family legends, memorates, and oral history compose the raw material for an account of Wisconsin farm life in Mitchell's monograph, "From Fathers to Sons: A Wisconsin Family Farm" (*Midwestern Journal of Language and Folklore* 10 [1984]). Some communities, such as Bowling Green, Indiana, have old settlers' reunions, which serve as extended family reunions. Activities dedicated to honoring the community's old people, symbols of the old settlers, include music, storytelling, tractor-pulling contests, and picnicking. Regional celebrations performed within the context of retirement communities serve some of the same functions, providing continuity and sense of place and shared history through stories, music, and other activities.

Although various national/ethnic, regional, and occupational groups brought with them the folklore of their countries, regions, and occupations, once settled in the Midwest they shared, borrowed, adapted, and blended the imported material to new settings and situations and created new stories inspired by historical circumstances, occupations, and the physical environment of the region. The Native American heritage; the transplantation, acculturation, and blending of various European, Asian, Southern, Yorker, Yankee, African American, and Hispanic cultures in a new environment; and the agricultural and industrial experience contributed to a body of folk narratives that we may term "Midwestern." Kessler and Ball's *North from the Mountains: A Folk History of the Carmel Melungeon Settlement, Highland County, Ohio* (2001) serves as a kind of microcosm of Midwestern folklore. Melungeon culture is not Native American, European, or Asian, but a mixture of these three groups. Though their folklore reflects their Southern heritage, Southern cultural features of their folklore intermingle with Northern features in Ohio. Likewise, there is not a uniform Midwestern folklore; various ethnic-religious-occupational combinations along with settlement history and environmental conditions formed a complex of diverse Midwestern folk cultures, not a unified folk cultural area. As a microcosm, Dorson's *Bloodstoppers and Bearwalkers: Folk Traditions of the Upper Peninsula* (1952) might even be more representative of Midwestern folklore, because he shows how Native American, European, and regional traditions intermingle and how various ethnic, religious, and occupational groups cohabit an area, sharing some traditions, such as local legendry, with other groups, and keeping other traditions, such as belief systems, to themselves. Indeed, Midwestern folklore reflects the motto of the United States: *e pluribus unum*—out of many, one.

Ron Baker

THE MIDWEST: BIBLIOGRAPHY AND OTHER RESOURCES

Bibliography

History and Study

470. Allen, Michael. *Western Rivermen, 1763–1861: Ohio and Mississippi Boatmen and the Myth of the Alligator Horse.* Baton Rouge: Louisiana State University Press, 1990. xiii, 261p. Illus. Index. Bibliographic Essay. Appendix of Two Songs and a Poem. 90-5860. 0-8071-1561-4.

Flatboatmen who navigated flatboats on the Ohio and the Mississippi rivers for a wage—professional river men—are the focus of Allen's work. Much of his material is factual, based on the more than eighty first-person accounts he discovered, written by the river men themselves

in letters, journals, and memoirs and on such primary sources as newspaper reports, travelers' journals, court records, customs records, and government documents. He pieces together the life of the river man, which, although hard and lonely, was envied by more settled townsmen and was being built into myth even as it was lived.

This mythology is the other part of Allen's presentation. He discusses contemporary accounts of the river man's life, which glamorized his job, and shows how this worker became an American archetype. He writes about Mike Fink, the "king of the western boatmen," (p. 6) who was a legend both to nineteenth-century Americans and to 1950s children, through the Walt Disney Davy Crockett movies and television show, and about the description of the river man as "half alligator, half horse."

This treatment of the river man is similar to Hauck's study of Davy Crockett, *Davy Crockett, A Handbook.*

471. Carpenter, Inta Gale, ed. *Folklore of the Calumet Region.* New York: Arno Press, 1980. 97–228p. Reprinted from *Journal of the Hoosier Folklore Society*, vol. x, no. 2, 1977. (Folklore of the World). 71-635756. 0-405-13300-6.

The first article in this reprint from the *Journal of the Hoosier Folklore Society* is by Richard M. Dorson. He contrasts the folklore project detailed in the succeeding chapters with a project he undertook in the 1940s, in the Upper Peninsula of Michigan (*Bloodstoppers and Bearwalkers*, repr., Cambridge, MA: Harvard Univ. Press, 1972). In that project, he examined the folklore of a rural, isolated area. In this newer project, a group of folklorists explored the folklore of what is known as

"De Region," an area of northwest Indiana that includes Gary.

Articles in this special issue of the journal concern the steel industry, ethnic folklore, black folklore, folk medicine, and crime. Most of the articles give detailed methodology. In addition, two articles specifically discuss the methods of collecting modern, urban folklore: "Coordinating an Urban Folklore Team Project," and "Hardware and Software in the Urban Field." These should be helpful to anyone thinking of exploring the folklore of their own city.

472. Hoffman, Daniel. *Paul Bunyan: Last of the Frontier Demigods.* New York: Temple University Publications, 1952. xiv, 213p. Motif Index. Name and Subject Index. Bibliog. 66-14159.

Not a retelling of the tales, this book sets out to explore the development of the legend of Paul Bunyan in oral folktale, in popular literature, and in the modern poetry of W. H. Auden, Carl Sandburg, and Robert Frost.

473. Martin, Philip. *Farmhouse Fiddlers: Music and Dance Traditions in the Rural Midwest.* Mount Horeb, WI: Midwest Traditions, 1994. 128p. Illus. Bibliog. Notes. 94-78042. 1-883953-06-5pa.

No actual songs, words, or music are presented here. Instead, this book is a look at the tradition of fiddling in the rural Midwest. It traces its homegrown development, with fiddlers teaching younger people the songs they themselves played. It shows the home dances, or "kitchen sweats," which were major pastimes for a society whose entertainment was limited by horse-drawn transportation to what it could produce locally. Finally, it shows the change in the tradition, brought about both by increased car ownership and by the radio, to a more commercial, less home-centered activity. Dance halls replaced the kitchen as the place to dance, and hired bands replaced the local fiddler. Many local fiddlers present their own stories in their own words in these pages. Both their words and the accompanying photographs bring back the times.

474. Rosa, Joseph G. *Wild Bill Hickok: The Man and His Myth.* Lawrence: Univ. Press of Kansas, 1996. xxiv, 276p. Illus. Index. Bibliog. Notes. 95-54015. 0-7006-0773-0.

This book does for Wild Bill Hickok something similar to what Michael A. Lofaro's *Davy Crockett: The Man, the Legend, the Legacy, 1786–1986* (Univ. of Tennessee Press, 1985) or Richard Boyd Hauck's *Davy Crockett, a Handbook* (Univ. of Nebraska Press, 1982) do for Davy Crockett. It shows both what is known of Hickok's actual life and discusses the legend that grew up around him, even during his own lifetime.

Treasuries

475. Allen, John W. *Legends and Lore of Southern Illinois.* Carbondale: Southern Illinois Univ., 1963. xx, 404p. Illus. Index.

Allen's preface states that this book is "about southern Illinois, its lore, legends, sometimes strange beliefs and bits of its history." (p. xiii) His avowed purpose is to make residents more aware of their history and to allow outsiders a glimpse of it. Some of the material here concerns real people and events. He includes some actual folk tales, as well as snippets of folk belief on marriage, home remedies, and farming. A substantial section is devoted to information about early life in Illinois—education in one-room schools, business activities, and travel methods.

476. Gard, Robert E., and L. G. Sorden. *Wisconsin Lore: Antics and Anecdotes of Wisconsin People and Places.* New York: Duell, Sloan and Pearce, 1962. x, 368p. Appendix of Place-Names. 62-12168.

Of course tales and legends of lumberjacks occupy pride of place in this compendium of Wisconsin lore. But there are also stories of ghosts, buried treasure, and the circus; information about folk cures, and superstitions; and listings of jokes, sayings, and proverbs.

This is similar to Benjamin Botkins's compilations of regional folklore: *A Treasury of New England Folklore, A Treasury of Southern Folklore,* etc.

477. Koch, William E. *Folksong, Folklore, Folklife and Some History.* Manhattan: Kansas State Univ., 1985. 275p. Illus. Bibliog.

Koch was a professor of English and folklore at Kansas State University for many years. At the end of his career, he compiled this compendium of all the articles and professional papers he contributed to the field. Many of the papers, given at conferences, had never been published; the articles are from various journals.

Articles are on a wide variety of topics: folk music, cowboys, place-names, various ethnic groups and their folk customs, tall tales, and farming. There are even newspaper articles about Koch included. It is an extremely eclectic collection.

Although the production is amateurish, with muddy black-and-white photographs and crooked pages, much of the material is still fresh and of interest today. It shows how small snippets of information (some of the articles are only a page or two) can pack much information.

478. Pound, Louise. *Nebraska Folklore.* Lincoln: Univ. of Nebraska Press, 1959. x, 243p. 59-9868.

Most of Pound's career centered on teaching and speaking. She did, however, produce some writings on folklore; the University of Nebraska Press has collected some of them here.

She presents folk legends surrounding caves, snakes, rain, lovers' leaps, Nebraska pioneers, and hoaxes. She also writes a chapter on folk customs, including holidays, death customs, sports and games, social customs, and food. This last chapter is a compendium of customs as varied as the "shivaree," or celebration of a marriage, and the water fights that were often part of holiday entertainment on such days as Memorial Day or the Fourth of July.

479. Sackett, S. J., and William E. Koch. *Kansas Folklore.* Lincoln: Univ. of Nebraska Press, 1961. xi, 251p. Index of Songs. Bibliog. Appendix: Motif Analysis. 61-11628.

All types of folklore are included here: tales and legends, crafts and customs, superstitions and beliefs, recreation and music. Chapter headings include Folktales; Legends; Beliefs, Superstitions, and Sayings; Proverbs and Riddles; Dialect; Folk Verse; Folksongs and Ballads; Customs; Dances and Games; and Recipes. The tales include some on those legendary Kansas critters, the hoop snake and the sandhill dodger.

480. Welsch, Roger L. *A Treasury of Nebraska Pioneer Folklore.* Lincoln: Univ. of Nebraska Press, 1966. xviii, 391p. Illus. by Jack Brodie. Title Index of Songs and Tales. Bibliog. Motif Analyses. 66-10876.

The first section of Welsch's compilation of Nebraska consists of songs and dances, many with music transcribed. Most have noted the name of the collector and the circumstances of its collection.

Part 2 is a collection of folk tales, subdivided into "White Man's Tales" and "Indian Tales." The white man's tales are of cowboys and settlers, including the character Febold Feboldson, a larger than life character similar to Paul Bunyan. The Indian tales are from a variety of tribes.

Part 3 consists of a collection of folk beliefs and superstition on such subjects as foods, weather, courting customs, and beliefs surrounding death.

Tales and Legends

481. Anderson, Bernice G. *Trickster Tales from Prairie Lodgefires.* Nashville: Abingdon, 1979. 94p. "As told to Bernice G. Anderson by Ingaglueh-Whoo-Tongah of the Poncas and by Maunkee Blackbear Tahbone of the Kiowas." Illus. by Frank Gee. 79-10198. 0-687-42620-0.

Anderson heard these tales from the elders of various tribes. They all concern Trickster, a character common to the stories of all tribes of the Plains. Trickster, according to Anderson, is as likely to do bad as good; his unexpectedness is his main characteristic. He is a "prankster and a cheater . . ." but he could be as well "a helper and a healer" (p. 14). The only thing you could be sure of in dealings with Trickster is that eventually he would fool you.

482. Anderson, Dale, ed. *Folktales of the High Plains.* Needham Heights, MA: Ginn, 1992. xvi, 273p. Illus. by Charlie

Norton. Bibliog. Endnotes to each section. 0-536-58243-2.

The High Plains of western Kansas and eastern Colorado are the setting for all these tales, which Anderson collected from a variety of informants, some of them third- and fourth-generation residents of the area. Some of the tales are not strictly folk tales, but more exactly are true reminiscences or family stories. Although some have been changed or embellished over the years, owing either to memory lapses of the teller or to a wish on the teller's part to respond to a particular audience, Anderson maintains that whether the story is true or not, it can still qualify as a folk tale. Each of the tales, he says, "has value as a folk action-oral tradition being passed down to the next generation" (p. xv).

Tales concern early settlers, Indians, animals, weather, cowboys—and cowgirls as well—bad men and sheriffs, jokes and pranks, and place-names. One chapter is devoted to tall tales.

The endnotes to each chapter contain information about the collection of the tale, the teller, and the tale's history.

483. Baker, Ronald L. *From Needmore to Prosperity: Hoosier Place Names in Folklore and History.* Bloomington: Indiana Univ. Press, 1995. 371p. Bibliog. 94-44707. 0-253-32866-7. 0-253-20955-2pa.

According to Baker, place-names can tell a great deal about a place's unofficial history. Although many places are named for famous people, or for geographic landmarks, others are named for local characters who never make the history books but are remembered in legends. Even the places named more conventionally often have stories attached to them of a more fanciful nature. Thus, although

Bloomfield, Indiana, was named for Bloomfield, New York, local legend says it was so named because early settlers saw blooming fields.

Baker lists hundreds of place-names, often giving the local legends that surround them.

His introduction discusses the importance of a knowledge of place-names in understanding the history of a place.

484. ——. *Hoosier Folk Legends.* Bloomington: Indiana Univ. Press, 1982. xix, 264p. "Sources and Notes" to the legends. 81-47568. 0-253-32844-6.

Many of the legends told here are comparatively modern and are common throughout the country. Some are legends concerning the automobile, such as the one about the couple sitting in a parked car in an area reportedly terrorized by a serial killer who wore a hook to replace a missing hand. The lovers became uneasy and drove away—and later found the hook hanging from their door handle. Some are common ghost stories, such as the perennial one about the two young men who pick up a young girl hitchhiking, only to have her disappear just as they arrive at her home. Upon inquiry, they discover that she had been recently killed in an accident and that her ghost never ceased trying to return home. In all versions, the young men find some proof that the girl had indeed been in the car; in this version, the backseat was wet where the girl had sat, because she had been standing in the rain.

Other legends, including some of Johnny Appleseed, are more local in nature.

Many of the legends concern death, often in a horrible fashion.

485. ——. *Jokelore: Humorous Folktales from Indiana.* Bloomington: Indiana University Press, 1986. xliii, 234p. Bibliog. Notes on tales. 84-43174. 0-253-33163-3.

Baker defines the "folk" as any group with something in common—residence in a particular locale, ethnicity, profession, or trade. He define "lore" as information in any format (written, spoken, artifact) that is passed from person to person. He considers jokes a particularly telling part of folklore.

In this book, he collects jokes from many groups of "folk." Ethnic groups are one, including Blacks, Poles, Jews, and Irish; categories of workers are another, including salesmen, farmers, politicians, medical personnel, teachers, and preachers. Also included are golfers, married couples, drunks and sloths, and Kentuckians. Tall tales and shaggy dog stories round out the collection.

Baker's introduction is a lengthy discussion of the place of humor and jokes in folklore.

486. Barnouw, Victor. *Wisconsin Chippewa Myths and Tales and Their Relation to Chippewa Life.* Madison: Univ. of Wisconsin Press, 1977. 295p. Based on folktales collected by Victor Barnouw, Joseph B. Casagrande, Ernestine Friedl, and Robert E. Ritzenthaler. Maps. Motif index. Subject index. Bibliog. Appendices. 79-53647. 0-299-07310-6.

The folktales told here are from a variety of informants, many of whose life stories are told in Appendix B. Some of the tales are creation myths, with Wenebojo, as a major character. Wenebojo's father was the sun; his mother was a young Indian girl. Up until his birth, his mother and her mother had been the only people on the earth.

Other tales concern animals and magic.

Appendix A gives information on the use of *Amanita muscaria,* a hallucinogenic mushroom, by the Chippewa.

Barnouw gives the name of the collector of each tale.

487. Boyer, Dennis. *Driftless Spirits: Ghosts of Southwest Wisconsin.* Madison, WI: Prairie Oak Press, 1996. xiii, 184p. 96-43649. 1-879483-35-1pa.

A sense of place and local flavor were the two qualities Boyer was looking for when he culled these ghost stories from the hundreds he collected.

He arranges his tales by county:

Iowa County
Grant County
Crawford County
Sauk County
Lafayette County
Richland County
Vernon County
Dane County
Green County

488. ——. *Giants in the Land: Folktales and Legends of Wisconsin.* Madison, WI: Prairie Oak Press, 1997. xiii, 157p. Illus. 97-35598. 1-879483-45-9pa.

Boyer also wrote *Driftless Spirits: Ghosts of Southwestern Wisconsin* (Madison, WI: Prairie Oak Press, 1996), a book of ghost stories. This book, divided into three sections, is more varied. The first section is on heroes and larger-than-life characters, with such names as Poker Run Pete and Haystack Hilda. Next comes a section on mythical wild creatures: the Willky Wooly, the Little Hodag, and the Dwarf Mastodons of Boaz, among others. Finally is a brief section on some creation myths of Native American tribes.

489. Brown, Dorothy Moulding. *Indian Legends of Historic and Scenic Wisconsin.* Madison, WI: n.p., 1969. 69p.

The legends in this book are extremely brief, perhaps a page or less. They all have to do with the natural world: legends of Wisconsin springs, waterfalls, trees, caves, rocks, and hills. Most concern the spirits—usually benevolent—that inhabit them.

490. ——. *Wisconsin Indian Place-Name Legends.* Wisconsin Centennial Issue. Madison, WI: n.p., 1948. 30p.

Brown chose to include stories of places throughout Wisconsin. Some of the stories and legends naming the places are of Native American origin. Names come from disasters in which many people were killed; from battles and wars; from stories of gods; and of course from stories of doomed lovers.

491. Coady, John P. *The Legends and Story of the Michigan Indian.* Cedar Springs, MI: Cedar Springs Historical Society, 1993. vi, 114p. Illus. pa.

A high school principal in Morley, Michigan, in the 1930s, Coady was given a manuscript of these legends by the mother of one of his pupils. They concern natural things, such as stars, trees, and land, as well as the daily activities of the Indians: hunting, fishing, and cultivation. The stories are from many tribes, among them Iroquois, Ojibway, and Ottawa.

492. Dorson, Richard M. *Bloodstoppers and Bearwalkers.* Cambridge, MA: Harvard Univ. Press, 1952; repr., 1972. ix, 305p. Index. 52-5394.

Dorson has collected lore from a very specific area of the country, the Upper Peninsula of Michigan. His tales are from many sources, some of Native American origin, some from European settlers such as Finns and Swedes, and others from occupational groups such as lumberjacks and miners. His tales include those of tricksters and healers, love potions and lynchings.

In this book he includes folklore from the many strains that make up American society, rather than from just one. His point is that such varying strains of folklore exist side by side in many communities and that all are worth exploring.

493. ——. *Negro Folktales in Michigan.* Cambridge, MA: Harvard Univ. Press, 1956. 245p. Illus. Bibliog. Index of Informants. Index of Motifs. Index of Tale Types. 56-6516.

Dorson collected these tales in various towns in Michigan where African Americans had settled over the years. Some of the areas were settled before and during the Civil War by people escaping slavery, or by freedmen. Others saw an increase in the number of African American citizens after the Civil War, during the great migration north of southern Blacks. Towns include Callvin Township, Benton Harbor, Covert, Idlewild, Inkster, and Mecosta. Dorson's intent was to discover if the storytelling traditions of African Americans in the South had been transplanted to areas in the North. He did find and record numerous tales, but found that the storytelling tradition was rooted in the South, and knowledge of such tales dwindled as individuals adapted to the North.

The tales include animal tales, fairy tales, tales of curses and hoodoo, tales of witches, and tales of spirits and hants.

494. Eastman, Mary Henderson. *Dahcotah, or Life and Legends of the Sioux around Fort Snelling.* 1849; repr., Afton, MN: Afton Historical Press, 1995. xxxi, 197p. Illus. 95-077777. 0-9639338-5-x.

Mary Henderson Eastman spent seven years at Fort Snelling, near present-day Minneapolis, as the wife of the commander of the post, Captain Seth Eastman. While there, she became fascinated with the ways of the Indians living nearby and talked to them often, asking them for their stories. They told her the stories that were precious to them, of the Great Spirit, other gods, their ceremonies, and their ways of medicine.

Her book was first published in 1849, and is here reproduced with only some obvious typos corrected. The illustrations are watercolors done by Captain Eastman.

495. Elm, Denus, and Harvey Antone. *The Oneida Creation Story.* Lincoln: Univ. of Nebraska Press, 2000. x, 172p. Translated by Floyd G. Lounsbury and Bryan Gick. Glossaries. Bibliog. 00-024446. 0-8032-6742-8pa.

The Oneida creation myth is told in both the Oneida language and, in facing columns, in English. Glossaries explain the Oneida language.

496. Everett, Lawrence. *Ghosts, Spirits and Legends of Southeastern Ohio.* Haverford, PA: Infinity, 2002. vii, 109p. Illus. 0-7414-1025-7pa.

Most of the tales told here are quite brief, only a page or two in length. Some have no attribution, but are traditional to the region, told by many people. Others are specific to a family or an individual; for these Everett adds the name of the person who told him the tale.

Ghosts are seen in cemeteries and on country roads; they are felt in an empty house or in a dark bedroom. Some simply make their presence known by activity—a piece of clothing moved or a rocking chair that gently rocks although no one is sitting in it.

497. Felumlee, Gary. *Ghosts in the Valley!: Ghost Lore of Muskingum, Morgan, Coshocton, Guernsey, and Tuscarawas Counties, Ohio.* Baltimore, MD: Gateway Press, 1998. 103p. Illus. Bibliog. 98-73210.

Eastern Ohio is the region spotlighted in this book; some of the tales date back to the 1700s. Felumlee collected them between 1995 and 1998.

Felumlee includes very early stories, stories set during the Civil War, stories about haunted houses, tales of witches and witchcraft, and stories set in graveyards.

Tales are extremely short, most only a page or less.

498. Gilmore, Melvin R. *Prairie Smoke.* New York: AMS Press, 1929; repr., 1966. xiii, 208p.

Gilmore retells many of the tales of the Indians of the Great Plains. He tells stories of animals and the Indians' relation with them, love stories, tales of children growing up and being instructed in the ways of their people, and tales showing the importance of various plants. Gilmore gives no attribution for any of the stories he tells.

499. Griffith, Cecil R. *The Missouri River: The River Rat's Guide to Missouri River History and Folklore.* Leawood, KS: Squire Publishers, 1974. 96p. Illus. 74-76554.

Griffith uses a geographical organization for this book, tracing the Missouri River from Rulo, Nebraska, to Saint Louis, Missouri. He relates snippets of history and folklore related to various places along the river's route.

500. Gringhuis, Dirk. *Lore of the Great Turtle: Indian Legends of Mackinac Retold.* Mackinac Island, MI: Mackinac Island State Park Commission, 1970. v, 89p. Illus. by Dirk Gringhuis. Index. Bibliog. 911872-11-6pa.

Gringhuis retells here various tales of the Mackinac area, first collected and written down by Henry Rowe Schoolcraft in the nineteenth century. They concern various supernatural beings that watch out for the Ojibway people. Some of the tales are creation stories, telling how various geographic landmarks came to be, or how the seasons first developed.

501. Heitz, Lisa Hefner. *Haunted Kansas: Ghost Stories and Other Eerie Tales.* Lawrence: Univ. Press of Kansas, 1997. xiii, 215p. Index. Bibliog. 97-17327. 0-7006-0865-6.

When asked if she believes in ghosts, Heitz replies that she believes in ghost stories. She believes that such stories perform several functions: exerting parental or social control, bonding individuals together, and fostering an interest in family history.

The tales she has collected are in the following categories:

Haunted houses and buildings
Ghosts in forts
Ghosts in schools and theaters
Graveyard ghosts
Ghosts in rural areas
Ghosts specific to Atchison, Kansas

502. Jagendorf, M. A. *Sand in the Bag, and Other Folk Stories of Ohio, Indiana, and Illinois.* New York: Vanguard Press, 1952. 192p. Illus. by William T. Utter. 52-11125.

Like the stories in Jagendorf's *New England Bean-Pot: American Folk Stories to Read and to Tell,* these are more stories than folktales, stories based on a folktale but embellished and enlarged for a more connected and more modern telling. The stories are of the early settlers of Ohio, Illinois, and Indiana, some of whom are characters, some plain folk, but all of whom are memorable. Jagendorf writes many of the stories in dialect.

Stories are of faithful animals who save their master's lives, of rogues and the people who unmask them, and of ghosts. Some of the stories are of the time when slavery still existed and people of the Midwest resisted it.

503. Jansen, William Hugh. *Abraham "Oregon" Smith: Pioneer, Folk Hero, and Tale-Teller.* Ph.D. thesis; Indiana University, 1949; repr., New York: Arno Press, 1977. xv, 354p. Index. Bibliog. (International Folklore). 77-70602. 0-405-10101-5.

Similar to Mody C. Boatright's *Gib Morgan: Minstrel of the Oil Fields* (Texas Folk-Lore Society, 1945) and Moritz A. Jagendorf's *The Marvelous Adventures of John Darling* (Vanguard Press, 1949), this book about Oregon Smith sets out to examine Smith as both a historical figure and a folk hero. Jansen researched the figure of Oregon Smith in court records, newspapers, and church documents, as well as by talking to people with a store of Abe Smith stories.

Oregon Smith was a tall tale-teller of gigantic talent. In fact, descendents of Smith to whom Jansen spoke often referred to any stretch of the truth as being "like Abe." His stories include one in which he performed surgery on his own wife, replacing part of her intestines with those of a sheep. According to Abe, she recovered completely, except that always afterward she wanted to eat grass.

This edition is a reprint of Jansen's Ph.D. thesis at Indiana University. Stith Thompson was his advisor.

504. Johnston, Basil. *The Manitous: The Spiritual World of the Ojibway.* New York: HarperCollins, 1995; repr., St. Paul: Min-

nesota Historical Society Press, 2001. xxiii, 247p. Glossary. 95-9274. 0-06-0171188-5.

The Ojibway lived in Canada in Ontario, Saskatchewan, and Manitoba; and in the United States, in Michigan, Wisconsin, and Minnesota. During Johnston's childhood, he listened to the stories of the manitous as told by tribal elders and developed a fascination with them. His stories of the manitous, first published as a hardback in 1995, is now reprinted as a paperback.

Johnston tells the stories of the manitous, those spirits of the Ojibway that influence community and individual life: life, guardianship, healing, leading, and teaching. From these manitous come help in all human endeavors, as long as humans live in accord with their environment and with each other. Other manitous preside over animals, over plants, over such things as creative talent, law, language, and wisdom.

Here is the story of the creation of the world by Kitchi-Manitou, the story of Muzzu-Kummik-Quae, or Mother Earth, and the stories of the four sons of Ae-pungishimook: Maudjee-kawiss, Pukawiss, Cheeby-aub-oozoo, and Nana'b'oozoo.

505. Judson, Katharine Berry. *Native American Legends of the Great Lakes.* Chicago: McClurg, 1914; repr., DeKalb: Northern Illinois Univ. Press, 2000. 204p. Index. 00-52766. 0-87580-250-8.

Judson first published this book in 1914, as part of a series on the literature and oral traditions of Native Americans. She was one of the few people of the time who saw these stories as more than myths, but as the true record of a people. Her belief was that Western society's bias toward a written rather than an oral record prejudiced them toward stories that had been handed down by mouth over generations.

Many of these stories are those of creation and of how the natural world came to be. There are tales here from the Winnebago, Chitimacha, Wyandot, Biloxi, Ojibwa, Mandan, Menomini, Ottawa, Cherokee, Sioux, Knisteneaux, Choctaw, Natchez, and Fox.

506. Katz, Michael Jay. *Buckeye Legends: Folktales and Lore from Ohio.* Ann Arbor: Univ. of Michigan Press, 1994. ix, 222p. Bibliog. 94-2379. 0-472-06558-0.

The legends presented here are from the early days of European settlement in Ohio. They are of both Native Americans and of European settlers. Some are ghost stories; some are stories of local eccentrics, including John Chapman, the famous Johnny Appleseed; some are stories of animals who help the people who care them, like the wolf cub adopted and cared for by a woman, that eventually saved that woman's child from being kidnapped.

There is no editorial material explaining the origin of any of the stories.

507. Kearney, Luke Sylvester. *The Hodag, and Other Tales of the Logging Camps.* Wausau, WI: n.p., 1928. 158p.

Kearney recounts tales of the Hodag, that beast that rose from the cremated remains of an ox, as well as of the Hide Behind, the Sidehill Gouger, and the Hoop Snake. These were the tales told by loggers in their camps.

508. Laird, Charlton Grant. *Iowa Legends of Buried Treasure.* Lincoln, NE: Foundation Books, 1990. xiv, 173p. Index of Names. Bibliog. Endnotes. 90-19777. 0-934988-23-4pa.

Laird collected these legends in the 1920s and wrote them up as his master's thesis in 1927. Here they are published for the first time as a book.

All concern legends of buried treasure in Iowa, most gathered firsthand, some collected through solicitation for letters on the subject in a newspaper. He groups his legends into three main sections: Treasure Lost during Transport, Treasure Lost through Violent Means, and Treasure Associated with a Particular Person.

Notes at the beginning of each legend give a brief look at its origin and how it was collected. The author's introduction gives a feel for the early days of Iowa, when the treasures he writes about were lost.

509. Liebert, Robert M. *Osage Life and Legends: Earth People/Sky People.* Happy Camp, CA: Naturegraph Publishers, 1987. 139p. Illus. Bibliog. Appendix A: Osage Cosmology. Appendix B: Ancient Tribal Order of the Osage. 0-87961-168-5. 0-87961-169-3pa.

Liebert retells the *wi-gi-es,* the stories of the Osage that have been told orally for thousands of years by the elders. Translated literally as "to make live," these *we-gi-es* tell the story of creation and the story of man's place in the universe.

510. Marriott, Alice. *Saynday's People.* Bison Book Edition. Lincoln: Univ. of Nebraska Press, 1963. xvi, 223p. Illus. Bibliog. for Illustrations. 63-10928.

These stories were collected in the mid-1930s. The book is divided into two sections: Winter-Telling Stories and Indians on Horseback.

Winter-Telling Stories are the stories told by the Kiowa in the evening or in the winter, when, according to tradition, the outside work was finished. They are all about Saynday, the "one, they say, who got lots of things in our world started and going" (p. 1). He brought the sun to his people, gave them the buffalo, and changed the appearance of many animals into what they are today.

Indians on Horseback tells of the everyday life of the Kiowa: their shelters, their clothing, their medicine, their recreation.

511. Marriott, Alice, and Carol K. Rachlin. *Plains Indian Mythology.* New York: Thomas Y. Crowell, 1975. xiii, 194p. Illus. Bibliog. 75-26554. 0-690-00694-2.

Myths and tales from the Pawnee, Osage, Arapaho, Crow, Kiowa, Cheyenne, Apache, Sioux, Shoshoni, and Comanche are retold here. They include creation stories, stories of animals, stories used to teach and explain. Some of the stories are somewhat modern in origin, even a tale about a young man who saw service in Vietnam and was given all the old sacred songs in a dream.

512. Matson, Elizabeth, and Stuart Stotts. *The Bookcase Ghost: A Storyteller's Collection of Wisconsin Ghost Stories.* Mt. Horeb, WI: Midwest Traditions, 1996. 87p. Notes on the Stories. 96-28978. 1-883953-16-2pa.

Ghost stories from all over Wisconsin are the subject of this book. All are told in the first person, with the storyteller claiming to have experienced the events in the story, or to know the person who did. All are told in the rhythm of the storyteller and are meant to be read or told aloud rather than simply read silently.

At the end of the book the authors add a section of hints on how to memorize and effectively tell a story.

513. McCutchan, Kenneth P. *Old Tales Retold: An Ohio Valley Decameron.* Evansville, IN: K. McCutchan, 1997. i, 212p. Illus.

The one hundred tales in this volume are short, only a page or two. Although they are based in fact, they have been embellished over the years and have attained folklore status. There are natural disasters here, as well as man-made ones, such as fires. Both ordinary people and more famous ones are included. Even John James Audubon is here, along with the persistent legend that he was the illegitimate son of the last King of France.

The tales told here first appeared in McCutcheon's column in the *Evansville [Indiana] Sunday Courier,* and concern Indiana.

514. Neely, Charles. *Tales and Songs of Southern Illinois.* Menasha, WI: G. Banta, 1938; repr., Norwood, Pa.: Norwood Editions, 1973. xix, 270p. Index.

Neely collected the material in these pages between 1935 and 1937. He died in 1937, and the material was then edited into its final form by John Webster Spargo. Neely collected both tales and songs, his only limitation being that the material must come from someone resident in the area of Illinois known as Egypt, the southernmost part of the state.

Tales are divided into the following categories:

Local legends
Humorous tales
Graveyard stories
Ghost stories
Witchcraft
Treasure troves
European folk tales

The second section of the book contains songs, often with music transcribed. Songs are divided into the following:

British ballads
Other imported ballads
American ballads
Western songs
Nursery and game songs
Love
Childhood and temperance
Local-interest ballads

Notes to each chapter give some information on the informant and on the history of a particular story or song.

515. Owen, Mary Alicia. *Voodoo Tales, as Told among the Negroes of the Southwest.* New York: G. P. Putnam's Sons, 1893; repr., New York: Negro Universities Press, 1969. xiv, 310p. Illus. by Juliette A. Owen and Louis Wain. 0-8371-1395-4.

Owen collected these stories in Missouri. She uses the same convention as Joel Chandler in his Uncle Remus tales, of having the tales told by a narrator, in this case several elderly Negro women. Unfortunately, the use of heavy dialect makes the tales not only difficult to read but also offensive to modern attitudes.

Many of the tales have animal characters, similar to those in the Uncle Remus tales.

516. Parks, Douglas R. *Traditional Narratives of the Arikara Indians.* Lincoln: Univ. of Nebraska Press, 1991. vol. 1 xxxiv, 684p.; vol. 2 xiv, 660p; vol. 3 xxiv, 468p; vol. 4 xv, 432p. (Studies in the Anthropology of North American Indians). 90-12889. vol. 1 0-8032-3691-3; vol. 2 0-8032-3692-1; vol. 3 0-8032-3694-8; vol. 4 0-8032-3695-6. Set 0-8032-3698-0.

The first two volumes of the set tell the tales in interlinear fashion—each tale is printed in both Arikara and English, one line of Arikara followed by one line of English. The tales are of creation, animals, the supernatural—all the tales that the Arikara told to make sense of their world. Tales are from a variety of tellers.

Parks's introduction gives detailed information on Arikara history, the central place the stories hold in Arikara life, and on the method of collecting these tales.

Volumes 3 and 4 retell the same tales as those that appear in the first two volumes, but in English only and in a more literary style.

This is a major work of scholarship.

517. Saunders, Don. *When the Moon Is a Silver Canoe: Embracing the History, the Legends, the Music, and the Poetry of the Wisconsin Dells, the Haunt of the Mighty Winnebago and His Woodland Gods.* Sun Prairie, WI: Royle Publishing, 1946; repr., 1968. 109p. Illus.

Legends of the Winnebago Indians, including creation legends, are told here. Many of the tales are told in verse.

518. Schoolcraft, Henry R. *The Myth of Hiawatha; and Other Oral Legends, Mythologic and Allegoric, of the North American Indians.* Philadelphia: J. B. Lippincott, 1856; repr., AuTrain, MI: Avery Color Studios, 1984. xxiv, 343p. 84-70272. 0-932212-35-2pa.

In the first half of the nineteenth century, Henry R. Schoolcraft served as Indian agent for the Upper Great Lakes. He became interested in the Chippewa language and culture and eventually published a vast six-volume work, *Historical and Statistical Information Respecting the History, Condition, and Prospects of the Indian Tribes of the United States* (Philadelphia, 1851–1857), which contained many legends and tales. He published as well various shorter works of Indian legends. Most of these are out of print and difficult to find. This paperback edition makes at least one of his works more readily available.

Among the legends told here is the story of Hiawatha. It was Schoolcraft's works that inspired Henry Wadsworth Longfellow to write his version of the story *Hiawatha*.

The introduction to this volume contains biographical information on Schoolcraft.

519. Smith, David Lee. *Folklore of the Winnebago Tribe*. Norman: Univ. of Oklahoma Press, 1997. xi, 180p. 97-21663. 0-8061-2976-x.

Winnebago Tribe historian David Smith received his introduction to and training in storytelling from his father. Here he recounts for the average reader the great stories of his people. Stories are divided into four groups: the creation stories; trickster stories; myths, all of which explain some natural happening such as why ducks have red eyes; and legends, or tales of the great historical happening of the group.

These tales are readable for today's audience.

520. Taylor, Troy. *Haunted Illinois*. Alton, IL: Whitechapel Productions Press, 1999. 288p. Bibliog. 1-892523-01-9pa.

Troy divides his ghost stories into both cities and regions of Illinois. He has chapters on the ghosts of Chicago, Decatur, Springfield, and Alton; and on the northern part of Illinois and the prairie. In addition, he includes an entire chapter on ghosts stories related to Abraham Lincoln.

521. Tholl, Josephine Bissell, comp. and ed. Ohio Federation of Women's Clubs. *Ohio Legends*. Distributed by Marionettes Club of the Ohio Federation of Women's Clubs, 1984. 548p.

Poetry, prose, and a few short plays mingle in this volume. The legends told in these varied formats concern the early days of Ohio. Although each selection has an author indicated, there is no information given as to where the legend originated or how accurate the retelling is.

522. Thomas, Rosemary Hyde. *It's Good to Tell You: French Folktales from Missouri*. Columbia: Univ. of Missouri Press, 1981. viii, 246p. Illus. by Ronald W. Thomas. Index. Bibliog. 81-50530. 0-8262-0327-2.

In the 1930s, Joseph Medard Carriere wrote down a number of Missouri folktales in French. This book is a translation of these tales into English. The Thomases worked with older people from the Old Mines area of Missouri who still remembered the old French dialect; they discovered that working with the tales actually improved these peoples' remembrance of and facility with the language.

The tales are all fairy tales, some with animals as characters, and they are presented in both French and English.

523. Voices, Davis Many. *Turtle Going Nowhere in the Plenty of Time*. Happy Camp, CA: Naturegraph Publishers, 1996. 39p; 23p. Illus. 96-31387. 0-87961-244-4pa.

You get two books in one in this collection of Native American tales of the Midwest and Southwest. First comes a collection of tales of the natural world, telling such stories as how Rabbit lost his tail; why Raccoon washes his food; and how bluebonnets were introduced into the world.

On the flip side of the book, bound in the opposite direction, comes the story of the monarch butterflies, who are said to carry prayers to heaven on their wings.

The Turtle of the title signifies the essence of these tales—"going everywhere, going nowhere. Turtle is going nowhere in the plenty of time" (Introduction, p. 7).

All the tales are illustrated with line drawings.

524. Welsch, Roger L. *The Liar's Corner: A Garland of Humor Columns from the Pages of the Nebraska Farmer, Fall, 1985–Fall, 1988.* Dannebrog, NE: Plains Heritage, 1988. xxiii, 150p.

The Nebraska Farmer sponsored a contest for tellers of tall tales and published the winners. Many of the tales center around farming, the weather, fishing, and other rural issues.

525. ——. *The Liar's Corner: The Saga Continues: Another Two and a Half Years of Laughter from the Nebraska Farmer's Liar's Corner, Fall 1988–Winter 1991.* Lincoln, NE: J & L Lee, 1993. 110p. 0-934904-32-4.

This is the next installment of prize-winners from *The Nebraska Farmer*'s tall tale contest. Again the focus is on rural pursuits, including a story about prairie dogs that dig up their holes and take them with them when they move.

526. ——. *Omaha Tribal Myths and Trickster Tales.* Athens: Ohio Univ. Press, 1981. 285p. Bibliog. 80-22636. 0-8040-0700-4.

Trickster tales, about Rabbit, Coyote, and Ictinike—the not quite animal, not quite human, ultimate trickster—make up the bulk of this book. Other tales are about adventurers and culture heroes, the animal world, animals and man, and creation and origin.

527. ——. *Shingling the Fog and Other Plains Lies.* Chicago: Swallow Press, 1972; repr., Lincoln: Univ. of Nebraska Press, 1980. 160p. Motif index. Notes. Appendix: List of informants. 79-18730. 0-8032-4709-5. 0-8032-9700-9pa.

Many of the tall tales and "lies" collected here are from a column that ran in the *Nebraska Farmer* in 1924 and 1925. Others Welsch collected from various informants.

The tales concern the land of the Great Plains, mostly Nebraska: the weather, the land itself and its difficulties and vagaries, and the animals that inhabit it, including some mythical ones. The lies are short, often just a line or two.

Notes indicate where the tale was collected. The motif index, based on Stith Thompson's *Motif-Index of Folk-Literature*, indicates when possible the motif of a particular tale.

528. Williams, Mentor L., ed. *Schoolcraft's Indian Legends.* East Lansing: Michigan State Univ. Press, 1956. xxii, 322p. Bibliog. Appendices. 55-11688.

Henry Rowe Schoolcraft first published the Indian legends he collected in the 1820s and 1830s. Since then, they have been reprinted, adapted, and discussed. Longfellow used the legends to create his *Hiawatha.* Here Schoolcraft's legends are reprinted, with a scholarly introduction and discussion. The legends include creation myths, the legend of Manabozho, and stories of animals.

The appendices contain other tales and legends collected by Schoolcraft and a selection of other works by Schoolcraft, including some correspondence.

529. Woodyard, Chris. *Spooky Ohio: 13 Traditional Tales.* Beavercreek, OH: Kestrel Publications, 1995. 84p. Illus. by Jessicca Wiesel. Index. Bibliog. Glossary. 91-75343. 0-9628472-3-2.

In these stories you'll find among others a deserted bride who dies of a broken heart and haunts the graveyard, a soldier escorted home from war by the ghost of his dead brother, and a protective mother who keeps suitors away from her daughter even after the mother's death. In addition to the stories themselves, the author appends a glossary of old-fashioned words; historical notes on the tales, such as information on battles; and a bibliography of other sources.

The stories are written in language simple enough for older children to read and understand.

530. Wyman, Walker D. *Stories about Hunters and Hunting in Wisconsin and the North Country: Ninety-one Yarns Told in Deer Camps, Taverns and Cafes in the Cutover Country of the Great Lakes Region.* River Falls: Univ. of Wisconsin–River Falls Press, 1987. 66p. Illus. pa.

The author of *Wisconsin and North Country Stories about Fish and Fishermen: Sixty Yarns Told about Fishing Bass, Muskies, Trout, and Other Species by Truth-Telling Outdoorsmen,* here tells similar tales about hunting. Paul Bunyan is again a figure in some of the brief tales.

531. ——. *Wisconsin and North Country Stories about Fish and Fishermen: Sixty Yarns Told about Fishing Bass, Muskies, Trout, and Other Species by Truth-Telling Outdoorsmen.* River Falls: Univ. of Wisconsin-River Falls Press, 1986. v, 42p. Illus. pa.

Tall tales about fishing abound. Here are sixty brief ones, including a few about Paul Bunyan. At one point he attached fishhooks to cows' tails, and drove the cows back and forth across a river. The cows caught fish to feed the men in Paul's lumber camp.

532. ——. *Wisconsin and North Country Wolf and Bear Stories: Seventy-Five Stories Told by Pioneer Settlers, Lumberjacks and Other Yarn Spinners.* River Falls: Univ. of Wisconsin–River Falls Press, 1984. iv, 68p. Illus. pa.

Many of the stories told here are anecdotes of individual's encounters with bears. Others, however, are of the tall tale variety, and some are myths, such as how the bear got his short tail and why bears hibernate.

Folk Music

533. Beck, Earl Clifton. *Lore of the Lumber Camps.* Rev. and enlarged. Ann Arbor: Univ. of Michigan Press, 1948. xii, 348p. Index of Ballads and Songs. Index of Music and Tunes. Bibliog.

The bulk of this book consists of songs from Michigan lumber camps, 118 in all. Songs are divided into categories:

Life in the Lumbering Camps
The Lumberjack and the Lumberjill
Dialect Songs
Tragedies in the Woods
Bunkhouse Ballads
Names in the Timberlands

A few of the songs have music transcribed.

Beck adds a section of tall tales and a lengthy introduction that gives the history of lumbering in Michigan, including names of specific lumberjacks and lumbering companies.

534. ——. *Songs of the Michigan Lumberjacks.* Ann Arbor: Univ. of Michigan Press, 1941. xi, 296p. Illus. Index of Ballads and Songs. Index of Tunes. Bibliog. Appendix of tall tales. (University of Michigan Studies and Publications).

Beck states in his introduction that he

did not intend for this to be a scholarly collection and explanation of the music of lumberjacks, but rather "to preserve here, as one species of Americana, the folk songs of the Michigan lumberjack" (p. 7). Nevertheless, he has included information on the origin and history of most of the songs, in headnotes. Most of the songs are transcribed without music.

Beck presents 104 songs, divided into the following categories:

"A-Lumbering Go" songs
Shantyman's Life
The Day's Work
Men at Play
Love and the Lumberjack
Death and the Shanty Boy
Moniker Songs
French-Canadian Songs
Bunkhouse Ballads
"The Greatest Logger in the Land"
(Paul Bunyan)

An appendix tells a few tall tales, such as one from a man who tamed two fish. They became so tame that they sat on the porch with him in rocking chairs, and he taught them to whistle. When he fell into the water and was in danger of drowning, these fish whistled to call up their friends. The fish banded together and pushed the man to shore.

535. Belden, H. M., ed. *Ballads and Songs Collected by the Missouri Folk-Lore Society.* 2d ed. Columbia: Univ. of Missouri, 1940; repr., 1955. xx, 532p. Index. (University of Missouri Studies, v. 15, no. 1). 55-7519.

Some one hundred people were involved in collecting these songs. Most were collected in the first decade of the twentieth century, but a few were contributed later. In all, Belden spent about forty years on this work, soliciting contributions from collectors and editing the collection. He includes 287 songs, for the most part without music transcribed. Headnotes with each song indicate the contributor and give a history of the song.

536. Brewster, Paul G. *Ballads and Songs of Indiana.* Bloomington: Indiana Univ., 1940. 376p. Index of Titles. Index of First Lines. Index of Tunes. Preface by Stith Thompson. (Indiana University Publications, Folklore Series.)

Brewster collected and presented one hundred ballads and songs of the region, many with numerous variations. He included tunes for fourteen of them.

As Stith Thompson wrote in his preface to the volume, residents of Indiana can find here "a part of their traditional life that might otherwise have perished" (p. 5).

537. Eddy, Mary O., ed. *Ballads and Songs from Ohio.* New York: J. J. Augustin, 1939; repr., Hatboro, PA: Folklore Associates, 1964. xxvii, 330p. Index to Contributors. Index to Titles. Index to First Lines.

This is considered the major collection of Ohio folk songs in existence. It is limited mainly to the area of northern Ohio. Most were gathered through personal contact, although Eddy also examined a number of old manuscript sources, including booklets of favorite songs handwritten by various schoolchildren. The songs are not arranged by category.

Eddy includes tunes for many of the songs.

538. Gardner, Emelyn Elizabeth, and Geraldine Jencks Chickering. *Ballads and Songs of Southern Michigan.* Ann Arbor: Univ. of Michigan Press, 1939; repr., Hatboro, PA: Folklore Associates, 1967. xviii,

501p. Illus. Index of Tunes. Index of Ballads and Songs. Bibliog. List of informants.

In 1937, Emelyn Elizabeth Gardner published *Folklore from the Schoharie Hills* (Ann Arbor: Univ. of Michigan Press, 1937). This slightly later volume concentrates on folk songs, rather than the mixture of legends, tales, superstitions, and songs that filled her earlier work.

She divides her songs into the following categories:

Unhappy Love
Happy Love
War
Occupations
Disasters
Crimes
Religion
Humor
Nursery

Headnotes give the name of the informant of a particular song, as well as a history and a discussion of variants.

539. Hicks, John Edward. *When Mother Sang: A Book of Folksong, Folklore and Childlore.* Kansas City, MO: Indian Creek Books,1997. v, 152p. Illus. Index. Bibliog.

Written mostly as a loving tribute to his mother, Hicks's book interweaves stories of the old days and songs. The songs are integrated into the stories of his mother; he always presents the context in which they were sung.

Although the book is entertaining, and contains endless snippets of information about daily life in early twentieth century Midwest, its format makes it difficult to locate either specific information or specific songs.

No music is transcribed with the songs.

540. Martin, Phil. *Across the Fields: Fiddle Tunes and Button Accordian Melodies.* Dodgeville, WI: Wisconsin Old-Time Music Project, 1982. 48p. Illus. with photographs by Lewis Koch and historical photographs. Index. pa.

A companion to the LP *Across the Fields* (FVF 201), this booklet presents traditional tunes and songs from the Norwegian American communities in rural Wisconsin, particularly the "coulee country" of west central Wisconsin. The tunes were played at dance parties in the area during the early part of the century. It is the first time many of these songs have been recorded or written down. Biographical sketches of the musicians accompany many of the songs.

The introduction chronicles the development of this music, from its origins in Norway through its adaptation to the American environment, and the photographs, both historical and contemporary, give a flavor of the landscape and of the musicians.

541. Peters, Harry B., ed. *Folk Songs out of Wisconsin: An Illustrated Compendium of Words and Music.* Madison: State Historical Society of Wisconsin, 1977. 311p. Illus. Index of Song Titles. 77-1793. 0-87020-165-4.

About two hundred songs—with music transcribed—are included in this volume. They were collected over a long period of time, most in the 1920s, 1930s, and 1940s, by a variety of people. Many of the songs reflect Wisconsin's geographic placement, with their emphasis on waterways, either the Great Lakes or the Mississippi River Basin. Others concern working life, work on boats or on railways, work in the lumber camps or on farms. And of course there are the usual themes of folk music: courtship and love, death and loss, patriotism, friendship, war, and recreation.

Peters includes headnotes to many songs, giving the history of the song, if known, and some information about how and where it was collected. He also includes portions of a journal written by Franz Rickaby, one of the prime collectors of this material, while working in the field in 1919. This journal gives a great flavor of the times and of the conditions under which a folk music collector worked. Also contributing to this flavor are the ample photographs throughout the book.

542. Rickaby, Franz. *Ballads and Songs of the Shanty-Boy.* Cambridge, MA: Harvard Univ. Press, 1926. xii, 244p. Illus. Glossary. Notes. Index of Titles. Index of First Lines. 26-11830.

The glossary of this work defines *shanty-boy* as "a member of a logging crew. A lumber-jack." The songs preserved here are the ones the shanty-boys sang at work and at play. Rickaby includes "all obtainable variants and fragments" (p. viii) and also transcribes the music.

Folk Belief and Ritual

543. Cook, Marshall, ed. *Wisconsin Folklife: A Celebration of Wisconsin Traditions.* Madison: Wisconsin Academy of Sciences, Arts and Letters, 1998. 64p. Illus.

Old and new folklore are blended here in this celebration of Wisconsin ways. There are chapters on the polka, on dairy farming, on birch-bark canoes made by the Ojibwe, on sturgeon fishing, and on church suppers. Also celebrated are the

Harley and the Green Bay Packers, more recent icons around which people rally.

544. Hodge, Robert A. *Some Madstones of Kansas.* Emporia, KS: Robert A. Hodge, 1997. 39p. Maps. Index. References. pa.

Madstones are objects believed to have the power of identifying a wound made by a venomous animal such as a snake or scorpion, sticking to it until the venom is neutralized, then dropping off. Hodge has collected numerous tales of these madstones and collects them here.

He arranges his stories according to the county in Kansas where they took place, and provides hand-drawn maps indicating each county. Stories are documented by newspaper accounts of the events.

545. Hyatt, Harry Middleton. *Folk-Lore from Adams County Illinois.* New York: Alma Egan Hyatt Foundation, 1935. xvi, 723p. Index. (Memoirs of the Alma Egan Hyatt Foundation).

This volume is similar in format and content to Annie Weston Whitney's *Folk-Lore from Maryland* (New York: American Folklore Society, 1925; repr., New York: Kraus Reprint, 1969). It is more than tales, including sayings, customs, superstitions, folk medicine, children's rhymes, weather lore—all the sayings and beliefs of "the folk." It is arranged by category, with a subject index. It consists primarily of brief, pithy sayings and beliefs, such as "If you sneeze before three o'clock, it means you are going to receive a letter."

Although the information was collected from an extremely small geographic area (within a ten-square-mile area around Quincy, Illinois), many of the sayings and beliefs were or are known and believed over a much wider range.

546. *Iowa's Early Home Remedies.* Sioux City, IA: Quixote Press, 1990. xi, 179p. Index. 1-878488-29-5pa.

Collected by high school students through interviews with their parents, grandparents, other relatives, and family friends, this small book gathers together folk remedies from times when "doctors were not sent for unless there was an extreme emergency and the drugstore was a rarity" (p. ix). Remedies are grouped by type of ailment.

547. Kessler, John S., and Donald B. Ball. *North from the Mountains: A Folk History of the Carmel Melungeon Settlement, Highland County, Ohio.* Macon, GA: Mercer Univ. Press, 2001. xvi, 220p. Illus. Index. Bibliog. Appendices. 00-052549. 0-86554-700-9; 0-86554-703-3pa.

The Melungeon are a people of mixed heritage: Native American, Asian, and European. Historically, they lived in Appalachia, in Tennessee, and Virginia. This study looks at a group living in a very small area of Ohio.

Although most of the book examines the history and origins of the people, a major section describes everyday life. The authors describe such everyday artifacts and activities as housing, laundry, clothing, foodstuffs, and plants used. Another section looks at rituals and customs around medicine, birth and death, child rearing, and marriage.

548. Koch, William E. *Folklore from Kansas: Customs, Beliefs, and Superstitions.* Lawrence: Regents Press of Kansas, 1980. xvii, 467p. Appendices. 79-20197. 0-7006-0192-9.

Like *Folk-Lore from Adams County, Illinois* (New York: Alma Egan Hyatt Foundation, 1935), this is a compendium of folk belief, arranged by category. In it one can find beliefs related to courtship, weddings, death, illness and injury, dreams, luck, the weather, plants, animals, and hunting and fishing.

In his introduction, Koch acknowledges his debt to Wayland D. Hand, who edited similar volumes for the multivolume collection of North Carolina folklore, *Frank Brown Collection of North Carolina Folklore* (Durham, NC: Duke Univ. Press, 1952–1964).

The information here is in the form of brief sentences or phrases, without annotation or explanation.

Students of folklore at Kansas State University collected the information during the 1960s. The complete collection, noted on 3 x 5 file cards, is housed at the Kansas State Historical Society Library.

549. Marimen, Mark. *Haunted Indiana 2.* Grand Rapids, MI: Thunder Bay Press, 1999. 146p. Notes. 1-882376-71-4pa.

Poltergeists, haunted mansions, and even the ghost of Amelia Earhart inhabit the pages of this collection of Indiana ghost stories.

550. Meckstroth, Glenna. *Tales from Great-Grandpa's Trunk: A Lighthearted Look at Rural Life.* New Knoxville, OH: G. Meckstroth, 1998. ix, 528p. 0-7880-1410-2.

Meckstroth's reminiscences of her childhood, as well as stories that her parents and grandparents told her of their own, make up this book. It contains much information about daily domestic life in the early part of the twentieth century: cooking, laundry, transportation, farming, and education. In addition, there is some reference to customs surrounding birth, marriage, and death.

The lack of an index makes it difficult to locate specific information, but, on the whole, this is an interesting read.

551. Thomas, Rosemary Hyde, ed. *Tra-*

ditional Uses of Wild Plants in Missouri. Special Issue of *Missouri Folklore Society Journal.* Vol. X, 1988. Columbia: Missouri Folklore Society, 1988. vi, 110p. Illus. Most of the articles have a bibliography.

A variety of topics are explored in this issue of *Missouri Folklore Society Journal* devoted to uses of plants. Two of the articles are biographical; one concerns George Engelmann (1809–1884), the other Julian Steyermark (1909–1988), both early Missouri botanists. Other articles concern medicinal uses of plants, uses within the Native American community, food uses, and uses in dying.

552. *Wisconsin's Early Home Remedies.* Sioux City, IA: Quixote Press, 1991. xi, 172p. Index. 1-878488-55-4pa.

This is similar to *Iowa's Early Home Remedies* (Sioux City, IA: Quixote Press, 1990), in that it is a listing of remedies for everything from cuts and scrapes to measles and sinus problems. As with remedies in the earlier book, high school students collected these through interviews with relatives and friends.

553. Wolf, Robert, ed. *Village Voices: Stories from the Amana Colonies.* Lansing, IA: Free River Press, 1996. 101p. (Free River Press Folk Literature Series). 1-878781-12-Xpa.

Some dozen residents of the Amana Colonies in Iowa tell their stories here. Not strictly folklore, these stories are of the old ways that are disappearing, even in these traditional communities: planting, beekeeping, singing, worship, getting married, and giving birth.

Material Culture

554. Arpy, Jim. *The Magnificent Mississippi.* Grinnell: Iowa Heritage Gallery/ Publications, 1983. 134p. Illus. 0-910381-07-0.

Fact and legend are mingled in this book. Lavishly illustrated with black-and-white photos, this depicts such disparate professions as rafting and rafters, the steamboat world of Mark Twain, and the circus. It depicts, too, the natural world of floods and earthquakes.

The copious illustrations, combined with the informal, reportorial style of writing, make this an engaging book.

555. Dégh, Linda. *Indiana Folklore: A Reader.* Bloomington: Indiana Univ. Press, 1980. viii, 311p. Illus. Bibliog. Index to the Bibliography. 79-2970. 0-253-20239-6.

Many people contributed to this reader; each chapter is written by a different person. Sections include:

Old Crafts and Skills (dry stone walling, covered bridges, quilting)
Place-Names and Oral History
Folk Belief, Medicine, and Magic
Horror Stories
Ghosts

Many of the chapters include a bibliography.

556. Dufur, Brett. *The Best of Missouri Hands: Profiles of the State's Fine Artists and Craftsmen.* Columbia, MO: Pebble Publishing, 1996. vii, 135p. Illus. Index. (Show Me Missouri Series). 0-9646625-5-8pa.

Carvers, basket weavers, and furniture makers are just some of the artisans profiled here in short (one to two pages) profiles. Photographs of both the artisans and examples of their works are included.

Dufur also includes a list of craft shops that carry the artisans' work and an index to types of crafts, to assist the reader in locating craftspeople working in a particular medium.

557. Dvorachek, Dorothy Ann, and Rochelle H. Saltzman. *Iowa Folklife Resource Directory: Performing Arts, Material Culture, Occupations, Display Events, Ethnic and Regional Museums and Cultural Organizations, Researchers/Consultants.* Des Moines: Iowa Folklife Program, Iowa Arts Council, Dept. of Cultural Affairs, 1997. iv, 58p. Illus. pa.

Individuals who maintain the old traditions are listed here, with contact information. Performing artists, craftspeople, cooks, and architects working in the vernacular tradition are all listed. Also included are names of people who work in traditional occupations: auctioneers, blacksmiths, cabinetmakers, carpenters, woodworkers, farmers, firefighters, butchers, horse trainers, meat packers, and makers of musical instruments.

Other chapters list museums and annual events.

558. *Festival of Iowa Folklife.* Des Moines: Iowa Sesquicentennial Commission, 1996. 60p. Illus.

In 1996, Iowa celebrated its 150th anniversary of statehood. A four-day festival was held on the state capitol grounds in August, with exhibits, concerts, and demonstrations of such folk arts as quilting, basket weaving, and knot tying. There were also events and demonstrations that highlighted particular ethnic groups, such as the Danish or the Meskwaki culture. This publication was the program of the festival.

In addition, throughout 1996, various communities in Iowa celebrated the Sesquicentennial with numerous fairs, parades, festivals, and concerts; these are spotlighted throughout the program.

559. Garland, Hamlin. *A Son of the Middle Border.* 1917. Reprint, New York: Macmillan, 1962. xiv, 401p. Bibliog.

Garland describes his boyhood in a variety of farms and villages in the Midwest. His book has become a classic. Rural life, its duties, daily tasks, recreations, and social relationships, is described in detail and with feeling.

560. Kaufman, Stanley A. *Amish in Eastern Ohio.* Walnut Creek, OH: German Culture Museum, 1991. 52p. Illus. Bibliog. pa.

Many pictures fill this book about the Amish. Kaufman provides a brief history of the Amish in Ohio, along with discussions of furniture, architecture, and folk arts.

561. ——. *Germanic Folk Culture in Eastern Ohio.* Walnut Creek, OH: German Culture Museum, 1986. 52p. Illus. pa.

Similar to Kaufman's other books, this reveals the history of Germans in Ohio through an examination of their folk art and ornaments. Kaufman writes about architecture, furniture, quilts, coverlets, Fraktur, metalwork, costume, and household. The book is dense with illustrations.

562. ——. *Moravians in Ohio.* Walnut Creek, OH: German Culture Museum, 1987. 52p. Illus. Bibliog. pa.

This is similar to Kaufman's *Amish in Eastern Ohio* and *Germanic Folk Culture in Eastern Ohio* (see entries). Kaufman packs this slim volume with details about the way of life of the Moravians, the earliest Germanic group to settle in Ohio. He discusses—and illustrates with photographs—church architecture and furnishings, house architecture, furniture, music, Fraktur, metalwork, textiles, housewares, and toys.

563. Liffring-Zug, Joan, and John Zug. *Seven Amana Villages: Recipes, Crafts, Folk Arts from the Seven Amana Villages of East, Amana, Middle, High, West, South, and Homestead.* Iowa City, IA: Penfield Press, 1981. [34p.]. Illus. 0-9603858-7-8pa.

A guidebook for the seven Amana villages, this small booklet gives a brief overview—copiously illustrated—of various Amana traditional crafts, such as weaving, basket making, furniture, and clocks. Some recipes are included. Obviously not an exhaustive study, it is nevertheless an intriguing first look at these communities.

564. Nothdurft, Lillian. *Folklore and Early Customs of Southeast Missouri.* New York: Exposition Press, 1972. 77p. 0-682-47495-9.

Similar to Henry Middleton Hyatt's *Folk-Lore from Adams County Illinois* (New York: Alma Egan Hyatt Foundation, 1935), this does the same thing for a section of Missouri. It contains sketches of folk characters, folk sayings, beliefs, medicine, tall tales, and a host of information about everyday life, with vignettes of corn shuckings, church socials, quilting parties, picnics, and other activities.

565. *Ohio Folk Traditions: A New Generation.* n.p. A. Govenar, 1981. 22p. Illus. Bibliog.

Although small, this book has information in it hard to find elsewhere. It profiles four Ohio artists working in traditional folk crafts—and two working in crafts, which could become traditional. Each profile consists of a brief description of the artist's work, some information about how they came to work in the particular craft, and several illustrations. Traditional crafts are stone carving, quilting, wood carving, and rag rug weaving; new traditions are chain saw carving and tattooing

566. Perkins, Stan. *Lore of Wolverine Country.* Swartz Creek, MI: Broadblade Press, 1984. xii, 244p. Illus. 0-940404-08-7pa.

Perkins presents brief vignettes of rural life in Michigan. Life at the one-room schoolhouse, on the farm, and in the workplace are all included. He also has stories on rural sports and leisure pastimes, such as hunting, fishing, and county fairs; on various modes of transportation, such as horse cars and steamboats; and information on medicine and religion. All in all, it is a varied book that gives an idea of many aspects of rural life a century ago.

567. Pond, Samuel W. *Dakota Life in the Upper Midwest.* St. Paul: Minnesota Historical Society, 1986, repr. 2002. xxi, 192p. Index. 2002-32598. 0-87351-455-6pa.

First published in 1908, under the title "The Dakotas or Sioux in Minnesota as they were in 1834," in *Collections of the Minnesota Historical Society*, vol. 12, the material here was collected and written down by Samuel W. Pond in the 1870s. He and his brother, Gideon H. Pond, worked with the Dakota people near Prairie du Chien and eventually compiled a dictionary of their language, several books of the Bible in translation, and some hymnals. In the course of their work, they also compiled this ethnographic study.

The Ponds recorded information on the "Dakota material culture and social, political, religious, and economic institutions" (Introduction, p. xi). Information on everyday living, such as farming methods, tools, dress, housing, and personal appearance; on language; on the arts, such as poetry and music; on religion, ritual, and customs around death and immortality; and on medicine and healing are all included.

568. Schmeal, Jacqueline Andre. *Iowa Folk Artists*. Ames: Iowa State Univ. Press, 1998. x, 126p. Illus. Bibliog. 98-7575. 0-8138-2889-9.

Schmeal gives both biographical information and information about the artists' craft in this volume. Artists include carvers, potters, quilters, and those working with corn husks. Quaker traditions, as well as of those of the Amish and of the Amana communities, are profiled.

569. Welsch, Roger, and Solomon D. Butcher. *Sod Walls*. Broken Bow, NE: Purcells, 1968. xv, 208p. Illus. Index. Bibliog. 68-21835.

Solomon Butcher, born in 1856, developed early on a fascination with the sod houses of the prairie. He became a photographer and spent the years from 1886 to 1892 traveling in Nebraska and taking photographs of the people and the structures. He concentrated on Custer County, Nebraska.

Nearly a hundred years later, folklorist Roger Welsch discovered the archive of Butcher's photographs and began the project that resulted in this book. Many of the photos are reproduced here, with explanation. Welsch examines more than the actual building of sod houses. He discusses the life that went on inside them, furnishings, leisure activities, farming activities, and family relationships. He adds a chapter of folk songs associated with the prairie.

570. Whorrall, Bill. *Voices from the Hills: Oral History and Folk Tales from Martin County, Indiana and Surrounding Areas.*

Shoals, IN: Bill Whorrall, 1995. 270p. Illus. by David Alford. Index. 94-090697.

Whorrall has collected from longtime residents of Martin County, Indiana, their reminiscences and memories of life lived long ago. Some of the stories told here are stories the teller heard from an earlier generation. The stories are of everyday life in a rural community, of farm life and work, of church and school, of recreational pursuits, of courting, marriage, and death.

It is Whorrall's hope that these stories will inspire others to record their own family memories. As he says, in this age of television and video cameras, the art of telling stories is threatened with loss.

Whorral doesn't stand in the way of his storytellers. The book is not arranged by subject or theme, but by teller. Each storyteller simply tells the story, often with one subject blending into another, in his or her own voice. An index helps locate information on a particular topic, but it is by reading the stories all the way through that one receives an impression of the teller, and through that teller, of a way of life gone by.

Folklore for Children

571. Arnold, Caroline. *The Terrible Hodag*. San Diego, CA: Harcourt Brace Jovanovich, 1989. 32p. Illus. by Lambert Davis. 88-18724. 0-15-2847540-2.

Arnold has used both her imagination and her memories of stories told at camp to tell this tale of the terrible Hodag, the frightening looking beast created with the body parts of several different animals, including an ox and a bear. The Hodag proves not to be so terrible after all, when he helps the loggers outwit an unfair boss. In return, the loggers promise never to cut every tree, but to leave enough so that the Hodag will have a place to live.

572. Balcziak, Bill. *Paul Bunyan.* Minneapolis: Compass Point Books, 2003. 32p. Illus. by Patrick Girouard. Glossary. Index. Bibliog. (The Imagination Series: Tall Tales). 2002-15118. 0-7565-0459-7.

Balcziak tells the timeless tales of Paul Bunyan anew: his birth—which "took six strong storks to carry him to his new parents' home in Maine" (p. 8); his finding of Babe, the Blue Ox, in a snowstorm; and his life as a lumberjack.

Although a brief book, obviously written for children, this version of *Paul Bunyan* is structured like a book for older children or adults, with its glossary, index, and bibliography. It adds a touch of fun for the young readers, however—a recipe for Paul's pancakes.

The illustrations by Patrick Girouard are in full color.

573. Benton-Banai, Edward. *The Mishomis Book: The Voice of the Ojibway.* St. Paul, MN: Indian Country Press, 1979. v, 114p. Illus. pa.

From the creation of the earth and of the Ojibway people, through their final migration to an island in Lake Superior, at the northern end of Wisconsin, Benton-Banai tells the story of the Ojibway. Throughout the entire story, he emphasizes the respect with which the people have always treated the earth and their efforts to live in harmony with it.

He states in a brief paragraph of introduction that he "has been careful not to profane any of the Ojibway teachings" (p. ii).

574. Calhoun, Mary. *High Wind for Kansas.* New York: William Morrow, 1965. 48p. Illus. by W. T. Mars. 65-11776.

Several people built wind wagons during the period of Western migration, thinking to harness the wind to propel people to the West. This account, although fictional, is based on an incident that happened in Westport, Missouri, when a man built such a wind-powered vehicle. In this story, he overreaches himself by building such a huge wind wagon that he loses control of it and ends up capsizing on the plains. There are stories today of a ghostly wind wagon occasionally seen on the plains, still swooping with the wind.

575. Cavender-Gougé, Lorraine, ed. *Collection of Legends and Stories.* n.p.: n.p., 1983. xiii, 52p. pa.

Taken from *Wigwam Evenings: Sioux Folk Tales Retold* by Charles A. Eastman and Elaine Goodale Eastman (Eau Claire, WI: E. M. Hale, 1909), this retells some of the tales told in that text. They are Sioux folktales retold for children aged five and up. There are creation tales, animal tales, and, as the introduction puts it, "brave and fortunate heroes, and beautiful princesses, and wicked old witches, and magical transformations, and all the other dear old familiar material of fairy lore" (p. iv). The introduction also points out the parallels between these tales and tales of other cultures that deal with witches, tricksters, gnomes, and other fanciful creatures.

The original 1909 edition consisted of 252 pages; this obviously much briefer version tells only a few of the stories.

576. Eastman, Charles A., and Elaine Goodale Eastman. *Wigwam Evenings: Sioux Folk Tales Retold.* Eau Claire, WI: E. M. Hale, 1909. xvi, 253p. Illus. by Edwin Willard Deming.

These tales of animals, heroes, princes,

and princesses, have been retold many times, most recently in the 1983 publication, *Collection of Legends and Stories,* edited by Lorraine Cavender-Gougé.

577. Erdoes, Richard, ed. *The Sound of Flutes and Other Indian Legends, Told by Lame Deer, Jenny Leading Cloud, Leonard Crow Dog, and Others.* New York: Pantheon Books, 1976. 129p. Illus. by Paul Goble. 76-8660. 0-394-83181-0. 0-394-93181-5 (lib. binding).

The stories transcribed here by Richard Erdoes were told to him by various people from the Sioux, Cheyenne, and Crow Indians.

578. Grisdale, Alex, as told to Nan Shipley. *Wild Drums: Tales and Legends of the Plains Indians.* Winnipeg: Peguis Publishers, 1974. vii, 78p. Illus. by Jim Ellis. 75-68. 0-919566-11-1. 0-919566-35-9pa.

Grisdale heard these stories from his own parents and grandparents and told them in turn to his children and grandchildren. This book is his attempt to make them available to a wider audience. The book tells tales of the Assiniboines, Cree, Sioux, Saulteaux, and Blackfoot, all Plains Indians.

These are perhaps too difficult for very young children, but school-age children would enjoy having them read to them.

579. Larned, W. T. *America Indian Fairy Tales.* New York: Derrydale, 1998. 119p. Illus. 97-50637. 0-517-20300-6.

At the beginning of the nineteenth century, Henry R. Schoolcraft lived among the Native American peoples of the Great Lakes. He listened to and collected their stories of "when the world was young" (p. 7). Here are adaptations of these stories, told for a young audience. The illustrations are in full color.

580. McCormick, Dell J. *Paul Bunyan Swings His Ax.* Calwell, ID: Caxton Printers, 1936. 111p. Illus. by Dell J. McCormick.

Although stories of Paul Bunyan locate him throughout the United States (he was born in Maine, say some, and he dug Puget Sound in Washington), he is most often seen in the woods of Minnesota. In this book McCormick tells the well-known tales of Paul Bunyan for children.

581. ——. *Tall Timber Tales: More Paul Bunyan Stories.* Caldwell, ID: Caxton Printers, 1939. 155p. Illus. by Lorna Livesley.

McCormick here presents a second collection of the Paul Bunyan stories for children.

582. Sherman, Betty Carriveau. *Tales Papa Told.* New York: Vantage Press, 1981. x, 155p. Illus. by Dick Francis. 80-52572. 533-04757-0.

Carriveau's father was French Canadian; her mother was French. These are tales her father told her when she was a child, and some came from his French-Canadian family. Others were ones he heard in the bunkhouses of Wisconsin lumber camps. Most of the tales are filled with larger-than-life characters, witches, kings and princesses, but also with common people who cope with strange adventures. Most of the tales have a moral, with the good people rewarded and the evil getting their just desserts.

583. Spavin, Don. *Chippewa Dawn: Legends of an Indian People.* Bloomington, MN: Voyageur Press, 1977. 55p. Illus. by Jack Kraywinkle.

Spavin says of these legends, which he heard as a boy growing up on the White Earth Reservation in northwestern Minnesota, "these were our fairy tales" (p. 5). He goes on to say that all peoples, if not formally educated, need to explain natural phenomena. These legends were one attempt to do so.

The legends concern how certain natural landmarks were created ("How Leech Lake Was Formed"), how certain creatures acquired their identifying characteristics ("How the Rabbit Got Its Long Ears"), or how mankind developed certain skills ("How the Chippewa Got Fire"). More largely, they deal with the creation of the earth and the Chippewa's place on it.

584. *Wisconsin Folklore.* Madison: State Historical Society of Wisconsin, 1973. 64p. Illus. (Badger History, vol. 25, no. 2). 0005-3759pa.

Written for children, this slim booklet presents legends and stories of the Menomini, tall tales of Wisconsin, superstitions, weather folklore, and folk songs. These sections are interspersed with activities such as a crossword puzzle and vocabulary words. The end papers give suggestions on further activities—writing a poem based on a legend, drawing a mural, or asking a folksinger to come to a class.

Literary Authors: A Selected List

Below is a selected list of authors who reflect and interpret the history and atmosphere of their region. These are authors of novels, poems, short stories, or reminiscences. Through reading the works of these authors, one can acquire knowledge of the history, people, and flavor of the region. This is not a complete list, either of authors, or of their works, but rather one calculated to start readers exploring and discovering their own favorites.

Aldrich, Bess Streeter, 1881–1954

A Lantern in Her Hand
The Rim of the Prairie

Anderson, Sherwood, 1876–1941

Major Fiction of Sherwood Anderson
Tar: A Midwest Childhood
Winesburg, Ohio

Cather, Willa, 1873–1947

Lucy Gayheart
My Antonia
O Pioneers!

Clemens, Samuel (Mark Twain), 1835–1910

The Adventures of Huckleberry Finn
The Adventures of Tom Sawyer
The Celebrated Jumping Frog of Calaveras County and Other Sketches
Life on the Mississippi

Dell, Floyd, 1887–1969

Homecoming: An Autobiography
Moon-Calf

Dreiser, Theodore, 1871–1945

An American Tragedy
The Financier
Newspaper Days
Sister Carrie

Dunbar, Paul Laurence, 1872–1906

Candle-Lightin' Time
The Heart of Happy Hollow
In Old Plantation Days

Eggleston, Edward, 1837–1902

The Graysons: A Story of Illinois
The Hoosier School-Boy
The Hoosier School Master: A Story of
  Backwoods Life in Indiana

Ferber, Edna, 1887–1968

Cimarron
Giant

Garland, Hamlin, 1860–1940

Boy Life on the Prairie
A Daughter of the Middle Border
The Forester's Daughter: A Romance of the
  Bear-Tooth Range
Prairie Folks
A Son of the Middle Border

Howells, William Dean, 1837–1920

Dr. Breen's Practice
The Kentons
My Year in a Log Cabin
The Rise of Silas Lapham

Hughes, Langston, 1902–1967

The Big Sea: An Autobiography
The Collected Poems of Langston Hughes
Mule Bone: A Comedy of Negro Life
Short Stories
Simple's Uncle Sam

Lane, Rose Wilder, 1887–1968

Let the Hurricane Roar
On the Way Home: A Diary of a Trip
  from South Dakota to Mansfield,
  Missouri, in 1894

Lewis, Sinclair, 1885–1951

Arrowsmith
Babbitt
Cass Timberlane: A Novel of Husbands
  and Wives
Elmer Gantry
Main Street: The Story of Carol Kennicott

Lindsay, Vachel, 1879–1931

Collected Poems
The Poetry of Vachel Lindsay
The Prose of Vachel Lindsay

Masters, Edgar Lee, 1868–1950

The Enduring Legacy: Edgar Lee Masters'
  Uncollected Spoon River Poems
The New Spoon River
Spoon River Anthology

Mencken, H(enry) L(ouis), 1880–1956

The Bathtub Hoax and Other Blasts and
  Bravos from the Chicago Tribune
The Diary of H. L. Mencken
Thirty-Five Years of Newspaper Work: A
  Memoir

Richter, Conrad, 1890–1968

The Awakening Land: The Trees, The
  Fields, The Town
The Light in the Forest
The Sea of Grass

Riley, James Whitcomb, 1849–1916

The Complete Poetical Works of James
  Whitcomb Riley
The Poems and Prose Sketches of James
  Whitcomb Riley

Rølvaag, Ole Edvart, 1876–1931

The Boat of Longing
Giants in the Earth: A Saga of the Prairie

Sandburg, Carl, 1878–1967

Abraham Lincoln: The Prairie Years
Chicago Poems
More Rootabagas
Rootabaga Stories
Slabs of the Sunburnt West

Sinclair, Upton, 1878–1968

American Outpost: A Book of
   Reminiscences
Autobiography
The Jungle
The Metropolis

Smiley, Jane, 1949–

Moo
A Thousand Acres

Stegner, Wallace, 1909–1993

Angle of Repose
Conversations with Wallace Stegner on
   Western History and Literature
Crossing to Safety
The Gathering of Zion: The Story of the
   Mormon Trail

Stratton-Porter, Gene(va Grace),
1863–1924

A Girl of the Limberlost
The Harvester
Her Father's Daughter

Suckow, Ruth, 1892–1960

Country People
Iowa Interiors
A Ruth Suckow Omnibus
Some Others and Myself: Seven Stories
   and a Memoir

Tarkington, Booth, 1869–1946

The Gentleman from Indiana
The Magnificent Ambersons
Penrod
Penrod and Sam
Seventeen

Wilder, Laura Ingalls, 1867–1957

By the Shores of Silver Lake
Dance at Grandpa's
Farmer Boy
Little House in the Big Woods
Little House on the Prairie
The Long Winter
These Happy Golden Years

Museums of the Region: A Selected List

Museums that feature everyday life abound in all regions of the country. Through the display of clothing, farm implements, household goods, industrial tools, or entire houses, workshops, and communities, these museums can help people of today understand and appreciate the lives lived by those who came before. The list below is not a complete list of museums in the region, but by browsing through it, one can get a glimpse of the richness of museum offerings. Explore on your own and discover even more fascinating museums.

Illinois

Aurora

Blackberry Historical Farm-Village
Barnes Road
Aurora, Illinois 60506
630-892-1550
http://www.ilohwy.com/b/blackhfv.htm

Schingoethe Center for Native American
   Cultures
Aurora University
347 South Gladstone Avenue
Aurora, Illinois 60506
630-844-5656
http://www.aurora.edu/museum/

Bishop Hill

Bishop Hill Heritage Museum
103 North Bishop Hill Street
Bishop Hill, Illinois 61419
309-927-3899
http://www.bishophill.com/links.html

Chicago

DuSable Museum of African American
   History
740 East 56th Place
Chicago, Illinois 60637
773-947-0600
http://www.dusablemuseum.org

Polish Museum of America
984 North Milwaukee Avenue
Chicago, Illinois 60622
312-384-3352
http://pma.prcua.org/

Lafox

Garfield Farm Museum
Garfield Road
Lafox, Illinois 60147
Mailing address:
P.O. Box 403
Lafox, Illinois 60147
630-584-8485
http://www.garfieldfarm.org

Lerna

Lincoln Log Cabin State Historic Site
400 South Lincoln Highway Road
Lerna, Illinois 62440
Mailing address:
P.O. Box 100
Lerna, Illinois 62440
217-345-1845
http://www.lincolnlogcabin.org

Naper

Naper Settlement Museum Village
523 South Webster Street
Naper, Illinois 60540
630-420-6010
http://www.napersettlement.org

Vandalia

The Little Brick House
621 St. Clair Street
Vandalia, Illinois 62471
618-283-0024
*http://www.vandaliaillinois.com/tourism/
   brickhouse.html*

Indiana

Cambridge City

Huddleston Farmhouse Inn Museum
U.S. 40
Cambridge City, Indiana 47437
765-478-3172
*http://www.historiclandmarks.org/things/
huddleston.html*

Elkhart

Midwest Museum of American Art
429 South Main Street
Elkhart, Indiana 46515
574-293-6660
http://midwestmuseum.us

Greenfield

James Whitcomb Riley Birthplace and
Museum
250 West Main Street
Greenfield, Indiana 46140
317-462-8539
*http://www.greenfieldin.org/parks/rileyhouse.
htm*

Nashville

International Blacksmith Museum
96 West Washington Street
Nashville, Indiana 47448
812-988-6811

New Harmony

Historic New Harmony, Inc.
Main and Church Streets
New Harmony, Indiana 47631
Mailing address:
P.O. Box 579
New Harmony, Indiana 47631
800-231-2168
*http://www.ulib.iupui.edu/kade/
newharmony/home.html*

Peru

Circus City Festival Museum
154 North Broadway
Peru, Indiana 46970
765-472-3918
http://www.perucircus.com/museum.htm

Iowa

Amana

Museum of Amana History
4310 220th Trail
Amana, Iowa 52203
319-622-3567
*http://www.cr.nps.gov/nr/travel/amana/
mah.htm*

Burr Oak

Laura Ingalls Wilder Park and Museum,
Inc.
3603 236th Avenue
Burr Oak, Iowa
563-735-5916
http://www.lauraingallswilder.us

Cedar Rapids

Czech and Slovak Museum and Library
30 16th Avenue SW
Cedar Rapids, Iowa 52404
319-362-8500
http://www.ncsml.org

Decorah

Vesterheim, Norwegian-American
    Museum
523 West Water Street
Decorah, Iowa 52101
Mailing address:
P.O. Box 379
Decorah, Iowa 52101
563-382-9681
http://www.vesterheim.org

Le Claire

Buffalo Bill Museum of Le Claire, Iowa,
    Inc.
200 North River Drive
Le Claire, Iowa 52753
http://www.buffalobillmuseumleclair.com

Oskaloosa

Nelson Pioneer Farm and Crafts
    Museum
2294 Oxford Avenue
Oskaloosa, Iowa 52577
Mailing address:
P.O. Box 578
Oskaloosa, Iowa 52577
641-672-2989
*http://www.villageprofile.com/iowa/
    oskaloosa/03his/topic.html*

Princeton

Buffalo Bill Cody Homestead
28050 230th Avenue
Princeton, Iowa 52768
563-225-2981
*http://www.scottcountyiowa.com/
    conservation/buffalobill.html*

Kansas

Ashland

Pioneer-Krier Museum
430 West Fourth (Highway 160)
Ashland, Kansas 67831
620-635-2227
http://skyways.lib.ks.us/towns/Ashland/

Baldwin City

Old Castle Museum
5th Street, Elm and Freemont
Baldwin City, Kansas 66006
Mailing address:
P.O. Box 65
Baldwin City, Kansas 66006
785-594-6809
*http://baldwincitychamber.com/
    attractions.html*

Dodge City

Boot Hill Museum, Inc.
Front Street
Dodge City, Kansas 67801
316-227-8188
http://www.boothill.org

Goessel

Mennonite Heritage Museum
200 North Poplar Street
Goessel, Kansas 67053
Mailing address:
P.O. Box 231
Goessel, Kansas 67053
620-367-8200
http://skyways.lib.ks.us/museums/goessel/

Hillsboro

Pioneer Adobe House Museum
501 South Ash Street
Hillsboro, Kansas 67063
316-947-3775
http://www.ohwy.com/ks/p/piadhomu.htm

Sedan

Emmett Kelly Historical Museum
204 East Main Street
Sedan, Kansas 67361
620-725-3470
http://www.emmettkelly.com

Wellington

Chisholm Trail Museum
502 North Washington
Wellington, Kansas 67152
620-326-3820
*http://skyways.lib.ks.us/towns/Wellington/
   museum.html*

Wichita

Indian Center Museum

650 North Seneca
Wichita, Kansas 67203
316-262-5221
http://www.indians.org/color/293.htm

Michigan

Caspian

Iron County Historical Museum
Brady at Museum Road
Caspian, Michigan 49915
Mailing address:
P.O. Box 272
Caspian, Michigan 49915
906-265-2617
http://www.ironcountymuseum.com

Copper Harbor

Fort Wilkins Historic Complex
Fort Wilkins Historic State Park
U.S. Highway 41 East
Copper Harbor, Michigan 49918
Mailing address:
P.O. Box 71
Copper Harbor, Michigan 49918
906-289-4215
*http://www.michigan.gov/hal/0,1607,7–16
   0–17447_18595_18604–,00.html*

Dearborn

Henry Ford Museum and Greenfield
   Village
20900 Oakwood Boulevard
Dearborn, Michigan 48124
313-982-6100
http://www.hfmgv.org

Detroit

Museum of African American History
315 East Warren Avenue
Detroit, Michigan 48201
313-494-5800
http://www.maah-detroit.org/

Frankenmuth

Frankenmuth Historical Museum
Frankenmuth Historical Association
613 South Main Street
Frankenmuth, Michigan 48734
989-652-9701
http://frankenmuth.michigan.museum/

Hastings

Historic Charlton Park Village and
    Museum
2545 South Charlton Park Road
Hastings, Michigan 49058
269-945-3775
http://www.charltonpark.org/Default.htm

Mackinac Island

Mackinac State Historic Parks–
    Fort Mackinac and Mackinac Island
    State Park
Mackinac Island (accessible by ferry)
Mailing address:
P.O. Box 873
Mackinaw City, MI 49701
231-436-4100
http://www.mackinacparks.com/

Marshall

Honolulu House Museum
107 North Kalamazoo Avenue
Marshall, Michigan 49068
269-781-8544
http://www.marshallhistoricalsociety.org/
    honohouse.htm

Northville

Mill Race Historical Village
Off Main Street on Griswold Road
Mailing address:
P.O. Box 71
Northville, Michigan 48167
248-348-1845
http://www.northville.lib.mi.us/community/
    groups/history/

Minnesota

Brainerd

Lumbertown, USA
Highway 77
Brainerd, Minnesota 56401
http://www.ohwy.com/mn/l/lumbtusa.htm

Duluth

Canal Park Marine Museum
Canal Park District
Duluth, Minnesota 55801
Mailing address:
Lake Superior Marine Museum
    Association
P.O. Box 177
Duluth, Minnesota 55801

218-727-2497
http://www.boatnerd.com/museums/cpmm/

Minneapolis

American Swedish Institute
2600 Park Avenue
Minneapolis, Minnesota 55407
612-871-4907
http://www.americanswedishinst.org/

Northfield

Norwegian-American Historical
    Association
1510 St. Olaf Avenue
Northfield, Minnesota 55057
507-646-3221
http://www.naha.stolaf.edu/

St. Paul

Gibbs Museum of Pioneer and Dakotah
    Life
2097 West Larpenteur Avenue
St. Paul, Minnesota 55133
651-646-8629
http://www.rchs.com/gbbsfm2.htm

Walnut Grove

Laura Ingalls Wilder Museum and
    Tourist Center
330 Eighth Street
Walnut Grove, Minnesota 56180
507-859-2358
http://www.walnutgrove.org/museum.htm

Missouri

Altenburg

Perry County Lutheran Historical
    Society, Inc.
H.C.R. 61
Altenburg, Missouri 63732
573-824-5542
http://www.perryvillemissouri.com/
    perrycountyhistoricalsociety.htm

Defiance

Historic Daniel Boone Home and
    Boonesfield Village
1868 Highway F.
Defiance, Missouri 63341
636-798-2005
http://www.lindenwood.edu/boonehome/
    Boonesfield.htm

Florida

Mark Twain Birthplace State Historic
    Site
37352 Road
Florida, Missouri 65283
573-565-3449
http://www.mostateparks.com/twainsite.htm

Hannibal

Mark Twain Home and Museum
208 Hill Street
Hannibal, Missouri 63401
573-221-9010
http://www.marktwainmuseum.org/

Nevada

Bushwacker Museum
231 North Main Street
Nevada, Missouri 64772
417-667-5841

St. Joseph

Jesse James House Museum
Pony Express Historical Association
12th and Penn
St. Joseph, Missouri 64502
Mailing address:
P.O. Box 1022
St. Joseph, Missouri 64502
816-232-8206
http://www.stjoseph.net/ponyexpress/
museums.shtml

Nebraska

Brownville

Meriwether Lewis Dredge Museum
Brownville State Recreation Park
Brownville, Nebraska 68321
Mailing address:
Captain Meriwether Lewis Foundation
P.O. Box 145
Brownville, Nebraska 68321
402-825-4131
http://www.meriwetherlewisfoundation.org/

Chadron

Museum of the Fur Trade
6321 U.S. Highway 20
Chadron, Nebraska 69337
308-432-3843
http://www.furtrade.org/index.php

Gothenburg

Pony Express Station
Ehman Park
Gothenburg, Nebraska 69138
308-537-3677
*http://www.ci.gothenburg.ne.us/attractions_*
lodges.htm

Lincoln

Museum of American Historical Society
of Germans from Russia
631 D Street
Lincoln, Nebraska 68502
402-474-3363
http://www.ahsgr.org/visit_ahsgr.htm

Minden

Harold Warp Pioneer Village Foundation
138 East Highway 6
Minden, Nebraska 68959
Mailing address:
P.O. Box 68
Minden, Nebraska 68959
308-832-1181
http://www.pioneervillage.com/

Omaha

Great Plains Black Museum
2213 Lake Street
(Webster Telephone Exchange Building)
Omaha, Nebraska 68110
402-345-2212
http://www.omaha.org/oma/black.htm

Red Cloud

Willa Cather Historical Center–
   Nebraska State Historical Society
P.O. Box 326
Red Cloud, Nebraska 68970
http://www.nebraskahistory.org/sites/cather/
   index.htm

Ohio

Archbold

Sauder Farm and Craft Village
225611 Street, Route 2
Archbold, Ohio 43502
800-590-9755
http://www.saudervillage.com/home/
   default.asp

Bath

Hale Farm and Village
2686 Oak Hill Road
Bath, Ohio 44210
Mailing address:
P.O. Box 296
Bath, Ohio 44210
330-666-3711
http://wneo.org/halefarm/

Coshocton

Roscoe Village
Roscoe Village Foundation
381 Hill Street
Coshocton, Ohio 43812
740-622-9310; 800-877-1830
http://www.roscoevillage.com/

Marietta

Ohio River Museum
601 Second Street
Marietta, Ohio 45750
740-373-3717; 800-860-0145
http://www.ohiohistory.org/places/ohriver/

Oxford

William Holmes McGuffey House and
   Museum
Oak and Spring Streets
Oxford, Ohio 45056
513-529-2232
http://www.lib.muohio.edu/mcguffey/
   museum.php

Portsmouth

Southern Ohio Museum and Cultural
   Center
825 Gallia Street
Portsmouth, Ohio 45662
614-354-5629
http://www.ohwy.com/oh/s/soohmucc.htm

Wilberforce

National Afro-American Museum and
   Cultural Center
1350 Brush Row Road
Wilberforce, Ohio 45384
Mailing address:
P.O. Box 578
Wilberforce, Ohio 45384
937-376-4944; 800-752-2603
http://www.ohiohistory.org/places/afroam/
   #location

Wisconsin

Clintonville

Oneida Nation Museum
County Road EE
Clintonville, Wisconsin 54929
800-236-2214
*http://www.oneidanation.org/enterprises/
    museum/museum.shtml*

Eau Claire

Paul Bunyan Logging Camp
1110 Carson Park Drive
Eau Claire, Wisconsin 54702
Mailing address:
P.O. Box 221
Eau Claire, Wisconsin 54702
715-835-6200
http://www.paulbunyancamp.org/

Menomonee Falls

Old Falls Village
County Line and Pilgrim Roads
Menomonee Falls, Wisconsin 53051
262-532-4775
*http://www.menomonee-falls.org/
    old_falls_village.htm*

Rhinelander

Rhinelander Logging Museum
Pioneer Park
Business U.S. 8 (Oneida Avenue)
Rhinelander, Wisconsin 54501
715-369-5004
*http://www.rhinelanderchamber.com/
    museum/museum.htm*

West Salem

Hamlin Garland Homestead
357 West Garland Street
West Salem, Wisconsin 54669
608-786-1399
*http://www.westsalemwi.com/wshist.htm#
    garland*

Journals in Folklore of the Region: A Selected List

The journals in the list below publish articles on folklore of the region. Some are scholarly; others are more popular. Many other journals and newsletters exist. Often, these are smaller, of more local interest, and published by museums, historical societies, folklore organizations, community groups, and schools. Explore your own area to see what other publications of folklore exist.

Mid-America Folklore
Midwestern Folklore

Web Sites: A Selected List

Below is a list of a few Web sites dealing with folklore of the region. You can find other Web sites by doing an Internet search on a search engine such as Google or Yahoo!, or by looking for the Web sites of various folklore organizations with which you are familiar.

*Folklore Institute, Indiana University at
    Bloomington, http://www.indiana.edu/
    ~folklore/*
Information about the institute, including programs.

Johnny Appleseed, http://www.appleseed. org/johnny.html
Information about John Chapman, or Johnny Appleseed. Links to various sites.

Kansas Heritage Center, http://www. ksheritage.org/
Offers for sale Kansas-related books and teaching materials. Lists materials on Kansas history, folklore, and government.

The Southwest

Arizona, New Mexico, Oklahoma, Texas

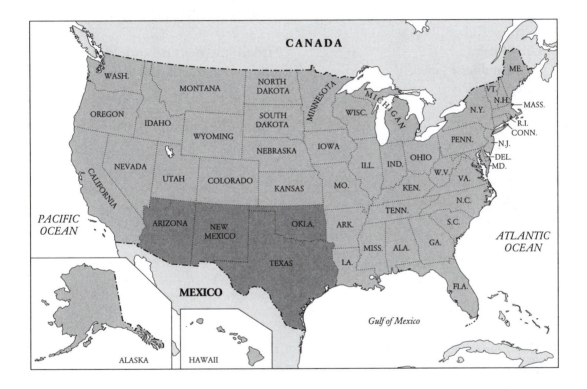

The Southwest: Checklist

Look for tales on:

Penitentes
Buried treasures and lost mines
Our Lady of Guadalupe
Oil fields
Outlaws

And for characters such as:

Billy the Kid
Gib Morgan
Frank and Jesse James
Belle Starr
Doc Holliday

Look for collections and works by:

Mody Boatright
Aurelio M. Espinosa
Arthur L. Campa
J. Frank Dobie
Elsie Clews Parsons
Rudolfo Anaya

Find music collections by:

Alan Lomax
John Lomax

Introduce children to:

Juneteenth
Pecos Bill
La Llorona
Yellow Corn Woman
Blue Corn Woman
The Alamo
Maasaw
Yaponcha, Wind God of the Hopis

Explore the rich literature of the region with:

Willa Cather
Tony Hillerman
Barbara Kingsolver
N. Scott Momaday

Consult journals:

The Arizona Quarterly
Publications of the Texas Folk-Lore
    Society
Southwest Folklore

THE SOUTHWEST: INTRODUCTION

The mention of the American Southwest immediately conjures a multitude of images: the magnificent, breathtaking Grand Canyon; the arid, dry desert landscapes of Arizona and New Mexico; a large, solitary saguaro cactus; the delicate springtime flowering of the Texas bluebonnets; the desolate, dusty landscape of Oklahoma's Indian Territory; the lonesome cowboy herding his cattle on their long journey north; the Native American artisan carefully crafting objects of beauty and pride; the Hispanic farmer diligently cultivating his crops; a Native American storyteller enchanting a ring of children around the winter's fire. Each of these images represents an almost mythic American Southwest, timeless in its historical appeal.

Accompanying these historical images are the vibrant images of the modern Southwest: a New Mexico low-rider slowly cruising and hopping in his bedazzling artistic automobile; Native Americans singing and dancing, celebrating their history and heritage at the Gathering of the Nations, the Indian Powwow; cowboy ranchers busting broncos and roping cattle at a local rodeo; Hispanic artisans selling their traditional devotional art at the Spanish Market in Santa Fe; African Americans celebrating their days of freedom at a Juneteenth city festival; urban Latinos remembering their heritage at a Dia de los Muertos ceremony.

Each of these modern images directly reveals the vitality of Southwestern culture and folklore. Every image represents the powerful role of folklore in the lives of the people of the Southwest. For some, folklore is an interesting curiosity, an area of academic interest. For others, folklore is the most important part of their lives, a profound connection to their ancestors and a central part of their individual and family experiences.

In order to keep their culture identity, people of the Southwest, especially Native Americans and Hispanics, have recently been especially active in reviving and preserving their folklore and cultural traditions. This essay will emphasize Native American and Hispanic folklore, as these are two of the primary cultural groups of the region. They are also the two oldest cultures in America.

The American Southwest is blessed with an abundance of living folklore. Southwestern folklore is what gives this region its identity. Since the early twentieth century, the Southwest has been a tourist destination, a place to see real "cowboys and Indians" and a place to witness nature's grandest spectacle and beauty. In addition to its folklore and stunning landscape, the Southwestern area of the United States is famous for its proud history and its diverse people.

For the purposes of this volume, the Southwest contains the states of Arizona, New Mexico, Oklahoma, and Texas. With a vast geography that can be barren and desolate, this region is home to four cultural groups: Hispanic, Native American, Anglo European, and African American. Each of these groups has a distinct historical folklore that enriches the region and the lives of its people.

Southwestern folklore is truly multicultural and diverse. This chapter will present several representative aspects of Southwestern folklore. Folklore is such a vast experience in people's lives that a short essay such as this cannot cover all of its facets. It is possible, however, to present the region's most well-recognized folklore areas and to give the reader a true impression of the richness, variety, and beauty of Southwestern folklore.

Our main questions and explorations are the inquiries of the scholar, the historian, and the folklorist: Why does this type of folklore exist here? Who are the people who live this folklore? What does their folklore look like?

Regional History

In this introductory overview of Southwestern folklore, an understanding of the region's history is important, because it will illustrate the historical sources of Southwestern folklore. Our Southwestern history story has two parts: the story of the region's original inhabitants, the Native Americans, and the story of the region's immigrant settlers, the Hispanic, Anglo European, and African American settlers.

Native Americans were the original inhabitants of the Southwest. For thousands of years Native Americans lived in harmony with their natural environment before the appearance of Europeans. The Southwestern Native Americans were part of two different cultural groups. The states of Arizona, New Mexico, and south Texas are part of the Southwestern cultural group. Oklahoma and Upper Texas are part of the Southern Great Plains cultural group.

These cultural group distinctions, however, are not absolute. Native Americans migrated throughout neighboring tribal territories, and tribal territories were ever changing. Nevertheless, Native American tribes within cultural areas did share

lifestyles and folklore that help identify distinct cultural groupings. For example, the nomadic tribes of the Southern Great Plains area were very different from the settled Pueblo culture of the Southwest. These cultural distinctions are very important to Native Americans, and they also determine differences in their folklore traditions.

The Plains culture was nomadic and changed significantly after the first European contact and the introduction of the horse. Using the tipi as its primary housing structure, Plains Indians lived a culture focused around the buffalo. Their life was a nomadic hunting life, lived following the vast buffalo herds.

The Southwestern Pueblo culture was a village-based culture. From the canyon and rock houses of the Anasazi Indians to the Taos Pueblo multitiered adobe houses, Pueblo culture was a farming existence. Their primary crop was corn, and their lives were greatly dependent on weather and rain for their cultivation success.

A listing of the tribal populations of our four Southwestern states contains representatives of the region's most well-known Native American tribes: the Navajo, Hopi, the Zuni in Arizona; the Tewa, the Tiwa and Apache in New Mexico; the Comanche, Apache and Wichita in Texas; the Osage, Kiowa and Cherokee in Oklahoma. Of course, many other tribes live in these states and tribes live in more than one state; but for our overview, these are the representative primary tribes and their territories.

Although many of these tribes were indigenous to their territory, others were foreign to it and came to the region under forced relocation by the United

States government. Forced relocation especially changed the Native American populations in Oklahoma and Texas. As each tribal nation became settled in its new lands, it quickly established its folklore and customs as well.

One example of this forced relocation is the story of the Cherokee journey to Oklahoma. Oklahoma territory was part of the United States' Louisiana Purchase from France in 1803. Soon after this purchase the American government began to move tribes from the Southeast to Oklahoma. The Indian Intercourse Act of 1834 designated this land set aside for Native Americans as Indian Territory. The government moved the Five Civilized Tribes, the Cherokee, the Chickasaw, the Choctaw, the Creek, and the Seminole to Indian Territory in Oklahoma. These tribes were known as the Five Civilized Tribes because of their advanced systems of government, education, and law. The Cherokee removal to Indian Territory became known as "The Trail of Tears," because so many Cherokee perished in the journey.

A children's ditty, "In 1492, Columbus sailed the ocean blue," marks the beginning of European history colliding with Native American history. When the Spanish and Anglo European settlers arrived in the Southwest, they found Native Americans throughout the region, living in fully established, mature civilizations teeming with an abundance of folklore.

When the Spanish arrived on the shores of the New World, they imported their total culture: their language, their religion, their government and law, their food, their animals, and their folklore. In their domination and conquest of the New World, they quickly became masters of what came to be known as New Spain. For our purposes the most important part of this history is that the states of Texas, New Mexico and Arizona were part of New Spain. In 1821, when Mexico won its independence from Spain, these states were the northern frontier of Mexico. These states became part of the United States after the War of 1848 between the United States and Mexico.

The strong presence of Mexican/Hispanic culture and folklore in the Southwest exists because at one time Texas, New Mexico, and Arizona were part of Mexico. A common sentiment from the time when this territory suddenly became part of the United States was one man's statement that "I didn't cross the border. The border crossed me." Original settlers in the Southwest, Hispanic people never lost their Spanish cultural heritage, and they nurture their folklore to preserve this heritage.

Southwestern folklore is also strongly marked by cowboy/ranch culture. The American cowboy is one of America's strongest mythic images. The image of the cowboy, honest, self-reliant, and hardworking, is one of America's strongest and most important images.

Along with all the other aspects of their culture, the Spanish brought two important animals to the New World, the horse and the cow. They also brought their centuries-old knowledge of how to work with horses and cattle on the open range. For almost two hundred years the Spanish worked with cattle and horses in the Southwest before Anglo European settlers began to move into the area.

In the early 1800s, when Anglo settlers began to move into south Texas, they quickly learned that the Spanish/Mexican vaquero was the master of "riding and roping."

The Anglo settlers quickly adopted every aspect of Spanish/Mexican cattle culture. What was once vaquero soon became cowboy. Modern cattle and ranch culture as we know it, the language, the dress, the tools of the trade, the techniques of breaking horses and the strategies of herding cattle on long drives, all came from the Spanish/Mexican vaquero.

Eventually, Anglo settlers evolved their own cattle and ranch culture. By the end of the Great Trail Drives in the 1880s, Anglo cowboys, cattlemen, and ranchers had established a ranch culture that continues to sustain cowboy folklore more than a century later.

The history of African Americans in the Southwest mirrors their history in America in general. The role of African Americans in the settlement of the West is an important one, only recently recognized by scholars and historians. African Americans were present at every aspect of the settlement of the West. Like other immigrant cultural groups, African Americans established their folklore wherever they migrated.

African Americans were present in the New World and the Southwest from the earliest arrival of the Spanish. First brought to the New World by the Spanish, Africans were at the bottom of Spanish society. Spanish society was very hierarchal. At the top were the *peninsulares,* pure Spaniards born in Spain. At the bottom were *zambos* who were mixed African and Native American.

Even during the days of the Great Trail Drives, African Americans made up almost one-quarter of the cowboys going up the trail. After the end of the Civil War, ex-slaves migrated into the Southwest in greater numbers. They came as laborers, farmers, trappers, mountain men, homesteaders, and cowboys. The descendants of these African American pioneers live throughout the Southwest, contributing their own folklore to the richness of Southwestern life.

Now the first part of our folklore journey is complete. The story of why folklore exists in any particular region is always the story of discovery, exploration, migration, and settlement. Folklore exists in a region because it is important in people's lives. Wherever people settle, they use their folklore traditions to give meaning to their daily activities and to enrich their spiritual lives. By following the historical journeys of Native American, Hispanic, Anglo European, and African American into the Southwest, we are ready to glimpse the rich folklore they established in the region.

Worldview

An intense spirituality characterizes the world outlook of the Native American and the Hispanic people of the Southwest. This spirituality infuses their lives and folklore with profound meaning.

Native Americans believe that all nature is one and that their lives must be lived in harmony with nature. Their religious beliefs contain a multitude of gods and spirits, and their songs, dances, and prayers all reflect a deep spirituality.

One example of this spirituality is the Southwestern worshipping of the Corn Goddess. Planting and harvest prayers, songs, and dances send the prayers of the Native American people to the Corn Goddess in order to ensure a plentiful harvest.

Another example is the relationship the Plains Indians had with the buffalo. To them, the buffalo was a gift from their gods. Before a hunt and before the slaughter, the Plains Indians pray and give thanks to their gods and the buffalo's spirit for the gift of life the buffalo gave them.

The worldview of the Native Americans did not contain the concept of landownership. To them the land, as well as the air, the wind, and the water belonged to everyone. They were stewards of the earth and had the responsibility of caring for the earth and all living creatures on it. This concept of shared responsibility for land stewardship was one of the central sources of conflict with the Europeans, who held landownership as one of their most important tenants.

Another important Native American concept was the primacy of the tribe. Individuals were responsible to the tribe as their first allegiance, and in an elegant reciprocity, the tribe was responsible to the tribe's individuals for their care and well-being. From childhood, parents taught their children about the importance of communal living and their responsibilities to the tribe.

Hispanic settlers also brought a deep spirituality to their communities. When the Spanish soldiers and missionaries arrived in new lands, they brought both the sword and the cross. Among the first structures built in a new Spanish village was the church. The church was the center of village communal life, and the priest was the spiritual leader of the community.

The Spanish also brought their concept of *la familia* to the New World. The family was the most important part of Spanish life. A large extended family gave support and guidance to every member of the family. The central importance of family in Spanish life is one of the culture's primary characteristics.

In the harsh, demanding environment of the Southwest, spirituality, tribe, and family were often the determining factors in life or death. The communal support of the tribe and the family helped people band together for the greater good, and their religious beliefs sustained them through their struggles.

Oral Traditions

The folklore of Native American culture is renowned for the extent of its oral traditions. Every tribe had its own creation myths and trickster tales. The various tribes each had their own religious tales to explain the natural world. For the Native Americans, oral traditions were the stories that passed on tribal history, explained their tribe's place on earth, and passed on tribal wisdom and values to successive generations.

An example of the melding of oral tradition and spirituality is of the Hopi Indian creation myths of Spider Woman. The Hopi had the kiva as their religious meeting place. *Kiva* was a Hopi word meaning underground. It was an underground room reserved for religious activities. At the center of the room was a hole in the floor called the *sipapu,* which was the connection between the spiritual world and the real world. The Hopi believed that their spirits came to the real word through the *sipapu.*

One of the Hopi creation myths tells of how Spider Woman brought the Hopi ancestors into the real world through the *sipapu.* From that time the Hopi have lived and prospered in the world.

The Comanche and Apache tribes tell a story about how the buffalo came to roam the world. In their story the coyote tricked the keeper of the animals into freeing the buffalo to roam the earth. From that time on, the Plains Indians have had the buffalo to sustain their lives.

Southwestern Hispanics also have an extensive oral tradition. Like the Native Americans, they use oral traditions to pass on cultural values, explain their place in the world, give expression to their religious beliefs, and to entertain themselves.

An especially delightful part of Hispanic oral traditions are *dichos*, Spanish proverbs. *Dichos* are small nuggets of wisdom passed down through the generations expressing the hard-earned wisdom of one's ancestors. Here are several examples of these traditional *dichos*:

* *Un gato viejo, ratón tierno:* An old cat, a young mouse. (He is an old man who likes young girls.)
* *Andar por las ramas:* Walking through the branches. (He is wasting his time. He is beating around the bush.)
* *En boca cerrada, no entra mosca:* In a closed mouth, no fly enters. (Keep quiet, and you will not make trouble for yourself. Keep your own counsel.)
* *De tal palo salta la estilla:* From such a log comes the splinter. (He is a chip off the old block.)
* *Las canas no quitan ganas:* Gray hair does not end desires. (You are as old as you feel.)
* *No hay rosa sin espinas:* There is no rose without thorns. (Nothing comes easily.)
* *Cada oveja con su pareja:* Each sheep with his partner. (Birds of a feather flock together.)
* *De tal palo tal astilla:* From such wood such a splinter. (Like father, like son.)

Southwestern cowboy ranch culture also has a rich oral tradition that keeps the stories of the Old West alive. Cowboys use their cowboy songs, tall tales, and poetry to keep the rough and ready spirit of the cowboy alive for the modern ranch hand as well as "city slickers."

One of the most important aspects of cowboy culture is the cowboy's code of honor. The cowboy's code of personal honor was critical to his character and reputation. Cowboys had innumerable sayings that reflected various aspects of their code of honor:

* A cowboy does not bother another man's horse.
* A cowboy asks before borrowing another man's horse.
* A cowboy has courage.
* A cowboy keeps his word.
* A cowboy is respectful to women.
* A cowboy offers friendship to strangers.
* A cowboy shares his grub with strangers.
* A cowboy does not complain.
* A cowboy is loyal.
* A cowboy will risk his life to save his partner.
* A cowboy never asks another cowboy about his past.
* A cowboy does not cut in front of another rider on the trail.
* A cowboy never talks rudely in front of a woman and always tips his hat.

More cowboy folklore concerns their colorful sayings. Even though the American cowboy has the image of being strong and silent, with the emphasis on silent, and of being a man of few words, the words he does say live in history as some of the most expressive ever spoken. Some were humorous, some insulting, and some wise. Here are several examples of the wit and wisdom of cowboys:

* He rides tall in the saddle.—A compliment said of a first-rate, righteous, top hand cowboy.
* He likes to change hats.—Said of someone who keeps changing from good to bad.
* Don't squat with your spurs on. —A warning to be careful and stay aware at all times.
* He'll take the slack out of your rope.—Said of someone who can teach you a lesson.
* She's a pistol packing mama.—Said of a rough and tumble woman.
* There's not a horse that can't be broke or a man that can't be thrown.
* You can spread it around, now let's see what you can do when it's all gathered up.—You can talk a good story but can you back it up.
* He couldn't see through a barbed wire fence.—Said of someone who is not too smart.
* He's trying to scratch his ear with his elbow.—Said of a cowboy who is trying to do something impossible.

The oral traditions of the Southwest are immensely diverse. They can be profound or humorous. They can be religious or worldly. But they all reflect the unique worldview of the Southwestern people.

Material Culture

The arts and crafts of Southwestern culture represent an abundant creativity at the service of necessity and spirituality. Neither the traditional Native American nor Hispanic culture had an active concept of an artist class creating objects of art. In both cultures, people made objects for use in their daily lives. Only later, with the creation of the tourist experience in the Southwest, the development of folk art as a collectible market, and the emergence of museum collections, did specific individuals become identified as cultural artists. A folk proverb about these traditional cultures states that they had no arts or artists, because everything they did was artistic.

Further study in museums, books, and on-line research will reveal the beauty and artistry of the Pueblo Indian kachina dolls, dolls made to represent their supernatural beings; the intricate designs of the Hopi baskets; the beautiful craftsmanship of Zuni and Santa Domingo jewelry; the geometric complexity of Navajo weaving and textiles; the colorful patterns of Apache beadwork; the majestic beauty of the Plains warrior eagle feather headdress; and the careful exactness of Navajo sacred sandpainting.

Each of these objects of art from Native American cultures represents a specific need for the tribes. Baskets were for carrying goods. Religious dolls were to be used in sacred rituals and for teaching children spiritual lessons. Woven blankets and clothing were for warmth and protection. Headdresses were symbols of bravery and leadership. Sandpaintings were part of important healing ceremonies.

In Native American tribes, men and women generally had different artistic domains. Men created objects for war, hunting, and ceremonies, whereas women created objects for clothing and household items. The artistic truth of Native American arts is that the arts were ever present and Native American people lived lives surrounded by beautiful objects.

Southwestern Hispanic culture similarly had a well-developed folk arts tradition based on the utilitarian needs of the people. Hispanic woodworkers made furniture decorated with simple geometric designs that define Spanish colonial style. Tinworkers made mirrors, furniture decoration, and religious images that also reflected Spanish colonial graphic design. Woodworkers, called *santeros,* made religious images, *retablos* and *bultos,* two- and three-dimensional carvings that served the religious ceremonies of the Catholic Church and needs of individual families for religious images in the family home.

Cowboy and ranch culture also had a well-defined artistry at the service of a cowboy's work. Leather tooling decorated saddles, chaps, and horse tack with marvelous scrolling designs. Metalworkers and blacksmiths created complex designs on spurs and metal horse tack to add a beautiful decorative quality to everyday work tools.

Celebrations

A people's celebrations are clear representations of their spirituality, their artistry, and their communal rituals. At one time these communal celebrations were solely for the needs of the tribe, village, or community. Today many of these celebrations are artificially staged events for the purpose of economics and tourism. The goal of modern celebrations is to somehow bridge the worlds of traditional ritual and modern commerce in order to give their participants the transcendent experience that is at the heart of all communal ceremonies.

Modern celebrations do serve several important functions. First, they re-create important traditional rituals. Second, they keep alive traditional knowledge. Finally, they serve educational purposes for both traditional communities trying to preserve their cultural ways and for tourists who wish to get a glimpse into traditional cultures.

The most important Native American ceremony is the powwow. At native powwows, also called the Gathering of Nations, tribes celebrate their traditional culture with singing, dancing, and chanting. Powwows also feature teaching, praying, and traditional rituals. Games and exhibits can also be part of powwows.

Southwestern powwows traditionally took place in the warm weather of the summer or fall, but with the availability of indoor arenas, they can now occur throughout the year.

Powwows, especially the larger ones, feature the customs of many tribes displayed in one place, at one time. These large cultural gatherings are ultimately very educational, because they help widely scattered tribes revive their cultural identity, and they help younger generation Native Americans learn about their cultural heritage.

Hispanic culture features a multitude

of community and family celebrations. In the Southwest, Cinco de Mayo has become the primary celebration of Hispanic cultural pride. Large and small city-wide celebrations feature traditional dancing, music, food, and arts and crafts.

Hispanic religious celebrations include Dia de los Muertos, the traditional Mexican celebration of the family's deceased ancestors, and various Christmas celebrations. The Christmas season also includes the Feast of Our Lady of Guadalupe, the patroness of Latin America.

One of the most important family celebrations is the Quinceañera, the celebration of a young girl's fifteenth birthday. Both a religious ceremony and a coming of age celebration, a girl's Quinceañera is one of the most joyous and memorable events of her life.

African Americans in the Southwest celebrate Juneteenth, which is the observance of African American Emancipation Day, June 19, 1865, when the African Americans in Galveston, Texas, learned that slavery had ended. The celebration of Juneteenth also commemorates African American education and achievement. For more than one hundred years African Americans in Texas, and now throughout the world, have celebrated the progress African Americans have made. For Juneteenth many Southwestern cities sponsor festivals featuring the richness of African American traditional culture and arts.

Cowboy and ranch culture of course has the rodeo. The modern rodeo developed from the Spanish/Mexican vaquero games and contests played during their cattle hunts. The Spanish word for the cattle hunts was *rodeo,* which meant to round up or surround. The Spanish and Mexican vaqueros created entertaining contests to show off their cowboy skills during these rodeos. Anglo cowboys witnessed the vaquero rodeos and developed their own versions of the contests. They adopted the Spanish word *rodeo* and used it to name their own cowboy contests, the rodeo.

The modern rodeo first appeared in the late 1800s. It quickly became a successful substitute for the trail drive experience for all the out-of-work trail drive cowboys. By the early 1900s the rodeo was established as both a contest of cowboy skills and a Western entertainment experience. Today the rodeo is both a celebration of cowboy and ranch traditional culture and a major aspect of American sports entertainment.

Conclusion

The Southwestern region of the United States is home to many of the richest cultural traditions in America. These traditions have sustained generations of Southwestern individuals, families, and communities in their struggles to shape their lives in a very demanding environment. Southwestern culture and folklore has produced a strong tourist industry as well as museum and scholarly interest.

For the people of the traditional Southwestern cultures, however, their folklore is a deeply personal experience. Through their cultural activities they keep alive the history and values of their ancestors. Today, these traditions continue with the efforts of cultural artists and activists who value traditional folklore and know its importance to modern life.

Angel Vigil

The Southwest: Bibliography and Other Resources

Bibliography

History and Study

585. Abernethy, Francis Edward, ed. *Juneteenth Texas: Essays in African-American Folklore*. Denton: Univ. of North Texas Press, 1996. xi, 364p. Illus. Chapter notes. Index. (Publications of the Texas Folklore Society, LIV). 96-21854. 1-57441-018-0. l

The Juneteenth of the title refers to the African American celebrations of the ending of slavery, traditionally held in June. Juneteenth celebrates many things, various days when slavery was outlawed in different places, and the day in June 1865 that African Americans in Galveston, Texas, were first aware of Lincoln's Emancipation Proclamation.

Essays by various authors fill this volume, covering various aspects of folklore. Some are based on personal experience and reminiscence; some are genre based, with essays on folk music such as zydeco and bebop. Some concern performers of folk songs, such as Lightnin' Hopkins, or jazz musicians, whereas others are concerned with a particular occupation, for example, the black cowboy and blacksmithing. One essay concerns the work of black folklorist J. Mason Brewer.

Two appendices round out the collection: one on the Texas African American Photography Collection and Archive in Dallas and the other on the African American Museum, also in Dallas.

Illustrations are black-and-white photographs.

586. Boatright, Mody C. *Folk Laughter on the American Frontier*. Gloucester, MA: Peter Smith, 1971. 191p. Notes. Index.

Boatright discusses the various types of frontiersmen and frontierswomen and the humor that has grown up around these archetypes. Here are the greenhorn, the liar, the tall tale artist, the con man, the country lawyer, and the preacher.

He shows how these myths have become part of our national character.

587. ———. *Mody Coggin Boatright, Folklorist: A Collection of Essays*. Austin: Published for the Texas Folklore Society by the Univ. of Texas Press, 1973. xxvi, 198p. Index. Bibliog. 73-6908. 0-292-75007-2.

Boatright's shorter essays are collected here. Three main themes are the American frontier, the cowboy, and the oil industry.

588. Brown, Lorin W. *Hispano Folklife of New Mexico: The Lorin W. Brown Federal Writers' Project Manuscripts*. Albuquerque: Univ. of New Mexico Press, 1978. xiii, 279p. Notes. Bibliog. Index. 78-51578. 0-8263-0475-3.

Brown was born in New Mexico, worked there as a schoolteacher, and later worked for the WPA collecting information on Hispano culture. This is an edited version of some of his manuscripts from the 1930s.

He himself says, in his 1977 foreword, that the way of life portrayed in his manuscripts was gone, replaced by a "modern era of rock and roll, new cars, and a fast pace unknown thirty years back" (p. x).

Most of the information in his manuscripts shows that way of life, a life paced more to the rhythm of the seasons than it is today.

The first section of this book is an account of Brown's life.

589. Espinosa, Aurelio M. *The Folklore*

of Spain in the American Southwest. Norman: Univ. of Oklahoma Press, 1985. xiii, 310p. Edited by J. Manuel Espinosa. Illus. Notes. Bibliog. of Aurelio M. Espinosa's Works. Bibliog. of works of Hispanic-American Literature. 85-40473.0-8061-1942-X.

J. Manuel Espinosa, the son of noted folklorist Aurelio M. Espinosa, here presents an edition of some of his father's unpublished manuscripts, as well as an account of his life and his collecting career. Espinosa was an early folklorist, one of the first to collect and study the Spanish folklore of northern New Mexico and southern Colorado.

The material here includes ballads and songs; hymns, prayers, and other religious expressions; proverbs; folk tales; and folk drama, both religious and secular; in short, in the words of the preface, "the highlights of all the major types of traditional Spanish folk literature found in the region, illustrated with extensive examples in Spanish and English translation" (p. xii).

590. Heisley, Michael. *An Annotated Bibliography of Chicano Folklore from the Southwestern United States.* Los Angeles: The Regents of the Univ. of California. Produced for and distributed by the Center for the Study of Comparative Folklore and Mythology, Univ. of California, 1977. vi, 188p. Index.

Books, periodical articles, and theses are included here. Heisley divides the bibliography into the following sections:

Bibliographies, Indexes, and General Works
Narrating Traditions
Singing, Dancing, and Musicmaking Traditions
Traditional Speech
Traditional Customs, Rituals, Healing Practices, and Beliefs
Traditional Drama and *Teatro*
Traditional Games, Play, and Play Rituals
Traditional Art, Architecture, Technology, Foodways, and Clothing

The material he indexes and annotates concerns folklore in Colorado, California, Arizona, New Mexico, and Texas. Sources collected are in both English and Spanish, although most of them are in English.

591. Speck, Ernest B., ed. *Mody Boatright, Folklorist: A Collection of Essays.* Austin: Published for the Texas Folklore Society by the Univ. of Texas Press, 1973. xxvi, 198p. Bibliography of Boatright's works. Index. 73-6908. 0-292-75007-2.

Thirteen of Boatright's essays appear in this volume. Some are on folk characters: Gib Morgan, Pecos Bill, the cowboy, and the oil promoter, or con man. Others are discussions on folklore itself and its meaning, such as the one on tall tales or that on the nature of myth.

A biographical essay on Boatright himself by Harry H. Ransom fills out the volume.

592. Villarino, José, and Arturo Ramírez, eds. *Aztlán Chicano Culture and Folklore: An Anthology.* New York: McGraw-Hill, 1997j. xvi, 269p. Bibliog. 0-07-014381-1pa.

Literature, culture, and history are intertwined in this study. Contributors discuss the legend of La Llorona and its significance; various folk heroes from real life, such as Pancho Villa, César Chávez, and Juan Soldado; and literary works, such as *The Milagro Beanfield War.* Also included are sections on Chicano folk music, including Tejano music, the role of women in Chicano culture, and a chile festival in New Mexico.

593. Weigle, Marta, and Peter White. *The Lore of New Mexico*. Albuquerque: Univ. of New Mexico Press, 1988. xiv, 523p. Illus. Notes. Place Index. Person Index. Subject Index. (Publications of the American Folklore Society). 88-1345. 0-8263-0991-7; 0-8263-1047-8pa.

In their introduction, Weigle and White describe their book this way: "it is part history, ethnography, and folklore and part anthology, exhibition catalogue, and guidebook" (p. ix). It is indeed a compendium of folklore information statewide.

Part I analyzes from a New Mexican perspective various forms of folklore, exploring what the stories, songs, artifacts, and rituals that developed in New Mexico say about the state, and how the geography, climate, history, and people of the area influenced that development. Part II looks at domestic architecture as an expression of folk art; rituals; apparitions, particularly religious visions; place-names; humor; political proverbs; and such musical expressions of folklore as cowboy songs, hoedowns, and agricultural songs. Part III looks at occupations such as trading, mining, and ranching; different cultural groups (healers, missionaries, lawmen); individual folk figures such as Billy the Kid; customs such as marriage rites and food rituals; and fiestas and festivals.

This is not a collection of actual folk material (no stories or songs are told in their entirety). Rather, it is a study of the development and expression of folklore in one region.

594. Winniford, Lee. *Following Old Fencelines: Tales from Rural Texas*. College Station: Texas A & M Univ. Press, 1998. xviii, 262p. Illus. Bibliog. Notes. 97-34586. 0-89096-802-0.

Winniford not only tells old tales here, but also explicates them, sets them in context, and shows how the tales influence a society, many times to effect behavior or to emphasize and encourage a code of conduct.

She presents three major categories of tales: those set on a farm; tales of tornadoes; and tales set in graveyards.

Illustrations are black-and-white photographs.

Treasuries

595. Castro, Rafaela G. *Dictionary of Chicano Folklore*. Santa Barbara, CA: ABC-CLIO, 2000. xvii, 332p. Illus. Index. Bibliog. 00-022477. 0-87436-953-3.

The length of the entries in this work make it more of an encyclopedia than a dictionary. Entries range from one or two paragraphs, to more than a page, and are on everything from food (fajitas and tortillas) to culture (low riders and urban youth, or *Pachucos*) to tales and legends (La Llorona and *The Tale of the Lost Mine*). Religion and the arts are also represented.

This is a look at Chicano history, folklore, and culture.

596. Hale, Duane K., ed. *Turtle Tales: Oral Traditions of the Delaware Tribe of Western Oklahoma*. Anadarko: Delaware Tribe of Western Oklahoma Press, 1984. 72p. Illus. Delaware dictionary.

A grant from the National Endowment for the Humanities in 1983 provided the funding for this project. Through it, young people from the Delaware Tribe interviewed the tribal elders and recorded their stories. The chapters in this book transcribe these stories. Chapters are

Stories Medicines, Foods, and
   Remedies
Clothing, Customs, and Crafts
History and Genealogy

Many of the stories illustrate a virtue, and were told to encourage proper behavior. The History and Genealogy section contains memories of historic events, such as the signing of a treaty with William Penn.

597. Lea, Aurora Lucero-White, ed. *Literary Folklore of the Hispanic Southwest.* San Antonio, TX: Naylor, 1953; repr., 1976. xv, 247p. Bibliog. Index.

Plays, ballads, folk stories, customs, and proverbs, in both Spanish and English, are presented in this compendium. Many items are religious in nature. Many of the stories have parallels in Grimm's fairy tales, and the section on customs includes information on weddings, wakes, fiestas, and dances.

598. West, John O., ed. *Mexican-American Folklore: Legends, Songs, Festivals, Proverbs, Crafts, Tales of Saints, of Revolutionaries and More.* Little Rock, AR: August House, 1988. 314p. Illus. Notes. Motif and Tale Type Index. Ballad Index. General Index. Bibliog. (The American Folklore Series). 88-3367. 0-87483-060-5; 0-874884-059-1pa.

West includes the following types of folklore:

Folk speech
Proverbs
Riddles
Rhymes

Tales
Ballads and songs
Beliefs and superstitions
Customs and festivals
Drama and dance
Games
Architecture
Foods
Arts and crafts

He includes both examples and explanations of these forms of folklore, centered in Northern New Mexico.

Tales and Legends

599. Archer, Jane. *Texas Indian Myths and Legends.* Plano: Republic of Texas Press, 2000. xiii, 231p. Bibliog. 00-051935. 1-55622-725-6pa.

Tales of various Native American cultures are collected here and retold for today: Caddo Confederacies, the Lipan Apache, the Wichita Confederacy, the Comanche, and the Alabama-Coushatta. Many of the tales are creation stories; there are also trickster stories, stories of man's place in nature, and tales of animals.

600. Arnold, Oren. *Ghost Gold.* 4th ed., revised and enlarged. San Antonio, TX: Naylor, 1967. x, 84p. 67-13400.

Superstition Mountain in Arizona is the setting for an enduring legend of a lost treasure that was presumably discovered and immediately lost in the mid-nineteenth century. It has attracted treasure seekers ever since. A German immigrant named Jacob Walz rediscovered it in the 1870s, killed several people to maintain his claim, and died himself without leaving accurate information as to the mine's whereabouts. No one has since found the purported gold.

Some of the language in this book, originally published in 1934, particularly characterizations of various ethnic groups, is offensive today.

601. Atencio, Paulette. *Cuentos from Long Ago*. Albuquerque: Univ. of New Mexico Press, 1999. 131p. 99-29204. 0-8263-2064-3pa.

Love, supernatural happenings and ghost visits, and holidays are some of the themes in these stories. The tales are told in both English and Spanish, on facing pages. All the stories are set in New Mexico, Arizona, Colorado, and northern Mexico. They are traditional tales, handed down from generations past; Atencio is the latest teller.

602. *Bella Starr, the Bandit Queen, or The Female Jesse James*. New York: Richard K. Fox, 1889; facsimile repr., Austin, TX: Steck, 1960. iv, 64p. Illus.

According to the preface of the 1960 reprint, this little 1889 publication on Belle Starr is the major source of much of the myth and folklore that surround Belle. Although facts are few and far between, the dramatic stories of Belle's adventures—many on the wrong side of the law—did much to enshrine Belle in American myth.

603. Boatright, Mody C. *Folklore of the Oil Industry*. Dallas, TX: Southern Methodist Univ. Press, 1963. vii, 220p. Illus. by William D. Wittliff. Notes. Index. 63-21186.

Oil folklore from Pennsylvania, West Virginia, Ohio, Kansas, Oklahoma, and Texas appears in this book, but it is Texan folklore that dominates. There are legends and superstitions on finding oil, widespread in the days before computers and seismographs, but still half believed today; stereotypical stories of such oil field characters as the landowner, the geologist, and the driller; and tall tales and songs.

604. ——. *Gib Morgan, Minstrel of the Oil Fields*. El Paso: Texas Folk-Lore Society, 1945. xi, 104p. Illus. by Betty Boatright. (Texas Folk-Lore Society Publication, XX).

Gib Morgan belongs to the same category as Davy Crockett: a real man with a true biography whose deeds have been exaggerated into folklore. There is a true body of literature about him, a body of legend, and a body of tall tales—some of which he manufactured and told himself.

The real Gilbert Morgan was born in 1842 in Pennsylvania. He became an oil driller who traveled throughout the country working at his trade.

Boatright's book tells the biography of Gib Morgan, as well as the legends and tall tales, both those others told about him and those that Morgan told about himself.

605. ——. *Singers and Storytellers*. Dallas, TX: Southern Methodist Univ. Press, 1961. vi, 298p. Edited by Wilson M. Hudson and Allen Maxwell. Index. 60-15894.

Stories from many sources make up this book. Here are tales of well-known characters such as Belle Starr; of folk types such as the trickster, the miner, and the cowboy; here are ghost stories, tall tales, and stories of folk belief and folk medicine. There are twenty-nine essays and stories in all, told by a variety of storytellers.

606. ——. *Tall Tales from Texas Cow Camps*. Southwest Press, 1934; repr., Dallas, TX: SMU Press, 1982. xxxiv, 105p. Illus. by Elizabeth Keefer Boatright. 82-3186. 0-87074-181-0.

Boatright first collected these stories in the 1930s and earlier, either while growing up on ranches in west Texas or while teaching at the University of Texas. All concern the cowboy, the tall-tale-telling, legendary, Western character. Here are cowboys who can shoot a prairie dog in the eye, then run fast enough to reach the creature before the bullet hits, and snatch them before they run away; cowboys who know the whiffle-poofle, that strange cross between an eel and a Gila monster that lives at the bottom of a lake; and cowboys who defend themselves against rattlesnakes by tickling them.

Here, too, are the stories of Pecos Bill, who killed a panther when he was three, who roped a train and nearly wrecked it in the process; and who rode a cyclone.

Front matter of this new edition includes some biographical material on Boatright.

607. Brett, Bill. *There Ain't No Such Animal, and Other East Texas Tales.* College Station: Texas A&M Univ. Press, 1979. 111p. Illus. 78-21777. 0-89096-069-2.

These tales are slight but charming, told in Texas dialect. The book has no introduction or explanatory material, just the tales themselves. Obviously it is useful for those seeking tales of east Texas, but for those seeking a discussion or history of them, this will not satisfy.

608. Brewer, John Mason. *Dog Ghosts, and Other Negro Folk Tales; and The Word on the Brazos: Negro Preacher Tales from the Brazos Bottoms of Texas.* Austin: Univ. of Texas Press, 1976. *Dog Ghosts:* xiv, 124p. *Word on the Brazos:* xv, 109p. *Dog Ghosts:* illus. by John T. Biggers. *Word on the Brazos:* illus. by Ralph White Jr. 76-14082. 0-292-71512-9pa.

Originally published in 1958 and 1953, respectively, by the University of Texas Press, *Dog Ghosts* and *The Word on the Brazos* are here reprinted in one volume.

Brewer was an African American folklorist who collected African American folklore in Texas in the 1950s, when the memory of slavery was still strong. The tales often concern the dog ghost, a benign spirit of a dog that appears in times of need. Other spirits also inhabit his tales, interacting in everyday life.

The preacher tales also often contain the supernatural and often have a moral or lesson.

All the tales are told in dialect.

609. Bullock, Alice. *Living Legends of the Santa Fe Country.* Santa Fe, NM: Sunstone Press, 1985. 124p. Illus. Index. 72-90583. 0-913270-06-7.

A very unusual guidebook, this tells of the legends of the Santa Fe, Albuquerque, and Taos areas of New Mexico. For the most part, the legends center on the small villages and pueblos like Chimayo and Nambe, not on the larger, more urban areas. Through this book you can find the church where you can be healed through application of holy soil; locate the place where two Eagle Dancers, the flower of Indian young manhood, actually became eagles and flew away; or find a buried treasure at Abiquiu, which is said to carry a curse for anyone daring to disturb it.

It is a book that will help you learn a bit of unusual history of this part of the country.

610. ——. *The Squaw Tree: Ghosts, Mysteries, and Miracles of New Mexico.* Santa Fe, NM: Lightning Tree, 1978. 96p. Illus. 77-86728. 0-89016-041-4. 0-89016-040-6pa.

Another book of Santa Fe legends by the author of *Living Legends of the Santa Fe Country.* This one concentrates on ghosts and supernatural happenings.

611. Campa, Arthur L. *Treasure of the Sangre de Cristos: Tales and Traditions of the Spanish Southwest.* Bibliog. Index.

Campa collected these stories naturally, while growing up and living in west Texas. During those years, he spent much time simply visiting and talking with neighbors and friends, whose stories these are. Many of the stories concern mining and treasure.

612. Carson, Xanthus. *Treasure!: Bonanzas Worth a Billion Bucks.* San Antonio, TX: Naylor, 1974. xii, 182p. Illus. 74-26855. 0-8111-0545-8.

Although some of the tales in this book are about treasures lost in Colorado, the bulk of the treasures are in Texas and especially New Mexico. Tales are of lost mines, stolen and subsequently abandoned shipments of gold and jewels, and lost army payrolls. Carson gives the details that are known about these lost treasures and as specific as possible locations for them.

He ends with a treasure tale from the Caballo Mountains, south of Truth or Consequences, New Mexico, which is a treasure that, at the time of the book's writing, still enticed people to search for it.

613. Courlander, Harold. *People of the Short Blue Corn: Tales and Legends of the Hopi Indians.* New York: Harcourt Brace Jovanovich, 1970. 189p. Glossary. Notes on sources. 75-115756. 0-15-260525-8.

Courlander's initial chapter, "The Land of the Hopis," describes the content of the stories: "the people still tell the old stories of adventure, of magic and sorcery, of courage and great deeds. They tell of men turned into animals and animals turned into men, of human wisdom and stupidity, and of the unending foolishness of the clown named Coyote. And they tell of the origin of all things, and how the Hopis left their former world below the surface of the earth to come to the place where they now live."

614. Cuevas, Lou. *In the Valley of the Ancients: A Book of Native American Legends.* Albuquerque, NM: Petroglyph National Monument, funded by a grant from the National Park Foundation with support from Pew Charitable Trusts, 1996. 58p. Illus. by Jim Fuge.

For all its brevity, this book is a charmer. It tells eleven southwest Native American legends in simple prose and illustrates them with effective black-and-white drawings. The legends have been told before in many places—the story of Corn Woman is particularly widespread—but this current presentation is worth a look.

615. Cushing, Frank Hamilton. *Zuñi Folk Tales.* New York: Knopf, 1931; repr., Tucson: Univ. of Arizona Press, 1988. xxix, 474p. Illus. 85-28960. 0-8165-0986-7pa.

Initial publication of this collection of Zuni folk tales predates the 1931 publication date shown. It was first published in 1901, with an introduction by John Wesley Powell. Cushing accompanied Powell on Powell's 1879 expedition through the Southwest and remained at the Zuni pueblo in northern New Mexico more than five years. Living there he participated in or observed the rituals and storytelling sessions in which he heard these tales.

The folk tales are of the natural world, and many contain animal characters, including Coyote, that trickster character seen so often in folk stories.

616. Dobie, J. Frank. *Apache Gold and Yaqui Silver.* New York: Bramhall, 1939;

repr., 1960. xv, 366p. Illus. by Tom Lea. Bibliog. on scalp hunters.

In this book, Dobie adds to the tales of lost mines and buried treasures that he wrote about in his earlier book, *Coronado's Children* (Univ. of Texas Press, 1978). He concentrates here on the numerous searches for two mines, the Lost Adams Diggings and the Lost Tayopa Mine.

617. ——. *Coronado's Children: Tales of Lost Mines and Buried Treasures of the Southwest.* Austin: Univ. of Texas Press, 1978. xxii, 329p. Illus. by Charles Shaw. Notes. Glossary. (Barker Texas History Center Series, No. 3). 78-58925. 0-292-71050-x; 0-292-71052-6pa.

First published by the Southwest Press in 1930, *Coronado's Children* tells the story of the inheritors of Coronado's search for the fabled Seven Cities of Ci'bola, the legendary cities whose palaces were trimmed with jewels and whose residents possessed uncounted gold. His children search for the lost mines and buried treasures of the Southwest. Dobie pieces together the records they left, in both writings and legends, and celebrates their hard work, their tenacity, and above all their unending optimism and hope.

618. ——. *I'll Tell You a Tale.* Boston: Little, Brown, 1931; repr., 1960. xvii, 362p. Selected and arranged by the author and Isabel Gaddis. Illus. by Ben Carlton Mead. Glossary.

Some tales of cowboys and ranchers, some love stories, some ghost stories, some mining adventures, some stories of animals, this melange is a collection of Dobie's work over the years.

619. ——. *Tales of Old-Time Texas.* Boston: Little, Brown, 1955; repr., Austin: Univ. of Texas Press, 1984. xii,

336. Illus. by Barbara Latham. Notes. Index. 0-292-78069-9pa.

Dobie wrote extensively about Texas traditions and tales. Here he presents a collection of traditional tall tales set in Texas. Some concern farming and how certain crops came to be associated with Texas, others concern weather, historical personages, and phantom presences. All give a flavor of Texas and the Texas character.

620. ——. *Tongues of the Monte.* Austin: Univ. of Texas Press, 1975. xiv, 301p.

Dobie tells the ghost stories and spirit stories he heard from the Mexicans who worked on his father's ranch in Texas before World War I, and later the ones he met on a ranch that he managed.

621. Dobie, J. Frank, ed. *Tone the Bell Easy.* Austin: Texas Folklore Society, 1932; repr., facsimile edition, Dallas, TX: Southern Methodist Univ. Press, 1965. 199p. Illus. Index. (Texas Folklore Society Publication Number X). Many threads make up the composition of this book: There are African American tales from Texas, collected from people who lived through the terrible days of slavery; several tales of witches from New Mexico; tales of Texan folk healers; some treasure legends; and some stories about the legendary Texan giant Strap Buckner. Some British ballads collected in Texas and some camp-meeting religious songs round out the collection.

The title comes from Dobie's interpretation of the saying "I number but the hours that are serene." He contends that it is only in those serene hours, when people are relaxed and easy, that the truth can be found—and that truth is found in the old traditional stories and songs.

622. Dobie, J. Frank, Mody C. Boat-

right, and Harry H. Ransom, eds. *Coyote Wisdom*. Austin: Texas Folklore Society, 1938; repr., facsimile edition, Dallas: Southern Methodist Univ. Press, 1965. 300p. Index. (Texas Folklore Society Publication Number XIV).

"Coyote is the hero of this book." This sentence is in the introduction to this volume (p. 6), and Coyote stories fill the first half. The stories show Coyote as trickster, as cunning survivor, and as rescuer.

A second section of the book contains Pueblo versions of old-world tales, such as "Cinderella" and "Beauty and the Beast." Whether these stories are modern-day adaptations of the European tales, or are ancient tales indigenous to the Pueblo is a matter of scholarly dispute.

Still a third section consists of essays on a variety of folklore-related topics. Among the subjects are comic preacher stories, the fool killer, Christmas customs, and party games.

623. Dorsey, George A. *The Mythology of the Wichita*. Norman: Univ. of Oklahoma Press, 1995. xi, 353p. Abstracts of tales. 95-2857. 0-8061-2778-3.

First published in 1904 by the Carnegie Institution, this is the result of interviews Dorsey had with the Wichita in the early twentieth century. The tales center around creation, stories about the natural world, about war and heroism, and about Coyote, the trickster character.

624. Eppinga, Jane. *Arizona Twilight Tales: Good Ghosts, Evil Spirits, and Blue Ladies*. Boulder, CO: Pruett Press, 2000. xi, 157p. Bibliog. 00-032353. 0-87108-901-7.

People are not the only ghosts in this collection of Arizona hauntings. There are also a train, a ship, and a church.

Among the people are Native Americans, some of whom appear to aid lost and weary travelers; settlers; soldiers; and miners. Capping off the collection is the story of Our Lady of Guadalupe, a figure powerful both to religion and to folklore, in both Mexico and the United States. Our Lady of Guadalupe commanded a poor peasant to visit the bishop of New Spain and ask that a church be built in her honor. As a sign that this request came from the Lady herself, she caused roses to bloom in the winter, which the peasant could deliver to the bishop.

625. Espinosa, Carmen Gertrudis. *The Freeing of the Deer, and Other New Mexico Indian Myths. Se Da Libertad al Venado y Otras Leyendas de los Indios de Nuevo México*. Albuquerque: Univ. of New Mexico Press, 1985; repr., 1999. x, 83p. 0-8263-0840-6; 0-8263-2085-6pa.

These tales are told in both English and Spanish, on facing pages. They were collected while Espinosa was on an archaeological dig in New Mexico. Many of them involve animals and the discovery of and raising of crops, such as how watermelon first came to the Navajo. The title story, "The Freeing of the Deer," relates how deer were once held captive by one people while others were starving; and how Ahayutah, the Warrior God, freed them so that all might share.

626. Everett, Donald E. *San Antonio Legacy: Folklore and Legends of a Diverse People*. San Antonio, TX: Trinity Univ. Press, 1979; repr., San Antonio, TX: Maverick, 1999. vii, 135p. Illus. Index. 00-052386. 1-893271-11-0; 1-893271-12-9pa.

Many of the stories here are true stories of historical figures. One is of the San Antonio man who invented barbed wire and thus changed the face of the Southwest; another is of the man who first created the ice cream soda. Others are more truly folkloric in nature: a tale of love set in the Alamo, stories of ghosts, even a story of a young widow who remains faithful to the memory of her dead husband—and who thinks he has returned in the body of a turkey!

627. Hallenbeck, Cleve, and Juanita H. Williams. *Legends of the Spanish Southwest.* Glendale, CA: Arthur H. Clark, 1938. 342p. Bibliog. Index. Map.

Legends of New Mexico, Arizona, California, and Texas, all of Spanish derivation, are compiled in this book. Many have religious themes.

628. Harwell, Thomas Meade. *Studies in Texan Folklore—Rio Grande Valley. Lore I. Twelve Folklore Studies with Introductions, Commentaries and a Bounty of Notes.* Lewiston, NY: Edwin Mellen Press, 1997. x, 162p. 97-947. 0-7734-4208-1.

Harwell, a college teacher, gathered these essays from his freshman students as part of a class project. Most deal with healing and medicine, including some essays on the Evil Eye. Others deal with La Llorona, or the Weeping Woman, and with weather lore. All together there are twelve studies of "the evil eye, shock, *recetas* and *curanderos,* ghosts, owl-lore, and weather-lore" (p. vii).

Harwell plans three more volumes of Texas folklore.

629. Havenhill, Jackye. *From the Big Red to the Rio Grande: Texas Legends.* Unionville, NY: Royal Fireworks Press, 1997. 168p. Illus. Bibliog. 0-88092-354-7.

Most of the stories told here are ghost stories, from all corners of Texas. Here are a headless horseman, a vanishing nun, a Robin Hood character, and—of course—a woman who is often seen walking by a lake. Also included are some stories of the natural world, such as the story of the will-o'-the-wisp and an explanation of how bluebonnets were first created.

630. Hazen-Hammond, Susan. *Spider Woman's Web: Traditional Native American Tales about Women.* New York: Berkley, 1999. xi, 242p. Index. Bibliog. 99-35823. 0-399-52546-7pa.

Tales that show women's power to influence the world are presented here. Tales are from a variety of Native American cultures. There are creation stories here, stories of the trickster character so common in storytelling, and stories of human relationships.

Hazen-Hammond adds to each story a section called "Connections," in which she presents questions to ponder, in an attempt to help the reader get a deeper meaning out of the stories. She also suggests keeping a journal while reading these tales and using the tales as a way to gain insight into one's own life.

631. Hinton, Leanne, and Lucille J. Watahomigie, eds. *Spirit Mountain: An Anthology of Yuman Story and Song.* Tucson: Sun Tracks and the Univ. of Arizona Press, 1984. xii, 344p. Illus. 84-112. 0-8165-0843-7; 0-8165-0817-8pa.

The stories and poems transcribed here are from the Yuman tribes of Hualapai, Havasupai, Yavapai, Paipai, Diegueño, Mojave, Maricopa, and Quechan. They tell the story of human origin according to the Yuman tradition and of the traditional way of life.

Stories and poems are presented both in English and in the original language, transcribed into the Roman alphabet.

632. James, Ahlee. *Tewa Firelight Tales.* New York: Longmans, Green, 1927. 247p. Illus.

San Ildefonso, a pueblo about twenty-five miles northwest of Santa Fe, New Mexico, is where James collected these tales in the 1920s.

Like so many Indian tales, these were told for education as well as entertainment. Some of them are similar to European fairy tales, such as the one reminiscent of the Cinderella story known in so many cultures.

633. Jameson, W. C. *Buried Treasures of Texas: Legends of Outlaw Loot, Pirate Hoards, Buried Mines, Ingots in Lakes, and Santa Anna's Pack-Train Gold.* Little Rock, AR: August House, 1991. 202p. Maps. Bibliog. 91-31771. 0-87483-178-4pa.

Arranged by region of Texas, this tells the tales of various lost treasures throughout the state. Regions are

The Trans-Pecos Desert
The Panhandle
North Texas
Central Texas
South Texas Brush Country
The Gulf Coat
East Texas Piney Woods

634. Kilpatrick, Jack F., and Anna G. Kilpatrick. *Friends of Thunder: Folktales of the Oklahoma Cherokees.* Dallas, TX: Southern Methodist Univ. Press, 1964. xviii, 197p. Illus. Notes. 64-16633.

The Kilpatricks collected these tales from Cherokees in Oklahoma during the 1960s; both authors are Cherokees themselves. Stories are divided into categories:

Bird stories
Animal stories (including stories of Br'er Rabbit)
Stories of Uk'ten', the serpent of the Cherokee paradise

Monster stories
Little People stories
Stories of Tseg'sgin', the Trickster
Humorous stories
Stories concerning customs
Historical stories

When a song is part of a story, the music is transcribed.

635. Kraul, Edward Garcia, and Judith Beatty. *The Weeping Woman: Encounters with La Llorona.* Santa Fe, NM: The Word Process, 1988. xii, 107p. Illus. by Tony Sanchez. 88-50347. 0-945937-06-7pa.

La Llorona as a character in Southwest folklore goes back to before the days of Cortés. She appears in many guises, but always as a woman looking for her lost children. The children may be lost, drowned, kidnapped, or killed by La Llorona herself, but she always looks for them. The people she appears to are always changed by their encounter, and always for the better.

Some of the encounters described by people in this book are contemporary ones.

636. Link, Margaret Schevill. *The Pollen Path: A Collection of Navajo Myths.* Walnut, CA: Kiva, 1956; repr., 1998. 205p. Bibliog. Index. Appendix. 98-66271. 1-885772-09-2pa.

In the 1920s, Margaret Schevill, a young wife of a University of California professor, felt drawn to the myths and religion of the Navajos. The death of her son made her question her own beliefs. She traveled into the West, living on Indian reservations, participating in and observing ceremonies, talking to elders about the traditions and stories that intrigued her. This book is her retelling of the creation and life myths of the Navajo.

In later years, she underwent therapy with C. G. Jung; the stories she tells are thus retold from a Jungian perspective.

The appendix is her story of her experiences.

637. Lomatuway'ma, Michael, Lorena Lomatuway'ma, and Sidney Namingha. *Hopi Animal Stories.* Lincoln: Univ. of Nebraska Press, 2001. xxxi, 261p. Edited by Ekkehart Malotki. Illus. Glossary. 00-050937. 0-8032-8271-0pa.

The three authors, as well as an additional anonymous author, are the narrators of these tales; Ekkehart Malotki is the editor who transferred them from the spoken word into print. All concern animals, all were told not only for their entertainment value but also for the purpose of transmitting cultural values. Many of the tales involve the trickster Coyote.

638. Malotki, Ekkehart, ed. *The Bedbugs' Night Dance and Other Hopi Sexual Tales: Mumuspi'yyungqa Tuutuwutsi.* n.p. Northern Arizona Univ., 1995. xxiv, 398p. Glossary. Appendix: Hopi alphabet. 95-17656. 0-8032-3190-3.

The stories told here are told both in English and in Hopi, on facing pages. They concern the fertility god and other sexual gods of the Hopi culture. Several narrators tell the stories; Malotki has collected and edited them. An introduction by E. N. Genovese explains the importance of this symbolism in Hopi religion and society.

639. ———. *Hopi Tales of Destruction.* Lincoln: Univ. of Nebraska Press, 2002. xii, 230p. Glossary. Bibliog. 2002-3601. 0-8032-8283-4.

Seven tales of the destruction of seven different Hopi villages are the stuff of this book. The villages are Hisatsongoopavi, Qu'ätaqtipu, Pivanhonkyapi, Sikyatki, Huk'ovi, Hovi'itstuyqa, and Awat'ovi. A variety of disasters destroyed these villages, some natural such as earthquakes, others the product of strife between and within villages.

Malotki gathered these tales from people whom he calls "story rememberers," those who remember and tell the tales of their peoples. The storytellers here are Michael Lomatuway'ma, Lorena Lomatuway'ma, and Sidney Namingha Jr.

Each tale is preceded by an introduction that sets the tale in context and gives information about how much is historically known about the event.

640. Malotki, Ekkehart, and Ken Gary. *Hopi Stories of Witchcraft, Shamanism, and Magic.* Lincoln: Univ. of Nebraska Press, 2001. lvii, 290p. Illus. Glossary. 00-050316. 0-8032-3217-9.

Malotki spent much time during the 1980s on the Hopi reservation in Arizona. While there, he made a study of many stories and tales, taping and transcribing them. Here he presents thirty-one of them, all related to shamanism and magic.

641. Malotki, Ekkehart, and Michael Lomatuway'ma. *Stories of Maasaw, a Hopi God.* Lincoln: Published in Collaboration with Lufa-type and the Museum of Northern Arizona by the Univ. of Nebraska Press, 1987. ix, 347p. Illus. by Petra Roeckerath. Glossary. (American Tribal Religions, volume 10). 87-164. 0-8032-3117-2. 0-8032-8147-1pa.

Maasaw is the omnipresent and multifaceted god in the Hopi tradition. Stories in this volume see him as a character, a person. He is portrayed both in heroic situations—as one who destroyed the enemies of the Hopi—and in more mundane ones—as one who courts and wins a wife.

Malotki collected the tales in the mid-1980s.

The tales here are presented on facing pages both in English and in the Hopi language.

642. Miles, Elton. *Stray Tales of the Big Bend*. College Station: Texas A&M Univ. Press, 1993. 186p. Photographs by Bill Wright. Notes. Index. 92-39729. 0-89096-534-x; 0-89096-542-0pa.

Stories of ghosts, buried treasure, and mysterious dreams appear in this book about the Big Bend country in west Texas. Many of the tales, of course, are about the pioneering days in the state.

643. Montana, Sybil. *Doc Holliday's Travels and Alluring Tales*. Rogersville, MO: S. Montana, 1997. 106p. Illus.

John Henry, or Doc Holliday, was surely a man of legend. In this small paperbound book, Montana tells what is known—or believed—about Holliday. She states that some of the stories told about him are not documented, although they might be true. Certainly he was a gambler, gunman, rover, and true resident of the Wild West.

644. Nequatewa, Edmund. *Truth of a Hopi: Stories Relating to the Origin, Myths and Clan Histories of the Hopi*. Flagstaff: Northland Pub., in cooperation with the Museum of Northern Arizona, 1990. Originally issued in 1936 as Bulletin No. 8 of the Museum of Northern Arizona. 136p. Edited by Mary-Russell F. Colton. Notes. Bibliog. pa.

Stories from several clans of the Hopi are included in this collection. The stories discuss clan origins, how they came out of the underworld, how they came to settle where they did, and their relationships with the Spaniards and the missionaries and with later groups. There are also stories of Yaponcha, the Wind God, and of various dances and festivals.

645. Nusom, Lynn. *Billy the Kid Cook Book: A Fanciful Look at the Recipes and Folklore from Billy the Kid Country*. Phoenix, AZ: Golden West, 1998. 108p. Illus. Index. 1-885590-32-6pa.

Interspersed with recipes reminiscent of the Wild West (Buttermilk Biscuits, Green Chile Stew, Tortilla Soup) are snippets of information about the life and legend of Billy the Kid. Here is information about his early days working in a butcher shop, the time he presumably spent in Mexico, and about his criminal escapades. Nusom reprints various newspaper stories of the day, reporting Billy's exploits.

This is more cookbook than folklore, but its presentation of folklore is very entertaining.

646. O'Bryan, Aileen, ed. *Navaho Indian Myths*. New York: Dover, 1993. vii, 187p. Myths told by Sandoval, Hastin Tiotsi hee (Old Man Buffalo Grass) to Aileen O'Bryan in late November 1928. (First published as *The Dîn'e: Origin Myths of the Navaho Indians* as Bulletin 163 of the Smithsonian Institution Bureau of American Ethnology, U.S. Government Printing Office, Washington, DC, 1956). Illus. Bibliog. 93-9688. 0-486-27592-2pa.

According to O'Bryan, she took down these stories as closely as possible in the way they were told to her by Sandoval, or Old Man Buffalo Grass, in 1928. They concern the origin of the world as believed by the Navajos and the relationships among all creatures in it.

O'Bryan was living in Mesa Verde National Park in Colorado when Sandoval came to her with the desire that these stories and beliefs be written down for future generations. Mesa Verde is believed to be the center of the old civilizations and is called "The Place of the Ancients."

647. Opler, Morris Edward. *Myths and Tales of the Chiricahua Apache Indians*. New York: American Folklore Society, 1942; repr., Lincoln: Bison Book Edition by the Univ. of Nebraska Press, 1994. xxvi, 114p. Appendix: Apache and Navaho Comparative References. Bibliog. (Sources of American Indian Oral Literature). 94-12396. 0-8032-8602-3pa.

Opler worked and lived with the Chiricahua people in New Mexico during the 1930s and collected these stories then. His presentation is divided into six parts:

Stories of when the world was young, how it was created, and how it was made safe for human habitation

The story of how daylight came into being

Stories of Coyote and other animals with human qualities. Coyote was often the trickster, but almost as often he was a being who did great kindnesses to humans

Stories of spirits and supernatural beings

Stories of Foolish People, told both for entertainment and to educate children

Miscellaneous stories

The stories have extensive footnotes of interest of folklore scholars, but can also be read simply for their narrative appeal.

648. Parsons, Elsie Clews. *Taos Tales*. New York: J. J. Augustin Publisher, 1940; repr., New York: Dover, 1996. 185p. List of references. Originally published as Vol. XXXIV of *Memoirs of the American Folk-Lore Society*, 1940. 95-45565. 0-486-28974-5pa.

First published in 1940, this reprint of a classic brings back almost one hundred Taos Indian tales collected by Elsie Clews Parsons. Characters include Blue Corn Woman, Yellow Corn Woman, and Coyote, the trickster character.

Most of the tales are extremely brief, a page or two.

Parsons's introduction gives background and some information on the culture that produced these tales.

649. ———. *Tewa Tales*. New York: American Folklore Society, 1926. 304p. Bibliog.

According to Parsons's introduction, in the early nineteenth century, part of the Tewa Tribe of New Mexico migrated to Arizona, invited by the Hopi Tribe. These two divisions of the Tewa developed different myths and folktales. Here Parsons has collected folktales of "emergence and migration" from both the divisions of the tribe.

650. Pepper, Choral. *Treasure Legends of the West*. Salt Lake City, UT: Gibbs Smith, 1994. 90p. Illus. Maps. Bibliog. 94-18062. 0-87905-611-8.

Books about lost treasures are numerous. Pepper provides an extra in this one—colorfully drawn foldout maps that show the area around which each lost treasure is thought to be. Armchair treasure hunters will find it interesting to use the full-color, foldout maps to attempt to solve the mystery of the lost treasures.

Treasures described are in Arizona, Montana, California, Montana, and Texas.

651. Rider, Rowland W., as told to Deirdre Paulsen. *Sixshooters and Sagebrush*. Provo, UT: Brigham Young Univ. Press, 1979; repr. as *The Roll Away Saloon: Cowboy Tales of the Arizona Strip*. Logan: Utah State Univ. Press, 1985. xviii, 114p. Illus.

79-15715; 85-29531. 0-8425-1696-4pa; 0-87421-124-7pa.

Rider was both a cowboy and a storyteller. He was a cowboy in the early 1900s, in the borderlands between Utah and Arizona. He was a storyteller in the latter years of his life, regaling audiences both in person and on television and radio. In between he attended college, was an engineer, owned a garage, served as city marshal of Kanab, Utah, and served in the U.S. Army during World War I.

The stories he tells here—transcribed by his granddaughter, Deirdre Paulsen—are rooted in truth and tell of his cowboy days. They tell of the everyday life of the cowboy and of some unusual incidents, including the times he met Theodore Roosevelt and Zane Grey. Some of the tales have evidently been embellished over the years and can rightly be called tall tales. In one, cowboys move a "rolling saloon" back and forth across the Arizona-Utah border, in order to evade the authorities. In another, Rider rides three times around a perching ground owl. The owl follows Rider's movements to his own detriment—after the third revolution of both cowboy and owl's head, the owl's head falls off.

652. Robe, Stanley L., ed. *Hispanic Folktales from New Mexico: Narratives from the R. D. Jameson Collection.* Berkeley: Univ. of California Press, 1977. ix, 223p. Bibliog. Register of Tale Types. Register of Motifs. (Univ. of California Publications. Folklore Studies: 30). 76-52036. 0-520-09570-7.

Some 204 tales make up this volume, collected in the early 1950s by students of R. D. Jameson at New Mexico Highlands University in Las Vegas. Jameson died before the study was complete, but always envisioned a book as the result of the study and collection. This is that result.

The tales for the most part are told by the elder relatives of the student collectors, people whose families had lived in the area for generations and who retained the old ways of their Spanish, Mexican, and Indian forebears.

Most tales include a note about the collector and the informant. Animal tales and jokes are the two most important categories of material collected in this volume.

653. Sharp, Jay W. *Texas Unexplained: Strange Tales and Mysteries from the Lone Star State.* Austin: Texas Parks and Wildlife Press, distributed by Univ. of Texas Press, 1999. vii, 134p. Illus. Bibliog. 1-885696-34-5pa.

Mysteries of Texas are the subject of this book: mysterious apparitions, ghosts, buried treasure, lost ships, monsters, mysterious crimes. All but one are based in Texas lore, retold by the author. One is based on an experience of the author's grandmother.

Black-and-white sketches illustrate the volume.

654. Stevens, Reed. *Treasure of Taos: Tales of Northern New Mexico.* Santa Fe, NM: Mariposa, 1992. 121p. Illus. by Janice St. Marie. Bibliog. 0-933553-08-0pa.

Five tales are told here, all reflecting the Hispanic culture of northern New Mexico. Many of them deal with the supernatural, and many emphasize the responsibility of individuals to their community.

655. Turner, Allan, and Richard Stewart. *Transparent Tales: An Attic Full of Texas Ghosts.* Lufkin: Best of East Texas Publishers, 1998. 156p. Illus. Index. 1-878096-51-6.

Tales of mysterious apparitions, haunted houses, and haunted restaurants all appear in this volume of ghost stories. All of the stories are documented, and information about the people who experienced the unusual happenings is included.

Illustrations are black-and-white photographs of the individuals whose stories are told, or of the sites at which the mysterious events happened.

656. Usner, Don J. *Benigna's Chimayó: Cuentos from the Old Plaza.* Santa Fe: Museum of New Mexico Press, 2001. 153p. Illus. 00-048972. 0-89013-381-6; 0-89013-382-4pa.

Most of the tales in this book came from the Old World centuries ago. They came to this book through Benigna Ortega Chávez, who told them to her family in the early part of the twentieth century. Eventually she wrote them down, in Spanish, and her daughter transcribed them into English. It is her grandson, Don Usner, who then reworked them for today's readers.

The tales are timeless ones of love, of magic, and of the natural world. Many are stories of a poor person who attains wealth and lives happily ever after. Usner spends time exploring the way in which such ancient folktales can illuminate today's world.

Several of the tales are told in both English and Spanish.

657. Vigil, Angel. *The Corn Woman: Stories and Legends of the Hispanic Southwest. La Mujer del Maiz: Cuentos y Leyendas del Sudoeste Hispano.* Englewood, CO: Libraries Unlimited, 1994. xxxi, 234p. Illus. Glossary. Bibliog. (World Folklore Series). 94-2091. 1-56308-194-6.

Many of the tales told here are told both in English and in Spanish. There are traditional *cuentos,* stories from the Aztec tradition, stories that blend the Indian and the Spanish cultures of the Southwest, religious stories, stories of magic and transformation, animal stories, and some stories from modern storytellers.

658. Williams, Brad, and Choral Pepper. *The Mysterious West.* Cleveland, OH: World Publishing, 1967. 192p. Illus.

Unlike many books that recount–or discount–mysteries of the West, this one avoids tales of lost treasure. It retells instead more unusual stories and attempts to present facts to dispute the legends. Many of the legends center on the "discovery" of various areas, for example, the story that Phoenicians discovered New Mexico, or that Romans settled Arizona.

659. Williams, Docia Schultz. *Best Tales of Texas Ghosts.* Plano: Republic of Texas Press, 1998. x, 394p. Illus. Bibliog. Index. 98-13263. 1-55622-569-5pa.

Arranged by geographic area, this has tales of ghosts seen in east Texas, San Antonio and south Texas, the south Texas coast, and the west Texas plains. Many of the tales are of gentle, sad ghosts rather than frightening ones.

Illustrations are black-and-white photographs, showing the venues of the ghostly visitations.

660. ——. *Phantoms of the Plains: Tales of West Texas Ghosts.* Plano: Republic of Texas Press, 1996. xv, 272p. Illus. Bibliog. Index. 95-24493. 1-55622-397-8pa.

Ghosts in public places, at cavalry posts, in hotels and restaurants, in schools, and in houses are the subjects of this volume. In addition, Williams tells tales of ghost animals and ghost lights. Many of the incidents are told either by the person who experienced the ghostly phenomenon or by a person who heard of it from a friend.

Illustrations are black-and-white photographs, often of the place at which the haunting happened.

661. ——. *When Darkness Falls: Tales of San Antonio Ghosts and Hauntings.* Plano: Republic of Texas Press, 1997. xiii, 344p. Illus. Sources. Index. 97-9192. 1-55622-536-9pa.

As in one of her other volumes of ghosts, *Phantoms of the Plains* (Plano: Republic of Texas Press, 1996), Williams here tells tales of ghosts and hauntings in hotels, restaurants, public buildings, schools, and houses. She also has a section of tales on strange happenings, such as ghostly vehicles and haunted portraits. Again as in the other volume, she documents all her stories with brief information about her informant and the individual's actual encounter with the supernatural.

Illustrations are black-and-white photographs of the various haunted places.

662. Williams, Harry. *Texas Trails: Legends of the Great Southwest.* San Antonio, TX: Naylor, 1932. vii, 269p. Illus. by Hans Reuter. Index.

First written for the *San Antonio Light,* between 1927 and 1931, these are tales of both real and fictitious Texans, although even the real tales have been embellished through retelling. The stories are of bad men and heroes, of gunfights and horse races, and of the fierce elements that all early Texans had to overcome.

663. Wilson, Steve. *Oklahoma Treasures and Treasure Tales.* Norman: Univ. of Oklahoma Press, 1976. xiii, 325p. Illus. Notes. Bibliog. Index. 74-15912. 0-8061-1240-9.

French, Spanish, and Indian treasures are all described in this book, with accounts of the legends that surround them; tales of the efforts to recover them; and maps, both old and new, of some of the sites. Illustrations also include photographs of the sites.

Frank and Jesse James make an appearance; they buried a substantial stolen treasure somewhere along the Chisholm Trail, only part of which has been found.

664. Yracébûrû, Maria. *Legends and Prophecies of the Quero Apache: Tales for Healing and Renewal.* Rochester, VT: Bear and Company, 2002. ix, 181p. Illus. 2002-688. 1-879181-77-0.

Thirteen tales from the Apache appear here. Yracébûrû heard them first from an old man important to her in her childhood, Ten Bears, who in turn had learned the stories—and their meaning—from his mother. The stories "are prayers and celebrations. They are given in joy for Earth Mother and for our healing" (Introduction, p. 7).

The stories concern creation, the battle between good and evil, healing, marriage, the importance of family, and the necessity of being one with Mother Earth.

665. Zeplin, Zeno. *Great Texas Christmas Legends.* Canyon Lake, TX: NELMAR, 1987. 137p. Illus. by Judy Jones. 87-7675. 0-9615760-3-0.

Zeplin presents these Southwestern legends as Christmas legends, but they are more suitable for a land of sunshine and warmth than are the more traditional snow and fur Christmas stories. One of the legends even proves that Santa Claus exists—he is the spirit of generosity in all of us.

Folk Music

666. Abernethy, Francis Edward. *Singin' Texas.* Dallas, TX: E-Heart Press, 1983.

xviii, 183p. Illus. Title and First Line Index. 83-080205. 0-935014-07-1; 0-935014-04-7pa.

Not only songs that originated in Texas, but songs that "passed through that state during the course of their eternal ramblings" (p. ix) are included here. Even the ones that just "passed through" have a Texas flavor, as they were changed and adapted by local musicians. Abernethy includes children's songs, dance songs, love songs, songs of the land, cattle trail songs, church songs, and modern day songs.

Many of the songs have music transcribed.

667. Allen, Jules Verne. *Cowboy Lore.* San Antonio, TX: Naylor, 1933; repr., 1971. xv, 174p. Illus. by Ralph J. Pereida. 70-110441. 0-8111-0358-7.

The latter half of this book comprises cowboy songs, usually with music transcribed. In the first half, Allen presents information on a cowboy's daily life, on cattle brands, and on cowboy vocabulary.

Allen was considered the original "singing cowboy." He recorded for RCA-Victor and was appointed the "singing cowboy" and official singer of cowboy songs of New Mexico in 1929 by New Mexico's then governor, R. C. Dillon.

668. Giglio, Virginia. *Southern Cheyenne Women's Songs.* Norman: Univ. of Oklahoma Press, 1994. xxi, 243p. Illus. Bibliog. Index. Cassette tape index. Cheyenne glossary. 93-23221. 0-8061-2605-1.

Both songs of everyday life and songs of ritual and unusual events are included here, for both types are considered important in the Cheyenne culture. Here are lullabies and children's songs, hand game songs, spiritual songs, and war songs.

Giglio provides music as well as words and a list of cassettes on which this music is recorded.

669. Lomax, John A., and Alan Lomax. *Cowboy Songs and Other Frontier Ballads.* New York: Macmillan, 1938. xxxviii, 431p. Index to Titles.

Although cowboys certainly worked in states other than Southwestern ones, the great cattle drives originated in Texas. It is for that reason that this book is included in the chapter on Southwest lore.

John A. Lomax collected the majority of these songs for the first edition of *Cowboy Songs and Other Frontier Ballads*, published in 1910. He collected them at the source, traveling by horseback and by train through the Western states and talking to the men who had ridden the range and sung these songs. With the help of his son, Alan, he added more newly discovered songs for this revised and enlarged edition.

The songs are arranged into sections:

Up the Trail
The Round-Up
Dodge City, the End of the Trail
Campfire and Bunkhouse
Off Guard
Son of a Gun
Way Out West

Many well-known favorites are included here, such as "Sweet Betsy from Pike," "The Old Chisholm Trail," "Bury Me out on the Prairie," and "The Santa Fe Trail," as well as lesser-known ones.

Many of the songs have music transcribed.

When the book was published in 1910, it was one of the very first copyrighted collections of American ballads. It is no less valuable today.

Music for some of the songs is included.

670. Moore, Ethel, and Chauncey O. Moore. *Ballads and Folksongs of the Southwest: More than 600 Titles Collected in Oklahoma.* Norman: Univ. of Oklahoma Press, 1964. xv, 414p. Illus. Bibliog. Index of Titles. Index of First Lines. Subject Index. 64-11329.

The Moores collected most of these 600 songs from the Tulsa area of Oklahoma. Each song is prefaced with information on its origin and the person who contributed it.

671. Robb, John Donald. *Hispanic Folk Songs of New Mexico, with Selected Songs Collected, Transcribed and Arranged for Voice and Piano.* Albuquerque: The Univ. of New Mexico Press, 1978. 83p. M54-2171.

Both religious and secular songs are transcribed here, most with music.

The introduction provides a history and discussion of folk music in New Mexico.

The songs are written in both English and Spanish.

672. Sedillo-Brewster, Mela C. *Mexican and New Mexican Folkdances.* 2d ed., revised and enlarged. Albuquerque: Univ. of New Mexico Press, 1938. 47p. Illus.

Music, steps, even costumes are shown in this small book for folk dances of Mexico and New Mexico. Steps are described in detail, so that the present-day reader can reconstruct the dance. Costumes are shown in small line drawings.

Folk Belief and Ritual

673. Anderson, John Q., comp. and ed. *Texas Folk Medicine: 1,333 Cures, Remedies, Preventives, and Health Practices.* Austin, TX: Encino Press, 1970. xix, 91p. Illus. by Barbara Mathews Whitehead.

Students in Anderson's folklore classes in the 1960s collected more than 6,000 items of folk medicine throughout Texas; from that massive collection, Anderson culled the 1,300 items in this book.

It is arranged similarly to other books of folk medicine, alphabetical by complaint—acne to whooping cough—and contains brief snippets of information under each heading.

In this book you can learn that to cure a sore throat you can pour turpentine on bacon and tie the concoction around your neck, or that chicken pox can be cured by leading the patient three times around the chicken house.

674. Campa, Arthur. *Hispanic Culture in the Southwest.* Norman: Univ. of Oklahoma Press, 1979; repr., 1993. xii, 316p. Illus. Bibliog. Index. 78-58135.0-8061-2569-1pa.

Much of this book relates the history of the Southwestern United States, with emphasis on the different groups that influenced it. But the latter half more specifically concerns folklore. There are chapters on superstition and witchcraft, on the Penitentes, on folk drama, folk singing and dancing, arts and crafts, and food preparation.

675. Curtin, L. S. M. *Healing Herbs of the Upper Rio Grande: Traditional Medicine of the Southwest.* Santa Fe, NM: Library of Anthropology, 1947; rev. ed. Santa Fe, NM: Western Edge Press, 1997. xviii, 236p. Illus. Bibliog. Glossary. Index. 97-060440. 1-889921-01-7pa.

Alphabetically arranged by the name of the plant, this gives a description of each plant and information as to its efficacy in healing. Some history of the use of a plant is included. Line drawings illustrate many of the entries.

676. Jameson, W. C. *Bubba Speak: Texas Folk Sayings.* Plano: Republic of Texas Press, 1998. ix, 195p. Illus. 98-14817. 1-55622-616-0pa.

Arranged alphabetically like a dictionary, *Bubba Speak* lists folk sayings from Texas under each word. Among the offerings under the word *dumb,* for example, are "So dumb, he spits upwind," and "He carries his brains in his coat pocket." Under *stare* comes "He could stare a hole in a stone wall."

Illustrations are cartoons.

677. Jordan, Charlie. *Charlie Jordan's West Texas Weather and Lore.* Abilene, TX: C. Jordan, 1997. ii, 152p.

About ten pages of this brief book are devoted to folk sayings about weather, such as "When the ants work late at night, it's a good sign that rain or snow is near." The rest of the book recounts stories of weather disasters such as tornadoes. Many of these are tall tales.

678. Mullen, Patrick B. *I Heard the Old Fishermen Say: Folklore of the Texas Gulf Coast.* Austin: Univ. of Texas Press, 1978; repr., Logan: Utah State Univ. Press, 1988. xxx, 183p.; repr.: xxxviii, 183p. Illus. Appendix A: List of the Magic Folk Beliefs. Appendix B: List of the Empirical Folk Beliefs. Notes. Bibliog. 78-33. 88-27684. 0-292-73813-7; 0-87421-139-5pa.

First published in 1978 in hardcover, this paperback edition was intended to give the material wider circulation, particularly for folklore courses. Mullen collected the information during the late 1960s and early 1970s.

Much of the material he collected is concerned with magic and superstition; much else concerns stories of buried treasure.

679. Robe, Stanley L., ed. *Hispanic Legends from New Mexico. Narratives from the R. D. Jameson Collection.* Berkeley: Univ. of California Press, 1980. xi, 548p. Registry of Motifs. (Univ. of California Publications. Folklore and Mythology Studies: 31.) 79-64490. 0-520-09614-2.

A professor at New Mexico Highlands University, Las Vegas, New Mexico, Raymond De Loy Jameson and his students during the early 1950s collected an extensive amount of folklore material. Some, the actual folktales, was published as *Hispanic Folktales from New Mexico* (Berkeley: Univ. of California Press, 1977).

This collection, however, is not made up of formal folktales, but of legends. Almost all concern the supernatural, and an ordinary person's encounter with some manifestation of the supernatural while going about ordinary tasks. Legends collected are divided into the following categories:

Omens
Curses
Death and the Dead
Ghostly Apparitions
The Devil
Witchcraft
Giants
Dwarfs and Goblins
Unusual Animals
Natural Phenomena
Magic
Belief
Treasures

Informant's name, informant's location, collector's name, and date are given for all legends.

680. Silverthorne, Elizabeth. *Legends and Lore of Texas Wildflowers*. College Station: Texas A&M Univ. Press, 1996. xvii, 240p. Notes. Bibliog. Index. 95-45245. 0-89096-702-4.

Alphabetically arranged by the name of the flower, this book tells the legends and folk stories associated with each. For example, under the bluebonnet, Silverthorne recounts the story of the young Indian girl, who, hearing that the Great Spirit was angry with her tribe and demanded that the tribe's most precious possession be sacrificed, decided to sacrifice her beloved doll. Only the doll's bonnet survived, in the guise of the bluebonnet.

Other legends concern healing properties of various flowers.

Material Culture

681. Bahti, Tom. *Southwestern Indians: Arts and Crafts, Tribes, Ceremonials*. Las Vegas, NV: KC Publications, 1997. 215p. Illus. Index. Bibliog. Glossary. 97-070258.

The first section of this book concerns crafts: baskets, bead making, fetishes, kachinas, weaving, sandpainting, pottery, silverwork, and turquoise. Information includes techniques, where certain crafts are practiced, and where to purchase examples. Full-color photographs are plentiful.

The second section is on particular tribal groups: Acoma, Apache, Chemehuevi, Chochiti, Cocopa, Havasupai, Hopi, Hualapai, Isleta, Jemez, Kaibab Paiute, Laguna, Maricopa, Mohave, Nambe, Navajo, Picuris, Pima, Pojoaque, San Felipe, San Ildefonso, San Juan, Sandia, Santa Ana, Santa Clara, Santo Domingo, Taos, Tesuque, Tohone O'od-

ham, Ute, Yaqui, Yavapai, Ysleta del Su, Yuma, Zia, and Zuni. Their history, their current way of life, and their practice of the ancient crafts are all described.

682. Boatright, Mody Coggin. *Tales from the Derrick Floor: A People's History of the Oil Industry*. Garden City, NY: Doubleday, 1970; repr., Lincoln: Univ. of Nebraska Press, 1982. xv, 268p. Bibliog. Index.

Most of the material in this book is composed of brief quotations—a paragraph or two—from people who worked in the oil fields and oil field towns in the early part of the century. Vignettes concern looking for oil, oil strikes, life in the boomtowns, law, dangers and accidents, and women in the oil fields.

One chapter is devoted to the jargon of the oil fields.

683. Cleaveland, Agnes Morley. *No Place for a Lady*. Boston: Houghton Mifflin, 1941. ix, 356p. Illus.

Morley writes of growing up in the Territory of New Mexico in the late nineteenth century. She writes of ranch work, of home remedies, of schooling, and of child rearing—everyday life in rural New Mexico.

684. Fannin, Jerry W., and Angela Farris Fannin. *Johnnies, Biffies, Outhouses, Etc.* Burnet, TX: Eakin Press, 1980. viii, 95p. Illus. 0-89015-259-4.

This book proves that almost anything can be the subject of an interesting book, because its subject is the outhouses of Texas. The Fannins (Jerry Fannin took the photographs and Angela Farris Fannin wrote the accompanying text) photographed some seventy-five outhouses. The text describes the outhouses and includes some of their design details.

Also included are some reminiscences

of people who grew up with this form of "convenience."

As the Fannins state, their purpose was to "preserve a part of Texas's past that will soon be nonexistent."

685. Fischer, John. *From the High Plains.* New York: Harper and Row, 1978. 181p. Illus. 78-437. 0-06-011269-7.

Fischer's family was among the early settlers of the High Plains, in the Panhandles of Texas and Oklahoma. As he puts it in his prologue, he grew up seeing "the last of the Old West slide around the corner of history" (p. 2). He writes of the real cowboy rather than the televised version, who "shambled across the prairie" rather than galloped, because cattle that were moved slowly did not lose as much weight; of the dugouts, or soddies, that were the first dwellings the settlers prepared; of the everyday life he lived growing up, which included chopping wood, stoking the furnace, mowing lawns, and a summer spent as a cowboy when he was only ten.

Fisher's book reflects the life in one small corner of the country at a time of intense change.

686. Griffith, James S. *Hecho a Mano: The Traditional Arts of Tucson's Mexican American Community.* Tucson: Univ. of Arizona Press, 2000. xxi, 104p. Illus. Notes. Bibliog. Index. 0-8165-1877-7; 0-8165-1878-5pa.

An exhibition of traditional arts at the University of Arizona Museum, November 2, 1996, through January 14, 1997, was the impetus behind this volume; the works described and pictured were part of it. Three levels of artwork are described and pictured. First are items that are primarily functional and secondarily visual objects, such as piñatas, grave markers, and boots. Although the items of this type in the exhibition are finely designed and made, their first reason for being is their function. Next comes a level where the visual function is more important, although the article is still functional, such as gardens and altars. The third level consists of objects that exist mainly because of their visual attractiveness, such as murals. Although the interplay between function and beauty changes, all of these objects possess both.

According to the curators of the exhibition, all objects also serve to interpret the community that made them to the larger, outside world.

Much of the artwork here is religious in nature; there is much work in textiles, in leather, and even in bread.

Illustrations are both black-and-white photographs and color plates.

687. Rosenak, Chuck, and Jan Rosenak. *Navajo Folk Art: The People Speak.* rev., 1st softcover edition. Flagstaff, AZ: Northland, 1998. xiii, 162p. Illus. Bibliog. Glossary. Gallery Guide. 97-36557. 0-87358-565-8; 0-87358-693-xpa.

First published in 1994 as a hardback, this has been reissued in softcover. The Rosenaks explore the folk art scene of the Four Corners region—where Arizona, Colorado, New Mexico, and Utah come together—dividing the area into eastern, central, and western regions. The Rosenaks describe the art of various artists within each region: woodcarvers, bead artists, weavers, potters, and those who work in mixed media. Color illustrations show many of the works.

An introduction describes how the culture of the Navajo informs their art: religion, clan relationships, and the concept of taboo all continue to influence artists. An appendix tells the Navajo creation story.

688. Sewell, Ernestine P., and Joyce Gibson Roach. *Eats: A Folk History of Texas Foods.* Fort Worth: Texas Christian Univ. Press, 1989. xiv, 257p. Illus. Bibliog. Index. 88-20158. 0-87565-032-5; 0-87565-035-xpa.

Holidays, celebrations, food descriptions, and recipes coexist in this trip through Texas by way of its food. The book is divided regionally—northeast, deep east, central, south, and west Texas—and also seasonally, with sections on spring eating, summer eating, harvest recipes, and end of the year.

Stories are told about why and when people eat certain foods and the customs that go along with them. Illustrations are plentiful, of early twentieth-century Texas and Texans.

Folklore for Children

689. Anaya, Rudolfo. *Maya's Children: The Story of La Llorona.* New York: Hyperion Books for Children, 1996. unpaged. Illus. 95-41973. 0-7868-0152-2 (trade); 0-7868-2124-8 (lib. binding).

La Llorona is a woman of legend, a woman who killed her own children and who wanders forever looking for them. Generations of parents in Latin America have used this legend to make their own children behave: "Be good or La Llorona will come to get you."

In this rendition, Rudolfo Anaya retells the legend without La Llorona as a villain. Rather, she loses her children to Time, through deception and trickery. She still wanders forever seeking them, but the image of mother as killer is gone.

The illustrations are in full color.

690. ——. *My Land Sings: Stories from the Rio Grande.* New York: Morrow Junior Books, 1999. 176p. Illus. Glossary. 99-19040. 0-688-15078-0.

All the stories here are set in New Mexico. They are the traditional tales, retold for children. Among them are the tale of La Llorona, the tale of the coyote and the raven, and tales of rural life.

691. Anderson, Bernice G. *Indian Sleep Man Tales.* NY: Bramhall House, 1940; repr., NY: Greenwich House, 1984. 145p. Illus. by Sears Frank and Bernice G. Anderson.

Like many Indian tales for children, these are meant both for instruction and entertainment. These are the tales of the Otoe and deal with the natural world, how various animals received their characteristics, and the traditions and celebrations of the tribe.

692. Baylor, Byrd. *And It Is Still That Way.* Santa Fe, NM: Trails West Publishing, 1976. 83p. 76-42242. 0-939729-06-7pa.

In his introduction, Baylor says, "Arizona Indian children made this book" (n.p.). He listened to children telling each other the legends of their own tribe or clan and encouraged them to remember more of those stories. This book is the result.

Legends came from children of the Navajo, Hopi, Papago, Pima, Apache, and Quechan. They deal with animals, the natural world, heroes, magic, and the ubiquitous Coyote.

Baylor notes that these legends are never told in the summer, because the belief is that snakes, which are crawling about in the summer, do not like hearing these legends and will seek out and bite the storyteller. He hopes that people reading the book will in turn honor the tradition and wait for winter to read the tales.

693. ——. *Way to Make Perfect Mountains: The Native American Legends of Sacred Mountains.* El Paso, TX: Cinco Puntos Press, 1997. 62p. Illus. Bibliog. 96-40531. 0-938317-26-1.

Creation stories make up one section of this small but lovely book about the mountains held sacred by Native Americans of the Southwest. Other stories are of supernatural beings that inhabit the mountains, of mysterious happenings there, and of ceremonies meant to respect them. Stories are from the Papago, the Apache, the Navajo, the Zuni, the Twea, the Yaqui, and the Yuma.

Illustrations are in black and white.

694. Bierhorst, John. *Doctor Coyote: A Native American Aesop's Fables.* New York: Macmillan, 1987; paperback repr., New York: Aladdin paperbacks, 1996. Unpaged. Illus. by Wendy Watson. 86-8669. 0-02-709780-3; 0-689-80739-2pa.

In the 1500s, a book of Aesop's fables came to the Americas. The Aztecs retold them, using Coyote as the main character. Here they are retold for modern audiences.

Illustrations are in full color.

695. Bowman, James Cloyd. *Pecos Bill: The Greatest Cowboy of All Time.* Chicago: Albert Whitman, 1967. 296p. Illus. by Laura Bannon.

Here are the stories of Pecos Bill, cowboy hero of the Southwest. They detail his upbringing in a pack of coyotes; tell of his exploits—from inventing cowpunching to gentling the devil's cavalry; describe his meeting with Slue-Foot Sue; and finally relate how he disappeared

from view, only to show up once more as legend.

696. Curry, Jane Louise. *Hold Up the Sky and Other Native American Tales from Texas and the Southern Plains.* New York: Margaret K. McElderry Books, 2003. 159p. Illus. by James Watts. 2002-16519. 0-689-85287-8.

Curry tells for modern readers the tales of the Kitkehahki, Osage, Kiowa, Kiowa-Apache, Wichita, Caddo, Comanche, Kitsai, Kadohadacho, Waco, Tawakoni, Bidai, Lipan Apache, and Tonkawa peoples. Creation stories, animal tales, and trickster tales are all here.

As with many Native American tales and stories, these are meant to teach and guide.

697. Dobie, J. Frank. *On the Open Range.* Dallas, TX: Banks, Upshaw, 1931. xii, 312p. Illus. Bibliog. Glossary.

In his preface, Dobie asserts that Americans "are inheritors of a vast body of tales about cunning coyotes, matchless mustangs, fabulous mines, gigantic bears, phantom stampedes, daring riders, and scores of other phenomena" and that "we do not have to go to the Eskimos or to Grimm for folk tales any more than the Grimm brothers themselves had to go outside Germany for theirs" (pp. x–xi).

He attempts to prove his point with this volume of frontier stories told for children. He tells of the longing to go West, of cattle and of horses, branding sessions, and bear hunting.

698. Dutton, Bertha, and Caroline Olin, eds. *Myths and Legends of the Indians of the Southwest.* Santa Barbara, CA: Bellerophon Books, 1978. Unpaged. Illus. Two volumes. Volume 1: Navajo, Pima, Apache. Volume 2: Hope, Acoma, Tewa,

Zuni. vol. 1: 0-8838-8049-0pa. vol. 2: 0-8838-8062-8pa.

Many things are covered—although briefly—in these two volumes. In addition to legends retold in simple language for children, the authors give information on customs and traditions, such as farming methods, dances, and ceremonies, and on arts and crafts, such as sandpainting, basket making, and pottery. The illustrations are black and white but quite clear, almost like illustrations in a coloring book.

699. Felton, Harold W. *Pecos Bill.* New York: Knopf, 1949. 177p. Illus. Bibliog.

Pecos Bill's life is told here, in the guise of "a faithful account," from his birth to his death or disappearance. The stories are told in a style suitable for children.

700. Hayes, Joe. *The Day It Snowed Tortillas.* Santa Fe, NM: Enchanting Land Books: Mariposa Publishing, 1982. 73p. Illus. by Lucy Jelinek. 0-933553-00-5.

Ten stories, or *cuentos,* of New Mexico are told here for children. They are stories that came originally from Spain, and traveled to New Mexico through Mexico. Some are reminiscent of Grimm's fairy tales. One of the stories is about La Llorona, or Crying Woman, who wanders about looking for her lost children.

701. ——. *La Llorona: The Weeping Woman.* El Paso, TX: Cinco Puntos Press, 1987. 32p.. Illus. by Vicki Trego Hill. 0-938317-02-4pa.

Hayes tells here the story of La Llorona, or Crying Woman, a well-known Hispanic folktale about a woman who loses her children—some versions, including this one, say she kills them—and walks through eternity searching for them and weeping. People often meet with her ghost.

Here the tale is told both in English and in Spanish.

702. Marriott, Alice Lee. *Winter-Telling Tales.* New York: Thomas Y. Crowell, 1947; repr., 1969. 84p. Illus. 73-78264.

Marriott tells the stories of the Kiowa people. The main character of the stories, Saynday, is the one who made things happen in the world. He caused the sun to be in the sky and to shine on both sides of the world; he brought the buffalo to his people; and when deer were eating all his people, he devised a way to grind the deers' teeth down, so that they became vegetarians. His cleverness and resourcefulness solved many problems.

703. McKee, Louise. *Dusty Desert Tales.* Caldwell, ID: Caxton Printers, 1941. 191p. Illus. with photographs and with drawings by J. Powell Scott.

Stories from the Pima, Apache, Hopi, and Yuma Indians are told here for children. Many of the stories have animal characters.

There are numerous black-and-white photographs depicting the everyday life of these people.

704. Morgan, William. *Coyote Tales.* Washington, DC: U.S. Indian Service, 1949; repr., Walnut, CA: Kiva, 2000. 31p. Illus. by Andrew Tsihnahjinnie. English adaptation by Hildegard Thompson. 99-089876. 1-885772-18-1pa.

During the 1940s, the Bureau of Indian Affairs was instrumental in having collected various children's stories and poems. The ones in this book were collected by William Morgan and illustrated by Andrew Tsihnahjinnie. He did both a Navajo version and an English translation. Hildegard Thompson did a further adaptation into English at that time.

The tales, presented once again for a

modern audience, feature the trickster Coyote.

705. Newcomb, Franc Johnson. *Navajo Bird Tales Told by Hosteen Clah Chee.* Wheaton, IL: Theosophical Publishing House, 1970. xiii, 125p. Edited by Lillian Harvey. Illus. by Na-Ton-Sa-Ka. 71-108760. 0-8356-0017-3.

In his introduction to this volume, Newcomb divides the lore and legends of the Navajo into three groups:

> the historical legend, the religious myth and the folk tale. The historical legend attempts to explain the origin of the Navajo tribe and describes the various tribal journeyings and migrations that took place in the past and which finally brought them to their present homeland. The religious myth tells of prophets who had contact with the Gods and wise men who taught them the rites, the chanted prayers, and the ceremonies that compose the Navajo religion of the present time. The folk tale comes from an earlier period when animals, birds, and men all lived at a common level and spoke a common language (p. xii).

Newcomb relates here tales in all three categories, told by the wise elder Hosteen Clah Chee to his grandchildren. The tales tell of the tribe's origin, their beginning days, and their relationships with animals and birds.

706. Roessel, Robert A., Jr., and Dillon Platero, eds. *Coyote Stories of the Navajo People.* Phoenix, AZ: Navajo Curriculum Center Press, 1974. 118p. Illus. by George Mitchell. 68-9678. 0-89019-005-4pa.

These fourteen stories are of "trotting coyote," which according to the introduction of this book represents "socially unacceptable behavior" (p. viii). Trotting Coyote usually gets his comeuppance in these stories, which makes them vehicles for teaching children the value of proper behavior.

The appealing illustrations give the impression of being colored with crayons.

707. Sauvageau, Juan. *Stories That Must Not Die.* Austin, TX: Oasis Press, 1975. vol. 1: 44p. vol. 2: 52p. vol. 3: 56p. Illus. Vocabulary lists. vol. 1: 0-916378-000-4; vol. 2: 0-916376-01-2; vol. 3: 0-916378-02-0.

Each paperback book contains ten folk tales written for children. Each story is written in both Spanish and English, is illustrated, and is followed by questions (again in both Spanish and English) on the text. Many of the stories have animals as characters; many others are stories of the supernatural.

708. Sevillano, Mando. *The Hopi Way: Tales from a Vanishing Culture.* Flagstaff, AZ: Northland Press, 1986. xx, 91p. Illus. by Mike Castro. Bibliog. 86-61067. 0-87358-413-9pa.

Most of the tales told here have animal characters, and most are teaching tales, with a moral.

In the introduction, Sevillano explains that the Hopi are reluctant to share their stories with outsiders, afraid that the stories will be used wrongly and disrespectfully. However, mindful of the fact that many stories are already lost, and many others are only imperfectly remembered, some were willing to share their knowledge in the hope that the stories would not become extinct.

Literary Authors: A Selected List

Below is a selected list of authors who reflect and interpret the history and atmosphere of their region. These are authors of novels, poems, short stories, or reminiscences. Through reading the works of these authors, one can acquire knowledge of the history, people, and flavor of the region. This is not a complete list, either of authors, or of their works, but rather one calculated to start readers exploring and discovering their own favorites.

Anaya, Rudolfo, 1937–

> *Albuquerque*
> *Bless Me, Ultima*
> *Heart of Aztlan*

Dobie, J. Frank, 1888–1964

> *Brush Country*
> *Coyote Wisdom*
> *Some Part of Myself*

Hillerman, Tony, 1925–

> *The Blessing Way*
> *Coyote Waits*
> *Finding Moon*
> *Hunting Badger*
> *Sacred Clowns*
> *Skinwalkers*
> *A Thief of Time*

Kingsolver, Barbara, 1937–

> *The Bean Trees*
> *High Tide in Tucson: Essays from Now*
>   *or Never*
> *The Poisonwood Bible*

Momaday, N. Scott, 1934–

> *A Coyote in the Garden*
> *House Made of Dawn*

Museums of the Region: A Selected List

Museums that feature everyday life abound in all regions of the country. Through the display of clothing, farm implements, household goods, industrial tools, or entire houses, workshops, and communities, these museums help people understand and appreciate the lives lived by those who came before. The list below is not a complete list of museums in the region, but by browsing through it, one can get a glimpse of the richness of museum offerings. Explore on your own and discover even more fascinating museums.

Arizona

Douglas

Slaughter Ranch Museum
6153 Geronimo Trail,
Douglas, Arizona 85608
Mailing Address:
P.O. Box 438
Douglas, Arizona 85608
520-558-2474
http://www.vtc.net/~sranch

Flagstaff

Arizona Historical Society Pioneer
  Museum
2340 North Fort Valley Road
Flagstaff, Arizona 86001
520-774-6272
http://www.arizona.edu/~azhist

Riordan Mansion State Historic Park
409 Riordan Road

Flagstaff, Arizona 86001
520-779-4395
http://www.pr.state.az.us

Mesa

Mesa Southwest Museum
53 North Macdonald
Mesa, Arizona 85201
480-644-2169
*http://www.ci.mesa.az.us/parksrec/msm/ind
ex.html*

Page

John Wesley Powell Memorial Museum
6 North Lake Powell Boulevard
Page, Arizona 86040
Mailing address:
Box 547
Page, Arizona 86040
928-645-9496
http://www.powellmuseum.org

Parker

Colorado River Indian Tribes Museum
Route 1
Box 23-B
Parker, Arizona 85344
520-669-9211

Phoenix

Phoenix Museum of History
105 North Fifth Street
Phoenix, Arizona 85004
602-253-2734
http://www.pmoh.org

Pioneer Arizona Living History Museum
Pioneer Road
Exit 225, Interstate 17
Phoenix, Arizona 85086
623-465-1052
http://www.pioneer-arizona.com

Tempe

Arizona Historical Society Museum
Central Arizona Division
1300 North College Avenue
Tempe, Arizona 85281
480-929-9499
http://www.tempe.gov/ahs

Tucson

Arizona Historical Society–Fort Lowell
   Museum
2900 North Craycroft Road
Tucson, Arizona 85710
Mailing address:
949 East 2nd Street
Tucson, Arizona 85719
520-885-3832
*http://www.oflna.org/fort_lowell_museum/
   ftlowell.htm*

Sosa-Carrillo-Fremont House Museum
151 South Granada
Tucson, Arizona 85701
520-622-0956
http://www.arizonahistoricalsociety.org

Wickenburg

Desert Caballeros Western Museum
21 North Frontier Street
Wickenburg, Arizona 85390

520-684-2272
http://www.westernmuseum.org

New Mexico

Albuquerque

Albuquerque Museum
2000 Mountain Road, N.W.
Albuquerque, New Mexico 87104
505-243-7255
http://www.cabq.gov/museum

Artesia

Artesia Historical Museum and Art
    Center
505 Richardson Avenue
Artesia, New Mexico 88210
505-748-2390
http://www.nmohwy.com/h/himuarce.htm

Aztec

Aztec Museum and Pioneer Village
125 North Main Avenue
Aztec, New Mexico 87410
505-334-9829
http://www.aztecnm.com/musuem/
    museum_index.htm

Cimarron

Old Mill Museum
220 West 17th Street
Cimarron, New Mexico 87714
Mailing address:
P.O. Box 62
Cimarron, New Mexico 87714
505-376-2417

http://www.nmculture.org/cgi-bin/
    instview.cgi?_recordnum=OMIL

Deming

Deming Luna Mimbres Museum
301 South Silver Street
Deming, New Mexico 88030
505-546-2382
http://www.cityofdeming.org/sights.html

Fort Sumner

Billy the Kid Museum
1601 East Sumner
Fort Sumner, New Mexico 88119
Mailing address:
Route 1
Box 36
Fort Sumner, New Mexico 88119
505-355-2380
http://www.southernnewmexico.com/
    BusinessDirectory/Museums/
    BillytheKidMuseum.html

Hobbs

Lea County Cowboy Hall of Fame and
    Western Heritage Center
5317 Lovington Highway
NMJC Campus
Hobbs, New Mexico 88240
505-392-1275
http://www.nmohwy.com/l/lecocoha.htm

Las Cruces

New Mexico Farm and Ranch Heritage
    Museum
4100 Dripping Springs Road

Las Cruces, New Mexico 88011
505-522-4100
http://www.nmculture.org

Pueblo of Acoma

Acoma Tourist and Visitation Center
Corner of I-38 and I-23
Pueblo of Acoma, New Mexico 87034
Mailing address:
P.O. Box 309
Pueblo of Acoma, New Mexico 87034
800-747-0181
http://www.nmohwy.com/a/acomapue.htm

Roswell

Historical Center for Southeast New
    Mexico
200 North Lea Avenue
Roswell, New Mexico 88201
505-622-8333
http://www.dfn.com/hcsnm/

Santa Fe

El Rancho de las Golondrinas Museum
334 Los Pinos Road
Santa Fe, New Mexico 87505
505-471-2261
http://www.golondrinas.org

Institute of American Indian Arts
    Museum
108 Cathedral Plaza
Santa Fe, New Mexico 87501
505-983-8900
http://www.iaiacad.org

Museum of International Folk Art
706 Camino Lejo

Santa Fe, New Mexico 87505
Mailing address:
P.O. Box 2087
Santa Fe, New Mexico 87504
505-476-1200
http://www.moifa.org

Palace of the Governors
On the Plaza
Santa Fe, New Mexico 87501
Mailing address:
P.O. Box 2087
Santa Fe, New Mexico 87504
505-476-5094
http://www.palaceofthegovernors.org/

Taos

Millicent Rogers Museum of Northern
    New Mexico
1504 Museum Road
4 miles north of Taos
Taos, New Mexico 87571
Mailing address:
P.O. Box A
Taos, New Mexico 87571
505-758-2462
http://www.millicentrogers.org

Oklahoma

Aline

Sod House Museum
Route 1
Aline, Oklahoma 73716
Mailing address:
P.O. Box 28
Aline, Oklahoma 73716
580-463-2441
http://www.ohwy.com/ok/s/sodhoumu.htm

Anadarko

Southern Plains Indian Museum
Highway 62, East
Anadarko, Oklahoma 73005
405-247-6221
http://www.ohwy.com/ok/p/plaindmu.htm

Blackwell

Top of Oklahoma Historical Museum
303 South Main Street
Blackwell, Oklahoma 74631
580-363-0209
http://www.members.aol.com/tommuseum/

Chandler

Lincoln County Historical Society
   Museum of Pioneer History
717 Manvel Avenue
Chandler, Oklahoma 74834
405-258-2809
http://www.ohwy.com/ok/y/ylincomu.htm

Clinton

Oklahoma Route 66 Museum
2229 West Gary Boulevard
Clinton, Oklahoma 73601
580-323-7866
http://www.route66.org

Durant

Fort Washita
15 miles east of Madill
Durant, Oklahoma 74701
580-924-6502

*http://www.texoma-ok.com/troopoer/
   1842.htm*

Elk City

National Route 66 Museum and Old
   Town Complex
2717 West Highway 66
Elk City, Oklahoma 73644
Mailing address:
P.O. Box 5
Elk City, Oklahoma 73648
405-225-6266
*http://www.elkcitychamber.com/route66.
   asp*

Fort Gibson

Fort Gibson Historic Site
907 North Garrison Avenue
Fort Gibson, Oklahoma 74434
Mailing address:
P.O. Box 457
Fort Gibson, Oklahoma 74434
918-478-4088
*http://www.geocities.com/
   fortgibsonhistoricsite*

Gate

Gateway to the Panhandle
Main Street
Gate, Oklahoma 73844
Mailing address:
P.O. Box 27
Gate, Oklahoma 73744
405-934-2004
*http://www.ohwy.com/ok/g/gatpanmu.
   htm*

Guthrie

Oklahoma Territorial Museum
402 East Oklahoma Avenue
Guthrie, Oklahoma 73044
405-282-1889
http://www.guthriemuseumcomplex.tripod.
   com/guthriemuseums/id2.html

Kingfisher

Chisholm Trail Museum
605 Zellers Avenue
Kingfisher, Oklahoma 73750
405-375-5176
http://www.ok-history.mus.ok.us

Oklahoma City

Oklahoma Heritage Center
201 N.W. 14th Street
Oklahoma City, Oklahoma 73103
405-235-4458
http://www.oklahomaheritage.com

Pawnee

Pawnee Bill Ranch
1141 Pawnee Bill Road
Pawnee, Oklahoma 74058
Mailing address:
P.O. Box 493
Pawnee, Oklahoma 74058
918-762-2513
http://www.ohwy.com/ok/p/pawbilmu.htm

Tahlequah

Cherokee National Museum

TSA-LA-GI-Cherokee Heritage Center
Willis Road
Tahlequah, Oklahoma 74465
Mailing address:
P.O. Box 515
Tahlequah, Oklahoma 74465
918-456-6007
http://www.cherokeeheritage.org

Tulsa

Gilcrease Museum
1400 Gilcrease Museum Road
Tulsa, Oklahoma 74127
918-596-2700
http://www.gilcrease.org

Texas

Alice

South Texas Museum
66 South Wright Street
Alice, Texas 78332
Mailing address:
P.O. Box 3232
Alice, Texas 78333
512-668-8891
http://www.ohwy.com/tx/s/soutexmu.htm

Austin

Jourdan-Bachman Pioneer Farm
11418 Sprinkle Cut Off Road
Austin, Texas 78754
512-837-1215
http://www.pioneerfarm.org

Texas Governor's Mansion
1010 Colorado

Austin, Texas 78701
512-463-5518
http://www.txfgm.org

Bandera

Frontier Times Museum
510 13th Street
Bandera, Texas 78003
Mailing address:
P.O. Box 1918
Bandera, Texas 78003
830-796-3864
*http://www.texasguides.com/frontiertimes.
html*

Big Spring

Heritage Museum and Potton House
510 Scurry
Big Spring, Texas 79720
915-267-8255
*http://www.museumsusa.org/data/
museums/TX/185333.htm*

Canyon

Panhandle-Plains Historical Museum
2410 Fourth Avenue
Canyon, Texas 79015
Mailing address:
WTAMU
Box 60967
Canyon, Texas 79016
806-651-2244
http://www.wtamu.edu/museum

Colorado City

Heart of West Texas Museum

340 East 3rd Street
Colorado City, Texas 79512
915-728-8285
http://www.ohwy.com/tx/h/hewetxmu.htm

Corsicana

Navarro County Historical Society,
   Pioneer Village
912 West Park Avenue
Corsicana, Texas 75110
903-654-4846
*http://www.museumsusa.org/data/
museums/TX/186740.htm*

Dallas

Old City Park: The Historical Village of
   Dallas
Dallas County Heritage Society
1717 Gano
Dallas, Texas 75215
214-421-5162
http://www.oldcitypark.org

Fort Bliss

Fort Bliss Museum
Pleasanton and Sheridan Roads
Fort Bliss, Texas 79916
Mailing address:
ATSA-MM
Fort Bliss, Texas 79916
915-568-6940
http://www.ohwy.com/tx/f/forblimu.htm

Fort Sam Houston

Fort Sam Houston Museum
1210 Stanley Road

Fort Sam Houston, Texas 78234
210-221-1886
*http://www.cs.amedd.army.mil/dptmsec/
    mnsc.htm*

Fort Worth

Log Cabin Village
2100 Log Cabin Village Lane
Fort Worth, Texas 76109
817-926-5881
http://www.logcabinvillage.org

Galveston

Texas Seaport Museum
Pier 21, Number 8
Galveston, Texas 77550
Mailing address:
502 20th Street
Galveston, Texas 77550
409-763-1877
http://www.tsm-elissa.org

Henderson

The Depot Museum Complex
514 North High Street
Henderson, Texas 75652
903-657-4303
http://www.depotmuseum.com

Houston

The Heritage Society
1100 Bagby
Houston, Texas 77002
713-655-1912
http://www.heritagesociety.org

McKinney

Collin County Farm Museum
7117 County Road 166
McKinney, Texas 75070
972-548-4793

Panhandle

Carson County Square House Museum
Texas Highway 207 at Fifth Street
Panhandle, Texas 79068
Mailing address:
P.O. Box 276
Panhandle, Texas 79068
806-537-3524
http://www.squarehousemusuem.org

Pecos

West of the Pecos Museum
First at Cedar (U.S. 285)
Pecos, Texas 79722
Mailing address:
Box 1784
Pecos, Texas 79772
915-445-5076
http://www.westofthepecosmuseum.com/

San Antonio

The Alamo
300 Alamo Plaza
San Antonio, Texas 78205
Mailing address:
P.O. Box 2599
San Antonio 78299
210-225-1391
http://www.thealamo.org

Witte Museum
3801 Broadway

San Antonio, Texas 78209
210-357-1881
http://www.wittemuseum.org

Tyler

Goodman Museum
624 North Broadway
Tyler, Texas 75702
Mailing address:
P.O. Box 2039
Tyler, Texas 75710
903-531-1286
*www.cityoftyler.org/41a4aa1fe7884239
   bade2d776d6ee47b/default.html*

Wimberley

Pioneer Town
333 Wayside Drive
Wimberley, Texas 78676
512-847-3289
http://www.ohwy.com/tx/p/piontown.htm

Journals in Folklore of the Region: A Selected List

The journals in the list below publish articles on folklore of the region. Some are scholarly; others are more popular. Many other journals and newsletters exist. Often, these are smaller, of more local interest, and published by museums, historical societies, folklore organizations, community groups, and schools. Explore your own area to see what other publications of folklore exist.

*AFF word. (Arizona Friends of Folklore)
The Arizona Quarterly; A Journal of
   Literature, History, Folklore*

*The New Mexico Folklore Record
Perspectives in Mexican American Studies
Publications of the Texas Folk-lore Society
Southwest Folklore*

Web Sites: A Selected List

Below is a list of a few Web sites dealing with folklore of the region. You can find other Web sites by doing an Internet search on a search engine such as Google or Yahoo!, or by looking for the Web sites of various folklore organizations with which you are familiar.

*Images of the Southwest, http://dizzy.library.
   arizona.edu/images/folkarts/*
Images of the Southwestern United States. Churches, folk arts, and maps. Information on the War Relocation Authority camps, USS *Arizona*, and Hispanic and Chinese populations.

*Rio Grande Folklore Archive, http://www.
   panam.edu/dept/folklore/index.html*
Catalog of the Rio Grande Folklore Archive at the University of Texas–Pan American Library, concentrating on Mexican American folklore.

*Texas Folklife Resources, http://www.
   texasfolklife.org*
Information on arts and culture of Texas, such things as quilting, leather work, dance, and carving. Includes links to a calendar of events.

*Wyatt Earp Historical Homepage,
   http://oldwesthistory.net/page43.html/*
Information on Wyatt Earp and the famous gunfight in Tombstone, Arizona. Includes a bibliography and links to other resources on Earp.

The West

California, Colorado, Nevada, Utah, Wyoming

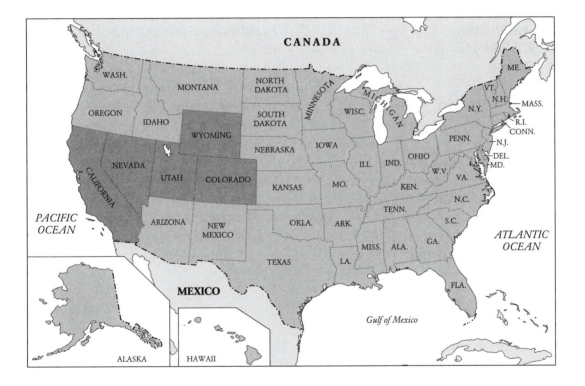

Look for tales on:

The Pony Express
The Mormon migration
Lost treasures

And for characters such as:

Bigfoot
Belle Starr
Doc Holliday
Wild Bill Hickok
Outlaws
Pioneers
The Forty-niners
Prospectors

Look for collections and works by:

Benjamin Botkin
Austin Fife

Find music collections by:

Austin Fife
John Lomax

Alan Lomax
N. Howard Thorpe

Introduce children to:

The jackalope
Cowboys
Bill Pickett
Mountain men

Explore the rich literature of the region with:

Owen Wister
Louis L'Amour
Zane Grey
Max Brand

Consult journals:

Western Folklore
UCLA Folklore Annals

THE WEST: INTRODUCTION

History

The West, for the purposes of this volume, is the central West, a vast stretch of land extending from the western part of the Great Plains, across the Rockies and the Great Basin, and on to the Pacific Ocean. The central West is closely related historically and culturally to surrounding regions: the Great Plains, the Northwest, and the Southwest.

The West is culturally diverse, but it is also brought together by a rugged environment: vast, arid (except for the far west coast), mountainous, spectacular. It is also linked by great historical themes: the conquest, subjugation, and revival of Native American cultures; settlement by peoples with roots in Mexico, Europe, Asia, and the eastern United States; occupations and lifestyles based on use (or abuse) of the land, including ranching, farming, logging, and the fossil fuels industries; and, increasingly, the concentration of Westerners into cities. The West has also been the source of one of the major popular myths held by Americans: the myth of the cowboy and the Western frontier.

The Native American cultures of the West were, and are, extremely diverse. They include the classic horse cultures of the Great Plains, such as the Arapaho, who originally followed the buffalo over the Northern Plains in alliance with the Cheyenne and Lakota, but were confined to reservations in Wyoming and Oklahoma; mountain cultures such as the Utes, confined to two reservations in southwestern Colorado, and the Sho-shone, now spread over a number of reservations throughout the Great Basin and intermountain West; Great Basin tribes such as the Paiutes, and a huge variety of California tribes, including the Yoruk, Mohave, and Karok. Some of the Western tribes, especially in California, were completely annihilated; most underwent cultural revivals in the twentieth century and continue to have rich but evolving traditions of religious ceremonies, storytelling, crafts, music, dance, foodways, and other types of folklife.

The European presence began with the Spanish forts and missions of California in the 1760s, leading to a hacienda (ranch) system based on the labor of Native American peons. (Spanish settlement in New Mexico was even earlier, beginning around 1600.) The Spanish/Mexican hacienda system later became the basis for ranch and cowboy culture throughout the West. In the San Luis Valley of southern Colorado, Spanish-speaking settlers came up from New Mexico in the eighteenth century, to establish a community that still thrives. Although the Treaty of Guadalupe Hidalgo drove Mexico out of what is now the western United States in 1848, the Hispanic presence has continued to be important.

Explorers, fur trappers, and mountain men from France and the eastern United States were active in the area throughout the early and mid-nineteenth century. Military forts and settlers soon followed, and by the 1840s trails, including the Oregon Trail, were being established through what had been Indian country. Western settlement was propelled by a number of factors, perhaps most dramatically by gold rushes, including those in California beginning in 1848 and Colorado in the 1860s. Also important was the Homestead Act of 1862, which promised 160 acres to anyone who settled on and developed unclaimed Western land, and the coming of the railroads during the 1860s–1880s.

Of particular note was the great western movement of members of the Church of Jesus Christ of Latter Day Saints (Mormons) in the 1840s–1850s, to escape persecution in the Midwest, and to found the state of Deseret. Utah is still the thriving heartland of Mormon culture, the goal of Mormon pilgrims and immigrants from all over the world, rich with distinctive traditions of legendry, song, dance, craft, and foodways.

The frontier is traditionally considered to have closed in 1890, the year of the massacre at Wounded Knee, South Dakota, and the confinement of all Native American tribes to Indian reservations. By this time the Homestead Act had already failed to a considerable extent, because the aridity of the West made 160-acre homesteads inadequate; instead, very large ranches, such as that of the Kendricks in Wyoming's Powder River Basin, had become the norm. With the growth of large ranches came the culture of cowboys; the classic cowboy culture celebrated in Western films was a phenomenon of the late nineteenth century, although today cowboys continue to work as hired hands on ranches. Cowboy culture is still quite active with traditions of saddle making, rawhide braiding, and many other crafts, as well as storytelling, songs, poetry, barn dances, and rodeo. Sheepherding has also been important in the West, attracting substantial numbers of Basque immigrants to parts of Wyoming, Utah, Nevada, and California.

By the late nineteenth century and into the twentieth, new themes enter the history and culture of the West, including the growth of public lands: The National Park Service, Forest Service, Bureau of Land Management and other federal land agencies (including the military) now account for well over half of all land in the West, as high as 86 percent in Nevada. Another theme is the rise and continual boom and bust of the resource extraction industries made possible by the public lands: not only ranching but logging, coal, silver, gold, copper, oil, natural gas, and uranium. All of these industries attracted migrants to the region and developed distinct occupational cultures.

The aridity of the West has made the struggle for water a constant theme. The twentieth century was marked by the growth of vast federal water projects: huge dams, vast reservoirs, hydroelectric power lines, canals, and pipelines. This made possible the rise of irrigated farming on immense corporate farms in places like California's San Joaquin Valley, which in turn attracted large numbers of Asian and Latino laborers. The need for labor in the West made California in particular one of the country's most ethnically diverse states; Angel Island in San Francisco Bay became the Ellis Island of the West, the entry point for large numbers of immigrants, primarily from Asia, from 1910 to 1940.

Western water projects also made possible the rapid growth of cities: Los Angeles, San Diego, Las Vegas, Salt Lake City, and Denver. By the late twentieth century, the West was the most urban region of the country: A substantial majority of Westerners now live in cities or suburbs. Western cities are as culturally and economically diverse as any in the United States. Much of the rural West remains sparsely inhabited, including large areas of Wyoming, Nevada, and Colorado's western slope.

The other great theme of the twentieth century West was recreation. With vast public lands and ever improving transportation (railroads, highways, air flight), the West became America's playground for sight-seeing, camping, hunting, fishing, hiking, dude ranching, and, in Nevada, gambling. By the mid-twentieth century, most Westerners lived in the city and went to the countryside to camp and fish; at the same time, large numbers of tourists from all over the country and world filled to overflowing such sites as Yellowstone, Yosemite, and Arches National Parks. The Western myth became a tourist draw, as Jackson, Wyoming, Virginia City, Nevada, and many other towns began to redesign themselves as Hollywood stage sets, complete with gunfights, gartered barmaids, and wooden false front saloons. Tourist sites drew not only from Hollywood but also from the mythic heroes of the West: fur trappers, mountain men, prospectors, cavalrymen, cowboys, outlaws, lumberjacks, stereotyped Indians.

Folklore

The folklore of the West is, of course, an outgrowth of its cultural history, and reflects the same great themes: immigration, occupation, urbanization, recreation, and both the conflict and coming together of cultures.

Pioneers and settlers told stories and sang songs reflecting their origins in Europe or the eastern United States and their experiences of westward migration. Many European cultural forms can be found in the West, brought in by immigrants: Norwegian log construction in the mountains of Colorado, Swedish fiddle tunes at barn dances in Wyoming, Basque accordion music and Italian stone masonry in Nevada. Distinct regional traditions developed: tall tales (and tongue-in-cheek creatures such as jackalopes) on the Great Plains, Mormon immigration songs, cowboy ballads and poetry. The craft of Western saddle making, for example, came north from Mexico but developed very different traditions of form and decoration in Wyoming (Northern Plains saddles), Nevada (Buckaroo saddles), and California. In Mormon areas, conservative gender roles have been a factor in the continued vitality of women's domestic crafts, such as quilting and lace making.

Outdoor occupations in the West also developed very distinct cultures, including not only ranchers but loggers, miners, oil workers, and public lands managers (rangers, game wardens). Each occupation had, and in most cases still has, its own set of occupational skills and jargon, jokes, even songs and craft traditions: for instance, legends of lost gold mines told by prospectors, chainsaw sculptures made by loggers, stories about numskull tourists told by park rangers. The recreation industries have also produced their share of folklore: A noteworthy example is the culture of gambling in Nevada, which includes the occupational folklore of croupiers and prostitutes (among others) and craft traditions such as the making of neon signs. Any consideration of occupational cultures would not be complete without a consideration of unions: union songs spread by the Industrial Workers of the World and others are still sung at rallies, and important events such as the massacre of strikers at Ludlow, Colorado, in 1917 are still commemorated. More recently, the formation of labor unions among immigrant farmworkers in California has produced *corridos* (ballads) and skits based closely on Mexican folk theater, for performance at union meetings, demonstrations, and strikes.

Mexican American traditions of all kinds continue to thrive throughout the West: Mariachi, Norteño, and Chicano Rock bands; Folklorico dancing; holiday and ceremonial traditions such as Day of the Dead celebrations, Las Posadas processions at Christmas, and Quinceañera ceremonies (coming-out celebrations when girls turn fifteen); craft traditions such as rawhide braiding, piñata making, neighborhood murals, and many others; foodways such as posole and tamales; and rich traditions of humor and storytelling, including the ubiquitous legend of La Llorona (the Weeping Woman, who haunts waterways lamenting her murdered children).

Ethnic diversity, always a major theme in Western history, has only increased with the passage of time. Many African Americans migrated to the West in search of new opportunities after the Civil War; in the twentieth century, Western cities saw rapid increases in African American populations as a result of the Great Migration out of the South. This gave rise to such traditions as Juneteenth (Emancipation Day) celebrations in many parts of the West and a distinct West coast style of blues music in California. Such events as the Chinese Exclusion Act of 1882 and

the internment of Japanese Americans during World War II have not, in the long run, been serious deterrents to the arrival of immigrants. Almost all Western cities and many smaller towns now have celebrations for Chinese or Southeast Asian New Years Days. Hmong embroidery and Indian Mehendi body decorations are now common features of many neighborhood festivals, next to the Bosnian and Filipino food booths and just down the street from the stage featuring cowboy poetry, Jewish klezmer bands, Armenian oud music, and polka dancing.

Native American folklife also continues to thrive, including very active traditions of storytelling. Stories vary, of course, from tribe to tribe, but there are common factors such as the ubiquitous trickster coyote, and the almost universal Star Husband Tale, about a young woman who falls in love with a star and climbs into the sky to marry him. Native families also pass down stories of massacres, forced migrations, and the struggle to keep traditions alive in spite of the outlawing of most aspects of tribal language and culture in the early days of Indian reservations. There is also a huge variety of active Native crafts, including basket making in the Great Basin; paintings on rawhide on the Great Plains; beadwork, feather work, woodcarving, quilting and the making of dance regalia throughout the West. Of particular note is the growth of powwows in the second half of the twentieth century, with their complex interplay of music and dance, art and ceremony, sacred and secular, local and national, competition and cooperation. Grass dancing, fancy dancing, and other intertribal dances represent the emergence of a broad Native American ethnic identity that complements, but does not supplant, local and tribal identities.

Many modern Western folk traditions are no different from those in other parts of America. Global markets and modern technology have brought in high-tech industries; urban legends are spread on the Internet; inner city youth rap, break dance, and spray paint elaborate tags on trains and walls; families pass on stories about the immigration of ancestors from El Salvador, Ethiopia, or Vietnam. It is likely that the distinct natural environment of the West will continue to be a unifying thread in a unique Western culture; the only safe prediction, however, is that Western folk traditions will continue to evolve.

Timothy H. Evans

THE WEST: BIBLIOGRAPHY AND OTHER RESOURCES

Bibliography

History and Study

709. Cheney, Thomas E. *Lore of Faith and Folly.* Salt Lake City: Univ. of Utah Press, 1971. ix, 274p. Notes. 78-161486. 0-87480-067-6.

Many folklorists are represented in this book of essays. Among them are Austin Fife and Alta Fife, authors or editors of *Ballads of the Great West* (Palo Alto, CA: American West Publishing, 1970), *Heaven on Horseback: Revivalist Songs and Verse in the Cowboy Idiom* (Logan: Utah State University Press, 1970), and *Saints of Sage and Saddle: Folklore among the Mormons* (reprint Salt Lake City: Univ. of Utah Press, 1980) and Wayland D. Hand, author of the authoritative *Popular Beliefs and Superstitions from Utah* (Salt Lake City: Univ. of Utah Press, 1984).

Essays focus on a variety of topics: local history and memoirs, family history, polygamy, cultural heroes, superstitions, and supernatural happenings. Naturally, since the history of the Mormons is so inextricably interwoven into the history of Utah, some of these essays deal with Mormon traditions.

710. Cunningham, Keith, ed. *The Oral Tradition of the American West: Adventure, Courtship, Family, and Place in Traditional Recitation.* Little Rock, AR: August House, 1990. 264p. Notes. Index of Authors and Performers. Index of Titles and First Lines. 90-43180. 0-87483-150-4; 0-87483-124-5pa.

A belief that traditional folklorists have neglected the area of folklore recitations led Cunningham to the compilation of this work. In it he brings together recitations from a variety of people from Arizona, New Mexico, Texas, and Utah. Some of the recitations the performer wrote; others the performer found in a book and memorized; still others the performer learned from another person. Recitations concentrate on common themes—love, courtship, home, children, and adventure.

711. Eberhart, George M. "Humanoids in North America." In *Monsters, a Guide to Information on Unaccounted for Creatures, Including Bigfoot, Many Water Monsters, and Other Irregular Animals*, pp. 151–195. New York: Garland, 1983. xiv, 344p. Author Index. Periodical Index. (Garland

Reference Library of Social Science, vol. 131). 82-49029. 0-8240-9213-9.

One chapter of this bibliography concerns humanoids in North America, specifically Bigfoot, or Sasquatch. Eberhart lists hundreds of books and magazine articles about this supposed denizen of the forest.

712. Etulain, Richard W. *Myths and the American West*. Manhattan, KS: Sunflower Univ. Press, 1998. 112p. Illus. Chapter notes. Index. 98-209196. 0-89745-224-0pa.

Etulain's thesis is that the "unknown" quality of the American West, from the beginnings of its exploration, contributed to a mythological quality. Ever since Europeans first started pushing into it, the West was invested with a larger-than-life quality, full of both promise and threat. Here he explores that mythological quality both through some of the mythical figures that came out of it and through the authors who documented it. Historical figures explored include Davy Crockett, Calamity Jane, Wild Bill Hickok, and Doc Holliday, as well as collective characters such as the wife and mother as civilizing influence, and Native Americans. Authors include Owen Wister and Laura Ingalls Wilder.

In addition, Etulain explores the effect of the landscape itself on our attitudes toward the West.

713. Ramsey, Jarold. *Reading the Fire: The Traditional Indian Literatures of America*. Rev. and expanded. Lincoln: Univ. of Nebraska Press, 1983; repr., Seattle: Univ. of Washington Press, 1999. xxvii, 332p. Index. Bibliog. Notes. 99-13656. 0-295-97787-6pa.

First published under the title *Reading the Fire: Essays in the Traditional Indian Literatures of the Far West*, this is an expanded and updated version. Ramsey discusses the creation and origin stories of several western Native American groups as well as the trickster character that appears in so many stories. He then explores how these stories have been changed and adapted through the Native American interaction with Anglo culture and how modern Native American writers use and explore the same themes.

714. Rosenberg, Bruce A. *The Code of the West*. Bloomington: Indiana Univ. Press, 1982. 213p. Illus. Notes. 82-47014. 0-253-31387-2.

Rosenberg examines several common themes of Western history, showing how each has become part of folklore, of our entrenched attitudes toward the West, and so, part of our national identity. His examples are mountain men, prospectors, the journey west, the Mormon journey with handcarts, Custer's last stand, the Pony Express, a riverboat race, the building of the railroad, outlaws, Indians, and wild horses.

715. Shirley, Glenn. *Belle Starr and Her Times: The Literature, the Facts, and the Legends*. Norman: Univ. of Oklahoma Press, 1982. xi, 324p. Illus. Notes. Bibliog. Index. 81-14683.

Belle Starr is a western legend, much like Billy the Kid or Doc Holliday. Like them, much of what is believed about her is false. In this book, Shirley attempts to construct the true Belle Starr from among the legends.

716. Steckmesser, Kent Ladd. *Western Outlaws: The "Good Badmen" in Fact, Film, and Folklore*. Claremont, CA: Regina Books, 1983. 161p. Bibliog. 83-2854. 0-941690-07-5; 0-941690-08-3pa.

The Robin Hood legend begins this book—hardly a Western American tale. But Steckmesser goes on to profile American outlaws and to compare their legends with the one about Robin Hood.

Treasuries

717. Botkin, Benjamin A. *A Treasury of Western Folklore.* Revised. New York: Crown, 1975. xxii, 613p. Index. 74-28471. 0-517-51684-5.

Many of the tales and anecdotes told here are of occupations: cowboys, ranchers, farmers, miners, and loggers. Others are of the tall tale variety or the folk hero. Botkin also includes folk songs in this addition to his compilations of regional folklore.

718. Erdoes, Richard, ed. *Legends and Tales of the American West: Tales from the American Frontier.* 1991; repr., New York: Pantheon Books, 1998. xix, 443p. Illus. Notes. Bibliog. (Pantheon Fairy Tale and Folklore Library). 90-53436; 98-15793. 0-394-51682-6; 0-375-70266-0pa.

First published in 1991 as *Tales from the American Frontier,* it reappears here as a paperback titled *Legends and Tales of the American West. The West* is a somewhat loose term in the title, moving with the moving frontier. The first chapter contains tales from Ohio—the west of the eighteenth century. Later chapters have tales of Davy Crockett and Daniel Boone in the west of their time. And still later chapters cover tales from the far west, from Colorado, New Mexico, and Utah. Tales concern cowboys, miners, Indians, ghosts, preachers, and gunslingers, all the characters that make up the Western mythology. Some of the characters, like Daniel Boone, are real historical personages, with the mythlike qualities that they acquired over time.

Many of the tales are written in language that would make for good reading aloud.

719. Fife, Austin E. *Exploring Western Americana.* Ann Arbor: UMI Research Press, 1988. xviii, 279p. Edited by Alta Fife. Index. Bibliog. Chapter Notes. (American Material Culture and Folklife). 87-30225. 0-8357-1857-3.

Fife concentrates on the folklife of Mormons in the American West. This is not a general survey but a series of in-depth articles on specific topics. Topics include tales of spectral wanderers, folk medicine, architecture, artifacts such as fences and hay derricks, and folk songs.

Tales and Legends

720. Alexander, Kent. *Legends of the Old West: Trailblazers, Desperadoes, Wranglers, and Yarn-Spinners.* New York: Friedman/Fairfax, 1994. 120p. Illus. Index. 94-8758. 1-56799-109-2.

Lavishly illustrated with contemporary photographs and drawings, this book tells the stories of a variety of Western characters, designated in the title. Alexander contends in his introduction that he attempts to look at both the good and the bad sides of his characters. He contends further that he tries to emphasize the heroic qualities they possessed, those qualities that contributed to their becoming legends.

People described include explorers, soldiers, cowboys, outlaws, entertainers, writers, artists, and social commentators.

721. Altrocchi, Julia Cooley. *The Old California Trail.* Caldwell, ID: Caxton Printers, 1945. 327p. Illus. Index. Bibliog.

Cooley traveled the California Trail, from Springfield, Illinois, to San Francisco, talking to those who traveled it as pioneers and to those who knew them, as she writes, "ninety years after the forty-niners" (p. 23). Much of what she writes is factual, but some is fanciful, the legends and stories that grew up around the trail.

Bandits, battles, and lost treasures are in these pages, "ancient memories of old-timers who themselves had actually come to their settlements in covered wagons, and the enlarged fables of the younger generation." (p. 22)

722. Black, Jack. *Western Treasures Notebook of Lost Mines and Buried Treasure.* Tarzana, CA: Ames, 1966. 96p. pa.

Black has collected stories of lost treasure from Arizona, California, Colorado, Idaho, Nevada, New Mexico, Oregon, Utah, Washington, Wyoming, and Mexico. The stories are brief, only a paragraph or two, and give the bare outline of the lost treasure.

Many of the stories were first printed in *Western Treasures* magazine.

723. Burnett, Claudine. *Strange Sea Tales along the California Coast.* Long Beach, CA: Historical Society of Long Beach, 2000. i, 194p. Illus. Bibliog. Index. 0-9610250-9-3.

Legends of sea serpents abound in this book. Some proved to be whales, sea otters, seals, sharks, or oarfish, but others were never explained. Other tales are of treasure ships, shipwrecks, and pirates.

724. Davidson, Levette J., and Forrester Blake, eds. *Rocky Mountain Tales.* Norman: Univ. of Oklahoma Press, 1947. xiv, 302p. Illus. by Skelly. Index.

Most of the tales are brief vignettes. They tell of the early days of Colorado. There are stories of mining claims, much information about the early towns, stories of ranching, and some tall tales. All

of them capture the flavor of an earlier day.

725. Eberhart, Perry. *Treasure Tales of the Rockies.* 3d. rev. ed. Chicago: Swallow Press, 1969. 315p. Bibliog. Index. 61-14373. 0-8040-0295-9.

More than one hundred legends appear here, of lost mines in Colorado and of the people who found them, lost them, and often spent the rest of their lives attempting to rediscover them. Sixteen legends were added to this third revised edition.

726. Fife, Austin, and Alta Fife. *Saints of Sage and Saddle: Folklore among the Mormons.* Bloomington: Indiana Univ. Press, 1956; repr., Salt Lake City: Univ. of Utah Press, 1980. xvii, 367p. Index. Notes. 56-1197. 0-87480-180-x.

The Fifes in their preface state that this book is a mixture of folklore and history. Some of the stories in it are considered history, but have been changed over the years to fit whatever time they are told in. They have acquired the status of legends within the Mormon Church.

The book is a look at the cultural history of a particular geographic area, changed and adapted over the years.

727. Gifford, Edward Winslow, and Gwendoline Harris Block. *Californian Indian Nights: Stories of the Creation of the World, of Man, of Fire, of the Sun, of Thunder, etc.; of Coyote, the Land of the Dead, the Sky Land, Monsters, Animal People, etc.* Glendale, CA: A. H. Clark, 1930; repr., Lincoln: Univ. of Nebraska Press, 1990. x, 323p. Illus. 90-33808. 0-8032-7031-3.

First collected in the early part of the century by Gifford and Block, these tales tell myriad stories of creation and formation. Many versions of the same tale are here, as different groups and tribes had their own tales, explaining the same phenomena.

Gifford and Block's original introduction is here, which explains much about the condition of Native Americans at the time, as is a newer introduction that updates some of that information.

728. Greenway, John. *Folklore of the Great West*. Palo Alto, CA: American West, 1970. 449p. Illus. Index. 74-88202.

Folklore of the Great West is a collection of articles published during eighty-three years by the *Journal of American Folklore*. They cover a broad range of topics: essays on life in the "good old days"; Indian legends; stories from miners, farmers, and ranchers; songs; and stories of ghosts and witches.

They cover, too, a broad range of folklore scholarship, sometimes showing the bias of the author. But this is a good source for a wide look at Western folklore, with stories of Paul Bunyan mixed with cowboy songs and Native American creation myths. The stories in the section titled "The Good Old Days" tell of an America no longer seen.

729. Jameson, W. C. *Buried Treasures of California: Legends from California's Mountains, Deserts, Beaches, and Cities*. Little Rock, AR: August House, 1995. Bibliog. 94-42466. 0-87483-406-6.

The subtitle says it all: These are tales of lost treasures throughout California. All the stories are supported by some documentation.

Jameson provides very simple outline maps to pinpoint the various treasures.

730. Judson, Katharine Berry. *Myths and Legends of California and the Old Southwest*. Chicago: A. C. McClurg, 1912; repr., Lincoln: Univ. of Nebraska Press, 1994. 193p. Illus. 93-46686. 0-8032-7580-3pa.

Judson mined the work of earlier ethnologists to reconstruct these tales of Native Americans in California, New Mexico, and Arizona. Groups represented are Zuni, Achomawi, Shastika, Pima, Sia, Gallinomero, Pai Ute, Maidu, Miwok, Nishinam, Ashochimi, Tolowa, Karok, Yurok, Hopi, Walpi, Yokuts, Navajo, and Patwin. As with so many Native American tales, these are creation stories and tales of animals, particularly of Coyote, the trickster.

The introduction to this 1994 edition gives a brief biography of Judson and places her work in the tradition of ethnological, anthropological, and folklore research.

Illustrations are black-and-white photographs, mostly of the places written about.

731. La Pena, Frank, Craig D. Bates, and Steven P. Medley, comps. *Legends of the Yosemite Miwok*. 2d, rev. ed. Yosemite National Park, CA: Yosemite Assoc., 1993. xii, 89p. Illus. by Harry Fonseca. Bibliog. 93-2158. 0-939666-57-xpa.

The compilers of these legends made every effort to trace each tale to a Native American storyteller, handed down from one to another, thus ensuring its authenticity. Tales concern the natural world, the naming of creatures and places, and the legends that have grown up around places.

Illustrations are in full color.

732. Latta, Frank Forrest. *California Indian Folklore*. Shafter, CA: Latta, 1936. 209p. Illus.

Latta explains in a brief introduction that he heard all these stories from Native Americans, elderly residents of California, and that he added nothing to them. The stories are divided into categories:

Creation Stories
Fire Stealing Stories
Origin Stories, or stories of how
    various natural phenomena came
    to be
Mythical Stories
Stories of Yosemite, such as how
    El Capitan grew
Stories of the Heavens
Hero Stories
Creation of Man

Latta adds some explanation concerning how various Indian words and names are pronounced.

Illustrations are black-and-white photographs of places and people.

733. Lee, Hector. *Heroes, Villains, and Ghosts: Folklore of Old California.* Santa Barbara, CA: Capra Press, 1984. 189p. 0-88496-223-7pa.

The title describes this book well: The tales are of heroes, villains, and ghosts. Among the heroes are a stagecoach driver and an early settler; the villains include murderers; and the ghosts include La Llorona, a ghost ship, and a lady who walks by a lake. Interspersed are tales of monsters, Bigfoot, and a caravan of camels given to California by Jefferson Davis. They still haunt the California desert where they performed military duties.

734. Luthin, Herbert W., ed. *Surviving through the Days: Translations of Native California Stories and Songs, A California Indian Reader.* Berkeley: Univ. of California Press, 2002. xxi, 630p. Illus. Index. Bibliog. 2000-31630. 0-520-22269-5; 0-520-22270-9pa.

Tales are divided into those from northwestern, north-central, south-central, and southern California. Groups represented are Cupeno, Atsugewi, Yurok, Tolowa,

Karuk, Hupa, Chimariko, Northern Yana, Achumawi, Yahi, Wintu, Nomlaki, Maidu, Eastern Pomo, Southern Pomo, Cache Creek Pomo, Lake Miwok, Ventureno Chumash, Chawchila Yokuts, Yowlumni Yokuts, Tübatulahbal, Ineseno Chumash, Serrano, Luiseno, Mojave, and Quechan.

This is an excellent anthology for those who want to begin exploring the rich literature of Native Americans.

Tales were collected and translated by a variety of individuals.

735. Merriam, C. Hart. *The Dawn of the World: Myths and Tales of the Miwok Indians of California.* Cleveland, OH: Arthur H. Clark, 1910; repr., Lincoln: Univ. of Nebraska Press, 1993. 273p. Illus. Index. Bibliog. 92-42566. 0-8032-3164-4; 0-8032-8193-5pa.

First published in 1910, with the title *The Dawn of the World: Myths and Weird Tales Told by the Mewan Indians of California,* the tales are republished here. Merriam worked for some thirty years with the Miwok Indians in California, during the late nineteenth and early twentieth centuries. He recorded their daily way of life and also their stories. According to the introduction to this edition, he collected and recorded information about "many aspects of California cultures, language, settlement patterns, religion, boundaries and material culture (especially basketry). The most important data collected by Merriam included detailed descriptions of rituals and other aspects of the cultural behavior practiced at the time that he was visiting" (p. 3).

He also recorded various stories. Since he was by profession a naturalist, most of the stories he asked about and recorded concerned the natural world, how various birds, animals, and places were named, and why various places were used for the things they were. Also included are stories about healing, ghosts, and powerful beings. Merriam included listings of scientific names of animals, trees, and other plants. Illustrations are black-and-white drawings.

736. Niemann, Greg. *Baja Legends: The Historic Characters, Events, and Locations That Put Baja California on the Map.* San Diego: Sunbelt Publications, 2002. xi, 260p. Illus. Index. Bibliog. 2001-49564. 0-932653-47-2pa.

Most of the material here is historical and factual rather than legendary. However, some of the history has shaded into legend, particularly that pertaining to the early explorations of the area. There are stories here about the early missionaries, about pirates, and about mutineers.

Chapters on the later history of the area are more factual and documented.

737. O'Connor, Richard. *Western Treasure Tales.* Niwot: Univ. Press of Colorado, 1998. xiii, 130p. Illus. Index. 97-48731. 0-87081-489-3pa.

Read this book if you yearn to find long lost treasure. It tells the stories not only of those who lost treasures but also of some of the latter-day treasure seekers who succeeded in discovering them. The treasures described are in Arizona, California, Colorado, Nevada, New Mexico, Oregon, and Utah.

738. ——. *Wild Bill Hickok.* New York: Doubleday, 1959; repr., New York: Konecky and Konecky, 1996. 282p. Bibliog.

O'Connor attempts in this biography to debunk some of the myths that have grown up around Hickok, notably the one concerning the number of men he is purported to have killed. One chapter also discusses the intersection of Hickok's legend with that of other Western characters such as Calamity Jane.

739. Pierce, Richard A. *Lost Mines and Buried Treasures of California: Facts, Folklore and Fantasy Concerning 110 Sites of Hidden Wealth Succinctly and Accurately Described, with a Map for the Guidance of Treasure Seekers.* 4th, rev. ed. Berkeley, CA: R. A. Pierce, 1961. 56p. Illus. Index to Treasure Maps.

According to the author of this slim typescript, all the tales here either have a factual base, or have "acquired a certain substance by being believed, transmitted or acted upon" (p. 2). Pierce gives what facts exist about the various treasures and also gives directions to the sites.

The treasure map Pierce provided was missing from the copy examined.

740. Shipley, William, ed. *Maidu Indian Myths and Stories of Hánc'ibyjim.* Berkeley, CA: Heyday Books, 1991. x, 181p. 0-930588-52-5.

Creation stories, coyote tales, and tales of other animals make up this volume. They are the stories of the Maidu people, from northern California.

How this book came to be is as interesting a tale as the stories it tells. Shipley spent time in the early 1950s with the Maidu, and particularly with Maym Benner Gallagher, a woman fluent in both English and Maidu. She taught Shipley the Maidu language, and together they translated some of the stories in a 1912 publication of Maidu stories. Some years later, Shipley rediscovered the original book from which they had translated, was delighted to realize that his knowledge of Maidu was sufficient to continue the work, and so translated the rest of the tales.

741. Smith, Anne M., coll., assisted by Alden Hayes. *Ute Tales*. Salt Lake City: Univ. of Utah Press, 1992. xxviii, 175p. Illus. (Univ. of Utah Publications in the American West, vol. 29). 92-53607. 0-87480-404-3pa.

Anne Smith made several visits to the land of the Northern Utes in 1936 and 1937, collecting some 700 myths. She analyzed these and compared them with the tales from other groups in her 1939 doctoral dissertation. Here 102 of the tales are reprinted. The tales are from the Uinta, the Uncompahgre, and the White River.

Smith herself described the tales as being mostly about animal characters in a world before humans inhabited it. Many of the tales concern the trickster figure, usually in these tales, the coyote. Many of the tales, too, contain sexual references.

742. Smith, Anne M., ed. *Shoshone Tales*. Salt Lake City: Univ. of Utah Press, 1993. xxxv, 188p. Illus. (Univ. of Utah Publications in the American West, vol. 31). 93-2944. 0-87480-405-1.

Smith did graduate work at Yale in the mid-1930s. After receiving her doctorate, she returned to the field of her studies, in eastern Utah, to record stories and tales. She recorded tales from some twenty different narrators during that study. She didn't prepare the tales for publication until late in her life, during the 1970s and 1980s.

These tales include creation tales, trickster tales, tales of conquests and tests, and hero tales.

743. Stewart, George Emery, Jr. *Tales from Indian Country: Authentic Stories and Legends from the Great Uintah Basin*. Sandy, UT: M. Gardner, 1997. ix, 315p. Illus. 97-69111. 1-57636-044-x.

Many of the stories in this volume are accounts of the history of Utah, including first settlements and the opening of lands for homesteading. The first section, however, is composed of Ute Native American tales and legends.

744. Szasz, Ferenc Morton, ed. *Great Mysteries of the West*. Golden, CO: Fulcrum, 1993. xxi, 266p. Index. Bibliog. 93-2230. 1-55591-111-0.

All sorts of mysteries are retold here. Tales include those of mysterious creatures such as Sasquatch and sea serpents; archaeological finds that tell of ancient, lost peoples; presumed alien contact such as that in Roswell, New Mexico; and lost treasures.

745. Thornton, Bruce. *Searching for Joaquín: Myth, Murieta, and History in California*. San Francisco: Encounter Books, 2003. xii, 185p. Notes. Index. Bibliog. 2002-192718. 1-893554-56-2.

Joaquín Murieta was a bandit who was shot down by Texas Rangers in 1853. According to legend, his head was then severed from his body and preserved and displayed. Since then, myth and reality have intertwined, as they have with other historical characters who have become legends–Daniel Boone, Paul Revere, and Wild Bill Hickok, to name a few. His story has also become mingled with the myths of the American West: westward migration and the opportunities it provided, the freedom from the strictures of society, the admiration of lives lived outside the bounds of convention.

Thornton retells the story of Murieta, attempting to separate historical fact from legend, and goes on to explain the meaning his story has for the modern age.

746. *Thunder of the Mustangs: Legend and Lore of the Wild Horses*. San Francisco:

Sierra Club Books, 1997. 119p. Illus. 97-16759. 0-87156-974-4.

For the most part, these stories are of real horses and the people who love them. There are, however, two sections that are more legend—one about the Wind-Drinker, the spirit horse that can't be caught, and one about the Woman Who Married a Horse.

The photographs are in full color, full page, and are stunning.

747. Vestal, Stanley. *Mountain Men.* Boston: Houghton Mifflin, 1937. x, 296p. Illus. Notes. Bibliog.

Based on fact, these tales tell of men who have become legendary: the trappers and traders who preceded the soldier and the settler into the American West. Here are Jim Bridger, Thomas Fitzpatrick, Jedediah Smith, David E. Jackson, James P. Beckwourth, Etienne Provost, William Sublette, Robert Campbell, John Colter, Bill Williams, John Fremont, William Bent, Joseph L. Meek, and "Uncle" Dick Wootten.

748. Walker, Dale L. *Legends and Lies: Great Mysteries of the American West.* New York: Forge, 1997. 308p. Illus. Index. Bibliog. 97-20792. 0-312-86311-x.

In lengthy chapters—twenty pages or more—Walker presents various and conflicting accounts of how a number of legendary figures in Western history died. In most cases, one account has become the accepted and believed version; but Walker often has an alternative proven one to dispute the conventional wisdom. The deaths of Davy Crockett at the Alamo; Meriwether Lewis; Sacagawea; Jesse James; Billy the Kid; Black Bart; John Wilkes Booth; Ambrose Bierce; George Custer; and Crazy Horse are all described here.

749. Williams, Brad, and Choral Pepper. *Lost Legends of the West.* 1970; repr., New York: Promontory Press, 1996. xii, 192p. Illus. 70-80368. 0-88394-093-0.

First published in 1970, the reissue proves that legends are always popular and never completely lost. These legends concern lost mines, lost towns, lost treasures, and even lost monsters—both sea serpents and Bigfoot. All the legends are rooted in fact, although somewhat embellished over the years.

750. ——. *Lost Treasures of the West.* New York: Holt, Rinehart and Winston, 1975. 184p. 74-5127. 0-03-013186-3.

West, Southwest, and Northwest all yield treasures to this book, for the tales here are of treasures in California, Oregon, Washington, Nevada, Idaho, Utah, Arizona, Montana, Wyoming, Colorado, and New Mexico. Most of the tales concern monetary treasure—either a lost mine or a sunken ship—but some involve lost graves and even lost mission churches. The authors thoughtfully provide a map of the region, with the locations of the purported treasures marked, for those who wish to make their own attempts at finding the treasures.

751. Wilson, Herbert Earl. *The Lore and the Lure of the Yosemite: The Indians; Their Customs, Legends and Beliefs; Big Trees; Geology, and the Story of Yosemite.* San Francisco: Schwabacher-Frey Stationery, 1925. 135p. Illus.

Wilson begins by telling the creation story of the Yosemite. He continues with information on daily life: diet, dwellings, weapons, and clothing. His next section is on religious rites and ceremonies. Before his final chapter, Legends of the Yosemite, he adds much information about the topography and geology of the

Yosemite area, with descriptions of such natural wonders as Half Dome and Bridal Veil Falls.

In his brief introduction, Wilson says that he gained his information from the work of earlier ethnologists. Whether he has transcribed the tales accurately or not is not known.

Folk Music

752. Daughters of Utah Pioneers. *Pioneer Songs.* Salt Lake City, UT: Daughters of Utah Pioneers, 1932. iv, 324p.

The first song in this book is "Come, Come, Ye Saints," which was composed on the plains in 1847, during a trip westward. Other songs gathered here, all with music transcribed, include "Little Brown Jug," "The Campbells Are Coming," and "Polly Wolly Doodle." All are said to have been sung in the early days of the settlement of Utah.

753. Fife, Austin, and Alta Fife. *Ballads of the Great West.* Palo Alto, CA: American West, 1970. 271p. Glossary. Title and First Line Index. Subject Index. 70-119002. 0-910118-17-5.

In this book, the Fifes record the words of 113 ballads of the West. Songs are about the physical environment or landscape of the West, cowboys, and dramatic happenings or events, such as the cattle drive or a stampede. Characters, some real and some mythical, include Pecos Bill, General Custer, Billy the Kid, and such archetypes as the schoolmarm.

754. ——. *Heaven on Horseback: Revivalist Songs and Verse in the Cowboy Idiom.* Logan: Utah State Univ. Press, 1970. vi, 114p. Index of Titles and First Lines.

All the songs here are religious in na-ture, songs about religion in general, Christian songs, songs about death, prayers, and hymns. One section contains parodies of cowboy songs.

Most of the songs include the music.

755. Hubbard, Lester A. *Ballads and Songs from Utah.* Salt Lake City: Univ. of Utah Press, 1961. xxi, 475p. Illus. Index of Titles. Index of First Lines. Bibliog.

All the ballads and songs here have music transcribed. Hubbard divides the songs into the following chapters:

Versions of Ballads Collected by
    Francis J. Child
Love and Courtship
Youth and Childhood
Domestic Relationships
Crimes and Criminals
War
Songs of the West
Miscellaneous Songs
Nursery Songs
Utah and the Mormons

Two hundred fifty songs and ballads are recorded in this book, many with more than one version.

756. Lomax, John A. *Songs of the Cattle Trail and Cow Camp.* 1919; repr., New York: Duell, Sloan and Pearce, 1950. xiii, 189p. Illus.

Working with a grant from Harvard University, Lomax collected the cowboy songs that he collated into the book *Cowboy Songs and Other Frontier Ballads.* This later book contains songs he collected at that time, but which he did not include in the first volume, as well as songs sent to him later by cowboys, poets, songwriters, and collectors. Although he says in his introduction that he knows the collection is not complete, he hopes it is complete enough that readers "may sense, at least in some small measure, the service, the glamour, the romance of that knight-errant of the plains–the American cowboy" (p. xiii).

The title page notes that the book is illustrated "with 78 drawings and sketches by famous Western artists"; these include Frederic Remington and Charles Russell.

No music is included in this volume.

757. Thorp, N. Howard. *Songs of the Cowboys.* New York: Bramhall House, 1966. 346p. Variants, Commentary, Notes, and Lexicon by Austin E. Fife and Alta S. Fife. Bibliog. Lexicon. Index of Titles. Index of First Lines. Subject Index.

N. Howard "Jack" Thorpe first collected cowboy songs in the late nineteenth century, when he himself was riding the range; he published a collection of twenty-three songs in 1908. Later, in 1921, he published an expanded collection of 101 songs.

In this edition, the Fifes expand on Thorpe's collection and add a lexicon of cowboy words and terms, a commentary on Thorpe's life and work, and indexes. They also expand on the songs themselves, adding variants of a song, and in some cases, a melody line.

A facsimile of Thorpe's original 1908 edition is appended.

758. Vestal, Stanley. *Fandango: Ballads of the Old West.* Boston: Houghton Mifflin, 1927. 66p.

Twenty ballads fill the pages of this slim volume. Only the words are included; no music is transcribed. A few of the ballads concern characters of the Old West, such as Belle Starr and Kit Carson. Vestal arranges the book geographically, with headings for the Santa Fe Trail, California, the Plains, New Mexico, the Plains Indians, Oklahoma, and Colorado.

759. Wagner, Chris. *Where the Deer and the Jackalope Play: Music of Wyoming's History.* Columbus, OH: Chris Wagner, 1998. 52p.

Many of the classic songs of the West are included in this slim, spiral bound volume. "Clementine," "Sweet Betsy from Pike," Good-Bye Old Paint," and others are here. All songs have their music transcribed.

Folk Belief and Ritual

760. Alexander, Bill. *Everything You Always Wanted to Know about Jackalope: But Didn't Think You Oughtta Ask.* Evanston, WY: Alexander Ragtime, 1980. 49p.

The mythical jackalope is a cross between an antelope and a jackrabbit, with the speed of one and the appearance of the other. It is most commonly found in Wyoming. Alexander gives all the known information about the jackalope, in the form of questions and answers.

761. Hand, Wayland D., and Jeannine E. Talley, eds. *Popular Beliefs and Superstitions from Utah.* Salt Lake City: Univ. of Utah Press, 1984. xxxix, 491p. Collected by Anthon S. Cannon, with the help of Jan Harold Brunvand, Austin E. Fife, Alta S. Fife, Wayland D. Hand, Hector H. Lee, William A. Wilson, and others. Bibliog. Index. 84-5286. 0-87480-236-9.

The editor of this volume, Wayland Hand, also edited the scholarly *Popular Beliefs and Superstitions from North Carolina, 1961–64.* This present volume resembles the earlier one in format and content and resembles, too, *Folk-lore of Adams County, Illinois, 1935,* edited by Henry Middleton Hyatt. It contains brief bits of folklore on a wide variety of subjects—foods, wedding customs, death customs and beliefs, medicine, travel—divided into categories. An extensive index helps locate beliefs on a particular subject.

The earliest material in the collection comes from the 1930s, with the bulk of information having been collected in the 1950s and 1960s.

762. Jewell, Donald P. *Indians of the Feather River: Tales and Legends of the Concow Maidu of California.* Menlo Park, CA: Ballena Press, 1987. vi, 184p. Illus. Bibliog. 87-13561. 0-87919-111-2.

In the early 1960s, Jewell was working on an archaeological site in northern California. While there, he spent some time with elderly members of the Maidu tribe, people who remembered the stories their own grandparents told of the days before interaction with westward bound settlers.

Much of what Jewell learned had to do with cultural change and the differences that mingling with other groups made. He also learned about various beliefs and customs, fertility customs, and death customs, and a great deal about everyday life in those early days.

763. Roeder, Beatrice A. *Chicano Folk Medicine from Los Angeles, California.* Berkeley: Univ. of California Press, 1988. v, 377p. Index. Bibliog. (University of California Publications: Folklore and Mythology Studies, vol. 34). 88-23426. 0-520-09723-8pa.

Between October 1975 and April 1976, the Chicano Heritage Project, sponsored by the Center for the Study of Comparative Folklore and Mythology at the University of California, collected data on Chicano arts and oral history. This book is a presentation and discussion of the data collected on folk medicine. It in-

cludes a survey of the literature, a look at the way traditional medicine was being applied at the time of the survey, remedies that had come from Mexico and were in use in the Chicano sections of Los Angeles, the role of traditional healers, and whether the influence of traditional medicine decreases as families stay longer in the United States and are more separated from their original culture.

Material Culture

764. Bragg, William Frederick. *Wyoming: Rugged but Right.* Boulder, CO: Pruett Press, 1979. 196p. Foreword by Robert W. (Red) Fenwick. 79-3527. 0-87108-539-9; 0-87108-540-2pa.

Bragg divides his book into eight parts:

First Citizens
Pathfinders and Pioneers
The Army
Cowboys and Cattlemen
Both Sides of the Law
Colorful Characters
Wheels and Rails
Places

Within each section he presents brief vignettes about the people and places of Wyoming: the handcarts used by the Mormons to travel the Oregon Trail; the days when cattle were king and fences not allowed; stories of Wyatt Earp, Wild Bill Hickock, Tom Horn, and the Hole in the Wall Gang; glimpses of rodeos and stagecoach holdups. He gives the reader a look at old-time Wyoming.

765. Dary, David. *Cowboy Culture: A Saga of Five Centuries.* Lawrence: Univ. Press of Kansas, 1989. xii, 384p. Illus.

Notes. Bibliog. Index. 88-30449. 0-7006-0390-5pa.

Although Dary describes his book as a history of the cowboy in the Western hemisphere, encompassing its Spanish roots, some of his chapters verge on folklore. In addition to chapters titled Ranch House Culture and Bunkhouse Culture, Dary includes several chapters which describe life on a cattle trail. His book contains information, in his words, on "the cowboy's culture—his horse and saddle, his lariat whistling in the air, the red-hot branding iron, the smell of burning hair and flesh on a calf being branded, sleeping under a blanket of stars, the taste of dust on a long trail drive, the smell of hot coffee on a cold morning, a new pair of handmade boots, or the fine wines served to wealthy cattlemen in the Cheyenne Club" (p. xi). All these have contributed to our current perception of the cowboy.

766. Evans, Timothy H., and Patricia A. Kessler. *Wyoming Folk Arts Handbook.* Cheyenne: Wyoming State Museum, 1993. 71p. Appendices.

Even if you're not from Wyoming, you might find this book useful. The authors give much information about collecting folklore and putting on a folk festival. They begin with a discussion of types of folklore that people might search for, such as crafts, folk beliefs, or dance and music. They continue with information about how to collect, how to conduct an interview, how to use a tape recorder, and how to create videotapes. This is followed with hints about coordinating a local festival and a lengthy section on integrating folk education into schools. They finish up with some suggestions about how to obtain funding.

Appendices are copies of forms that might help gatherers of folklore: a Photo Log, an Informant Data Form, a Folk Arts Collection Form, and an Architectural Form.

767. Jordan, Terry G., Jon T. Kilpinen, and Charles F. Gritzner. *The Mountain West: Interpreting the Folk Landscape.* Baltimore: Johns Hopkins Univ. Press, 1997. xii, 160p. Illus. Notes. Bibliog. Index. 87-1270. 0-8018-5431-8.

The West of the title includes the west of Canada as well as of the United States. In their introduction, the authors state that they have largely avoided libraries and archives in their research for the book, preferring instead to examine the West in the field, allowing the West to speak for itself through its artifacts. Their contention is that by finding the similarities in building styles, they will discover—and let the reader discover—something of the flavor of the West and how it differs from other regions.

They examined and photographed such remnants of the old West as log cabins, fences, and outbuildings. Their descriptions and photographs of these artifacts is their attempt to share the "messages of the cultural landscape" (p. 9).

768. Margolin, Malcolm, and Yoland Montijo, eds. *Native Ways: California Indian Stories and Memories.* Berkeley, CA: Heyday Books, 1995. 127p. Illus. Index. Bibliog. 0-930588-73-8pa.

Margolin and Montijo tell the story of today's Native Americans in California by telling about some of the old ways that are still being followed. They explain and give examples of music and dance, arts such as basket making, and rituals and customs. They also write about native and traditional foods, modes of transportation, and dwelling places. Throughout the book, contemporary Native Americans are interviewed; their voices speak of how these traditions are still alive today and enrich and define their lives.

Black-and-white photographs of people, places, and artifacts are abundant.

769. Reedstrom, Ernest Lisle. *Ernest L. Reedstrom's Scrapbook of the American West.* Caldwell, ID: Caxton Printers, 1991. xx, 259p. Illus. Notes. Bibliog. Index. 90-43034. 0-87004-303-x.

Information on a variety of customs and activities of the Old West is contained in this volume: clothing, such as moccasins and snowshoes; tools, such as skinning knives; and weapons, such as the bow and arrow. You'll find information on the Stetson, on holsters, on the burro as an essential part of the miner's outfit, on the Concord stage, on structures, such as the soddie, and on pioneer recipes. A potpourri at the end even gives tips on poker playing.

This is an excellent source for quick information on a variety of topics related to the West.

770. Shippey, Lee. *It's an Old California Custom.* New York: Vanguard, 1948. 292p.

One of a series of books on customs of various states and cities, this one treats California's to a somewhat lighthearted look. Shippey connects present-day customs with the history of the state. Thus the California development of drive-ins for everything from food service to banking is linked to the early days when settlers had no houses—or at most possessed a one-room adobe structure that could not accommodate the entire family—and slept on the ground. He traces the interest in pageants and theater he saw in California in his own day to the days of Spanish influence and their love for festivals and celebrations and the later exuberance of the Gold Rush era.

This is a slight book, with little organization, but it does give a look at bygone days and customs of the times.

Folklore for Children

771. Curry, Jane Louise. *Back in the Beforetime: Tales of the California Indians.* New York: Macmillan, 1987; repr., New York: Aladdin Paperbacks, 2001. 134p. Illus. by James Watts. 86-21339. 0-689-50410-1; 0-689-84048-9pa.

Curry retells twenty-two tales from California Indian tribes. Some are tales of creation, others are tales of the trickster. Many of the tales have a moral or lesson.

Illustrations are black-and-white drawings.

772. Miller, Robert H. *Reflections of a Black Cowboy.* Englewood Cliffs, NJ: Silver Burdett Press, 1991. Illus. vol. 1: 0-382-24079-0. vol. 1: 0-382-24084-7pa. vol. 2: 0-382-24080-4. vol. 2: 0-382-24085-5pa. vol. 3: 0-382-24081-2. vol. 3: 0-382-24086-3pa. vol. 4: 0-382-24082-0. vol. 4 0-382-24087-1pa.

Miller's *Reflections of a Black Cowboy* consists of four separate, brief volumes: *Cowboys, The Buffalo Soldiers, Pioneers,* and *Mountain Men.* Each explores the contributions that African Americans had on the settling of the West. He includes information on such legendary figures as Dead Wood Dick, Cherokee Bill, and Bill Pickett.

773. *Stories of Our Ancestors: A Collection of Northern-Ute Indian Tales.* n.p.:

Uintah-Ouray Ute Tribe, 1974. x, 109p. Illus. by Clifford Duncan.

The tales in this book were first published in a variety of journal sources. Some were first collected by John Wesley Powell and were either unpublished or published in the *First Annual Report of the Bureau of American Ethnology;* others were first published in the *Journal of American Folklore.* They have been slightly revised for use in public schools.

Most of the tales involve animals, including the coyote. Many of them were told to model and encourage acceptable behavior; they were used as teaching tools.

774. Strang, Clara, Gerlad Strang, and John M. Weatherwax. *The Coming of the Animals: Bird and Animal Stories of the California Indians.* Los Angeles: Suttenhouse, 1934. 163p. Illus. by Marguerite Boyd.

Many of the stories told here speak of death, cruelty, and suffering. Stories concern many different animals and birds.

Illustrations are black-and-white line drawings.

775. Wukovits, John. *Legends of the West: Butch Cassidy; The Gun Slingers; Jesse James; Annie Oakley; The Black Cowboys; Wyatt Earp.* Philadelphia: Chelsea House Publishers, 1996; 1997. 64p. ea. Illus. Index. Chronology. *Oakley:* 97-009106; 0-7910-3906-4. *Earp:* 97-003941; 0-7910-3852-1. *Cassidy:* 97-013191; 0-7910-3857-2. *James:* 96-038468; 0-7910-3876-9. *Gunslingers:* 96-043112; 0-7910-3876-9. *Black Cowboys:* 97-002620; 0-7910-3907-2.

Each of these small books, written for children, focuses on a different character of the Old West. Not strictly folklore, they each tell enough stories about the character—or group—to indicate why these people became legends.

Each book is well illustrated, with contemporary photographs as well as a number of stills from modern-day films about the West.

Literary Authors: A Selected List

Below is a selected list of authors who reflect and interpret the history and atmosphere of their region. These are authors of novels, poems, short stories, or reminiscences. Through reading the works of these authors, one can acquire knowledge of the history, people, and flavor of the region. This is not a complete list, either of authors or of their works, but rather one calculated to start readers exploring and discovering their own favorites.

Brand, Max, 1892–1944

The Bells of San Carlos and Other Stories
The Legends of Thunder Moon
Max Brand's Best Western Stories
Valley Thieves

Clark, Walter Van Tilburg, 1909–1971

The Ox-Bow Incident
The Track of the Cat

Grey, Zane, 1872–1939

The Call of the Canyon
The Code of the West
The Dude Ranger
The Last of the Great Scouts
The Lost Wagon Train
Riders of the Purple Sage
To the Last Man
West of the Pecos

Harte, Bret, 1836–1902

> *The Best of Bret Harte*
> *The Best Short Stories of Bret Harte*
> *The Luck of Roaring Camp, and Other*
>   *Sketches*
> *Tales of Trail and Town*

L'Amour, Louis, 1908–1988

> *The Haunted Mesa*
> *The Lonesome Gods*
> *Valley of the Sun: Frontier Stories*
> *West of Dodge: Frontier Stories*

London, Jack, 1876–1916

> *Adventure*
> *The Call of the Wild*
> *Short Stories*
> *White Fang, and Other Stories*

McMurtry, Larry, 1936–

> *Boone's Lick*
> *Cadillac Jack*
> *Comanche Moon*
> *Desert Rose*
> *Lonesome Dove*
> *Streets of Laredo*

Morris, Wright, 1910–1998

> *Ceremony in Lone Tree*
> *The Territory Ahead*
> *Will's Boy: A Memoir*

Norris, Frank, 1870–1902

> *A Deal in Wheat: And Other Stories of*
>   *the New and Old West.*
> *McTeague: A Story of San Francisco*
> *The Octopus: A Story of San Francisco*

Shepard, Sam, 1943–

> *Geography of a Horse Dreamer*
> *Paris, Texas*
> *The Unseen Hand and Other Plays*

Stegner, Wallace, 1909–1993

> *Angle of Repose*
> *Conversations with Wallace Stegner on*
>   *Western History and Literature*
> *Crossing to Safety*
> *The Gathering of Zion: The Story of the*
>   *Mormon Trail*

Steinbeck, John, 1902–1968

> *Cannery Row*
> *Grapes of Wrath*
> *Of Mice and Men*
> *Travels with Charley*

Wister, Owen, 1860–1938

> *The Virginian: A Horseman of the Plains*
> *The West of Owen Wister: Selected Short*
>   *Stories*

Museums of the Region: A Selected List

Museums that feature everyday life abound in all regions of the country. Through the display of clothing, farm implements, household goods, industrial tools, or entire houses, workshops, and communities, these museums can help people of today understand and appreciate the lives lived by those who came before. The list below is not a complete list of museums in the region, but by browsing through it, one can get a glimpse of the richness of museum offerings. Explore on your own and discover even more fascinating museums.

California

Carpinteria

Carpinteria Valley Historical Society and
  Museum of History
956 Maple Avenue
Carpinteria, California 93013
805-684-3112
http://www.caohwy.com/h/histmuse.htm

Chino

Yorba-Slaughter Adobe Museum
17127 Pomona Rincon Road
Chino, California 91710
Mailing address:
C/o San Bernardino County Museums
2024 Orange Tree Lane
Redlands, California 92374
909-597-8332
http://www.co.san-bernardino.ca.us/museum

City of Industry

Workman and Temple Family
  Homestead Museum
15415 East Don Julian Road
City of Industry, California 91745
626-968-8492
http://www.homesteadmuseum.org

Fort Bragg

The Guest House Museum

343 North Main Street
Fort Bragg, California 95437
Mailing address:
P.O. Box 71
Fort Bragg, California 94537
707-964-0902
*http://www.museumsusa.org/data/
  museums/CA/11052.htm*

Fresno

Kearney Mansion Museum
7160 West Kearney Boulevard
Fresno, California 93706
559-441-0862
http://www.valleyhistory.org

Glendale

Casa Adobe de San Rafael
1330 Dorothy Drive
Glendale, California 91202
Mailing address:
Parks, Recreation and Community
  Services Division
613 East Broadway, Room 120
Glendale, California 91206
818-548-2000
*http://www.museumsusa.org/data/
  museums/CA/8235.htm*

Lancaster

Western Hotel/Museum
557 West Lancaster Boulevard
Lancaster, California 93534
661-723-6260
*http://www.coflancasterca.org/parks/
  museumgallery.htmwesternhotel.htm*

Los Angeles

Southwest Museum
234 Museum Drive
Los Angeles, California 90065
Mailing address:
P.O. Box 41558
Los Angeles, California 90041
323-221-2164
http://www.southwestmuseum.org

Wells Fargo History Museum
333 South Grand Avenue
Los Angeles, California 90071
Mailing address:
Historical Services
420 Montgomery Street
San Francisco, California 94163
213-253-7166
http://www.caohwy.com/w/wefahmla.htm

Martinez

John Muir National Historical Site
4202 Alhambra Avenue
Martinez, California 94553
925-228-8860
http://www.nps.gov/jomu

Monterey

Monterey State Historic Park
20 Custom House Plaza
Monterey, California 93940
831-649-7118
http://www.mbay.net/~mshp/

Pacifica

Sanchez Adobe Historic Site

1000 Linda Mar Boulevard
Pacifica, California 94044
650-359-1462
http://www.ci.pacifica.ca.us/Sanchez.html

Sacramento

Governor's Mansion State Historic Park
1526 H Street
Sacramento, California 95814
916-322-4775
http://www.cal-parks.ca.gov

San Diego

Historical Shrine Foundation of San
    Diego County
2482 San Diego Avenue
San Diego, California 92110
619-298-2482

San Francisco

Museum of Craft and Folk Art
Building A, Fort Mason Center
San Francisco, California 94123
415-775-0991
http://www.mofca.org

San Jose

San Jose Museum of Quilts and Textiles
110 Paseo de San Antonio
San Jose, California 95112
408-971-0323
http://www.sjquiltmuseum.org

San Simeon

Hearst Castle
750 Hearst Castle Road
San Simeon, California 93452
805-927-2020
http://www.hearstcastle.org

Colorado

Arvada

Arvada Center for the Arts and
    Humanities
6901 Wadsworth Boulevard
Arvada, Colorado 80003
303-431-3080
http://www.arvadacenter.org

Aurora

Aurora History Museum
15001 East Alameda Drive
Aurora, Colorado 80012
303-739-6660
http://www.ohwy.com/co/a/auhimuse.htm

Boulder

Boulder Museum of History
1206 Euclid Avenue
Boulder, Colorado 80302
303-449-3464
http://www.bcn.boulder.co.us/arts/bmh

Brighton

Adams County Museum Complex
9601 Henderson Road

Brighton, Colorado 80601
303-659-7103

Central City

Gilpin History Museum
228 East High Street
Central City, Colorado 80427
Mailing address:
P.O. Box 247
Central City, Colorado 80427
303-582-5283
http://www.coloradomuseums.org/gilpin.htm

Denver

Black American West Museum and
    Heritage Center
3091 California Street
Denver, Colorado 80205
303-292-256
http://www.coax.net/people/lwf/
    bawmus.htm

Colorado Historical Society
1300 Broadway
Denver, Colorado 80203
303-866-3682
http://www.coloradohistory.org

Four Mile Historic Park
715 South Forest Street
Denver, Colorado 80222
303-399-1859
http://www.fourmilepark.org

Molly Brown House Museum
1340 Pennsylvania Street
Denver, Colorado 80203
303-832-4092
http://www.mollybrown.org

Fairplay

South Park City Museum
100 4th
Fairplay, Colorado 80440
Mailing address:
P.O. Box 634
Fairplay, Colorado 80440
719-836-2387
http://www.southparkcity.org

Fort Garland

Old Fort Garland
South of U.S. 160 on Highway 159
Fort Garland, Colorado 81133
719-379-3512
*http://www.museumtrail.org/
    FortGarlandMuseum.asp*

Golden

Buffalo Bill Memorial Museum
987 ½ Lookout Mountain Road
Golden, Colorado 80401
303-526-0747
http://www.buffalobill.org

La Junta

Bent's Old Fort National Historic Site
35110 Highway 194 East
La Junta, Colorado 81050
719-383-5010
http://www.nps.gov/beol

Leadville

Heritage Museum and Gallery
102 East Ninth Street
Leadville, Colorado 80461
Mailing address:
P.O. Box 962
Leadville, Colorado 80461
719-486-1878
http://www.ohwy.com/co/h/herimuse.htm

Littleton

Littleton Historical Museum
6028 South Gallup
Littleton, Colorado 80120
303-795-3950
http://www.littletongov.org

Sterling

Overland Trail Museum
Junction I-76 and Highway 6E
Sterling, Colorado 80751
P.O. Box 4000
Sterling, Colorado 89751
970-522-3895
http://www.sterlingcolo.com

Winter Park

Cozens Ranch
77849 U.S. Highway 40
Winter Park, Colorado 80482
Mailing address:
P.O. Box 165
Hot Sulphur Springs, Colorado 80451
970-726-5488
http://www.grandcountymuseum.com

Nevada

Carson City

Bowers Mansion
4005 U.S. 395, North
Carson City, Nevada 89704
702-849-0201
*http://www.cr.nps.gov/nr/travel/nevada/
bow.htm*

Fallon

Churchill County Museum and Archives
1050 South Maine Street
Fallon, Nevada 89046
775-423-3677
http://www.ccmuseum.org

Henderson

Clark County Heritage Museum
1830 South Boulder Highway
Henderson, Nevada 89015
702-45-7955
http://www.co.clark.nv.us

Reno

Nevada Historical Society
1650 North Virginia Street
Reno, Nevada 89503
775-688-1191
*http://www.clan.lib.nv.us/docs/museums/
hist/soc.htm*

Utah

Brigham City

Brigham City Museum-Gallery
24 North 300 West
Brigham City, Utah 84302
Mailing address:
P.O. Box 583
Brigham City, Utah 84302
435-723-6769
*http://www.brigham-city.org/services/
museum.html*

Fairfield

Camp Floyd/Stagecoach Inn State Park
18035 West 1540 North
Fairfield, Utah 84013
Mailing address:
P.O. Box 288
Cedar Valley, Utah 84065
801-768-8932
*http://www.stateparks.utah.gov/park_pages/
camp.htm*

Farmington

Pioneer Village
375 North Lagoon Lane
Farmington, Utah 84025
Mailing address:
P.O. Box 696
Farmington, Utah 84025
801-451-8050
*http://www.sonsofutahpioneers.org/
p7400.htm*

Ogden

Ogden Union Station Museums
25th and Wall Avenue, Room 212
Ogden, Utah 84401
801-621-4808
http://www.theunionstation.org/

Saint George

Brigham Young's Winter Home
67 West 200 North
Saint George, Utah 84770
Mailing address:
490 South 300 East
Saint George, Utah 84770
435-673-2517
*http://www.stgeorgetemplevisitorscenter.org/
    byounghome.html*

Salt Lake City

Beehive House
67 East South Temple
Salt Lake City, Utah 84111
801-240-2681
http://www.utohwy.com/b/beehhous.htm

Chase Home of Utah Folk Arts
Center of Liberty Park
Salt Lake City, Utah 84102
Mailing address:
C/o Utah Arts Council
617 East South Temple
Salt Lake City, Utah 84102
801-533-5760
http://www.utahfolkarts.org

Daughters of Utah Pioneers Pioneer
    Memorial Museum
300 North Main Street

Salt Lake City, Utah 84103
801-538-1050

Utah State Historical Society
300 Rio Grande Street
Salt Lake City, Utah 84101
801-533-3500
http://www.history.state.ut.us

Wellsville

American West Heritage Center
4025 South Highway, 89–91
Wellsville, Utah 84339
435-245-6050
http://www.americanwestcenter.org

Wyoming

Buffalo

Jim Gatchell Museum
100 Fort Street
Buffalo, Wyoming 82834
Mailing address:
P.O. Box 596
Buffalo, Wyoming 82834
307-684-9331
http://www.jimgatchell.com

Casper

Fort Caspar Museum
4001 Fort Caspar Road
Casper, Wyoming 82604
307-235-8462
http://www.fortcasparwyoming.com

Cheyenne

Cheyenne Frontier Days Old West
  Museum
4610 North Carey Avenue
Cheyenne, Wyoming 82001
Mailing address:
P.O. Box 2720
Cheyenne, Wyoming 82003
307-778-7290
http://www.oldwestmuseum.org

Historic Governors' Mansion
300 East 21st Street
Cheyenne, Wyoming 82001
Mailing address:
Department of State Parks and Cultural
  Resources
122 West 25th Street
1st Floor NE, Herschler Building
Cheyenne, Wyoming 82002
307-777-7878
http://wyoparks.state.wy.us/govern1.htm

Wyoming State Museum
Barrett Building
2301 Central Avenue
Cheyenne, Wyoming 82002
307-777-7022
http://wyomuseum.state.wy.us/

Cody

Buffalo Bill Historical Center
720 Sheridan Avenue
Cody, Wyoming 82414
307-587-4771
http://www.bbhc.org

Douglas

Wyoming Pioneer Memorial Museum
Wyoming State Fairgrounds
400 West Center Street
Douglas, Wyoming 82633
Mailing address:
P.O. Box 911
Douglas, Wyoming 82633
307-358-9288
http://wyoparks.state.wy.us/
  Pioneer%20Museum%20stuff/

Fort Bridger

Fort Bridger State Museum
37000 Business Loop, I-80
Fort Bridger, Wyoming 82933
Mailing address:
P.O. Box 35
Fort Bridger, Wyoming 82933
307-782-3842
http://www.fortbridger.com

Fort Laramie

Fort Laramie National Historic Site
Fort Laramie, Wyoming 82212
Mailing address:
HC 72, Box 389
Fort Laramie, Wyoming 82212
307-837-2221
http://www.nationalparks.org/guide/parks/
  fort-laramie–1986.htm

Lander

Fremont County Pioneer Museum
636 Lincoln Street
Lander, Wyoming 82520

307-332-4137
http://www.ohwy.com/wy/f/fremontm.htm

Laramie

Wyoming Territorial Park
975 Snowy Range Road
Laramie, Wyoming 82070
307-745-3733
http://www.wyoprisonpark.org

Pinedale

Museum of the Mountain Man
700 East Hennick
Pinedale, Wyoming 82941
Mailing address:
P.O. Box 909
Pinedale, Wyoming 82941
307-367-4101
http://www.museumofthemountainman.com

Journals in Folklore of the Region: A Selected List

The journals in the list below publish articles on folklore of the region. Some are scholarly; others are more popular. Many other journals and newsletters exist. Often, these are smaller, of more local interest, and published by museums, historical societies, folklore organizations, community groups, and schools. Explore your own area to see what other publications of folklore exist.

California Indian Storytelling Times
From the Sourdough Crock: A Newsletter
   from the California Folklore Society
Newsletter: California Folklore Society
Newsletter of the Colorado Folklore Society

New West: The Newsletter of Country
   Western Dance and Folklore
UCLA Folklore Annals
University of California Publications:
   Folklore and Mythology Studies
Utah Folklife Newsletter
Western Folklore

Web Sites: A Selected List

Below is a list of a few Web sites dealing with folklore of the region. You can find other Web sites by doing an Internet search on a search engine such as Google or Yahoo! or by looking for the Web sites of various folklore organizations with which you are familiar.

California Gold: Folk Music from the Thirties,
   http://www.lcweb2.loc.gov/ammem/
   afcchtml/cowhome.html
An on-line exhibition of photographs, drawings, documents, and recorded music, including the music of various ethnic groups.

California Gold: Northern California Folk
   Music from the Thirties, http://www.
   memory.loc.gov/ammem/afcchtml/
   cowhome.html
Description of the Work Projects Administration California Folk Music Project collection, which includes sound recordings, photographs, drawings, and documents. Different ethnic communities of northern California are featured. Some material is accessible on-line; for other material, access information is provided. Subject searching is possible.

Charles Todd and Robert Sonkin Collection,
   http://www.lcweb.loc.gov/spcoll/242.html
Charles Todd and Robert Sonkin did field

research of the songs of people living in migratory camps in the early 1940s. This is a description of the collection.

Hispano Music and Culture of the Northern Rio Grande: Juan B. Rael Collection, http://www.memory.loc.gov/ammem/ rghtml/rghome.html
A Library of Congress presentation of on-line folk drama, wedding songs, and dance tunes, recorded in New Mexico and Colorado.

Max Bertola's Southern Utah: Kokopelli, http://www.so-utah.com/feature/kokopeli/ homepage.html
Kokopelli is a mythical figure of the Anasazi, usually depicted playing a flute.

Here is information about the figure, along with links to other resources.

University of California at Los Angeles, Ethnomusicology Archive, http://www. ethnomusic.ucla.edu/archive/
Descriptions and access information on the material in the archive, including recordings of folk and ethnic music.

University of California at Los Angeles: Folklore and Mythology Archives, http://www.humnet.ucla.edu/humnet/ folklore/archives/
Description of student projects and individual collections at the UCLA Folklore and Mythology Archives. Many collections are of California folklore.

The Northwest

Idaho, Montana, North Dakota, Oregon, South Dakota, Washington

Look for tales on:

The Nez Percé
The Clackamas
The Kootenai
Outlaws
Lakes and rivers

And for characters such as:

Dirty Dan Harris
Shamans
Calamity Jane
Hathaway Jones

Look for collections and works by:

Ella E. Clark
Jame Walker
Katharine Berry Judson
Melville Jacobs

Introduce children to:

Animal tales
Coyote, the trickster
Lewis and Clark
Sacagawea

Explore the rich literature of the region with:

O. E. Rølvaag
Wallace Stegner

Consult journals:

Northwest Folk Directory and Resource Guide
Northwest Folklore

THE NORTHWEST: INTRODUCTION

Defining the region that we call the Northwest has never been a simple task. Finding common elements in its folk culture is daunting. When Charles Haywood assigned regions to Volume 1 of his 1951 *Bibliography,* he credited Howard Odum's definitive work on American regions. However, Odum's Northwest is quite different from that of Haywood, as it includes Kansas, Utah, and Wyoming, but not Oregon or Washington, which he assigned to a region he called the Far West. In Volume 2 of Haywood's *Bibliography,* which focused on Native American folklore, he used a different set of regions based on cultural affinity. This division was advanced by anthropologist Clark Wissler in the early twentieth century and is still in general use today.

Looking at the history of the United States as a republic, and at its nonindigenous majority population, there are regions that clearly share a common history and culture, including folk culture. New England, the South, and the Mormon West are three examples. Other regions, such as the Mid-Atlantic states, the Midwest, and the Great Lakes, are more ambiguous, often overlapping, or leaving some states, such as West Virginia and Oklahoma, hard to categorize. What do Washington, Idaho, Montana, North Dakota, and South Dakota share that make them a region? Many, including Odum, would not put those five states together. A look at a physical map of the United States shows five states of Haywood's Northwest traversed by the Great Plains (the Dakotas and eastern Montana), the Rocky Mountains (western Montana and much of Idaho), the

plateaus of the Intermountain West (the central and eastern parts of Oregon and Washington, and southern Idaho), and the Northwest Coast (the western parts of Oregon and Washington). Looking at the folklore, as well as the history, economics, literature, and arts of these areas, one can easily see the effect that physical geography and consequent natural environment has on all that is human in them.

Physical geography and natural environment are not necessarily related to political boundaries. Thus Great Plains culture, both Native and non-Native, can be found from well north in Canada's Prairie Provinces south into Texas. The Intermountain West, the Rocky Mountains, and the Northwest Coast's regional cultures transcend national and state boundaries. The Northwest Coast extends south into northwestern California's redwood coast and north to include both coastal British Columbia and the Alaska Panhandle.

There are, however, significant historical factors shared by a Northwest region that include the Dakotas and Washington and the states in between. In the 1991 anthology *The Centennial West* (Seattle: Univ. of Washington Press, 1991), its editor, historian William Lang, defines "the Northern Tier States." They include five of the six states of Haywood's Northwest together with Wyoming, but not Oregon. Recognizing the area's geographical diversity (he calls it "a region of regions" p. 3), Lang begins with the observation that the six Northern Tier States were all admitted to the Union during a nine-month period, in 1889–1990. (Oregon had attained statehood in 1859.) In Lang's words, the admission of the six states was "the largest addition to the

Union since the transformation of the original thirteen British colonies." (p. 4) The subsequent settlement of the Northern Tier was the last great expansion of population into a previously "empty" (at least of non-Native people) region of the United States.

The Northwest includes most of two great river basins, the Missouri and the Columbia-Snake. It was first explored via its rivers, as by Lewis and Clark in 1805–1806. The Oregon Territory, in particular the Willamette Valley and points north that later became Washington, were first settled primarily via the Oregon Trail in the mid-nineteenth century. Most of the rest of Haywood's Northwest was largely settled and developed as a result of the completion of the three northern transcontinental railroads. Once settlers were in the region, they often used the rivers to reach places of settlement and, when possible, to settle near a river.

There are distinctive aspects of life in the Northwest. To this day much of it is a vast, thinly populated land. Farming is highly dependent on an uncertain water supply. Aridity is an overwhelming feature of the landscape. The rural Northwest's economy has been based, since its original non-Indian settlement, on the extractive exploitation of natural resources, at times in a manner totally unconscionable, and always at the behest of European and Northeastern American capital. Logging and hard-rock mining alternately created and destroyed, and re-created and re-destroyed, communities in all five states. Even farming ("the only pursuit that is sure," to quote the well-known Northwest folk song "The Old Settler") has been extractive and totally dependent, first on railroads, later on

credit for machinery and chemicals. The railroads promoted the "dryland farming" that led to much of the regions' agricultural settlement. It turned out to be an uncertain enterprise for those families who risked everything to pursue it. Prices for metals, lumber, livestock, and dryland-farmed crops fluctuated wildly, leading to numerous small personal tragedies as farms and jobs came and went. Natural resources such as timber, ores, and topsoil were, in effect, plundered. German farmers from Russia settled the Great Plains and the Intermountain West, in part because of the similarity of those places to their homelands. The same can be said of the Scandinavian loggers and fishermen who settled on the Northwest Coast and the Basque sheepherders of the Rockies and the Intermountain West.

A distinctive phenomenon in the Northwest has been the involvement of the federal government. Land grants to the railroads, the Homestead Act, the removal of Native people to reservations, and the subsequent control of the reservations' inhabitants characterized the nineteenth century. The building of hydroelectric and irrigation installations and the management of national forests and grasslands and Bureau of Land Management lands for logging, mining, and grazing have characterized the twentieth century. When the Bureau of Reclamation opened irrigated lands in the Intermountain West and the northern plains, the area attracted Midwesterners who had failed at farming due to the Depression or the droughts of the 1930s.

The domination of the Northwest by outside capital and distant federal agencies has produced a mentality among many Northwesterners that is fraught with contradiction. People in logging, sawmill, and mining communities will go to great lengths to defend the practices of the very companies that have exploited their communities' natural wealth, because these industries have been the only game in town. People who have depended mightily on federally subsidized electricity, irrigation water, grazing improvements, timber and mining patent sales, and barge traffic decry federal interference and launch periodic "sagebrush rebellions" against the federal government's control. In the words of historian Bernard DeVoto, they have cried, "Get out, but give us more money." On the other hand, many Northwesterners have continued to believe in "next year country," that next year will be better because hard work and God's benevolence will surely bring back the good times.

An even greater paradox has been that, along with the often-eager acceptance of plunder as economic necessity, Northwesterners also revere the land, "the wide open spaces," and the heroic forests. Almost any member of a ranching or logging family can wax eloquent on the beauty of the environment in which he or she lives and works and its superiority to California or "back east" as a place to live, hunt, fish, and enjoy a spectacular nature. Any number of cowboy or logger poems (at least those written by ranch or timber folks) extol both untamed nature and its ultimate control, often taking a swipe at those who would preserve it in its pristine condition.

For the Native people of the Northwest, the march of history since the beginning of settlement has been ever downward. Before their contact with non-Indians and during the exploration and fur trading eras, the Native people had developed ways of life closely tied to the environments peculiar to the region. Both hunting and river valley agriculture flourished among the people of the plains. The introduction of the horse to the plains in the early eighteenth century developed a new culture based primarily on buffalo hunting and brought Siouan-speaking Native settlers out of the woods of Minnesota into the plains, where they became the formidable equestrian people so difficult for whites to subdue.

The Rocky Mountains were not a home for the Indian people, although they traveled through them to hunt and trade. West of the Rockies, the Plateau people hunted and gathered, even going east to hunt buffalo after the horse came their way in the late eighteenth century, but they depended most on the great salmon runs that came to the Columbia and its tributaries. West of the Cascades, the people of the Northwest Coast exploited the sea's resources, especially the salmon runs, but also other fish and shellfish. They lived a far more sedentary life than their eastern neighbors. They were among the most prosperous Native people in the Americas, and the leisure time that offered them allowed them to develop a complex social structure and a rich heritage of artistic and religious expression.

As non-Indians conquered the West, the Native people's resistance ended when they were relegated to reservations, ostensibly places where they could continue their traditional way of life. For many reasons that became impossible, and a downward cultural and economic spiral devastated the reservations' inhabitants. The reservation itself has become a powerful factor in the development of society and culture among Indian people. Today it is likely that the majority of Indian people identify more with "the rez" where they live or grew up than with their ancestral origins. Intertribal events, such as powwows and hand game tournaments, often but not always held on reservations, have come to be a powerful factor in defining modern Indian culture.

Folklore Collection and Study in the Northwest

Until recently, our knowledge of the culture and traditions of Indian people has been largely filtered through the lenses of non-Indian ethnographers—travelers and missionaries at first, later on anthropologists, folklorists, and photographers.

Systematic ethnographic research in the United States began with the Smithsonian's Bureau of American Ethnology's (BAE) researches on Plains tribes during the 1880s. Among the first collections of northern Plains Native tales were Lakota Sioux examples collected in the 1880s for the BAE's James Owen Dorsey by Lakota tribesman George Bushotter. Using Edison's new technology, Frances Densmore collected Native songs and music from northern plains people in the 1890s and 1900s. Working for Franz Boas, who was the American Museum of Natural History's ethnologist, Alfred Kroeber collected and compiled Arapaho and Gros Ventre texts, and Clark Wissler did the same among Siouan, Blackfoot, and other northern Plains tribes. Also early in the twentieth century, David Duvall, a Montana Blackfoot, collected and published numerous Blackfoot tales. Well

into the middle of the twentieth century, the American Museum of Natural History, Columbia University, and the University of Chicago, dispatched numerous anthropology graduate students to Plains "field schools" to document all aspects of Native culture.

The Siouan tribes were pioneers in publishing traditional tales and other lore in literary forms of their native languages. Oglala Lakota Sioux Ivan Stars wrote down dozens of traditional Native narratives from his own repertoire during the 1920s. On the other hand, Black Elk, who was illiterate, dictated his spectacular autobiography, filled with Oglala traditional information, to non-Indian author John G. Niehardt, who published it in 1932 as *Black Elk Speaks*. It is the best-known and most widely read account of Plains Indian culture and history.

Pacific Coast cultures have been documented by a veritable "who's who" of scholars and other individuals. Myron Eells wrote and published one of the first systematic and reliable collections of Native American oral literature while serving as a missionary on Puget Sound during the late nineteenth century. Franz Boas, revered as the founder of modern cultural anthropology, began his fieldwork on the lower Columbia River in the 1890s. Because of Boas's interest in the Northwest and his emphasis on the collection of folklore, many of his students became leading researchers on Northwest Coast culture. Melville Jacobs, Erna Gunther, Viola Garfield, and Edward Sapir are only a few. Jacobs's own students included such luminaries as William Elmendorf, Wayne Suttles, and Pamela Amoss.

It is also important to note the work of photographer Edward Curtis, whose photographs and documentary filming exposed many Americans to the material culture and ceremonies of the Northwest Coastal peoples. Curtis also photographed and published photos of Plains, Plateau, Alaskan, and Southwest peoples.

In the Intermountain Northwest, Verne Ray, Gladys Reichard, James Teit, Leon Metcalf, and Dell Skeels collected and published lore of the Plateau tribes, especially the Nez Percé. Also in the Intermountain West, an Okanogan woman, Mourning Dove, collected and published traditional stories and, in 1927, wrote one of the first novels ever written by a Native American woman, *Cogewea: The Half-Blood,* a book rich in Okanogan stories and traditions. Emily Philips of the Spokane Tribe also collected and wrote down her people's stories, which were later edited and published.

Since the political struggles of the 1960s, many Indian individuals and tribal entities have been actively engaged in efforts of cultural conservation and revival. Language teaching, traditional skills, and traditional stories have become part of the curriculum of schools in Native communities, both on and off reservations. This emphasis has led to the publication of stories buried in archives. Repertoires of those living individuals who remembered stories and traditional skills, such as basket weaving, woodcarving, and indigenous food preparation, have been sought and shared. Recent books, such as Virginia Beavert's *The Way It Was,* Vi Hilbert's *Haboo: Native American Stories from Puget Sound,* and Nettie Kuneki-Jackson's *The Heritage of Klickitat Basketry* present Native culture from the Native perspective. Interest in Native culture on the part of non-Indians has also led to the publication of

stories from unpublished collections and to the collection and publication of previously unrecorded material, such as in compilations by Donald Hines and Jarold Ramsey.

By 1946, the population of the Northwest was sufficiently deeply rooted that a group of university scholars met in conference to define the distinctiveness of the Northwest's culture, including that of its non-Indian settlers. The conference's convener, V. L. O. Chittick, said, "the Northwest is ripe for a folklorists's services." Interestingly enough, many genres of folk culture found in the Northwest had been widely collected elsewhere in North America. Likewise groups such as fishermen, cowboys, farmers, ranchers, and miners had had their folklore collected and studied elsewhere in North America but not in the Northwest. Why are there more than a dozen published books of songs of lumberjacks from the Great Lakes states and the Northeast states, but only one folio of doubtful origins, *Elmore Vincent's Lumberjack Songs,* ever published of Northwest material? Some would argue that it is because singing had died out in lumber camp bunkhouses by the time logging was flourishing in the Northwest. This seems unlikely because folklorists were still collecting such songs in the East by the middle of the twentieth century, and Northwest loggers were writing poems, some of them of a lyrical nature, and submitting them to industry publications as late as the 1980s. A more likely explanation is that singing and song making in the Northwest woods had died out by the time people thought to look for it.

Because the Northwest was the last major region of the contiguous states to be settled, it has also had a reputation of provincialism to live down. Unlike Appalachia, where provincialism and even poverty were romanticized and considered remnants of Shakespearean English culture, the Northwest, at least before the advent of Microsoft, has always been considered a backwater. The elaborate cultural expressions of its Native people could be shared with the world, but its loggers, salmon fishermen, ranchers, farmers, and hard-rock miners were not as "noble" as Maine's lumberjacks and lobstermen, Texas's cowboys, Pennsylvania's coal miners, or the Midwest's farmers. It is quite likely that this inferiority complex led the Northwest to neglect its folklore during much of its culturally formative period. In the words of folklorist Barre Toelken, "the middle-to-upper-class descendants of the Northwest pioneers have tried continually to depict their grandparents as farsighted, godfearing folk who had no superstitions, sang no earthy songs, and who, if they had oral traditions, gave them up quickly as proof of their willingness to pull themselves up by their bootstraps."

Despite these tendencies, there have been a few individuals who have documented the Northwest's non-Native folk culture. Journalist James Stevens wrote columns in Northwest newspapers from 1942 through 1957. Journalist and local color writer Stewart H. Holbrook wrote about loggers and Northwest vernacular culture ("the lowbrow Northwest") from the 1930s through the 1960s. University of Oregon professor Randall V. Mills published articles during the 1940s and founded what later came to be named the Randall V. Mills Folklore Archive. Robert Alderson, who taught English at Port-

land's Reed College, and Robert Hitchman, who served as editor of the journal *Western Folklore* during the 1950s and 1960s, published articles on Northwest place names and their origins. Also beginning in the 1960s, two Seattle musicians, Phil Williams and Vivian Williams, began to collect and record Northwest instrumental folk music, eventually founding Voyager Recordings, which released many LPs (and later CDs) of the traditional fiddle music of the region, released with extensive notes.

Two professional folklorists came to the Northwest during the 1960s and began serious study of the region's folklore. They were Jan Harold Brunvand, who taught at the University of Idaho, and Barre Toelken, who spent much of his career at the University of Oregon. Brunvand's textbook, *The Study of American Folklore: An Introduction,* uses many examples from his years collecting folklore in Idaho. Toelken established the University of Oregon's graduate folklore program and founded the journal *Northwest Folklore.* Toelken also published many articles on Northwest folklore. His textbook, *The Dynamics of Folklore,* contains numerous Northwest examples, many from the Randall V. Mills Archive. Folklorist and architectural historian Louie Attebery of College of Idaho has specialized in the material culture of Idaho. During the 1970s, Suzi Jones, one of Toelken's students, conducted extensive surveys of folk culture in Oregon. In 1997, a team of geographers, led by Terry G. Jordan, published *The Mountain West,* which included the first comprehensive description of folk architecture and other aspects of the folk-built environment in the mountain Northwest.

During the early 1980s, folklorist Robert E. Walls of Seattle compiled the Northwest's only statewide-annotated folk culture bibliography, *Bibliography of Washington State Folklore and Folklife* (Seattle: Univ. of Washington Press, 1987). By no means are all listed articles or books specifically about folklore or folk culture. Its content includes, in its author's words, "anything relating to traditional expressions and way of life of ordinary Washingtonians, past and present" (p. v).

Beginning in the late 1970s, the National Endowment for the Arts' funding of public folklore programs brought public folk arts programs to all five states of Haywood's Northwest. Professional folklorists conducted extensive research in the Native and non-Native traditions, concentrating on folk artistic expression, including storytelling and folk poetry, as well as basket weaving, woodcarving, flytying, and embroidery. Idaho, Oregon, and Washington developed statewide folk arts exhibits and published books on folk arts in conjunction with statewide exhibitions.

Folk Culture in the Northwest

Looking first at Native American culture, there are numerous stories, variously called legends, myths, or folktales, that are indigenous to Indian people. Most have some kind of didactic function. They might explain the origin of a group of people or of a natural phenomenon. They might indicate acceptable bounds of behavior, often by example of a price paid for transgression. Most involve characters that are both animal and human, often referring either to a time "when the animals talked and walked like men" or when humans had the characteristics of their animal ancestors. Some of the stories are specific to a given tribal community in a given locality. Others are far more widespread, sometimes existing throughout a large culture area, and other times transcending culture areas. Coyote is a central character in numerous Native American stories throughout the Northwest, especially in its inland areas. In most cases, he is both a trickster and a facilitator.

In Plains cultures, there are two basic types of traditional tales: "true stories," which are conceptual history or religious myth, and "fictional stories" told for entertainment and amusement. Many of the "true stories" tell of tribal origins and migration or of great hunts. They might also contain or explain the concept of *wakan,* which is the sacred element of Plains culture. Even the "fictional stories" are often instructive in a way comparable to Old World fairy tales.

Along the Pacific Coast, especially farther north, there are numerous tales involving Raven, Eagle, Bear, Wolf, Killer Whale, and other creatures that both inhabit that environment and are ancestral beings in the traditional belief system of that area's Indian people. Salmon, who is the major food resource of both Coastal and Intermountain Plateau people, is also a leading figure in Native narrative. It is likely that every salmon-dependent Indian community has a tale of how, during ancestral times, the life of Salmon came to be closely entwined with that of humans, leading to the resource giving of itself for human nourishment.

The origin of a mountain range or of the Northwest Coast's effusive rain and the inland Northwest's aridity are subject matter for traditional Native stories. The eruptions of the Cascades' volcanic peaks are reflected in the stories told by people who live close to them. So are earthquakes and avalanches, especially those that have had a lasting effect on the landscape.

A form of Indian folklore rarely noticed outside the Native community is contemporary pan-Indian humor. Jokes and anecdotes about life on "the rez," about differences in culture among the tribal communities, and Indian-white man stories, are all a part of this genre. Coeur d'Alene/Spokane Indian author Sherman Alexie is one of the first literary figures to make use of this genre in his writing. The patter that powwow emcees use to fill in between events often incorporates this kind of humor. Contemporary Indian humor can also have a didactic or moral content when it refers with bitter irony to the problems of contemporary Indian life.

Native American material culture in the Northwest varies profoundly, For example, there is the purely portable tipi of the Plains Indians, originally made of hides. On the Intermountain Plateau, people lived in semipermanent lodges of tule reeds during the winter and in conical tule or hide tipis during their nomadic season. The permanent wooden-plank longhouses of the Northwest Coast impressed the early explorers, as did the Coastal people's mighty dugout canoes carved from the trunks of old-growth trees.

Artistic expression varies among Northwest tribal people. Horse gear and traditional outfits could be plain or elaborate. Porcupine quillwork was highly decorative. Beadwork was rare when only a sparse supply of beads from seashells was available, but once glass and ceramic beads arrived with non-Indians, it became a major Native art form. Basket weaving ranged form the purely practical to the elaborately artistic, and it used many different types of fiber. The ethnographic paintings by George Catlin and Karl Bodmer of nineteenth-century Plains people reveal a high degree of artistic elaboration, especially in ceremonial outfits.

The Northwest Coast people are internationally renowned for their carving skills, and they are popularly associated with the totem pole. However, the totem pole, which is a narrative heraldic device, was traditionally made by tribes farther north, in British Columbia and the Alaska Panhandle. Washington and Oregon's Coastal people carved large and small effigies, which often functioned as welcoming figures. In modern times, totem pole carving has spread southward, and there are now many Washington and Oregon totem pole carvers who incorporate motifs of their tribal communities into the poles that they carve. Masks, helmets, and numerous types of utensils are also elaborately shaped by Northwest Coast carvers.

The folk culture of the non-Indian people of the Northwest reflects their ethnic origins, their occupational culture, and the environment, both social and natural, in which they live or have lived. Each of the dominant rural industries has its own folk culture. Thus you can hear cowboy poetry at a cattlemen's banquet in Montana or "greenhorn-in-the-woods" stories told by the emcee at a logging show. Hard-rock mining, with its attendant dangers, is full of beliefs and practices associated with good and bad luck and stories that illustrate how transgression of a belief can lead to danger or tragedy. Stories about weather or about real or imagined conspiracies to lower commodity prices or raise the prices of transportation and supplies are common in diners where farmers gather for coffee. The lore of fishing and hunting guides is shared among the guides themselves and with their clients along the Missouri River in the Dakotas, on the Olympic Peninsula, and in many places in between.

The Northwest's occupational groups also have distinctive material folk culture. Some of it exists in the form of the tools and techniques of their work. It can also be found in celebratory events, such as agricultural fairs, logging shows, rodeos, and miners' drilling contests. There are carvers and painters who specialize in representations of work, and there are artists who use the tools of a specific occupation, such as the logger's chainsaw, to express themselves artistically.

Specific aspects of Northwest history that have led to genres of folk culture that transcend ethnic and occupational communities, such as stories, songs, and poems about outlaws, hobos, robber baron businessmen, and radical labor leaders. Songs and poems by radical labor organizer Joe Hill of the Industrial Workers of the World (IWW) and stories about Harry Bridges of the International Longshore and Warehouse Union (ILWU) or about the IWW and the ILWU's conflicts with management and authority are still part of the Northwest's labor lore.

The five states of Haywood's Northwest have a complex history of ethnic settlement. Although there are African Americans in the region, especially in its larger cities and in and near its military bases, its non-Native ethnic communities are primarily European, Asian, or Latin American in origin. Parts of the Dakotas are a mosaic of European ethnic settlements. Germans from Russia (including Mennonites and the communal Hutterite colonies), other Germans, Scandinavians (especially Norwegians and Swedes), and Slavs (especially Czechs), are locally predominant. The farming region of central and eastern Montana has many Germans (from Germany and Russia) and Scandinavians. The Métis communities along North Dakota and Montana's Canadian border are a unique mixture of French and Native American cultural influences. Mining communities in Montana's and Idaho's mountainous areas are even more complex mosaics with local concentrations of Irish, Germans, Slavs, Italians, Welsh, and Scandinavians. Basque sheepherders, ranchers, and innkeepers can be found in many parts of Idaho and Montana. Eastern Washington's farmlands also have many German-Russian (including Mennonite and Hutterite) and Scandinavian settlers.

Scandinavians, especially Finns, Norwegians, and Swedes, were numerous among the loggers and millworkers in both the coastal and inland Northwest's forests. Finns and Norwegians were also among the Northwest's leading commercial fishermen and boatbuilders. The descendants of Croatian and Greek immigrants are still well represented in the Northwest's maritime trades.

Asian settlement in the inland Northwest once consisted primarily of Chinese men who placer-mined or worked on the railroads. Idaho was once 10 percent Chinese. Anti-Asian hostility drove most of them away. Filipino farmhands in Washington's Yakima Valley eventually became farmers and orchardists. The urban areas of Oregon and Washington's Pacific Coast attracted settlers from China, Japan, and the Philippines, and many of the Japanese became produce farmers or fishermen in western Washington until they were interned at the beginning of World War II. Koreans, Vietnamese, and other East and Southeast Asians became very numerous in Oregon and Washington in the late twentieth century.

One of the most important migrations into the Northwest has been that of Latino Americans. First to come were Tejanos, U.S. citizens of Mexican heritage from Texas, who came to work as farmhands in the orchards and farms of the Intermountain West. Later, a series of successions of immigrants and temporary workers from Mexico, and in most recent years from Central America, have arrived. Although many were and still are migrants, there is now a significant population of Latino Americans who have settled in the Intermountain West, some of whom are farmers and small businessmen. By the end of the twentieth century, Mexican and Central American immigrants dominated non-timber work in the Northwest's forests

The boom in high tech in the Seattle and Portland areas spawned another influx of highly skilled immigrants from Europe and Asia, the latter most notably from China and India. The collapse of the Soviet Union brought in Russians and Ukrainians, who are now numerous in pockets all over the Intermountain and Coastal Northwest. New opportunities also drew new African and Middle Eastern immigrant communities into parts of the urban Northwest.

The ethnic complexity of the present-day Northwest means there is a huge body of folk culture, oral and material, that has scarcely been collected or studied. A few examples are in order here: Immigrants from the Hmong tribe of Laos can be found making exquisite traditional baskets and playing unique styles of music in Seattle's suburbs. On the Columbia Plateau and in the Yakima Valley there are Mexican musical ensembles whose fame has spread all the way back to Mexico. Latino non-timber workers on the Olympic Peninsula sing *corridos* about immigration and the vicissitudes of their economic condition. Hutterite congregations from South Dakota to Washington sing 500-year-old hymns and recite religious proverbs and tales of old world-martyrdom in an archaic German dialect. Asian Indian immigrants in the Portland area make elaborate costumes for their community celebrations. The people of refugee communities, whether from Europe, the Middle East, or Asia, share stories of horror and heroism derived from the experiences that caused them or their parents to leave their homelands.

Conclusion

The great cities of Seattle and Portland characterize the Northwest as much as do its vast prairies and forests and barely settled mountain ranges. Oral and material culture of the Native people varies as much as or more than that of many of the settler communities. In terms of both Native and non-Native folk culture, there are cases in which the environment has been the overriding influence. In other cases, place of origin still dominates a folk group's culture. In yet others, the experiences that settlers and their descendants had upon arriving in the Northwest have most strongly shaped their culture. Perusing the titles in this section of the bibliography reveals that the Northwest has as much diversity as it has similarity. A drive from Sioux Falls, South Dakota, to Cape Flattery on the Pacific Coast takes the traveler through landscapes as varied as any in North America. In those places where the cultural landscape is visible, it also displays remarkable diversity. Were you to meet people along the way and have them share their traditions, you would come away amazed by the cultural richness of this region. The cultural and environmental diversity of these six states may be the most important quality that the region holds in common.

Jens Lund

THE NORTHWEST: BIBLIOGRAPHY AND OTHER RESOURCES

Bibliography

History and Study

776. Lévi-Strauss, Claude. *The Story of Lynx.* Chicago: Univ. of Chicago Press, 1995. xvii, 276p. Translated by Catherine Tihanyi. Index. Bibliog. Notes. 94-34811. 0-226-47471-2.

Lévi-Strauss explores the notion of twinship, and how the understanding of that notion differs between Native American and Anglo cultures. To accomplish this exploration, he uses the stories of the Northwest Coast people as illustrations.

Treasuries

777. Jones, Suzi. *Oregon Folklore.* Eugene: Univ. of Oregon, 1977. Illus. Index. Notes. 78-100792. 0-87114-077-2.

Jones describes this book as a "crazy quilt, pieced from fabric of random sizes, shapes, and colors in an incoherent and asymmetrical pattern, yet with a character all its own" (p. 7). She includes stories, tall tales, jokes and riddles, snippets of folk medicine, songs, and information on crafts and home industries. The first few chapters each treat a region of the state (The Oregon Coast, The Willamette Valley, East of the Cascades). Other chapters are thematic, concentrating on work, storytelling, celebrations, folk belief, and music.

The book is illustrated with black-and-white photographs.

Tales and Legends

778. Bagley, Clarence. *Indian Myths of the Northwest.* Brighton, MI: Native American Book Publishers, 1930; repr., 1991. Index. 1-878592-34-3.

Coyote appears in this collection, as do Loon, Crayfish, and other animals common to Native American mythology. There are also creation stories and stories of how various places came to be.

Unfortunately the brief introduction was written at a time when Native American mythology was considered not in religious terms but as fanciful stories of simple people. The stories themselves, however, have universal themes.

779. Bailey, Robert G. *River of No Return (the Great Salmon River of Idaho). A Century of Central Idaho and Eastern Washington History and Development Together with the Wars, Customs, Myths, and Legends of the Nez Perce Indians.* rev. ed. Lewision, ID: R. G. Bailey Printing, 1947. xxix, 754p. Illus. Bibliog.

Part history, part guidebook, part folklore, this book traces a century of Idaho history. It includes information about the Lewis and Clark expedition, about early mining camps, about early ranching days, about the early days of statehood. It also contains information about the daily life of that time, both among native populations and the newcomers—miners and ranchers.

A section of tales of the Nez Percé Indians follows.

Bailey arrived in Montana in the 1890s and spent time in frontier towns and mining camps, making the acquaintance of Calamity Jane, among others. He ran several newspapers in a variety of mining camps, during gold rush times. He later worked for the Idaho State Historical Society, and in that guise met many of the people who shaped the early history of the area, listening to their stories and learning from them the ways of the Old West.

780. Baumler, Ellen. *Spirit Tailings: Ghost Tales of Virginia City, Butte, and Helena.* Helena: Montana Historical Society Press, 2002. Illus. Index. Bibliog. 2002-3741. 0-917298-91-8pa.

All the ghost stories here relate to mining and mining camps, hence the "tailings" of the title.

The illustrations are black-and-white photographs of many of the places where the ghosts have been seen.

781. Beavert, Virginia. *The Way It Was: Yakima Legends.* n.p.: Franklin Press, 1974. Illus. Glossary. 74-33971.

Tribal elders from a number of bands within the Yakima Tribe contributed legends to this compilation. Legends and tales were transcribed in the original language, then translated into English, in order to preserve more of the full flavor and meaning of each.

Legends concern the creation, the natural world, life lessons, and various places.

782. Beckham, Stephen Dow, ed. *Tall Tales from Rogue River: The Yarns of Hathaway Jones.* Corvallis: Oregon State Univ. Press, 1974; repr., 1990. 178p. Illus. by Christina Romano. Notes and Sources. Bibliog. (Northwest Reprints). 90-41875. 0-87071-512-7.

Hathaway Jones was a tale teller in the tradition of the Münchhausen tales. Born in 1870, he lived in the Rogue Country, a hundred-mile-long canyon of the Rogue River in southeastern Oregon; he died in 1937. He became a contract mail carrier in the area in 1898, and carried his tales with him as well as the mail.

His tales either had himself as the main character, or his father, William, or grandfather, Ike. They are all tall tales, full of exaggeration and humor.

Beckham's introduction gives what information is known about the life of Hathaway Jones and discusses his tale telling as part of the genre of Münchhausen, or tall tales.

783. Boas, Franz. *Chinook Texts.* Washington, DC: Government Printing Office, 1894. (Bulletin. Smithsonian Institution. Bureau of American Ethnology, 20.)

Boas collected these texts in the summers of 1890 and 1891, in Clatsop County, Oregon. He worked with Charles Cultee, one of only two people who at that time spoke the Chinook language.

The myths and tales are presented both in English and Chinook. They encompass creation stories, animal stories, stories of adventure, and stories of spirits.

784. ——. *Kathlamet Texts.* Washington, DC: Government Printing Office, 1901. (Bulletin. Smithsonian Institution. Bureau of American Ethnology, 26.)

As with the *Chinook Texts,* Boas collected these texts in the summers of 1890 and 1891, as well as during December 1894. He worked again with Charles Cultee, one of only three people who at that time spoke the Kathlamet dialect, and the same person who helped him transcribe the tales in *Chinook Texts.*

The myths and tales are presented both in English and Kathlamet. Like those of the Chinook, they encompass creation stories, animal stories, stories of adventure, and stories of spirits.

785. Boas, Franz, ed. *Folk-Tales of Salishan and Sahaptin Tribes.* Lancaster, PA: Published for the American Folklore Society by G. E. Stechert, 1917. (American Folklore Society, Memoirs, v. 11).

Several people collected the various tales told here: James A. Teit, Marian K. Gould, Livingston Farrand, and Herbert J. Spinden. They were collected during the late nineteenth and early twentieth centuries.

Coyote figures prominently in the tales, as do Raven and other animals. All tales are from the Salishan or Sahaptin tribes of the Northwest.

786. Bruseth, Nels. *Indian Stories and Legends of the Stillaguamish, Sauks and Al-* lied *Tribes.* Fairfield, WA: Ye Galleon Press, 1977. Illus. 0-877700-78-8.

As a child in the 1880s and 1890s, Bruseth spent time in various camps of the Stillaguamish and Sauk Tribes. He listened to their stories, many of which he transcribes here.

At the beginning of the book, before the actual tales, Bruseth gives some scant information on the way of life during this time of the Stillaguamish and Sauk.

787. Bullchild, Percy. *American Indian Genesis: The Story of Creation.* Berkeley, CA: Seastone Press, 1998. xv, 92p. 98-30543. 1-56975-156-0.

Bullchild, a Blackfoot, tells here the story of creation, how the peoples of the earth dispersed into the four directions, and how the buffalo came.

788. Clark, Ella E. *Indian Legends of the Pacific Northwest.* Berkeley: Univ. of California Press, 1953. viii, 225p. Bibliog. Glossary. 0-520-00243-1.

Clark collected these tales from the Indians of Washington and Oregon. They center around the natural elements of the land, and Clark divides them accordingly: myths of the mountains; myths of the lakes; myths of rivers, rocks, and waterfalls; and myths of creation, the sky, and stars. Each section begins with an introductory chapter giving background information about the tales.

789. Dooling, D. M., ed. *The Sons of the Wind.* New York: Parabola Books, 1984; repr., San Francisco: HarperCollins, 1992. (Society for the Study of Myth and Tradition). 91-58396. 0-06-250234-4pa.

Dooling here retells the mythology of the Ogallala Lakota. The tales told here concern the beginning of the world, the creation of such things as the four directions, animals, and the world itself.

They are a retelling in a more popular form of tales heard and collected by Dr. James Walker on the Pine Ridge Reservation in the late 1800s. He listened to many of the shamans of the Ogallala, gleaning stories from all of them. When he died, he left behind a collection of unpublished and to a great extent unorganized typescripts. These were transcribed for scholars in *Lakota Myth* (Univ. of Nebraska Press, 1983) by Elaine Jahner. This current edition is for those who wish to learn and enjoy the stories.

790. Frey, Rodney, ed. *Stories that Make the World: Oral Literature of the Indian Peoples of the Inland Northwest as Told by Lawrence Aripa, Tom Yellowtail, and Other Elders.* Norman: Univ. of Oklahoma Press, 1995. xix, 264p. Illus. Bibliog. Index. Glossary. Notes. (The Civilization of the American Indian Series, v. 218). 94-39935. 0-8061-2710-4.

Frey became interested in the differences between a spoken or told story and a written version of the same when he reviewed texts for a language arts curriculum committee in Coeur d'Alene, Idaho. He realized then how much the spoken word depended on, and was enhanced by, the performance of the speaker. The audience became more engaged in the stories and the characters than a lone reader did. This collection of tales told by various Coeur d'Alene elders is the result of his conviction.

In addition to the telling the tales, Frey includes here various photographs of the area, meant to make the reader experience the story more deeply and understand more thoroughly what it is about. He includes also various questions and study hints, designed to make the reader a more active participant in the stories than the passive reader would be.

Tales are those told traditionally by the Coeur d'Alenes.

791. Green, John. *On the Track of the Sasquatch.* Surrey, B.C.: Hancock House, 1994. Illus. C94-910261-X. 0-88839-341-5.

Washington, Oregon, California, and British Columbia are the places where the sightings of Sasquatch, or Bigfoot, which are described in this book, took place. Green includes transcriptions of interviews with or statements by people who reported encounters with Sasquatch, as well as numerous photographs of plaster casts of footprints.

792. ———. *Year of the Sasquatch.* Agassiz, B.C.: Cheam, 1970. Illus. 72-182690.

Here Green continues his account of sightings of Bigfoot, or Sasquatch, that he began in his earlier book *On the Track of the Sasquatch.* Again he concentrates both on sightings of the creature itself and on the finding of footprints or tracks, and again his recorded sightings center in British Columbia, California, Oregon, and Washington.

He illustrates the book with photographs of tracks, photographs of individuals who have reported seeing Sasquatch, and maps of various areas where sightings have occurred.

793. Hilbert, Vi. *Haboo: Native American Stories from Puget Sound.* Seattle: Univ. of Washington Press, 1985. Illus. Bibliog. 85–40397. 0-295-96270-4pa.

Vi Hilbert grew up in western Washington, hearing the old stories of her people. In her turn, she told them to others, in an effort to preserve both their culture and language. Stories of the creation and development of the world and stories of animals are two main themes of this collection.

794. Hines, Donald M. *Celilo Tales: Wasco Myths, Legends, Tales of Magic and the Marvelous.* Issaquah, WA: Great Eagle Publishing, 1996. 265p. Illus. Notes. Index to Motifs. Bibliog. 96-094025. 0-9629539-5-4pa.

This volume begins with a description of the Wasco Indians, their villages, and way of life. They lived near the mouth of the Deschutes River in Oregon. It continues with short biographies of three ethnographers who worked and studied there, Jeremiah Curtin, Edward Sapir, and Lucullus Virgil McWhorter.

The bulk of the book consists of the tales, arranged in the following categories:

Tales of the origins of man, animals,
  and plants
Legendary tales
Tales of magic
Tales of conflicts and adventures

795. ——. *Tales of the Nez Perce.* Fairfield, WA: Ye Galleon Press, 1984. 232p. Illus. Notes. Bibliog. Index of Motifs and Tale Types. 83-19659.0-87770-311-6.

Hines divides the tales into six sections: tales of the origins of plants and animals, and of natural phenomena; tales of the coyote as trickster; two sections on tales of marvelous happenings; tales of adventures; and tales that correspond to the European tale type, the Märchen.

The index of tale types is in accordance with the Stith Thompson divisions.

Hines includes a lengthy introduction, which is an overview of the Nez Percé history and culture.

796. Hitchman, Robert. *Place Names of*

Washington. Tacoma: Washington State Historical Society, 1985. 85-24683. 0-917048-57-1.

Hitchman spent years researching Washington state history, including place names. Indian tribes, explorers, fur traders, farmers, and ranchers all contributed to the naming of various places and geographic landmarks. Most of what Hitchman discovered comes under the rubric of local history, but some of the names are so old that the stories associated with them have become folklore.

797. Hunter, Don, with René Dahinden. *Sasquatch/Bigfoot: The Search for North America's Incredible Creature.* Buffalo, NY: Firefly Books, 1993. C93-093171-8. 1-895565-28-6.

René Dahinden spent some forty years tracking Sasquatch/Bigfoot in the Northwest and is convinced of Sasquatch's reality. Here, with Don Hunter, he describes his research methods and details many sightings of the mysterious creature.

Most of the sightings documented were reported in British Columbia, Washington, Oregon, and northern California.

798. Jacobs, Melville. *Clackamas Chinook Texts.* Bloomington: Indiana Univ. Research Center, 1958. vol. 1: 293p. vol. 2: 294–663p. Notes. (Publication of Indiana Univ., Research Center in Anthropology, Folklore, and Linguistics).

Jacobs spent four months listening to Mrs. Victoria Howard of West Linn, Oregon, in the summer of 1929 and in early 1930. At that time, she was one of only three or four speakers of the Clackamas dialect of Columbia River Chinook.

Jacobs concentrated on transcription of myths, tales, and songs that Mrs. Howard remembered. The myths and tales are of both the Clackamas group and of the Molale.

Although Jacobs was interested primarily in the preservation of the language and transcribed these tales in both English and the Clackamas language (both reproduced in these volumes), he succeeded as well in preserving the stories and tales of the culture.

Many of the tales concern animals and natural phenomena.

799. ——. *Content and Style of an Oral Literature: The Clackamas Chinook Myths and Tales*. Chicago: Univ. of Chicago Press, 1959. Index. 58-5617.

Eight tales of the Clackamas make up the first part of this book, tales of Coyote, other animals, and mythical figures. Jacobs then goes on in the second part of the book to discuss these tales. He discusses relationships within the tales, various personality types to be found in them, how humor is used, how the tales present a certain worldview, and the various literary devices used.

Jacobs's stated objective is to make the tales appealing and understandable to a broad audience, made up of people from a different sociocultural group than the original tale-tellers.

800. Jones, Suzi, and Jarold Ramsey. *The Stories We Tell: An Anthology of Oregon Folk Literature*. Corvallis: Oregon State Univ. Press, 1994. Illus. Index. Bibliog. (The Oregon Literature Series, 5.) 94-5078. 0-87071-379-5; 0-87071-380-9pa.

One of six books in the Oregon Literature Series, *Stories We Tell* concentrates on traditional literature from many groups. The editors define folk literature as "the collective traditional verbal art of a community" (p. xix). By community, they mean any group, be it cultural, linguistic,

geographic, or political. Folk literature, they continue, usually began as spoken or told literature and evolved into the written form. Such literature not only is helpful in teaching us about a common identity but also continues to be used by modern authors to inform their own writing.

The editors divide this literature not by culture, ethnicity, or genre, but by theme. Thus they assemble chapters of material on the following areas:

Creation stories and stories of place
Stories of encounters and first
    contacts
Folk heroes and characters
Stories of hunting and fishing
Trickster stories
Stories of work
Treasure stories
Monsters and fabulous creatures
Ghosts and spirits
Family stories
Stories of husbands, wives, and lovers
Retold stories

Among the folk heroes and characters are stories of Hathaway Jones and Münchhausen. Trickster stories include Coyote as a character, and stories of work include Paul Bunyan tales. Among the monsters are both sea serpents and Bigfoot, and ghost stories include variations of some tales told in many parts of the country. The retold stories include some stories from the Christian Bible retold to suit Native American audiences.

The editors state that they have included "some folk texts whose language and underlying attitudes may be offensive to modern readers, on racial, ethnic, or sexual grounds" (p. xxi). They explain the inclusion of such stories as being necessary to present a true picture of the history and development of Oregon literature, to maintain a link to the past, and to help modern populations avoid the "prejudices and errors of those who came here before us" (p. xxi).

801. Judson, Katharine Berry. *Myths and Legends of the Pacific Northwest.* Chicago: McClurg, 1997; repr., Lincoln: Univ. of Nebraska, 1997. 145p. Illus. 96-39239. 0-8032-7597-1 pa.

Judson makes no claim that this work is original; on the contrary, she gives credit to the storytellers from whom she obtained the tales. She has limited the collection to creation stories, stories of the origin of the people of the area, stories of the discovery of fire, and stories connected with the physical features of the area. Together they represent the wisdom of a people passed on to every generation.

Her love for the Pacific Northwest is evident in her preface to the second edition of this work, published in 1912.

802. Kootenai Culture Committee, Confederated Salish and Kootenai Tribes. *Ktunaxa Legends.* Pablo, MT: Salish Kootenai College Press, 1997. xvi, 380p. Illus. 97-67052. 0-295-97660-8pa.

These are tales told by the Ktunaxa, or Kootenai, people, in western Montana, northern Idaho, and British Columbia. About half the stories include the trickster character, Coyote. Many of the stories are used to encourage certain behavior in children—sharing, honesty, and a respect for all life.

Illustrations are black-and-white line drawings.

803. *Kootenai Legends.* Flathead Indian Reservation, Elmo, MT: Confederated Salish and Kootenai Tribes' Kootenai Culture Committee, 1984. viii, 382p. Illus.

These tales are both entertaining and instructive—they traditionally are used to teach children about the respect they should have for the earth and all its aspects. About half the tales involve Coyote, that clever, resourceful character who meets challenging situations and always solves whatever problem he encounters. The remaining stories involve other animals and nature's powers.

804. Linderman, Frank. *Indian Why Stories: Sparks from War Eagle's Lodge-Fire.* New York: Scribner's, 1915; repr., Lincoln: Univ. of Nebraska Press, 2001. 00-051193. 0-8032-7998-1pa.

Trapper, miner, politician, and newspaperman, Frank Linderman had an adventurous life. During his trapping days, in the late nineteenth century, he lived among the Cree and Chippewa people. He listened to their stories and learned some of their language, saying that the elders of the tribe were as careful in "handling" the stories as he was in receiving them (p. x). The tales told here, in a book reprinted from the 1915 publication, concern how the natural world became the way it is. Such tales as "Why the Kingfisher Always Wears a War-Bonnet" and "Why the Night-Hawk's Wings Are Beautiful" are typical.

805. MacDonald, Margaret Read. *Ghost Stories from the Pacific Northwest.* Little Rock, AR: August House, 1995. Notes. Index of Ghostly Motifs. Subject Index. Location Index. Bibliog. (American Folklore Series). 95-34554. 0-87483-436-8; 0-87483-437-6pa.

Both public and private ghosts appear in this volume. With the exception of the category hitchhikers, MacDonald arranges the stories by where the sightings occurred. Ghost stories are collected in the following places:

Private houses
Neighborhoods
Rural areas
Hotels
Restaurants
Museums
Theaters and movie houses
Schools and colleges
Shops
Public buildings such as fire stations
Parks and golf courses
Hitchhikers
Lighthouses
Ships

There are also stories about ghosts of pets and other animals.

The Index of Ghostly Motifs allows the reader to seek out stories on a certain theme.

806. Marshall, Joseph. *The Lakota Way: Stories and Lessons for Living.* New York: Penguin Compass, 2001. Index. 2001-1035225. 0-670-89456-7.

Old tales of the Lakota are retold here to illustrate the character traits that the Lakota hold dear: humility, perseverance, respect, honor, love, sacrifice, truth, compassion, bravery, fortitude, generosity, and wisdom. Marshall, who heard many of the tales from his grandparents, adds commentary that makes the tales relevant to modern times.

807. Matson, Emerson N. *Longhouse Legends.* Camden, NJ: T. Nelson, 1968. Illus. by Lorence Bjorklund. Bibliog. 68-22747.

Thirteen legends of the Swinomish Indians, outlined by Swinomish chief Mar-tin J. Sampson, are included in this book. Some are love stories; others concern the natural world, such as the one explaining how the first solar eclipse came to be. Most have a moral or lesson.

In his introduction, Matson describes the longhouse and discusses its importance in Native life, as cultural center, town hall, and place of celebration.

Illustrations are mostly black-and-white drawings used to illustrate the tales. Also included are several color photographs of totems.

808. McLaughlin, Marie L. *Myths and Legends of the Sioux.* Bismarck, ND: Tumbleweed Press, 1974. Illus. 74-84646pa.

McLaughlin lived many years on an Indian reservation in the Dakota territory, where her husband was an Indian agent. She grew up in Minnesota, also in Indian territory. In her foreword, written in 1913, she says that the stories she relates "were told me by the older men and women of the Sioux, of which I made careful notes as related" (p. 10). Stories concern animals and the natural world.

McLaughlin compares the power and importance of folklore to music, believing that both the music and the stories of a people can convey "the qualities of that people's heart" (p. 10).

809. Oneroad, Amos E., and Alanson B. Skinner. *Being Dakota: Tales and Traditions of the Sisseton and Wahpeton.* St. Paul: Minnesota Historical Society, 2003. Edited by Laura L. Anderson. Map. Illus. Index. Bibliog. 2002-151743. 0-87351-453-x.

In the early twentieth century, Amos Oneroad attended and graduated from the Bible Teacher's Training School and School of Divinity of Columbia University. While there, he met two anthropologists, Alanson Skinner and Robert H. Lowie. Along with several other anthropologists, the three worked together to record information about Oneroad's traditional culture. Various circumstances prevented the group from developing a finished product from their manuscript; Laura Anderson has performed this service.

Anderson divides the information gathered and organized by Oneroad and Skinner into two major areas: Sisseton and Wahpeton Traditions and Customs, and Sisseton and Wahpeton Tales and Folklore. Under customs come chapters on ceremonies, naming customs, customs centered around adolescence and coming of age, courtship and marriage customs, death and burial customs, dress, dwellings, games, and household implements.

Tales include those about animals and a series of stories about the character of Iktomi, an adolescent who must leave his home and make his own place in the world. Most of the tales end with a moral.

810. Phillips, Emily M. *Red Dawn (Monatyei): Plateau Indian Legends.* Spokane, WA: Spokane Indian Education Program, Spokane Public Schools, 1989. 82p. Edited by M. Jean Hauge. Illus. by Martina Ramos.

The stories told here were collected and told by Emily Phillips, a woman of the Spokane Tribe, in the early part of the twentieth century. They were then edited by M. Jean Hauge. It is Miss Phillips who was named Monatyei, or Red Dawn.

Many of the tales concern the natural world, animals and plants, and how things came to be.

811. Ramsey, Jarold. *Coyote Was Going There: Indian Literature of the Oregon Country.* Seattle: Univ. of Washington Press,

1977. Illus. Index. Notes. 76-49158. 0-295-95441-8.

Ramsey includes some 500 tales from native groups in Oregon. He arranges the tales by region: Northeastern Oregon, the Columbia, the Willamette Valley, the Coast, Southwestern Oregon, and the Great Basin. Groups represented are Nez Percé, Wanapum, Cayuse, Umatilla, Bannock, Wishram, Wasco, Lower Chinook, Warm Springs, Clackamas Chinook, Santiam Kalapuya, Atfalati Kalapuya, Mary's River Kalapuya, Molale, Nehalem Tillamook, Chinook, Alsea, Coos, Klamath, Modoc, Takelma, Shasta, Joshua-Tututni, and Northern Paiute.

Ramsey compiled this anthology in response to an essay written in 1962 by Melville Jacobs, who used the essay as a call to action, accusing Oregonians of not caring about their native literary heritage and challenging them to begin preserving it. Ramsey scoured various academic journals and series for stories and tales originally collected by Jacobs and other anthropologists. He states that his versions are purer and truer to the original than many versions printed in later "romanticized" collections.

Coyote of course figures largely in these stories, as do other animals, natural elements, and heroic deeds.

812. Salmonson, Jessica Amanda. *Phantom Waters: Northwest Legends of Rivers, Lakes, and Shores.* Seattle: Sasquatch Books, 1995. xi, 210p. Notes and commentaries on the tales. 95-18588. 1-57061-018-5pa.

All the tales here, from the Pacific Northwest, have water as their setting and their theme. Here are stories of falls—Multnomah Falls, Spokane Falls; of rivers—the Snoqualmie River, the St. Joe

River, the Necanicum River; of bays—Willapa Bay, Coos Bay; of Sauvie Island; the Seattle waterfront; of the Moses Coulee; of parks—Glacier National Park, Stanley Park; and of lakes—Lost Lake, Lake Sutherland, Lake Crescent, Mason Lake, Snow Lake, Horsethief Lake, Crater Lake, Wallowa Lake, and Red Fish Lake.

Salmonson has taken the traditional tales of these places and rewritten them for a modern audience.

813. Schultz, James Willard. *Blackfeet Tales of Glacier National Park.* Helena, MT: Riverbend Pub., 1916; repr., 2002. Illus. (Western History Classics). 1-931832-14-5.

At age eighteen, James Willard Schultz, originally from Boonville, New York, visited his uncle in St. Louis. During this visit, he was engulfed by the adventure and romance promised by the West. He went to Montana, where he lived for many years, marrying a woman of the Blackfeet and working as a fur trader and rancher. He listened to and recorded many stories from the Blackfeet, many of which he published in newspapers and magazines. These are transcribed here, in a book first published in 1916.

Many of the stories are of adventure and triumph. Others involve the spiritual beliefs and ceremonies of the Blackfeet, or their relationship with and deep respect for the natural world. Many have a moral and are used to teach younger members of the tribe.

814. Seaburg, William R., and Pamela T. Amoss. *Badger and Coyote Were Neighbors: Melville Jacobs on Northwest Indian Myths and Tales.* Corvallis: Oregon State Univ. Press, 2000. x, 310p. Illus. Index. Bibliog. (Northwest Readers Series). 00-008046. 0-87071-473-2pa.

Melville Jacobs was a student of Franz Boas, who spent much time in the field in Oregon and Washington, recording the language and tales of various people there. This new edition of some of his works concentrates on his work with the Clackamas Chinook, Klikitat Sahaptin, Miluk Coos, Upper Cowlitz Sahaptin, Hanis Coos, and Santiam Kalapuya.

The book is divided into three parts. Part one reprints five of Jacobs's theoretical essays, concentrating on the oral traditions of the Clackamas Chinook. Part two prints nine of Jacobs's translations of tales, along with interpretations. Part three presents eleven additional stories, from a variety of cultures.

815. Sullivan, Michael Sean. *The Fairhaven Folktales of Dirty Dan Harris.* Bellingham, WA: Ink Slinger Publishing, 1981. 74p. Illus. 81-85084. 0-941956-00-8pa.

Dan Harris moved to the north coast of Puget Sound from Long Island and lived there during the mid- and late nineteenth century. He went to sea as a whaler, did some smuggling—not really considered smuggling in those days—and was in the freight business. He also was a storyteller.

The stories he told concerned the area: a fire that destroyed the town center, stories of sailing and of steamboats, even a story about meeting a "wild man of the woods." All the stories had Dan as the main character, which is why not only his stories survive, but why he himself has survived as a folk character.

816. Walker, Deward E. *American Indians of Idaho.* Moscow: Univ. of Idaho, 1973. Illus. Glossary. (Anthropological Monographs of the Univ. of Idaho, no. 2). 73-179200.

The first half of this book is a discussion of the culture and way of life of various Indian groups. The second half transcribes tales of the Kutenai, Kalispel, Coeur d'Alene, Nez Percé, Shoshone-Bannock, and Northern Paiute.

817. ——. *Myths of Idaho Indians*. Moscow: Univ. Press of Idaho, 1980. 204p. Illus. Bibliog. 79-57484.

In his introduction, Walker speaks of myths as what "impart[s] the basic values and beliefs of a society and give[s] moral instruction to its members." (p. 7) Myths often tell the stories of creation, or explain what is good or bad in behavior.

These myths, from many different groups of Idaho, tell these stories. Many of them have a trickster character, whose behavior is used to point out the necessity of abiding by conventional behavior. Others explain how certain physical attributes of the area—mountains or rivers—got their shapes and their names.

Myths are from the Kutenai, the Kalispel, the Coeur d'Alene, the Nez Percé, the Shoshone, and the Northern Paiute.

818. Wilson, Gary A. *Outlaw Tales of Montana*. Havre, MT: High-Line Books, 1995. xvi, 211p. Notes. Bibliog. 95-61348. 0-9632240-0-x.

Although the characters whose stories are told here are real people, they have become characters of folklore because of their participation in the larger myth of the American West's "bad guy." Here are stories of Con Murphy, Henry Thompson, Henry Ieuch, George Parrott, Kid Curry, and Abe Gill. Horse thieves, gold thieves, and killers, they have become local legends.

Folk Music

819. Allen, Linda. *The Rainy Day Song Book*. Bellingham, WA: Whatcom Museum of History and Art, 1978. Illus.

Both traditional and contemporary songs make up this volume. Songs are divided into chapters:

Early Explorers, Settlers, and Native Americans
Songs of Protest and Struggle
Folk Heroes
True Love, Fun, and Nonsense
Tragedies
Work Songs
By Land and by Sea
Beautiful Northwest Country

All songs have music transcribed. Illustrations are black-and-white photographs of people and of traditional activities such as fruit picking and logging.

820. Sorrels, Rosalie, comp. *Way Out in Idaho: A Celebration of Songs and Stories*. Lewiston, ID: Confluence Press, 1991. xxii, 250p. Illus. Bibliog. 90-083710. 0-917652-83-5.

In 1987, a project team headed by folk singer Rosalie Sorrels began traveling the state of Idaho, talking to people and collecting their songs. The songs collected here represent, according to Sorrels, the "state's various regions and the diversity of our people in terms of their occupations and backgrounds" (Foreword, p. xiii).

Songs are divided into chapters representing the native peoples of Idaho; settlers and immigrants, railroaders; miners; ranchers, cowboys, and sheepherders; the struggles of workers; religions; dance; women; and children.

A few tales are interspersed among the songs. Also included are many photographs of the people who sang the songs and the places and activities they sang about.

821. Thomas, Philip J. *Songs of the Pacific Northwest*. Saanichton, B.C.: Han-

cock House, 1979. Illus. Index. Bibliog. C78-002200-0. 0-919654-89-4; 0-88839-040-8pa.

Most of the songs transcribed here originated in British Columbia, but some are from the state of Washington. Songs concern early settlement of the area, mining, logging, transportation, fishing, and ranching.

Shirley A. Cox transcribed the music.

Folk Belief and Ritual

822. Hines, Donald M. *Frontier Folksay: Proverbial Lore of the Inland Pacific Northwest Frontier.* Norwood, PA: Norwood Editions, 1977.

Riddles, proverbs, Wellerisms, and puns make up this book. It is a collection of such jokes and sayings, all collected in the Pacific northwest.

823. McKechnie, Robert Edward. *Strong Medicine: History of Healing on the Northwest Coast.* Vancouver: J. J. Douglas, 1972. Index. Bibliog. Notes. 74-166882. 0-88894-011-4.

The early medicine of both Native American and white traditions is the subject of McKechnie's book. He discusses shamanism, the use of spices and herbs as medicine, and the role of spirits. His book continues into the early twentieth century, when modern practices and medicines began to replace the old ways.

824. Medcenter One College of Nursing. *Folk Medicine on the Prairie: Natural Methods of Curing and Preventing Disease According to the People of the Prairie.* Bismarck, ND: Medcenter One, 1989. 24p. Ill. Bibliog.

Written by students in a biology class at the Medcenter One College of Nursing, this slim volume is "an approved project of the North Dakota Centennial Commission." The students interviewed various people as well as consulting medical books, recipe books, and almanacs.

The diseases or conditions included here are divided into three categories: short-term, often self-curing conditions, such as warts; chronic conditions, such as tuberculosis or asthma; and maladies with a mental component. Diseases or conditions within each category are listed along with their attendant remedies.

825. Nash, Tom, and Twilo Scofield. *The Well-Traveled Casket: A Collection of Oregon Folklife.* Eugene, OR: Meadowlark Press, 1999. x, 181p. Illus. by Don Adkins. Index. Bibliog. 92-53609. 0-87480-390-x.

Recipes, folk cures, superstitions, songs, customs, and a few tales make up this book. It is divided into six geographic regions: the Oregon Coast, the Willamette Valley, Southern Oregon, Central Oregon, Northeastern Oregon, and Southeastern Oregon.

Here you can discover that "If you plant a cedar tree, when it grows large enough to shade a grave, someone in the family will die" (p. 45); that the devil's kitchen is "cracks or caves in the snow, spouting steam or sulphur fumes" (p. 116); and that when a woman wears two feathers in her hair, it "signifies a marriage or a relationship." (p. 128) You can also hear the voices of early residents talking about their regions and discover a bit of the history of various towns.

826. Vossler, Ronald J. *Lost Shawls and Pig Spleens: Folklore, Anecdotes, and Humor from the Oral Traditions of Germans from Russia in the Dakotas.* Fargo, ND: Germans from Russia Heritage Collection, North Dakota State Univ. Libraries, 2002. Illus. by Joshua Vossler and Andrea Trenbeath. 2002-112477. 1-891193-41-4.

Some eighty-nine very brief anecdotes make up this book. Much is humorous, jokes, and riddles, and much is black humor, trading on the hard lives lived by these immigrant farmers. Some of the stories touch on the hard times they'd left behind in the Old Country, and others touch on the hardships in their new land.

A few of the anecdotes reflect the superstitions common to the group, such as forecasting the weather according to the size of a butchered pig's spleen.

Material Culture

827. Ashwell, Reg. *Coast Salish: Their Art, Culture, and Legends.* Seattle, WA: Hancock House Publishers, 1978. Illus. C78-002069-3. 0-88839-009-2.

Ashwell includes no legends in this slim volume, only a brief discussion of what Salish legends were like and what purpose they served. The bulk of the volume is on Salish art, crafts, and way of life: food, dress and ornament, occupations, religion, the potlatch, customs surrounding death, and housing.

Illustrations are photographs, both black-and-white and color.

828. Attebery, Louie W., ed. *Idaho Folklife: Homesteads to Headstones.* Salt Lake City: Univ. of Utah Press, 1985. Illus. Bibliog. Notes. 84-17341. 0-87480-240-7.

The distinguished Wayland D. Hand wrote the introduction to this volume of essays. He makes the comment that folklore is more than tales and stories. In addition to what people say, "what they *do*, and they *make* are, in every sense, meaningful expressions of the creative energy of man" (p. vii).

Essays are on a variety of subjects: material culture, ethnic groups and the process of acculturation, early farm life, folk song, folk narrative, folk speech, and natural history.

J. Sanford Rikoon contributes an annotated bibliography on Idaho folklife.

829. Baird, Genevieve. *Northwest Indian Basketry.* Tacoma: Washington State American Revolution Bicentennial Commission, 1976. Illus. Bibliog. Appendices. 76-29125. 0-917048-01-6.

Various types of Indian basketry are compared: Aleutian, Eskimo, Northwood Indian, Tlingit Haida, Tsimshian, Wakashan, Clallam and Quinault, Skokomish, British Columbia, Western Washington, Nez Percé, and Wasco. Baird discusses various inspirations for basket designs, how baskets are made, and the way in which basketry has changed with changes in lifestyles.

Baird includes numerous appendices:

Maps
Glossary of basket-weaving terms
List of botanical materials used in basket weaving
List of societies known for basket making
List of families in the area known for basket making
Description of the cataloguing system used by the Washington State Historical Society Museum
Listing of major basket collections at the museum
Description of the museum's basket collection
Information on the care of baskets

830. Etulain, Richard W., ed. *Basques of the Pacific Northwest.* Pocatello: Idaho State Univ. Press, 1991. Illus. Chapter notes. 0-937834-30-0.

Etulain begins this book with an essay

on the history of Basque settlement in the region. He follows this with essays by others that touch on the language, customs, names, and worklife of the Basques in the Northwest. Two essays give extensive accounts of two specific people; another deals with folklore.

Illustrations are black-and-white photographs.

831. Gueldner, R. M. H. *German Food and Folkways: Heirloom Memories from Europe, South Russia and the Great Plains.* Fargo, ND: Germans from Russian Heritage Collection, North Dakota State Univ. Libraries, 2002. Illus. Glossary. Index. Bibliog. 00-134927. 1-891193-16-3.

The bulk of this book consists of recipes for German dishes. The introduction, however, gives a brief history of the migration of German and Russian people to the United States, information on the German and the Russian kitchen, and information about German names.

832. Harrison, Bruce. *The Basques: A Sporting Introduction.* Boise, ID: Baldwin, 1971. Illus. Appendices. Bibliog.

Originally written as a master's thesis, this presents information about Basque sport and recreation—hunting, racing, dancing, and the game of pelota.

Perhaps the most useful portion of this thesis is Appendix XIII, which is a "mini-dictionary" of Basque and English words.

833. Holm, Bill. *The Box of Daylight: Northwest Coast Indian Art.* Seattle, WA: Seattle Art Museum, 1984. Illus. Bibliog. 83-50231. 0-932216-13-7.

During the summer and fall of 1983, three Seattle institutions—the Burke Museum, the Pacific Science Center, and the Seattle Art Museum—mounted exhibits of the art of the Plains or the Northwest Coast Indians. *The Box of Daylight* is the exhibit catalog.

Included is art from the Salish, Kwakiutl, Westcoast, Northern Wakashan, Bella Coola, Haida, Tsimshian, and Tlingit.

Lavishly illustrated, the catalog includes chapters on various types of art and artifacts, from masks and headdresses to boxes, blankets, and beadwork. Each chapter, on a different type of object, begins with a discussion of the art form and includes detailed descriptions of various items, along with photographs.

Five brief essays, also illustrated, round out the exhibition catalog: on shamanic art, silver, basketry, a nineteenth-century pipe carver, and masks.

834. ——. *Spirit and Ancestor: A Century of Northwest Coast Indian Art in the Burke Museum.* Seattle, WA: Burke Museum, 1987. Illus. with photographs by Eduardo Calderón. Index. Bibliog. (Thomas Burke Memorial Washington State Museum Monograph, 4). 87-8298. 0-295-96509-6; 0-295-96510-xpa.

After a brief history of the collections at the Burke Museum, Holm presents information on the art and artifacts of various cultures:

The Lower Columbia River People
The Coast Salish
The Westcoast People
The Kwakiutl
The Bella Coola and Bella Bella
The Tsimshian
The Haida
The Tlingit

The photographs are often in full color, and the descriptions of such objects as bowls, masks, robes, baskets, and chests are detailed.

835. Jones, Suzi. *The Folk Art of the Oregon Country.* Salem: Oregon Arts Commission. 1980. Illus.

Suzi Jones curated this exhibition of folk arts produced by the Oregon Arts Commission, with participation by the University of Oregon Museum of Art, the Oregon Historical Society, and the Renwick Gallery. It includes the artifacts of daily living, such as cradles, chairs, baskets, and pottery. In addition, a section titled "Ethnic Arts" includes arts from various ethnic groups: Swiss, Finns, Estonians, Russians, Mexican-Americans, Nez Percé, Klamath, and Chinook.

An introductory essay by Barre Toelken gives a history of folk art in the region and discusses its importance and influence on life.

836. Jones, Suzi, ed. *Pacific Basket Makers: A Living Tradition: Catalog of the 1981 Pacific Basketmaker's Symposium and Exhibition.* Fairbanks, AK: Published for Consortium for Pacific Arts and Cultures, Honolulu, Hawaii, by the Univ. of Alaska Museum, 1983. Illus.

Eighteen basket makers from both the eastern and western edges of the Pacific Rim participated in this symposium and lent their art works to this exhibit. Participants were from the Commonwealth of the Northern Marianas, Hawai'i, Guam, California, American Samoa, and Alaska.

The catalog is illustrated with photographs both of the baskets and of the basket makers.

An introductory essay discusses the importance that basket making had in various cultures.

837. Kuneki, Nettie, Elsie Thomas, and Marie Slockish. *The Heritage of Klickitat Basketry: A History and Art Preserved.* Portland: Oregon Historical Society, 1982. Illus. Bibliog. 81-86185. 0-87595-106-6pa.

The authors give step-by-step, illustrated directions for making traditional baskets—including information about gathering the raw materials. An introductory essay gives a sense of the importance of this art form to the Klickitats.

838. Lund, Jens, and Elizabeth Simpson, eds. *Folk Arts of Washington State: A Survey.* Tumwater, WA: Washington State Folklife Council, 1989. Illus. Index. Bibliog. Appendix. 89-16696. 0-9623539-0-6pa.

Two exhibits of folk art, in 1987 and 1988, and the research that went into them form the basis for this book. Four essays discuss the many cultural origins of the folk art of Washington, show examples of folk art, and give information about many local artists. One chapter discusses folk art that grew out of various occupations.

The book is profusely illustrated with both color and black-and-white illustrations of various examples of the art.

An appendix presents a list of resources: organizations, film and video distributors, museums and historical societies, and festivals in the area.

839. Mattila, Walter. *The Pioneer Finnish Home.* Portland, OR: Finnish American Historical Society of the West, 1971. Illus. (Finnish Emigrant Studies Series, vol. 6, no. 2).

Mattila describes the craftsmanship that went into building cedar log homes in the Northwest. Built by Finns, these often included a separate structure for use as a sauna. Many were built by homesteaders in the late nineteenth century.

In addition to the description and photographs of the actual structures, Mattila provides much information about the process that many dedicated people participated in, to save these structures from deterioration and encroachment by development.

840. Mattila, Walter, ed. *The Finnish*

Paul Bunyans. Portland, OR: Finnish American Historical Society of the West, 1973. Illus. (Finnish Emigrant Studies Series, vol. 8, no. 2).

Mattila chronicles the life of the Finnish American loggers during the early part of the twentieth century. He discusses their immigration to the United States, their push westward to homestead and work in the logging industry, and their loyalty to workers' rights and to trade unions. Most of the narrative of this book is a history of the Finns in America. However, the illustrations and reprints from journals and newspapers give a good idea of life in logging camps of that time. Customs such as the sauna are chronicled here, as are old-time crafts such as canoe building.

841. Seattle Art Museum. *The Spirit Within: Northwest Coast Native Art from the John H. Hauberg Collection*. New York: Rizzoli International, 1995; pa: Seattle: Seattle Art Museum, 1995. 303p. Illus. Index. Bibliog. 94-069971. 0-8478-1847-0; 0-932216-45-5pa.

For more than thirty years, John H. Hauberg collected Native art from the state of Washington, southeast Alaska, and British Columbia. In 1991, he gave his collection to the Seattle Art Museum, which has since added to it. The result is a collection of textiles, baskets, weapons, carvings, and metals. Much of the collection is described and photographed here.

The text not only describes the objects, but in many cases offers comparisons of the works of various native cultures.

842. Siporin, Steve. *Folk Art of Idaho: "We Came to Where We Were Supposed to Be."* Boise: Idaho Commission on the Arts, 1984. Illus. Bibliog. 84-228796.

Between August 1984 and May 1986, several Idaho museums hosted an exhibition of folk art. *Folk Art of Idaho* is the catalog of the exhibition.

The catalog is divided into four sections:

Beauty in the Home
Working on the Land
Whimsey and Recreation
Ceremony and Celebration

Objects typifying each of these sections range from tablecloths and handbags to models of agricultural equipment, baskets, whirligigs, games, and articles of clothing.

Of course the catalog is lavishly illustrated with photographs, both black-and-white and color, of many of the items exhibited.

843. Wardwell, Allen. *Tangible Visions: Northwest Coast Indian Shamanism and Its Art*. New York: Monacelli Press, 1996. vii, 336p. Illus. Bibliog. 95-24157. 1-885254-16-4.

Amulets, masks, drums, and rattles are some of the artifacts described and illustrated here. The book is a lavishly illustrated catalog of the objects used by the shamans of the Northwest Coast tribes, specifically the Haida, Tlingit, and Tsimshian tribes. Shamans operated as healers and communicators with the spirit world.

The book also discusses shamanism of this area in relation to practices and beliefs in other parts of the world.

The catalog of objects is divided into the following categories:

Masks
Amulets
Soul Catchers

Cups, Combs, and Crowns
Staffs
Drums
Rattles
Clothing
Boxes and Chests
Figures

Folklore for Children

844. Arlee, Johnny. *Coyote Stories of the Montana Salish Indians*. Pablo, MT: Salish Kootenai College Press and Montana Historical Society Press, 1999. 62p. Illus. 99-24153. 0-917298-61-6pa.

There are more pictures than text in this brief book, appropriate for a book written for grade school children. Here are the stories about Coyote and Raven, told by the Salish people of Montana. Most of the stories, in addition to being entertaining, point out a moral or encourage acceptable behavior.

Illustrations are black-and-white line drawings.

845. Buchanan, Joan, and Sandra Davies. *Music in Our Lives: The Pacific Northwest Coast Indians: Music, Instruments, Legends*. Vancouver, British Columbia: Western Education Development Group, 1980. Illus. by Lyle Wilson. Bibliog. 81-190530. 0-88865-012-4pa.

Teachers and parents of school age children will be able to use this book to teach about Northwest Indian music. Included are songs, with music transcribed, instructions for making simple versions of traditional instruments, and poetry.

The book is a curriculum guide for fourth grade.

846. Finley, Debbie Joseph. *How Marten Got His Spots, and Other Kootenai Indian Stories*. Helena: Montana Historical Society Press, 2002. Developed by the Kootenai Culture Committee, Confederated Salish and Kootenai Tribes. Illus. by Debbie Joseph Finley and Howard Kallowatt Jr. 2002-75925. 0-917298-92-6pa.

Four stories from the Kootenai culture of western Montana are in this book: How Marten Got His Spots, Coyote and Trout, Little Weasel's Dream, and Tepee Making. The first two are at the third grade reading level; the second two are at the fourth grade level.

Illustrations are black-and-white drawings.

847. Griffin, Trenholme James, ed. *Ah Mo: Indian Legends from the Northwest*. Blaine, WA: Hancock House, 1990. 64p. Illus. by Margaret Chodos-Irvine. Bibliog. 0-88839-244-3pa.

Trenholme Griffin is the great-grandson of Judge Arthur E. Griffin, the man who first collected these stories. They were told to Judge Griffin by various people in Washington State, between 1884 and 1947. They are retold here for children.

Animals are the main characters of the stories: the loon, clam, octopus, crane, coyote, robin, sea gull, and fish duck. Also present are other natural elements, the sun, moon, river, and wind.

Stories are from the Chinook, Kittitas, Lummi, Puyallup, Skagit, Snohomish, Snoqualmie Suquamish, and Twana peoples.

The title Ah Mo comes from the fact that, because these stories were told to children, the children were required to indicate their attention by saying this phrase at intervals. As the frequency of response diminished, the children were deemed sleepy enough to be put to bed.

848. Martin, Fran. *Nine Tales of Coyote.* New York: Harper and Brothers, 1950. Illus. by Dorothy McEntee. 50-10860.

Tales from the Nez Percé, the Sahuptian and the Salishan tribes are included here, all featuring the character Coyote.

849. Rudolph, Nancy Lyn. *Paper Animal Masks from Northwest Tribal Tales.* New York: Sterling, 1996. 79p. Illus. Index. 95-39222. 0-8060-4383-1.

Seventeen animals, spiders, and bugs significant to the people of the Northwest Coast are profiled here: porcupine, coyote, eagle, bear, frog, raven, mountain goat, lynx, deer, mouse, salmon, rattlesnake, owl, spider, beaver, skunk, and mosquito. Each one-page profile tells a story about the creature, indicating its significance to the people. Along with the story are full-color photographs of the animal.

Each story is also accompanied by illustrated instructions on how to construct a mask of the animal head.

Literary Authors: A Selected List

Below is a selected list of authors who reflect and interpret the history and atmosphere of their region. These are authors of novels, poems, short stories, or reminiscences. Through reading the works of these authors, one can acquire knowledge of the history, people, and flavor of the region. This is not a complete list, either of authors, or of their works, but rather one calculated to start readers exploring and discovering their own favorites.

Carver, Raymond, 1938–1988

The Stories of Raymond Carver

Where I'm Calling From: New and Selected Stories

Doig, Ivan, 1939–

Ride with Me, Mariah Montana
This House of Sky: Landscapes of a Western Mind

Dorris, Michael, 1945–1997

The Broken Cord
A Yellow Raft in Blue Water

Erdrich, Louise, 1954–

The Antelope Wife
The Birchbark House
The Last Report on the Miracles at Little No Horse
Love Medicine

Harrison, Jim, 1937–

Legends of the Fall
Off to the Side: A Memoir
Plain Song

Kesey, Ken, 1935–2001

The Sea Lion: A Story of the Sea Cliff People

Rølvaag, O. E., 1876–1931

The Boat of Longing
Giants in the Earth: A Saga of the Prairie

Stegner, Wallace, 1909–1993

Angle of Repose
Conversations with Wallace Stegner on Western History and Literature
Crossing to Safety

The Gathering of Zion: The Story of the Mormon Trail

Welch, James, 1940–

The Death of Jim Loney
The Indian Lawyer
Winter in the Blood

Museums of the Region: A Selected List

Museums that feature everyday life abound in all regions of the country. Through the display of clothing, farm implements, household goods, industrial tools, or entire houses, workshops, and communities, these museums can help people understand and appreciate the lives of those who came before. The list below is not a complete list of museums in the region, but by browsing through it, one can get a glimpse of the richness of museum offerings. Explore on your own and discover even more fascinating museums.

Idaho

Boise

Idaho State Historical Museum
610 North Julia Davis Drive
Boise, Idaho 83702
208-334-2120
http://www.state.id.us/ishs/index.htm

Clayton

Custer Museum
Yankee Fork Ranger District

Clayton, Idaho 83227
http://www.ohwy.com/id/y/yanfrkgd.htm

Coeur d'Alene

Museum of North Idaho
115 N.W. Boulevard
Coeur d'Alene, Idaho 83814
Mailing address:
P.O. Box 812
Coeur d'Alene, Idaho 83816
208-664-3448
http://www.museumni.org/

Lewiston

Luna House Museum
Nez Perce County Museum
306 Third Street
Lewiston, Idaho 84501
208-743-2535
http://www.ohwy.com/id/l/lunahhmu.htm

Moscow

McConnell Mansion
110 South Adams
Moscow, Idaho 83843
Mailing address:
327 East Second Street
Moscow, Idaho 83843
208-882-1004
http://www.moscow.com/resource

Spalding

Nez Perce National Historical Park
39063 U.S. Highway 95
Spalding, Idaho 83540

Mailing address:
Route 1
P.O. Box 100
Spalding, Idaho 83540
208-843-2261
http://www.pigpen.itd.nps.gov/nepe

Montana

Anaconda

Copper Village Museum and Arts Center
    of Deer Lodge County
401 East Commercial
Anaconda, Montana 59711
406-563-2422
*http://goldwest.visitmt.com/listings/
    3142.htm*

Billings

Moss Mansion Historic House Museum
914 Division Street
Billings, Montana 59101
406-256-5100
http://www.mossmansion.com

Western Heritage Center
2822 Montana Avenue
Billings, Montana 59101
406-256-6809
http://www.ywhc.org

Browning

Museum of the Plains Indian
Junction of Highway 2 and 89 West
Browning, Montana 59417
Mailing address:
P.O. Box 410
Browning, Montana 59417

406-338-2230
http://www.iacb.doi.gov

Butte

World Museum of Mining
West End of Park Street
Butte, Montana 59702
Mailing address:
P.O. Box 33
Butte, Montana 59703
406-723-7211
http://www.miningmuseum.org

Choteau

Old Trail Museum
823 Main Street
Choteau, Montana 59422
406-466-5332
http://www.oldtrailmuseum.org

Culbertson

Northeastern Montana Threshers and
    Antique Association
P.O. Box 168
Culbertson, Montana 59218
406-787-5265
http://www.edgeta.org/brnch77.htm

Deer Lodge

Grant-Kohrs Ranch National Historic
    Site
210 Missouri Avenue
Deer Lodge, Montana 59722
Mailing address:
P.O. Box 790
Deer Lodge, Montana 59722

406-846-2070
http://www.nps.gov/grko

Fort Benton

Museum of the Northern Great Plains
20th and Washington
Fort Benton, Montana 59442
Mailing address:
P.O. Box 262
Fort Benton, Montana 59442
406-622-5133
http://www.fortbenton.com/museums/
agmuseum.htm

Kalispell

Conrad Mansion National Historic Site
    Museum
Between Third and Fourth Streets and
    Woodland Avenue
Kalispell, Montana 59901
Mailing address:
P.O. Box 1041
Kalispell, Montana 59903
406-755-2166
http://www.conradmansion.com

Missoula

Historical Museum at Fort Missoula
Building 322
Fort Missoula, Montana 59804
406-728-3476
http://www.montana.clom/ftmslamusseum

Poison

Miracle of America Museum, Inc.
58176 Highway 93

Poison, Montana 59860
406-883-6804
http://www.cyberport.net/museum

Wolf Point

Wolf Point Area Historical Society, Inc.
220 2nd Avenue South
Wolf Point, Montana 59201
Mailing address:
P.O. Box 977
Wolf Point, Montana 59201
406-653-1912
http://www.ohwy.com/mt/w/wolfpoin.htm

North Dakota

Abercrombie

Fort Abercrombie Historic Site
P.O. Box 148
Abercrombie, North Dakota 58001
701-553-8513
http://www.state.nd.us/HIST/abercrombie/
abercrombie.html

Bismarck

Former Governors' Mansion State
    Historic Site
320 Avenue B East
Bismarck, North Dakota 58501
Mailing address:
State Historical Society of North Dakota
North Dakota Heritage Center
612 East Boulevard Avenue
Bismarck, North Dakota 58505
701-255-3819
http://www.discovernd.com/hist

State Historical Society of North Dakota
North Dakota Heritage Center
612 E. Boulevard
Bismarck, North Dakota 58505
701-328-2666
http://www.discovernd.com/hist

Cavalier

Pioneer Heritage Center
13571 Highway 5
Cavalier, North Dakota 58220
701-265-4561
http://www.ndparks.com/parks/ISP.htm

Epping

Buffalo Trails Museum
Main Street
Epping, North Dakota 58843
Mailing address:
P.O. Box 22
Epping, North Dakota 58843
701-859-4361
http://www.wsc.nodak.edu/webcontest/
　　Museums/Buffalo%20Trails%20Museum
　　.html

Fort Totten

Fort Totten State Historic Site
Building 14
Fort Totten, North Dakota 58335
Mailing address:
P.O. Box 224
Fort Totten, North Dakota 58335
701-766-4441
http://www.state.nd.us/hist//totten/totten.
　　htm

Jamestown

Frontier Village Association, Inc.
17th Street S.E.
Jamestown, North Dakota 58401
Mailing address:
P.O. Box 324
Jamestown, North Dakota 58402
701-252-7492
http://www.ohwy.com/nd/f/fronvill.htm

Stanton

Knife River Indian Villages National
　　Historic Site
County Road 37
Stanton, North Dakota 58571
Mailing address:
P.O. Box 9
Stanton, North Dakota 58571
701-745-3300
http://www.nps.gov/knri

Watford City

Pioneer Museum
104 Park Avenue West
Watford City, North Dakota 58854
Mailing address:
P.O. Box 302
Watford City, North Dakota 58854
701-842-2990
http://www.ohwy.com/nd/p/pionmuse.htm

Williston

Fort Union Trading Post National
　　Historic Site
15550 Highway 1804

Williston, North Dakota 58801
701-572-7321
http://www.nps.gov/fous

Oregon

Astoria

Columbia River Maritime Museum
1792 Marine Drive
Astoria, Oregon 97103
503-325-2323
http://www.crmm.org

The Heritage Museum
1618 Exchange Street
Astoria, Oregon 97103
503-325-2203
http://www.clatsophistoricalsociety.org

Baker City

National Historic Oregon Trail
　　Interpretive Center
Oregon Highway 86
Baker City, Oregon 97814
Mailing address:
P.O. Box 987
Baker City, Oregon 97814
541-523-1845
http://www.or.blm.gov/nhotic

Bend

The High Desert Museum
59800 South Highway 97
Bend, Oregon 97702
541-382-4754
http://www.highdesert.org

Grand Ronde

Confederated Tribes of Grand Ronde
　　Cultural Program
Confederated Tribes of Grand Ronde
9615 Grand Ronde Road
Grand Ronde, Oregon 97347
503-879-2248
http://www.grandronde.org

Haines

Eastern Oregon Museum on the Old
　　Oregon Trail
3rd and Wilcox
Haines, Oregon 97833
Mailing address:
P.O. Box 182
Haines, Oregon 97833
541-856-3233
http://www.hainesoregon.com/eomuseum

Newport

Oregon Coast History Center
545 S.W. Ninth
Newport, Oregon 97365
541-265-7509
*http://www.newportnet.com/coastshistory/
　　home.htm*

Pendleton

Umatilla County Historical Society
　　Museum
108 S.W. Frazer
Pendleton, Oregon 97801
Mailing address:
P.O. Box 253

Pendleton, Oregon 97801
541-276-0012
http://www.umatillahistory.org

Portland

Oregon Historical Society
1200 S.W. Park Avenue
Portland, Oregon 97205
503-222-1741
http://www.ohs.org

Saint Paul

Robert Newell House, Dar Museum
8089 Champpeg Road N.E.
Saint Paul, Oregon 97137
503-266-3944
http://www.ohwy.com/or/r/rnewelhm.htm

South Dakota

Aberdeen

Dakotah Prairie Museum
21 South Main Street
Aberdeen, South Dakota 57402
Mailing address:
P.O. Box 395
Aberdeen, South Dakota 57401
605-626-7117
http://www.brown.sd.us/museum

Brookings

State Agricultural Heritage Museum
South Dakota State University
925 11th Street

Brookings, South Dakota 57007
Mailing address:
SDSU P.O. Box 2207C
Brookings, South Dakota 57007
605-688-6226
http://www.agmuseum.com

Chamberlain

Akta Lakota Museum and Cultural
    Center
St. Joseph's Indian School
Box 89
Chamberlain, South Dakota 57325
605-734-3452
http://www.stjo.org

Frankfort

Fisher Grove Country School
17250 Fishers Lane
Frankfort, South Dakota 57440
Mailing address:
17268 Fishers Lane
Frankfort, South Dakota 57440
605-472-1212
*http://www.state.sd.us/gfp/sdparks/fisher/
    fisher.htm*

Geddes

Geddes Historic District Village
Box 97
Geddes, South Dakota 57342
605-337-2501
*http://www.geddessd.org/historicalvillage.
    html*

Huron

Dakotaland Museum
State Fair Grounds
P.O. Box 1254
Huron, South Dakota 57350
Mailing address:
1616 1st Street S.W.
Huron, South Dakota 57350
605-352-4626
http://www.museumsusa.org/data/
museums/SD/78826.htm

Madison

Prairie Village
West Highway 34
Madison, South Dakota 57042
Mailing address:
P.O. Box 256
Madison, South Dakota 57402
605-256-3644
http://www.prairievillage.org

Philip

Prairie Homestead
Exit 131 off State Highway 90
Philip, South Dakota 57567
605-433-5400
http://www.prairiehomestead.com

Pierre

South Dakota State Historical Society
900 Governors Drive
Pierre, South Dakota 57501
Mailing address:
Cultural Heritage Center

900 Governors Drive
Pierre, South Dakota 57501
605-773-3458
http://www.state.sd.us/deca/cultural

Rapid City

Minnilusa Pioneer Museum
222 New York Street
Rapid City, South Dakota 57701
605-394-6099
http://www.sdsmp.edu/journey/

Sioux Falls

Siouxland Heritage Museums
200 West 6th Street
Sioux Falls, South Dakota 57104
605-367-4210
http://www.siouxlandmuseums.com/depts/
siouxland/siouxland_museums/index.asp

Yankton

Dakota Territorial Museum
Westside Park
610 Summit Street
Yankton, South Dakota 57078
Mailing address:
P.O. Box 1033
Yankton, South Dakota 57078
605-665-3898
http://www.museumsusa.org/data/
museums/SD/79798.htm

Washington

Chinook

Fort Columbia House Museum
Fort Columbia State Park
Highway 101
Chinook, Washington 98614
Mailing address:
P.O. Box 488
Ilwaco, Washington 98624
360-777-8221

Cle Elum

Carpenter Home Museum
221 East 1st Street
Cle Elum, Washington 98922
509-674-5702

Eatonville

Pioneer Farm Museum and Ohop Indian
    Village
7716 Ohop Valley Road East
Eatonville, Washington 98328
360-832-6300
http://www.pioneerfarmmuseum.org

Fort Lewis

Fort Lewis Military Museum
Building 4320
Fort Lewis, Washington 98433
Mailing address:
P.O. Box 331001
Fort Lewis, Washington 98433
256-967-7206
http://www.lewis.army.mil/DPTMS/
    POMFI/museum.htm

Ilwaco

Lewis and Clark Interpretive Center
Fort Canby State Park
Ilwaco, Washington 98624
Mailing address:
P.O. Box 488
Ilwaco, Washington 98624
360-642-3029
http://www.parks.wa.gov/lcinterpctr.asp

Pasco

Sacajawea Interpretive Center
Sacajawea State Park
2503 Sacajawea Park Road
Pasco, Washington 99301
509-545-2361
http://lewisandclarktrail.com/section4/
    wacities/tricities/SacajaweaCenter/

Redmond

Marymoor Museum of Eastside History
6046 West Lake Sammanish Parkway
    N.E.
Redmond, Washington 98073
Mailing address:
P.O. Box 162
Redmond, Washington 98073
425-885-3684
http://www.eastsideheritagecenter.org

Seattle

Burke Museum of Natural History and
    Culture
University of Washington Campus
Seattle, Washington 98195

Mailing address:
University of Washington
Box 353010
Seattle, Washington 98195
206-543-7907
http://www.burkemuseum.org

Nordic Heritage Museum
3014 N.W. 67th Street
Seattle, Washington 98117
206-789-5708
http://www.nordicmuseum.com/

Wing Luke Asian Museum
407 Seventh Avenue South
Seattle, Washington 98104
206-623-5124
http://www.wingluke.org

Snoqualmie

Northwest Railway Museum
38625 S.E. King Street
Snoqualmie, Washington 98065
Mailing address:
P.O. Box 459
Snoqualmie, Washington 98065
425-888-3030
http://www.trainmuseum.org

Tacoma

Camp 6 Logging Museum
Point Defiance Park
North End of Pearl Street
Tacoma, Washington 98407
Mailing address:
P.O. Box 340
Tacoma, Washington 98401
253-752-0047
http://www.camp–6–museum.org

Toppenish

Toppenish Museum
One South Elm
Toppenish, Washington 98949
509-865-4510
http://www.ohwy.com/wa/t/toppenhm.htm

Wenatchee

Wenatchee Valley Museum and
Cultural Center
127 South Mission
Wenatchee, Washington 98801
509-664-3340
http://www.museum.wsd.wednet.edu

Yacolt

Pomeroy Living History Farm
20902 N.W. Lucia Falls Road
Yacolt, Washington 98675
360-686-3537
http://www.pacifier.com/~pomeroy

Yakima

Yakima Valley Museum and Historical
Association
2105 Tieton Drive
Yakima, Washington 98902
509-248-0747
http://www.yakimavalleymuseum.org

Journals in Folklore of the Region: A Selected List

The journals in the list below publish articles on folklore of the region. Some are scholarly; others are more popular. Many other journals and newsletters exist. Often, these are smaller, of more local interest, and published by museums, historical societies, folklore organizations, community groups, and schools. Explore your own area to see what other publications of folklore exist.

Journal of the Folklore Society of Greater Washington
Northwest Folk Directory and Resource Guide
Northwest Folkdancer
Northwest Folklore
SFS (Seattle Folklore Society) Flyer
The Wash.Board: The Newsletter of the Washington State Folklife Council

Web Sites: A Selected List

Below is a list of a few Web sites dealing with folklore of the region. You can find other Web sites by doing an Internet search on a search engine such as Google or Yahoo!, or by looking for the Web sites of various folklore organizations with which you are familiar.

Adams Museum and House,
http://adamsmuseumandhouse.org/
The Adams House is in Deadwood, South Dakota. It contains folk art.

Idaho Symbols, http://www2.state.id.us/gov/fyi/symbols/index.htm
Information about such things as the state flag, flower, and animal, as well as folk dance.

Lakota Sioux, http://www.littlesioux.org
Much information about the Sioux, including information about their legends, stories, art, music, dance, and traditions. Some stories are on-line.

Sacred Buffalo, American Indian Stories and Poems, http://www.homestead.com/WhiteBuffaloMiracle/SacredWhiteBuffaloStories.html
Full text of many traditional Native American stories.

Seattle Folklore Society (SFS),
http://www.seafolklore.org/
The Web site for the society, including information about membership, governance, and events.

The Tree Leaves Folk Fellowship,
http://www.treeleaves.com/
Information on folk art, folk music, folkways, and folklore in general of the Northwest.

University of Oregon (UO): Folklore Program, http://darkwing.uoregon.edu/~flr/
As well as giving information about the folklore program at the University of Oregon, this site provides links to other folklore sites.

Alaska

Alaska: Checklist

Look for tales on:

The Tlingit
The Inupiaq
The Haida
Fishing
Mining

And for characters such as:

Qayaq
Daagoo

Bird Girl
Raven

Introduce children to the tales of:

Ticasuk

ALASKA: INTRODUCTION

Alaska: The Great Land, the Last Frontier, is the largest state in the United States and one-fifth the size of the rest of the country combined, yet its people[1] make up fewer than 627,000–less than one-fourth of a percent–of the total U.S. population. Alaska is a sparsely populated land of immense natural beauty with more than three thousand rivers (ten of which are longer than 300 miles), more than two million lakes, nineteen mountains higher than 14,000 feet, and more than half the world's glaciers.

Most of Alaska's population is located in four urban centers: Anchorage, Fairbanks, Juneau, and Ketchikan. The rest of Alaska's 220 communities are scattered throughout the land, mostly along major rivers or near the coast. Only a few of the rural communities are connected to a road system; many are accessible only by boat or by plane.

Alaska Natives, the indigenous residents of the Great Land, represent about 16 percent of the state's population. They include Inupiaq and Yupik Eskimos, Aleuts, Alutiiq, Athabaskans, Tlingits and Haidas. The remaining population is a mixture of white, Asian, Hispanic, Pacific Islanders, African American, European, and Middle Eastern. Most of the adults living now in Alaska who are not descended from native cultures came to the state from somewhere else.

Despite Alaska's geographic dispersal and demographic diversity, Alaskans consider themselves one people. Rather than emphasizing commonality, however, Alaskans often relate to one another based on contrasts between "outsiders" and residents, newcomers and old-timers, or sourdoughs, urbanites and villagers, Alaska Natives and non-Natives, and developers and environmentalists.

Folklore in Alaska is a living process that changes as the state's people change and as its physical, political, social, and cultural environment varies. Although Alaska is made up of a variety of people from many cultural backgrounds, Alaskans possess a common body of traditions associated with living in a northern climate. This folklore encompasses the everyday knowledge of what it takes to live in the Last Frontier. It is passed on by imitation or word-of-mouth from one person to another, over generations and across a wide territory.

Folklore forms include verbal arts (myths, jokes, personal narrative stories), festivals and celebrations, material culture (folk arts and crafts, foods, clothing, and architecture), as well as beliefs and worldviews. The incredibly varied folklore Alaska reflects the cultural backgrounds of Alaska's people. Eskimo dancing, totem pole carving, bead working; potlatches, banyas (saunas), log cabins, Athabascan spirit houses, dog sleds, ivory carvings, caches, smokehouses; Scandinavian folk songs, Russian Christmas (starring), muktuk (whale blubber), Tlingit oratory, akutaq ("Eskimo ice cream"), and curried salmon are all part of the Alaska folklore repertoire.

Alaskans belong to folk groups based on shared traits such as ethnicity and occupations. For example, folk groups that share common ethnicity are Scandinavians, Filipinos, Koreans, Japanese, Russians, and Inupiaq Eskimos. Folk groups sharing a common occupation or activity include commercial fishermen, cannery workers, subsistence hunters, loggers, oil workers, dog mushers, mountain climbers, bush pilots, homesteaders, and gold miners.

Although they belong to several different cultural and language groups, Alaska's indigenous people are collectively known as Alaska Natives. They share a common history that continues to shape their contemporary existence. Today Alaska Natives have blended their cultural traditions to maintain a strong commitment to their indigenous ways as well as accepting some changes. Many Alaska Natives continue to speak their ancestral languages, perform ancestral dances, tell traditional stories, and practice age-old values handed down through generations.

The land now known as the state of Alaska has been continuously inhabited by Native peoples for thousands of years. Each of these culture groups is well known for its own distinct traditions. Perhaps their art forms are most familiar to outsiders. The Tlingit, Haida, and Tsimshian of the southeastern coastal rainforest are known for their totem poles. The Athabascan tribes of the interior are recognized for their detailed beadwork. The Aleut people of the Aleutian Chain and Pribilof Islands are renowned for their intricate grass basketry. The Yupik people of the Yukon-Kuskokwim Delta and coastal southwest Alaska are recognized for their Eskimo dolls. The Inupiat of the northern coast of the Chukchi and Beaufort seas are well known for their ivory carvings.

The other major group of people in Alaska is composed of non-Native immigrants to the state. A common first greeting among non-Native Alaskans is "Where are you from?" Alaska's immigrant population is made up of different types of people who came to Alaska for many different reasons. For example, the early "sourdoughs," came to Alaska seeking their fortunes and eventually settled down to establish homes and families. Some Alaskans came originally on military assignment, recognized Alaska's unique offerings, and put down roots. Residents of the Matanuska Valley[2] arrived during the bleak days of American's Great Depression and ended up building family farms and the community of Palmer. Modern-day adventure and fortune seekers continue to arrive steadily, lured by tales of grandeur, oil wealth, and high wages. As with any frontier society, a certain number of "on the edge" people are lured to Alaska—the reclusives, the individualists, the radicals, and those who stay a scant step ahead of the law. Some, after leaving the Lower 48 rat race behind seek out a self-reliant lifestyle. Many new Alaskans find themselves unable to adjust to the extremes of weather and the country's demands; they soon leave empty-handed and disillusioned.

Today and in the past, what these immigrants share is that they bring to Alaska their cultural traditions and their desire to start a new life in the last frontier. Alaska's folklore is the result of blending the cultural traditions of its diverse immigrant and native populations. Over the past 250 years Alaska's history has been punctuated by a series of boom-and-bust cycles, which has brought European and American immigrants to Alaska in search of fur, whales, gold, copper, salmon, and oil.

The first newcomers to arrive in Alaska were the Russian fur traders in the 1700s, who established a colony and forced

Aleuts and Alutiiqs to hunt sea otter for the lucrative fur trade. The initial impact of the Russian regime on Alaska Natives was devastating. The Alaska Native population was severely reduced, partly through hardship, but mainly through European-introduced smallpox and other diseases. Over time, however, through acculturation, Russian language, foods, customs, and possibly most importantly, the Russian Orthodox religion became an integral part of Alaskan culture.

The next wave of outsiders came in the mid-1800s, when the northern coast of Alaska was occupied by Yankee whalers in search of whale oil and baleen. The commercial whaling industry nearly decimated the bowhead whale population in the Beaufort and Chukchi seas. After gold was discovered in the early 1900s, Alaska was rapidly transformed by the onslaught of hundreds of thousands of immigrants. For the first time in Alaska's history, Euro-Americans outnumbered Native people in the state.

During World War II, bases and airstrips were built and thousands of troops were stationed in Alaska. The military presence resulted in new roads, airstrips, and harbors along with the bases. Many soldiers remained after the war to homestead or live in cities. The U.S. military was also active during the 1950s Cold War. Because of Alaska's strategic location and the growing economic prospect of oil development, Congress was prompted to approve Alaska's statehood in 1958. Although the Russian fur traders, Yankee whalers, gold miners, and World War II troops all brought changes to Alaska, nothing impacted that state as much as the population explosion of newcomers associated with the Trans-Alaska Pipeline construction and the subsequent "oil boom" of the 1970s.

As a group, Alaskans are an independent breed with diverse backgrounds. One trait that ties Alaskans together is their strong connection to their environment. Poet laureate John Haines believes that for Alaskans it is the land that creates the person. It is the environment that challenges and inaugurates the settler into the Alaskan community and the landscape that bonds Alaska Natives to their ancestral home.

What makes Alaska unique is that it is a land of places—in fact, there exist more places than people in Alaska. Alaska's landscape includes lush rain-drenched forests and barren windswept tundras. It boasts of lofty mountains and endless swamps—along with a handful of highrise buildings and uncountable numbers of one-room cabins. With an average of 1.2 square miles (3 km) of land for each resident, Alaskan geography possesses an abundance of diversity. A small sample of Alaska's unique places includes: the confluence of the Talkeetna, Susitna, and Chulitna rivers, a glacier in the Alaska Range, the migratory path of the Porcupine caribou herd, an isolated village located on a volcanic island in the Bering Sea, and a few square blocks in Anchorage.

Alaska, however, is more than just a collection of places. It's a state of mind. Using folklore forms, Alaskans create meaning out of place. Wilderness becomes peopled through folklore, and place-based relationships are expressed through stories, names, material culture, and music. For Alaskans, perception of place is both geographic and cultural. For example, the 1990s statewide Communities of Memory project raised questions about the nature of community and the importance of folklore in maintaining community. During one of the project's storytelling workshops, Aleut storyteller Barbara Svarny Carlson emphasized the geographic aspect of her connection to place: "For me, the place of Unalaska, the rocks, the animals, the plant life, the weather, the view of the constellations and such are unequivocally at least as important as the people when I think of that community" (Morrow, in press). For the Matanuska colony storytellers participating in the Communities of Memory project in Wasilla in 1993, culture played an important role in defining sense of place when they talked about what was required of them to adapt to Alaska. When the colonists arrived, many of them found that they had to develop radical farming and gardening innovations to adjust to harsh winters and a short summer growing season with twenty-four hours of daylight at its peak.

Alaskan folklore is dynamic and varies from person to person, yet it maintains certain qualities that make it familiar and recognizably Alaskan. For example, an Alaskan log cabin builder who came to Alaska in his adult life designs a log house by mimicking local convention. He might use local materials (spruce) and draw on local design that includes a door in the gable while also adding a distinct flare to his notching technique that he learned from a Swedish master log builder. Over time the Swedish notching techniques become incorporated into the community's repertoire of designs.

To be an Alaskan is to learn from first-hand experience, by word of mouth, observation, and imitation. For example, a young Inupiaq Eskimo boy learns to hunt seals first by watching his grandfather, father, and other male relatives hunt, then after assisting his elders on hunts and listening to them he learns to hunt for himself. A young Alaskan child might grow up watching her mother prepare smoked salmon year after year and later remember how to make smoked salmon for her own children.

Folklore serves many functions in Alaska. For example, a secondary science teacher in western Alaska draws on a Yupik legend to enhance their science curriculum to instruct students about the moon and tide. Residents in Talkeetna organize a festival celebrating moose droppings for the purpose of entertaining Alaskans and tourists. Elaborate Tlingit oratory makes kinship and cultural ties public.

Verbal Arts

Verbal arts are a folklore form transmitted in words. The range of verbal arts used in Alaska includes traditional tales, myths legends, personal narratives, jokes, and oratory. Each of the ethnic and occupational groups in Alaska has its own verbal arts. Some stories and narratives are common to many Alaskans. For Alaska Native people, myths and legends act as a communal reservoir for societal values and beliefs. The tradition of storytelling is intrinsic to all Alaska Native cultures. It has been used since ancient times to tell about mythology and family histories, teach life lessons, offer valuable role models, and provide entertainment. Many Alaska Native stories explain how humans were created and changed, and they set forth many rules for the ways people should behave. Among these rules are the taboos people should follow to respect the spiritual power of natural things like plants, animals, or the earth itself. For the Koyukon Athapaskan people, for example, the Distant Time stories serve as a guide to understanding the surrounding world and how to live in it in the right way. English speakers usually think of these stories as only for entertainment, but for contemporary Koyukon, the stories function as a way to validate both Christian and traditional teachings. As does the bible, traditional Koyukon stories explain how the world began, where animals and humans came from, and how all of creation changed as time passed (Attla 1983). According to Koyukon master storyteller Katherine Attla, the stories describe the role of the Raven whose powers are likened to God's, although the Raven had poor manners and was full of trickery. The stories also recalled the Bible's description of a flood that covered the world; in the Koyukon version, plants and pairs of animals survived when the Raven took them onto a raft. Koyukon storytellers often compare this ancient Koyukon story with the Genesis flood to show how much it is like the Bible and as evidence that each tradition supports the truth of the other.

The narratives from the immigrant population focus on different themes and genres than those of the Alaska Native. For example, the story of how a person came to Alaska is a typical immigrant narrative. In contrast to the Alaska Native narratives, Alaska's immigrants share personal narratives that describe their acceptance into the local culture, adapting to the climate and natural environment, the creation of community, outside friends

and relatives' misperception about Alaska, a woman arriving in a white pantsuit and high heel boots to join her already acclimated boyfriend, and the escapades of local folk heroes. These themes are familiar and formulaic and reflect the common traits that Alaskans have chosen to identify as their own, implying that to become Alaskan one must adopt certain Alaskan-specific values, experiences, and understandings.

Jokes are another highly developed verbal genre that non-Natives have developed. Jokes reflect Alaskan attitudes and experiences that validate one's Alaskan status and include misperceptions that people in the Lower 48 have about Alaskans along with boasting and exaggerations about the extreme cold, the wildlife, and living conditions.

Jokes about misperceptions of Alaska by people from the Lower 48:

* You have taken a trip "outside" and tried to cash a traveler's check, from an Alaskan bank, and the cashier asked you the current exchange rate in Alaska.
* You have called an 800 number to order something from a catalog and then were told "Alaska? Oh, we don't ship out of the United States."
* All of your relatives refer to you as that crazy person that lives up north in an igloo.

Extreme cold and weather:

* The trunk of your car doubles as a deep freeze.
* When it warms up to -35 degrees (Fahrenheit) and you go out in your shirtsleeves to wash your car.

* When you drive for a mile on square tires on a -65-degree morning before they eventually become normal.
* When you have to set your alarm every three hours to go start your car and let it run for twenty minutes in hopes that it will start in the morning so you can go to work.
* Instead of plugging in your freezer, you just move it to the front porch!
* You know that the term *break up*[3] has more to do with the weather than personal relationships.

Insects bigger than life and living conditions:

* The most effective mosquito repellent is a shotgun.
* The mosquitoes have landing lights.
* You put up with the pain of a toothache until the Permanent Fund[4] Dividend checks come out in October.
* You open your freezer to take out something for dinner, and are faced with many choices: pink salmon, silver salmon, red salmon, king salmon, smoked salmon, or halibut.
* You're buying a house, and you have to ask for water and electricity as options.

Festivals and Celebrations

Cabin fever, in Alaskan folk terminology, is characterized by restlessness resulting from long dark winters and isolation. As a way to fight off cabin fever, a number of winter festivals and celebrations are organized statewide. One major celebration is the Fur Rendezvous. The Fur Rendezvous is a ten-day-long celebration of Alaska's fur trapping and trading heritage held in Anchorage each February. This event includes a snow sculpture contest, sled dog races, the Miners and Trappers Ball, a parade, fireworks, and a carnival.

Alaska's best-known celebration is the Iditarod, the 1,100-mile sled dog race from Anchorage to Nome that is held each spring. The race begins on a Saturday in early March in downtown Anchorage. The mushers start on Fourth Avenue on streets covered with snow for the event, and then the teams move onto trails that wind through the city and out into the country. Although the first day's race attracts crowds, it is only a ceremonial event. The real racing starts on Sunday after a restart in Wasilla, about fifty miles northeast of Anchorage. During the next week and a half Alaskans keep track of their favorite mushers' progress via TV, radio, and newspaper, as the dog teams cross a thousand miles of wilderness and small checkpoints on their way to Nome on Alaska's northwest coast.

Other Alaska celebrations include Talkeetna's Wilderness Woman competition and Bachelor Ball. Talkeetna is a small community whose proximity to Mt. McKinley makes it a starting point for mountain climbers and flight-seeing tours. This combined festival brings women from all over the country to Talkeetna to test their wilderness skills and later to bid on a bachelor. Another winter festival is the Polar Bear Jump Off Festival held in Seward. For the Polar Bear Plunge, folks dress up in outlandish costumes and dive into Seward's harbor. Seward is the northernmost ice-free seaport in North America, but the water isn't much above freezing.

In the summer there are numerous festivities around the state, especially honoring summer solstice. Each August for many years, residents in Kodiak recalled their Russian heritage with an outdoor pageant, *Cry of the Wild Ram,* a drama that depicts the Alaskan theme of one man's effort to turn a wilderness into a community—it is the story of determination, adversity, treachery, and love, complete with pyrotechnics. The "Wild Ram" was Alexander Baranov, who once headed the Russian-American Company in the United States. The play was discontinued in about 1996 after complaints that the pageant demeaned Alaska Natives and glorified their Russian oppressors.

Material Culture

The creation of material culture is a dynamic process that changes over time. Alaskans are guided to create by their cultural traditions and physical needs. As a result, the purpose of objects can be transformed. For example, although at one time an Inupiaq carved harpoon head and a Chilkat blanket were important for daily and ceremonial use, today they no longer serve this role. Instead they are prized by private art collectors and museums.

Folk traditions are shaped, changed, and created according to the needs and desires of the artists and their surrounding community. One particular folk tradition, caribou masks, started in 1950 in Anaktuvuk Pass. Almost all the residents of Anaktuvuk Pass are Nunamiut, Inupiaq Eskimos who live inland and traditionally relied very heavily on caribou herds. The masks were eventually considered "high-end" tourist art but initially did not possess a cultural significance beyond their souvenir status (Blackman 2001).

In order for an object to be considered a folk craft it must be made for practical use in everyday activities. Ulus are examples of such a craft. An ulu, or woman's knife, is a tool found in most Inupiaq kitchens and used daily to fillet fish and cut up meat. Generally, an ulu is made of a steel blade and a bone or ivory handle. Yet this "craft" item also functions as an icon of Alaskan Native culture and is marketed to tourists in fancy packaging with the handles made from materials not found in Alaska.

Acculturation refers to the borrowing of cultural components by one group from another group as a result of prolonged contact. Spirit houses are an example of the process of acculturation. Spirit houses are located near Anchorage in Eklutna, at the site of the oldest continually inhabited Athabascan community in Alaska. Colorful and decorated spirit houses have been built over the graves of deceased relatives at Eklutna Cemetery. Dating back as far as the 1700s, the crafting of spirit houses results from the melding of Athabascan and Russian Orthodox beliefs and practices. Often a family identifies its clan by using specific colors in their spirit houses. Each grave is also covered with a Russian orthodox cross.

Alaska Native people are able to live directly from the land through hunting, fishing, and gathering. This lifestyle is made up of cultural and spiritual values of respect, sharing, and love of the land. By sharing special foods with one another such as akutuq ("Eskimo ice cream") Yupik people are able to feel a strong connection to the food they eat. Akutaq is a favorite traditional recipe, made by mashing berries together with ingredients that may include seal oil, Crisco (shortening or lard), dried fish, salmon eggs, sugar, and potatoes. Other common Alaska Native foods are smoked and fermented salmon, both of which are gathered, prepared, and consumed in a traditional manner contrasting sharply with mass-produced foods.

Clothing serves several functions. Although garments offer protection from everyday elements, they also communicate information about the person wearing them. Traditional Inupiaq clothing, ingeniously designed to meet the most demanding and inhospitable climatic conditions in the world, is also among the most intricate and aesthetically appealing creations of the worlds' indigenous cultures. Today, Eskimo seamstresses continue to make attractive fur clothing sometimes using new materials, styles, and techniques or sewing garments to be worn in new contexts. Fur clothing has become a key symbol of Eskimo identity and is worn at political meetings, weddings and other formal occasions to stand for Eskimo's ongoing struggle for political, economic, and cultural viability. Clothing can also be seen as a symbolic map of the wearers' social standing. In the past, for example, a chief's elegant fox or sea otter parka marked his station, as did the slave's plain coat of bird skin or seal. Styles of decoration and design reflected the village, gender, and age of the wearer (Lee 2001).

Among nonnatives in Alaska, living in the Last Frontier means more opportunity for individualism. Talkeetna is a community where there are no zoning restrictions, and the average person is free to build unconstrained. As a result, Talkeetna's house types symbolize the relationship among individuals, community conventions, and the physical environment. Talkeetnans make a strong commitment to place, by building houses that fill their cultural landscape with meaning.

Although there has always been a certain degree of variation in Talkeetna's house types, the basic components that make up the homes there have remained invariable over the years. This is due in part to the fact that people in Talkeetna continue to perpetuate the same lifestyle as their predecessors. Their freewheeling lifestyles evolve into an increasing level of permanence as individuals use Talkeetna as a hub from which to operate for seasonal work. Over time the builders make a commitment to the place, and as a result, the house takes on more permanence. The basic cabin design in Talkeetna is the trapper, or sourdough, cabin. Its characteristics are simple and functional, using a box floor plan with low walls and a roof designed to accommodate the weight of the snow or to allow for the snow to slide off. The typical version of this form in Talkeetna is a square or rectangular floor plan with a door and a window in the gable end. Modifications can be adapted from the basic square floor plan to create other shapes as well. Roofs are made of flattened out metal fuel cans painted red, and the chinking between logs consists of whatever is available to the builder: socks, underwear, or moss.

Today Talkeetna's population hovers around six hundred. The community remains an outpost for miners, trappers, climbers, slope workers, weekenders, adventure seekers, and dog mushers. Its simple design of log and frame businesses and homes typify an early twentieth-century trade town. Talkeetna has maintained this colorful mixture up to the present day.

Worldview and Beliefs

A worldview is a system of beliefs that provides a person with a fundamental understanding of how the world works. For Alaska Native people, this system of beliefs is reflected in their close connection to the land, along with shared language, traditions, values, beliefs, and kinship. Alaska Natives' traditional knowledge is handed down from previous generations through oral tradition. This traditional knowledge is the cornerstone of native cultural identity. Some aspects of traditional knowledge are common and shared throughout the Alaska. Other aspects are more localized and specific to certain communities, families, and even individuals.

However, native knowledge is not merely traditional. Alaska Natives also possess knowledge that does not have its origin in traditional lifestyles, spirituality, philosophy, social relations, customs, cultural values, and so on. In other words, Alaska Natives have obtained an extensive body of nontraditional knowledge through direct exposure (e.g., cultural interaction and formal schooling) and indirect exposure (e.g., television and other media) to non-Native values, attitudes, ways of thinking, philosophies, institutions, and the like. Together, these two sources of knowledge, traditional and nontraditional, articulate to produce a frame of understanding and validation that gives meaning to the world around them.

Today in Alaska there is heightened pride in Alaska Native birth and a revival of native culture. Native languages, art, and subsistence skills are now taught in the schools, and the Alaska Native voice is growing stronger in Alaskan politics. Although this is a period of great change for Alaska Natives, for many, the future has never held more promise. Opportunities are now endless for those who manage the precarious balance between two cultures.

Alaska Native religion provides an example of how culture changes over time. The Alaska Native groups who were encountered by the Russians beginning in the eighteenth century adopted Russian customs, language, and Orthodox religion. One religious holiday that combines both Alaska Native and Russian customs is Selaviq, which is celebrated in Russian Orthodox communities in the Yukon-Kuskokwim Delta and elsewhere in Alaska. Communities vary a great deal in how they celebrate this holiday, yet the basic form is the same. The celebration always begins on January 7, Christmas Day according to the Julian calendar. Selaviq contains a mixture of Russian Orthodox (specifically Ukrainian) and American indigenous customs. Traditional Yupik ceremonies in their pure form were discouraged by the Russian priests. Although some people in southwest Alaska identify Selaviq with both Yupik and Orthodox parts, in practice, it is a dynamic, new tradition, unlike any of its Yupik, Russian, or American predecessors and more than the sum of its parts. Modified from decade to decade since its introduction during the 1930s, it remains a strong expression of the values placed on "the teachings of our ancestors" at the same time it creatively reestablishes and reaffirms the integrity of the contemporary Yupik community.

Today the celebration of Selaviq brings together Russian Orthodox, Ukrainian, American, and indigenous systems of knowledge and practice. All contribute to the event that the Yupik people of western Alaska have constructed and continued to modify as a new Yupik tradition. Yupik Eskimos believe Selaviq to be an important part of their own history, which includes but is by no means controlled by their interaction with Russian Orthodox clergy. In fact many Yupik people perceive the Russian Orthodox Church as the repository of traditional Yupik values. The songs they sing, whether in Slavonic or Yupik, are considered to have been passed down from their ancestors. Moreover, the intra- and inter-village feasting associated with Selaviq involves both native and nonnative peoples from all over the region, and is considered typically Yupik (Fienup-Riordan 1990).

Exploring the context of stories, objects, songs, and other folklife traditions in Alaska provides unique insights into Alaska as more than just a place, but rather a state of mind. Alaska's people are independent, adventurous, romantic, and hardworking, but not necessarily in traditional ways. Alaska is a place with a rich history inhabited by people who have impacted its traditions, tradition bearers, folk groups, communities, and distinct regions. By examining the background of Alaska's people, processes, and artifacts, we can understand why certain traditions continue.

In conclusion, Alaska culture is a particular way of life that is learned and acquired by its members, who share certain distinct attitudes, customs, and symbols with one another. Alaskan folklore is a product of historical, geographic, and environmental processes. Alaskan folklore consists of those traditional aspects of our state's culture, which are learned within communities and passed on from generation to generation. Because it is a product of environment and history, Alaskan folklore, in its many facets, uniquely reflects the personality of the state and its communities.

Amy Craver

NOTES

1. According to the 2000 U.S. Census figures.

2. The program's goal was to provide farmers from the Midwest an opportunity to develop agriculture in Alaska.

3. *Break up* is characterized by melting snow and muddy conditions and occurs around March and April.

4. The 1980 Alaska Legislature created the Permanent Fund Dividend Program to distribute a portion of the income of the Permanent Fund each year to eligible Alaskans as a dividend payment. In October 2002, $1540.30 was distributed to every qualified Alaska man, woman, and child.

REFERENCES CITED

Attla, Catherine. *Sitsiy Yugh Noholnik Ts'in': As My Grandmother Told It: Traditional Stories from the Koyukuk.* Fairbanks, AK: Yukon-Koyukuk School District and Alaska Native Language Center, 1983.

Blackman, Margaret. *Faces of the Nunamiut: Maskmaking in Anaktuvuk Pass, Alaska.* Anchorage, AK: Panel of the American Folklore Society Conference, 2001.

Fienup-Riordan, Ann. *Eskimo Essays.* New Brunswick, NJ: Rutgers University Press, 1990.

Lee, Molly. *The Political, Aesthetic and Functional Dimensions of Arctic Clothing.* Anchorage, AK: Panel American Folklore Society Conference, 2001.

Morrow, Phyllis, ed. *Communities of Memory.* Fairbanks: University of Alaska Press, forthcoming.

ALASKA: BIBLIOGRAPHY AND OTHER RESOURCES

Bibliography

Tales and Legends

850. Attla, Catherine. *Bakk'aatuniy: Stories We Live By.* Nenana, AK: Yukon Koyukuk School District and Alaska Native Language Center, 1989. vi, 408p. Told by Catherine Attla. Transcribed by Eliza Jones. Translated by Eliza Jones and Chad Thompson. Illus. by Cindy Davis. 89-14905. 1-55500-025-8pa.

This is Attla's second collection of transcribed stories from the Koyukon people. As before, these tell stories of how the world came to be and developed. Many times the stories are told to influence or shape present-day behavior.

Like the earlier volume, this one presents the stories in both the Koyukon text and in an English translation.

851. ——. *Sitsiy Yugh Noholnik Ts'in': As My Grandfather Told It: Traditional Stories from the Koyukuk.* Nenana, AK: Yukon Koyukuk School District and Alaska Native Language Center, 1983. vi, 408p. Told by Catherine Attla. Transcribed by Eliza Jones. Translated by Eliza Jones and Melissa Axelrod. Illus. 89-14905. 1-55500-025-8pa.

Catherine Attla heard these stories of "the time of long ago" in her childhood. In her turn, she retold them, using them as they have been used in all generations: to explain the past and the present, to teach what is sacred, to teach good behavior, and to guide people in right living.

Many of the stories concern the beginning of the world and the creation of the world's creatures. Others set out rules for human behavior.

The stories are told both in the Koyukon text and in an English translation.

852. Beck, Mary L. *Heroes and Heroines of Tlingit/Haida Legend.* Anchorage: Alaska Northwest Books, 1989. xiii, 113p. Illus. Bibliog. 89-14931. 0-88240-334-6pa.

Stories of southeast Alaska are told here. Beck states in her foreword that the tales "deal . . . with significant events in tribal, clan or family history, with adventures and misadventures of folk heroes, with supernatural forces, and with relationships and interchanges between human and nonhuman beings" (p. ix). She points out that these tales, like all folklore tales, are made up of truth and fiction, metaphors for the truths of the society which created them.

853. Laguna, Frederica de, ed. *Tales from the Dena: Indian Stories from the Tanana, Koyukuk, and Yukon Rivers.* Seattle: Univ. of Washington Press, 1995. xx,

352p. Illus. by Dale DeArmond. Index. List of Sources. 94-41285. 0-295-97429-X.

These tales were collected and recorded in 1935 by Frederica de Laguna, the editor of the present volume, and Norman Reynolds, while on an archaeological expedition to the Yukon Valley. The two recorded the tales in longhand, often both transcribing the same tale from the same teller. The written accounts combine the transcriptions of both.

The editor indicates in her preface that she knows some of the transcriptions are inaccurate, owing to her own youth and inexperience and unfamiliarity with native languages. However, the tales are still absorbing.

The first seventy pages of the book consist of discussions of the lifestyle of the Dena (population, hunting, tools, and so on) and various customs (funeral, clothing, and religion). The last section, about fifty pages, comments on the myths and stories, offering comparisons of these tales with tales told by other groups. In between is the bulk of the book, about two hundred pages of brief tales from the Dena people. The tales are divided up by the geographic area of origin: Nenana, Tanana Mission, Ruby, Koyukuk Station, and Nulato.

The illustrations by Dale DeArmond are black-and-white, in the style of woodcuts.

854. Long, Orma F. *Eskimo Legends and Other Stories of Alaska.* Hicksville, NY: Exposition Press, 1978. 70p. Illus. 0-682-49089-X.

A schoolteacher born in 1886 in North Dakota, Mrs. Long taught in Alaska for a number of years in the early part of the twentieth century. Her slim volume is a mixture of native tales about animals and the natural world; mining and gold rush stories; and more modern-day episodes, such as the story of Wiley Post's and Will Rogers's deaths in an airplane crash.

She also includes some snippets of natural history.

855. Oman, Lela Kiana. *The Epic of Qayaq: The Longest Story Ever Told by My People.* Ottawa: Carleton Univ. Press, 1995. Published simultaneously by the Univ. of Washington Press, Seattle. xx, 119p. Illus. C95-900224-3; 95-51536. 0-88629-267-0 (Canada); 0-295-97531-8 (U.S.) pa.

This traditional epic of the Inupiat tells the story of Qayaq, possessor of supernatural powers, who was charged by his mother with the task of "saving the human race from evil." The epic is the story of his travels. It includes a creation story, a story of a great flood, and a story that mirrors that of Jonah and the Whale.

Oman heard these stories from Inupiat miners and travelers in the mining town of Candle, Alaska, in the 1940s.

Illustrations are of Inupiat art and artifacts, from the Priscilla Tyler and Maree Brooks Collection of Inuit Art, at Carleton University Art Gallery.

856. Oquilluk, William A., with the assistance of Laurel L. Bland. *People of Kauwerak: Legends of the Northern Eskimo.* 2d ed. Anchorage: Alaska Pacific Univ. Press, 1981. xviii, 242p. Maps. Glossary. 0-935094-07-5pa.

These are the old stories of the Inupiat, their stories of creation and of heroic feats, such as the discovery of fire. They were told to William A. Oquilluk, born in 1896, by his grandfather and other elders familiar with the traditions of their people.

857. Smelcer, John E. *The Raven and the Totem: Traditional Alaska Native Myths and Tales.* Anchorage: Salmon Run, 1992. 149p. Illus. Index. Bibliog. 92-146504. 0-9634000-0-2pa.

Smelcher's impetus in collecting and publishing these tales was only partly to preserve the tales themselves, although in his preface he mentions the many inferior and inaccurate collections that have been published. He also wanted to help preserve the various languages of Alaska, and to this end, he collected many of the tales from native speakers. Thus, he feels that these versions are authentic.

Most of the tales concern animals, especially Raven, who made the land, created man, and gave him fire.

858. Swanton, John Reed. *Tlingit Myths and Texts.* Washington, DC: GPO, 1909. viii, 451p. (Smithsonian Institution, Bureau of American Ethnology, Bulletin 39).

Dr. John R. Swanton collected these stories in Sitka and Wrangell, Alaska, in 1904. He presents them here without commentary or explanation. Half of the stories are told only in English; the other half are told with an accompanying text in the native language.

Stories are of animals, humans with supernatural powers, of the importance of following customs and rules, or simply of earlier times.

This is not easy reading and is suitable for those wishing a scholarly study.

859. Wendt, Ron. *Strange, Amazing, True Tales of Alaska.* Wasilla, AK: Goldstream Publications, 1995. 64p. Illus. Bibliog. 95-081491. 1-886574-10-3pa.

Some of the tales told in this paperback are only a paragraph long; others are a page or two. All are of the tall tale variety, the "strange but true" tales of the frontier. Titles include "Man Falls 17,000 Feet and Lives!," "Airplane Flies toward Siberia without Pilot," and "Sea Swallows Men Near Point Hope while Villagers Watch." Tales of mining and fishing abound.

The bibliography is brief, composed mostly of titles of local newspapers, which presumably presented some of these tales. All in all, this is a fun, quick read, of the pamphlet variety.

Folk Music

860. Enrico, John James, and Wendy Bross Stuart. *Northern Haida Songs.* Lincoln: Univ. of Nebraska Press, 1996. xii, 519p. Notes. Index. Bibliog. (Studies in the Anthropology of North American Indians). 96-4211. 0-8032-1816-8. Northern Haida songs are presented in this very scholarly work. The social meaning, the language, and the music are all analyzed. Music is transcribed for many of the songs.

861. Roderick, Barry, ed. *Panhandler's Songbook: Folksongs of Southeast Alaska and the Yukon.* Juneau: Archipelago, Inc., 1979. 95p. Illus.

The seventy-five songs transcribed here were collected by a variety of singer/songwriters in southeast Alaska and the Yukon. The songs deal with occupations (fishing, mining, foresting, oil exploration), with love, and with the land itself. All songs have music transcribed. All are headed by a brief paragraph quoting the singer/songwriter's own thoughts on the song and what it means.

The personalities of the singers come through. Most people feel that folk music belongs to and is created by everyone, not by individuals, and indeed, this book is written by "the people of Southeast [Alaska] and the Yukon," with the help of Roderick and various other editors.

Folk Belief and Ritual

862. Salisbury, O. M. *The Customs and Legends of the Thlinget Indians of Alaska.* New York: Superior Publishing Co., 1962. xii, 275p. Illus. 62-14494.

Most of this book is devoted to a description of everyday life in the tiny village of Klawock, in southeastern Alaska in the early 1920s. The author's parents, Oliver Maxson and Alma Salisbury, were the school principal, schoolteacher, and government advisor to the native peoples there. It was a time when native culture was giving way and being changed by the imported culture of the United States.

Some of the life described involves religious rituals and customs, local medicine, food, holiday celebrations, witchcraft, and marriage.

The author states that his parents' writing "gives insight into the thoughts, the dreams, the joys and the sorrows of both oldsters and moderns . . . , bridging the gulf between the old and the new" (Foreword, p. xii).

Material Culture

863. Chandonnet, Ann. *Alaska's Arts, Crafts, and Collectibles.* Anchorage: Chandonnet Editing & Research, 1998. xiii, 193p. Illus. Index. 98-92499. 0-9662999-0-6.

Everything from dolls to totem poles is described in this book. It is arranged by category and works somewhat like a shopping guide. Each category (beadwork; cedar; gold nugget jewelry, e.g.) contains information about the craft, lists museums where examples can be found, and lists contemporary artisans who are practicing the craft. Illustrations are plentiful.

864. Chaussonnet, Valerie. *Crossroads Alaska: Native Cultures of Alaska and Siberia.* Washington, DC: Arctic Studies Center, National Museum of Natural History, Smithsonian Institution, 1995. 112p. Illus. Maps. Bibliog. 95-804.

Thirteen native groups from Siberia and Alaska are profiled here. They are Inupiaq, Yupik, Alutiiq, Aleut, Athapaskan, Tlingit, Native peoples of the Russian Far East and Chukotka, Siberian Yupik, Chukchi, Koryak, Even, Amur River, and Nivkh. Each profile covers one or two pages of this lavishly illustrated book and includes information on politics, history, ceremonies, and daily life.

Following the group profiles comes the meat of the book: an illustrated catalog of artifacts. This catalog is divided into subject categories: Home; Children: Dolls and Toys; Fashion; Spirits; Cuisine: Food for People, Food for Spirits; People, Animals, and the Land; People, Animals, and the Sea; and Strangers: War, Trade, Contact.

Both the descriptions and the illustrations show how connected the peoples of these two continents are.

865. Graburn, Nelson H. H., Molly Lee, and Jean-Loup Rousselot. *Catalogue Raisonné of the Alaska Commercial Company Collection, Phoebe Apperson Hearst Museum of Anthropology.* Berkeley: Univ. of California Press, 1996. xix, 582p. Illus. Index. Bibliog. (Univ. of California Publications

in Anthropology, v. 21). 95-42187. 0-520-09783-1pa.

The Alaska Commercial Company was founded in 1868. Among its activities were harvesting fur seals and supplying the gold rush miners. The company also collected various artifacts that represented the various native cultures of Alaska. The company donated this vast collection to the University of California in 1897; it is this collection that is photographed and described—item by item—here.

The collection is divided into the following categories:

Hunting and fishing
Transportation
Domestic equipment and
   manufacturing tools
Warfare
Clothing
Dwellings and furnishings
Ritual and ceremonial equipment
Music and musical instruments
Tobacco and snuff
Games, sports, and gambling
Novelties and models made for sale
Child-rearing equipment
Toys
Raw materials and unfinished artifacts

Descriptions and information concerning each artifact is very brief, only a line or two. The index makes it possible to locate a specific item or items used for a specific purpose.

866. Jacobsen, Johan Adrian. *Alaskan Voyage, 1881–1883: An Expedition to the Northwest Coast of America.* Chicago: Univ. of Chicago Press, 1977. xii, 266p. Translated by Erna Gunther. Glossary of Place Names. Index. Bibliog. 77-78066. 0-226-90433-4.

Jacobsen's 1881 exploration of North America is translated here by Erna Gunther. Although it is essentially an anthropological discussion, there is much information about artifacts of daily life—hunting, fishing, and ceremonies. Jacobsen's interaction with the people of the area caused him to learn much about their customs and daily living, including medical procedures, rituals, and religion.

867. Jones, Suzi, ed. *Eskimo Dolls.* Anchorage: Alaska State Council on the Arts, 1982. Illus. Bibliog. 82-620026. 0-910615-00-4.

In the mid-1980s, a traveling exhibit of Eskimo dolls, featuring the work of eighteen doll makers, visited many Alaskan communities. The catalog gives not only descriptions of many of the dolls, with photographs, but also biographical information about the artists, photographs of the artists, and information about the process of doll making.

An essay by Susan W. Fair discusses the history, tradition, and meaning of Eskimo doll making.

868. Osgood, Cornelius. *Ingalik Material Culture.* 1940; repr., New Haven: Human Relations Area Files Press, 1970. 500p. Illus. Bibliog. Index of Manufacturers. 77-118248.

Osgood presents meticulous descriptions—and many line illustrations—on various implements and artifacts of daily life among the Ingalik Indians in Alaska. His notes on each implement include information on material, construction, where and when made, use, method of use, and ownership (usually, man, woman, or child). This is not a book for reading, but for reference.

869. Oswalt, Wendell H., ed. *Modern Alaskan Material Culture.* Fairbanks: Univ.

of Alaska Museum, 1972. 130p. Map. "Project reports under grant no. PO-60-70-3762." pa.

In 1970–1971, the National Endowment for the Humanities funded a study of Native American material culture in Alaska. Some five field investigators and four field assistants visited five sections of Alaska. They collected and described various artifacts used by the people there, including indigenous forms, modified indigenous forms, and items introduced by outsiders.

Aside from the one map of the area that is included, there are no illustrations. Illustrations would have made this more accessible to the more casual student. As it is, this is a scholarly discussion.

Folklore for Children

870. Cothran, Jean, ed. *The Magic Calabash: Folk Tales from America's Islands and Alaska*. New York: David McKay Co., 1956. viii, 88p. Illus. 56-9093.

Stories from Alaska, Hawaii, Puerto Rico, and the Virgin Islands are all included in this book. Many of the stories involve the natural world and its origins; many are about how wit and trickery can outmaneuver strength.

871. Gilham, Charles E. *Eskimo Folk-Tales from Alaska*. London: Batchworth Press, 1955. 142p. Illus.

Gilham spent two summers with the native peoples of Hooper Bay, south of Nome. He heard most of these tales from one of the elders, a man who had studied the ways of the Medicine Man. Many of the tales have a lesson or moral.

872. Johnston, Thomas F., and Tupou L. Pulu, compilers. *Yup'ik Eskimo Songs.*

Anchorage: National Materials Development Center, Rural Education, University of Alaska, 1982. viii, 84p. Illus.

Written for use in the classroom, this small book includes dance songs, story songs, and game songs. An introduction provides ideas for teachers. All the songs have music transcribed, and each contains an explanation of the story it tells, or of the game or dance that accompanies it.

Many of the songs are illustrated with line drawings.

873. Rasmussen, Knud. *The Eagle's Gift: Alaska Eskimo Tales*. Garden City, NY: Doubleday, Doran and Co., 1936. xiv, 235p. translated by Isobel Hutchinson. Illus. by Ernst Hansen.

Short tales, mostly concerning animals, fill this volume. They are illustrated with both black-and-white and color sketches.

874. Ticasuk. *Tales of Ticasuk: Eskimo Legends and Stories*. Fairbanks: Univ. of Alaska Press, 1987. xxv, 134p. Illus. 87-081286. 0-912006-24-2.

The story of the author/teller of these tales is as fascinating as the tales themselves. Ticasuk, daughter of a Russian American-Eskimo father and an Eskimo mother, was born in 1904 and raised in the frontier of Alaska. Education was her passion; she acquired several degrees, including a posthumous Doctorate of Humane Letters, and was still studying at the time of her death.

Her distress at the loss of her culture because of the increasing pressures of civilization on Alaska inspired her to try to preserve as much of it as she could. She transcribed legends collected from her eldest neighbors, worked on a dictionary of the Malimiut dialect of the Inupiaq language, helped develop a curriculum guide for teaching the Inupiaq language and culture, and worked on an encyclopedia of Eskimo life and culture.

These tales, told simply enough for children, deal with animals, people who change into animals, tricksters, and heroes.

875. Wallis, Velma. *Bird Girl and the Man Who Followed the Sun: An Athabaskan Indian Legend from Alaska.* Fairbanks: Epicenter Press, 1996. 224p. Illus. 96-32679. 0-945397-34-8pa.

Daagoo and Bird Girl, a boy and girl belonging to different tribes, both were different from other members of the group—restless and wandering, wanting to follow no rules but their own. In this twentieth-century retelling of the tale for children, Wallis adds many events to the bare bones of the story. The two leave their home groups, travel widely to the Land of the Sun, but in the end find that they must go home and reconcile with their traditions, even while their travels have left them richer.

Literary Authors: A Selected List

Below is a selected list of authors who reflect and interpret the history and atmosphere of their region. These are authors of novels, poems, short stories, or reminiscences. Through reading the works of these authors, one can acquire knowledge of the history, people, and flavor of the region. This is not a complete list, either of authors, or of their works, but rather one calculated to start readers exploring and discovering their own favorites.

Barbeau, Marius, 1883–1969

The Indian Speaks

Pathfinders in the Northern Pacific
The Tree of Dreams

Leopold, Aldo, 1886–1948

For the Health of the Land: Previously Unpublished Essays and Other Writings
The River of the Mother of God and Other Essays

Michener, James, 1907–1997

Alaska

Muir, John, 1838–1914

Letters from Alaska
Mountaineering Essays
Muir among the Animals: The Wildlife Writings of John Muir
My First Summer in the Sierra
The Story of My Boyhood and Youth
Travels in Alaska

Woodward, Caroline, 1952–

The Alaska Highway Two-Step
Disturbing the Peace

Museums of the State: A Selected List

Museums that feature everyday life abound in all regions of the country. Through the display of clothing, farm implements, household goods, industrial tools, or entire houses, workshops, and communities, these museums can help people of today understand and appreciate the lives lived by those who came before. The list below is not a complete list of museums in the region, but by browsing through it, one can get a glimpse of the richness of museum offerings. Explore on your own and discover even more fascinating museums.

Anaktuvuk Pass

The Simon Paneak Memorial Museum
341 Mekiana Road
Anaktuvuk Pass, Alaska 99721
Mailing address:
P.O. Box 21085
Anaktuvuk Pass, Alaska 99721
907-661-3413
*http://www.nsbsd.k12ak.us/villages/akp/
    museum/paneak.htm*

Anchorage

Anchorage Museum of History and Art
121 West Seventh Avenue
Anchorage, Alaska 99501
907-343-6172
http://www.ci.anchorage.ak.us

Oscar Anderson House Museum
420 M Street
Anchorage, Alaska 99501
907-274-2336
http://alaskan.com/akencinfo/oscar.html

Dillingham

Samuel K. Fox Museum
Seward and D Streets
Dillingham, Alaska 99576
Mailing address:
P.O. Box 273
Dillingham, Alaska 99576
907-842-5610
http://www.nushtel.com/~dlgchmbr

Fairbanks

Dog Mushing Museum
535 2nd Avenue
Coop Plaza
Fairbanks, Alaska 99708
Mailing address:
P.O. Box 80136
Fairbanks, Alaska 99701
907-456-6874

Haines

Alaska Indian Arts
Historical Building #13
Fort Seward
Haines, Alaska 99827
Mailing address:
P.O. Box 271
Haines, Alaska 99827
907-766-2160
http://www.alaskaindianarts.com

Sheldon Museum and Cultural Center
11 Main Street
Haines, Alaska 99827
Mailing address:
P.O. Box 269
Haines, Alaska 99827
907-766-236
http://sheldonmuseum.org

Juneau

Alaska State Museum
395 Whittier
Juneau, Alaska 99801
907-465-2901
http://www.museums.state.ak.us

House of Wickersham State Historical
    Site

213 Seventh Street
Juneau, Alaska 99801
Mailing address:
400 Willoughby Avenue
Juneau, Alaska 99801
907-465-4563
http://www.dnr.state.ak.us/parks

Kake

Kake Tribal Heritage Foundation
422 Totem Way
Kake, Alaska 99830
907-785-3258

Ketchikan

Totem Heritage Center
601 Deermount
Ketchikan, Alaska 99901
Mailing address:
629 Dock Street
Ketchikan, Alaska 99901
907-225-5900
http://www.city.ketchikan.ak.us

Metlakatla

Duncan Cottage Museum
501 Tait Street
Metlakatla, Alaska 99926
Mailing address:
P.O. Box 8
Metlakatla, Alaska 9926
907-886-441

Sitka

Sheldon Jackson Museum
104 College Drive

Sitka, Alaska 99835
907-747-8981
http://www.museums.state.ak.us

Wrangell

Wrangell Museum
318 Church Street
Lower Level
Wrangell, Alaska 99929
Mailing address:
P.O. box 1050
Wrangell, Alaska 99929
907-874-3770
http://www.wrangell.com

Journals in Folklore of the State: A Selected List

The journals in the list below publish articles on folklore of the region. Some are scholarly; others are more popular. Many other journals and newsletters exist. Often, these are smaller, of more local interest, and published by museums, historical societies, folklore organizations, community groups, and schools. Explore your own area to see what other publications of folklore exist.

> *Alaskan Folklorian*
> *Forget-Me-Not*

Web Sites: A Selected List

Below is a list of a few Web sites dealing with folklore of the region. You can find other Web sites by doing an Internet search on a search engine such as Google or Yahoo!, or by looking for the Web sites of various folklore organizations with which you are familiar.

Alaska Folk Dance, http://www.folkdancing. org/alaska.html
Linked from the homepage of the Folk Dance Association, this is specific to events, performers, performances, classes, and groups to join in Alaska.

Alaska Folk Festival, http://www.juneau. com/aff/
Home page for the Folk Festival, with links to its schedule, newsletter, and events from past festivals.

Alaskan Folk Music and More, http://www. mosquitonet.com/~gcn/
Links to events and happenings in the world of folk music, including specific performances as well as festivals.

American Folklore: Alaska, http://www. americanfolklore.net/folktales/ak.html
A link from the American Folklore Website (www.americanfolklore.net) allows you to choose a state for its folklore. The Alaskan offering is "The First Tears," about the origin of tears.

Legends and Folklore of the Northern Lights, http://stories.freeweb-hosting.com/ webdoc96.htm
Folklore which derives from the fascination with the northern lights, or Aurora Borealis, much of which attempts to explain the origins of the lights.

LitSite Alaska, http://litsite.alaska.edu/uaa/
Contains information on Alaskan traditions, and traditional tales.

Hawaii

Look for tales on:

Fishing
Tricksters
Kapu
Individual islands

And for characters such as:

Pele
Maui
Captain James Cook
Kama-pua'a
Kamehameha
Kane
Ku

Look for collections by:

W. D. Westervelt
Mary Kawena Pukui

Laura Green
Thomas Thrum

Introduce children to:

Menehune
Maui

Explore the rich literature of the state with:

James Michener
Jack London
Helen M. Swanson

HAWAII: INTRODUCTION

Aloha![1] The realm of ancient Hawaiian myths and legends abounds with supernatural beings, such as gods and goddesses, *aumakua* (family guardian-spirits), *mo'o* (lizard-beings), mythical *menehune* (little people), and many more. Stories about these magical beings help us to gain a better insight into the mysteries of ancient Hawaiian culture. In doing so, we gain a better understanding of not only contemporary Hawaiian culture but also that of the world at large. The worldview reflected in the oral traditions of Hawaii reveals a tropical island culture that was once based on surviving in an environment with limited natural resources. This meant living in harmony with nature, which often also meant maintaining a harmony with the spiritual realm. Thus even the simple act of drinking water meant more than just a basic function for physical survival, but could also be understood as the partaking of a blessing from the gods Kane and Kanaloa (Beckwith 1970, 64; Pukui 1994, 94). The Hawaiian belief that all natural and human-made objects possessed *mana,* or spiritual energy, further indicated the strong interrelationship between the physical and spiritual worlds.

The aim of this essay is to help the reader of the sources listed in Terry Ann Mood's bibliography to better use Hawaiian folklore in our everyday lives. Perhaps by making some rudimentary connections between traditional Hawaiian folklore and our complex lives in today's society, we can better appreciate the value of folklore in helping us to enrich the quality of our lives. In particular, by learning how the early Hawaiians re-spected physical nature along with its spiritual dimensions, we might learn how to better cope with the stress and anxieties experienced in today's sometimes fast-paced world.

The Early Polynesians

Scholars suggest that the word *hawaii* means "the little Java" or "the burning Java" and may have its roots in "the modern Zaba or Saba on the Arabian seacoast" (Westervelt 1926, 37). The Lapita people, ancestors of the Polynesians, spread eastward into the Pacific from their homelands in northwestern Melanesia, perhaps as early as 1600 B.C.E. (Abbott 1992, 1). The Lapita first arrived in the western Polynesia islands of Tonga roughly around 1000 B.C.E., and in Samoa about 1200 B.C.E. By the beginning of the Christian era, when settlers from Samoa landed in the Marquesas Islands, the transition from Lapita to Polynesian culture was well under way (Abbott 1992, 3). Marquesan voyagers arrived in Hawaii sometime between 300 and 750 C.E. and the Tahitians followed later, arriving between 1000 and 1250 C.E. (Mitchell 1992, 11). Most scholars today would agree on the general pattern of Polynesian settlement, but the dates are still being negotiated. A uniquely Hawaiian culture is believed to have been established by approximately 1100 C.E. (Abbott 1992, 10).

One aspect of the uniqueness of Hawaiian culture lies in the excellence, innovation, and creativity of its arts and crafts or "material culture." This is not to say that the arts and crafts of other Polynesian groups bear less merit, but rather that many Hawaiian artifacts stand out even in a field of other rich and notewor-thy Polynesian counterparts. Some of the areas in which Hawaiians excelled in-clude: featherwork (Young 1999, 49), *kapa* barkcloth (Buck 1964, 166), and plaited *makaloa* sedge sleeping mats (Mitchell 1992, 104). Even the *auwai* aqueduct sys-tem (Abbott 1992, 9) of the Hawaiians was notable. Thus Hawaiian culture flour-ished in spite of the precariousness of is-land living.

The Value of Folklore in Establishing Our[2] Identity

The role that oral traditions (stories, songs, proverbs, etc.) play in contempo-rary society can be compared to the re-flections we see on shiny surfaces, such as mirrors, glass, water, and so on. Reflected images are "real" because they exist, but they are not tangible; they are not the source objects themselves. Oral traditions are the same way; they exist all around us, but because they are not tangible, we often look right through them or do not even see them at all. But the value of *mo'olelo* (oral traditions) is that they re-flect our past, our heritage, and by so do-ing, they help us to know who we are (see Oring 1994). As our own reflections in a mirror help us to groom our self-image by allowing us to put on our makeup, comb our hair, and so forth, folklore also helps us to shape our identity. Our reflec-tions in the mirror are not really us, but they help us to see what our merits and deficiencies are. Folklore serves the same purpose as our own reflections in a mir-ror; they are not us physically, but oral traditions help us to see who we are and from where we came.

If we understand the values of our an-cestors, we can more clearly see how our past affects our present as well as our fu-ture. The shaping of our individual and collective identity is conceivably a matter of choice to a certain degree. Do we con-sciously choose to embrace our cultural heritage, weigh its highlights and darker moments, and incorporate the balance into our lives? Or do we choose to look right through *mo'olelo* traditions and not enjoy the rich associations between the sweet fragrance of *maile* (*Alyxia olivae-formis*) and the enchanting music of the ti-leaf flute of Kahalaomapuana still echoing in the rainforest of Paliuli? (See Beckwith 1970, 526; Colum 1925, 137; Pukui 1994, 158; Wichman 1998, 120.)

Two Values of Traditional Hawaiian Culture: Conservation and Generosity

Two basic concepts of traditional Hawai-ian fishing culture were the conservation of fish resources and the fair and gener-ous distribution of the fish catch (Kawa-harada 1992, *xii*). One can safely extend these two concepts to Hawaiian culture in general. Abiding by these two precepts meant survival in a time before the con-venience and stability of canned or flash-frozen foods. The consequences could be fatal for not obeying the rules of conser-vation, or the *kapu* system (see introduc-tion to Kawaharada 1992). The virtue of being "generous" with certain resources, especially to strangers, is exemplified in the following narrative:

The Springs of Ko'olau Loa

Two strangers came to Ko'olau Loa on O'ahu, two tall fine-looking men. The eye-ball of the sun was sinking in the west, and the men were thirsty and tired. "Here are good houses," said one, "and over there is a spring. Let us ask here for drink and rest."

"E!" the men called. "Have you water for thirsty travelers?"

Two old people came to the doorway. "We have no water for strangers," said the man. The travelers glanced toward the spring which bubbled out and formed a little stream. "That is only enough for ourselves," the old man added quickly.

"Be on your way!" called the old woman. "We want no strangers here." And the two stood blocking their doorway.

Without a word the tall men walked away. Close to the shore they found another home. "These houses are small," one of the men remarked. "No room for strangers here! And I don't see any spring."

"Aloha!" called a friendly voice. "You are welcome! Come and eat." An old man hurried toward them from the little home.

"We are thirsty," said the travelers, "but you have no spring."

"Oh yes, we a have a spring," the old man answered. "It is in the ocean's edge, and the water is a little salty, but better than none. I'll fill the water gourds." He led the strangers to his eating house, brought water, and set food before them.

When they had eaten, he led them to the sleeping house. "Your mats are ready," he told them.

The two looked about. "Those are your mats," they answered. "Where shall you sleep?"

"Right here," said the old woman quickly, showing them a mat laid on the floor. "We like a cool place when the night is warm."

"You are kind," the tall men told her. "We hope you will not feel the hardness of the pebbles underneath your mat."

The old folks did not feel the pebbles. They slept well and when they woke their guests were gone. "Why did they leave so early?" asked the man in disappointment. "I should have given them food." He went to fill the water gourd and gave his wife a drink.

She tasted, then looked at him in surprise. "Where did this water come from?"

"From our spring, there in the ocean's edge. Is the water very salty?"

"It is not salty at all," she told him. "Taste it. It is cool and fresh." He tasted, and the two looked at each other wondering.

Later they heard that the spring nearer the mountains had turned salty in the night. That was the spring of which the owner said, "Its water is only enough for ourselves."

"Our visitors were two gods," the kind man said to his wife. "It was well I gave them drink and food."

"You did for them what you do for all who come," his wife replied. "Now we shall have good water for our guests."

—From the *Tales of the Menehune*, Pukui, pp. 90–92.

In essence, the above tale exemplifies the "aloha spirit." The kind old couple can be seen as the embodiment of the "ideal Hawaiian," because of their generous act of sharing what little they had with their visitors—gods or mortals alike. The lesson in the above narrative is similar to the moral of many biblical passages, which arguably could have influenced Hawaiian mythology (see Thrum 1917, 15). One such example is the parable of the widow's mite, in which the poor widow gives to the temple the only money on which she has to live. She is praised for her generosity, not because her monetary contribution was greater than those of the other worshippers, but because the proportion of her offering compared to her few assets was much greater than those who gave from their vast stores of wealth. The moral of the parable and the Hawaiian tale is to be as generous as we can to others. In contemporary Hawaiian society, people living in urban areas would think we were *pupule* (crazy) if we yielded our house and home to total strangers or to the *hale pule* (place of worship). But the lesson of simply being generous to others is still applicable in our world today. Human beings will likely always respond to the kindnesses shown us; generosity begets generosity, whether in the mythical past or in times present. As stated in the introduction to Padraic Colum's *At the Gateways of the Day,* "All human desire is the same" (1924, xv). And Kawaharada sums up the lesson by saying, "stinginess makes human life, which is intrinsically communal, impossible" (1992, xxvii). The lessons taught in old Hawaiian folklore still have great relevance today.

A Note on the Term *Folklore*

At this juncture, a brief discussion on the meaning of *folklore* might prove helpful. The common understanding of the term *folklore* generally denotes *oral traditions* such as myths, legends, folktales, ghost stories, and the like. However, professional and academic folklorists define the scope of folklore in a broader way. As Mood points out in the introduction to this book, various scholars and sources define the term differently, but most would agree that the items of folklore are based on "tradition," oral transmission, and change or adaptation. The juxtaposition of *tradition* and *change* might seem contradictory at first but the concept becomes clearer when we look at how some traditional-style sailing canoes, such as the Hokule'a, are now being built of plywood, fiberglass, and resin rather than traditional natural materials such as koa wood (Voyaging Traditions Web site; Chun 1995, 65). The design or process may stay the same (tradition), but the materials may differ (change).

Most folklorists today also tend to make a distinction between *folklore* and *folklife*. When doing so, *folklore* usually refers to oral traditions, and *folklife* denotes activities such as building *imu* ovens, dancing the hula, practicing *la'au lapa'au* (native Hawaiian medicine), and so on. *Folklife* also includes the resulting or related products from such activities (*kulolo* pudding, *pahu* drums, *lomi* sticks, etc.). These objects are called *material culture*. But, for convenience sake, folklorists also use the word *folklore* as an umbrella-term to denote *folklife* and all its subcategories such as *material culture, folk medicine, folk belief, folk dance, folk music, folk games,* and so on. Thus, in general, folklorists define and use the term *folklore* in a much broader way than just meaning the oral traditions of myths, legends, folktales, and the like, but also include the areas of *folklife* as well.

Two more important points concerning *folklore* deserve to be mentioned here.

First, the term *folklore,* while referring to the items of folklore itself, also refers to the study or profession of folklore as well. Sometimes clarification is necessary to distinguish whether an author is referring to the items of folklore or to the scholarly discipline, but usually the intent is clear from the context. Folklore, as a discipline, is very similar to anthropology, but folklorists tend to gather data by using fieldwork techniques, in other words, interviewing knowledgeable practitioners of a folklore tradition. Along with this fieldwork base, folklorists tend to focus on "tradition"—to study the ways that a tradition is generated, assessed, modified, and transmitted. Folklorists also tend to focus on the individual aesthetic expression in relation to its greater community or to start with a particular tradition then situate it in its larger cultural context (see Glassie 1999).

To illustrate the above example, folklorists might look at how *kapa* (barkcloth)-maker Pua Van Dorpe, in the early 1980s, successfully reproduced a *kilohana* (decorated bedcover) through painstaking research and experimentation. A folkloristic approach would probably follow a method similar to that used by ethnobotanist Isabell Aiona Abbott in her treatment of *kapa*-making (Abbott 1992, 49–58), or that of David Young (1999, 42–48). But, along with culturally oriented accounts of *kapa*, which cover its historical production and use, folklorists would probably also interview Van Dorpe to document her trial-and-error learning process. Folklorists would also inquire about the aesthetics of *kapa*-making: Do modern-day *kapa*-makers still strive to meet the standards of old, which considered well-made *kapa* to be "clearer than moonlight; clearer than the snow on the mountains" (Kamakau 1976, 113). Also, folklorists would be interested in the modifications to the traditional process or materials necessary to produce modern-day *kapa*. Inquiries would be made as to whether new materials were being incorporated into the traditional process, much like the construction of the Hokule'a sailing canoe. Current folkloristic research would also discuss the tension resulting from issues surrounding the significance of *kapa*-making to contemporary Hawaiian culture. The issues are many: the integrity of revival art, politics of culture, identity politics, race and gender concerns, cultural versus environmental conservation, repatriation, sovereignty, and so on. Essentially, folklorists today, as well as other ethnologists, tend to focus on how people make sense of the world by understanding the people's ethos or identity. But the folkloristic approach usually looks at a specific aesthetic expression, such as *kapa*-making, through a variety of lenses, such as oral tradition, history, art history, linguistics, literature, religion, politico-economics, archaeology, and science. The resulting composite perspective gives us a broader understanding of the values of Hawaiian culture, both past and present, and the place of *kapa* in it. The aforementioned characteristics of the folklore discipline: favoring fieldwork-based research techniques, brokering tradition, and focusing on the individual aesthetic expression in relationship to the larger community are just a few distinctions of the discipline. But as Mood begins the introduction to this book, "There are probably as many definitions of folklore as there are folklorists." (p. xiii).

The second point regarding folklore concerns the word *tradition*. In recent decades scholars have reexamined the concept of *tradition*. No longer does the term refer only to a process handed down through time, but now it also refers to the spatial repetition of a process. A good example of this is the circulation of urban legends over the Internet. Within a rather short span of time, the distribution or repetition of an urban legend, can encompass the globe. So folklore isn't just "old" traditions anymore, but also "new" ones (pop culture) as well. And the *folk* in *folklore* doesn't necessarily refer just to the people of a bygone era, rural locality, or tribe, but rather, it can refer to those of us still living today. Thus, folklorists who are interested in pop culture could conceivably study the "traditions" of current Hawaiian aesthetic expressions, such as the "Eddie Would Go" big-wave surf contests[3], Protect Kaho'olawe Ohana activities[4], Jawaiian music[5], *li hing* powder recipes[6], and so on. Potential folklore material constantly fills the pages of Honolulu's two daily newspapers, especially the "Island Life" or "Today" sections.

The Sourcebook Bibliography

The sourcebook bibliography is probably best used as a basic foundation on which to expand one's own research on Hawaiian folklore. New readers will likely discover favorite items on the list and perhaps be led to other items of interest. However, informed readers might be puzzled at the omission of certain indispensable items from the list or question the inclusion of others. But as Mood states in the introduction to this book, "None of these supplementary lists is meant to be complete. The field is simply too vast to make that claim. They are, rather, representational . . ." (p. xvi). The bibliography offers the reader a broad spectrum of sources with which to further pursue

one's own interests. The listings of books, authors, Web sites, and museums offer a variety of information from the consecration of human sacrifice (Valeri 1985, 49) to the sleep-inducing qualities of *liliko'i* (passion fruit) flower tea (Corum 1985a, 105).

The observant reader will notice that the items listed on the sourcebook bibliography travel along two axes of Hawaiian culture: traditional and cosmopolitan. The majority of the items deal with traditional Hawaiian culture, such as the oral traditions or material culture peculiar to Hawaii or Polynesia: legends of the fire-goddess *Pele,* using *ti* leaves (*Cordyline fruticosa*) as a protective amulet, and catching octopus with *leho* (cowrie shell) lures. Cosmopolitan Hawaiian culture reflects the eclectic mixing of different immigrant traditions in contemporary Hawaii, such as the widespread Chinese custom of "playing firecrackers" on New Years' Day, the Japanese etiquette of taking off one's footwear before entering people's homes, or the Filipino *bitor* tradition of offering money to the newlywed couple during the first dance at wedding receptions (Clarke 1994, 46).

One of the features of the sourcebook bibliography is its emphasis on "accessibility." For readers living in Hawaii, the items listed (books and audiotape material) are all accessible through the Hawaii State Library system. The references and bibliographies contained in many of these books will likely lead the reader to other related sources that may be more specialized or less accessible. Another good strategy to find a wealth of related material is to visit one's local library and peruse the Hawaiian section. The reference librarians are generally quite helpful and knowledgeable in finding specific information.

Critics of the sourcebook bibliography might remark on the heavy emphasis on the oral traditions of Hawaiian folklore rather than items of folklife. But these traditional *mo'olelo* provide a secure understanding of the Polynesian roots of Hawaiian culture; the legends of the god Maui are an excellent example of an oral tradition that is shared by all Polynesian cultures (Beckwith 1970, 226; Colum 1924, 7; Pukui 1994, 18; Westervelt 1987, vii). The different Polynesian versions help us to see the commonalities within a large triangle of related Pacific island cultures: Tonga, Samoa, Tahiti, Aotearoa (New Zealand), Rapa Nui, Hawaii, and so on. However, according to Beckwith, it is the legends of the fire goddess Pele, rather than the Hawaiian versions of the Maui legends, that help us to see the uniqueness of Hawaiian culture (1970, 4). Thus this comparative aspect of oral traditions, as well as material culture, adds a new dimension to the reflections of Hawaiian culture: It leads us to see beyond the immediacy of Hawaiian culture into a greater network of Polynesian lineage.

The reader interested in Hawaiian folklife will find the topic addressed under the categories of *Folk Belief and Ritual* and *Material Culture*. But sometimes these categories of folklore may be confusing or misleading because of the porous boundaries between the genres that allow for great crossover. For example, the sourcebook bibliography appropriately lists *hula pahu* (drum dances) under *folk music;* but we could also conceivably list it under *tales and legends* because of its narrative chants, under *folk belief and ritual* because of its use and function, and also under *material culture* because of the many objects connected with its performance. Nonetheless, these genres of folklore are helpful in organizing the material in a useable and systematic way. And, although the sourcebook bibliography does emphasize oral traditions, the *mo'olelo* can lead us to other genres of folklore, as in the case of hula.

Another feature of the sourcebook bibliography is the combination of both serious scholarship as well as items of humor for both children and adults. The annotations by Mood for each item will help the reader to discern the academic nature or content of the items. The first two items on the list are particularly noteworthy for the intensity of their scholarship: Martha Beckwith's *Hawaiian Mythology* and Valeri Valerio's *Kingship and Sacrifice.* Notable books on the other end of the spectrum that offer lighter reading are Ann Kondo Corum's two cosmopolitan works *Folk Remedies from Hawaii* and *Folk Wisdom from Hawaii* . A practical feature of the sourcebook bibliography is the inclusion of the section on children's folklore; what better way to promote and perpetuate folklore than by awakening our children's excitement of it?

Conclusion

Martha Warren Beckwith (1871–1959), a folklorist, published *Hawaiian Mythology* in 1940. Her body of work continues to serve as a reliable source for those studying Hawaiian and Polynesian folklore. The thoroughness of her scholarship and the importance placed on documenting oral traditions in the native Hawaiian language reflects her training under Franz

---

**ABRIDGED GUIDE TO THE PRONUNCIATION
OF HAWAIIAN WORDS**

Unstressed Vowels	*Stressed Vowels*
a = *a* as in *above*	a,a = *a* as in *far*
e = *e* as in *bet*	e = *e* as in *bet*
i = *i* as in *city*	e, e = *ay* as in *pay*
o = *o* as in *sole*	i, i = *ee* as in *see*
u = *u* as in *moon*	o, o = *o* as in *sole*
ʻ = a glottal stop, as in *oh-oh*	u, u = *oo* as in *moon*

Based on the *Hawaiian Dictionary* (Pukui 1986, xvii)

Boas, one of the founders of the American Folklore Society (Beckwith 1970, ix). Regarding the relationship of Hawaiian oral traditions to that of the rest of Polynesia, Beckwith writes, "A close comparative study of the tales from each group should reveal local characteristics, but for our purpose the Polynesian race is one, and its common stock of tradition, . . . repeats the same adventures among similar surroundings and colored by the same interests and desires" (Beckwith 1997, 297).

Thus, Beckwith sees Hawaiian oral traditions as displaying more similarities than differences with other Polynesian repertories. More so than Hawaiian material culture with its many unique developments, Hawaiian oral traditions can be seen to maintain the "common stock" of their Polynesian origins.

Beyond this connection between Hawaiian and Polynesian oral traditions Beckwith also draws a further connection to the world at large:

In theme the body of Polynesian folk tale is not unlike that of other . . . story-loving people. It includes . . . philosophy—stories of cosmogony and of heroes who shaped the earth; . . . annals—migration stories, tales of culture heroes, of conquest and overrule . . . romance—tales of competition, of vengeance, and of love; . . . wit—of drolls and tricksters; and . . . fear in tales of spirits and the power of ghosts. These divisions are not individual to Polynesia; they belong to universal delight; but the form each takes is shaped and determined by the background, either of real life or of life among the gods, familiar to the Polynesian mind. (1997, 299)

By understanding this universal connection of Hawaiian and Polynesian folklore to that of all humankind, we can more clearly see that we as human beings are more similar than different. In this way, folklore, both the traditions themselves and the discipline, can be incorpo-

GLOSSARY OF HAWAIIAN TERMS

aloha–a greeting of friendship or love

aumakua–family or personal god

auwai–ditch mainly for irrigation and sometimes for household purposes

hale pule–church, chapel, *Lit. house (of) prayer*

Hokule'a–the name of the first replica of an ancient Polynesian voyaging canoe built in 1974 by the Polynesian Voyaging Society

hula–the dance tradition of Hawaii basically classified as either ancient (*kahiko*) or modern-style

imu–an underground oven

Ka-hala-o-mapuana–the youngest sister below the four maile sisters; *Lit. the wafting fragrance of the pandanus fruit*

Kanaloa–one of the four great gods; constant companion of Kane, who together found water in many places

Kane–a god of sunlight, creation, fresh water, forests; the leading god of the Hawaiian pantheon

kapa–tapa; barkcloth; *Lit. the beaten thing*

kapu–sacred; forbidden

kilohana–the decorated top-sheet of usually a five-layered barkcloth quilt

koa–the largest of native forest trees known for the beauty of its wood; *Acacia koa*

Ko'olau Loa–a district name on O'ahu island

kulolo–a sweet pudding made of baked or steamed grated taro and coconut milk

la'au lapa'au–medicine, *Lit. curing medicine*

leho–general name for cowrie shell

liliko'i–passion fruit; grows on a vine and after straining its many seeds, the juice is used to flavor desserts and beverages; *P. edulis f. flavicarpa*

lomi–to rub; to massage, a lomi stick is designed for self-massage purposes

maile–a sweet-smelling native shrub used for decoration and lei; *Alyxia olivaeformis*

makaloa–a perennial sedge used to make fine mats on the island of Niihau; *Cyperus laevigatus*

mana–spirit, energy, power

menehune–Legendary race of small people who worked at night, building fish ponds, roads, temples

mo'o–lizard, reptile, dragon; water spirit

mo'olelo–story, tale, history, tradition, legend

na–particle indicating a plural, as in *na mo'olelo* (stories, tales, etc.)

ohana–family; related

pahu–a drum with a base usually carved out of a coconut trunk and covered with cured shark skin

Paliuli–paradise; traditionally believed to be located in the upland forests of Puna

Pele–the volcano goddess

pupule–crazy, insane

ti–the various parts of this versatile plant has many uses as food, clothing, shelter, decoration, and the like; *Cordyline terminalis* rated into our daily lives to illuminate our past, identify ourselves in the present, and inform our future. Folklore can help us to alleviate the pressures of daily living simply by showing us how other people, both past and present, have learned to cope under similar conditions. If we are able to look beyond the specifics of a tradition, that is, to see how Polynesia is related to the seven other U.S. regions covered in this book and also to the rest of the world, folklore can be very useful in a curative way. Don't many of the testimonies emanating from the 9-11 tragedies bear witness to the lesson of generosity expressed earlier in "The Springs of Ko'olau Loa"? Thus folklore can be quite useful in our contemporary lives despite any seeming contradictions, confusing symbolisms, or apparent irrelevance to the world in which we live.

Reflected in the folklore of Hawaii are the universal principles governing a people conscious of the interrelationship between the natural environment, material culture, and the spiritual world. Let us apply this worldview of the early Hawaiians to help us to better understand our own identity, whether Hawaiian or otherwise, and our place in the world at large.

Alfred Kina

NOTES

1. See Abridged Guide to the Pronunciation of Hawaiian Words on page 414; a glossary of Hawaiian terms appears on page 415.

2. The term *our* is used in the broad sense throughout this essay to include "Hawaiians-at-heart."

3. The Quicksilver In Memory of Eddie Aikau Big Wave Invitational, originated in 1986, commemorates the legendary figure who lost his life in an ill-fated Hokule'a voyage. Eddie Aikau (1946–1978) was noted for his skill and enthusiasm in riding the big waves (forty feet) on O'ahu's North Shore. He lost his life in 1978 when attempting to paddle for help off the coast of Lana'i Island after the Hokule'a, on which he was a crewmember, had swamped. "Eddie would go" refers to his reputation: "when no one else would or could, only Eddie dared." The surf contest is held at Waimea Bay sometime between December and February, when the proper conditions of minimum twenty-foot swells permit. It has only been completed a handful of times since its inception. The twenty-four invited contestants from all over the world usually consider this surf contest the ultimate in the sport (see http://starbulletin.com/98/03/09/features/story1.html).

4. The Protect Kaho'olawe 'Ohana is a community based, islands-wide, grassroots organization committed to protecting Kaho'olawe Island from bombing and desecration by the U.S. Navy. Members of the 'Ohana first touched the 'aina in 1976 through a series of occupations. In 1994, Kaho'olawe was turned over to the state of Hawai'i (see http://www.k12.hi.us/~waianaeh/HawaiianStudies/kaho.html).

5. Jawaiian music is a combination of Jamaican and Hawaiian music that began to get popular in the early 1990s. Also called Hawaiian Reggae, or Island Hawaiian music (see http://www.arts.auckland.ac.nz/ant/234/Lecutre%203B%20Hawaii.htm).

6. *Li hing powder* is a blend of spices and seasonings such as anise, licorice, and Chinese five-spice that was once used primarily for flavoring Chinese-style preserved seeds. The red powder, with its salty-sweet taste, now flavors many popular items from gummy-bears to tequila (see *http://www.hawaiiandelica-seas.com/MM008.ASP?pageno*

=46). *Li hing mui* translates to "traveler's plum," referring to the preserved seed once used as a food for travelers on the road (see *http://the.honoluluadvertiser.com/2000/Aug/16/816islandlife1.html*).

REFERENCES

Abbott, Isabella Aiona. *La'au Hawai'i: Traditional Hawaiian Uses of Plants.* Honolulu, HI: Bishop Museum Press, 1992.

Beckwith, Martha. *Hawaiian Mythology.* Reprint, Honolulu: University of Hawaii Press, 1970 (1940).

——. *Ka Mo'olelo O La'ieikawai: The Hawaiian Romance of Laieikawai.* Honolulu, HI: First People's Productions, 1997 (1919).

Buck, H. Peter (Te Rangi Hiroa). *Arts and Crafts of Hawaii.* Honolulu, HI: Bishop Museum Press, 1964.

Chun, Naomi. *Hawaiian Canoe-Building Traditions.* Rev. Honolulu, HI: Kamehameha Schools Press, 1995.

Clarke, Joan. *Family Traditions in Hawaii: Birthday, Marriage, Funeral and Cultural Customs in Hawaii.* Honolulu, HI: Namkoong Publishing, 1994.

Colum, Padraic. *At the Gateways of the Day.* Vol. 1 of *Tales and Legends of Hawaii.* New Haven, CT: Published for the Hawaiian Legend and Folklore Commission by the Yale University Press, 1924.

Corum, Ann Kondo. *Folk Remedies from Hawaii.* Honolulu, HI: Bess Press, 1985a.

——. *Folk Wisdom from Hawaii: Or Don't Take Bananas on a Boat.* Honolulu, HI: Bess Press, 1985b.

Glassie, Henry. *Material Culture.* Bloomington: Indiana University Press, 1999.

http://starbulletin.com/98/03/09/features/story1.html. Eddie Riding on the Crest of the Myth, March 6, 1998. Accessed 8–15–02.

http://the.honoluluadvertiser.com/2000/Aug/16/816islandlife1.html. Future looks delicious for crack seed in Hawai'i. Accessed 8–17–02.

http://www.arts.auckland.ac.nz/ant/234/Lecutre%203B%20Hawaii.htm. Jawaiian Music-Andrew Weintraub. Accessed 8–16–02.

http://www.hawaiiandelica-seas.com/MM008.ASP?pageno=46. Hawaiian Terminology/Pidgin. Accessed 8–17–02.

http://www.k12.hi.us/~waianaeh/Hawaiian Studies/kaho.html. Kaho'olawe, May 16–18, 1997. Accessed 8–16–02.

Kamakau, Samuel Manaiakalani. *The Works of the People of Old* (Na Hana a ka Po'e Kahiko). Honolulu, HI: Bishop Museum Press, 1992 (1976).

Kawaharada, Dennis, ed. *Hawaiian Fishing Legends: With Notes on Ancient Fishing Implements and Practices.* Honolulu, HI: Kalamaku Press, 1992.

Mitchell, Donald D. Kilolani. *Resource Units in Hawaiian Culture.* Rev. ed. Honolulu, HI: Kamehameha Schools Press, 1992 (1969).

Oring, Elliot. "The Arts, Artifacts, and Artifices of Identity." *Journal of American Folklore* 107 (1994): 211–247.

Pukui, Mary Kawena, and Samuel H. Elbert. *Hawaiian Dictionary: Hawaiian-English, English Hawaiian.* Rev. ed. Honolulu: University of Hawaii Press, 1986.

——. *Tales of the Menehune.* Rev. ed. Honolulu, HI: Kamehameha Schools Press, 1994.

Valeri, Valerio. *Kingship and Sacrifice: Ritual and Society in Ancient Hawaii.* Chicago: University of Chicago Press, 1985.

Westervelt, W. D. *Hawaiian Historical Legends.* 3d. ed. New York: Fleming H. Revell Co., 1926.

——. *Myths and Legends of Hawaii.* A. Grove Day, ed. Honolulu, HI: Mutual Publishing, 1987.

Hawaii: Bibliography and Other Resources

Bibliography

History and Study

876. Beckwith, Martha. *Hawaiian Mythology.* New Haven, CT: Yale Univ. Press for the Folklore Foundation of Vassar College, 1940. Reprint, Honolulu: Univ. Press of Hawaii, 1970. xxxiii, 571p. New Introduction by Katharine Luomala. Index. Bibliog. 70-97998. 0-8248-0514-3.

Beckwith describes her book (in a letter asking Katharine Luomala to begin work on a revision) in these terms: "I conceive [it] to be the province of a true mythology—not merely a series of tales, but, with the tales as major illustration or formal expression, to point out the ideas of the relation of man to the world he lives in, geographic, historic, social and political, which result in such expression, and to connect the particular forms of expression developed in Hawaii to those common with his throughout the known Polynesian area."

This Beckwith did, producing both a collection of tales and a study of them. Each chapter deals with a theme of folklore, discusses that theme, and presents tales that illustrate it. In many cases the tales are as told by a variety of cultures.

Themes discussed are Gods, the Children of Gods, the Chiefs, and Heroes and Lovers.

877. Valeri, Valerio. *Kingship and Sacrifice: Ritual and Society in Ancient Hawaii.* Chicago: Univ. of Chicago Press, 1985. xxviii, 446p. Index. Bibliog. Notes. 84-23991. 0-226-84559-1; 0-226-84560-5pa.

Much of the material presented as folklore by early ethnologists and preservers of Hawaiian culture is in reality the Hawaiian religion. Here Valeri presents a scholarly study of some of the elements of Hawaiian religion, including the concept of kapu, the role of priests, and the role of sacrifice. No tales are retold here.

Tales and Legends

878. Colum, Padraic. *At the Gateways of the Day,* vol. 1 of *Tales and Legends of Hawaii.* New Haven, CT: Published for the Hawaiian Legend and Folklore Commission by the Yale University Press, 1924. xxvii, 217p. Illus. Notes.

In 1923, Colum was invited by the Commission on Myth and Folklore to survey the tales and legends of island folklore and mythology that had been collected over the years, and to edit them for children. He enlisted the help of Hawaiian elders, who knew or had known the stories, in shaping and preparing them for publication.

The stories in volume 1 (volume 2 is titled *The Bright Islands*) treat of the beginnings of the Hawaiian Islands, how they came to be, of Maui, the hero who discovered fire, and of many romances.

Illustrations are line drawings.

879. ——. *The Bright Islands,* vol. 2 of *Tales and Legends of Hawaii.* New Haven, CT: Published for the Hawaiian Legend and Folklore Commission by the Yale University Press, 1925. xiv, 233p. Illus. Notes.

Volume 1 of this two-volume set is titled *At the Gateways of the Day.* This second volume is also a collection of tales prepared by Colum at the behest of the Commission on Myth and Folklore. Although the stories in volume 1 are mythological, those in this volume are based on historical fact. Many concern the great kings of Hawaii.

880. Grant, Glen. *Glen Grant's Chicken Skin Tales: 49 Favorite Ghost Stories from Hawai'i*. Honolulu, HI: Mutual, 1998. viii, 184p. Illus. 98-68055. 1-56647-228-8pa.

Grant presents more ghost and supernatural tales with Hawaiian roots. Some come from previous studies of Hawaiian ghostlore; others come from Grant's own experiences in leading ghost tours, and the participants' desire to share with him their own encounters with the supernatural realm.

881. ——. *Obake Files: Ghostly Encounters in Supernatural Hawai'i*. Honolulu, HI: Mutual, 1996. xxiii, 277p. Illus. Bibliog. (Chicken Skin Series). 96-78339. 1-56647-100-1pa.

In addition to being a college teacher, Grant also hosts a radio program on Hawaiian lore; conducts ghost and history tours in Honolulu, and appears as a storyteller. During his tours, many people would share with him their own experiences with the supernatural. Many of the stories here were collected in this way.

He divides his book into three parts: types of ghosts, including ancestral ghosts, graveyard ghosts, visions of Pele, choking ghosts, wandering ghosts, and faceless ghosts; places that are haunted, including natural places, buildings, and houses; and a collection of photographs that purport to be of supernatural happenings.

Grant also adds an essay on his own spiritual journey and how he came to believe in the importance of the supernatural.

882. ——. *Obake: Ghost Stories in Hawai'i*. Honolulu, HI: Mutual, 1994. 178p. Illus. 97-194818. 1-566470-72-2.

When Glen Grant published this book, he had spent twenty-five years collecting the ghost stories of the Hawaiian Islands. The stories come from students in his classes, from elders, and from newspaper accounts. Many of the ghosts in these stories are malevolent, reaching out to hurt the living.

883. Green, Laura C. S., and Mary Kawena Pukui, colls. and trans. *The Legend of Kawelo, and Other Hawaiian Folk Tales*. Honolulu, HI: n.p., 1936. 185p.

Most of the stories here deal either with the origin of natural things (stones, springs, vegetation), or with romance. They were collected by Green on Oahu, and by Pukui from her native district on Hawaii.

An eighty-five-year-old storyteller told the legend of Kawelo, who became the ruler of Kauai, to Mrs. Pukui's husband, who gave it directly to the collectors.

This collection is a classic in the field.

884. Kamakau, Samuel Manaiakalani. *Tales and Traditions of the People of Old: Na Mo'olelo a ka Po'e Kahiko*. Honolulu, HI: Bishop Museum Press, 1991. 184p. Translated by Mary Kawena Pului. Edited by Dorothy B. Barrère. Notes. Glossary. Index. Bibliog. 89-62482. 0-930897-44-7.

These translations of Kamakau's newspaper articles of the late 1800s are made up of the stories of mythical and legendary chiefs of Hawaii. He includes the genealogy of various chiefs.

Many of these stories were used later as the basis for collections of legends compiled by other writers, among them W. D Westervelt and Thomas G. Thrum.

885. Kawaharada, Dennis, ed. *Hawaiian Fishing Legends, with Notes on Ancient Fishing Implements and Practices*. Honolulu,

HI: Kalamaku Press, 1992. xxviii, 126p. Illus. Bibliog. Notes. Glossary. 91-060407; 0-9623102-3-9pa.

The ancient fishermen of Hawaii are celebrated here: Ku'ula'kai, 'Ai'Ai, Nihooleki, Puniakai'a, Kalamainu'u,l, and Punia. All were famous for their ability to bring in large catches, often overcoming the supernatural powers of such creatures as the shark and the octopus. This ability was greatly respected, as fish was the mainstay of the people's diet.

Kawaharada also discusses some of the traditions and customs of fishing, such as the ancient practice of making certain fish *kapu* at certain times of the year, to ensure a continuance of supply.

This book is both a collection of delightful, readable tales, and a scholarly discussion of them.

886. Loebel-Fried, Caren. *Hawaiian Legends of the Guardian Spirits.* Honolulu, HI: Univ. of Hawaii Press, 2002. 109p. Illus. Bibliog. 2002-2822. 0-8248-2537-3.

In her preface, Loebel-Fried states that she offers these legends as "illuminated, sacred texts." These are the texts that demonstrate how tied the early Hawaiians were to nature, how grateful they were to it for its bounty, and how they tended it. Loebel-Fried offers tales revolving around five gifts of nature, vital to the Hawaiians' survival: the breadfruit, the plover, the shark, the gourd, and the owl.

The illustrations are woodcuts by the author.

887. Manu, Moses. *Keaomelemele: "He Mooleleo Kaao no Keaomelemele."* Honolulu, HI: Bishop Museum Press, 2002. viii, 176p. Illus. (Legacy of Excellence). 2001-6617. 1-58178-015-x; 1-58178-016-8pa.

Moses Manu was an author in the late 1800s. The tale he tells here was first pub-

lished as a serial newspaper column in the Hawaiian language paper *Ka Nupepa Kuokoa,* in 1884 and 1885. It tells the story of creation, of the beginnings of the human race, and of how the gods provided for humans. It tells, too, of the importance of the priest, of worship, and of the sacred hula.

Keaomelemele was one of the ancient ones. It was she who first was given the hula and who in turn imparted it to the rest of Hawaii, making it the sacred dance that it is.

The text is presented first in Hawaiian, as it was published in the newspaper, and then in an English translation by the noted scholar of Hawaiian culture, Mary Kawena Pukui.

888. Martin, Blanche R. *Wonder Stories of Old Hawaii.* Santa Rosa, CA: n.p., 1978. 158p. Glossary. pa.

Many of these tales are fragments, or shortened versions of longer ones meant to be told aloud. Most have to do either with the natural world or with how certain implements such as the drum or the canoe sail were first made.

889. Pukui, Mary Kawena. *Tales of the Menehune.* Rev. ed. Honolulu, HI: Kamehameha Schools Press, 1994. xii, 130p. Illus. Index. 0-87336-010-9.

The Menehune are little people, only two or three feet tall, with gruff voices. They work at night, and any project they undertake must be completed in one night or be abandoned. All over Hawaii can be found unfinished walls and other projects that people say are the work of the Menehune.

People who mistreat the Menehune are punished; those who are good to them benefit from their help.

The legends collected in this volume

include those of how the islands came to be and stories of Pele.

890. Pukui, Mary Kawena, comp. *Hawai'i Island Legends: Pikoi, Pele and Others.* Honolulu, HI: Kamehameha Schools Press, 1996. Previously published as *Pikoi and Other Legends of the Island of Hawaii*, 1949. vi, 242p. Illus. Glossary. 0-87336-032-xpa.

First published in 1949, these stories are now retold for a modern audience by Caroline Curtis. Some of the stories are about great chiefs and some about the gods and goddesses of ancient Hawaii. Curtis indicates in her preface that she, too, has made changes in the old stories, in accordance with story-telling tradition.

The illustrations are black-and-white, in woodcut style.

891. ——. *Folktales of Hawaii = He Mau Kaao Hawaii.* Honolulu, HI: Bishop Museum Press, 1995. xiv, 160p. Illus. Bibliog. 93-74561. 0-930897-43-9.

Most of the tales told here are presented both in English and in Hawaiian. Tales are of the gods, the great chiefs, and of the land itself.

This volume was published as a tribute to Mary Kawena Pukui on the hundredth anniversary of her birth. Pukui was a famed storyteller in Hawaii, whose efforts were instrumental in preserving Hawaii's culture. The tales are told mostly in her words and rhythms, with some updating for a modern readership.

892. Rivenburgh, Viola K. *Tales of the Menehune, the Little Pixie Folk of Hawaii.* Port Angeles, WA: Peninsula, 1980. 48p. Illus. Guide to pronunciation. 0-918146-19-4pa.

Nine tales of the Menehune, the little people of Hawaii who perform prodigious amounts of work in a single night,

are retold here. Tales are from several Hawaiian islands.

893. Thrum, Thomas G. *Hawaiian Folk Tales: A Collection of Native Legends.* 3d ed. Chicago: A. C. McClurg, 1917. xi, 284p. Illus. Glossary of Hawaiian words.

In the preface to this edition, Thrum decries the fact that so little effort had been made to preserve the ancient stories and traditions of the Hawaiians before contact with the wider world destroyed or changed them. Here he brings together stories collected from many native Hawaiians, as well as some preserved by early scholars of the tradition. Stories concern the gods of Hawaiian tradition, the origins of the islands, the Menehune, or industrious little people of legends, and the creation and naming of places and creatures.

Kawelo, Ku-ula, the Fish God of Hawaii, and Pele are featured in tales here.

Thrum's work is considered a classic.

894. Westervelt, W. D. *Hawaiian Historical Legends.* 3d ed. New York: Fleming H. Revell Co., 1926. 218p. Illus.

This is the sixth volume of Hawaiian legends that Westervelt published. Most of the tales are based on traditional Hawaiian legends and chants and tell the stories of the gods and ancient peoples. Some, however, tell of the beginnings of contact with other peoples, stories of the first printing in Hawaii and of Hawaii's first constitution. Thus this volume presents both the ancient stories and a look at the beginnings of the changes that came to the islands.

895. ——. *Legends of Gods and Ghosts (Hawaiian Mythology).* Boston: Press of Geo. H. Ellis, 1915. Reprint, under the title *Hawaiian Legends of Ghosts and Ghost-Gods*, Rutland, VT: Charles E. Tuttle Co.,

1963. x, 263p.; xvii, 262p. (reprint). Illus. Index to Hawaiian terms used.

Westervelt is considered one of the foremost early collectors of Hawaiian legends and tales, one of the first to take the spoken tale and record it. In this book, he concentrates on the spirit world, gods and goddesses, both beneficial to mankind and harmful.

Maui is here, the god who pulled the Hawaiian Islands up from the ocean depths while on a fishing trip, and who taught the secret of fire. There are also Pele and her husband, Kamapuaa, who influence the lava flows and the ocean. Fairies and gnomes inhabit this world, as do cannibal ghosts.

896. ———. *Myths and Legends of Hawaii.* Selected and edited by A. Grove Day. Honolulu, HI: Mutual Publishing, 1987. ix, 267p. 0-935180-86-9.

According to A. Grove Day, who selected these tales from the body of work by W. D. Westervelt, Westervelt was as important to the preservation and dissemination of the mythology of Hawaiians as Thomas Bulfinch was to that of the Greeks. Between 1919 and 1923, Westervelt published several books of Hawaiian legends, among them *Legends of Ma-ui, Around the Poi Bowl, and Legends of Paao, Legends of Old Honolulu,* and *Legends of Gods and Ghosts.*

Day has selected from these to compile a book of legends on the gods and goddesses, heroes and heroines, of Hawaii. Here are stories of Kane, the father of all; Ku, god of war; Kaneloa, ruler of the afterworld; and Lono, god of growing things. In addition, there are stories of Pele, the goddess of volcanoes; Hina, the goddess of women's work; and Kuula, the god of fishermen.

This is a concise, readable collection from some of the major works on Hawaiian mythology.

897. Wichman, Frederick B. *Kaua'i: Ancient Place-Names and Their Stories.* Honolulu: Univ. of Hawaii Press, 1998. xi, 202p. Illus. Index. Bibliog. Notes.97-45775.0-8248-1943-8pa.

Wichman admits in his preface that "there are countless more place-names on Kaua'i than are contained in this volume" (p. x). His book is a record and explanation of the ancient place-names given to valleys, mountains, beaches, and ridges on the island by the Polynesians, the first inhabitants. Wichman makes an attempt here to record these names before they are replaced (as they are being now) by a new culture with its own names.

Wichman's preface gives information on his sources, which will be useful to someone wanting to pursue this topic in more depth.

898. ———. *Polihale and Other Kaua'i Legends.* Honolulu, HI: Bamboo Ridge Press, 1991. 182p. Illus. 91-24204. 0910043-24-8.

Eighteen legends make up this book, all from the island of Kaua'i. Many concern the natural world and the islanders' place in it: how fire was discovered, how the stars in Orion's belt were created, why the Spouting Horn roars, how the first trees came to be.

The titles of these legends, listed in the table of contents, are written in Hawaiian, which makes it more difficult to locate a particular legend.

The book is illustrated with delicate line drawings.

Folk Music

899. Beamer, Winona. *Na Hula O Hawaii: The Songs and Dances of the Beamer*

Family. An Island Heritage Limited Edition. Norfolk Island, Australia: Island Heritage, 1976. 195p.Illus. 75-24136.

Winona, or Nona, Beamer grew up in a family that treasured and taught the hula. She continued the tradition. Here she tells the stories of various hulas in narrative form, as well as stories of her own life as a dancer of this tradition. She also includes music to many of the dances.

She also gives some insight into the philosophy of hula: The dancer's body represents all of nature, with the waistline representing the horizon; the lower part of the body, the land and sea; the upper part of the body, the sea and sky. The hula itself is about more than telling a story, it is also about interpreting emotions.

Many of the illustrations are in color; both photographs and drawings are included.

900. Kaeppler, Adrienne L. *Hula Pahu: Hawaiian Drum Dances.* Volume 1, *Ha'a and Hula Pahu: Sacred Movements.* Honolulu: Bishop Museum Press, 1993. xv, 289p. Illus. Index of Chant Titles. Subject Index. Bibliog. Notes. (Bishop Museum Bulletin in Anthropology, 3). 91-073874. 0-930897-55-2pa.

The history, development, and meaning of the hula are the subjects of this book and of the sequential volume, Volume 2, *The Pahu, Sounds of Power.* In Volume 1, Kaeppler discusses the importance of hula to the history and traditions of Hawaii, tells the stories of many of the dances, and gives information about some of the people who performed the dances and kept the tradition alive. She also provides diagrams of many of the dances and a wealth of black-and-white photographs of dancers in performance.

901. Kelly, John M. *Folk Music Festival in Hawaii: Folk Songs from Asia, the Pacific*

and America. Boston: Boston Music Company, 1965. 96p. Illus. Index by country. Pronunciation guide.

Collected here are folk songs from many different countries of the world, the countries that have contributed to the culture of Hawaii. Kelly gives a brief introduction to each song, giving some of the background and story surrounding it.

All songs have music transcribed.

902. *Musics of Hawaii: An Anthology of Musical Traditions in Hawaii.* Honolulu, HI: State Foundation on Culture and the Arts, Folk Art Program, 1997. 152p. Illus. Bibliog. Glossary of Musical Terms. Profiles of Musicians. pa.

Written for use by teachers in the classroom, to introduce the rich tradition of music in Hawaii, this book contains a discussion of many of the different strains that have contributed to Hawaiian music. Sections on Hawaiian chant, Pacific Island church music, African American gospel music, Pacific Island song, Japanese music, Okinawan classical and folk music, Chinese music, Korean music, Southeast Asian music, Puerto Rican music, Portuguese music, Filipino music, Native American music, and music of North America and Europe are all included. Each section discusses the music itself as well as its influence on Hawaii.

The book is accompanied by five sound discs.

903. *On Hawaiian Folk Music.* An Island Heritage Limited Edition, 2d ed. Norfolk Island, Australia: Island Heritage, 1965. 68p. Illus. 77-173474.

On Hawaiian Folk Music is presented in three parts. First comes a long story song, told in the rhythm of ancient Hawaiian chant, and telling of the beginnings of Hawaii. Next comes a reminiscence by an old man who knew and loved the songs of Hawaii's history and who participated in their preservation. And last is a description, with illustrations, of the instruments used in Hawaii's music, bamboo tubes, the gourd whistle, rhythm sticks, the drum, the stringed bow, the split bamboo rattle, pebble castanets, the bamboo nose flute, the gourd rattle, the triton trumpet, the coconut drum, the rhythm board, leg ornaments, and gourd drum.

Illustrations for the first section of the book are full-page black-and-white photographs of Hawaiian Islanders in the early part of the century.

904. Tatar, Elizabeth. *Hula Pahu: Hawaiian Drum Dances.* Volume II, *The Pahu, Sounds of Power.* Honolulu, HI: Bishop Museum Press, 1993. xvii, 358p. Illus. Index of Chant Titles. Subject Index. Bibliog. Notes. (Bishop Museum Bulletin in Anthropology 3). 91-072828. 0-930897-54-4pa.

Volume I of *Hula Pahu: Hawaiian Drum Dances, Ha'a and Hula Pahu: Sacred Movements,* concentrates on the dance. Volume II concentrates on the drum itself. Construction, use, history, and significance are all discussed and illustrated. The two volumes together form a significant history of the role of dance in Hawaii.

Folk Belief and Ritual

905. Clarke, Joan. *Family Traditions in Hawaii: Birthday, Marriage, Funeral, and Cultural Customs in Hawaii.* Honolulu, HI: Namkoong, 1994. 110p. Illus. Index. Bibliog. 94-68763. 0-9643359-0-5pa.

The traditions of the varied cultures of Hawaii are the subject of this book. Clarke begins with background information on these various cultures that make

up the population of Hawaii: Hawaiians, Chinese, Portuguese, Japanese and Okinawans, Koreans, Filipinos, Samoans, Tongans, Vietnamese, and Laotians. She then offers chapters on birthday celebrations, marriage customs, and funeral traditions, as well as one of annual celebrations maintained by all these cultures. She includes both adult and children's traditions.

Color photographs show some of the artifacts used in the various traditions and celebrations.

906. Corum, Ann Kondo. *Folk Remedies from Hawaii.* Honolulu, HI: Bess Press, 1985a. v, 137p. Illus. Bibliog. 86-70672. 0-935848-37-1pa.

Remedies for everything from childbirth pains to stomach problems are included here. The presentation is humorous, with cartoons of sufferers used to illustrate the various remedies. Some of the remedies are based on plants; some are active remedies, such as making a lei, putting it on, and swimming out to sea. The action of the sea in washing off the lei also washes away the illness.

Corum also includes an illustrated listing of plants used for medicinal purposes.

907. ——. *Folk Wisdom from Hawaii, or, Don't Take Bananas on a Boat.* Honolulu: Bess Press, 1985b. vi, 114p. Illus. 84-73554. 0-935848-32-0pa.

Like Corum's other book, *Folk Remedies from Hawaii,* this one is a lighthearted look at various customs of the islands. Again like the other book, it is illustrated with cartoons that illuminate each point. The book's chapters deal with practical advice ("When you want unwanted guests to go home, stand a broom on its handle"); plants (bless a house with ti leaves); animals (don't kill a black moth—

it is the returned soul of a departed loved one); fish (to ensure good luck when fishing, throw back the first fish caught); the body ("Specks on your fingernails mean you will be getting a present soon."); and birth and death (ghosts that float are harmful; ghosts that walk are not). Lighthearted and humorous, this is an enjoyable way to pick up on local beliefs and superstitions.

908. Kaaiakamanu, D. M., and J. K. Akina. *Hawaiian Herbs of Medicinal Value Found among the Mountains and Elsewhere in the Hawaiian Islands, and Known to the Hawaiians to Possess Curative and Palliative Properties Most Effective in Removing Physical Ailments.* Rutland, VT: Charles E. Tuttle, 1922. Reprint, Honolulu: Pacific Book House, 1977. 74p. (reprint edition). Translated by Akaiko Akana. 76-177367. 0-8048-1019-2pa.

Alphabetically arranged, this lists various native plants, provides a physical description of each, and indicates for what ailments the plant is useful.

909. Kamakau, Samuel Manaiakalani. *Ka Po'e Kahiko: The People of Old.* Honolulu, HI: Bishop Museum Press, 1964. ix, 165p. Chapter notes. Index. Bibliog. (Bernice P. Bishop Museum Special Publication 51). 66-5392.

Kamakau wrote a series of articles on Hawaiian history and culture for weekly Hawaiian newspapers between 1866 and 1871. The series of articles on cultural topics was translated by various scholars. Articles concern the religious system of the Hawaiians, including the creation story, medical practices, stories of spirits, and stories of sorcery.

910. Malo, David. *Hawaiian Antiquities (Moolelo Hawaii).* 2d ed. Honolulu, HI: Bishop Museum Press, 1951. xxii,

278p. Index. Chapter notes. (Bernice P. Bishop Special Publication 2). 51-5835.

Malo was born around 1793. During his early life he was steeped in the traditions and history of Hawaii. His father was a follower of Kamehameha; he himself was connected with the court of the queen. In the words of the brief biography that introduces this work, Malo had "an intimate acquaintance with the history, traditions, legends and myths of old Hawaii, as well as with the *mele, pule,* and *oli* that belong to the hula" (p. vii).

Much of this book concerns rites and beliefs: eating under the kapu system, conduct, rites concerning circumcision, rites concerning the dead, public ceremonies, and healing practices. Other parts concern customs and daily activities: the house and furniture, games and sports, and fishing.

In addition to this book, Malo also wrote a history of the king, Kamehameha.

911. Pukui, Mary Kawena. *Olelo No'eau: Hawaiian Proverbs and Poetical Sayings.* Honolulu: Bishop Museum Press, 1983. xix, 351p. Illus. by Dietrich Varez. General Index. Index to Place Names. Index to Personal Names. Index to Birds. Index to Fishes and Other Aquatic Animals. Index to Plants. (Bernice P. Bishop Museum Special Publication, no. 71). 83-72688. 0-910240-92-2; 0-910240-93-0pa.

Mary Kawena Pukui spent her life collecting and preserving the language and the culture of the Hawaiian people. Among her other works is the standard *Hawaiian-English Dictionary.*

This collection of proverbs, jokes, riddles, chants, aphorisms, and other spoken sayings is arranged alphabetically. Pukui adds annotations, illuminating the context in which a certain saying would be used. Subject access is provided through the general subject index. The index to places includes mythical places, and the index to people includes the names of gods and other spiritual beings.

912. Williams, Rianna M. *Deaths and Funerals of Major Hawaiian Ali'i.* Honolulu, HI: R. M. Williams, 2000. 217p. Illus. Bibliog. Glossary. pa.

Full-page black-and-white photographs of the funerals of various prominent ali'i, or rulers, of Hawaii illustrate this book. The book itself is basically divided into two parts. First come lengthy descriptions of specific funerals, including that of King Kamehameha V and of Queen Li-li'uokalani. Second is a discussion of various funeral customs, such as the use of death masks, flower symbolism, and various royal paraphernalia.

Material Culture

913. Abbott, Isabell Aiona. *La'au Hawai'i: Traditional Hawaiian Uses of Plants.* Honolulu, HI: Bishop Museum Press, 1992. xii, 163p. Illus. Index. Bibliog. Notes. 91-073874. 0-930897-62-5.

More than the medicinal uses of plants is the study of this book; other cultural uses are also explained and illustrated. Religious uses, use in clothing, in household furnishings and houses themselves, in fishing, in music and ceremonies, in warfare, and in ceremonial costume are all included, as well as medicinal uses.

The author knew the eminent Hawaiian historian and ethnologist Mary Kawena Pukui and received some of her information and knowledge from that source. Uses of plants from many of the Hawaiian Islands are included and compared.

914. Kamakau, Samuel Manaiakalani. *The Works of the People of Old: Na Hana a ka Po'e Kahiko.* Honolulu, HI: Bishop Museum Press, 1976. viii, 170p. Translated by Mary Kawena Pukui. Edited by Dorothy B. Barrère. Notes. Glossary. Index. Bibliog. (Bernice P. Bishop Museum Special Publication 61). 75-21315. 0-910240-18-3.

A sequel to Kamakau's *Ka Po'e Kahiko: The People of Old,* this collection of his newspaper articles focuses on material culture. Here is information on food cultivation, fishing, crafts, worship, and ritual.

915. McDonald, Marie A. *Ka Lei: The Leis of Hawaii.* Honolulu, HI: Topgallant, 1978. 187p. Illus. Index. Bibliog. 78-19082. 0-914916-32-7pa.

In her introduction, McDonald states "In every part of the world where man has lived and lives, he has made for himself a lei, a necklace, a crown of various materials to adorn his body, to ward off evil spirits, to bring good fortune, to please his gods, to denote rank among men, to give as tokens of love, and for pure and simple enjoyments" (p. 1). She refers to the Aztec and Mayan crowns and garlands of gold and of flowers, to the Greek laurel leaves that rewarded achievement, and to Christ's crown of thorns.

McDonald discusses materials used to make leis, methods of construction, and the traditions that surround different types of leis, made and given for different occasions. She includes diagrams for making leis and many color photographs.

916. Young, David. *Na Mea Makamae: Hawaiian Treasures.* Kailua-Kona, HI: Palapala Press, 1999. x, 109p. Illus. Bib-

liog. Notes. Glossary. 99-74449. 1-883528-09-7; 1-883528-10-0pa.

Heavily illustrated with both drawings and photographs, this book gives information on the construction and use of shelter, textiles, clothing, game artifacts, artifacts for travel, musical instruments, weapons, and ornaments. Young also discusses food and religion.

Folklore for Children

917. Chun, Naomi N. Y. *Hawaiian Canoe-Building Traditions.* Rev. Honolulu, HI: Kamehameha Schools Press, 1995. v, 86p. Illus. Bibliog. 0-87336-043-5.

Children are the intended audience for this book; it is designed as an activity book for use in the schools. While reading this book, children can do crossword puzzles, take true-or-false tests, answer questions based on illustrations, or work their way through a maze to the launching place for canoes. Illustrations are in black-and-white.

918. Dolch, Edward W., and Marguerite P. Dolch. *Stories from Hawaii.* Champaign, IL: Garrard, 1960. 167p. Illus. (Folklore of the World). 60-9707.

Elementary school children are the target audience for this collection of folktales. They are written in simple language, so children can read them for themselves, and are illustrated with full-page, color drawings.

Tales include those of Maui, who found fire, of princes and princesses, and of Pele, the goddess of the volcano.

Dolch adds a list of Hawaiian words with a guide to their pronunciation.

919. Lee, Robin Koma. *Legends of the Hawaiian Waters.* Honolulu, HI: Maka-pu'u Press, 1998. Unpaged. Illus. 98-91233. 0-9604182-1-0pa.

These twelve tales are written in a simple enough way to be readable to children yet retain enough complexity to appeal to adults. The tales concern various personalities of Hawaii, particularly Maui, who discovered fire; Pele, the goddess of the volcano; and Kama-pua'a, who could change shapes at will.

The book is beautifully illustrated in color, and the tales are printed in a typeface resembling hand printing.

920. Metzger, Berta. *Tales Told in Hawaii.* New York: Frederick A. Stokes, 1929. xii, 116p. Illus.

Tales from throughout the Pacific as well as tales specifically from Hawaii are in this book. Most concern the natural world—how the Hawaiian Islands came to be in a row, why the sun and moon travel through the sky separately rather than together, why flowers wilt at night.

Illustrations are in black and white.

921. Thompson, Vivian L. *Hawaiian Legends of Tricksters and Riddlers.* New York: repr. Honolulu: Holiday House, repr. Kolowalu, 1969, repr. 1990. 103p. Illus. Bibliog. Glossary.

Like so many cultures, the Hawaiian culture has stories of tricksters as part of its folklore. Thompson believes that these trickster stories arose because in ancient times Hawaii was a mysterious and dangerous place, filled with unknown animals; only the clever trickster can cope with such menace.

Riddles were also an important part of Hawaiian culture. Riddlers were respected for their wit.

This collection presents many of the classic tales of Hawaiian folklore, written for children.

922. ——. *Hawaiian Tales of Heroes and Champions.* Repr. Honolulu: Univ. of Hawaii Press, 1971; Honolulu: Univ. of Hawaii Press, 1990. 128p. Illus. by Herbert Kawainui Kane. Bibliog. Glossary. (A Kolowalu Book). 72-151757. 0-8248-1076-7.

Like her earlier book, *Hawaiian Legends of Tricksters and Riddlers,* this one retells for children the tales of old Hawaii. Here Thompson offers twelve tales of shape changers and other supernatural heroes of Hawaii. She includes Kana, who could stretch his body as tall as a tree; and Shark Man of Ewa, who could change from man to shark or other creatures. She includes, too, those with supernatural weapons. All used their powers at various times to help.

Literary Authors: A Selected List

Below is a selected list of authors who reflect and interpret the history and atmosphere of their region. These are authors of novels, poems, short stories, or reminiscences. Through reading the works of these authors, one can acquire knowledge of the history, people, and flavor of the region. This is not a complete list, either of authors or of their works, but rather one calculated to start readers exploring and discovering their own favorites.

Bonehill, Ralph (pseudonym of Edward L. Stratemeyer), 1862–1930

Off for Hawaii, or, The Mystery of a Great Volcano

Keller, Nora Okja, 1965–

Fox Girl

Michener, James, 1907–1997

Hawaii

Museums of the State: A Selected List

Museums that feature everyday life abound in all regions of the country. Through the display of clothing, farm implements, household goods, industrial tools, or entire houses, workshops, and communities, these museums can help people of today understand and appreciate the lives lived by those who came before. The list below is not a complete list of museums in the region, but by browsing through it, one can get a glimpse of the richness of museum offerings. Explore on your own and discover even more fascinating museums.

Hana, Maui

Hana Cultural Center
4874 Uakea Road
Hana, Maui, Hawaii 96713
Mailing address:
P.O. Box 27
Hana, Maui, Hawaii 96713
808-248-8622
http://www.hawaiimuseums.org/mc/ismaui _hana.htm

Honolulu, Oahu

Bishop Museum
1525 Bernice Street
Honolulu, Oahu, Hawaii 96817
808-847-3511
http://www.bishopmuseum.org

Hawaii Maritime Center
Pier 7
Honolulu Harbor
Honolulu, Oahu, Hawaii 96813
808-523-6151

Iolani Palace
King and Richards Streets
Honolulu, Oahu, Hawaii 96813
Mailing address:
P.O. Box 2259
Honolulu, Oahu, Hawaii 96804
808-522-0822
http://www.iolanipalace.org/

Mission Houses Museum
553 South King Street
Honolulu, Oahu, Hawaii 96813
808-531-0481
http://www.lava.net/~mhm/main.htm

Kailua-Kona, Oahu

Hulihee Palace
75–5718 Alii Drive
Kailua-Kona, Oahu, Hawaii 96740
808-329-1877
http://www.huliheepalace.org

Lahaina, Maui

Lahaina Restoration Foundation
120 Dickenson
Lahaina, Maui, Hawaii 96761
808-661-3262
http://www.lahainarestoration.org

Lihue, Kauai

Kauai Museum
4428 Rice Street

Lihue, Kauai, Hawaii 96766
Mailing address:
P.O. Box 248
Lihue, Kauai, Hawaii 96766
http://www.kauaimuseum.org

Journals in Folkore of the State: A Selected List

Other journals and newsletters besides the one listed below exist. These are often smaller and more local, published by museums, historical societies, folklore organizations, community groups, and schools. Explore on your own to see what other publications on folklore exist.
Journal of Hawaiian and Pacific Folkore and Folklife Studies

Web Sites: A Selected List

Below is a list of a few Web sites dealing with folklore of the region. You can find other Web sites by doing an Internet search on a search engine such as Google or Yahoo!, or by looking for the Web sites of various folklore organizations with which you are familiar.

Legends of Maui: A Demi-God of Polynesia and of His Mother Hina, *http://www.sacred-texts.com/pac/maui/index.htm*
Presents legends of Maui, compiled by W. D. Westervelt.

Voyaging Traditions, *http://leahi.kcc.hawaii.edu/org/pvs/L2traditions.html*
Resources on both Hawaiian and Polynesian voyaging traditions and stories. Links to a bibliography.

Index

Numbers in bold type and brackets, for example, **[999]**, refer to works cited in the bibliography section of each chapter, *by item number*. All other references are to page numbers.

A

Abbott, Isabell Aiona, **[913]**

Abenaki people. *See* Wabanaki

Abernethy, Francis Edward, **[585]**, **[666]**

Abraham "Oregon" Smith (Jansen), **[503]**

Abrahams, Roger D., **[306]**

Abrams, Ann Uhry, **[108]**

Acadians. *See* Cajuns

Achomawi people, **[43]**, **[730]**, **[734]**

Acoma people, **[43]**, **[681]**, **[698]**

Across the Fields (Martin), **[540]**

Adams, Charles J., III, **[131]**, **[132]**

Adams, Richard C., **[133]**

Adirondack Mountains, **[126]**, **[161]**, **[217]**, **[220]**

Adirondack Tales (Early), **[161]**

Adirondack Voices (Bethke), **[220]**

The Adventures of High John, the Conqueror (Sanfield), **[464]**

Aesop's fables, **[694]**

Africa, West, **[350]**

African American Folktales (Abrahams), **[306]**

African American Museum (Dallas), **[585]**

African Americans, **[13]**, **[423]**, 222, 225, 270, 275, 316

    museums and historic sites on, 27, 31

    music of, **[78]**, **[103]**, 155–156

    tales and legends of, **[4]**, **[5]**, **[8]**, **[30]**, **[42]**, **[44]**, **[46]**, **[53]**, **[54]**, **[471]**, **[585]**, **[621]**, **[772]**

    tales and legends of South on, **[306]**, **[318]**, **[321]**, **[382]** 156–157

    as women, **[53]**, **[63]**

    See also Black cowboys

Afro-American Folk Lore (Christensen), **[321]**

Ah Mo (Griffin), **[847]**

Alabama, **[466]**

    folk belief and ritual of, **[415]**, **[425]**, **[446]**

    folk music of, **[394]**, **[412]**

    history and study of folklore in, **[5]**, **[285]**

    material culture of, **[446]**, **[841]**

    museums of, 207

    tales and legends of, **[316]**, **[320]**, **[333]**, **[334]**, **[384]**, **[387]**, **[389]**

Alabama (Windham), **[446]**

Alabama people, **[60]**, **[324]**, **[350]**, **[353]**, **[599]**

Alabama's Favorite Folk Tales (Tackett), **[387]**

The Alamo, **[17]**, **[454]**, **[626]**, **[748]**

Alaska, **[17]**, 383–404

    festivals and celebrations of, 390–391

    folk beliefs and ritual of, **[860]**, **[862]**

    folk music of, **[860]**–**[861]**

    folklore for children on, **[870]**–**[875]**

    history and study of, 383–394

    journals of, 403

    literary authors on, 401

    material culture of, **[836]**, **[863]**–**[869]**, 391–393

French Canadians, **[118]**, **[534]**, **[582]**
Frey, Rodney, **[790]**
Friends of Thunder (Kilpatrick), **[634]**
Frietchie, Barbara, **[300]**
Fritz, Jean, **[266]**
From My People (Dance), **[29]**
From Needmore to Prosperity (Baker), **[483]**
From the Big Red to the Rio Grande (Havenhill), **[629]**
From the High Plains (Fischer), **[685]**
Frontier, American, **[39]**, **[587]**, **[669]**, **[718]**
Frontier Folksay (Hines), **[822]**
The Frontiersman (Derr), **[325]**
Fruits, **[94]**, **[303]**
Fullman, Lynn Grisard, **[333]**
Further Tales of Uncle Remus(Lester), **[458]**
Fussell, Fred C., **[401]**

G

Games, **[3]**, **[5]**, **[27]**
   of Alaska, **[865]**, **[872]**
   of Hawaii, **[910]**, **[916]**, 410
   of Midwest, **[478]**, **[566]**
   of Northeast, **[114]**, **[124]**, **[125]**, **[250]**
   of Northwest, **[809]**, **[832]**, **[842]**
   of South, **[304]**, **[305]**
   of Southwest, **[598]**, **[622]**
Gard, Robert E., **[476]**
Gardner, Emelyn Elizabeth, **[167]**, **[438]**
Garland, Hamlin, **[559]**
Garrison, Webb B., **[334]**
Gaudet, Marcia G., **[417]**
Geller, L. D., **[168]**
Geography of folklore, **[5]**, **[17]**, **[150]**, **[593]**, **[767]**, 345–346, 385
Georgia, **[5]**, **[302]**, **[408]**, **[466]**
   folk belief and ritual of, **[416]**, **[420]**, **[422]**
   museums of, 208–209
   tales and legends of, **[55]**, **[318]**, **[334]**, **[346]**, **[391]**
Georgia Folklore Archives, **[318]**
German Americans, **[35]**, **[561]**, **[562]**, **[826]**, **[831]**, 222–223, 346, 353
German Food and Folkways (Gueldner), **[831]**
German-American Folklore (Barrick), **[35]**

Germanic Folk Culture in Eastern Ohio (Kaufman), **[561]**
Ghost Gold (Arnold), **[600]**
The Ghost of Peg Leg Pete (Jagendorf), **[273]**
Ghost Stories from the American South (McNeil), **[356]**
Ghost Stories from the Pacific Northwest (MacDonald), **[805]**
Ghost Stories of Pennsylvania (Asfar), **[136]**
Ghost Tales from the North Carolina Piedmont (Tanenbaum), **[388]**
Ghostly Tales and Legends along the Grand Strand of South Carolina (Floyd), **[330]**
Ghosts, **[25]**, **[27]**, **[44]**, **[49]**, **[62]**, **[64]**
   in Hawaiian folklore, **[880]**–**[882]**, **[895]**
   in Midwestern folklore, **[476]**, **[484]**, **[487]**, **[496]**, **[497]**, **[501]**, **[502]**, **[512]**, **[514]**, **[520]**, **[529]**, **[549]**, **[555]**
   in Northeastern folklore, **[121]**, **[122]**, **[136]**, **[152]**, **[155]**, **[185]**, **[212]**, **[218]**
   in Northwestern folklore, **[780]**, **[800]**, **[804]**, **[805]**
   in Southern folklore, **[296]**, **[303]**, **[310]**, **[316]**, **[323]**, **[328]**, **[332]**, **[333]**, **[339]**, **[348]**, **[354]**, **[356]**, **[360]**, **[361]**, **[369]**, **[371]**, **[372]**, **[374]**–**[380]**, **[384]**, **[387]**, **[388]**, **[421]**, **[424]**
   in Southwestern folklore, **[594]**, **[600]**, **[601]**, **[605]**, **[608]**, **[610]**, **[618]**, **[620]**, **[624]**, **[626]**, **[642]**, **[652]**, **[658]**–**[661]**, **[679]**
   in Western folklore, **[718]**, **[719]**, **[728]**, **[733]**
Ghosts, Spirits and Legends of Southeastern Ohio (Everett), **[496]**
Ghosts along the Cumberland (Montell), **[421]**
Ghosts and Goosebumps (Solomon), **[384]**
Ghosts in the Hills (Jump), **[348]**
Ghosts in the Valley! (Felumlee), **[497]**
Ghosts of the Carolinas (Roberts), **[375]**
Ghosts of the Southern Mountains and Appalachia (Roberts), **[376]**
Giants in the Land (Boyer), **[488]**
The Giants of the Dawnland (Mead), **[189]**
Gib Morgan, Minstrel of the Oil Fields (Boatright), **[604]**

About the Author

Terry Ann Mood is a librarian and professor emeritus at the University of Colorado of Denver, where she was an associate professor and the head of collection development and humanities bibliographer at the Auraria Library. Presently she is the coordinator of database purchasing at the Colorado Alliance of Research Libraries. Her previous publications include *ARBA Guide to Biographical Resources 1986–1997* (Englewood, CO: Libraries Unlimited, 1998), which she coedited with Robert L. Wick, and *Distance Education: An Annotated Bibliography* (Englewood, CO: Libraries Unlimited, 1995), as well as a number of articles in professional library journals. She holds a B.A. from Brown University, an M.S.L.S. from Simmons College, and an M.A. in literature from the University of Reading in Reading, England.

About the Contributors

Ron Baker authored the introduction to the chapter on the Midwest. He is a professor in the English department at Indiana State University, specializing in American folklore.

Amy Craver, who introduced the Alaska chapter, is a research associate at the Institute of Social and Economic Research, as well as an adjunct professor for the anthropology and humanities departments at the University of Alaska, Anchorage. She is a Ph.D. candidate in folklore from the Folklore Institute at Indiana University.

Timothy Evans contributed the introduction to the chapter on the West. Evans is a professor within the folk studies program of the modern language and intercultural studies department at Western Kentucky University. His specialties include American folklore, public and applied folklore, material culture, and the American West. He was formerly the Wyoming State folklorist.

Alfred Kina, author of the introduction to the chapter on Hawaii, is a Ph.D. student at Indiana University's Folklore Institute. He is a *hanai kanaka maoli*, or adopted native Hawaiian.

Jens Lund is the author of the introduction to the Northwest chapter. Dr. Lund's Ph.D. is in folklore and American studies from Indiana University. He is an independent researcher and consultant in folklore, folk arts, and oral history, and he travels extensively within the United Stated in that capacity. He has also served as director of the Washington State Folklife Council and has been on the faculty at the University of Washington.

W. K. McNeil, author of the introduction to the South and Southern Highlands chapter, is folklorist at the Ozark Folk Center State Park. He has published numerous books, including *The Arkansas Folklore Sourcebook*.

Richard Sweterlitsch wrote the essay introducing the chapter on the Northeast.

He holds a Ph.D. in folklore from the Folklore Institute of Indiana University. He has recently retired from the University of Vermont, where he taught English literature, including courses in folk narrative. He continues to lecture on Vermont folklore in various community venues.

Angel Vigil contributed the introduction to the Southwest chapter. Mr. Vigil is the chairman of the fine and performing arts department of the Colorado Academy in Denver, Colorado. In addition to being a published author, Mr. Vigil is a well-known storyteller in the area.